The Fourth of July Encyclopedia

JAMES R. HEINTZE

McFarland & Company, Inc., Publishers

Jefferson, North Carolina, and London

LIBRARY OF CONGRESS CATALOGUING-IN-PUBLICATION DATA

Heintze, James R.
The Fourth of July encyclopedia / James R. Heintze.
p.   cm.
Includes bibliographical references and index.

ISBN-13: 978-0-7864-2777-2
ISBN-10: 0-7864-2777-9
(illustrated case binding : 50# alkaline paper) ∞

1. Fourth of July — Encyclopedias.   I. Title.
E286.A1284   2007   394.263403 — dc22   2006033532

British Library cataloguing data are available

Cover art ©2006 Pictures Now

Manufactured in the United States of America

McFarland & Company, Inc., Publishers
Box 611, Jefferson, North Carolina 28640
www.mcfarlandpub.com

CONTENTS

ACKNOWLEDGMENTS

My appreciation is extended to the following individuals who have encouraged the writing of this book: Patricia A. Shifferd, for information on the American Composers Forum project, "Continental Harmony"; Alan C. Aimone, senior special collections librarian, West Point, New York, United States Military Academy, for information on the history of the academy; Kathy W. Hall, Nicholasville, Kentucky, for information on and photos regarding William Price; to George Arnold, reference librarian, American University, Washington, D.C., for his photographs and information on the Washington and Lafayette monuments in Paris, France; to Lisa A. Cramb, publicity director, New Boston, New Hampshire, Fourth of July Association, Inc., for information and photograph regarding the "Molly Stark Cannon"; Bryan Craig, research librarian, Monticello; Richard Edwards, Ella Wheeler Wilcox Society; Eric Brooks, curator, Ashland, Kentucky, The Henry Clay Estate; William D. Cissna, public relations director, and Nancy Thomas, director of interpretive resources and outreach, for information on the history of Old Salem, North Carolina; Rick Fowler, agent, Beach Boys; Heather Lanman, park interpreter, Palo Duro Canyon State Park, Canyon, Texas; David McCartney, archivist, and Denise Anderson, University of Iowa, for information on the "Old Capitol"; Gerry Strey, reference librarian, Wisconsin Historical Society, for celebrations in Wisconsin; to Helen S. Joseph for her gift of historic facsimile editions of the Declaration of Independence printed for the Coca-Cola Bottling Company and the Society of the Cincinnati of Maryland; Bridget P. Carr, archivist, Boston Symphony Orchestra, for information on the history of the BSO; Annie Armour, head of archives and special collections, Sewanee: The University of the South, for information on the university; Debra Adleman, assistant curator, Susquehanna County Historical Society, for information on the soldier's monument in Montrose, Pennsylvania; Robert Antill of the public library of Willoughby, Ohio, for information on Willoughby's Civil War monument; Cathy Roy, Reference Department, Niagara Falls (Ontario) Public Library, for a photograph and information on Niagara Falls; Juan Bastos for photographs of Los Angeles landmarks; Mary Finch, audiovisual archivist, George Bush Presidential Library and Museum, for assistance in obtaining a photograph of George Bush; Jim Crenshaw of St. Louis, for information on the Kaskaskia Island Liberty Bell and ceremonies held on that Illinois site; Diane B. Jacob, head of Archives and Records Management, Preston Library, Virginia Military Institute, for information and an illustration on the history of VMI; to Gerald Szymanski, circulation services librarian, Sibley Music Library at the Eastman School of Music, for information on the Fourth in Rochester, New York; to my son Terry Heintze for photographs taken by him at the Gettysburg National Cemetary, and my loving wife, Yolanda Aguirre Heintze, for her encouragement and support.

PREFACE

This is the first comprehensive reference work on the nation's most important holiday; it documents and promotes understanding of the history of Independence Day through the eyes and hearts of those who celebrate it across America and abroad. The entries in this work demonstrate the significance of the Independence Day celebration and focus on the holiday as it has been commemorated, starting with the first public readings of the Declaration of Independence in 1776.

The range of entries is broad and includes unique, unusual, and little-known events. Readers can expect to find information on fireworks, parades, orations, recitations, reenactments, immigrants and ethnic groups, associations, patriotic icons, cornerstone ceremonies, dedications of statues and monuments, artillery salutes, launchings of ships, construction of railroads, canals and other civic projects, social movements, and events representing the nation's milestones of progress, including the Centennial and Sesquicentennial Expositions in Philadelphia, in 1876 and 1926, respectively, and the World's Columbian Exposition in 1893 and the Bicentennial in 1976.

Also included are numerous entries on both prominent and lesser-known individuals who participated in some noteworthy manner on the Fourth, including all U.S. presidents and many other statesmen. Brief biographical information for each individual is provided to help provide a context for his or her participation in celebrations.

There are also articles on education, abolition, temperance, prohibition, prisons, electric light displays, labor disputes, ships, parades, circuses, amusement parks, and naturalization.

Entries are based primarily on historical newspaper reports, but are supported with key secondary print and online texts. A number of experts on specific topics and geographical areas of the country were consulted for additional information and are mentioned in the acknowledgments.

An excellent source the author turned to for biographical information on the presidents is "The Presidents of the United States," on The White House homepage <*http://www. whitehouse.gov/history/presidents/*>. Readers may wish to refer to the author's Web site, *Fourth of July Celebrations Database* <*http://gurukul.american.edu/heintze/fourth.htm*>, which has additional information on many of the topics presented in this volume.

Events that happened coincidentally on July 4 but were not connected in any way to a celebration are not included. Selections from speeches are provided both to reflect the theme of the addresses and to bring attention to memorable statements.

Entries are arranged alphabetically. General sources are listed in the bibliography; specific sources are listed following the articles and are cited in chronological order of publication. Cross references in **bold type** point to other entries that have additional information. Readers who are introducing themselves to the history of the Fourth of July may want to read the articles "Declaration of Independence" and "Fourth of July" first to understand the significance of the nation's founding charter and how the celebrations began.

The impact of the Fourth of July over its many decades of history has been considerable. The holiday has served as the genesis for thousands of civic projects, acts of legislation, establishment of associations, innumerable speeches, premieres of poetic and musical works, and advances in communication, utilities, commerce, technology, and science, along with many other efforts that have contributed to the advancement of the nation.

The holiday has also been one of unfortunate events due in part to the mishandling of artillery, fireworks, and other explosive devices that resulted in injuries, death, and destruction. The Mammarello fireworks explosion in Philadelphia (1900), for example, killed seven children, and in the Wanamie, Pennsylvania, explosion (1906) five children died. Due to the careless use of fireworks, a number of towns were destroyed or severely damaged, including Denton, Maryland (1865), Portland, Maine (1866), Pontiac, Illinois (1874), Harlem, New York (1886), Edwards, New York (1894), and Benton, Pennsylvania (1910).

Other tragic occurrences were the result of large crowds assembling on public streets without adequate law enforcement and on hastily constructed grandstands and platforms, many of which collapsed. Disparate groups roamed the streets and often crossed paths, which occasionally led to brawls and riots. See, for example, the **Annapolis riots of 1847 and 1853**, **Hibernian Societies riot** (1853) in New York, **New York riots of 1857**, **Marysville, Pennsylvania, riot** (1870), **Vicksburg, Mississippi, killings** (1875), **Hamburgh, South Carolina, massacre** (1876), **Butte, Montana, riot** (1894), and **Boston riot of 1895**.

Another hazard of the celebrations was the risk of eating food that had been left out too long in the hot July sun and the use of inappropriate serving containers such as those made out of lead or copper. See the articles

Lemonade and **Ice Cream** for examples of food poisoning in Harrisonville, Missouri (1881), and Coulterville, Illinois (1886).

Most Independence Day events were held on July 4, but if that date fell on the sabbath, events were typically held on the following day. The years that July 4 fell on a Sunday include 1779, 1784, 1790, 1802, 1813, 1819, 1824, 1830, 1841, 1847, 1852, 1858, 1869, 1875, 1880, 1886, 1897, 1909, 1915, 1920, 1926, 1937, 1943, 1948, 1954, 1965, 1971, 1976, 1982, 1993, 1999, 2004. Readers should be aware that information for events described in these years usually indicates that secular observances were held on the following Monday.

Many towns that were founded on or around the Fourth of July hosted centennial Independence Day celebrations, including Middlebury, Vermont (1866), New Haven, Connecticut (1884), Cincinnati, Ohio (1888), Quincy, Massachusetts (1892), Patterson, New Jersey (1892), Auburn, New York (1893), Kingsville, Texas (1904), Princeton, New Jersey (1913), and Peekskill, New York (1916).

The Fourth of July and its revelry and excitement also provided opportunities for individuals to seek attention for political or social causes or to simply garner personal attention. They did so by making speeches, dressing in costumes for parades and reenactment ceremonies, and performing daring feats. The balloon ascensions and trips over Niagara Falls on the Fourth, for example, drew numerous spectators but often proved fatal. In contrast, the nation's poets, writers, and orators were more sublime. Such personalities as Francis Scott Key, Ralph Waldo Emerson, Charles Sumner, Frederick Douglass, William Cullen Bryant, and John Greenleaf Whittier, among others, produced some of the best and most memorable pieces of America's literary and artistic work related to the Fourth.

Many of the ways the early Fourths were celebrated are still prevalent today — the barbecues, fireworks, parades, speeches, and trips to popular destinations. Some of the practices popular in the past, such as the decoration of homes and buildings with evergreens, the illumination of windows, and the artistically designed set pieces in fireworks displays, have now been replaced with equally appealing visual expressions such as the wearing of colorful T-shirts that exhibit patriotic icons in red, white and blue, and watching fireworks displays complemented by elaborately designed media productions.

Fourth of July celebrations in recent times have been no less poignant than in the past. Events such as the Oklahoma City bombing, the World Trade Center attack and Operations Desert Storm and Iraqi Freedom have weighed heavily on the minds of Americans and greatly affected Independence Day programs, not unlike the way Americans reacted, for example, at the onset of the War of 1812, the Civil War, and World Wars I and II.

THE ENCYCLOPEDIA

Aadne, Arnt A.

Composer of "Hurrah for the Fourth of July: A Song for Every Home in U.S.A. March Song" (Brooklyn: Arnt A. Aadne, 1905) for voice and piano. First line: "The best thriving nation in all the creation is truly said to be ours."

Abolition

Antislavery movement begun in the late 1820s, which gradually gained momentum leading to emancipation at the end of the Civil War. The Fourth of July was an opportunity for those opposing African-American slavery to voice their dissent, if not outrage, regarding its political and moral evils. Many Americans viewed Independence Day as a time for leisure and celebration. The freedoms implied by the celebrations, however, were not extended to African-Americans. The idea of inclusion and identity became a common theme, first expressed by **George Buchanan** in his address before the Maryland Society for Promoting the Abolition of Slavery on July 4, 1791, and later in numerous addresses throughout the first half of the nineteenth century. The Fourth of July also served as a catalyst for antislavery societies to assemble large audiences and to hear well-known speakers call for unification. It was in the Northern states that anti-slavery rhetoric was commonly heard. Key events that helped increase the popularity of the movement included the New York State Assembly's decision to ban slavery from that state, effective July 4, 1827, and the efforts of individuals such as William Lloyd Garrison and Arthur and Lewis Tappan, who established the American Anti-Slavery Society in Philadelphia in 1833, and Frederick Douglass, one of America's most popular orators at that time.

Believing that slavery represented a national tyranny and disgrace, those who spoke out on this issue raised the national consciousness for change and action. Some of these Independence Day orators included Lemuel Haynes, the first African-American to present a Fourth of July oration, in Rutland, Vermont, 1802; Austin Steward and Nathaniel Paul on the occasion of abolition of slavery in New York State, in Rochester, New York, 1827, and Albany, New York, 1827, respectively; William Lloyd Garrison, editor of *The Liberator* and one of the first white speakers to voice antislavery dissent, at Boston's Park Street Church, 1829; Frederick Douglass, "What to the Slave Is the Fourth of July," Rochester, New York, 1852; and Henry David Thoreau, "Slavery in Massachusetts," in Framingham, Massachusetts, July 4, 1854.

Notable meetings were held on the Fourth of July throughout New England and the Mid-Atlantic states. Some of these events included an American Colonization Society meeting in New York City on July 4, 1828; an "Anti-Slavery Society" meeting at the "Chatham Street Chapel," New York City, July 4, 1834; a meeting of the Anti-Slavery Society of Troy, Michigan, at which a set of resolutions called for immediate abolition and emancipation, July 4, 1838; a "Know Nothing Anti-Slavery Celebration," with several speakers, including Massachusetts Senator Henry Wilson, at Abington, Massachusetts, July 4, 1855; a meeting at Shiloh Church in New York City on July 4, 1856, on the occasion of the 28th anniversary of the abolition of slavery in New York, with speaker H.H. Garnet.

Sources: Nathaniel Paul, *An Address Delivered on the Celebration of the Abolition of Slavery* (Albany: John B. Van Steenbergh, 1827); *New York Enquirer*, 4 July 1828; *Evening Post*, 5 July 1834, 2; "A Bright Spot," *Colored American*, 18 August 1838; "In Abington," *Boston Daily Journal*, 5 July 1855, 2; "The Glorious Fourth," *New York Times*, 7 July 1856, 2; "Abolition Fifty Years Ago," *New York Times*, 5 July 1884, 5; James, "The Other Fourth of July," 160.

Acton Library, Saybrook, Connecticut

The Thomas C. Acton Library was dedicated on July 4, 1874. Acton provided the land for the library and was "chiefly instrumental in procuring funds for the erection of the building and in collecting books." The library, which cost $4000, was built on the main street of the town and was situated across the street from Acton's residence. At the ceremony, speeches were given by Jackson S. Schultz, James C. Carter, and George H. Chapman. The Declaration of Independence was read by John Acton, nephew of Thomas C. Acton. Agnes Acton read a poem composed for the occasion by George W. Bungay. The library has since been replaced with a more modern structure.

Source: "The Acton Library," *New York Times*, 6 July 1874, 2.

Adams, Charles Francis (1807–1886)

Younger son of **John Quincy Adams.** This highly regarded politician and historian was an active orator on the Fourth of July. Born in Boston, Adams was a member of the Massachusetts House of Representatives (1841–44) and state senate (1844–45). On July 4, 1843, he presented an oration in Boston's Faneuil Hall which, according to newspaper reports, was exceptional. "We have heard the Oration spoken of, in high terms of praise, by those who are fully competent to decide upon

its merits. It was characterized by strength of language, boldness of thought, and fearless independence. The venerable John Quincy Adams was present, and listened to the discourse of his son, with evident deep feeling and interest." (See also **Mrs. Lydia Howard Sigourney.**) At the onset of the Civil War, Charles resigned from Congress to accept an appointment by President Lincoln as minister to England, a post he held until 1868. According to Kinley Brauer, "Although conservative by nature, Adams led a revolutionary movement in Massachusetts politics in the 1840s, and his contribution to the nation as minister to Britain during the Civil War was brilliant."

Adams gave no less than four additional orations on the Fourth of July: one in Boston (1856) "before members of the schools," the second, an antislavery address, in Fall River (1860), the third in Boston (1872), and the fourth, titled "Progress of Liberty in a Hundred Years," in Taunton, Massachusetts (1876), the latter printed in the *Chicago Tribune* on the following day. The Boston oration received a favorable review in the *Springfield Republican.*

On July 4, 1887, as evidence of his popularity, a year after Adams died, orator William Everett (1839–1910) presented a speech titled "Address in Commemoration of the Life and Services of Charles Francis Adams" at the "Stone Temple" in Quincy, Massachusetts, on July 4.

Sources: *The Atlas*, 6 July 1843; *Springfield Republican*, 6 July 1872; *Chicago Tribune*, 5 July 1876, 3; Kinley Brauer, "Charles Francis Adams," *American National Biography* 1:74–77.

Adams, Charles Francis, Jr. (1835–1915)

Historian, civic leader, soldier, and son of **Charles Francis Adams,** who was an orator active on the Fourth of July. He was born in Boston and graduated from Harvard in 1856. Adams enlisted as a Union soldier in the Civil War and eventually attained the rank of brigadier general. He fought in the battles at Antietam and Gettysburg. After the war, his attention turned to history and he wrote several books, including *Railroads: Their Origin* *and Problems* (1878). His interest in railroads resulted in an appointment to the Massachusetts Board of Railroad Commissioners in 1869 and eventually to the position of president of the Union Pacific Railroad in 1884. It was during this period that he was most active on Independence Day. On July 4, 1872, he spoke in Boston, and his address was printed shortly after by the publishers Rockwell and Churchill. On July 4, 1874, he was in Weymouth, Massachusetts, where he gave a presentation, "Wessagusset and Weymouth, an Historical Address" (printed by the Weymouth Historical Society, 1905), on the occasion of the 250th anniversary of that town. He spoke about the first church there, where Abigail Adams attended as a youngster. His father, Charles Francis, Sr., was in the audience, which "warmly applauded" his speaking abilities.

After 1890 Adams was in Quincy, Massachusetts, devoting himself to various civic affairs. On Independence Day in 1892, on the occasion of the 100th anniversary of the town, he spoke in the First Church there. A newspaper quoted an excerpt of his speech:

> The time will never come when to secure good municipal government all citizens will have to do is to cast a ballot. In Chicago, Philadelphia, New York, Boston, and the other large cities municipal government is not in the hands of the citizens, but in those of interested parties.

Following the oration, a banquet was held at the Robertson House.

Adams' final years were spent as president of the Massachusetts Historical Society (1895–1915).

Sources: "A Town's Two Hundred and Fiftieth Anniversary," *New York Times*, 7 July 1874, 3; "Quincy's Centenary," *New York Times*, 5 July 1892, 1; *Webster's American Biographies*, ed. Charles Van Doren (Springfield, Mass.: G & C Merriam, 1984), 7–8.

Adams, George Washington (1801–1829)

The eldest son of **John Quincy Adams**, who was a member of the class of 1821 at Harvard University. On July 4, 1824, he presented an oration in the family's hometown of Quincy, Massachusetts. Two years later on the Fourth of July, on the occasion of a flag pres-

entation there, an ode he wrote to the tune of "Adams and Liberty" was performed.

Source: *Columbian Sentinel*, 22 July 1826, 1.

Adams, John (1735–1826)

Second president of the U.S. (1797–1800), who argued fervently on behalf of independence at the meetings of the Continental Congress and who was one of three presidents to die on the Fourth of July. Adams was the first significant figure to advocate celebrating the Fourth annually. Born in Braintree, now Quincy, Massachusetts, Adams graduated from Harvard in 1755, wrote articles against the Stamp Act in the *Boston Gazette* (1765) and was a delegate to the 1st and 2nd Continental Congresses (1774–78). He supported raising troops and recommended George Washington as commander of the Continental Army in 1775. After the Congress voted favorably for independence on July 2, 1776, Adams became the first person to acknowledge the importance of celebrating a national anniversary. On July 3 Adams wrote a letter to his wife Abigail expressing his thoughts on the importance of celebrating the occasion and said that he thought July 2 would be the anniversary of American independence celebrated each year:

> The Second Day of July 1776, will be the most memorable Epocha, in the History of America. I am apt to believe that it will be celebrated, by succeeding Generations, as the great anniversary Festival. It ought to be commemorated, as the Day of Deliverance by solemn Acts of Devotion to God Almighty. It ought to be solemnized with Pomp and Parade, with Shews, Games, Sports, Guns, Bells, Bonfires and Illuminations from one End of this Continent to the other from this Time forward forever more. You will think me transported with Enthusiasm but I am not. I am well aware of the Toil and Blood and Treasure, that it will cost Us to maintain this Declaration, and support and defend these States. Yet through all the Gloom I can see the Rays of ravishing Light and Glory. I can see that the End is more than worth all the Means. And that Posterity will tryumph in that Days Transaction, even altho We should rue it, which I trust in God We shall not.

Because the printed July 4 Dunlap edition of the Declaration was the principal one circulated to the states, it was that date and not July 2 that the public and future generations would adopt as the anniversary date. For the next 100 years Adams' letter was reprinted numerous times in newspapers across the country, beginning in the early 1790s, but by a curious turn of fate many of these reprintings, such as in the *National Intelligencer* (1810), *Poulson's American Daily Advertiser* (1839), *New York Herald* (1853), and *New York Times* (1873), had Adams' date that he wrote the letter printed as July 5 and the date Adams designated as the anniversary printed as July 4, the date the public recognized as the anniversary. In 1840, the *National Intelligencer* had printed the correct dates. On July 4, 1860, Edward Everett distinguished between the 2nd and 4th of July. Hon. B.C. Whitman, in his oration presented at Theater Hall in Carson City, Nevada, on July 4, 1876, cited the correct dates. The distinction between the dates was finally laid to rest by John H. Hazelton in his 1906 publication *The Declaration of Independence, Its History* when he declared "the 2d of July and not the 4th therefore was the day upon which America declared her independence."

In 1777 Adams was in Philadelphia for the Fourth and in a letter he wrote to his daughter on July 5 he described the "festivity and ceremony becoming the occasion." He had dinner with other members of Congress after he had visited the frigate *Delaware* with George Washington. The vessel fired a salute of thirteen guns which was answered by "thirteen others from each other armed vessel in the river." Throughout Philadelphia there was "a vast concourse of people, all shouting and hurrahing in a manner which gave great joy to every friend to this country and the utmost terror and dismay to every lurking tory."

An important Fourth for Adams was that in 1778 when he was in Passy, France, with Benjamin Franklin garnering support from the French for the American cause. According to Adams' diary, the two hosted a dinner that day for "the American Gentlemen and ladies, in and about Paris," and was the first celebration of the Fourth of July in continental Europe.

Although Adams' presidency never gained the popularity that Washington's had, nonetheless throughout the years he had a following of those that honored him in song, toasts, and speechmaking. For example, a popular air titled "Adams and Liberty," composed by **Robert Treat Paine, Jr.**, in 1798, was sung on the Fourth in Boston (1834) and Newburyport, Massachusetts (1837).

Adams retired from public life in 1801.

Sources: *National Intelligencer*, 13 July 1810, 3, and 4 July 1840, 3; *New York Herald*, 4 July 1853, 1; *New York Times*, 5 July 1873, 8; *Poulson's American Daily Advertiser*, 4 July 1839, 3; "Mr. Everett's Oration," *New York Times*, 7 July 1860, 1–2; "The Fourth in Carson," *Daily Territorial Enterprise* (Virginia City), 6 July 1876, 1; Charles Warren, "Fourth of July Myths," *William and Mary Quarterly* 2 (July 1945): 237–42; *Diary and Autobiography of John Adams* (Cambridge: Belknap Press of Harvard University Press, 1961); *The Book of Abigail and John: Selected Letters of the Adams Family, 1762–1784* (Harvard University Press, 1975), 142.

Adams, John Greenleaf (1810–1887)

Wrote an ode titled "Up! To the Winds of Heaven" that was sung at a temperance convention, July 4, 1844, on Boar's Head, Hampton Beach, New Hampshire.

Source: broadside (New Hampshire: Samuel Fabyan, Jr., 1844).

Adams, John Quincy (1767–1848)

Sixth president of the U.S. (1825–29), who was extensively involved in Fourth of July celebrations, both as a participant and spectator. Adams was born in Quincy (previously Braintree), Massachusetts, and studied in France and Holland (1778–80). He studied at Harvard, graduated in 1787 at the age of twenty and was admitted to the bar in 1790. He was elected as a U.S. senator in 1803. From 1809 to 1814 he was minister to Russia and from 1815 to 1817, minister to Great Britain. From 1817 to 1825 he served as secretary of state under James Monroe. Adams was elected to the presidency in 1824.

Adams enjoyed attending Independence Day celebrations and listening carefully to orations so as to develop his speaking skills and making notes about these events in his diary. On July 4, 1787, he heard two orations: one at the chapel in Boston, where he heard latter part of Thomas Dawes's oration, and the other at the "old brick meeting house," where he heard John Brooks speaking at the Society of the Cincinnati celebration. In the following year he again heard two orations: Harrison Gray Otis spoke at the "old South meeting house" and William Hull at the old brick meeting house. On Independence Day in 1793 he gave an oration in Boston "at the request of the [town's] inhabitants."

As secretary of state, Adams gave an oration at the Capitol on July 4, 1821. President Monroe was ill and Adams was asked to take his place. Adams read from an original copy of the Declaration of Independence and followed that with an address. He spoke about England and the development of power, rights, and freedom, and the purpose of the Declaration of Independence. His commentary was reviewed by the press, and three pamphlets were issued as responses to his address. In Boston William Spooner's *Review of an Address Delivered by Honourable John Quincy Adams, at Washington, on 4th of July, 1821* (Wells and Lilly) dealt with the content and rhetoric of the speech. In Virginia, three articles written under the signature "Servius Sulpitius" were published in the *Alexandria Gazette* on July 18, 19, and August 8, and were issued in the following year as a separate pamphlet (printed by J. Shaw, Jr.). In New York, a reviewer using the name "Vindex" also issued a pamphlet that was a response to Adam's piece. In an "extract of a letter to the editor of the *Franklin Gazette*," written on July 4, the writer had glowing praise for Adams' oration:

> This day has been celebrated here with great hilarity. Mr. Adams, the Secretary of State, delivered an oration to the most crowded audience I ever saw at the Capitol, except upon an inauguration of President. The Declaration of Independence was read from the original parchment. It is the first time I have seen Mr. Adams in the character of an orator. His expression was energetic, with which his action corresponded; and I think he gave ample satisfaction. Those who predicted that he would show himself a *tame* orator, were greatly and agreeably disappointed.

During his presidency, Adams continued to be active on the Fourth of July, either in hosting dinners at the Executive Mansion, giving orations, or being involved in civic and military parades. In 1825 Adams reviewed military troops in front of the Executive Mansion on the Fourth and then went to the Capitol to hear a reading of the Declaration of Independence and an oration presented by Asbury Dickens, clerk of the Treasury Office. Later he opened the president's residence for two hours of entertainment.

On July 4, 1826, he marched in a parade to the Capitol, where he heard Judge Joseph Anderson read the Declaration of Independence, an oration by attorney Walter Jones and speeches by Secretary of War James Barbour and Attorney General Richard Rush. Adams wrote in his diary that "Jones's oration was ingenious, and far wide from the commonplaces of the day. But he had written it in loose fragments, without much connection, and had not committed it to memory. So he read from his notes, and commented upon them extemporaneously, which made a desultory composition, full of interesting matter, but producing little effect as a whole." About Barbour and Rush, Adams wrote, "Barbour's address was the overflowing of a generous, benevolent, and patriotic heart, respectable even in its inefficiency," and "Mr. Rush spoke also very impressively, and with correct elocution."

One of Adams' favorite predilections were for developing internal improvements that he believed would lead to prosperity and thereby increased national union. In no address was this more evidenced than in his Fourth of July address in 1828 on the occasion of the groundbreaking ceremony for the excavation of the **Chesapeake and Ohio Canal** just above Georgetown. The president began the day by meeting a group of the directors of the C & O Canal Company. Accompanying Adams was his second son John, who was born on July 4, 1803. For the occasion the U.S. Marine Band played a medley of national airs. This was the first time a president played a prominent role in a Fourth of July celebration of such magnitude.

On July 4, 1831, Adams presented an oration in Quincy, Massachusetts. Before his speech, the following "psalm" he wrote specifically for that day was sung there in the church. Adams referred to it in his diary as his "own version of the 149th psalm":

I

Sing to the Lord, a song of praise
Assemble, ye who love his name;
Let congregated millions raise
Triumphant glory's loud acclaim.

From earth's remotest regions come;
Come greet your maker and your King;
With harp, with timbrel, and with drum,
His praise let hill and valley sing.

II

Your praise, the Lord will not disdain;
The humble soul is his delight;
Saints, on your couches, swell the strain;
Break the dull stillness of the night.

Rejoice in glory—bid the storm,
Bid thunder's voice his praise expand;
And while your lips the chorus form
Grasp for the fight, his vengeful brand.

III

Go forth in arms! Jehovah reigns!
Their graves, let foul oppressors find;
Bind all their scepter'd kings in chains,
Their peers with iron fetters bind.

Then, to the Lord shall praise ascend;
Then all mankind, with one accord,

And freedom's voice till time shall end,
In pealing anthems—praise the Lord.

On July 4, 1837, Adams spoke in the meeting house at Newburyport, Massachusetts. According to Adams, his oration "was listened to with deep attention and occasional applause."

Sources: *New York American*, 7 July 1821, 2; *National Intelligencer*, 5 July 1826, 2; *Alexandria Gazette*, 7 July 1828, 3; *Niles' Register*, 16 July 1831, 345–46; *Richmond Enquirer*, 19 July 1831, 4; Charles Francis Adams, ed., *Memoirs of John Quincy Adams*, 12 vols. (Freeport, New York: Books for Libraries Press, 1969); *Diary of John Quincy Adams* (Harvard University Press, 1981).

Adams, Samuel (1722–1803)

Born in Boston, Adams was a Revolutionary patriot, signer of the Declaration of Independence, and second cousin of John Adams (1735–1826). Adams presided over the cornerstone laying ceremony of the Massachusetts State House on July 4, 1795.

Adams was a graduate of Harvard, later working in a brewery business. He became a powerful spokesperson for opposition to the Sugar, Stamp and Townshend Acts (1764–67). He helped organize the Sons of Liberty (1765), created the Massachusetts Committee of Correspondence (1772), wrote the Boston declaration of rights (1772) and played a prominent role in the Boston Tea Party (1773). He served as a delegate to the state convention (1788) where he approved of the ratification of the federal Constitution and in 1794–97 was governor of Massachusetts.

On July 4, 1880, a statue in honor of Adams was unveiled on New Washington Street in Boston. Although there were no outdoor ceremonies, Robert D. Smith presented an oration on "the life and times of Adams" in the Boston Theatre. According to a newspaper report, the statue, now in front of Faneuil Hall, was "the work of Miss Anna Whitney," originally sat on the site of an old well, and stood ten feet high with a lower base of Quincy granite. The entire cost of the memorial was estimated at $10,000. The figure of Adams was described as "represented in the ordinary citizen's dress of the period, standing erect and with folded arms, the artist having seized for the posture the attitude of Adams at the moment of the close of his crowning argument, after the Boston massacre, before Gov. Hutchinson and his Council." Four inscriptions adorn the panels of the pedestal.

Through the years Adams was mentioned occasionally in Fourth ceremonies. On July 4, 1876, at the park in Port Richmond, New York, the orator for the occasion, George W. Curtis, referred to Sam Adams as "the father of the Revolution."

Sources: *Independent Chronicle*, 6 July 1795, as reported in Travers, *Celebrating the Fourth*, 119; "Staten Island Festivities" and "In Memory of Samuel Adams," *New York Times*, 5 July 1876, 10, and 6 July 1880, 1, respectively.

Admiral Nachimoff

Russian cruiser, moored in New York harbor on July 4, 1893, that was gaily decorated with bunting in honor of Independence Day. At 8:00 A.M., she fired a twenty-one gun salute and that evening her decks were "brilliantly illuminated from stem to stern with hundreds of electric lights. On the mainmast were the words, 'Fourth of July,' in letters fifteen feet high."

Source: "Admiral Nachimoff Celebrates," *New York Times*, 5 July 1893, 9.

African-Americans

The African-American heritage has contributed greatly to the history and traditions of the Fourth of July, through parades, speech-making, music, and other revelry. While in the early years attitudes often frowned upon participation of blacks in Fourth of July ritual, especially that which was exclusively reserved for whites, African-Americans gradually took on a more visible, if not prominent, role in Independence Day expression. They brought to the event their own history and experiences of festivals, first, according to Shane White, in "holiday activities organized by their masters" that they imbued "with new life and meanings," and later, when their events became more independently organized affairs. Around 1800 in Boston, blacks were generally left alone to assemble on the common for merriment, but in other cities, as blacks came together to express themselves in music, dance, and dress, their reception was not always favorable. The Philadelphia Fourth celebrations of 1804 and 1805 resulted in blacks and whites clashing on the streets. However, the emancipation of slavery in New York in 1827 helped greatly to provide opportunities for blacks to celebrate and to foster their July 5 counter-celebrations of the 1830s. On July 4, 1827, at the Zion Church in New York, black pastor William Hamilton spoke to a large group made up of New York's black associations, and on the following day several thousand African-Americans marched through the streets carrying banners and singing. In the 1830s as the **Abolition** movement gained momentum, celebrations by blacks increased in number. Many events took on an anti-slavery theme, yet combined that with typical Fourth of July entertainment. In Henrietta, New York, on July 4, 1848, friends of the anti-slavery cause met at the Presbyterian Church and heard speeches and sang antislavery songs.

In the South the African-American contribution to the Fourth following the Civil War was especially significant. Whereas whites expressed little interest in celebrating the Fourth following the surrender of General Lee's forces at Appomattox, the new black "freedmen" celebrations that took place throughout the South played a major role in assuring the Independence Day traditions of former times remained intact. On July 4, 1865, in Raleigh, North Carolina, a large African-American parade that included a brass band processed from Guion Hotel to the "African Church" where those assembled heard speeches and sang songs. In Newbern, North Carolina, on July 4, 1866, a parade hosted a "Freedman's Bureau" wagon "covered with an immense American flag."

Sources: Leslie Maria Harris, "Creating the African American Working Class: Black and White Workers, Abolitionists and Reformers in New York City" (Ph.D. dissertation, Stanford University, 1995); Shane White, "'It Was a Proud Day': African Americans, Festivals, and Parades in the North, 1741–1834," *Journal of American History* 81/1 (June 1994): 13–50; *North Star* (Rochester), 7 July 1848, 2; "The Celebration," *The Daily Standard*, 6 July 1865, 2; *Newbern Daily Times*, 5 July 1866.

Alabama State Capital, Montgomery

The cornerstone of the new capitol building was laid there on July 4, 1846. Now a national historic landmark, the building served as the first capitol of the Confederacy in 1861.

Source: *Charleston Courier*, 16 July 1846, 2.

Alaska

The first organized Fourth of July celebration in this state took place at the major settlement of Sitka on July 4, 1868, seven months after the purchase (18 October) of Alaska from Russia. The program, which included American citizens, Russians, and Native Americans, began in the morning with a mile-long canoe race in the harbor. That afternoon everyone processed to a grove adjacent to the Indian River and heard music and speeches, one by William S. Dodge, collector of the port and mayor of Sitka. Dodge spoke about the importance of the American ownership of the land, events of the last several months, and what the future held. William H. Wood read the Declaration of Independence. Of note in the procession was a young Russian lady dressed to represent the Goddess of Liberty, riding in a fire engine. The ceremony was followed by an artillery salute, dinner, and fireworks.

Alaska celebrated its first Fourth of July as a new state in the union on July 4, 1959. The first official raising of the 49-star flag occurred that day at **Fort McHenry** in Baltimore.

Sources: *Oration by Hon. Wm. Sumner Dodge Delivered at Sitka, Alaska, Saturday, July 4th, 1868*: "Liberty: Her Struggles, Perils and Triumphs" (San Francisco: Alta California Printing House, 1868); Valerie Stubbs Mecutchen, "Alaska's First Star-Spangled Fourth," *Journal of the West* 6/3 (1967): 433–39.

Albany, New York, affray

The capital of New York State was the site of the first death on the Fourth of July caused by political factions with opposing viewpoints. On July 4, 1788, a group of fifty Anti-Federalists who were "marching in procession to a vacant lot in the skirts of its town," burnt a copy of the Constitution. The Federalists who were also marching that day ran into the opposing group. "A general battle took place, with swords, bayonets, clubs, stones, etc., which lasted for some time, both parties fighting with the greatest rage." Some of the Anti-Federalists retreated to the house of Mr. Hilton. The Federalists attacked the house; many were injured and "one poor man, a cooper," was killed by a bayonet. Six Anti-Federalists were injured and twelve Federalists were also hurt.

Years later Fourth of July celebrations in the city had returned to a more tranquil state. On July 4, 1801, 300 spectators gathered peacefully to view 60 militia men, some dressed "in scarlet and mounted on horses of various descriptions," fire off artillery and volleys of small arms. The day ended with a dinner for the volunteers and militia officers.

On July 5, 1886, Albany held its bicentennial celebration amidst artillery salutes and fireworks. The highlight of the celebration was the opening of the Loan Exhibition in the Al-

bany Academy, which consisted of about 4,000 paintings and documents, including, for example, the Dongan Charter (after Thomas Dongan), "the grant of which by the Irish Governor of the Province of New York, on July 22, 1686, to a committee of Albanians composed of Peter Schuyler and Robert Livingston" and "the original draft in President Lincoln's handwriting of the Emancipation Proclamation." (See **Emancipation Proclamation**.) In the "picture gallery" spectators saw the portrait of Peter Schuyler, the first mayor of the city, painted by Sir Godfrey Kneller. As part of the ceremony that day, a bicentennial march composed by Frank E. Greene was performed by the Philharmonic Society, and J. Howard King presented the exhibition to the Citizens' Bicentennial Committee. Albany Mayor John Boyd Thacher accepted the exhibition on behalf of the city. A poem was read by William D. Morange and Leonard Kip delivered the oration.

Sources: *New York Daily Advertiser*, 10 July 1788, 2; *Connecticut Courant*, 14 July 1788, 3; *The Port-Folio* 1/29 (18 July 1801): 229; *New York Times*, 6 July 1886, 1; *Connecticut Courant*, 14 July 1788; *New York Daily Advertiser*, 10 July 1788; Appelbaum, *The Glorious Fourth*, 31; David Waldstreicher, *In the Midst of Perpetual Fetes: The Making of American Nationalism, 1776–1820* (Chapel Hill, N.C., 1997), 91, 93, 103–04.

Alexandria, Virginia, affray *see Mount Vernon*

Alexandria, Virginia, canal

A ground breaking ceremony for the Alexandria branch of the Chesapeake and Ohio Canal took place a mile north of Alexandria on July 4, 1831. The event began at noon with members of the Common Council of Alexandria and various military and civic organizations in attendance. A newspaper reported:

The Civic Escort, was an imposing part of the procession, composed of upwards of sixty citizens, mounted, with blue scarfs, under the command of Dr. Carson. On arriving at the ground designated, the procession formed in order. T. F. Mason, Esq. one of the directors of the Canal, then addressed the large concourse of citizens assembled in an animated speech. At its conclusion, the spade was presented to John Roberts, Esq. Mayor.

Roberts addressed the audience about the importance of the canal for Alexandria's economy:

> [It] will connect us with the interior of the parent State, by the noble waters which irrigate her extensive plains or wash the bases of her magnificent mountains; will open to us an interchange of trade and friendly communication, with the western, part of our neighboring state of Maryland; will lead us by a still water navigation to the sources of the upper Potomac, and finally, as we hope, even in our day, will connect us in commercial relations and social intercourse, with the immense waters of the Valley of the Mississippi.

Sources: *Alexandria Gazette*, 6 July 1831, 3; *Richmond Enquirer*, 15 July 1831, 4.

Allegheny City, Pennsylvania

A square and a half of buildings burned to the ground on July 4, 1874, with an estimated loss of $300,000. The cause was attributed to firecrackers tossed by boys into the carpenter shop of Cresswell and Burgoin. The location of the fire was principally on the west side of Federal Street, between Sampson Street and Marquette Alley, extending back to Arch Street. Three or four buildings on the east side of Federal Street were also totally destroyed.

At one time it was feared that the whole upper part of the city would be destroyed, as the supply of water was limited and a very high wind prevailed, carrying the sparks in all directions, and setting fire to houses two or three squares away. But with the united efforts of the Pittsburg and Allegheny City Fire Departments the flames were brought under control about 7 o'clock in the evening. Over 100 houses in all were destroyed, leaving many families homeless.

Source: "Losses by Fire," *New York Times*, 5 July 1874, 1.

Allen, Henry Watkins (1820–1866)

Governor of Louisiana (1864–65) who had a monument dedicated in his honor on July 4, 1885, at the state capitol. At the occasion Col. T.G. Sparks presented an address. Allen was elected Confederate governor on November 2, 1863, but was exiled to Mexico after the war. He died in Mexico City. His body was later brought back and now rests on the Old State Capitol grounds in Baton Rouge.

Source: *Address by Col. T.G. Sparks on the Life and Civil Services of Gov. Henry Watkins Allen ...* (Baton Rouge: Capitolian-Advocate Book and Job Print, 1885?).

Allied Veterans Association of Pennsylvania

This association dedicated a monument to Camp William Penn, a training camp for "Negro Civil War soldiers," in La Mott, Pennsylvania, on the grounds of the La Mott Community Center, on July 4, 1943. The monument has the engraving "Camp William Penn: 1863–1865. Training camp for colored troops enlisted into the United States Army." No less than eleven regiments were mustered at Camp Penn.

Source: "Program" (16 pp.) published in La Mott in 1943.

Almirante Barroso

This Brazilian cruiser took part in a Fourth of July celebration in New York harbor on July 4, 1892, by displaying a forty-foot American flag. "The vessel was anchored almost in the shadow of the statue [of Liberty], and was the object of much curiosity from the throngs of visitors to the statue."

Source: "Observed by the Navy," *New York Times*, 5 July 1892, 8.

Altoona, Pennsylvania

On July 4, 1882, the first public transportation system, the "City Passenger Railway Company of Altoona, Pa," was begun. The company operated eighteen horse cars, but in 1891 adopted electric service.

Source: History of AMTRAM Web site, <http://www.amtram.org/about/history.htm>.

"America," or "My Country 'Tis of Thee"

Patriotic song with words written by Samuel Francis Smith (1808–1895) in 1831 and first sung at Park Street Church in Boston on July 4 that year. Smith was born in Boston and graduated from Harvard College in 1829. He enrolled in the Andover Theological Seminary in 1830. While engaging in theological studies there he translated German songs for the composer and tunebook compiler Lowell Mason. One of the hymn tunes he selected happened to be a German version of the melody of the British tune "God Save the King." The patriotic German lyrics prompted Smith to write an American patriotic version. "My Country 'Tis of Thee" was inspired in part by a previous song of his, "The Children's Independence Day," which was premiered a year earlier on the Fourth of July. Some of the "America" text was borrowed from that song. The performance of "America" at the Park Street Church in 1831 was given on behalf of the Boston Sabbath School Union by a juvenile choir under the direction of Lowell Mason. The popularity of the song quickly catapulted the piece into the standard patriotic repertoire of the nineteenth century and it became a symbol of American freedom. The tune and text also inspired new lyrics that reflected those that spoke out against the shortfalls of America's political and social ideals. According to Robert James Branham and Stephen J. Hartnett, the song's popularity in various reform and political movements was due to its "musical simplicity, which enables even marginally talented poets to rewrite its lyrics without much efforts, while even the tone-deaf can learn quickly to sing along with its simple tune."

Some of the remarkable early Fourth of July performances of "America" included one at Ganiteville, South Carolina, 1858, sung to the words "Our land with mercies crowned" by the "factory girls" at a ceremony held at the School House; one at Georgetown, D.C., by Wither's Band at a Union Sabbath School celebration in 1858; one at Helena, Montana, 1876, by the Gesang Verein at Court House Square; one at Coney Island, New York, 1880, by a group of 300 men and women, conducted by P.S. Gilmore; one at Philadelphia in 1885, sung by the Veterans of the War of 1812 at the "Old Court House"; and one at the Pavilion in Los Angeles in 1889 by a chorus of 200 children.

Sources: *Charleston Courier*, 8 July 1858, 1; *Washington Evening Star*, 6 July 1858, 2; "1876," *Helena Daily Herald*, 5 July 1876, 3; "A Hot Day by the Sea," *New York Times*, 5 July 1880, 8; "Military Gatherings," *Philadelphia Inquirer*, 6 July 1885, 2; "The Exercises," *Los Angeles Times*, 5 July 1889, 2; Branham and Hartnett, *Sweet Freedom's Song: "My Country 'Tis of Thee" and Democracy in America.*

"America the Beautiful" *see* Bates, Katharine Lee (1859–1929)

American Association for the Recognition of the Irish Republic *see* Irish-Americans

"American Fair"

Phrase frequently used to represent women in toasts presented at Fourth of July dinners, collations, and other ceremonies during the eighteenth and nineteenth centuries. Although women were typically excluded from association ceremonies and dinners, they nonetheless held a special place of reverence, as men toasted them for their virtue, knowledge, and understanding. Toasts to women were typically presented last, and thereby as a tribute, in an often long and time consuming ritual of offerings. Although the "American Fair" were depicted, as one might expect, by men as important role models where home and hearth were concerned, for example, "The American fair — Always lovely, but more so when decked with homespun" (Richmond, 1810), male expectations about women often went far beyond that. Considerable evidence can be gleaned from these toasts as to the role of women in a typically male-dominated society and the fact that their virtue and honor were held in such high regard. Toasts show how women served as an inspiration for men and that men had high expectations regarding their judgment: "The American fair — May their charms be the incentive to virtue and their smiles its rewards" (Washington, 1803) and "The American fair — may they never give their hands but with their hearts, and their hearts never be given to traitors" (St. Louis, 1809). Other similar phrases used to represent women included "Daughters of Columbia" and "Daughters of America." Occasionally appropriate instrumental music was provided after the toast was offered. For example, at the Mathews, Virginia, Court House celebration on July 4, 1831, following a toast to "The

American Fair" at the dinner that afternoon, the popular tune "Come Haste to the Wedding" was played.

"The American Fair" as a topic of discussion in orations was far less common than their tributes in toasts. William Gibson, speaking in Augusta, Georgia, on July 4, 1856, closed his oration "with a touching tribute to the influence of woman in every noble cause, and a belief, that it would have a potent effect in cheering the sons of America in their struggle to maintain intact the liberties of their beloved country." See also **Women and the Fourth of July.**

Sources: *Maryland Herald, or Hager's-Town Weekly Advertiser*, 18 July 1810, 3; *National Intelligencer*, 6 July 1803, 3; *Missouri Gazette*, 12 July 1809, 2; *Richmond Enquirer*, 15 July 1831, 3; *Chronicle and Sentinel*, 6 July 1856, 2.

American Federation of Labor (AFL) building, Washington, D.C.

Dedicated on July 4, 1916, with President Woodrow Wilson presenting a speech at the ceremony there. The AFL was founded on December 8, 1886, in Columbus, Ohio, and Samuel Gompers was elected its first president. For the Washington celebration, 10,000 union workers paraded and Wilson said he was pleased with the results of the labor movement and the new building. "I am going to take the liberty of dedicating it to the thing I believe in most — the accommodation of the interest of various classes in the community by means of enabling those classes to understand one another and to cooperate with one another," he said.

Source: "Wilson Advises Calm Counsel," *New York Times*, 5 July 1916, 1, 3.

"American Festival"

A popular phrase and theme used for describing a Fourth of July celebration. "American Festival" was first used by the editor of the *Pennsylvania Gazette* in reference to the event held in Alexandria, Virginia, on July 4, 1793. Washington attended this celebration, which was held at John Wise's hotel. On display there was a cap of liberty with a canvas below that had a stanza of "O Liberty! Thou Goddess, Heavenly Bright" painted on it. A newspaper reported that "the presence of our distinguished and highly revered citizen, the president of the United States, gave an exquisite sublimity to the enjoyment."

During the 1990s, the phrase "American Festival" was used as the theme for the annual celebration held in San Jose, California, at the downtown Guadalupe River Park. That event was begun in 1991 and typically drew major headliners for concerts that represented the nation's diverse cultures. In 1994, for example, the salsa fusion Calenco band Sol y Luna performed as well as Cameroon-based Bikutsi rock band Les Tetes Brulees, which provided African music after the *Mercury News* fireworks show. In 2001, California governor Gray Davis spoke at the America Festival (sponsored by Calpine, an energy company), and pledged to "keep the lights on," a reference to the recent energy crisis that had plagued California. "Davis was introduced by Calpine chief executive Peter Cartwright — whose multimillion-dollar stock option cash-in made news last month — and San Jose Mayor Ron Gonzalez, who unsuccessfully opposed Calpine's planned 600-megawatt Metcalf Energy Center in Coyote Valley." On July 4, 2006, an "American Festival" was held inCenterville, Ohio.

Sources: *Pennsylvania Gazette*, 17 July 1793; Peter Stack, "Have a Blast," *San Francisco Chronicle*, 3 July 1994, 31; Suzanne Herel, "Davis Lauds California Generator," *San Francisco Chronicle*, 5 July 2001, A2; *Akron Beacon Journal*, Ohio.com, 21, March 2006.

American Indians *see* Native Americans

American Protective Association *see* Butte, Montana, riot

American Pyrotechnics Association (APA)

The APA is the leading trade association of the fireworks industry and supports and promotes safety standards for all aspects of fireworks. It has a diverse membership including regulated and licensed manufacturers, distributors, wholesalers, retailers, importers and suppliers of fireworks, and professional display firms. Additional information about the fireworks industry, facts and figures, the history of fireworks, and state laws can be found on APA's Web site at <*www.americanpyro.com*>.

American Revolution Bicentennial Commission

Established on July 4, 1966, through an act signed by President Lyndon Johnson. See **Bicentennial**.

American Revolution Society

A patriotic society in Charleston, South Carolina, that met annually on the Fourth of July from the 1790s to 1833. One of the first reported meetings occurred on July 4, 1794, when noted speaker **David Ramsay** gave an oration. Members typically assembled at the Carolina Coffee-House or William's Coffee House and paraded to St. Michael's Church where a "Divine Service" was held which usually included the presentation of an oration. The society followed the service with a meeting and dinner at the coffee house. Frequently the services held at St. Michael's Church were shared with other organizations, usually the State Society of the Cincinnati. In 1831 and 1832, in addition to the Revolution Society and the Cincinnati, the State Rights and Free Trade Party, '76 Association, and Young Men's Free Trade Association were present. From 1801 to 1832, under the sponsorship of the Revolution Society, at least 12 orations were published by local printers. In later years, meetings were held in other places, including Mr. Fayolie's Room. In 1833 the American Revolution Society merged with the '76 Association and was renamed the Whig Association, a nullification anti-Jackson organization.

Sources: *Columbian Herald*, 2 July 1794, 4; see *Charleston Courier* for years noted.

American Wind Symphony Orchestra

This world famous wind orchestra gave its first British concert on July 4, 1961, performing from a barge on the Thames River. Among the works performed was *Fanfare for the Common Man* by American composer Aaron Copland. Robert Austin Boudreau founded the orchestra.

Source: *New York Times*, 5 July 1961, 30.

"Americanization Day"

A national program organized in 1915 by the editors of *Immigrants in America Review* magazine with assistance by Frederic C. Howe, commissioner of immigration at Ellis Island, to foster a better understanding of the diversity of the races in the United States through Fourth of July programs. "If American ideals and purposes and opportunities are to be fully realized, the barriers that separate the newly naturalized citizen from the native born must be swept aside." Through a National Americanization Day Committee, cities across the country were encouraged to offer on Independence Day "Citizenship Receptions" and other programs that included "appropriate exercises in honor of our naturalized fellow-citizens and declarants." Howe addressed letters of encouragement to the mayors of American cities.

"Americanization Day" became the theme for many major Independence Day celebrations that year. In Kansas City, Missouri, 220 new citizens sang "America" and other patriotic songs. No less than "nineteen nationalities were represented among the new citizens." In St. Louis, events included speeches by Governor Elliot Woolfolk Major, ex-governor David R. Francis, and Speaker Champ Clark of the House of Representatives and one of the founders of the American Legion. Clark explained the meaning behind being an American citizen and cautioned, "Remember that no man can bear allegiance to two countries at the same time."

Sources: "Make the Fourth of July, 1915, 'Americanization Day,'" *American City* 12 (June 1915): 492–93; "Clark Asks Loyalty of New Americans" and "New Citizens Celebrate," *New York Times*, 5 July 1915, 14.

André, Major John (1750–1780)

British military officer who, during the Revolutionary War, was captured as a spy by three American militiamen and later executed at Tappantown, New York. At Tarrytown, New York, on July 4, 1853, a monument to the men who captured André was dedicated. James T. Brady was the chief orator and spoke about captors John Paulding, David Williams and Isaac Van Wart. Included in the event was an address by James C. Hamilton, son of Alexander Hamilton, a parade made up of militia representing various New York towns, and music by Dodworth's Band. At Tappan-town on July 4, 1876, after an oration presented in the Dutch Church where André stood trial and was condemned, the old Stone Tavern where he was imprisoned "was thrown open to the public by D.R. Stylens, the proprietor." See also **War of 1812.**

Sources: *New York Herald*, 6 July 1853; "The Celebration at Tarrytown — Monument to André," *New York Times*, 6 July 1853, 2; "Independence Day Elsewhere," *New York Times*, 5 July 1876, 5; James Thomas Flexner, "John André," *Encyclopedia Americana* 1: 821–22.

Annapolis riots of 1847 and 1853

On July 4, 1847, a riot occurred at Annapolis, Maryland, caused by a group of individuals that arrived aboard a steamship from Baltimore and whose final destination was St. Michaels on the Eastern Shore. Aboard were various military companies, their musical bands, and plenty of alcohol. The crowd of persons was so great that the captain decided not to risk crossing the bay, especially because of the presence of women and children. A local newspaper described what happened:

> He puts into Annapolis for safety. By the time of the boat's arrival there, many of the passengers are drunk and leave the boat looking for other sources of amusement. Liquor is found there, as elsewhere, and fresh potions are taken by those who "seek strong drink." Gardens are entered by rowdy feet, and what is not unsparingly and rudely "appropriated," is trampled under foot. Oaths and obscenities are heard on all sides. Fights are had in the open streets. The whole village becomes a scene of uproar and confusion, alarm and terror!
>
> When the Baltimoreans attempted to reboard the boat, brickbats and brandy bottles follow in angry exchange, accompanied by shouts of vengeance. Presently women and children are struck by the missiles, and seriously injured. Rifles are jerked and fired by infuriated husbands and fathers and brothers. Their balls take effect, and a number are wounded, some severely!

As the vessel departs, she was grounded "because of the hurried and confused attempt at departure. Some Annapolitans bring a cannon to the shore to fire upon the ship, but several men intercede and the cannon is not fired."

Another similar riot occurred on July 4, 1853, when approximately 500 citizens of Baltimore went on an excursion to Annapolis. They traveled on the steamer *Powhatan*. A "row" occurred between them and a group of Annapolitans, the latter firing muskets into the *Powhatan*. Two persons were killed, one from Annapolis, the other from Baltimore. Several others were injured.

Sources: *The National Era* 1/28 (15 July 1847), 3; *Washington Evening Star*, 5 July 1853, 3.

Annapolis Ugly Club

On July 4, 1808, the Ugly Club met "at Mr. Coolidge's to celebrate the day." The members of the group "of several years standing" numbered sixteen men, "as ugly … as have lived since the days of Thersites." It was reported that "his ugliness the president, and his homeliness the vice president, with the respective members, arranged in official order, sat down to an elegant dinner." They drank 17 toasts to varied recipients, including "The President of the United States — Ugliness no obstacle to an advancement to a high preeminence among our fellow citizens." Other toasts included one to the legislature of Maryland, "May it become a political ugly club," and one to the club members' female counterparts, ""Our sisters in ugliness — May they raise a generation worthy of them." For the occasion one of the members wrote and sang a song to the tune "Mason's March."

> (First stanza)
> Tho' the masons declare,
> They can tell to a hair,
> By a touch of the finger each other;
> And boast that they own,
> Some secret unknown,
> Which none can e'er learn but a brother.
> Yet no signs do they know,
> Half so certain I trow,
> As that which distinguishes this Sir;
> For in each member's face,
> There's some — ugly place,
> Which no man with his eyesight can miss, Sir.

Source: *Lady's Weekly Miscellany* 8/11 (7 January 1809): 167–68.

Annunzio, Gabriele D' (1863–1938)

This Italian poet wrote the poem "To America in Arms," for the Fourth of July in 1918.

Source: "All Italy Honors Our flag," *New York Times*, 5 July 1918, 9.

"Anthems" for the Fourth of July, 1842

Three anthems were performed at the Fourth of July celebration in Boston in 1842. The first lines, respectively, are: "For thee, my native land, for thee"; "For freedom, honor, and native land"; and "God bless our native land." The latter anthem was translated from German by Charles Timothy Brooks (1813–1883), John Sullivan Dwight (1813–1893), and William Edward Hickson (1803–1870).

Source: broadside, "Order of Exercises at the Celebration of the Sixty-Sixth Anniversary of American Independence ..." (Boston: J.H. Eastburn, 1842).

Anthony, E. (fl. 1855–1860)

Merchant and popular photographer located at 308 and later 508 Broadway who sold "instantaneous views" of places in New York City and elsewhere. At least three scenes of the Fourth of July were available for sale including "The Regatta, July 4th, 1859," "View of the Police on the Battery, July 4th, 1859," and "The Regatta, July 4, 1860." Anthony advertised that he photographed "objects in rapid motion" and that they "are depicted as sharply and distinctly as if they had been transfixed for the purpose."

Source: *Harper's Weekly*, 10 September 1859, 592.

"Appeal for Liberty"

A speech on suffrage written for the July 4, 1915, celebration in New York by Mrs. Carrie Chapinan Catt and Mrs. Charlotte Perkins Gilman. The "Appeal" was publicly read several times that day, at least once by British-born actress Margaret Wycherly at the Statue of Liberty, once at Claremont, another at Columbus Circle and no less than four more instances in a suffrage parade down Riverside Drive.

Five suffrage organizations of New York City — the New York State Woman Suffrage Party, the Collegiate League, the Woman Suffrage Party, the Equal Franchise Society, and the Men's League — had met to demonstrate on behalf of women's suffrage. The "Appeal" was signed by the heads of the five suffrage organizations. Margaret Wycherly, dressed as a Goddess of Liberty at the Statue of Liberty, spoke about "political discrimination against women." Addressing the men of New York, Wycherly read aloud:

> We therefore appeal to you, in the name of justice and fair play, for relief from the intolerable position in which we are placed.
> We protest that no Government is just which taxes and governs half its people without their consent.
> We protest that no government is efficient which is guilty of so absurd a discrimination as that of putting a vote in the hand of male paupers and denying that privilege to at least a third of its taxpayers; of counting the opinion of illiterate males, and denying that count to the 41,000 women, teachers of the State.
> We protest that no Government is sound which pretends to secure the highest welfare to its people, yet pays no heed to what half its people want.
> We protest that no Government is logical which elevates half its people regardless of qualifications to sovereignty and condemns the other half to political subjection.
> Justice gave you the vote. In the name of that same great virtue, we ask you to give it to us!

Later that day members of the group met near Claremont to hear Wycherly's reading of the "Appeal" followed by May Peterson, draped in an American flag, singing the "Star-Spangled Banner." The group paraded along Riverside Drive. A Liberty Float was drawn by four white horses, "bearing the Goddess of Liberty (Miss Wycherly).... At the head of each horse marched a woman in white with a palm branch. They were four women sculptors of the city. The posing of the women on the Liberty Chariot was done by Miss Janet Scudder, the sculptor." Included in the march were a number of men, a military band of twenty pieces, and "Mrs. Alice Burke and her yellow suffrage automobile."

Source: "Women Ask Votes at Liberty's Feet," *New York Times*, 6 July 1915, 9.

"Appeal for Peace"

On July 4, 1861, at the onset of the Civil War, a broadside was printed by the "Women of Maryland" and "sent to Lieut. Gen. [Winfield] Scott" calling for an end to national hostilities. The appeal mentioned the opposing officers as the "sons of your training" and the "comrades of your battles" and said that "the petty spirit of party jealousy" must be cast aside. "Can the emblazoned record of any victory confer a greater glory than this legacy of Peace?" they asked. The women, in claiming "no distinction in party broils," claimed their natural rights of not having their husbands, sons, and brothers "torn from our homes, and incarcerated in the decaying atmosphere of a military prison, each day taking from us all that supports life! We implore you by all you value in Time's great Past, or hope for in unwritten Future, to stay the sorrows of our souls!"

Source: *An American Time Capsule*, Library of Congress Web site.

Apprentices' Library, Brooklyn, New York *see* Lafayette, Marquis de

"Aquafest"

Popular name of Fourth of July celebrations used by towns near bodies of water. One of the earliest Aquafest Independence Day celebrations occurred in Rice Lake, Wisconsin, in 1964. It was reported that Jack Moullette coined the term. On July 4, 2001, an Aquafest celebration took place in Tampa, Florida. The Florida Aquarium hosted the event, billed as "a celebration of America's birthday and a salute to Florida's seafood industry and marine resources."

Source: Lea Iadarola, "Aquafest is Tampa's New Fourth Fete," *St. Petersburg Times*, 28 June 2001 (Week End Online).

Armory, Brooklyn, New York

The cornerstone of this building at the corner of Pineapple and Henry Streets was laid on July 4, 1858. Present at the ceremony were the mayor of New York and other major dignitaries. The stone was described by a local reporter as a "brown one, two feet square, containing the contents of the old one, the Records of the City, the names of all the city and county officers, newspapers of the day, Bible, etc. etc." After the ceremony, the participants and spectators went to the City Hall

to hear a reading of the Declaration of Independence, followed by an address by Henry Ward Beecher. Beecher spoke about the original armory, whose cornerstone was laid with Lafayette present. "Lafayette," he said, "was there — one of the few men whom now we could all afford heartily to praise — not his head at the expense of his heart, nor his heart at the expense of his head, but the whole man — head, heart and all. He was a man who stood with Washington, and whose name it was a pleasure to associate with his."

In 1930, the armory was torn down and workmen discovered the armory cornerstone, which contained records indicating that the cornerstone "had previously been used for the foundation of the Apprentice's Library, located on the site of the armory." Other items included "a small piece of cable, patterned after that which was to span the Atlantic," various city records, the by-laws of the Poached Egg Club and Pastime Baseball Club, "a steel engraving of President James Buchanan," and a copy of the Brooklyn City Charter. With the armory being dismantled, according to a newspaper report, the cornerstone was to be used again in a "modern apartment building" which was planned on the site. See also **Lafayette, Marquis de**.

Sources: "The Celebration in Brooklyn" and "Unearth Records of Early Brooklyn," *New York Times*, 6 July 1858, 1, and 12 October 1930, 28, respectively.

Army of the Potomac Society

Formed on July 5, 1869, in New York City, this society met occasionally on the Fourth of July. The officers of the society met at Steinway Hall during the morning and elected General Philip Henry Sheridan (1831–1888), a distinguished Union officer, as president. That evening the society convened its first meeting, with Sheridan presiding over 400 attendees. Participating was a prominent group of military officers, with no less than 27 generals, including George B. McClellan (1826–1885), George Meade (1815–1872), and **Ambrose E. Burnside**. Also present was Admiral David Glasgow Farragut (1801–1870). The orator was General Joshua L. Chamberlain, governor of Maine. He spoke about the

Army of the Potomac and said, "the bravery it had displayed, the hardships it had undergone, the battles it had fought, the victories it had won, were themes to which justice could never be done." Chamberlain complimented General Ulysses S. Grant, "the mention of whose name was loudly cheered." He ended his speech saying that "the oft-quoted phrase may be repeated with truth, 'All quiet on the Potomac.'" On July 3–4, 1890, the society met in Portland, Maine. The initial ceremony took place at city hall. Speakers included **Hannibal Hamlin**, Gen. **William Tecumseh Sherman**, and Gen. F.A. Walker. Walker presented a touching address about the past days of glory that were past and gone. "Yes comrades, our stay is over," he said. "Mustered out of service, enfeebled by years, disabled by wounds, we are no longer to be counted even among the military reserves of the country. Another war, should it occur, would have to be fought by younger and stronger hands than ours." Society members also reviewed a parade that day that included 700 men from naval vessels and other military units from Lincoln Park, and in the afternoon they gathered at Little Chebeague Island for a clambake and additional entertainment.

On July 4, 1891, members of the Army of the Potomac were in Buffalo celebrating. There was a grand parade through city streets ending at the Soldiers Monument at Lafayette Square, followed by a banquet at Music Hall.

Sources: *New York Times*, 6 July 1869, 1; "A Comparison of Armies" and "Army of the Potomac," *New York Times*, 4 and 5 July 1890, 1 and 2, respectively; "Army of the Republic," *New York Times*, 5 July 1891, 2.

Arthur, Chester A. (1830–1886)

Twenty-first president of the U.S. (1881–85). Arthur seemed to avoid the boisterous Independence Day celebrations. He was born in Fairfield, Vermont, and graduated from Union College in 1848. He served in the Civil War as a quartermaster and later was elected vice president under James Garfield. He became president after the death of Garfield in September 1881. On July 4, 1885, Arthur went to New York City to stay at the Fifth Avenue Hotel. According to a newspaper report, "he made the trip now because he could be away from the capital better on the Fourth of July than earlier, as he had been very busy."

Source: "The President in Town," *New York Times*, 3 July 1883, 8.

Artillery accidents

The practice of using artillery for providing Fourth of July salutes became a serious problem after the Revolutionary War had ended. By the 1790s as Fourth of July celebrations increased across the country, many of the old Revolutionary guard who had been called on to discharge the cannons had forgotten the drills that were necessary to fire them safely. In addition, adding to the risk of serious accidents, many of the cannons may not have been properly maintained over the years. Some of the men participating in town rituals may have already toasted heavily on the day of celebration, and alcohol combined with poor judgment frequently resulted in tragic results. It was not uncommon that scores of persons each year lost limbs and had other injuries while others lost their lives. One of the earliest instances of a tragic ending to an artillery salute occurred at Fort Constitution in Portsmouth, New Hampshire, on July 4, 1809. According to a local newspaper, "Two chests of powder, and a number of loose cartridges, which were placed near, took fire." The explosion wounded or killed between fourteen and twenty soldiers and citizens, "besides doing much other essential damage." By the 1820s artillery accidents had become so acute that in New York in 1827, for example, it was reported by a journalist that "so many sacrifices of lives and limbs are calculated to turn a day of rejoicing into one of mourning."

Many of the reports of accidents describe in some detail how the accidents occurred. For example, in Whitehall, Vermont, on July 4, 1823, "a man had both arms blown off" by the discharge of a cannon. It is said that in his zeal to keep up the "roar of artillery" in commemoration of the days when powder was not thrown away, he attempted to re-load the piece, at the "very moment when the match was touched to the last charge.'"

On July 4, 1827, in Wilmington, Delaware, it was reported that

[t]wo young men, who assisted in firing the cannon, and were actually engaged in ramming down the cartridge, when the gun accidentally went off, were dreadfully torn and bruised; one of them, Mr. Brady, had a large wound made in his forehead, one side of his face taken off, and a part of his breast taken away. The other, a Mr. Hyatt, had his right hand literally torn to pieces (and has since undergone amputation of the arm) besides other wounds — for the former there is very little hope of recovery; the latter, should the weather keep cool a few days it is expected will recover, but the loss of his right arm will be likely to render his remaining days extremely painful.

On July 4, 1837, at the Northampton, Massachusetts, Woolen Factory, a keg of powder held by an individual exploded, severely injuring twelve persons, while on that same day in Annapolis, Maryland, two persons were injured, one losing his arm, when a cannon exploded during the morning artillery salute.

On July 4, 1850, in New Haven, Connecticut, the celebration there was marred by this tragic artillery accident:

A young man named George Palmer, was mortally wounded by the explosion of a cannon on the morning of the 4th. The piece was loaded up to the muzzle, and a slow match applied; but as it did not go off so soon as expected, the unfortunate man stepped up close to it, and when in the act of applying a lighted match to the priming, the piece exploded and a large fragment of it struck his leg. Dr. Jewett was at once summoned, who amputated the leg and did everything possible to alleviate the sufferings of young Palmer, but after lingering in great distress during the day and following night, he expired on the morning of the 5th.

The Molly Stark Cannon with members of the New Boston Artillery Company. This cannon was captured on August 16, 1777, at the battle of Bennington, Vermont, by American troops under the command of General John Stark. The cannon, cast in Paris, France, has been under the care of the citizens of New Boston, New Hampshire, for generations, and is fired annually on the Fourth. Photograph (July 4, 2004) courtesy of Lisa A. Cramb, with permission of Brent Armstrong, New Boston Artillery Company.

After the Civil War, injuries and deaths from artillery firings gradually diminished on the Fourth as cannons were withdrawn from use and others left in disrepair.

Sources: *New Hampshire Gazette*, 11 July 1809, 3; *Poultney Gazette*, 9 July 1823, 3; *Frederick-Town Herald*, 21 July 1827, 3; *Poulson's American Daily Advertiser*, 11 July 1837, 3; *New York Herald*, 6 and 7 July 1850, 1 and 1, respectively.

Artillery salutes

An important component of Fourth of July celebrations that began shortly after the signing of the Declaration of Independence on July 4, 1776. Cannons and artillery salutes were at first a symbolic representation of the new and unified nation. The firing of artillery was ceremonial and was commonly heard in many towns at sunrise to signal the start of the holiday. Artillery was not only occasionally fired at noon, but also a volley often sounded the conclusion of the day's events. Towns situated on major ports enjoyed the sound of salutes fired from ships moored in harbors. In Philadelphia's first Fourth celebration in 1777, thirteen cannons were fired in honor of the new thirteen states by each of the ships and galleys in the adjacent waters. Throughout the day there were "triple discharges of cannons." On July 4, 1801, the American frigate *Boston* moored in the harbor fired an artillery salute in honor of the day while on that same day a frigate in the Potomac River fired salutes in tandem with celebratory toasts being drunk at a dinner held there.

George Washington had inspired his troops on July 4, 1778, when, from his headquarters in Brunswick, New Jersey, he ordered a thirteen-piece artillery salute followed by "a single Cannon which will be a signal for a running fire to begin on the right of the Army and be continued to the left with Musquetry and Cannon." The Continental Congress also encouraged the tradition of using artillery at Independence Day ceremonies in Philadelphia when, in 1785, it resolved by order that on July 4 "two cannon with apparatus for firing salutes" be furnished for the purposes of conducting appropriate salutes in support of the dinner for fifty persons at the "coffee house."

Some individual cannons have been closely connected with the Fourth of July. For example, a new cannon with the word "Federal" inscribed on it was presented to the Federal Society in Carlisle, Pennsylvania, as a symbolic gesture for the ratification of the Constitution. The new cannon was cast in Carlisle, Pennsylvania, by Michael Ege's furnace and was used to accompany the presentation of ten toasts given at Letart Springs by Federalists on July 4, 1788.

Occasionally there were 100-gun salutes, the earliest reported occurrence having been on July 4, 1815, at the cornerstone ceremony for the Washington Monument in Baltimore. Most of the 100-gun salutes occurred, however, at a number of 1876 centennial celebrations. One of the early instances of artillery being fired with the singing of a national anthem occurred in Boston on the Common in 1858 when the "Light Artillery" heightened the effect during the singing of "Hail Columbia."

Occasionally old cannons were brought back into service especially for Independence Day ceremonies. On July 4, 1891, in Newark, New Jersey, a cannon used in the War of 1812 was fired, and in recent years the Revolutionary War "Molly Stark" cannon fired annually at the New Boston, New Hampshire, celebrations. After the Civil War, artillery firings on the Fourth gradually diminished as cannons were either withdrawn from use or left in disrepair.

Sources: *Virginia Gazette*, 18 July 1777; *Pennsylvania Packet*, 14 July 1778; *Carlisle Gazette*, 9 July 1788, as reported in Appelbaum, *The Glorious Fourth*, 31; *New-England Palladium*, 3 July 1801, 3; *National Intelligencer*, 6 July 1801, 2; *Frederick-Town Herald*, 15 July 1815, 3; "Massachusetts," *New York Times*, 6 July 1858, 2; *New York Times*, 4 July 1891, 2; *The Writings of George Washington from the Original Manuscript Sources, 1745–1799*, ed. John C. Fitzpatrick (Washington: Government Printing Office, 1934), 12:154–55; *Journals of the Continental Congress, 1774–1789*, 29 June 1785, 485–86 as reproduced in *American Memory: A Century of Lawmaking, 1774–1873* Web site.

Atchison, Kansas

On July 4, 1854, Senator David R. Atchison and some Platte County friends dedicated this town.

Source: Hennig Cohen and Tristram Potter Coffin, eds., *The Folklore of American Holidays*, 3rd ed. (Detroit: Gale, 1999), 278.

Atlantic and St. Lawrence Railroad

The groundbreaking ceremony for this railroad, also known in the early years as the Portland and Montreal Railroad, occurred on July 4, 1846, at a place of close proximity to the town of Portland, Maine. For the occasion, Portland was decorated with American flags and the hotels were full with visitors from far and wide. Following a parade and dinner, the ceremony included "remarks from Judge Prebble, of Portland." The groundbreaking was announced by "the roaring of cannons and the ringing of church bells." Present were Governor Hugh J. Anderson and "members of the Legislature."

Source: "Commencement of the Portland and Montreal Railroad," *Baltimore Sun*, 9 July 1846, 1.

Attucks, Crispus (1723–1770)

One of five American patriots killed by the British in the Boston Massacre on March 5, 1770. Attucks, a former slave, was cited as the first man killed, and this fact was disputed by whites during the nineteenth century. In one instance, a confrontation between whites and blacks occurred on July 4, 1875, and resulted in death and injury (see **Vicksburg, Mississippi, killings**). Throughout the nineteenth century Attucks was honored by African-Americans throughout the country. In Boston, Crispus Attucks Day was celebrated by abolitionists on March 5, 1858, and during the nineteenth century, the patriot was celebrated in verse by anti-slavery poets. Stephen James described Attucks as an important example in the "tradition of American national and racial identity formation." On July 4, 1976, in Philadelphia, Rev. Jesse Jackson recalled the life of Attucks, stating, "Two-hundred years ago when Crispus Attucks was killed, we became free of King George and slaves of George Washington."

Sources: James, "The Other Fourth of July," 1–29; Lawrence Meyer, "America Joyfully Toasts Birth of a Nation," *Washington Post*, 5 July 1976, A14.

Auburn, New York, Centennial

Site for an unusual July 5 Independence Day black protest celebration at Sandford Hall in 1856. Using July 5 as a symbol of protest by African-Americans was generally abandoned by the 1840s. Participants included Austin A. Steward, Jermain Wesley Loguen, Henry Highland Garnet, Lucretia Mott, and Frederick Douglass. On July 2–4, 1893, Auburn celebrated its centennial anniversary of its settlement. Events included "historical sermons," an oration by Jacob G. Schurman, president of Cornell University, a historical address by John W. O'Brien, a military and civic parade 100-gun salute, and fireworks.

Sources: James, "The Other Fourth of July," 161; "Auburn's Centennial Celebration," *New York Times*, 4 July 1893, 8.

Augusta, Maine, State House

The cornerstone of the "New State House" was laid on July 4, 1829. Maine entered the Union in 1820, and the legislature first met in the new State House in 1832.

Source: *Columbian Sentinel*, 15 July 1829, 1.

Austin, Samuel (1760–1830)

Clergyman, president of the University of Vermont who delivered three Fourth of July orations. Born in New Haven, Connecticut, Austin studied law at Williams College and later entered Yale, receiving a degree in 1783. His attention subsequently turned to religion and he pursued theological studies under Jonathan Edwards, son of the elder. From 1805 to 1842 he published a number of sermons, addresses, and books. Some of his writings were politically controversial, for example *A Sermon Preached at Worcester on the Annual Fast, April 11, 1811* (1811) which criticized Thomas Jefferson, and *The Apology of Patriots, or the Heresy of the Friends of the Washington and Peace Policy Defended* (1812) which questioned the political policies of the party in power.

Austin was described as "tall, erect, well-proportioned and courtly in appearance with a face quickly expressive of his emotions, widely informed and with unusual command of language, animated and often vehement in delivery, ... [and] known as one of the ablest preachers of his day." One of his Fourth of July orations was pronounced at Worcester in 1798 (Worcester: Leonard Worcester, 1798); another was delivered at Newport in 1822 (Newport: William Simons, 1822); and yet another was given at Worcester in 1825 (Worcester: W. Manning, 1825?), the latter "before an assembly convened for the purpose of celebrating this event religiously."

Sources: *Appletons' Cyclopaedia of American Biography* (New York: D. Appleton, 1887), 1:120–21; *Dictionary of American Biography*, ed. Allen Johnson (New York: Charles Scribner's Sons, 1928), 1:436–37.

Automobiles

First took part in Fourth of July parades at the turn of the nineteenth century. In Dyersville, Iowa, on July 4, 1899, "horseless-carriages" were in the celebration. An early parade that included automobiles in Washington, D.C., occurred on July 4, 1909, when 100 vehicles decked out in flowers and flags and sponsored by the *Washington Post* newspaper were driven through city streets. The newspaper reported the event as "spectacular."

Sources: *Dubuque Daily Times*, 6 July 1899, 3; "Day Pleases Official," *Washington Post*, 6 July 1909, 2; "Taft for a Sane Fourth," *New York Times*, 6 July 1909, 3.

Ayliffe, James E. (fl. 1860s–1870s)

Bell ringer who maintained the tradition that began annual Fourth of July ceremonies in New York City during the 1860s–1870s by sounding out popular and patriotic tunes using the bells in the steeple of Trinity Church. The Trinity bells were usually rung by Ayliffe at 8 A.M. and again at noon, but these times occasionally varied. Typically, crowds gathered on the church grounds to hear the bells up close. Usually about fifteen tunes were sounded, and their titles were printed in local newspapers. On July 4, 1868, the following melodies were heard in this order:

1. Ringing the chimes of eight bells
2. "Hail Columbia"
3. "Yankee Doodle"
4. "Blue Bells of Scotland"
5. Airs from "Child of the Regiment"
6. "Red, White and Blue"
7. "Evening bells"
8. "On to the Field of Glory"
9. "The Soldier's Return"
10. "Columbia, the Gem of the Ocean"
11. "Spanish Melody"
12. "The Eclipse Polka"
13. Scotch Melody from *Guy Mannering*
14. "The Chimes Quadrile"
15. "Yankee Doodle"

Many of these tunes were selected for performance every year, but occasionally Ayliffe replaced some of these with new and different melodies. On at least two occasions, Ayliffe engaged noted New York composer George F. Bristow to write a new work to be played. In 1864, Bristow wrote a "*Rondo*, with major and minor keys" and in 1865 a "*Grand National Fantasia*, in honor of our great victories." The latter work was made up of arrangements of "Vive l'America," "Bound Soldier Boy," "Old Folks at Home," "Coming through the Rye," "Hail Columbia," and "The Campbells Are Coming," etc. Reports about the ringing of Trinity's bells occurred also in the 1890s. See, for example, "Old Trinity's Bells," *New York Herald*, 5 July 1896, 7.

Balloon ascensions

One of the most popular spectator events on the Fourth of July in the nineteenth and early twentieth centuries. A balloon ascension represented the rise of America as a nation. It was a dangerous sport, often resulting in injury or death to those who participated. The individuals who operated the balloons were considered well educated in the sciences and typically were referred to as "professors." In Buffalo, New York, on July 4, 1870, a balloon ascension was a success. Professor King, accompanied by reporters from the *Commercial Advertiser* and *Boston Advertiser*, flew the balloon, and they landed near Lockport. Another successful flight occurred in Los Angeles, on July 4, 1886, when a "monster balloon" called the *Monitor* was sent aloft with three persons inside. The balloon reached an altitude of 7200 feet and drifted about for over an hour. It finally landed "at the schoolhouse on Richardson's ranch at Glendale."

Others were not so successful. At Ionia, Michigan, near Detroit, on July 4, 1873, Professor Lafontaine of Brooklyn, Michigan, was instantly killed by falling 500 feet from his balloon. "The ropes passed from under the basket, and the Professor came down 100 feet from where he ascended, to the horror of ten or twelve thousand spectators." At the town of

Riverview, Illinois, in 1894, Professor Jones of Bloomington attempted a balloon ascension and parachute fall but that day the wind was blowing strong and the ropes broke, sending the balloon out of control. Jones hung on but later fell out of the balloon, tumbling to the ground 40 feet below. He suffered numerous broken bones and internal injuries.

Sometimes the balloons escaped and were lost. In Chicago in 1855, a balloon ascension by S.M. Brooks took the "aeronaut" up "about a mile." The balloon ran into trouble six miles out and was caught in a telegraph wire, when the car containing Brooks fell to the ground. Brooks offered a reward of fifty dollars for the recovery of his balloon, which "mounted into the heavens like a freed bird."

Some balloon ascensions were carried out at night as was the case in Cohoes, New York, in 1848. Dr. C.F. Goss managed to get his balloon off without mishap and "the people were astonished and gratified at the unusual sight of a balloon ascension by night."

Balloons were commonly decorated and some launched amidst the sounds of music. In 1838 in Salem, Massachusetts, a "grand balloon ascension" was given by Mr. Lauriat, with a background "martial music."

Some balloons never made it off the ground due to excessive weight or unexpected mishaps. In Chicago in 1858, a "monster balloon" called the *Spirit of '76* attempted a liftoff with a heavyset dignitary aboard: "When the time for starting arrived it was found that with all the gas the aerial vehicle would hold, it would not lift the corpulent Doctor higher than the fence." In Hartford, Connecticut, in 1864, a balloon named the "'Stars and Stripes,' which had been undergoing the process of gas-filling on Central row, came in contact with a staging near it, and was badly torn, all the gas escaping."

In addition to the *Spirit of '76* and *Stars and Stripes*, other balloons also had colorful names, such as the balloon named *Young America* that went aloft from the Common in Boston on July 4, 1856, and traveled some 14 miles distant to South Braintree, and the balloon *Comet* that was sent aloft from Pittsfield, Massachusetts, on July 4, 1859.

In 1892 there were three balloon ascensions on the Fourth of July that failed, resulting in the death of two persons. In Boston, George Augustus Rogers of Malden, Maine, and his assistant Thomas Fenton were killed, when their balloon took off from the Common and plunged into the sea off Thompson's Island. A third passenger, Delos E. Goldsmith, a representative of the City Press Association, survived. In Augusta, Maine, a balloon ascension there resulted in aeronaut Madam Patti of Boston nearly being killed when the vessel fell into the Kennebec River. In Waltham, Massachusetts, Frank P. Shattuck's balloon got caught in telegraph wires above the Park Theatre Building. About 10,000 persons saw him pulled from the basket by a group of persons who were watching the spectacle from the roof.

At least two marriages in balloons were reported in newspapers. On July 4, 1883, A.D. Davis of Chicago and Rose Kennedy of Springfield, Illinois, were married in a balloon that was sent aloft in Cleveland. Their "aerial wedding trip" lasted for four miles, after which they safely landed. On July 4, 1890, in Lowell, Massachusetts, Professor J.K. Allen took to the air in his balloon carrying with him Charles G. Stowell and Miss Lottie E. Anderson, "who were married in the presence of upward of 10,000 persons by the Rev. W.W. Downs of Boston. The balloon sailed away in a northerly direction and its landing has not yet been reported."

In the early 1900s interest in balloon ascensions continued. In Bowling Green, Ohio, 8,000 persons witnessed the death of 18-year-old Clarence Crosby who fell 500 feet from his balloon at the Wood County Sunday School Association's picnic on July 4, 1913.

It was common as well to launch unmanned balloons. On July 4, 1829, an illuminated balloon, 15 feet in diameter, was sent aloft. Sometimes a number of small balloons were let go to the delight of the spectators. For example, in New York in 1857, it was reported that rose colored balloons were flown from the roof of City Hall:

At noon one hundred little India Rubber balloons were sent up by the Common Council

Committee, much to the delight of the youngsters as well as of children of a larger growth, attached to each of them was a paper specifying the time and place of its ascent, and persons who discover them in any part of the country are requested to send accounts to the newspaper offices of the time and place of their discovery, the experiment being expected to develope [sic] some interesting facts relative to the currents of air and the conditions by which they are governed.

In New York City on July 4, 1913, paper fire balloons were sent aloft to the delight of spectators. One of the balloons landed on a 100-foot awning over the playground of the Hebrew Orphan Asylum at 136th Street and set it on fire. "The flames illuminated the neighborhood and there was some excitement in the houses surrounding it." Another fire that took place as the result of a "fire balloon" sent aloft occurred on July 4, 1902, in Bar Harbor, Maine. A local newspaper reported, "A burning balloon sailing eastward from one of the summer cottages on the shore ... drifted against a parapet and fell upon the shingle roof" of the Hotel Rodick, a towering 100-foot-high structure with 400 rooms. It was built in 1881 and was once considered "the most famous hotel on the Eastern coast." Fortunately the blaze was limited to the roof and the local fire department extinguished it in time.

At least one piece of music, the "Star-Spangled Banner," was composed to honor the "Aeronaut" Samuel A. King on July 4, 1864. This "National Ode" was signed "H. F. D" and its first line, "Like the bird of our banner I soar on high," was appropriately descriptive.

Sources: *Daily Cincinnati Gazette*, 4 July 1829, 1; *Gloucester Democrat*, 3 July 1838, 2; *New York Times*, 6 July 1857, 2; *New York Weekly News*, 11 July 1857, 1; *Hartford Daily Courant*, 6 July 1864, 2; *Washington Evening Star*, 5 July 1870, 1, and 5 July 1894, 1; *Daily Press*, 6 July 1855, 3; *Washington Evening Star*, 7 July 1856, 1; *Daily Chicago Times*, 7 July 1858, 3; *Pittsfield Sun*, 7 July 1859, 2; *Chicago Daily Tribune*, 5 July 1873, 8; "The Fourth," *Los Angeles Times*, 6 July 1886, 4; "Married in Midair," *New York Times*, 5 July 1890, 1; "Three Balloon Accidents," *New York Times*, 5 July 1892, 1; "Married in the Air," *San Francisco Chronicle*, 6 July 1883, 3; "Fire in Bar Harbor Hotel," *New York Times*, 5 July 1902, 1; "8,000 See Balloonist Killed" and "Great Awning Burns," *New York Times*, 5 July 1913, 2; Arthur H. Masten, *The History of Cohoes, New York, from Its Earliest Settlement to the Present Time* (Albany: J. Munsell, 1877), 110.

Baltimore and Ohio Railroad

The laying of the first stone for the B & O railroad occurred on July 4, 1828, at a spot slightly over two miles from the center of Baltimore. The event began in downtown Baltimore on Market Street, with a procession of city trades with highly decorated coaches, wagons, and floats, all containing tradesmen in their respective costumes. There was a printers' vehicle which "was a beautiful quadrangular Temple, containing a complete Printing establishment, with an elegant Press in operation, issuing copies of the Declaration of Independence." Another car drawn by four horses contained cordwainers "manufacturing a pair of shoes for **Charles Carroll**, of Carrollton," who presided over the ceremony. Yet another vehicle "decorated with green branches of cedar" contained cedar coopers "engaged in the different parts of their occupation — one of them turned a butter churn, and, during the procession, made eight pounds of butter."

At the sight for the dedication was a "handsome canopy" with seating provided for Charles Carroll, the railroad directors, Baltimore Mayor Jacob Small, the city council and invited guests. Also present were numerous members of Masonic lodges representing Maryland, Pennsylvania, Delaware, and Virginia. In a highly ceremonial affair, John B. Morris, a member of the board of directors, spoke about the advantages of the railroad and how it was to be "justly considered a work of national importance." He told his audience that the railroad symbolized the nation's independence and freedom and would "perpetuate the Union of the American states." Shortly after, Carroll, with a "spade" in hand, performed the ceremony of laying the cornerstone. Inside the block was "a glass cylinder, hermetically sealed, containing a copy of the Charter of the Company and a scroll containing the words of the commemoration of the day." After the firing of a national salute, a procession was again formed and returned to the city by way of Pratt Street. Two days later

Harpers Ferry, West Virginia. Master Armorer Benjamin Mills' house (left) was completed on July 5, 1859, and served as the headquarters for various Union officers during the Civil War. The Baltimore and Ohio Railroad advertised excursions on the Fourth that carried hundreds of visitors during the 1880s and after to this town, known for its history and exceptional scenery. Photograph by author.

Carroll sent a note of gratitude to the bookbinders of Baltimore thanking them for an "elegantly bound" book, "containing the Report of the Engineers' Surveys of the B & O Railroad." Carroll wrote, "May the Almighty bless the undertaking and increase the prosperity of Baltimore, of Maryland, and of the U. States."

Another noteworthy event connected to the B & O Railroad was the construction of the 700-foot Thomas Viaduct (named after Philip Thomas of the railroad) at Elkridge, Maryland, which was completed in two years — July 4, 1833, to July 4, 1835. The creation of the B & O Railroad remained dear to the hearts of Marylanders. On July 4, 1900, the *Baltimore Morning Herald* retold the story of the 1828 event and described the exact place where the ceremony for the laying of the first stone took place: "a field two and a quarter miles from town, south of the Frederick Turn-pike road, and near the upper Carroll's Mill on Gwynn's Falls."

Sources: *Alexandria Gazette*, 10 July 1828, 3; "The Fourth of July at Baltimore," *National Intelligencer*, 8 July 1828, 2; "Beginning the B & O," *Baltimore Morning Herald*, 4 July 1900, 8.

Baltimore and Susquehanna Railroad

On July 4, 1832, six miles of the railroad were opened for travel. The cars were drawn by mules until 1833, when mule-power was exchanged for steam.

Sources: "The Fourth of July," *Harper's Weekly*, 7 July 1894; Robert I. Vexler, ed., *Baltimore, a Chronological and Documentary History, 1632–1970* (Dobbs Ferry, N.Y.: Oceana Publications, 1975), 33.

Bandot, Pere Seraphin

The first Fourth of July oration printed in a foreign language was in French and presented by Reverend Pere Seraphin Bandot in Philadelphia on July 4, 1779. According to Stephen Elliot James, the work was an "acclaim of the celebration of God's handiwork, the glorious revolution ... and its promise to much of mankind."

Sources: Seraphin Bandot, *Discours pronounce le 4 juillet, jour de l'anniversaire de l'independence, dans l'Gglise catholique* (Philadelphia, 1779); James, "The Other Fourth of July," 48–49.

Barnum, Phineas Taylor (1810–1891)

Born on July 5, this showman and impresario, born in Bridgeport, Connecticut, moved to New York City and bought Scudder's American Museum and Peale's Museum in 1841. Advertised as Barnum's American Museum, the showman frequently staged elaborate productions on Independence Day, including on July 4, 1856, a performance of the drama *New-York Patriots; or the Battle of Saratoga*, that included "costumes and continental uniforms, thrilling scenes and startling incidents." On July 4, 1853, Barnum was in Norwalk, Connecticut, at Fajrwell's Amphitheatre giving a speech before several thousand persons. The town enjoyed a mile-long parade. Barnum spoke about religious liberty and the free press in America. In 1871 he opened his circus, billed as "The Greatest Show on Earth" and in 1881 established the popular Barnum and Bailey Circus. On July 4, 1893, a bronze statue of Barnum made by Thomas Ball was unveiled in Bridgeport, Connecticut. Starting in the mid-1940s, the City of Bridgeport held an annual P.T. Barnum Fourth of July festival, frequently extending over a twelve-day period or longer and ending on the Fourth of July. At the 1973 celebration Senator Lowell P. Weicker, Jr., was there.

Sources: "The Fourth—The Day at Norwalk," *New York Times*, 6 July 1853, 2, 4 July 1856, 5, and 5 July 1893, 4; Eleanor Charles, "Homespun Parties for the 4th of July," *New York Times*, 2 July 1978, CN1.

Bartlett, Joseph (1762–1827)

Writer, actor, lawyer, and politician whose unusual life and witty, keen, and attention-getting perspectives were reflected in three Fourth of July orations he gave in 1805, 1809, and 1823. Bartlett was born in Plymouth, Massachusetts, and was a graduate of Harvard in 1782. He studied law and taught school and in 1783 moved to London. His escapades there landed him in debtor's prison, but he earned his release by raising funds for a play he wrote and later staged. He returned to America, studied and practiced law in Boston and Woburn, respectively, but earned a reputation as a drunkard, a characteristic he carried most of his life. He moved to Cambridge in the 1790s and served in the Massachusetts House of Representatives from 1799 to 1802. In 1803, Bartlett moved to Saco, Maine, and was elected a state senator in 1804–1805. He lost his seat in 1806 due to his political leanings, and was publicly ridiculed by an editor of a local newspaper. Bartlett sued him and won, the verdict resulting in a prison sentence for the editor, but Bartlett was compelled to leave Maine due to public disfavor caused by his legal actions.

On July 4, 1805, Bartlett delivered an oration in Biddeford, a town located a few miles south of Saco. Although some of his presentation consisted of what his audience expected to hear—for example, praise and gratitude to Washington and Jefferson for making freedom and liberty possible and a statement that the Declaration of Independence was "stampt with the arms of freedom"—much of what he had to say was startling to his audience, as he launched a scathing attack on those persons of both political parties that he "considered as a scourge to any nation." In doing so, his oration reflected his particular Federalist viewpoint; he asked his listeners to vigorously support the Constitution of the United States and to be aware of partisans who "wickedly violated" the nation's charter:

A few unprincipled demagogues, of both political parties of our country, think, they have a right, which the citizens generally do not possess, to kill and make alive at pleasure. They send forth their mandates, like the edict of a Pope, and cursed is the man, who dares to disobey, think or act for himself.... They talk of "liberty and equality"; yet consider the citizens as spokes in the political ladder, by which they may mount to the first offices of government. They inflame the passions of the honest citizens by misrepresentation and direct falsehood, merely that they may rise by the destruction of others.

To Bartlett's credit he called for "liberty of the press" and said that the press must be held "sacred in all free governments." He also asked that agriculture and commerce be supported and that the militia be held in high regard, rather than a permanent standing army. "In war they saved our nation — in peace they secure us from civil discord — they guard us against foreign invasion — they keep from our land that scourge of civilization, that curse of Liberty, a permanent Military Establishment, which have, and ever will, wherever maintained, annihilate every free government."

On July 4, 1809, Bartlett was in Portsmouth, New Hampshire, where he delivered an oration before the Republican citizens there. Bartlett's oration was a slightly reworded version of his 1805 text. To satisfy the citizens of Portsmouth he added the name of John Adams as another patriot to revere, and also included references to James Madison. A newspaper reported on the oration: "The applause with which it was received by a numerous audience testified their satisfaction. Instead of the declamatory rant with which the people are too often insulted on such occasions, the orator noticed, in a cursory manner, the prominent events in our political history, the different administrations of our government, etc. in a language energetic, manly and chaste."

By 1823, Bartlett had moved to Boston. His life was in its decline. His inebriation continued to plague him and he was housed through charity. Nonetheless he was invited to give the Fourth of July oration that year. He spoke at the Exchange Coffee-House Hall on the evening of July 3. The title of his address was "The Fourth of July Anticipated," and he included an "Ode" and two poems, one of which prophetically portended his approaching death and the other, titled "New Vicar of Bray," being a gleeful deference to Boston and local politician Josiah Quincy:

J. Quincy now by all admir'd
Our city's pride and glory;

May He the difference never know,
'Twixt Federalist and Tory.

Barlett's text for this oration was essentially the same as that presented in 1809, except now, in order to bring it up to date, he included references to James Monroe and John Quincy Adams. Bartlett died in Boston four years later.

Sources: Joseph Bartlett, *An Oration Delivered at Biddeford* (Saco, Maine: Weeks, 1805); *New-Hampshire Gazette*, 11 July 1809, 3; Joseph Bartlett, *An Oration Delivered at the Request of the Republican Citizens of Portsmouth, N.Y., on the Fourth July, 1809* (Portsmouth, N.H.: W. Weeks, 1809); Joseph Bartlett, *The Fourth of July Anticipated: An Address, Delivered at the Exchange Coffee-House Hall* (Boston: Ebenezer K. Allen, 1823); William Pencak, "Joseph Bartlett," in *American National Biography*, 2:279–80.

Bartlett, Josiah (1729–1795)

On July 4, 1888, a statue to Bartlett, the first signer of the Declaration of Independence, was unveiled in his hometown of Amesbury, Massachusetts.

The statue was the gift of local citizen J.R. Huntington and stood in Huntington Square, "at the junction of Main, School, and Sparhawk streets." It was described as made of bronze, over 8 feet in height and weighing 1,300 pounds. "It stands on a beautiful pedestal of polished granite, the whole being 21 feet in height. The statue is the work of Karl Gerhardt." The ceremony included a military and civic procession in the morning, a reading of a poem by **John Greenleaf Whittier** by Prof. Churchill of Andover and an oration by Robert T. Davis. Governor Oliver Ames officially accepted the statue on behalf of the state of Massachusetts from the donor.

Sources: *New York Times*, 4 and 5 July 1888, 5 and 4, respectively.

Bates, Katharine Lee (1859–1929)

Educator, writer, and poet who is remembered chiefly for her poem "America the Beautiful," which was inspired, in part, by an excursion to the summit of **Pike's Peak**, **Colorado**, in 1893. Bates was born in Falmouth, Massachusetts, but after the early death of her father, moved to Wellesley, Massachusetts, which became her permanent home for the remainder of her life. She received a degree from Wellesley College in 1880, taught in both public and private schools, and later returned to Wellesley, where she taught English and literature for the next forty years. Bates gained a reputation as a poet and writer, publishing several noteworthy collections of poems, including *The College Beautiful and Other Poems* (1887) and *America the Beautiful and Other Poems* (1911).

Bates is best remembered today for "America the Beautiful," written in 1895 and later set to music composed by **Samuel Augustus Ward** by an unknown individual. The writing of "America the Beautiful" was the result of a tour of America in 1893 that led Bates to Chicago and points west. On July 4 she was in Kansas and wrote in her diary "Fertile prairies" and "A better American for Such a Fourth." On July 22 she was at the summit of Pike's Peak and noted: "Most glorious scenery I ever beheld." She began writing "America," which was later published in three revised versions: the first on July 4, 1895, in the weekly church publication *The Congregationalist*, the second on November 19, 1904, in the *Boston Evening Transcript*, and third and final one in her book *America the Beautiful and Other Poems* (1911). According to Lillian Robinson, "the poem is representative of her style in its adherence to mainstream nineteenth-century poetic conventions — the line of John Greenleaf Whittier, say, over that of Walt Whitman — and in its paired invocation of natural beauty and spiritual or national brotherhood." Through the years "America the Beautiful" was entrenched as a patriotic song, a quasi-national anthem comparable to the "Star-Spangled Banner," and was frequently performed on the Fourth of July.

On July 4, 1993, an "American the Beautiful" plaque was installed on the top of Pike's Peak to commemorate the 100th anniversary of the Bates poem.

Sources: Lillian S. Robinson, "Katharine Lee Bates," *American National Biography* 2:333–34; Lynn Sherr, *America the Beautiful: The Stirring True Story Behind Our Nation's Favorite Song* (New York: BBS Public Affairs, 2001).

Battle of Brandywine

Billed as a great "national drama," this show took place at Purdy's National Theatre in New York City on July 4, 1856.

Source: *New York Times*, 4 July 1856, 8.

Battle of Our Nation

A patriotic production that took place in Chicago in 1899 and was advertised as the "grandest war spectacle."

Source: Bob Kurson, "July Fourth — Then and Now: 1899 Festivities Had Flair Similar to Today's," *Chicago Sun-Times*, 4 July 1999, 13.

Battle reenactments

One of the popular traditions on the Fourth of July, with one of the earliest such events occurring during the Revolutionary War. Reenactments, sometimes referred to as "mock engagements" or "sham battles," assured the public of the capability and readiness of the military and served as entertainments that heralded the patriotic deeds of the citizen soldier. In the antebellum period, the combatants represented were typically the British and Americans. The descriptions of these engagements showed the American soldiers as undaunted and courageous, "winning the battle, in honor of the day." Typically, following a mock battle, participants received the accolades of the spectators and then retired without the least animosity to the local tavern or hotel to share dinner and to drink toasts to the victors. One of the earliest mock battles occurred on July 4, 1779, in Boston, portrayed by the town's militia, commanded by Col. Match. Other regiments that participated that day included Col. Tyler's Independent Company and another company commanded by Captain Davis. According to a newspaper report, the "mock engagement [was] highly entertaining to a vast concourse of spectators." Following the event 100 gentlemen dined in a tent, followed that evening by a display of "rockets, and a variety of curious fireworks."

Another example of a "sham battle" took place on July 4, 1855, at Whippy Swamp, in Prince William's Parish, South Carolina, by local militia troops before an assemblage of spectators. "The spirit of '76 was rekindled in many bosoms present, when they heard the roar of musketry, tramping of steeds and clashing of swords in sham battle."

Following the Civil War, many of the battle reenactments that occurred were derived from the memories and events of that war. For example, on the occasion of the nation's centennial in 1876 a great sham battle was staged by military and naval units before a crowd of 100,000 at the Presidio, San Francisco Bay and surrounding forts. Following a dress parade, the land engagement began with soldiers firing blank cartridges. "Supporting batteries at Black Point and on the heights of the presidio thundered a hearty approval as the infantry advance." Although the land battle was considered a success, batteries at Fort Point and Alcatraz failed to hit their targets in the bay and the crowd considered the event a "fizzle." Disappointed in the lack of military training and the "failure of the Army and Navy to sink a scow in San Francisco Bay in 1876," Brian McGinty "pointed out the glaring vulnerability of Western coastal defenses."

Another celebrated event occurred at the "State Camp," near Peekskill, New York, on July 4, 1883. The reenactment known as the battle of Round Mountain consisted of two armies of several companies commanded by Col. Austen and Col. H.B. Gates, respectively, depicting several skirmishes, complete with artillery and field maneuvers. Two years later on July 4 in Jamestown, New York, another mock Civil War battle was fought, and on July 4, 1890, at Marysville, California, a battle was staged by military companies from Chico, Colusa, and Marysville. On July 4, 1895, a sham battle took place at the fair grounds in Hagerstown, Maryland, between the Chambersburg Company, Douglas Guards, and a Baltimore battalion. "For about an hour the battle waged fiercely, each side alternately advancing and retreating." On July 4, 1903, in Lindale, Georgia, the Atlanta 5th Regiment engaged in a sham battle there.

Mock battles were frequently depicted in imaginative ways. For example, the USS *Constitution*'s engagement with the *Guerrière* in 1812 was reenacted in 1821 (See **USS *Constitution***) and two pyrotechnic reenactments between the ironclad vessels *Monitor* and *Merrimac* took place, one in New York on July 4, 1862, and the other in San Francisco on July 4, 1876. Another interesting reenactment occurred in Cleveland on July 4, 1873, and was advertised as a "miniature naval bombardment on the lake."

Not all reenactments were undertaken without mishaps. In a sham battle held in Youngstown, Ohio, on July 4, 1891, a seven-year-old girl was killed and two other youngsters injured by a signal rocket, while a third youth was killed after having been shot accidentally by a soldier using live ammunition.

Occasionally black companies fought in reenactments. On July 4, 1890, three units from Richmond and Norfolk fought three others from Richmond, Manchester, and Petersburg at the exposition grounds. A local newspaper reported humorously, "the bravery of the various officers in standing in front of their troops while firing was remarkable, and would certainly, if carried out in actual warfare, place rapid promotion within the reach of the lowest private."

One of the longest running and grandest Civil War reenactment traditions, begun as early as the 1880s, is that commemorating the Battle of Gettysburg fought on July 3–5, and now taking place each year on farm land adjacent to the actual Gettysburg battlefield. Typically involving thousands of reenactors from all parts of the country, the principal battles during the three days have grown in popularity through the years and are now staged in nearly perfect authenticity. In 1888 on the Fourth a "sham battle" was given after dark and an early reenactment of Pickett's Charge, one of the most popular skirmishes, occurred on July 3, 1913. An unusual skirmish was that of July 4, 1922, when a complement of U.S. Marines staged Pickett's Charge using modern World War I armaments. In 2004, the reenactment included 3,500 soldiers before 25,000 spectators.

Recently, at the Richard Nixon Library in Yorba Linda, California, a Revolutionary era battle reenactment of Lexington and Concord took place on July 4, 1997. The day's events included an encampment that represented everyday life two hundred years ago. According to a local newspaper, there was "free apple pie for the first 200 visitors, a display of an 1830 copy of the Declaration of Independence, a National Bell Ringing Ceremony," and a "Betsy Ross Flag Raising Ceremony with musket salute."

Another reenactment of a sham Revolutionary War battle, staged between "The New Regiments of the Continental Line," led by Jeff Lambert, captain of the 1st Virginia Old Guard Regiment and Fife and Drum Corps, and the "Crown Forces," took place on Pennsylvania Avenue directly in front of the National Archives Building in Washington, D.C., on July 4, 2000. See also **Fort McHenry**.

Sources: *Boston Gazette*, 12 July 1779, 3; *Charleston Mercury*, 19 July 1855, 2; *Chicago Daily Tribune*, 5 July 1873, 8; "A Sham Battle," *New York Herald*, 5 July 1883, 4; *New York Times*, 5 July 1885; "End of the Reunion," *Baltimore Morning Herald*, 5 July 1888, 4; "All Over the State," *Los Angeles Times*, 5 July 1890, 5; *Richmond Daily Dispatch*, 5 July 1890, as reported in Roger D. Cunningham, "'They Are as Proud of Their Uniform as Any Who Serve Virginia': African American Participation in the Virginia Volunteers, 1872–99," *Virginia Magazine of History and Biography* 110/3: 318–19; "Killed in a Sham Battle," *Houston Daily Post*, 6 July 1891, 2; "News of the State," *Baltimore Morning Herald*, 5 July 1895, 7; *Atlanta Journal*, 5 July 1903, 5 and 9; "Pickett's Charge Fifty Years After," *New York Times*, 4 July 1913, 3; "Modern Gettysburg to Be Staged Today," *New York Times*, 4 July 1922, 4 and 5 July 1922, 7; Brian McGinty, "The Great Sham Battle," *American History Illustrated* 13/6 (October 1978): 18–24; Benjamin Epstein, "Patriot Games: From a Revolutionary War Battle Reenactment to Fireworks," *Los Angeles Times*, 3 July 1997, F6; "Independence Day 2000," *Washington Post*, 5 July 2000, A8; "Pickett's Charge Provides Traditional Finale, *Evening Sun* (Hanover, Pa.), 5 July 2004.

Beach Boys

Icon of enduring American musical groups that performed, often for free, on the Fourth of July in Washington, D.C., and elsewhere. The Beach Boys (Brian, Carl, and Dennis Wilson, with Mike Love and Al Jardine) gave their first momentous Fourth of July concert abroad, in Leningrad in 1978. On July 4, 1980, the group began the tradition of Independence Day pop concerts on the Washington, D.C., National Mall. They drew 200,000 fans that year by performing hit music they had made famous since 1961, when they began giving concerts. This particular event was filmed on six cameras. They appeared again on the Mall in 1981.

In 1983 James Watt, secretary of the interior, banned the Beach Boys from performing in Washington on July 4 that year in order to dissuade "the wrong element"—drug and alcohol consuming youths—from attending the celebration. The Beach Boys were replaced by singer Wayne Newton and the U.S. Army Blues Band. The uproar from the public that resulted from the ban was enormous. To many the Beach Boys were considered an important part of the American musical tradition. Even Vice President George Bush responded, "They're my friends and I like their music." Undaunted, the group gave a free Independence Day concert that year in Atlantic City before thousands.

In 1984 they were back on the Mall on July 4 highlighting a star-studded performance that included Three Dog Night and the O'Jays, George Jones, and Roy Clark before a crowd of 200,000. In 1985 they gave two concerts on Independence Day, the first in Philadelphia during the afternoon on a stage built at the front steps to the city's art museum and the second in Washington on the Mall later that evening. Their Philadelphia performance was almost cancelled. Contractual and financial issues were resolved only at the last moment when American Airlines agreed to act as a co-sponsor. Probably recalling the 1983 Washington affair, Mayor W. Wilson Goode went on television and assured Philadelphia citizens that the concert would take place. Appearing with them in those concerts were Jimmy Page, the Oak Ridge Boys, Southern Pacific and others.

On July 4, 1986, the group performed in Manor, Texas, as part of Farm Aid II with **Willie Nelson**. On the Fourth of July in 2000 and 2001, the group performed in Houston, Texas (see **"Power of Freedom"**). On July 4, 2001, "An All-Star Tribute to Brian Wilson," a show that had been taped at Radio City Music Hall on March 29, was aired on television. The Beach Boys were inducted into the Rock and Roll Hall of Fame in 1988.

Sources: Richard Harrington, "The Fourth: Good Vibrations at the Beach Party on the Mall," *Washington Post*, 5 July 1980, B1; Phil McCombs and Richard Harrington, "Watt Sets Off Uproar with Music Ban," *Washington Post*, 7 April 1983, A1; "By Chuck Conconi," *Washington Post*, 5 July 1983, C3; "Parades, Patriotism and Pyrotechnics," *New York Times*, 5 July 1984, B16; Chuck Conconi, "Personalities,"

Washington Post, 4 July 1985, D3; "An Indoor Guide to a Fabulous Fourth," *Baltimore Sun*, 4 July 2001, 8G; Nancy H. Evans, "The Beach Boys," in *Contemporary Musicians*, ed. Michael L. LaBlanc (Detroit, Mich.: Gale Research, 1989).

Beaufort, North Carolina, Court House

On July 4, 1786, the court house in Beaufort burned to the ground as a result of an errant artillery shell fired at the Independence Day celebration there. A newspaper reported that the fire

> appeared upon the shingles. Apprehending it might be some part of the cartridges blown from the field pieces, they tore away the shingles where the smoke appeared, when instantly the flames broke out most furiously, which gave it the appearance of design, and the court-house was unfortunately burnt down. The inhabitants have since very generally and liberally subscribed to the immediate rebuilding an elegant court-house, which in all probability, will be ready the ensuing court.

Source: *Pennsylvania Gazette*, 9 August 1786.

Bechet, Etienne Marie (d. 1798)

Officer in the Continental Army, who served with distinction in the Revolutionary War. On July 4, 1921, ceremonies were held at his tomb in St. Paul's Church, in New York. Present were "two companies of the Twenty-Second Infantry and a detachment of sailors [who] marched up broadway to the church, followed by members of the Sons of the American Revolution, a detachment bearing the flag of the American Legion and a delegations from the French War Veterans." Brig. Gen. Oliver B. Bridgman conducted the ceremonies and addresses were given by Brig. Gen. Charles J. Bailey, "commanding the Second Coast Artillery area," Rear Admiral Harry P. Huse "of the Third Naval District," and Gaston Liebert, French consul general. A band played "The Marseillaise," and the ceremony ended with a military salute.

Source: "Honors for General Bechet," *New York Times*, 5 July 1921, 2.

Bement, Illinois, Area Veterans' Memorial

Dedicated on July 4, 1998.

Source: *Dedication of the Veterans' Memorial*, videorecording (Bement, Ill., 1998).

Benton, Pennsylvania, fire

Most of this town, located in Columbia County, was burned to the ground on July 4, 1910, when a firecracker "lodged" in a barn. According to one report, "the Benton-Argus plant, a hotel, a bank, the principal stores, and twenty-five dwellings" were destroyed. Another account cited sixty buildings destroyed and thirty families homeless.

Sources: "Exploding Cracker Causes $300,000 Fire," *Atlanta Journal*, 5 July 1910, 1; *New York Times*, 5 July 1910, 8.

Berceau

In honor of the American Independence Day, this French corvette vessel was to fire an artillery salute on July 4, 1801, in Boston harbor.

Source: *New-England Palladium*, 3 July 1801, 3.

Bible

Referred to frequently in numerous Fourth of July orations and sermons. Throughout the history of the Fourth of July celebrations, divine intervention was credited, in part, with the inspiration of the framers of the nation's charters and the rise of America's greatness. Scripture from the Bible typically served as a source and inspiration for sermons given on July 4 or 5, when either of those days fell on a Sunday. On July 4, 1793, Samuel Miller (1769–1850), a Presbyterian minister, preached at the meeting of the Tammany Society in New York and based his sermon on II Corinthians 3:17 ("And where the Spirit of the Lord is, there is Liberty"). Leonard Bacon gave a sermon based on Mark 12:34 ("Thou art not far from the Kingdom of God") twice on Sunday, July 4, 1824, in Boston, "first in the afternoon at the Union Church on Essex Street and again that evening at the First Baptist Church on Back Street."

On Sunday, July 5, 1846, Matthew 28:6 ("He is not here: for he is risen, as he said, Come, see the place where the Lord lay") was the source for "Rev. Mr. Baker's" sermon given in Congress in the Hall of the House of Representatives. President **James Knox Polk** was there and recorded the event in his diary.

On July 4, 1861, the sermon at St. Paul's Church, "Third Street, below Walnut," in Philadelphia given by the rector there, was based on Romans 13:1 ("Let every soul be subject to the higher power"). In New York City, on July 4, 1880, Rev. J.P. Newman preached on "The Responsibilities of American Citizenship" at Central Methodist Episcopal Church, located at Seventh Ave. and 14th Street. He based his sermon on Exodus 18:21 ("Moreover thou shalt provide out of all the people able men, such as fear God, men of truth, hating covetousness; and place such over them, to be rulers of thousands, and rulers of hundreds, rulers of fifties, and rulers of tens").

Sources: Samuel Miller, *A Sermon, Preached in New-York, July 4th, 1793* (New York: Thomas Greenleaf, 1793), printed in *Political Sermons of the American Founding Era, 1730–1805* (Indianapolis: Liberty Fund, 1998), 2:1149–67 ; *The Press*, 5 July 1861, 3; "The Duties of Citizenship," *New York Times*, 5 July 1880, 8; "Sermon from Mark XII, 34," Bacon Family Papers, Yale University Library, printed in Henry A. Hawken, *Trumpets of Glory: Fourth of July Orations* (Granby, Conn.: Salmon Brook Historical Society, 1976), 57–59.

Bicentennial

Marked the 200th anniversary of the founding of the nation and the largest number of local celebrations since the Centennial celebration in 1876. Over 5000 colorful and memorable events were staged across the nation. No less than 101 countries took part in the festivities. Thousands of Americans took advantage of a vast number of patriotic souvenirs marking the occasion, such as "flags, pillows, banners, balloons, bracelets, charms, postcards, [and] patches." The first celebration was a flag-raising early in the morning at Mars Hill Mountain, Maine, where daylight first occurs in the states. In New York, "Operation Sail" brought together the largest assemblage ever of tall ships, representing twenty-two nations. At the Graff House in Philadelphia, the temporary home of Thomas Jefferson in 1776 when he was writing the Declaration, a United States Park Service guide described the founder's life. Meanwhile, President Ford visited Valley Forge, presented a Bicentennial address before 100,000 spectators in Philadelphia and boarded the USS *Forrestal* in New York, where he reviewed a parade of square-riggers. In Boston a memorial service was presented in the Old North Church and the USS *Constitution* fired her cannons. In St. Louis, thousands of spectators watched an Independence Day air show. In Washington, D.C., the Declaration of Independence was read aloud on the steps of the National Archives while country music singer Johnny Cash hosted a musical extravaganza at the Sylvan Theater on the Mall. Bicentennial exhibits included the Museum of History and Technology's "A Nation of Nations" and the Arts and Industries "1876: A Centennial Exhibition."

The planning for the Bicentennial was officially launched in July 1966 when President Johnson signed a congressional resolution authorizing him to appoint a 34-member commission to "plan for public and private celebrations." In early July 1970 the American Revolution Bicentennial Commission (ARBA) recommended Philadelphia as the official city that would host the national celebration and in a report submitted to the president on the Fourth proposed three themes: "Heritage '76," in which groups would examine the nation's past; "Open House USA," which people from all over the world would be invited to attend; and "Horizons '76," whereby projects would be initiated by groups across the country as contributions to the future of America. From 1973 to 1975 ARBA inventoried thousands of events that were developed specifically for the Bicentennial.

Sources: Don Irwin, "President Signs Plans on July 4 Bicentennial," *Los Angeles Times*, 9 July 1966, 16; "The Nation: Philadelphia Favored for '76 Celebration," *Los Angeles Times*, 2 July 1970, B2; "Bicentennial Report Handed to President," *Los Angeles Times*, 4 July 1970, 2; "President Talks," *New York Times*, 5 July 1976, 1; Lawrence Meyer, "America Joyfully Toasts Birth of a Nation," *Washington Post*, 5 July 1976, A1, A14; *Comprehensive Calendar of Bicentennial Events* (Washington, D.C.: American Revolution Bicentennial Administration, 1975); Lynn Darling, "Bicentennial Wins Plaudits for Legacies to the Nation; Bicentennial Hailed for Its Legacies," *Washington Post*, 1 January 1977, A1.

"Bicentennial Minutes"

In commemoration of the nation's Bicentennial, Shell Oil Co. sponsored 732 one-minute TV spots on all aspects of American history that ran from July 4, 1974, to July 4, 1976. First Lady Betty Ford delivered the final "Bicentennial Minute" in place of President Ford because CBS, under requirement by the FCC "equal time" rule, would have had to allot 60 seconds to other presidential candidates. Other readers included Louis Jourdon, Jean Stapleton, Cleveland Amory, Lloyd Bridges, Leslie Caron, Richard Chamberlain, Glenn Ford, Valerie Harper, and Tony Randall.

Source: Judith Martin, "Spotting Trivia as History," *Washington Post*, 4 July 1974, E1–E2.

Bigelow, Edward Manning (1850–1918)

Civil engineer and director of the Public Works in Pittsburgh. A bronze monument in honor of him was unveiled in Schenley Park on July 4, 1895. Bigelow was born in Pittsburgh, attended Western University, and was appointed Pittsburgh City engineer in 1880. He was responsible for the creation of a public park system by acquiring 1,300 acres of land, and, as a result of his efforts, was recognized as the "father of Pittsburgh parks." At the base of the monument is the inscription "Edward Manning Bigelow, whose untiring efforts secured to the people of Pittsburgh Schenley and Highland Parks. Erected by public subscription during his lifetime, July 4, 1895." Some 100,000 persons were there for the unveiling, and they heard Pennsylvania governor Daniel H. Hastings deliver an address. Following his tenure as city engineer, Bigelow was appointed first state highway commissioner in 1910 and was credited with improving the highway system in Pittsburgh.

Sources: "Monument Unveiled at Pittsburg," *New York Times*, 5 July 1895, 5; "Edward Manning Bigelow," *National Cyclopaedia of American Biography*, 20:398.

Billings, William (1746–1800)

American Revolutionary War patriot, composer, and singing teacher who wrote popular patriotic pieces reflecting Revolutionary War themes. Born in Boston, Billings began teaching music around 1769 and held classes at various churches, including the Brat-tle Street Church, Old South Church, and others. He wrote over 340 works, many of which are found in a series of six tunebooks. Among his patriotic pieces are "Chester," "Lamentation over Boston," and "Independence," the latter an anthem composed for the 1783 Fourth of July celebration at the Brattle Square Church. "The States, O Lord, with songs of praise, / Shall in thy strength rejoice, / And, blest, with thy salvation raise / To heaven their cheerful voice."

Sources: J.I. Young, "The Pioneer of American Church Music," *Potter's American Monthly* (October 1876): 255–56; Karl Kroeger, "William Billings," *Grove Music Online* (Oxford, 2005).

Black Hawk (1767–1838)

Also known as Ma-ka-tai-me-she-kia-kiak, this Sauk tribal leader gave a Fourth of July speech at Fort Madison, Iowa, in 1838 that was printed in eastern seaboard newspapers. Black Hawk gained notoriety for leading his tribe and others in battle against Illinois militia and federal troops at Bad Axe River in August 1832. An 1804 treaty that required the Sauks to leave their settlement along the Rock River (now in Illinois) and move west of the Mississippi River was neglected by Black Hawk and some members of the tribe. Black Hawk was defeated at Bad Axe River, taken into custody and imprisoned in Missouri and Virginia. He was later taken to Washington, D.C., where he met President Andrew Jackson. In 1833 Black Hawk was permanently relocated to Iowa with the Sauk and Foxes tribes. In that year, he was invited to Fort Madison as an "illustrious guest" for the Fourth of July ceremony held there. A number of toasts were presented, with one offered to Black Hawk by J.G. Edwards: "May his declining years be as calm and serene as his previous life has been boisterous and full of warlike incidents. His attachment and present friendship to his white brethren [?] entitle him to a seat at our festive board." Black Hawk responded with a brief but touching speech expressing his pleasure for the day and asking that the past be forgotten but that also he will never forget the Mississippi River and his home. "Rock river was a beautiful country — I liked my towns, my cornfields, and the home of my people. I fought for it. It is now yours — keep it as we did — it will produce you good crops." Black Hawk died in October of that year near Des Moines River, Iowa.

Sources: *Alexandria Gazette*, 7 August 1838, 2; *Native North American Literature*, ed. Janet Witalec (New York: Gale Research, 1994), 59–60; Paula Sheil, "Native Pride," *Record* (Stockton, California), 4 July 2004, F1, F4.

Blair, Montgomery (1813–1883)

Postmaster general under Abraham Lincoln who hosted a unique Independence Day celebration at his summer estate in Silver Spring, Maryland, on July 4, 1867. Blair, eldest son of Francis Preston Blair, founder of the town of Silver Spring, Maryland, was an attorney who represented Dred Scott before the U.S. Supreme Court. In 1854, he built the summer manor called Falkland near the home of his father. Montgomery Blair's principal residence, known as Blair House, is located on Pennsylvania Ave across from the White House.

In Washington the trial of John S. Surratt, an associate of John Wilkes Booth, who assassinated Lincoln, was held in late June and early July 1867, at the Criminal Court House in Washington. Surratt was wanted by the law for his role in Lincoln's murder but had left the country. He was eventually captured abroad, returned and brought to trial. On Independence Day, the proceedings were adjourned, the court room having been promised to the **Oldest Inhabitants Association** for their celebration. The twelve jurors on the case wanted to celebrate the Fourth but had to do so sequestered. Accompanied by two bailiffs, the group left the city and went to the Silver Spring Blair mansion, located about six miles from downtown Washington. The details of the outing were reported in a local newspaper:

> Yesterday, the jury in the Surratt case, having received permission of the Court, spent the day on a picnic. They left their quarters at Seaton House in carriages, in the morning, and proceeded to the country residence of Hon. Montgomery Blair, at Silver Spring, and obtaining permission from that gentleman and his lady, located themselves on the farm, and enjoyed themselves in rambling through the beautiful groves on the place, etc. About noon

they assembled at the famous spring, where refreshments were spread out and demolished. The foreman of the jury, Mr. [W.B.] Todd, presided and made some happy remarks, and introduced Mr. George A. Bohrer, who read the Declaration of Independence, prefacing the reading with brief historical remarks, after which, under the leadership of Mr. Robert Ball, the company, composed of the twelve jurors and the two bailiffs, Messrs. Roes and Hughes, united in singing the "Star-Spangled Banner," making the old woods ring. The remainder of the day was spent in social converse, walks through the wood, etc., and they returned in the evening to their quarters, exceedingly gratified with their brief respite from court-house durance.

Falkland was burned by the Confederate troops during the Civil War. See also **Charles Sumner**.

Source: *Washington Evening Star*, 5 July 1867, 1.

"Blessings of Fredon"

This song was written for the Fourth of July, 1803, and was sung to the tune "Yankee Doodle." First line: "Come, celebrate your happy state."

Source: broadside (New York: G. and R. Waite, 1803).

Blyth, Stephen Cleveland (d. 1844)

Composed an "Ode on the Military Celebration at Salem of the Fourth of July, 1806."

Source: broadside (Salem, Mass.: 1806).

Boker, George Henry (1823–1890)

American poet and playwright who wrote "Hymn for the Fourth of July, 1863," printed in *Poems of the War* (Boston: Ticknor and Fields, 1864).

> (First stanza)
> Lord, the people of the land
> In Thy presence humbly stand;
> On this day, when Thou dist free
> Men of old from tyranny,
> We, their children, bow to Thee.
> Help us, Lord, our only trust!
> We are helpless, we are dust!

On July 4, 1865, his "Hymn for the Union League" of Philadelphia was premiered in that city.

Boombox Parade, Willimantic, Connecticut

An annual tradition beginning in 1986 and established as a result of Independence Day funding cuts. According to Kathy Clark, a subsidy coordinator for the Willimantic Housing Authority, who came up with the idea, "Willimantic was no longer able to support a high school marching band." The parade was greeted with some initial shock but was widely reported and quickly became one of the nation's popular events. Participants typically carry boombox radios with popular music blasting at full volume.

Source: "A Radio Active Parade," *Washington Post*, 5 July 2000, C1, C9.

Boston and Worcester Railroad

Opened on July 4, 1835, providing service from Boston to towns in western Massachusetts. This was one of three railways operating in the mid-1830s.

Source: *Massachusetts Historical Society* Web site, 24 September 2002, <http://www.masshist.org/>.

Boston Common

One of the oldest public parks in America and the principal outdoor site in Boston for Independence Day celebrations. Boston acquired the land, about 50 acres, in 1634 from William Blackstone. Independence Day celebration events have included military parades and drills, fireworks, food, games and exhibitions. The first fireworks took place on the Common on July 4, 1777. On July 4, 1805, a "pyrotechnical exhibition," with "transparencies of the National and States Arms" were displayed along with busts of Washington and Hamilton "from a stage in the centre of the Common." On July 4, 1818, the Charitable Mechanics Association sponsored a craft demonstration and contest, awarding prizes to the best coopers. Another noteworthy event occurred on July 4, 1856, when thousands witnessed a balloon ascension by "the son of the celebrated aeronaut, Mr. Wise" in a vessel named *Young America*.

Throughout its history, the Common was a popular site for numerous concerts by bands and other musical ensembles. On July 4, 1876, for example, Arthur Hall directed a group of eighty instrumentalists made up of Hall's First Regimental Band, Edmonds,' O'Connor's and the Metropolitan Bands during the hours of 8 A.M. and 10 A.M. that day. The Boston Common is designated as an important landmark of the **Freedom Trail**, consisting of seventeen historic Boston sites.

Sources: *Boston Gazette*, 7 July 1777, 6 and 8 July 1818; *New England Palladium*, 5 and 9 July 1805, 9 and 2, respectively; "The Fourth," *New York Times*, 7 July 1856, 1; "Boston Correspondence," *Westfield Republican* (New York), 8 July 1874, 2.

Boston Pops

Renowned orchestra whose tradition of performing patriotic music on the Fourth of July began in 1929 under the directorship of Arthur Fiedler at the Esplanade on the Charles River Basin. Over forty instrumentalists from the Boston Symphony Orchestra presented the ensemble's first Independence Day concert with selections by Otto Nicolai and Sigmund Romberg and concluding with a rendition of Victor Herbert's *American Fantasia*. On Saturday, July 6, 1929, the Boston Pops performed John Philip Sousa's *El Capitan March*. It was Fiedler's vision to combine classical and popular music programs in an outdoor setting. Through the years the Pops continued the tradition of performing popular American folk, Broadway, and classical works, as well as pieces representing the armed forces. All of the concerts were presented free of charge. On July 2, 1940, the dedication of the new Edward Hatch Memorial Concertorium took place. The Hatch Shell, with its improved acoustical qualities over previous structures used, was the site for the popular Esplanade concerts. Some of the American composers whose works were frequently programmed included Morton Gould, George Gershwin, Richard Rogers, Stephen Foster, Irving Berlin, and Leonard Bernstein.

Through the years a number of landmark dates for Esplanade concerts occurred, with the most notable on July 4, 1974, when the first performance of Tchaikovsky's *1812 Overture*, with accompaniment of live cannons and fireworks, took place. The idea to combine the sound of artillery and fireworks with music was the idea of Fiedler and his friend David Mugar, "entrepreneur and son of the founder of Star Markets." Attendance for the concerts had dwindled and this combination of sound and spectacle attracted larger audiences.

On July 4, 1976, a record-breaking crowd of 400,000 attended the concert and fireworks display. On July 4, 1977, the use of speaker towers for transmitting sound was eliminated "in favor of AM and FM radio broadcast of the entire program without commercial interruption." In 1991 the event was broadcast through the A & E cable network. In 1998 in commemoration of the 25th anniversary of the *1812 Overture* with cannons and fireworks, "60,000 copies of a 48-page program book" were printed.

In January 1980 noted film composer John Williams was appointed conductor of the Pops and continued the tradition of providing patriotic music and audience sing-alongs on the Fourth. On July 4, 1990, Williams' work *Celebrate Discovery!*, written for the 500th anniversary of the 1492 Columbus voyages, and a work titled *Celebrate America*, written by Cynthia Mann and Barry Weil, were premiered. In 1991 the Hatch Shell underwent a major renovation but was re-opened on July 2 in time for the annual Fourth concert. In 1995 Keith Lockhart succeeded Williams as conductor and in 2002 his Independence Day broadcast was nominated for an Emmy Award. Other conductors have included Harry Ellis Dickson, who first served as assistant conductor under Fiedler, and Seiji Ozawa. Notable headliners that have performed on the Fourth have included Marvin Hamlisch (1994), the Pointer Sisters and Mel Tormé (1995), Sandy Duncan and the Furman Singers (1996), Roberta Flack (1997), Melissa Manchester (1998), and Tracy Silva (2004), Pop-Search 2004 winner. On July 4, 2003, the Boston Pops performed with the Mormon Tabernacle Choir and celebrated the chorus's 75th anniversary tour.

Sources: "Official Guide to the Reopening of the Hatch Shell" and selected programs, Scrapbook Collection, Boston Symphony Orchestra; Richard Dyer, "25 Years of Pop," *Boston Globe*, 3 July 1998, D1; Nancy Rabinowitz, "Mormon Tabernacle Choir to Sing with Pops on Fourth," *Associated Press State and Local Wire*, 15 June 2003.

Boston Riot of 1895

On July 4, 1895, a patriotic parade known as "The Little Red Schoolhouse Parade" ended when a drunken crowd of men and women attacked the paraders, resulting in one person killed and others wounded. The parade started in the early afternoon in East Boston and was made up of about 1,200 men representing "A.P.A. [American Protective Association] lodges, the Patriotic Sons of America, Orange lodges, the Order of United Workmen, and kindred organizations." About three hundred policemen stood watch over the parade as a red schoolhouse, a representation of the regulation New England schoolhouse, was pulled along the streets. "The float was covered with red, white, and blue bunting, and the schoolhouse was surmounted by the Stars and Stripes." Some of those parading were dressed in costume, including "a tall figure clothed in military costume, representing **Uncle Sam**." At the rear of the parade was a carriage with men and women inside. A group of drunken women watching the parade suddenly converged on the carriage and a milk can was tossed into the carriage. Immediately insults were exchanged, several fights broke out, and one man was killed on the spot by a pistol shot.

Sources: "Rioting in Boston," *Baltimore Morning Herald*, 5 July 1885, 1; "Rioting in East Boston," *New York Times*, 5 July 1895, 1.

Boulder, Colorado, Court House

The cornerstone of the second county court house in Boulder, Colorado, was laid on July 4, 1882. It is located on Pearl Street, between 13th and 14th Streets. The cost of the finished building was $59, 950.

Source: *Boulder County Colorado Government Online*, <http://www.co.boulder.co.us/about.htm>.

Boulder Monument, Buffalo, New York

Dedicated on July 4, 1896, this monument in Park Meadow honors unknown soldiers of the War of 1812. The local Society of Sons of the Revolution, G.A.R. Union Veteran Legion, and "various civil and choral societies" sponsored the event. Commissioner Marcus M. Drake and Sherman S. Rogers, member of the New York State Senate, were the principal speakers.

Source: "In Memory of Soldiers," *Baltimore Morning Herald*, 5 July 1896, 3.

Boy Scouts of America (BSA)

Throughout the history of the organization, the scouts have actively participated in ceremonial events on Independence Day. One of the earliest took place in London, on July 4, 1926, when American ambassador to England Alanson B. Houghton presented a bronze statuette of a bison on behalf of the Boy Scouts of America to the Prince of Wales, who received the statuette on behalf of the Boy Scouts of Britain.

On July 4, 1937, a BSA jamboree with 27,000 scouts was held in Washington, D.C. One of the principal events was their participation in a memorial service at the Tomb of the Unknown Soldier in Arlington, Virginia. The ceremony was held in the Arlington Amphitheater and Ray O. Wyland, national director of education of the BSA, spoke on the "Heroes of Peace and War." On July 4, 1933, the members representing the Boy Scouts of Vermont placed a wreath at the grave of Calvin Coolidge in Plymouth. More than 5,000 scouts attended the event.

The second national jamboree was held at Valley Forge, Pennsylvania, on July 4, 1950, with 47,000 scouts in attendance. A pageant titled "Scouting across the Nation" was presented with 8,000 participants, many in costume. Later that evening a grand fireworks celebration, ceremonially begun by Dwight D. Eisenhower, took place. Included in the display was "a blazing likeness of the Statue of Liberty and one of the Boy Scout badge" and a large silk American flag shot skyward illuminated by aerial flares. On July 4, 1960, a "colorful tableau honoring the 50th anniversary of the founding of the Boy Scouts of America" was staged at the Rose Bowl in Pasadena, California.

Sources: *New York Times,* 5 July 1926, 1; "Coolidge's 61st Birthday Marked by Scout Wreath," *Washington Post*, 5 July 1933, 9; "Jamboree Grounds Jammed as Crowds Flock to See Scouts" and "Scouts Will Honor Unknown Soldier," *Washington Post*, 5 July 1937, 5; "Ike to Start Fireworks at Scout Session," *Washington Post*, 4 July 1950, 9B; "Circus, Fireworks on Tap at Bowl," *Los Angeles Times*, 3 July 1960, SG1.

Bradford, Vermont, Public Library Building

Dedicated on July 4, 1895. Josiah H. Benton delivered an address for the occasion.

Source: *Address of J.H. Benton, Jr.* (Boston: A.C. Getchell, 1896).

Brandt

Steam tugboat that was returning to Wilmington, North Carolina, on July 4, 1869, from an excursion for a large party of individuals and blew her boiler, killing at least one and injuring others. The mishap occurred "six miles below the city." Colonel Thomas D. Mears, son of W.B. Mears, drowned after he jumped overboard and attempted to swim to land. The steamer *Waccamaw* aided in the rescue of others.

Sources: *New York Times*, 6 July 1869, 8; "Sad Accident to an Excursion Party," *Washington Evening Star*, 6 July 1869, 1.

Bristol, Rhode Island

The site for one of the longest running Fourth of July celebrations, with the first observance occurring in 1785 under the direction of Henry Wight, a Revolutionary War soldier. Patriotic exercises were held throughout the years at various houses of worship, the town halls, opera house, the town common, the Hotel Belvedere, and in recent years at the Colt Elementary School. There have been only a few years when parades were omitted, such as in 1881, when the town was in mourning due to the shooting of President Garfield. Part of the tradition included an annual artillery salute, the first having been fired on the town common in 1790, the convening of an active Independence Day committee, the first such committee noted in the town council records of 1815, and fireworks, the first reported use in the town ceremonies in 1840. Since 1923, with the exception of only a few years, over 70 ships have sailed into Bristol's port to take part in the Independence Day events there. On July 4, 1976, in honor of the nation's Bicentennial, Governor Phil Noel presented an American flag to the town's Fourth of July committee.

Source: Richard V. Simpson, *Independence Day: How the Day Is Celebrated in Bristol, Rhode Island* (Middletown, R.I.: Aquidneck Graphics, 1989).

Brooklyn, New York, Board of Education

Likely the first local board of education in the country to adopt a resolution that the Declaration of Independence be read in all public schools on the last school day before the Fourth of July. The practice was begun in 1857 and usually other patriotic activities such as speeches were given to complement the readings.

Source: "Brooklyn Items," *New York Times*, 3 July 1858, 8.

Bryan, William Jennings (1860–1925)

Statesman and noted orator who presented profound statements on the Fourth of July on the progress of the United States and the world. Born in Salem, Illinois, Bryan, after practicing law, was elected to Congress in 1890. Not long after, he became a member of the Chautauqua lecture circuit and was in demand as a public speaker. Bryan lost a presidential election bid in 1896 to William McKinley, but later, after helping to secure the election of Woodrow Wilson, was appointed secretary of state (1913–15).

On July 5, 1897, Bryan spoke at Fiesta Park in Los Angeles, and a newspaper reporter noted that Bryan's presence would make for "one of the great days" for that city. A Fourth of July speech he gave at the Hotel Cecil in London in 1906 was titled "The White Man's Burden" and focused on a comparison of Western society with the Orient. Bryan, a religious fundamentalist, proposed that Christian nations were obliged to stimulate "inferior nations" towards self-development, but to do so using Western ideals as the objective. He cited "five great duties" that would be carried to the rest of the world: "education, knowledge of the science of government, arbitration as a substitute for war, appreciation of the dignity of labor, and a high conception of life."

On July 4, 1913, Bryan was in Washington, where Wilson had named him "Acting President of the United States." According to a newspaper report, "this title for years has been given popularly to the ranking officer of the Administration in Washington in the absence of the President and Vice President." Bryan delivered another Independence Day address on the topic of "Universal Peace" at the Panama-Pacific Exposition held in San Francisco in 1915. Bryan "discussed the solving of democratic problems, the true measure of greatness, and the methods we should employ in dealing with other nations." Speaking before a crowd of 122,000, the largest audience Bryan ever addressed, he said, "If the United States is to lead the world in the advance toward economic peace it must be guided by the principle that human rights come first.... The heart, overflowing with sympathy and animated by good will — this and this only — is equal to the delicate and difficult task for which a great nation has prepared itself."

On July 4, 1916, Bryan gave three addresses. First he spoke in Peekskill, New York, at the town celebration. He stressed the importance of the "unity of the country," and in offering our services to the warring countries of Europe, he said, "We are kin to all of them and we cannot be enemies to any of them." Later that day Bryan spoke to 1000 inmates at Sing Sing Penitentiary about patriotism and recommended "plans and specifications for leading a useful life." He also spoke at the annual meeting of the **National Educational Association (NEA)** at Madison Square Garden in New York. On Independence Day in 1924, Bryan was at the University of Virginia in Charlottesville giving a speech (see **Monticello**).

Sources: "Hon. William J. Bryan," *Los Angeles Times*, 5 July 1897, 10; "Bryan's July 4 Speech on White Man's Burden," *New York Times*, 5 July 1906, 5; "Bryan, Acting President," *New York Times*, 4 July 1913, 6; "122,000 Hear Bryan at Fair," *New York Times*, 6 July 1915, 9; "Bryan at Peekskill Praises Soldiers" and "Bryan Talks to Convicts," *New York Times*, 5 July 1916, 18.

Buchanan, George (1763–1808)

Anatomist, member of the American Philosophical Society, and the first person to address the issue of slavery of African-

Americans on Independence Day. His address on July 4, 1791, was titled "Oration Upon the Moral and Political Evil of Slavery" and was given at a public meeting of the Maryland Society for Promoting the Abolition of Slavery and the Relief of Free Negroes in Baltimore. Buchanan presented a strong statement of admonition that slavery is the cause of revolutions and there was great danger that an African-American revolution posed a real threat:

> What, then, if the fire of Liberty shall be kindled amongst them? What, if some enthusiast in their cause shall beat to arms, and call them to the standard of freedom? Would they not fly in crowds, until their numbers became tremendous, and threaten the country with devastation and ruin?

Buchanan set the theme for future speakers. He promoted "abolitionism without destroying American unity," the freedom of slaves without the need for a new revolution.

Sources: George Buchanan, "An Oration..." (Baltimore: Philip Edwards, 1793; Cincinnati: Robert Clarke, 1873); James, "The Other Fourth of July," 84–90.

Buchanan, James (1791–1868)

Fifteenth president of the U.S. Buchanan graduated from Dickinson College and served in Congress (1820–31), the U.S. Senate (1835–45), and as U.S. president (1857–61). On at least two occasions, Buchanan's preference for celebrating the Fourth was entertaining guests in the White House. In 1858 he was invited to attend the July Fourth "Democratic celebration in Independence Square" in Philadelphia, but declined, noting in his letter of regret that Americans should "keep alive from generation to generation the memory of the common sufferings and the common dangers which our fathers encountered in achieving our independence." When the Democrats of Harrisburg, Pennsylvania, invited Buchanan to their Independence Day celebration in 1865, he also declined and expressed in a letter that "peace has once more returned to bless our land," but that "our joy" is "tinged with a cloud of sorrow" regarding the death of Lincoln.

Sources: "Letter from President Buchanan" and "Letter from Ex-President Buchanan," *New York Times*, 9 July 1858, 3 and 14 July 1865, 6, respectively.

Buckline, Harry

Composed "Fourth of July, 1865. All Hail to Our Triumph: 'E Pluribus Unum,'" for solo and chorus. First line: "All hail to our triumph, ye loyal, ye true." Published, Chicago: H.M. Higgins, 1865.

Bull Run Civil War Battlefield, Manassas, Virginia

Site for a Fourth of July celebration in 1867 held by the Illinois State Association. Five railroad cars full of "excursionists, a large number of whom were ladies," traveled from Washington to a "luxuriant grove" in the vicinity of the battlefield. The day's festivities included speeches by officials of the association, music, provided by Heald's Band, and dancing "in the participation of which the ladies, by their dazzling beauty and graceful movements, won the admiration of the 'sterner sex.'"

The first principal battle of the Civil War took place on July 21, 1861, at Bull Run, south of Washington, D.C. It was there that the Confederate troops, under the command of Generals Joseph E. Johnston and Thomas J. "Stonewall" Jackson, routed General Irvin McDowell's Union troops, sending them in a panic back to Washington.

Source: "Celebration at Bull Run Battlefield," *Washington Evening Star*, 5 July 1867, 1.

Burlington College, Burlington, New Jersey

This institution was founded on Independence Day sparking annual celebrations that typically featured speeches presented by students, readings of the Declaration of Independence, and music. On July 4, 1853, for example, the event included addresses by Bishop George W. Doane, president of the college, and G.J. Burton, representing the senior class. According to a newspaper report, the Hall of the College was filled "with the citizens and ladies of Burlington, the young ladies of St. Mary's School, numbering 130" and "music helped to enliven the intervals in the business of the programme." William Dempster sang the "Star-Spangled Banner," and J.C. Garthwaite, Jr., read the Declaration of Independence. Doane encouraged the students to cultivate "moral excellence," to uphold the principles of the Constitution, and to cultivate their minds. On behalf of the students, Burton said, "We celebrate, to-day, a double festival; the anniversary of our Independence, and the founding of our College. We blend, to-day, in one, the two-fold character of the Christian and the Patriot. It was a happy co-incidence, that our College was first opened on the birthday of our liberty."

Sources: "Burlington College" and "The Young American," *New York Times*, 6 and 7 July 1853, 2 and 2, respectively.

Burnside, Ambrose E. (1824–1881)

On July 4, 1887, a statue of Union general Ambrose Burnside was unveiled in Exchange Place, Providence, Rhode Island. Burnside was born in Liberty, Indiana, and graduated from West Point in 1847. He served in the Mexican War and later became involved in some business ventures that almost drove him into debt. At the onset of the Civil War, he commanded the First Rhode Island Regiment and later was made commander of the Army of the Potomac. After the war Burnside served three terms as governor of Rhode Island, his adopted state.

The event for the unveiling of his statue drew militia from across Rhode Island, and some from other states in New England. Governor John W. Davis was appointed president of the day and made a brief address. Also present was Gov. Phineas C. Lounsbury of Connecticut, Launt Thompson, the sculptor of the monument, and Gen. **William Tecumseh Sherman**, "whose carriage was drawn by four heavy dappled grays." After the procession which lasted over an hour, the assembly arrived at a large stand that had been erected south of the monument "and covered with a canvas roof."

After a prayer from the Rev. Joseph J. Woolley, of Pawtucket, Gen. Lewis Richmond of Burnside's staff made a brief address, and then the statue was unveiled by Gen. Lewis Richmond, also of Burnside's staff, with the assistance of others.

Reports describe the statue as standing on a granite pedestal sixteen feet high, the figure of the general being nine feet high. "The aim was to represent Burnside as he appeared in the field. He is apparently upon an eminence, and is scanning manoeuvres at a distance, as a field glass is held in his right hand."

Gen. Horatio Rogers presented an oration (Providence: E.L. Freeman and Son, 1887) in which he discussed Burnside's military career. "The delivery of the statue to the city was by Col. Robert H.I. Goddard and Mayor [Gilbert F.] Robbins received it in the name of the city. The benediction and the 'American Hymn' by Reeve's Band closed the exercises at the monument."

Source: "A Statue of Burnside," *New York Times*, 5 July 1887, 1.

Burr-Hamilton Duel

Professional rivalry between Aaron Burr and Alexander Hamilton as lawyers and politicians led to a duel between the two which took place on the morning of July 11, 1804, at Weehawken, New Jersey. Burr shot Hamilton, who died the next day. Hamilton was buried on the grounds of Trinity Church and Burr was forced to flee New Jersey for the South. Ironically, Burr and Hamilton were at the same July 4 celebration held a few days previous at a dinner given by the New York Society of the Cincinnati. While Burr listened, Hamilton sang "an old military song," which was purported to be either "The Drum," according to his son John Church Hamilton, or "How Stands the Glass Around?," according to Alexander's grandson, Schuyler Hamilton.

Sources: *The Autobiography of Colonel John Trumbull*, ed. Theodore Sizer (New Haven, 1953), 237–38; "What Was Hamilton's 'Favorite Song'?" *William and Mary Quarterly* 12/2 (April 1955): 298–307.

Bush, George Herbert Walker (b. 1924)

Forty-first president of the U.S. (1989–93). Born in Milton, Massachusetts, Bush was dedicated to traditional American values and held political service in high esteem. His sentiments were frequently expressed in Fourth of July ceremonies. Bush graduated from Philips Andover Academy, served in World War II as a naval pilot, and later graduated from Yale in 1948. Bush's political career was varied, including serving two terms as Texas representative to Congress, as well as holding the positions of ambassador to the United Nations, chief of the U.S. Liaison Office in Beijing, China, and director of the Central Intelligence Agency.

On July 4, 1975, Bush presided over the first public celebration of U.S. independence in Bejing. The 500 guests, both Chinese and American, gathered at the U.S. liaison office for hot dogs and beer amidst the sounds of recordings of Johnny Cash and John Denver.

In 1980 he was elected vice president under Ronald Reagan. After Reagan's tenure, Bush was elected president after defeating his Democratic opponent, Governor Michael Dukakis of Massachusetts. Bush faced his greatest challenge as president when he vowed to liberate Kuwait after President Saddam Hussein of Iraq invaded the small country in August 1990. President Bush rallied the support of the United Nations. After a massive air campaign (January 1991), over 500,000 allied and U.S. troops sent over to Kuwait a month later successfully routed the Iraqi army. The battle, dubbed **Operation Desert Storm**, was celebrated across the country on the following Fourth of July.

In July 1983, Bush was in Europe bolstering NATO support for the employment of medium range missiles in Europe. On July 4 he spoke at the Rebild Festival near Aalborg, Denmark, cautioning Danes that peace "has to be built and it has to be protected.... all our people have had to live with the pressures and tensions involved in maintaining our freedom in a turbulent world." On July 4, 1988, Bush,

Vice President and Mrs. George Bush in the Fourth of July parade in Wyandotte, Michigan, 1988. Photograph used by permission of the George Bush Presidential Library.

campaigning for the presidency, visited a number of towns in the Midwest, sending a similar message. At Elmwood Park in Chicago, he spoke to a group of neighborhood residents reminding them that the peace they enjoyed was a result of the nation's strength. At Wyandotte, near Detroit, he joined a parade, and in St. Louis, he enjoyed hot dogs at the Veiled Prophet Fair. On the following two Fourths, Bush was at his summer retreat in Kennebunkport, Maine.

On July 4, 1991, Bush joined with all

Americans in celebrating the victory in the Gulf War. In Marshfield, Missouri, he and the First Lady reviewed a parade and spoke to a crowd, honoring the military. Later that day the Bushes were in Grand Rapids, Michigan, where they rode in the Freedom Parade. President Bush gave a brief speech. "We are very lucky to call America our home ... ," he said. "As Americans we share more than a magnificent land; we share values, we share commitments, experiences, beliefs and challenges.... Every one of us, every one of us feels proud to say, 'I am an American and I love my country.' And let's not be embarrassed to say so." Bush also presided over the official dedication of the **Mount Rushmore National Memorial**.

In 1992, Bush visited Faith, North Carolina, on the Fourth, where he praised family values in a speech at Faith Legion Park. "We meet in small-town America," he said, "in many ways the spiritual heart of all America." Earlier that day he was in Daytona, Florida, presiding over the start of the Pepsi 400 stock-car race and paying tribute to racing king Richard Petty.

Sources: "Beer and Hot Dogs in Peking on the 4th," *Washington Post*, 5 July 1975, A9; "Bush, Joining a Danish Fete on 4th, Stresses Need for New Missiles," *New York Times*, 5 July 1983, A8; Gerald M. Boyd, "Seeking Midwest Votes, Bush Stresses Positive," *New York Times*, 5 July 1988, B6; "White House Briefing," *Federal News Service*, 4 July 1991; "Bush Salutes Vets in Small-Town Parades," *USA Today*, 5 July 1991, 4A; Kathryn Tolbert, "Bush's 4th: Small Towns, Car Race," *Boston Globe*, 5 July 1992, 8.

Bush, George W. (b. 1946)

Forty-third president of the U.S. (2001–). Declared war on world-wide terrorism following the attacks of September 11, 2001, and rallied America's citizens on behalf of human freedoms in his patriotic Independence Day addresses. Born in New Haven, Connecticut, Bush spent his early years in Midland and Houston, Texas. He graduated from Yale University in 1968 and joined the Texas Air National Guard. After receiving a graduate degree from Harvard Business School in 1975, he participated in the purchase of the Texas Rangers baseball franchise. Bush was elected governor of Texas in 1994 and was re-elected

in 1998. He served two years of that term before being elected president in 2000.

On July 4, 2001, Bush and First Lady Laura were in Philadelphia at the Greater Exodus Baptist Church attending a "block party," where he encouraged faith-based and community organizations to reach out to children in need. He followed that with an address at Independence Hall, where he praised the nation's founders, the Declaration of Independence, and the "influence of faith in God." "The founding generation discerned in that faith the source of our own rights," he said. "Our nation has always been guided by a moral compass. In every generation men and women have protested terrible wrongs and worked for justice — for the abolition of slavery, the triumph of civil rights; for the end of child labor, the equal treatment of women, and the protection of innocent life." That day he also received from Philadelphia Mayor John Street a bible box made from wood of the last surviving liberty tree that was cut down on the campus of St. John's College in 1999.

In 2002 Bush was in Ripley, West Virginia, speaking before 1000 local residents, Governor Bob Wise and other officials. It was the first of three Independence Day visits Bush made to West Virginia. Bush reflected on the patriots of 1776, Pearl Harbor, September 11, and American troops engaging terror around the world. "We will take the battle to the enemy," he said, "wherever he hides and wherever he plans and wherever he dwells." Bush also publicly recited the Pledge of Allegiance in response to a federal appeals court that earlier had ruled the phrase "under God" unconstitutional.

In 2003 Bush visited Dayton, Ohio, where he joined others in celebrating the 100th anniversary of powered flight by Wilbur and Orville Wright. In his address he continued the themes of the previous year, heralding the military for their selfless commitment to the nation, and stressing how "the Declaration of Independence holds a promise for all mankind."

July 4, 2004, was marked by Bush's trip to Charleston, West Virginia, where he defended the war in Iraq in his address there to Mayor Danny Jones and residents of the area.

"Our immediate task in battle fronts like Iraq and Afghanistan and elsewhere is to capture or kill the terrorists," he said. Bush praised the progress in Afghanistan and Iraq. "We have promised to help deliver them from tyranny, to restore their sovereignty, and to set them on the path to democracy," he said. In 2005 Bush visited West Virginia for the third time on the Fourth. At West Virginia University he again called for support of his actions in Iraq. "We remember the band of patriots who risked their lives to bring freedom to a new colony," he said. "They kept their resolve, they kept their faith in a future of liberty."

Sources: Sonya Ross, "Bush Marks July 4th at Block Party," *Associated Press State and Local Wire*, 4 July 2001; Judy Kern, "USA Must Accept Terrorism Threat, Bush Says," *USA Today*, 5 July 2002, 2A; Jeff Zeleny, "Ripley Can Believe It: Bush Visits on the Fourth," *Chicago Tribune*, 5 July 2002, 1, 26; Jennifer Loven, "Bush Marks Fourth at Ohio Air Base," *Philadelphia Inquirer*, 5 July 2003, A4; Pete Yost, "Invasion Defensible, Bush Says," *Chicago Tribune*, 5 July 2004, 7; Vanessa Williams, "Bush Defends Iraq War in W. Va. Visit," *Boston Globe*, 5 July 2004, A2; Mark Silva, "Bush Defends Iraq War in W. Va. Speech," *Baltimore Sun*, 5 July 2005, 3A; Mark Silva, "Bush Hammers Theme of Resolve in Time of War," *Chicago Tribune*, 5 July 2005, 4; Web site, <www.whitehouse.gov>.

Butler County Soldiers, Sailors and Pioneers Monument

This monument officially opened on July 4, 1906, in Hamilton, Ohio, on the site of Fort Hamilton, built in 1791. The monument is dedicated to all Butler County military personnel and is a three-story structure topped off by a dome with a fourteen-foot bronze statue of a Civil War soldier standing on it. The statue was the work of Hamilton sculptor Rudolph Theim. The interior of the monument is ornamented with polished tablets of Tennessee marble with names of Butler County soldiers and sailors inscribed on them. The glass windows commemorate the contribution of women during the nation's wars.

Source: City of Sculpture, Web site, 24 September 2002, <http://www.cityofsculpture.org/sculpture.html>.

Butte, Montana, riot

On July 4, 1894, an American Protective Association (widely known by its initials A.P.A. and also referred to as American Proscriptive Association) riot broke out in Butte, Montana, with one person killed and several wounded. The incident was begun by two saloonkeepers who decorated their establishments for the Fourth of July with bunting forming the letters A.P.A. The militia was called out and all saloons and stores that sold ammunition were closed. "A crowd started to tear down" one of the saloons when the shootings occurred. The A.P.A. was an anti-Catholicism secret organization, founded in Clinton, Iowa, in 1887.

Sources: "An A.P.A. Riot in Montana" and "Secret Work of the A.P.A.," *New York Times*, 5 July 1894, 1 and 9, respectively; "Riot at Butte, Mont.," *Washington Evening Star*, 5 July 1894, 1.

Byrd, Richard E. (1888–1957)

U.S. rear admiral, explorer, and aviator who was honored in Boston on July 5, 1926, for his Arctic expedition and again in Paris on July 4, 1927, for his completion of a transatlantic flight. Byrd was born in Winchester, Virginia, and graduated from the U.S. Naval Academy (1912). He flew a dirigible across the Atlantic (1921), flew over the North Pole (1926), and with three associates, flew from New York to France (29 June–1 July 1927). He also made two expeditions to the Antarctic (1928–30 and 1933–35) and was credited with the discovery of a number of geological areas near the South Pole.

On Boston Common on Independence Day in 1926, 20,000 spectators honored him and two of his companions, pilot Floyd Bennett and flight engineer George O. Noville. Andrew J. Peters, former Boston mayor, presented an oration. He spoke on "A Citizen's Responsibility for Democracy." Following him was Francis Good, state commander of the American Legion, who told the audience the American Legion flag had been taken to the Pole by Commander Byrd. Byrd spoke as well and explained the difficulty of the trip. He also acknowledged the fifty other men that assisted him at the North Pole. "Getting our planes through the ice from ship to land and making a landing field was a colossal undertaking. Up in the bitter cold these men worked day and night, frequently in snowstorms, with their hands and feet frozen." About the future of aviation he commented, "It is my conviction that an era of aviation development lies just around the corner, so colossal that even the most enthusiastic, if they could read into the future, would be astonished. America is especially adapted to the commercial use of aviation, and progress will result from its development."

Also on July 5, 1926, an exhibition of Byrd's plane, the *Josephine Ford*, opened for viewing at the new Wanamaker Building at Eighth Street and Broadway, in New York, and Floyd Bennett was there to answer questions.

On July 4, 1934, Byrd was in the Antarctic at his base, Little America. He and his men set off fireworks in a storm with the temperature at 33 degree below zero, and this event was likely the first fireworks display in that part of the world. He also rang Philadelphia's **Liberty Bell** by a remote electrical device.

Sources: "20,000 Cheer Byrd on Boston Common" and "Byrd's Plane on View at John Wanamaker's," *New York Times*, 6 July 1926, 21; *New York Times*, 5 July 1927, 1; "Byrd Rings Liberty Bell by Electrical Impulse," *New York Times*, 5 July 1934, 10.

Caldwell, Joseph Blake (d. 1811)

Presented an oration (Worcester: Isaiah Thomas, Jr., 1808) at Barre, Massachusetts, on July 4, 1808, in which 14 "spirited resolutions" that condemned the policies of the government and the Embargo Act were proposed. The ceremony had 600 Federalists in attendance.

Calhoun, John C. (1782–1850)

Statesman and vice president under John Quincy Adams and Andrew Jackson who was a fervent supporter of states' rights, which earned him the respect of Southerners, especially those in his home state of South Carolina. Calhoun held a number of exemplary positions including that of secretary of war under Monroe (1817–25), U.S. senator (1832–43), and secretary of state under Tyler (1844–45). It was at his "South Carolina Exposition" of 1828 that he put forth his principles of states' rights. Calhoun saw the Fourth of July as an opportunity to express his sometimes controversial political views. On July 4, 1830,

in Pendleton, South Carolina, at an anniversary dinner celebration, he proposed a toast in which he said "consolidation and disunion" are "two extremes of our system" and that "they are equally dangerous, and ought both to be equally the object of our apprehension." His comments caused a quick editorial response by the *National Intelligencer* in Washington. Calhoun was in error, the article stated, since consolidation and disunion "are both beyond its extreme limits, and when either occurs the system no longer exists."

Another significant celebration he participated in was the fiftieth anniversary event in Washington in 1826. He joined in a procession there riding in a carriage immediately behind the president. The group left the Executive Mansion and made its way to the Capitol. After hearing an oration and reading of the Declaration of Independence, he returned to the president's residence to assist in meeting and entertaining visitors for several hours.

Calhoun's popularity and influence was long lasting both during and after his lifetime. He was recognized annually on the Fourth of July and honored through toasts and statements. In 1839, he was invited to speak at the **Tammany Society** meeting in New York on the Fourth, but declined. On July 4, 1842, at a meeting of the '76 Association in Charleston, South Carolina, a toast was presented to "J. C. Calhoun — our earliest choice — his claim to the support of the people is founded on his splendid talents, his eminent services and unwavering adherence to correct principles." Five years later on Independence Day the same association once again honored Calhoun: "His lofty virtues and talents are destined to maintain the constitutional rights and liberties of our whole country. The offerings of party, and the allurements of ambition, can never mislead him from the high purposes of his life." On July 4, 1845, in Lawtonville, South Carolina, at a dinner celebration, the following toast to Calhoun was presented: "John C. Calhoun: The first to throw himself in the breach against federal usurpation, may he live to see his principles predominate throughout the world."

On July 4, 1853, the Calhoun Monument

Association was established in Orangeburg, South Carolina, in his honor. This first meeting was held in the court house, J.J. Salley was elected president, and a constitution was drawn up. Article two in the document stated that a monument to Calhoun was to be erected.

Sources: Charles Francis Adams, ed., *Memoirs of John Quincy Adams*, 12 vols. (Freeport, New York: Books for Libraries Press, 1969); *National Intelligencer*, 22 July 1830, 3; *Alexandria Gazette*, 13 July 1839, 2; "'76 Association," *Charleston Courier*, 7 July 1842, 2, and 8 July 1847, 2; "Celebration of the 4th of July in St. Peter's Parish," *Charleston Courier*, 18 July 1845, 2; *Charleston Mercury*, 13 July 1853, 2.

Cambridge, Maryland

Celebrated the 200th anniversary of its founding on July 4, 1884, before a crowd of 5,000 with artillery salutes, parades, speeches, and fireworks. Included in the parade were "floats representing the trades, merchants and manufacturers, bands of music, and drum corps." The Declaration of Independence was read and an oration given by James Wallace on the court house lawn. He described the town's early history and "present prosperity" after which he "received much applause from the attentive listeners."

Sources: "Great Fun at Cambridge," *Baltimore Morning Herald*, 5 July 1884, 1; *New York Times*, 5 July 1884, 3.

Camp Hill, Pennsylvania

A Bicentennial Plaza was dedicated here on July 4, 1976.

Source: *Camp Hill Bicentennial Plaza Dedication July 4, 1976* (Camp Hill, Pa.: Bicentennial Committee, 1976).

Camp Release Monument, Montevideo, Minnesota

Located near Montevideo, this 51-foot-tall granite monument was dedicated on July 4, 1894, and commemorates "the release of 269 captives and the surrender of about 1200 Dakota people," following the Dakota Conflict of 1862. In the fall of that year, "Dakota tribes surrendered to Col. Henry Sibley on a bluff overlooking the valley and the present day site of Montevideo." The monument is inscribed with information about the Dakota battles.

Source: "Camp Release Monument," Western Minnesota Prairie Waters Web site, 11 September 2002, <http://www.prairiewaters.com/attractions/museums/crelea.php3>.

Canadian Riots of 1913

In Moose Jaw, Saskatchewan, and Winnipeg, American flags were trampled on and riots ensued on July 4, 1913. In both places Americans affronted Canadians by waving the Star-Spangled Banner. At Moose Jaw, "an American attempted to raise a flag on top of a lamp post. It was torn down and a free fight ensued. Earlier in the day fifty Americans, waving flags, had attempted to march up Main Street." Police turned them back. At Winnipeg, "a young man waving an American flag in the faces of the returning 100th Regiment of Winnipeg Grenadiers" and at the same time shouting "hurrah for the American eagle" caused that affray.

Source: "Trample Our Flag in Canadian Riots," *New York Times*, 5 July 1913, 1.

Canonicus

This iron-clad vessel was the first improved *Monitor*-style designed by John Ericsson. It was built in Boston and launched in 1863. She served admirably during the Civil War, first in the James River area of Virginia and later stationed off the coast of Charleston, South Carolina. From 1872 to 1877 she cruised the Atlantic coast and Gulf of Mexico. *Canonicus* fired a salute in honor of the Centennial, July 4, 1876, while on the Mississippi River at New Orleans, Louisiana.

Source: *New Orleans Republican*, 6 July 1876, 1.

Cape May, New Jersey, Naval Base

On July 4, 1916, the harbor was officially opened with a ceremony and events that included a naval display of cruisers and submarines in the harbor, a land parade of marines and sailors, and a military ball.

Sources: "Submarines in 4th Fete" and "Naval Base at Cape May," *New York Times*, 4 and 5 July 1916, 6 and 11, respectively.

"Capitol Fourth"

Popular name for the Fourth of July concerts that began on the grounds of the west lawn of the U.S. Capitol in 1981. The events featured popular headliners accompanied by the National Symphony Orchestra (NSO). Hosts have included E.G. Marshall, Joel Grey, Tony Danza, and Barry Bostwick. Conductors of the NSO have included Henry Mancini, Mstislav Rostropovich, Leonard Slatkin, Hugh Wolf, James Conlon, and Erich Kunzel. Performers have included Ray Charles, Amy Grant, Tony Bennett, and Kenny Rogers. In 2004 a special tribute was given to the late Ray Charles as well as a 150th birthday salute to **John Philip Sousa**.

On April 22, 1999, Congress passed a concurrent resolution (S. Con. Res. 29, 106th Congress, 1st Session), sponsored by C. Trent Lott (Rep. — Mass.), authorizing the National Symphony Orchestra to have concerts on the Capitol grounds three times a year, on Memorial Day, the 4th of July, and Labor Day, establishing that such concerts would be "free of admission charge and open to the public" and officially recognizing the use of that space at those specified times.

Source: A Capitol Fourth Web site, <http://www.pbs.org/capitolfourth/concert.html>.

Capitol of the United States *see* United States Capitol

Carlin, Thomas (1789–1852)

A monument to the sixth elected governor of Illinois (1838–42) was unveiled in Carrollton, Greene County, Illinois, on July 4, 1917. Carlin was born in Kentucky, served in the **War of 1812**, and was a state senator (1825–33). Carlin was instrumental in establishing Carrollton, the county seat.

Source: broadside, "Unveiling Exercises: Governor Thomas Carlin Monument...." (n.p., 1917).

"Carnival of the Confederacy" *see* Vicksburg, Mississippi, battle

Carroll, Charles (1737–1832)

The last surviving signer of the Declaration of Independence and an active participant in Independence Day celebrations in Baltimore. Carroll was born in Annapolis, Maryland, studied law abroad and returned to a life of public service. He opposed taxation

without representation and was elected to the Second Continental Congress on July 4, 1776. He favored ratification of the U.S. Constitution and was a member of the U.S. Senate (1789–92) and the Maryland Senate (1774–1804). Carroll was highly interested in the Fourth of July because it represented the achievements of the new nation.

On July 4, 1820, Carroll was invited by the Committee of Arrangement of Baltimore to attend their celebration that was to provide "a greater degree of interest than any ceremony that has been witnessed here on a similar occasion." Carroll, with his copy of the Declaration of Independence in hand, was accompanied by General Samuel Smith and Colonel John Eagar Howard, "two heroes of the revolution." The celebration took place in **Howard's Park**, and Carroll and the others sat on a platform. Above Carroll's head were displayed several American flags and a copy of Mr. Binns' printing of the Declaration "in an elegant gilt frame." Carroll handed his copy of the Declaration to Doctor T. Watkins, who read it to the crowd assembled there. He said, "Who could stand in the presence of the venerable patriot [Carroll], and not catch the influence of that holy flame, which filled, illumined, and inspired him, in '76?"

When **John Adams** and **Thomas Jefferson** died on July 4, 1826, only Carroll was left as a surviving signer of the Declaration of Independence, and the city council of New York realized the significance of the occasion. It requested that Carroll sign a copy of the Declaration of Independence "for deposit in the public hall in the city." The patriot of eighty-nine years signed the document on August 2, the anniversary of the day that he signed the original document in 1776. "I do hereby recommend to the present and future generations the principles of that important document as the best earthly inheritance their ancestors could bequeath to them, and pray that the civil and religious liberties they have secured to my country may be perpetuated to remotest posterity and extended to the whole family of man," he wrote.

On July 4, 1828, Carroll assisted in the laying of the "first stone" of the **Baltimore and Ohio Railroad**.

During his life, Carroll was honored in ceremonies and speeches across the country. At a dinner held on July 4, 1831, at Steward's Island, opposite the city of Pittsburgh, the following toast to him was offered:

> Charles Carroll of Carrolton — the surviving signer of the Declaration of Independence: —
> "'Tis the last rose of summer
> Left Blooming alone —
> All his noble companions
> Are faded and gone."

On July 4, 1876, at Druid Hill Park in Baltimore, Gen. Charles E. Phelps spoke about Carroll's life. His comments about the patriot were expressed "as to move many of his audience to emotion." At the Fourth celebration in Hagerstown, Maryland, in 1895, Joseph B. Updegraff read "a series of interesting reminiscences of the signing of the Declaration by Charles Carroll, of Carrollton." On July 4, 1932, the Charles Carroll General Assembly Degree of Patriotism of the Knights of Columbus staged a Fourth of July ceremony outside Federal Hall in Bryant Park, New York City.

Each year on the Fourth, tours of the Charles Carroll House (109 Duke of Gloucester Street), Annapolis, Maryland, are given.

Sources: *Federal Gazette*, 30 June 1820; *Frederick-Town Herald*, 8 July 1820, 2; *National Intelligencer*, 8 July 1820, 3; *Niles* XVII (8 July 1820), 329; *Virginia Herald*, 5 July 1820, 2; "Declaration of Independence," Charleston Courier, 9 July 1842, 2; *Maryland Journal and True American*, 16 July 1828, 2; "National Anniversary: Pennsylvania," *The [Washington] Globe*, 14 July 1831, 3; "The Nation's Birthday" and "Municipal Celebration at Druid Hill Park," *Baltimore Bee*, 5 July 1876, 4 and 5, respectively; "News of the State," *Baltimore Morning Herald*, 5 July 1895, 7; "Exercises at Federal Hall," *New York Times*, 4 July 1932, 12.

Carter, James E. "Jimmy" (b. 1924)

Thirty-ninth president of the U.S. (1977–81) and best known for his life-long work advocating human rights across the world. Carter's message to the nation on July 4, 1977, focused on freedom and stewardship. "The work of freedom can never be finished," he said, "for freedom is not a temple which is completed when the last stone is in place, but a living thing that each generation must complete anew."

In 1980 on the Fourth, President Carter spoke at the NAACP's 71st annual convention in Miami Beach. He pledged "fiscal austerity" and "warned that Ronald Reagan's election could mean a conservative overhaul of the Supreme Court and profound changes in the federal judiciary." He also spoke at Merced College in California that day on the partial grain embargo of the Soviet Union, immigration, and the American hostages being held in Iran.

On July 4, 1986, Carter was in Harare, Zimbabwe, where he led a walkout of "American officials, [and] diplomats from the British, West German and Dutch embassies" due to Zimbabwean "criticism of United States policy toward South Africa."

Sources: "President Reflects on Freedom in Special 4th of July Message," *Washington Post*, 3 July 1977, A20; Herbert Denton and Lou Cannon, "Reagan Would Turn Judiciary to Right, Carter Tells Blacks," *Washington Post*, 5 July 1980, A1, A4; "Carter Leads Walkout at Party in Zimbabwe," *New York Times*, 5 July 1986, 4.

Carusi, Gaetano (1760–1843)

Composer, conductor, impresario, and musical instrument dealer who lived in Philadelphia, Baltimore, and Washington and who actively participated in Fourth of July celebrations. In 1805 Carusi, his wife Philippa, and their three young sons, Samuel, Nathaniel, and Lewis, along with a group of Italian musicians, left Italy for America. For the next fifteen years, Carusi led an itinerant musical life, spending time in a number of cities on the Eastern Seaboard. On July 4, 1816, he was in Annapolis, where he and his band provided music for a celebration by the "Republican citizens" at the Assembly Room. Some of the works performed were "Washington's March," "Hail Columbia," and "Madison's March." Carusi settled permanently in Washington in 1822 and built the Washington Assembly Hall (known also as Carusi's Saloon), a spectacular building for concerts and other entertainments. For the next one hundred years the hall had the distinction of being one of the most popular gathering places in the city. In addition to presidential inaugural balls, Carusi hosted a number of Fourth of July dinners there. For example, on July 4, 1828, the city's Committee of Arrangements for Independence Day contracted with H. Rumpff's Hotel to provide a "handsome dinner" at the "spacious City Assembly Rooms of Mr. Carusi."

Sources: *National Intelligencer*, 24 June 1828, 1; *Washington Evening Star*, 3 July 1885, 2; James R. Heintze, "Gaetano Carusi: From Sicily to the Halls of Congress," in *American Musical Life in Context and Practice to 1865* (New York: Garland Publishing, 1994), 75–131.

Catholic Total Abstinence Fountain, Philadelphia

The ceremony for the dedication of this fountain located in Fairmount Park in Philadelphia occurred twice, the first for the Centennial on July 4, 1876, and again on July 4, 1877, because only two of the four statues planned for the design had been completed in time for the 1876 event. The fountain was located "immediately to the west of Machinery Hall" on the Centennial Exhibition grounds. It was conceived in 1873 at an annual convention of the society and cost $58,000. Herman Kirn was selected as the sculptor. "The design represents Moses after having struck the rock, his right hand pointing to Heaven, the source of the miracle, and his left hand holding the tables of the law." The memorial was completed in the following year, when the statue of Moses was placed in position and the water turned on.

An immense crowd gathered to witness the blessing of the fountain by Rev. James O'Reilly, band music, and two addresses, one by Rev. Patrick Byrne of Trenton, president of the Catholic Total Abstinence Society, and the other by John Lee Carroll, governor of Maryland.

At the second dedication before a crowd of 25,000, John H. Campbell officially transferred the fountain to the Park Commission, represented by David W. Sellers. Both John Lee Carroll and John F. Hartranft, governor of Pennsylvania, gave speeches, after which Philip A. Nolan, secretary of the Centennial Committee, "recited a poem appropriate to the occasion." On July 4, 1878, many returned to the fountain to decorate it "in honor of the Revolutionary heroes."

Sources: "Dedication of the Catholic Temperance Fountain," *New York Times*, 5 July 1876, 4; "The Total Abstinence Cause," *New York Times*, 5 July 1877, 1; "Observances at Other Points," *New York Times*, 5 July 1878, 3.

Centennial

The nation celebrated the 100th anniversary of the signing of the Declaration of Independence in 1876 with great joy, reflection, and expressions of aspirations and hope for the future. Events included magnificent parades, 100-gun salutes, orations, recitations of the Declaration of Independence, and dinners.

In Trenton, the town's parade included "two Centennial Cars, one of 1876 containing thirty eight young ladies dressed in modern style, and one of 1776 containing thirteen young ladies dressed in Continental costume." Towns were festooned in displays of flags and banners set against a background of church bells. In Jersey City, New Jersey, "whistles on all the railroad locomotives and factories in the city blew continuously" around the clock. In Bridgeport, Connecticut, "almost every public building, factory, and residence" was decorated. In Toledo, Ohio, the main streets were spanned "at prominent points" by "arches bearing appropriate mottoes and names of Revolutionary battles." San Francisco enjoyed a four-mile parade with 10,000 participants while Omaha, Nebraska, had a torchlight parade and "a grand electric display." In St. Paul, Minnesota, a 100-gun salute began a day filled with patriotic music by several bands, parades, and an address by Governor John Pillsbury. In Bristol, Rhode Island, a parade float named "Triumphal Car" saw 38 ladies and a "Goddess of Liberty" waving to the crowds along the streets. In Savannah, Georgia, a "Centennial tree" was planted at Schuetzen Park.

Americans everywhere feasted on a banquet of new music and poetry written especially for the occasion, while tributes poured in from around the world. In New York at the Academy of Music, William Cullen Bryant's "Centennial Ode" to music by J. Mosenthal was sung by the Centennial Sangerverbund after an address by Richard S. Storrs, who captivated his audience by the "magic charm of his word-painting and the interesting character of his historical allusions." At Port Richmond, New York, 500 children sang "Hail Columbia" and the "Star-Spangled Banner."

Events in Europe were festive and included a celebration dinner of the American Legation at the Westminster Palace Hotel in London. Toasts were presented to President Grant and Queen Victoria. In Frankfurt, Germany, a concert, a reading of the Declaration of Independence, speeches and fireworks were given. In Paris the morning newspapers featured articles on the Centennial and American flags that "were profusely displayed in the principal streets of the city." In Lisbon and Rome, private parties marked the occasion.

In many places the daytime events carried over well into the night. Fireworks were attended in most places by immense crowds. In Norwich, Connecticut, pyrotechnics were set off from barges in the center of the river. In Columbus, Ohio, "the dome of the Capitol was illuminated and a national salute was fired."

Important national events included the admission of Colorado to the Union and the **Centennial Exhibition** held in Philadelphia. Other highlights were cornerstone ceremonies (see **Quincy, Illinois, Court House**) and dedications of statues and other monuments (see **Catholic Total Abstinence Fountain** and **Centennial Fountain, Evanston, Illinois**).

Philadelphia began its celebration on the evening of December 31, 1875, outside of Independence Hall with a flag-raising and speech by Mayor William S. Stokley. On the morning after, church bells rang and fireworks were sent aloft. Preparations for the Centennial Fourth were typically planned weeks if not months ahead. The idea for a national Centennial Exhibition was first introduced in 1864. The fair officially opened to the public on May 10, 1876. Other towns held three-day celebrations, July 3–5.

Centennial celebrations helped to provide a catalyst for the healing and bonding of the nation following the Civil War. Although the North and West celebrated extensively, the white South, recovering from a devastating war and still harboring resentments, mainly offered tributes to the day. Large elaborate celebrations were few in number. The tension in some areas of the South was nowhere more evident than in **Hamburgh, South Carolina**, when a fight there resulted in the deaths of six blacks and one white. Nonetheless blacks celebrated fervently in many Southern towns, in honor of the nation and their new-found freedom. Richmond raised the Star-Spangled Banner in tandem with the Virginia state flag on top of the state capitol, the first time on the Fourth in sixteen years. The Richmond Grays, a black regiment, traveled to Washington and joined in celebrations there. Residents of Montgomery, Alabama, enjoyed a parade of firemen, a 37-gun salute, and a speech by ex-governor Thomas H. Watts. Neil Blue read from a copy of the Declaration of Independence. He was the only survivor of the group that voted for delegates to the territorial convention which adopted the Constitution under which Alabama was admitted into the Union in 1819. Orators appealed to the citizens of the nation to come together, and many stressed the importance of the common heritage. Representative William T. Avery (Dem.— Tenn.), speaking in Memphis, said, "This Fourth of July is a common heritage: it belongs to no North, no South, no East, no West. Men of the South as well as men of the North aided in establishing this empire of freedom. It is the united work of both."

Independence Day was also an event of considerable contrasts. In Washington, D.C., at the First Congregation Church in an act of celebration there, as Bayard Taylor read his poem "Centennial Bells," in Philadelphia, Susan B. Anthony and others belonging to the National Woman's Suffrage Association, in an act challenging those celebrating, read their "Declaration of Rights for Women." In Chicago, at the Turners and Socialists gathering, a revised Declaration of Independence from the socialist's standpoint was distributed while at the same time the nation's Centennial Exhibition at Fairmount Park in Philadelphia displayed the hand and torch of the Statue of Liberty before tens of thousands of citizens.

The orations presented on the Fourth reflected the sentiments of the nation regarding its history and progress. "It has been one of struggle, but one of prosperity," said Isaac W. Smith at the centennial celebration at Manchester, New Hampshire. Many of the addresses presented broad historical sweeps of time with lengthy descriptions of specific interesting events that occurred both in national and local context. "To note the landmarks in our history; to ever aim at the purity of the birth of the nation, is the safeguard of our destiny," exclaimed Col. J.H. Gilpatrick, speaking in Leavenworth, Kansas. George F. Talbot, speaking at Portland, Maine, perhaps best summarized the lessons that were gleaned from the Centennial. "The first century closes behind us," he said. "Let us enter upon the second with thankfulness for all that we have achieved, and with a determination to make our country worthier than ever of our highest love and holiest devotion." While many orators preferred to reminisce about the previous hundred years, Governor Thomas H. Watts, addressing an audience in Montgomery, Alabama, looked forward to the year 1976. He projected a country of 400 million inhabitants that stretched across 100 states!

> Indulge me one moment longer, fellow-citizens. Imagine that some one of us it may be some bright-eyed boy could witness our next Centennial anniversary, the celebration of the 4th of July, 1976. What a spectacle would ravish his sight! The beatific vision of St. John on the Isle of Patmos was scarcely more enrapturing, than this spectacle would be!
>
> If our people be true to the Constitution; if good will and internal peace prevail; if science continue its giant stride; if God be our God, and we be His people; judging the future by the past, the States composing the American Union will be multiplied to one hundred States; the population will be increased from forty to four hundred millions; our territory will extend to the Isthmus of Panama from the frozen lakes of the North; railroads, like a network, will connect all parts of this vast country, and intelligence will flash along innumerable telegraph wires from State to State, from city to city and from village to village! The school-house and the church will adorn every hill and beautify every valley! And these four hundred millions of people from one hundred free, separate, independent, and co-equal States, protected by the same Federal Constitution, speaking the same language, worshiping the same God, will unite their voices in anthems of praise and adoration to the Rulers of the Universe, and of gratitude to the patriots of two hundred years ago, for the blessings of American freedom.
>
> And then, when one hundred stars shall be emblazoned on our national flag, these four hundred millions of people may turn, as we to-day turn, and apostrophize that flag as the ensign of a great Confederate Republic.

Out of the hundreds of orators speaking on July 4, a handful were cited as the best and most outstanding by the local press. The *Boston Evening Transcript* named Charles Francis Adams (Taunton, Massachusetts), William M. Evarts (Philadelphia), and Robert C. Winthrop (Boston) as "possessing superior qualifications, by nature or attainments, to depict the grandeur and danger of the nation, its heroisms and its meannesses, its virtues and its faults, what it has accomplished and what remains for it to accomplish, with the shoals and quicksands lying in it future course, could not have been selected in America." The *St. Louis Globe-Democrat* thought Evarts' oration was the most "magnificent" presentation that "will go into history, not only as one of the most brilliant efforts of Mr. Evarts' life, but as by far the ablest oration, which the Centennial year has produced. In its paragraphs are exhibited the master thoughts of a profound philosopher." The *Springfield Daily Republican* agreed with Adams and Evarts as excellent choices but added Richard S. Storrs (New York) to the list: "Dr. Storrs' skillful rhetoric glows along the great triumphs of English liberty in a masterly style, and his fresh and vigorous thought, if less analytical, is not less buoyant than Mr. Evarts," the paper noted, and added, "Mr. Adams's oration is the most striking of all the boldness of design and quaintness of treatment."

George F. Talbot, speaking at Portland, Maine, seemed to best summarize lessons that were gleaned from the Centennial. "The first century closes behind us," he said. "Let us enter upon the second with thankfulness for all that we have achieved, and with a determination to make our country worthier than ever of our highest love and holiest devotion."

Sources: *Omaha Republican*, 4 July 1876, 4; *San Francisco Chronicle*, 4 and 6 July 1876, 3 and 1, respectively; *Washington Evening Star*, 5 July 1876, 1, 4; "A

Second Century Begun," "Independence Day Elsewhere," "All Around New York," "Greetings from Abroad," and "Staten Island Festivities," *New York Times*, 5 July 1876, 1, 5, 7, and 10, respectively; "Programme. City of St. Paul. Fourth of July [1876]," Chilson Collection, Library, University of South Dakota; Appelbaum, *The Glorious Fourth*, 102–15; Richard V. Simpson, *Independence Day: How the Day Is Celebrated in Bristol, Rhode Island* (Middletown, R.I.: Aquidneck Graphics, 1989), 26.

Centennial Exhibition, Philadelphia

A grand international fair that celebrated the hundredth birthday of the United States and attracted millions of visitors to Philadelphia's Fairmount Park to see displays representing the best of the arts, sciences, and industries of the time. No less than 20 nations participated, as did most of this country's 37 states. The exhibition was one of 10 great world's fairs of the 19th century and was instrumental in raising the image of America as a country of greatness and prosperity.

The idea for the exhibition was first introduced by John L. Campbell in February 1864, at a speech he gave at the Smithsonian Institution in Washington, D.C. Years later, with considerable persuasion, Congress passed legislation in March 1871 that created a United States Centennial Commission that later established "an International Exhibition of Arts, Manufactures, and Products of the Soil and Mine" in Philadelphia. Members of the commission included its president, Joseph R. Hawley, newspaper publisher and former congressman, John Welsh, a Philadelphia businessman, and Alfred T. Goshorn, a Cincinnati attorney. Numerous other individuals were appointed to oversee virtually every facet of the project, which spread over 284 acres and included 249 buildings and structures of all sizes. The transfer of Fairmount Park for use by the Centennial Commission in preparation for the International Exhibition and Centennial Celebration in 1876 took place on July 4, 1873. On July 4, 1874, a ground-breaking ceremony took place before numerous spectators.

The exhibition opened to the public on May 10, 1876, and over 186 thousand persons attended that day. President Grant and Mrs. Grant joined some 4,000 dignitaries on a grandstand erected in front of Memorial Hall. An orchestra under the direction of renowned conductor Theodore Thomas accompanied a chorus of 1000 voices singing **John Greenleaf Whittier**'s "Centennial Hymn," composed especially for the occasion. Other hymns composed for the opening ceremonies included "Welcome to All Nations," by **Oliver Wendell Holmes,** and "Our National Banner," by Dexter Smith (1839–1909). Also performed was "Centennial Inauguration March" by Richard Wagner and "Centennial Cantata" with words by Sidney Lanier and music by Dudley Buck. After speeches by Hawley and Grant, international flags were raised, 800 singers performed Handel's "Hallelujah" chorus, a 100-gun salute sounded, and President Grant and Emperor Dom Pedro II of Brazil turned on the giant Corliss steam engine in Machinery Hall that provided power to all of the exhibits. Some of the principal buildings included the Main Building of 20 acres, Machinery Hall, one of the most popular sites, Agricultural Hall, Art Gallery or Memorial Hall, and Horticultural Hall. The Women's Pavilion was a novelty, with the exhibits being facilitated only by women. There were 24 state buildings and 9 buildings constructed by foreign nations. The industries, arts, and humanities represented a broadest range of professions and products imaginable.

On July 4 one of the important ceremonies of the day was the unveiling of a statue of Baron Alexander von Humboldt, sponsored by the Humboldt Monument Association. The statue was made by Frederick Drake of Berlin and was nine feet in height, made of bronze, and cost $18,000. The location was near the Girard Avenue Bridge. Music was provided by a large chorus and speeches were presented by George K. Ziegler, G. Kellner, and Charles S. Keyser.

The Centennial Exposition closed on November 10. Ceremonies included a musical program, addresses and a flag ceremony. See also **Catholic Total Abstinence Fountain, Philadelphia.**

Sources: *New York Times*, 5 July 1873, 5; J.S. Ingram, *The Centennial Exposition* (Philadelphia:

Hubbard Brothers, 1876); "Exercises in Fairmount Park," *New York Times*, 5 July 1876, 4; Edith L. Markham, "Poetry Written for the Opening Exercises and the Fourth of July Celebration at the 1876 Centennial Exhibition in Philadelphia" (M.A. thesis, University of North Carolina, 1950); Robert C. Post, ed., *1876: A Centennial Exhibition* (Washington, D.C.: National Museum of History and Technology, Smithsonian Institution, 1976); Bruno Giberti, *Designing the Centennial: A History of the 1876 International Exhibition in Philadelphia* (Lexington: University Press of Kentucky, 2002).

Centennial Fountain, Evanston, Illinois

Dedicated on July 4, 1876. The fountain, located at the corner of Davis and Orrington Avenue, was "transferred" by J.H. Kedzie "to the municipality." Speeches were made by Gen. Julius White and E.S. Taylor.

Source: "Suburban: Evanston," *Chicago Tribune*, 5 July 1876, 3.

"Centennial Hymn" *see* John Greenleaf Whittier (1807–1892)

Chappaqua, New York, Monument

Officials of this town unveiled "a model of a monument to be erected here in memory of the World War veterans" on Independence Day in 1920. The monument was designed by Frederick Ginsberg and when completed was to be located in the park in the village center. "Speeches were made by Deputy Attorney General Berger, Supreme Court Justice Philip McCook and the Rev. Frank A. Clendenin, local pastor."

Source: "Unveiling at Chappaqua," *New York Times*, 6 July 1920, 4.

Charleston, West Virginia, train wreck

Occurred on July 4, 1891, on the Kanawha and Michigan Railroad, eight miles west of Charleston. The mishap was cited as "the worst wreck ever known in this part of the state." The train, whose final destination was Columbus, Ohio, had two carloads of Independence Day excursionists aboard, including members of the Order of United American Mechanics who were on their way to Poca. The accident occurred as the train was crossing a high trestle that had caught fire during the night. The engine, baggage and mail cars passed over safely, but the two passenger cars plunged over the bridge. At least seventeen died and fifty-eight were injured.

Source: "A Terrible Wreck," *Houston Daily Post*, 5 July 1891, 1.

Charlotte and South Carolina Railroad

The promotion ceremony for the creation of a railroad line from Charlotte, North Carolina, to Columbia, South Carolina, took place on July 4, 1847, in Chester, South Carolina. A ceremony included addresses by Edward J. Palmer of Fairfield, James Greggt and Joseph A. Black of Columbia, and F.W. Davie of Chester. According to a newspaper reporter, "Their remarks were all characterized by practical good sense, which rendered them highly acceptable to the citizens assembled, and contributed much to the promotion of the great scheme in which they were enlisted." In addition to a barbecue and music by the Cedar Shoals and Chesterville Bands, subscriptions were available for raising money for the railroad. The town of Chester had pledged a share of the funds required to support the venture.

Source: "Celebration of 4th July at Chester, S.C.," *Charleston Courier*, 16 July 1847, 2.

Chattanooga, Tennessee, "monster parade"

One of the most significant celebrations in the South after the Civil War occurred there on July 4, 1890, when two thousand Confederate veterans marched in a "monster parade." General John B. Gordon was commander of the procession which included three regiments of Tennessee State Guards and several military companies from other southern cities. Fifty thousand persons witnessed the men marching in their Confederate uniforms but "not a single Confederate flag was displayed, but every command carried the national colors." A reporter noticed that the soldiers who were in the Civil War "clearly indicated that it has been a long time since the close of the war. The men are gray-haired and nearly all infirm. Many of them appeared in their old tattered gray jackets."

An impressive group of military officers gave speeches to a crowd of 5,000 persons assembled in a large tent. They included Generals John B. Gordon of Georgia, W.S. Cabell, E. Kirby Smith, and George Thomas ("Tige") Anderson of Georgia. "The sentiments were patriotic and eloquent, and the wildest enthusiasm prevailed." General Gordon remarked to the crowd that "slavery was wrong, and consequently that the South had been on the wrong side of the fight." There were brass bands that played "national airs and 'Dixie,' 'Bonny Blue Flag,' and war tunes of both sides, and cheers greeted every air."

That evening Lookout Mountain and Missionary Ridge were "ablaze with bright lights, and on the Tennessee River and Cameron Hill" were "monster pyrotechnic displays." On the following day many of the veterans assembled on the Chickamauga battlefield, "the proposed national park," for a picnic. On July 3 the United Confederate Veterans' Association had been founded by Gordon, Smith, and others.

Sources: "Ex-Confederate Veterans" and "The Fourth at Chattanooga," *New York Times*, 4 and 5 July 1890, 5 and 2, respectively.

Chesapeake and Delaware Canal

Celebrated on at least two Fourth of July occasions for its importance in opening up inland waterway travel. In Easton, Maryland, on July 4, 1825, the canal was toasted at a dinner celebration held in the Easton Hotel as "a national work destined to produce incalculable national benefits." Governor Samuel Stevens, Jr., of Maryland and other dignitaries were in attendance. On July 4, 1829, the canal was completed, and the embankments at the summit were opened and water let in. In attendance was Philadelphia mayor Benjamin Wood Richards and various military personnel who marched along the towpath in "knee-deep" mud with "rain pouring in their faces." The first barge that day to pass through the canal was the *Chesapeake*, and its destination was Delaware City. On the same day another barge passed through the canal on its way from Worcester to Providence, Rhode Island.

Sources: "Celebration of the Fourth of July, 1825, in Easton," *Easton Gazette*, 9 July 1825, 3; *Independent Journal* (Downingtown, Pa.), 14 July 1829, 2; "Opening of the Chesapeake and Delaware Canal," *National Intelligencer*, 8 July 1829, 3.

Chesapeake and Ohio Canal

The groundbreaking ceremony for the C & O Canal took place on July 4, 1828, with President John Quincy Adams presiding. Early in the morning the directors of the C & O Canal Company, members of Congress, militaries officers, secretaries of executive departments, and foreign dignitaries met at Tilley's Hotel in Georgetown and marched in procession, accompanied by music from the U.S. Marine Band, to High Street Wharf. There they boarded steam boats and barges and proceeded up the Potomac River to a spot "one or two hundred yards East of the line of the present Canal. The President and other officials traveled on the steam boat *Surprize*, preceded by the band on its own barge, playing airs, now animated, now plaintive." The passengers gathered at a "spot marked by Judge Wright, the Engineer" of the canal company. A number of speeches were given before a crowd of thousands that included several military companies. President Adams spoke about the history of self-government and the duty of mankind "to subdue the earth" by command of "his creation." He said, "We hope and believe that its [the canal's] practical advantages will be extended to every individual in our Union." When the president attempted to cast the first shovel-full of dirt, his spade hit a root, but after several attempts he finally succeeded drawing "a loud and unanimous cheering" from the spectators. Later that day at a celebration held by the printers of Washington City, a toast was offered to "The Earth this day dug at the Canal Celebration. We look anxiously for the day when the united waters of three great streams shall rush through the spot it so lately occupied." The canal's route ran adjacent to the Potomac River and was completed at Cumberland, Maryland, in 1850.

The laying of the cornerstone for lock number 2 was scheduled for July 4, 1829, but was postponed due to severe rain. President Andrew Jackson and the U.S. Marine Band

Great Falls Tavern, in Maryland near Washington, D.C., built by the C & O Canal Company between 1828 and 1831 and now administered by the National Park Service. The Potomac River's majestic rapids served as a popular Fourth of July destination for canal travelers during the nineteenth century. In the early twentieth century, concerts were given there on the Fourth. The tavern, shown here sitting next to the canal and lock, provided meals and lodging. Photograph by author.

were supposed to be there, but Jackson remained in the Executive Mansion.

During the nineteenth century, the C & O Canal was a popular way of traveling west to Harper's Ferry for a Fourth of July excursion. On July 4, 1856, the packet boat *Argo* left Georgetown early in the morning for an Independence Day trip to Harper's Ferry.

On July 4, 2003, a reenactment of Adams' canal excursion took place, and included addresses, music by the Wildcat Regiment Band, the U.S. Marine Brass Quintet playing "Hail to the Chief," and other tunes, and a reading of the Declaration of Independence.

Sources: "Fourth of July, 1828" and "The Fourth of July," *National Intelligencer*, 4 and 7 July 1828, 3 and 2, respectively; "The Fourth of July," *National Intelligencer*, 7 July 1829, 3; *Evening Star*, 1 July 1856, 3; Stephen G. Callas, "Canal Trip Provided Memorable Holiday," *Northwest Current* (Washington, D.C.), 3, 10.

Chico State Normal School, Chico, California

On July 4, 1888, the cornerstone of Chico State Normal School (later California State University at Chico) was laid by the Lodge of Free and Accepted Masons of California with Hiram N. Rucker, Grand Master mason, officiating. "A temporary floor had been laid over the basement wall, an organ and choir were present with Miss Nellie Meade as organist." General John Bidwell presented a brief address. Items placed in the cornerstone included official documents, photographs, newspapers, and various coins. The Chico Normal School building burned to the ground in 1927.

Sources: "Fourth in Chico," *Chico Daily Enterprise*, 5 July 1888; Pam Herman Bush, *A Precious Sense of Place: The Early Years of Chico State* (Chico: Friends of the Meriam Library, California State University, 1991), 26–27.

Chile

This South American country declared July 4, 1925, a national holiday as a tribute to the United States.

Source: *New York Times*, 5 July 1925, 16.

Christ Church, London

Located at the junction of Westminister Bridge and Kensington Road, this church was dedicated on July 4, 1876. "In the center of the front rises the Lincoln Tower (named after our deceased President) to the height of 200 feet." Two thousand persons were present for the ceremony. "The Rev. Dr. Joseph P. Thompson, formerly of this city, responded on behalf of Americans. Three times three cheers were given for the President and people of the United States."

Source: *Harper's Weekly*, 5 August 1876.

Cincinnati Centennial

The centennial celebration of the founding of Cincinnati occurred on July 4, 1888, as the city opened an exposition beginning with ceremonies held in the Music Hall. A number of governors were present, including Joseph B. Foraker (Ohio), John M. Thayer (Nebraska), Isaac P. Gray (Indiana), and James Addams Beaver (Pennsylvania). Music was provided by the Cincinnati Orchestra and the May Festival Chorus. The signal for the start of the event was given by the widow of President James K. Polk, the oldest living first lady, from her home in Nashville, Tennessee. She threw an electric switch that operated a gong in the Cincinnati Hall, after which "the ponderous machinery of the exposition" was put in motion. The choir sang Handel's "Hallelu-

jah" chorus. The group then joined in a massive parade of floats and pageantry that traveled through the city's streets. "The visiting governors rode in carriages, each carriage drawn by four milk white steeds." Fireworks and artillery salutes rounded out the day.

Source: "Cincinnati's Centennial," *New York Herald*, 5 July 1888, 4.

Cincinnati, Societies of the

Federalist clubs active from the 1780s inspired by Cincinnatus and located in several states, including Connecticut, Georgia, Maryland, Massachusetts, New Jersey, New York, Pennsylvania, and South Carolina. Members included only veteran officers who fought in the Revolutionary War, as well as their elder sons.

Cincinnatus (519–439? bc) was a Roman general who symbolized virtue after having left his farm as a humble person to lead his military into battle. George Washington was heralded for his Cincinnatus-like virtue of similarly meeting his new country's call to arms and giving up power after the war. This was a common theme expressed in orations following the Revolutionary War. For example, on July 4, 1785, in Boston, John Gardiner spoke about Cincinnatus and how he disbanded his army and then "retired from his exalted publick station." In an oration delivered on July 4, 1788, to the Society of the Cincinnati in Boston, William Hull explained that Washington "cheerfully relinquished the splendid scenes of military command, and like the Roman Cincinnatus, retired to the cultivation of his farm, and the tranquil walks of domestic life." The charter of the Cincinnati recognized the right of eldest sons of society members to inherit the badge and titles of the incumbents, guaranteeing the perpetuity of the organizations.

The Fourth of July was adopted as the date for holding their annual meetings and dinners. In 1788 and 1789 societies worked towards the adoption of the Constitution and the inauguration of the new government. Their meetings were noted for pomp and splendor and usually included noteworthy speakers. An early example of a Cincinnati meeting occurred at the North Church in Hartford, Connecticut, on July 4, 1787, when Joel Barlow presented an oration there on behalf of the state society. From 1787 to 1800, the Federalists attempted to monopolize the celebration of Independence Day, particularly in Philadelphia and New England. Their "Federal" festivities, such as the toasts presented at Independence Day dinners, typically omitted the names of persons considered to be Anti-Federalists. The political climate began to change, however, with the election of Thomas Jefferson as vice president in 1797.

According to Stephen E. James, African-American veterans were not initiated as members but nonetheless "accepted the Cincinnati aesthetic," as evidenced by their use of military symbolism in their parades.

In the mid- to late nineteenth century society, meetings were routinely celebrated. On July 4, 1876, for example, the New York State Society of the Cincinnati was held in their library at 67 University Place with Hamilton Fish, president, presiding. Their annual dinner was at Delmonico's at 14th Street and Fifth Avenue, and toasts presented among the 52 participants included one drunk standing and in silence to George Washington.

The tradition of holding society meetings on the Fourth of July continued into the twentieth century. Issues discussed at the meetings focused on contemporary issues in politics and government. For example, on July 4, 1913, at a meeting of the Rhode Island Society of the Cincinnati in Newport, Professor William McDonald of Brown University gave an address on "An Aristocracy or a Democracy," in which he said that there is a lack of experts in public service and that government should consist of the "best men" and "not an aristocracy of vulgar wealth, of hereditary descent." Brown advocated for the enlistment in military service by young men to train them "in discipline of body and mind."

Sources: Charles Warren, "Fourth of July Myths"; John Gardiner, *An Oration Delivered July 4, 1785* ... (Boston, 1785), 32; William Hull, *An Oration Delivered to the Society of the Cincinnati ... July 4, 1788* (Boston: Benjamin Russell, 1788), 10, as reported in Martin, "Orations on the Anniversary of American Independence, 1777–1876," 103; "Society of the Cincinnati," *New York Times*, 5 July 1876, 7; *New York Times*, 5 July 1913, 1.

Circuses

Circus productions were popular attractions on Independence Day and often drew large crowds. An early event occurred on July 5, 1813, when in New York City, the circus on Broadway featured a "Grand military manoeuvre" on horses followed by fireworks. The cost for admission ranged from 50 cents to one dollar. An unusual stunt occurred in Norfolk, Virginia, on July 4, 1839, when an elephant "attached to the menagerie" there swam across the harbor from Town Point to Portsmouth and back. On July 4, 1866, Chiarini's Royal Spanish Circus presented three "exhibitions" to accommodate larger crowds. On July 5, 1875, the Howes and Cushing's Circus put on a show in Gloucester, Massachusetts, that included gymnasts, jugglers, and "Castello, the youthful bareback rider" as well as the popular "La Petite Frederika, who rode splendidly." Also, "Miss Pauline Lee's jugglery feat while standing on a horse driving around the ring was well executed. Last but not least, was Prof. Pierce's performances with the den of lions."

In Chico, California, on July 4, 1888, "Girard Leon's Monster Circus" at the "old Chico hotel lots on Second Street" held their circus in tandem with "Prof. Samwell's $10,000 troupe of educated horses, dogs, ponies, goats, monkeys and bears." There were trapeze artists, including a "Japanese troupe of acrobats and jugglers," and a brass band that provided the music. Tickets cost 25 and 50 cents.

See also **Phineas Taylor Barnum** and **Grandstands and platforms**.

Sources: *New York Statesman*, 5 July 1813, 3; *Baltimore Sun*, 10 July 1839, 2; *New York Times*, 3 July 1866, 7; *Gloucester Telegraph*, 30 June 1875, 3; *Chico Daily Enterprise*, 3 July 1888.

City of Brotherly Love Humanitarian Award, Philadelphia

The first Brotherly Love award was given to Elton John at Independence Hall, on July 4, 2005, for his efforts in raising millions of dollars on behalf of HIV/AIDS education, prevention, and treatment. This event replaced the Liberty Medal presentation of 2005 due to the absence of that award's recipient, Ukrainian president Viktor Yushchenko. Accompanying John at the ceremony was U.S. representative Barney Frank of Massachusetts and Philadelphia mayor John Street.

Source: Julie Stoiber, "He's All Keyed Up for Honor," *Philadelphia Inquirer*, 5 July 2005, B1.

Civil War, 1861–65

The single most significant historic event of the nineteenth century; it changed the way the Fourth of July was celebrated. Although the middle, northern and most western states celebrated the holiday with vigor and enthusiasm, the outlook regarding the meaning of the Fourth changed in certain respects. Both the North and South were preparing for war. July 4, 1861, was a pivotal date which reflected the deep sentiments and fears the entire nation shared. In Washington, D.C., some 20,000 to 30,000 troops assembled from all over the North to protect the city from the threat of secessionist incursions. Abraham Lincoln was extremely concerned for the future of the nation and had submitted his address to Congress in special session that day. The rest of the city enjoyed a festive mood with flag raisings, public addresses, and fireworks. At Camp Jackson near Pigs Point, Virginia, Louisiana and Georgia Confederate regiments formed into battle lines on the parade grounds as a brass band played patriotic tunes. "Nearly three thousand bayonets glistened in the bright sunlight of the morning" and fifteen artillery guns fired a volley in honor of the Southern states. In Baltimore, a silk flag was presented to the Sixth Massachusetts Regiment at the Relay House while a "grand Union demonstration" took place at Druid Hill Park. In many Southern towns the new Confederate flag was flown. In Milledgeville, Georgia, women assembled at the Milledgeville Hotel to assemble "three thousand cartridges for the confederate army," while citizens in South Danvers, Massachusetts, sang the "Star Spangled Banner." In Philadelphia military brigades marched as ships in the harbor there sounded their artillery. In Frederick, Mary-

land, and Alexandria, Virginia, women baked hundreds of pies for the Union and Confederate soldiers, respectively.

As the war progressed there were few, if any, celebrations in the South. There the Fourth of July was regarded as a Union event. Northern cities, however, continued to express their fervor and patriotism on the holiday. In 1862, Salem, Massachusetts, had a flag raising event. New York and Washington, D.C., had pyrotechnic displays. In Cincinnati, at Shires' National Theater, a patriotic drama titled *Fourth of July in the Morning* was presented. In Richmond, the editor of the *Daily Dispatch* referred to Abraham Lincoln as a "magnificent ass" and said that Union military plans to occupy that city on the Fourth of July were futile. Special celebrations for the wounded in Union hospitals were also commonly held. In 1863 many of Washington City's buildings were transformed into hospitals. According to a newspaper reporter, "At least 56 separate facilities in Washington were used as hospitals at some time over the course of the war." On July 4 celebrations were held in the following hospitals: Columbian, Carver, Armory Square, St. Aloysius, Douglas, Judiciary Square and Emory. "All of them were decorated with flags to a greater or less extent. Patriotic songs were sung, the Declaration of Independence was read, speeches were delivered, and letters from prominent men in the loyal States were received and read." A number of speeches were given, including those by Hon. Mr. Tabor, of Iowa at Columbian, J.A. Stoddard of the Treasury Department, and Rev. T.R. Howlett of the Calvary Baptist Church at Armory Square. At Judiciary Square there was a reading of the Declaration of Independence and patriotic addresses. According to General E.M. Lee, on July 4, 1864, a celebration by Union soldiers occurred in a prison in Macon, Georgia. As the prisoners finished singing the "national anthem" and "Forever Float that Starry Flag," Confederate guards broke up the event.

Following the war, celebrations in the North continued with great enthusiasm. In many towns and cities there were numerous military processions that honored those that fought and died and speeches that focused on the rationale of the war and the idea that the country now called for a time of healing. Military officers were honored for their services. In Washington on July 4, 1865, officers of the 16th New York Cavalry presented General N.B. Switzer "a valuable sword, belt, and sash" as an acknowledgment "of his successful career as commander of that regiment." In Springfield, Massachusetts, on July 4, 1867, Governor Alexander Hamilton Bullock of Massachusetts delivered an oration at city hall on the "'War of Vindication,' clearly and forcibly discussing the lessons and results of the war." Animosity in the South continued to carry on for many years. A reporter for *The Daily Standard* of Raleigh, North Carolina, noted on July 6, 1865, that it was simply too soon to muster up interest in celebrating the Fourth of July. By the 1870s interest in celebrating the Fourth gradually began to reemerge. Augusta, Georgia, military units celebrated for the first time since the war on July 4, 1875. In Richmond, Virginia, the U.S. flag was raised over the Capitol for the first time in sixteen years. On July 4, 1891, Cheraw, South Carolina, became the first town in that state to celebrate the Fourth of July in over thirty years.

The Spanish-American War, during which soldiers from the North and South fought together on the battlefield, helped to bring the country back together. Rev. H.M. Wharton, speaking at a Fourth celebration in 1898 at Druid Hill Park in Baltimore, said, "The war is a great blessing. It has united our country until we are one and inseparable now and forever. Our soldiers are now all under one flag. The most magnificent scene of the war was when, the other day while fighting near Santiago under the rays of a terrible sun the boys from the North and South united in singing 'The Star-Spangled Banner.'"

Sources: *Clarendon Banner* (Manning, South Carolina), 16 July 1861, 2; "The Fourth at Camp Jackson," *Daily Dispatch* (Richmond), 8 July 1861; *Evening Star*, 5 July 1861, 3; "The Fourth at Baltimore," *The Free Press* (Philadelphia), 5 July 1861, 2; *South Danvers Wizard*, 3 July 1861, 2; *Cincinnati Daily Gazette*, 4 July 1862, 4; *Richmond Daily Dispatch*, 4 July 1862, 2; *Washington Evening Star*, 6 July 1863, 3; "General Lee's Oration," *Rocky Mountain News*, 6 July 1870, 2; "Fourth of July Presentation," *Daily Morning Chron-*

icle, 6 July 1865, 4; "Military and Civic Parade in Springfield, Mass.," *New York Times*, 5 July 1867, 8; *The Daily Times* (Jackson, Miss.), 6 July 1875; *New York Times*, 5 July 1891, 8; "In the Park," *Baltimore Morning Herald*, 5 July 1898, 4; "Battle Stories of the Civil War: The War Day by Day Fifty Years Ago, July 4, 1861," *Los Angeles Times*, 4 July 1911, II/11.

Civil War Memorial Monument, Hamburg, New York

This monument, located in Memorial Park, was erected on July 4, 1914, and dedicated a month later. In 1998 a time capsule was discovered when the statue was being repaired. It contained numerous documents and Buffalo newspapers, and an "1888 medal worn by the president of the Women's Relief Corp., believed to be an auxiliary support for American soldiers."

Source: *Buffalo News*, 18 July 1998, 5C.

Civil War Monument, Derby, Connecticut

This twenty-one-foot-high ornamented monument consists of a full-size bronze figure mounted on a granite pedestal and was dedicated to the men in the area that served in the Union army. The base of the monument was dedicated on July 4, 1877, and the dedication of the bronze statue took place on July 4, 1883. The ceremony for the first dedication included music provided by the Bristol Brass Band. At the second dedication, an audience of 8,000 persons from New Haven, Bridgeport, and the surrounding towns heard Captain Wilbur F. Osborne, 1st Connecticut Volunteer Heavy Artillery, present an oration. A mounted bronze plaque has these words inscribed: "In memory of the men of Derby and Huntington who fell in the service of their country in the war of the rebellion, 1861–1865 as defenders of liberty and nationality."

Sources: *Daily Transcript*, 7 July 1883, and program of dedication ceremonies as quoted in "Civil War Monument" in *Civil War Monuments of Connecticut*, Web site, October 2005, <http://www.chs.org/ransom/023.htm>.

Civil War Monument, Havre de Grace, Maryland

Unveiled on July 4, 1900, by the Grand Army of the Republic in honor of the Union soldiers who died during the Civil War. The ceremony included music by the Aberdeen (Maryland) Band, a poem recited by Miss May Sitzler, and an oration by Capt. William M. Potter of Washington, D.C. The monument is "a ten-foot high shaft, four feet wide at the base."

Source: "To Union Dead," *Baltimore Morning Herald*, 5 July 1900, 3.

Clark, Willis Gaylord (1810–1841)

Composed a four-stanza ode that was sung to the melody of the "Star Spangled Banner" at the Athenian Society celebration at Bristol College on July 4, 1835.

(First stanza)
Hail, hail to the day, when with Memory's wand,
We waken the praises of worthies departed,—
Whose labors of valor delivered the land
From the fierce, open foe, and the traitor, false-hearted;—
Whose blood fell like rain,
In the ranks of the slain,
And cried from the ground, with a voice not in vain!
We hail the bright day, which reminds us of yore,—
Of the warriors that slumber, to battle no more!

Source: broadside, "Ode by Willis Gaylord Clark" (Burlington, [Vermont?]: J.L. Powell, 1835).

Clay, Henry (1777–1852)

Popular statesman, attorney, and candidate for president in 1824 who had a monument cornerstone dedicated to his memory at Ashland, the Henry Clay estate, in Lexington, Kentucky, on July 4, 1857, and who for many years was honored on Independence Day through songs and toasts. Clay was born in Hanover County, Virginia, studied law in Richmond and set up his practice in Lexington, Kentucky. Turning his attention to national issues, he was elected to the state legislature (1803–06), and served as speaker (1807–09), and congressman (1811–20, 1823–25). Clay was among the "hawks" that encouraged war with Britain in 1812. He was known for his adeptness in reaching compromises on sectional differences thereby pacifying the nation during the politically and socially turbulent times preceding the Civil War. He played a major role in framing the Missouri Compromise (1820). He offered his sponsorship for the compromise Tariff of 1833 and the Missouri Compromise of 1850. By 1833 his reputation had already been established as a peacemaker and by 1850 he had become known as the "Great Pacificator."

The cornerstone ceremony for the monument at Ashland included an oration by R.I. Breckenridge. "The festival concluded with an extensive barbecue." The memorial was designed by Julius W. Adams of Lexington and its cost was $58,000. The monument was officially completed on July 4, 1861. Clay's body was placed in the vault of the monument in April 1864, following the death of his wife, Lucretia Hart Clay. Through the years the monument suffered from a lack of attention but was fully restored in the mid-1970s.

Clay spoke on the Fourth of July at the Lexington, Kentucky, court house in 1800, before the military corps and citizens there. Following his address, the party dined at Maxwell's Spring. Clay occasionally attended celebrations on the Fourth of July, including one on July 4, 1832, at a National Republican dinner in Washington City. The affair was held "in a spacious Pavilion, erected for the purpose, on the lawn of the Mansion-house, on the bank of the Potomac." Clay's association with the Fourth of July is also remembered by the numerous times his name was honored in ceremonies. For instance, on July 4, 1833, in Philadelphia, among the toasts given at the public dinner of "The Friends of American Industry and the City Administration," was the following: "Henry Clay — the distinguished statesman, who met his country in turmoil and confusion, and said, let there be peace, and there was peace." On July 4, 1842, the *Alexandria (Virginia) Gazette* published information on a "Song — for the 4th of July," to the tune of "Auld Lang Syne," written as a tribute to Clay. On July 4, 1843, at a Whig Festival held in Philadelphia, another song, "Hurray for the Clay" (Philadelphia: J.C. Osbourn, 1843), was sung in honor of him. The piece was composed by J.C. Osbourn, and arranged for piano and voice.

In June 1849 Clay was invited to attend

an Independence Day gathering of Whigs at the Chinese Museum in Philadelphia but declined. In a letter he wrote which was read aloud to the Whigs gathered there on the Fourth, he expressed his political support: "Concurring entirely with you in the importance to the welfare and prosperity of the Union of maintaining Whig principles, by all fair and honorable means, I should be most happy, both for the pleasure of meeting my Whig fellow-citizens, and of assisting in the commemoration of the great epoch of our national birth, to be able to accept your kind invitation; but my distant residence deprives me of that satisfaction." The Philadelphia Whigs responded with a toast to Clay: "The sage of Ashland — One of the great men of the age. Generations yet unborn will 'lisp his name and hymn his praises.'"

Henry Clay died on June 29, 1852, in Washington, D.C. His death cast a gloom over many celebrations in many cities, from Albany, N.Y., to New Orleans. A number of tributes were expressed to him including one in Boston, when the Massachusetts Society of the Cincinnati meeting on the Fourth and under the leadership of Franklin Pierce drafted a resolution honoring the statesman. Copies were sent to Clay's relatives of note. Henry Clay, Jr., inherited his father's penchant for public speaking. As a cadet at **West Point** he presented an exemplary Independence Day address in 1830. His manner was described as "commanding, ... his voice was strong and well modulated."

Sources: *Kentucky Gazette*, 10 July 1800; "Fourth of July at West Point," *National Intelligencer*, 12 July 1830, 2; *National Intelligencer*, 4 July 1832, 3; "At Philadelphia," *National Intelligencer*, 13 July 1833, 3; *Alexandria Gazette*, 7 July 1842, 1; "Anniversary Festivities," *National Intelligencer*, 10 July 1849, 2; "The Massachusetts Society of Cincinnati and Henry Clay," *New York Times*, 7 July 1852, 1; "The Fourth Out West," *New York Times*, 7 July 1857, 4; Ashland, the Henry Clay Estate, Web site, <www.henryclay.org>.

Clay Library, East Jaffrey, New Hampshire

The Clay Library Building was dedicated on July 4, 1896, in memory of Susan B. Clay, a resident of Jaffrey. The building was de-

signed by H.M. Francis, architect of Fitchburg, Massachusetts. The ceremony for the building included a concert by the East Jaffrey Cornet Band, music by Gressinger's Orchestra, a dinner, readings of poetry, and various speeches, including a keynote address by Charles F. Richardson of Dartmouth College.

Source: *Dedication of the Clay Library Building at East Jaffrey, New Hampshire, Saturday, July 4, 1896* (Concord, N.H.: Republican Press Association, 1896).

Cleeves and Tucker Memorial Monument, Portland, Maine

Named after George Cleeves and Richard Tucker, Portland's first settlers, and unveiled on July 4, 1883. At the ceremony were Mayor John W. Deering and Governor Frederick Robie. An oration was delivered by William W. Thomas, "newly appointed minister to Sweden." The monument is located in Eastern Promenade Park.

Source: "A Monument to First Settlers," *New York Times*, 5 July 1883, 2.

Cleveland, Stephen Grover (1837–1908)

Twenty-second and 24th president of the U.S. (1885–89; 1893–97), less active as a participant on the Fourth of July than other presidents, but remembered for his participation at the Fourth of July celebration in Buffalo. He was born in Caldwell, New Jersey, and lived in New York State. Cleveland worked as an attorney in Buffalo and was elected mayor of that city in 1881 and then governor (1883–84).

As governor, Cleveland spoke at an evening banquet following the unveiling of a **Soldiers and Sailors Monument** at Buffalo on July 4, 1884. He expressed his thoughts about the Civil War and the thousands of New York "sons who fought and came home laden with the honors of patriotism, many of whom still survive and, like the minstrels of old, tell us of heroic deeds and battles won which saved the nation's life."

On July 4, 1885, Cleveland spent much of the day at the White House working on papers, then took a carriage ride to the northern part of the city at Tennallytown. Cleveland "was kept busy responding to salutations" by a number of "picnic parties" along the way. For the Fourth in 1890, Cleveland had been invited to the Tammany Society event in New York as a special guest, but he declined with a letter of regret in which he expressed his concerns over political partisanship. A local newspaper paraphrased Cleveland's thoughts expressed that day: "While the people would not revolt against their plan of government, they would revolt against the domination of any political party which abused its power and sought its own continuance by betraying the liberties of the people." On July 4, 1893, the president had arrived at Buzzard's Bay, Massachusetts, on the steam ship *Oneida*. He was confined to only a few activities due to his rheumatism. He prepared to write a message to Congress regarding the extra session of Congress that was called. On July 5, 1895, he and his family were at Gray Gables in Buzzard's Bay, Massachusetts, to see the fireworks which had been postponed from the previous night on account of foul weather. (See also **Pullman Strike**.)

Sources: "A Gala Day at Buffalo," *New York Times*, 5 July 1884, 2; "The Week in Society," *Washington Post*, 5 July 1885, 4; "Patriotism and Politics," *Washington Post*, 5 July 1890, 1; "News of the President" and "President Cleveland Ill," *New York Times*, 5 and 7 July 1893, 4 and 4, respectively; "The President Celebrated Last Night," *New York Times*, 6 July 1895, 1.

Clifton, Arthur (1784?–1832)

Wrote musical works expressly for the Fourth of July. On July 4, 1818, *The Carrollton March* (Baltimore: John Cole, 1828), for piano, which he dedicated to Charles Carroll of Carrollton, was performed "at the ceremony of commencing the **Baltimore and Ohio Railroad**." See also **"Grand National Jubilee."**

Clinton, De Witt (1769–1828)

Popular mayor of New York City and governor of New York who promoted the construction of the **Erie Canal** and **Ohio Canal**. The groundbreaking ceremonies occurred on July 4, 1817, and July 4, 1825, respectively.

Clinton, William Jefferson (b. 1946)

Forty-second president of the U.S. (1993–2001) whose major contribution to the Fourth was the Millennium celebration in 2000 and his efforts to further world peace and address both local and national issues. Born in Hope, Arkansas, Clinton graduated from Georgetown University, studied at Oxford University, and received a law degree from Yale University in 1973. He was elected Arkansas attorney general in 1976 and governor of that state in 1978. With his running mate, Tennessee senator Albert Gore, Jr., he won the presidential election in 1992. "He was the first Democratic president since Franklin D. Roosevelt to win a second term."

On July 4, 1993, Clinton presented Liberty Medals to Nelson Mandela and Frederik W. de Klerk outside Independence Hall. In his presentation, Clinton said the United States would assist South Africa as it moved toward a more democratic state. Clinton also went to Davenport, Iowa, that day where he visited this city, flood-raged as a result of Hurricane Andrew, and reassured citizens of the availability of financial aid. His radio address to the nation that day focused on the country's founders, "who created a durable and prosperous democracy, with broader liberties and greater opportunities for each succeeding generation, and they encouraged people all across the world to demand from their governments the same freedoms and possibilities that Americans enjoy."

In 1994, Clinton was in Warsaw, Poland, as a guest of President Lech Walesa. On July 4, 1996, the president was at the Patuxent Naval Air Station in southern Maryland, assisting in the release of an eagle named "Freedom" back into the wilds after the bird had been injured and nursed back to health. This expression of the president's commitment to environmental protection was sponsored, in part, by the U.S. Fish and Wildlife Service. On that same day, First Lady Hillary Rodham Clinton was at the main hall of Radio Free Europe in Prague giving a speech encouraging developing democracies.

In 1998 Clinton returned on July 4 from a trip to China where he met with President Jiang Zemin and in the following year was in the White House where he spent three hours communicating with Pakistani prime minister

Nawaz Sharif about the India and Pakistan conflict over the disputed territory of Kashmir.

The Millennium celebration in 2000 saw Clinton and his family in New York at the harbor viewing the largest maritime assemblage ever in this country and giving a speech on his final Fourth of July in office. He reviewed the military ships parade, "International Naval Revue 2000," from the missile cruiser USS *Hue City*, then boarded the carrier USS *John F. Kennedy* for the tall ships' "Parade of Sails." On the flight deck of the carrier, "Clinton issued citations to outstanding sailors, gave the oath of reenlistment to crew members, watched twenty men and women become American citizens during a naturalization ceremony led by Attorney General Janet Reno and joined them in the Pledge of Allegiance." His speech touched on American icons including the Statue of Liberty, Ellis Island, the Declaration of Independence, and George Washington. Regarding Manhattan, he said that "it was here where the [Continental] troops first pledged their lives, their fortunes, their sacred honor."

See also **Ship Parades**.

Sources: Lynne Duke and Al Kamen, "South African Leaders Receive Liberty Medal at Independence Hall" and Stephen Buckless, "Clinton Tours Flooded Midwest Areas, Pledges Aid," *Washington Post*, 5 July 1993, A6; "President's Fourth of July Message," *New York Times*, 5 July 1993, 7; Michael Abramowitz, "Symbolism Meets Reality on the Wing" and Christine Spolar, "First Lady Applauds E. Europe," *Washington Post*, 5 July 1996, A5 and A18, respectively; Lyndsey Layton, "Tall Ships, Navy Vessels Mark Fourth with Parade," *Washington Post*, 5 July 2000, A7; William J. Clinton Web site, <http://www.whitehouse.gov/history/presidents/bc42.html>.

Cody, William Frederick (1846–1917)

Cowboy, army scout and popular entertainer known as "Buffalo Bill" who produced the first rodeo-like event billed as the "Old Glory Blow Out" on July 4, 1882, in North Platte, Nebraska. Cody was born in Iowa but spent much of his early life in Kansas and Nebraska. His life's endeavors mostly reflected his love for the Western frontier and plains. He served as a scout with the 5th and 9th Kansas Cavalries and was a buffalo hunter for the Kansas Pacific Railroad; the thousands of buffalo he killed earned him the nickname of "Buffalo Bill." Cody was featured in a number of "Western" dime novels which increased his popularity, and eventually he was drawn into show business. He was one of the principal characters in a play, *Scouts of the Plains*, which toured Eastern cities in 1872. The "Old Glory Blow Out" featured riding and roping contests and was one of the first events of its kind to offer prizes. Not long after, Cody organized his "Wild West Show," which played to audiences in the East, as well as tours across Europe and Great Britain. The show's stars included Annie Oakley and Chief Sitting Bull. On July 4, 1894, Buffalo Bill's Wild West Show performed in Ambrose Park in South Brooklyn, New York. General admission was 50 cents. On July 4, 1887, Cody attended the Independence Day reception at the American legation in London.

On July 4, 1924, a bronze monument of Buffalo Bill was unveiled in Cody, Wyoming. The monument was designed by Mrs. Harry Payne Whitney and financed by the Buffalo Bill American Association.

Sources: *New York Times*, 1 July 1894, 12; "Buffalo Bill in Bronze Will Guard Wyoming Trail," *New York Times*, 18 May 1924, XX12; *Webster's American Biographies*, ed. Charles Van Doren (Springfield, Mass.: G. and C. Merriam, 1984); Rick Ewig, "William Frederick Cody," *American National Biography* 5:134–36.

Coffin, R.S.

Composed "Morn of the Fourth of July," for voice and piano. First line: "Behold from the brow of the mountain advancing, The Genius of Freedom appears to our view" (Baltimore: T. Carr's Music Store, n.d.).

Cold War

The intense rivalry that emerged between the USSR and the United States following World War II and lasted until the tearing down of the Berlin Wall in 1990 during the presidency of Ronald Reagan was reflected in Fourth of July celebrations and speechmaking. Frequently depicted as the "Free World" versus the "Communist Bloc," the two superpowers had a preponderance of nuclear weapons that kept both nations on a continued edge of suspicion, if not war. Beginning with President Truman, the U.S. policy was one of "containment," to prevent other countries from falling within the Soviet influence and to block Russian aggression. It is not surprising therefore that the Independence Day celebration came to serve as a reminder to Americans of the continual danger the nation faced. A sense of fear and urgency for readiness emerged in some of these events, through advertising and public statements. On July 4, 1950, a large advertisement ran by the American Heritage Foundation, titled "But how good are you in a cold war," stressed the importance of good citizenry on the Fourth of July, while in New York at J. Hood Wright Park, Representative Jacob K. Javits (Rep.) declared in a speech that "America's forces of production will win over Communism."

Some of the events designed to bring attention to the issue were extreme. In Baltimore on July 4, 1951, a mock atomic bomb explosion was set off before 25,000 spectators as a demonstration of the explosive devastation and its effect on civic life. "Smoke and flame mushroomed, two faked houses collapsed and water and gas mains burst," a newspaper reported. "'Wounded' civilians tried to deal with radiation-started fires."

Cold War concerns emerged in numerous other cities across the country on Independence Day that year. In Chicago, Senator Everett M. Dirksen (Rep.— Ill.) in a speech before the Chicago Junior Chamber of Commerce urged citizens to be vigilant against "marching Soviet military imperialism." The goal of communism, he said, is "to liquidate freedom." In Philadelphia that day James H. Duff (Rep.— Pa.) also carried the torch, saying, "The battle is on between oppression and freedom today as it was in 1776." Near Cincinnati, Charles P. Tuft, chairman of the Ohio segment of the Crusade for Freedom, spoke before a rally made of residents from Cheviot and Westword on the importance of the Bill of Rights. He commented that in a national survey, many teachers were afraid to teach what communism was "because they might be called communist."

From the early 1960s on, Soviet authorities frequently sent Fourth of July greetings to Americans to ease tensions but also to find fault with America's freedoms. American government's leaders often responded in kind. One of the first key messages occurred on July 4, 1961, when Soviet premier Khrushchev and Soviet president Leonid I. Brezhnev called for a joint effort for world peace. "In sending our greetings to you today, we wish to express the hope that the recent Vienna meeting, and the exchange of opinions on questions in the interest of both countries, will win the mutual efforts of both our governments for a speedy solution of the pressing problems left in the wake of the last war after the defeat of the aggressors." In 1962–63 similar messages were sent by Khrushchev. In 1962 Khrushchev "made a surprise visit" to the U.S. Embassy's Independence Day party and exchanged greetings with American jazz giant Benny Goodman. President Kennedy responded in 1963 on the Fourth with a message that was read by U.S. Minister Eugenie Anderson over government radio and television in Sofia, capital of Communist Bulgaria. Meanwhile First Deputy Premier Anastas Mikoyan was visiting an American Embassy Independence Day party where in responding to a reporter's question asking if his presence at the party signaled an easing in the cold war, said, "We are for easing the cold war. My presence signifies respect for the people of the United States. My country and people are for ending the cold war."

On July 4, 1977, Soviet leader Brezhnev sent "best wishes" to President Carter and encouraged "a stable development of relations between the U.S.A. and the U.S.S.R." Yet U.S. ambassador Malcolm Toon was not permitted to present a Russian television address because of "references to the human rights policy of Carter." On July 4, 1980, Ambassador Thomas J. Watson, Jr., was also not allowed to tape an address due to a reference to Afghanistan. Soviet troops were in Afghanistan in the prior year.

On the Fourth in 1984, Moscow officials barred U.S. ambassador Arthur A. Hartman from delivering an Independence Day television address there because as reported in the

New York Times, the text "was part of President Reagan's re-election campaign." In 1986 Soviet leader Andrei A. Gromyko sent President Reagan a telegram of congratulations while the Communist Party newspaper *Pravda* dismissed the Statue of Liberty celebrations as propaganda "for fanning up chauvinistic sentiments, and to justify before the eyes of Americans the aggressive militaristic course of Washington."

Sources: *Washington Post*, 4 July 1950, 5B; "Javits Speaks at Rally," *New York Herald Tribune*, 5 July 1950, 20; "Atomic Touch for 4th" and "Freedom of Choice Cited," *New York Times*, 5 July 1951, 16 and 18 respectively; *New York Times*, 5 July 1951, 8; "Khrushchev Sends July 4 Note to U.S.," *New York Times*, 4 July 1961, 11; "Khrushchev Sends JFK July Fourth Peace Note," *Washington Post*, 4 July 1962, A16; Theodore Shabad, "Khrushchev Visits U.S. Embassy Fete," *New York Times*, 5 July 1962, 1; "K. Sends U.S. Peace Wishes," *Washington Post*, 5 July 1963, A12; Reinhold Ensz, "Reds Tie New Test Ban Proposal Definitely to Nonagression Pact," *Washington Post*, 5 July 1963, A1; "Brezhnev Sends Note on Independence Day," *New York Times*, 4 July 1977, 2; "Moscow Bars a Speech on July 4th by Envoy," *New York Times*, 4 July 1984, A4; "Mixed Signals from Moscow," *New York Times*, 5 July 1986, 27.

Colleges and universities

Institutions of higher learning have played a significant role in the country's traditions in celebrating the Fourth of July. Activities include speeches, groundbreaking ceremonies, and general revelry. Colleges founded on Independence Day include University of the South (1857) (see **Sewanee: University of the South**), **Tuskegee University** (1881), and Randolph-Macon College (1890; see **Randolph-Macon Academy**). The United States Military Academy (see **West Point**) had its official opening on July 4, 1802. On July 4, 1853, the cornerstone of the new college building at Hillsdale College was laid and included a speech by college president Edmund Fairfield. On July 4, 1894, the cornerstone of **Denny Hall**, the first building at the University of Washington, was laid. Other cornerstone ceremonies of major campus buildings on the Fourth include the **Old Capitol** at University of Iowa (1840), Cornell College (1856), **Heck Hall** at Northwestern University (1867), and **Hardin-Simmons**

University (1891). An historic monument to Thomas Jefferson (see **Jefferson Monument**) was transferred from the grounds of Monticello and unveiled at the University of Missouri at Columbia on July 4, 1885.

Student parades were another important way in which colleges and universities marked the day. The first parade of students on the Fourth occurred on July 4, 1783, when individuals representing the University of Pennsylvania marched in honor of George Washington, who received an honorary doctorate from the institution that day. University of Pennsylvania students and faculty carrying a banner with the words "The rising generation" marched in the "**Grand Federal Procession**" in Philadelphia on July 4, 1788. In the South one of the first parades occurred on July 4, 1844, and consisted of faculty, trustees, and students from the College of Charleston who marched about the city streets there (see **Teachers and Scholars Parade**).

On Independence Day in 1841, St. Louis University celebrated at Concert Hall where students heard an oration and a sermon and "Hymn of Thanksgiving" in the cathedral. At times students simply gathered together on Independence Day to offer toasts in honor of the day. On July 4, 1804, Yale College students drank ten tankards. The University of Virginia was a major setting for Fourth of July ceremonies and speeches. One of the earliest occurred on July 4, 1827, when professors and students "attended an elegant dinner" there.

Throughout the history of the Fourth, college professors and students were frequently invited to speak. In Hanover, New Hampshire, Dartmouth student Daniel Webster gave his first Independence Day oration in 1800 in the town's meeting house. On Independence Day in 1817, Benjamin F. Allen addressed the students at Brown University in the college chapel (oration printed by Jones and Wheeler of Providence, R.I.). On July 4, 1853, G.J. Burton of the senior class addressed fellow students at Burlington College in New Jersey. A long standing tradition of orators speaking on the Fourth at District of Columbia colleges include at Columbian College, Malachi Bonham (1923), Baron Stow (1825), and John Boulivare (1826); and at Georgetown College, William H. Wikoff (1827), Hugh Caperton (1839), James Ryder (1840 and 1843), James H. Bevans (1842), Walter Smith Cox (1843), Julien Cumming (1846) and **George Washington Parke Custis**, the most frequent orator at that institution, with six appearances spanning 1837–57. On July 5, 1882, at Williams College in Williamstown, Massachusetts, U.F. Wilcox of Northboro gave "a philosophical oration" titled "American in 1982." Yet other Independence Day faculty addresses included Alexander R. Gates (University of Alabama, 1841) and Samuel G. Brown (Dartmouth College, 1865).

Student organizations commonly met on Independence Day. The Philodemic Society (Georgetown College) and Enosinian Society (Columbian College) held elaborate affairs during the 1820s. On July 4, 1839, the Peace Society of Amherst College met, and John Lord addressed the group, and on July 4, 1829, the Anti-Slavery Society of Williams College gathered to hear an oration by Giles B. Kellogg. On Independence Day in 1837, students of Oberlin College celebrated by holding anti-slavery meetings.

On Independence Day in 1837, College of William and Mary president Thomas Roderick Dew addressed his baccalaureate students who were graduating that day. On July 4, 1845, President John Tyler spoke at William and Mary. In 1847 Georgetown College celebrated the Fourth (a Sunday) on July 5. Several speeches were given and music was provided by the college band.

In the twentieth century the tradition continued. On Independence Day in 1916, Mount Rushmore sculptor Gutzon Borglum spoke at City College of New York. H. Hayes Yeager of George Washington University read the Declaration of Independence at the **Sylvan Theater** on the Mall in Washington, D.C., on July 4, 1930.

Recently Pennsylvania State University at University Park has held elaborate celebrations such as that in 2003 with huge fireworks shows and band concerts. Students and alumni at American University in Washington, D.C., have hosted campus barbecues and outings to the National Mall for the fireworks show. See also **Seton Hall College**.

Sources: *Freeman's Journal*, 9 July 1783; "Grand Federal Procession," *Pennsylvania Gazette*, 9 July 1788; "Anniversary of American Independence," *American Mercury*, 12 July 1804, 3; *Richmond Enquirer*, 13 July 1827, 2 and 4; John Lord, *An Address Delivered before the Peace Society of Amherst College, July 4th, 1839* (Amherst: J.S. and C. Adams, 1839); *Daily Missouri Republican*, 3 July 1841; *Charleston Mercury*, 4 July 1844, 2; *Richmond Enquirer*, 8 July 1845, 4; "Burlington College," *New York Times*, 6 July 1853, 2; "Williams College Exercises," *New York Times*, 6 July 1882, 5; Claude Moore Fuess, *Daniel Webster*, 2 vols. (Boston: Little, Brown and Co., 1930):1, 54; Edmond S. Meany, *A History of the University of Washington* (from Web site); *Washington Post*, 5 July 1930, 1; John Stewart Bryan, *Thomas Roderick Dew: An Address Delivered April, 3, 1939, at the Memorial Service for the Thirteenth President of the College of William and Mary in Virginia, Who Died in Paris, France, August 6, 1846* (Williamsburg, Virginia, 1939); Robert S. Fletcher, *A History of Oberlin College* (New York: Arno Press, 1971), 249; Megan Rooney, "Star-Spangled Campus Revelry," *Chronicle of Higher Education*, 4 July 2003, A8; Charles Milhauser, "College Hall 1857–1978" (Typewritten, Cornell College, Mount Vernon, Iowa, no date).

Colored State Normal Institute

The cornerstone for this school located in Chesterfield County, near Petersburg, Virginia, was laid "with imposing ceremonies" on July 4, 1883. Senator William Mahone of Virginia and other prominent state officials were present. R.T. Greiner of Washington, D.C., was the orator.

Source: "A Corner-Stone Laid," *Baltimore Morning Herald*, 5 July 1883, 4.

Colt, Samuel (1814–1862)

Inventor and developer of the legendary Colt revolver, who on July 4, 1842, in New York, unveiled a "sub-marine experiment" for blowing up enemy ships. He successfully tested his invention before a tremendous crowd of spectators lining the Battery, Castle Garden, "the shipping and the wharves, and roofs of the houses as far as the eye could reach." Colt was on board the USS *North Carolina* where he directed the experiment which had "a battery" placed on the vessel's hull. As the explosion occurred the vessel broke into hundreds of pieces and was sent up into the air a height "of from one to two hundred feet."

A local newspaper reported that "the view to the eye was beyond description with the pen; and as the spiral volume of water was descending, the crowd on the outer bulwarks of Castle Garden involuntarily shrunk back as though they expected to be enveloped in one shower of water, interspersed with fragments, although the vessel had been placed several hundred yards from the garden in anticipation of such a result."

Source: "The Fourth and Its Events," *New York Herald*, 6 July 1842, 2.

Columbia and Augusta Railroad

This railroad was officially completed to the town of Leesville, South Carolina, on July 4, 1868, and a celebration was held there with over 2500 spectators present. Several speeches were given including one by William Johnson, president of the railroad.

He congratulated African-Americans for their work on the railroad and told them "their labor was invaluable to the country at large."

Source: "The Rail Road Celebration at Leesville, S.C.," *Charleston Daily Courier*, 6 July 1868, 2.

Columbia's Independence; or, the Temple of Liberty

The drama, also titled *Independence of Columbia*, and consisting of singing, dancing, and recitations, was performed at the Washington Theatre in Washington City on July 4, 1809, 1810, and 1811.

Sources: *National Intelligencer*, 3 July, 1809, 3, 4 July 1810, 3, and 4 July 1811, 3.

Columbus, Ohio, Court House

The cornerstone for the building was laid on July 4, 1885. The structure was projected to cost $500,000.

Source: "In Other Towns," *Philadelphia Inquirer*, 6 July 1885, 2.

Columbus, Ohio, Turners riot

Occurred on July 4, 1855, when a parade of firemen, turners and other societies turned into a general riot, resulting in one dead and several injured. The event, which was widely reported, began with a dispute between one of the turners and a young boy. Shortly after, the turners assaulted various persons, threw stones

at people in the streets, and began firing their pistols. When it was over, the police arrested 24 turners "against whom public opinion is very decided."

Sources: *Alexandria Gazette*, 6 July 1855, 3; "Serious and Fatal Riot in Columbus, Ohio" and "The Riot in Columbus, Ohio, on the Fourth of July," *New York Times*, 6 and 9 July 1855, 4 and 6, respectively.

Columbus Statue Executive Committee

Presided over a groundbreaking ceremony at the Eighth Avenue plaza in New York City on July 4, 1892, in preparation for receiving a 76-foot statue of Christopher Columbus from Italy as a gift to the city. Flags of Italy and the United States were raised and members of local Italian societies, including Fraterna Amore, Exerciso Italiano, and Mutuo Socorso, were there to see 120 Italian laborers work on the site. C.A. Barattoni gave an address in which he reported:

> The monument which will shortly be conveyed to these shores, the gift to the City of New York from the Italians, has already been described and illustrated in the various metropolitan papers. The Royal Art Commission, appointed under the auspices of the Ministry of Fine Arts of Italy, at Rome, has pronounced is one of the finest products of the modern Italian sculptor's art, and we feel sure that, once erected on this square, a few months hence owing to its intrinsic artistic merits, it will command the admiration of all art-loving Americans.

A band played tunes representing both countries.

Source: "Foundation Work Begun," *New York Times*, 5 July 1892, 8.

Common Glory

A play by noted playwright Paul Green with a scene, "The Drafting of the Declaration of Independence," was presented on July 4, 1949, on the Washington Monument grounds. The play was in "its third full season at Williamsburg, Virginia." The event also included music by the U.S. Navy and Marine Bands, a speech by Gen. Jacob L. Devers, commander of the Army Field Forces.

Source: "250,000 Expected to See July 4 Show at Monument," *Washington Post*, 4 July 1949, B1.

Coney Island, New York

A popular resort area developed after the Civil War that drew thousands of persons who enjoyed a wide range of attractions on the Fourth of July, including public bathing, racetracks, sightseeing piers, and amusement parks. One of the popular traditions associated with Coney Island and which continues today was the introduction there of frankfurters in 1870 by Charles Feltman. By 1888 Brighton and Manhattan Beaches featured well known musical ensembles. On July 4 that year, Anton Seidl conducted an orchestra of seventy musicians from the Metropolitan Opera House at Brighton Beach, and Patrick S. Gilmore and his military band provided entertainment at Manhattan Beach.

On July 4, 1894, 300,000 persons visited Coney Island by way of six railroads, a flotilla of steamboats, and electric cars. John Philip Sousa's band performed at Manhattan playing a rendition of the "Star-Spangled Banner" accompanied by an artillery salute from an "old cannon on the lawn." The day also included fireworks and a performance by trained parrots in Hagenbeck's arena.

Three amusement parks were opened between 1897 and 1904, and they raised the island's commercial development dramatically. The mechanical rides provided at Steeplechase Park, Luna Park, and Dreamland dazzled the public and increased the reputation of Coney Island nationwide. On July 4, 1916, Nathan's annual Fourth of July hot dog eating contest was begun and has only missed two occasions: in 1941, "to protest the war in Europe, and in 1971, to protest the prevalence of the hippie lifestyle."

Manhattan Beach was the site for Independence Day performances by popular musical groups, such as Sousa's Band and the Frank Daniels Opera Company in 1899. Such concerts were followed typically by fireworks displays.

Sources: "A Sunday Out of Doors," *New York Times*, 5 July 1886, 5; "Coney Island Music," *New York Times*, 4 July 1888, 5; "Coney Island's Big Crowd," *New York Times*, 5 July 1894, 9; Stephen Weinstein, "Coney Island," *The Encyclopedia of New York City*, 272–74; Larry McShane, "The Fourth: Hot Dog!: Stomachs Vie for Immortality at Yearly Contest," *Newsday*, 2 July 1999, A41.

Connecticut State Capitol, Fourth of July Legislation

As a part of the official observance of Independence Day, appropriate ceremonies shall be held in the hall of flags of the State Capitol on July fourth in each year. The Governor shall issue a proclamation recalling to the citizens of the state the historic significance of Independence Day. The Governor shall designate a state official of a patriotic society or a state official of a veterans organization to plan and have charge of such ceremonies, in such manner that the conduct of such ceremonies shall be alternated from year to year between an official of a patriotic society and an official of a veterans organization. The necessary expense of such ceremony, not exceeding seven hundred and fifty dollars each year, shall be paid to the society or organization conducting the ceremonies.

Source: *General Statutes of Connecticut*, Title 1, Chapter 2: Legal Holidays and Standard of Time (1–5 Independence Day Celebrations).

Connecticut Street Armory, Buffalo, New York

Known also as the 74th Regiment Armory, the cornerstone of this building was dedicated on July 4, 1898, after a large Masonic parade that included soldiers of the 74th Regiment and Civil War veterans. In 1982 an extensive fire led to a restoration of its main hall. On July 4, 1998, the building was rededicated and "the aging military records, marksmen's badges, Masonic lodge mementos and city newspapers from the original time capsule" were reinterred along with a group of 1998 items. The building is currently used for civic celebrations and other events.

Source: "Celebrate a Milestone for a West Side Landmark," *Buffalo News*, 4 July 1998, 2C.

Continental Harmony

A community-based music commissioning program, begun as a millennial year celebration, with many musical works premiered on the Fourth of July. In 2000 the American Composers Forum, in partnership with the National Endowment for the Arts (NEA), sponsored composer residencies in all 50 states. Each composer was selected from a large group of applicants and worked with a community representative to carry out a residency and to premiere a musical composition written for local musicians. In toto, musical compositions in many genres — symphonic, chamber, opera, choral, ethnic — and for diverse combinations of musical forces were performed throughout the nation.

As appropriate to a national music celebration, many communities chose to perform their piece of music as part of their Independence Day observance. These included an elaborate pageant featuring the three cultures of New Mexico, a piece for chorus and band based on locally-submitted poetry in Wisconsin, and a work for gospel choir and woodwind quintet in Rhode Island. Of particular note were the works composed for San Francisco, California (*Freedom Dreams* for band, by Jennifer Higdon), Indianapolis and Carmel, Indiana (*Liberty for All* for orchestra, by James Beckel), and Gettysburg, Pennsylvania (*South Mountain Echoes* for band, by Rob Maggio). Gettysburg was celebrating its own bicentennial as well as the millennium, so Maggio's work evoked that community's important place in American history.

The success of the millennium year projects has led the American Composers Forum and the NEA to continue Continental Harmony as an on-going program.

Coolidge, Calvin (1872–1933)

Thirtieth president of the U.S. (1923–29) and the only chief executive born on July 4. Throughout his years as president he received birthday gifts at Independence Day ceremonies. Coolidge assumed office on August 2, 1923, on the death of President Harding. On July 4, 1924, Coolidge addressed the national convention of the **National Educational Association** in Washington, D.C. He spoke about the importance of education as a tool for promoting good citizenship and the value of teachers in public education. "The obligation which we all owe to those devoted men and women who have given of their lives to the education of the youth of our country that they might have freedom through coming into a knowledge of the truth is one which can never be discharged," he said. "They are enti-

tled not only to adequate rewards for their service, but to the veneration and honor of a grateful people." He later returned to the White House to be at the bedside of his ill son.

On Independence Day in 1925, Coolidge was at the "Summer White House" at White Court near Swampscott, Massachusetts, reading telegrams of congratulations and making arrangements to have his father in Plymouth Notch, Vermont, taken to Boston for a medical operation. Later that afternoon the president and Mrs. Coolidge boarded the presidential yacht *Mayflower* anchored in Marblehead Cove for a birthday dinner. On the day before, he had been in Cambridge, Massachusetts, giving a "memorial address reviewing Washington's place in history."

On July 4, 1926, Coolidge was on the South Jersey exposition grounds where he planted a tree, and later gave a speech in Philadelphia at the official opening of the **Sesquicentennial Exposition**. Coolidge also visited Independence Hall, where he sat in Washington's chair and signed the historic guest book. On the following day, at Christ Church, Coolidge read the names of seven signers of the Declaration of Independence on a bronze replica of a tablet that was unveiled there by six young women who were descendants of the signers.

On Independence Day in 1927, Coolidge was in Rapid City, South Dakota, celebrating his birthday and donning Western clothes as he accepted a gift horse and riding outfit from the Boy Scouts of America. At the ceremony there he was affectionately referred to as "Cal our pal."

On July 4, 1936, memorial exercises were held in Plymouth, Vermont, at the grave site of Coolidge. This has become an annual ceremony. Each year a Coolidge Birthday Parade takes place from the village green to the cemetery, which is now part of the President Calvin Coolidge State Historic Site. The event is sponsored by the Calvin Coolidge Memorial Foundation.

Sources: *New York Times*, 5 July 1924, 1 and 14, 5 July 1926, 5 and 13, 6 July 1926, 1 and 12, and 5 July 1936, 22; "Coolidge Shares Birthday with Boy," *New York Times*, 5 July 1925, 1 and 5; "Coolidge as Cowboy

Wins West's Heart," *New York Times*, 5 July 1927, 1 and 3; President Calvin Coolidge State Historic Site, Web site, <http://www.dhca.state.vt.us/HistoricSites/html/coolidge.html>.

Cooper, Samuel (1725–1783)

This clergyman, born in Boston, publicly read the Declaration of Independence in Boston on August 11, 1776. James Warren later commented that the reading was "attended to by the auditory with great solemnity, and satisfaction." Cooper was minister of the Brattle Street Church, Boston, and was noted for his eloquence in public speaking. In 1753 he was named chaplain of the Massachusetts House of Representatives. Although recognized for taking a stand for peace and reconciliation prior to the American Revolution, he possibly was the author of a number of political essays published in the *Boston Gazette* and *Independent Ledger* proposing "a return to an earlier period when Massachusetts was virtually independent." After the Revolutionary War began, Cooper was an ardent proponent in New England of a military and diplomatic alliance with France. Cooper's position that the slave trade be curtailed emerged in a letter he wrote to John Adams on August 14, 1776, about his reading of the Declaration on August 11: he wished that some of Jefferson's narrative about the slave trade had not been discarded by the Continental Congress.

Sources: *New England Chronicle*, 15 August 1776; *Records of the State of Massachusetts* E.I., reel 9, unit 3: 82. See also, "James Warren to John Adams, August 11, 1776" and "Samuel Cooper to John Adams, 17 August 1776," in *Papers of John Adams*, ed. Robert J. Taylor (Cambridge, Mass.: Belknap Press of Harvard University Press, 1977–96) 4: 446 and 458.

Copenhagen, Denmark

Throughout the twentieth century the people of Denmark have celebrated America's Fourth of July as an expression of the excellent relations the Danes and Americans share. One of the first noteworthy Fourth of July celebrations on Danish soil occurred in tandem with Denmark's National Exposition in 1909. The crown prince and princess of Denmark were in attendance, and a musical cantata titled *The Fourth of July*, the text by Ivar Kirkegaard of Racine, Wisconsin, and the music composed by Carl Busch of Kansas City, was performed. See also **Rebild National Park, Denmark.**

Source: *New York Times*, 5 July 1909, 2.

Courtland, Kansas

The town where a cornerstone for a proposed monument to mark the spot where the American flag was first raised (by Zebulon M. Pike in 1806) over the territory of Kansas was laid on July 4, 1901.

Source: *Colorado Springs Gazette*, 5 July 1901, 1.

Cox, Samuel Sullivan (1824–1889)

Congressman representing Democrats in Ohio and later New York who won the favor of the nation's mail carriers by advocating for increased pay, shorter hours, and paid vacations. In recognition of his efforts, letter carriers representing the "General Post Office" and its branches from across the country erected a statue of him in Astor Plaza, New York City, in 1892, and formally presented it to the city on July 4, 1895.

In the 1870s Cox had already brought attention to himself through his attacks on big government. On July 4, 1877, he spoke at **Tammany Hall** in New York and denounced President Hayes for taking office through a dishonest election and said that New York State politics had resulted in "wrongful legislation." He claimed that "'the recent tendency of Legislatures has been to aggrandize their power,' without consulting the Constitution." On July 4, 1884, again at Tammany, he spoke denouncing "the spirit of greed" and "legalized gambling."

On July 4, 1888, a parade of delegations of letter carriers from New York, Philadelphia, Newark, Albany, Baltimore, Worcester, and Boston took place in New York City. They gathered in part to honor Cox, who had helped pass the eight-hour work day law. About 500 men marched from the City Hall plaza to the residence of Cox where a number of distinguished officials were assembled to greet them. From there they marched to Union Square and later that evening to the Academy of Music. According to a reporter, Cox addressed the audience there, saying that "he had helped in Congress to recover some $85,000 back pay for the 'boys'; then he started out to get them a vacation, but before they had that in the shape they wanted it the eight-hour movement came up. He was proud to be able to stand before the boys and say he had helped to pass that law."

Cox was a popular orator throughout his career and frequently gave political speeches on the Fourth. For example, on July 4, 1872, he spoke at the Tammany Society celebration in New York. The last Independence Day event he attended was in Huron, South Dakota, in 1889. His address was published (Metropolitan Job Printers) shortly thereafter in New York.

On Independence Day in 1890, a national conference of letter carriers representing ten cities met in New York to discuss the new national association that was founded on August 30, 1889, in Milwaukee, and to encourage carriers in all cities to join the association. The principal resolution adopted at the meetings was in the form of recommendations for pay increases for the letter carriers.

The Cox monument ceremony on July 4, 1895, included speeches by several officials. Chairman George H. Newsom of the Statue Committee delivered the "presentation speech." Postmaster Charles W. Dayton was the orator of the day and Job E. Hedges accepted the statue on behalf of the mayor of New York. Two bronze tablets adorned the sides of the statue's pedestal. One was inscribed with a dedication to Cox and the other tablet "contained the names of the 187 cities in the United States whose letter carriers contributed to the fund for the erection of the statue." The statue was later moved to Tompkins Square Park.

Another popular cause that won Cox recognition was his work for improving the Life Saving Service for sailors whose boats had shipwrecked. Again his efforts focused on improving pay and benefits, as well as service. Appropriately, in the audience for the Fourth of July ceremony in 1895 was N.J. Kearney, assistant superintendent of the Life Saving Service.

Sources: "Tammany's Celebration," *New York Times*, 5 July 1877, 6; "Tammany Talks Patriotism," *New York Herald*, 5 July 1884, 8; "The Carriers' Parade," *New York Times*, 5 July 1888, 8; "Sunset Cox in Dakota," *Washington Post*, 5 July 1889, 1; "Uniting the Letter Carriers," *New York Times*, 5 July 1890, 2; "Cox Statue Presented," *New York Times*, 5 July 1895, 9; Allan Peskin, "Samuel Sullivan Cox," *American National Biography* 5:631–32.

Coyle, William H.

Composed "Firemen's Ode," dedicated to the firemen of Detroit, which was read on July 4, 1850.

Source: *Firemen's Ode* (Detroit: Dunklee, Wales, 1850).

Crafts, Col. Thomas, Jr.

Presented the first reading of the Declaration of Independence in Boston on July 18, 1776. Crafts was commander of the regiment of artillery responsible for defending Boston during the Revolutionary War. John Adams knew Crafts and referred to him as an excellent officer, "civil, sensible, and of prodigious merit." Crafts was highly regarded in the community, and his reading of the Declaration "was received with great joy, expressed by three huzzas from a great concourse of people assembled on the occasion." Crafts was married and together with his four children lived in Leominster, Massachusetts.

Sources: John Adams to James Warren, 3 December; Thomas Crafts, Jr., to John Adams, 16 December 1775, in *Papers of John Adams* (Cambridge, Mass.: Belknap Press of Harvard University Press, 1979), 3: 339 and 367, respectively; *New York Times*, 4 July 1871, 2; *Orderly Book of the Regiment of Artillery Raised for the Defence of the Town of Boston, Commanded by Col. Thomas Crafts, from June 1777, to Dec., 1778* (Salem, Mass.: Salem Press, 1876).

Cranford, New Jersey

Site where a tablet to mark Crane's Ford, which gave the town its original name, was unveiled on July 4, 1929, by Judge William W. Mengells, a 94-year-old Civil War veteran. The inscription on the marker, placed by the Cranford Historical Society, read: "Here light horsemen guarded while General Washington's army was encamped at Morristown."

Source: "Cranford Unveils Tablet," *New York Times*, 5 July 1929, 21.

Cuba

The Fourth of July has been enthusiastically celebrated by the Cuban people during the twentieth century as a demonstration of friendship for Americans. During the presidency of Fulgencio Batista, celebrations were held to demonstrate solidarity with the United States. On July 4, 1941, one of the largest parades in Havana occurred. Thousands marched "amid flags and banners [and] other thousands crowded the sidewalks and cheered the marchers." Along with Batista, U.S. ambassador George S. Messersmith and other members of the diplomatic corps reviewed the parade. Earlier that day "Batista broadcast a message of greeting to the United States, saying that 'the ideas which have served as the basis for the organization of the great American nation are the same as those for which all the nations of America have fought.'" Also that day, the National Tobacco Commission presented a wood cabinet filled with cigars and cigarettes to Messersmith, to be delivered to President Roosevelt "as a token of admiration and friendship from the Cuban people."

In the nineteenth century it was believed by some that Cuba would eventually be annexed as a state. As early as July 4, 1823, Charles P. Curtis expressed this sentiment in an oration presented in Boston. The American presence in Cuba on the Fourth of July during the nineteenth century was evidenced by American ships displaying flags and bunting in Havana Harbor. Also, it was a tradition for the American colony in Cuba to hold a traditional Fourth of July breakfast at the American Club. The American Legion frequently presented children's picnics on that day. An unusual incident occurred on July 4, 1897, in Havana, when American newspaper correspondents were barred from attending the Fourth of July celebration at the U.S. Consulate. On July 4, 1910, another celebration took place at the American Club and hundreds of Americans were present along with "representatives of all branches of the Cuban Government." On Independence Day in 1929, 5000 Americans celebrated, and the day began with an artillery salute from Cabanas Fortress, which, according to a newspaper report, was "answered by their United States cruisers *Wyoming* and *New York* in port here with 500 middies. American sailors also placed a wreath on the Maine memorial."

A notable Fourth of July celebration occurred in 2002 at the Karl Marx Theater where the communist government expressed their acknowledgment of Americans and their heritage. President Fidel Castro attended the event, which included a singer's rendition of "Old Man River" and a ballet set to George Gershwin's "I've Got Rhythm." Vicky Huddleston, chief of the U.S. Interests Section in Havana, praised the event as an example of the close friendships of the people of both countries. "We hope that Cuba continues to celebrate the Fourth of July," she said.

Since the nineteenth century, Cuban-Americans in the United States have expressed patriotic pride in their close connections to their homeland and fellow Cubans. New York has been a popular place for such celebrations. One of the earliest occurred on July 4, 1853, when Cuban residents of New York and members of the "Lone Star" assembled in front of the New York Hotel at 11 P.M. and serenaded the U.S. minister to Spain and set off fireworks. On July 4, 1869, 350 Cuban "patriot" residents of New York City paraded "to evoke sympathy for the Cuban revolutionary cause." Another colony of Cuban-Americans was founded in Newark, New Jersey. At Waverly Park there on July 4, 1896, a parade of civic and military organizations on behalf of Cuban interests occurred. Before a crowd of 2000 persons, Colonel Mulliken of Newark "made a rousing speech for the Cuban cause," as did Mayor James M. Seymour. Representative William Sulzer of New York in adding to the heightened sentiments "declared that the Spanish flag should be spit upon and trampled by every American." See also **Spanish-American War**.

Sources: "The Cuban Celebration in New York," *New York Herald*, 7 July 1853, 3; *New York Times*, 6 July 1869, 1, 6 July 1897, 2, and 5 July 1910, 8; "The Fourth in Havana," *New York Times*, 7 July 1874, 1; "Cuban-American Carnival," *New York Herald*, 5 July 1896, 7; "Celebration in Havana," *New York Times*, 5 July 1929, 7; "Big Parade in Havana," *New York Times*, 5 July 1941, 6; Anita Show, "Communist Cuba Pays Homage to America," *Associated Press State and Local Wire*, 5 July 2002.

Cumberland Road

In St. Clairsville, Ohio, ground was broken on July 4, 1825, for the continuation of the Cumberland Road west of Ohio. The Declaration of Independence was read and an oration delivered "after which, in the presence of a large assemblage of ladies, and the exulting roar of cannon, the first excavation was made by the superintendent of the road; the military in the mean time forming a hollow square, and cheering the laborers with loud, long and repeated huzzas."

Source: *Frederick-Town Herald*, 23 July 1825, 3.

Cunningham, A.F. (fl. 1834–1851)

Popular orator, resident of Washington, D.C., and clerk at the U.S. Treasury Department, who read a "Teetotallers' Declaration of Independence," a variation on the Declaration of Independence, at a temperance celebration in Washington, D.C., on July 4, 1849, and spoke at the laying of the cornerstone of the city's **Temperance Hall** on July 4, 1843. Cunningham presented five other Independence Day orations at other temperance and trade union celebrations from 1834 to 1851.

Sources: *National Intelligencer*, 4 July 1834, 3; 2 July 1835, 3; 6 July 1843, 3; 4 and 7 July 1851, 3 and 2, respectively.

Cushing, Caleb

Composed an original eight-stanza ode that was sung to the tune of "Perry's Victory" on July 4, 1824, in Newburyport, Massachusetts.

(First stanza)
Oh! sublime was the warning America gave,
When she rose, on this morning, the free and the brave,
Sent the blaze of her standard to flash on the eye,
And the war-cry of freemen to clash in her sky.
And pealed the loud anthem, at Victory's best,
To the Queen of the Main and Pride of the West.

Source: broadside, "Order of Exercises for the Celebration of the Forty-Eighth Anniversary of American Independence, July 1824" (Newburyport: W. and J. Gilman, 1824) as reproduced in *An American Time Capsule: Three Centuries of Broadsides and Other Printed Ephemera*, Web site.

Custis, George Washington Parke (1781–1857)

Step-son of George Washington and dilettante, who was the most popular speaker in Washington prior to the Civil War. Custis inherited a plot of land and designed and built a mansion named "Arlington House near Alexandria, Virginia" just across the Potomac River. In 1804 he married a daughter of Col. William Fitzhugh, a close friend of Washington. Arlington House was a favorite place for Independence Day celebrations.

Newspapers report seventeen speeches given by Custis spanning 1804–57. Some of his notable addresses include one at the presentation of a flag "adorned with the bust of the Father of the Country, and bearing the inscription 'Pro Patria Semper,'" to Capt. J.T. Minor's Company of Light Infantry in Alexandria, Virginia (1823), another at the groundbreaking of the **Alexandria, Virginia, Canal** (1831) and six at Georgetown College (1837, 1840, 1843, 1846–47, and 1857). Three of his addresses were published, one presented in 1804 at the Episcopal Church in Alexandria, Virginia (*Washington Federalist*, 16 July 1804, 2), another given at "Arlington House" (*Maryland Gazette*, 28 July 1825, 2), and the third at Monument Place in Washington, 1850 (Washington: H. Polkinhorn, 1850). Custis's popularity is reflected in the newspaper report referring to his 1843 address at Georgetown College as "one of his eloquent and patriotic speeches, during the delivery of which long, loud, and repeated bursts of applause resounded throughout the spacious hall." An obituary written at the time of his death on October 10, 1857, perhaps best describes his appeal as a speaker:

The whole country knew him — and his patriotism will long be remembered. Closely allied to the Washington family, fond of calling himself the child of Mount Vernon, he was never so much in his element as when he was talking or writing of the Great Chief, and the Men and Times of the Revolution.... Though Mr. Custis was never in public life, he was in his younger days an eloquent and effective speaker, and had a fondness for oratory as long as he was able to gratify those who constantly called on him to make public addresses.

Custis was a participant in other notable occasions. On July 4, 1826, he took part in the nation's "Fiftieth Jubilee" event by hosting a party following the celebration held in the

Capitol. He provided the original tent that Washington used during the Revolutionary War as a setting for the dinner that followed the ceremony. In the following year on the Fourth, a play he wrote, *The Indian Prophecy: A National Drama in Two Acts*, had its Philadelphia premiere at the Chestnut Street Theater. On July 4, 1848, on the occasion of the laying of the cornerstone of the Washington Monument, Custis rode in a carriage that represented the soldiers of the Revolution.

Sources: *Alexandria Gazette*, 8 July 1823, 2, and 12 October 1857, 3; *Washington Evening Star*, 4 July 1898, 11; Heintze, *Orations, Speeches, and Readings of the Declaration of Independence in Washington, D.C. and Surrounding Towns on the Fourth of July: 1801–1876*.

D'Annunzio, Gabriele *see* Annunzio, Gabriele D'

Dartmoor, England

Location of the Dartmoor Prison Museum, which houses exhibits reflecting the history of the prison which was used for incarcerating American prisoners during the War of 1812. On July 4, 1814, an Independence Day celebration by American prisoners took place and eighteen toasts were drunk.

Source: *New Hampshire Gazette*, 4 October 1814, 4.

David

This French ship under the command of Captain Baron arrived in Philadelphia from Bordeaux a few days before July 4, 1861, and participated in the Independence Day celebration there. Her cargo included wines and liquors that had not yet been unloaded. At 12 noon on July 4, Captain Baron fired a salute of thirty-four guns from the *David*, which was moored at the Lombard street wharf, and was answered by a twenty-one-gun salute fired by the inspector and other officers of the custom house who had procured a cannon. That afternoon the Americans were invited aboard the *David* "where the glorious Fourth was celebrated in a proper manner."

Sources: *The Press*, 5 July 1861, 2–3; *Richmond Daily Dispatch*, 8 July 1861.

Davis, Jefferson (1808–1889)

President of the Confederacy during the Civil War, who gave a Fourth of July speech in 1858 on board the steamer *Joseph Whitney* bound from Baltimore to Boston and declared "this great country will continue united." A newspaper reported that "in the course of his beautiful speech, Senator Davis passed a noble eulogium on our mother country, and dwelt on the many reasons why the most cordial friendship should be maintained with her." Another report noted that "Davis dwelt at some length on the right of search question; on the insulting claim which Great Britain made to a peace right to visit our ships." Davis said, "Let a foreign power, under any pretence whatever, insult the American flag, and it will find that we are not a divided people; but that a mighty arm will be raised to smite down the insulter."

Davis was born in Todd County, Kentucky, and graduated from West Point in 1828. He served in the Black Hawk War (1832) and the War with Mexico. He was elected U.S. senator (1847–51) and appointed secretary of war under Franklin Pierce. He was elected once again as senator (1857) but resigned on January 21, 1861, after Mississippi seceded from the Union. Following his resignation, Union sympathizers who previously regarded him highly came to despise him. In Flushing, New York, for example, on July 4 of that year, a number of citizens held a mock ceremony and burned Davis in effigy. On February 22, 1862, after serving as provisional president of the Confederacy, he was inaugurated as its president. With the surrender at Appomattox of the Confederate Army in April 1865, Davis announced the end of the Confederacy on April 24, 1865. Davis was later captured and spent two years in the Fortress Monroe, Virginia, prison. There were those, however, who believed that Davis deserved to be hung for his treasonous acts against the Union. On July 4, 1866, John Alexander Logan (1826–1886), Union general and U.S. senator, in a speech before a crowd of 25,000 in Salem, Illinois, said, "There ought to be an example made in this land, and for future generations, of Jefferson Davis and many others who were associated with him in the organization of treason. They ought to be tried, convicted and hung."

After his release from prison, Davis traveled abroad, lived in Beauvoir, Mississippi, and wrote *Rise and Fall of the Confederate Government* (1881).

Sources: "The Hon. Jefferson Davis Making a Fourth of July Speech at Sea," *New York Times*, 12 July 1858, 1; *Alexandria Gazette*, 12 July 1858, 2; "The Fourth in Flushing," *New York Times*, 6 July 1861, 3; "Our National Anniversary," *Weekly Missouri Democrat*, 10 July 1866, 1.

Dawes, Thomas (1757–1825)

Boston lawyer and judge who wrote an "Ode to Independence," which was set to music by William Selby (1738–1798), and performed at the chapel in Boston, July 4, 1787. Dawes also gave an oration (published by S. Hall, 1787). John Quincy Adams was in the audience, but having arrived late, heard only the last portion of the oration and the ode.

Source: *Worcester Magazine*, July 1787, 194.

"Declaration Day"

Name frequently used in place of "Fourth of July" in early turn-of-the-nineteenth-century celebration programs in Duluth, Minnesota, "to reinforce the social control concerns the word 'independence' challenges and which might stimulate manifestations of drunkenness, fighting, and incidents with firecrackers." Another theme for the day used was "Patriot's Day."

Source: Mary Lou Nemanic, "The Fourth of July on the Minnesota Iron Range: Small-Town America and Working Class Nationalism, 1892–1992" (Ph.D. dissertation, University of Minnesota, 1996), 46.

Declaration of Independence

The nation's founding charter and most cherished symbol of liberty. The Declaration symbolizes the birth of a new nation and the determination of American colonists to shed the rule of English tyranny. Adopted on July 2, 1776, after a vote taken by delegates of the Second Continental Congress meeting in Philadelphia, the Declaration was printed in multiple copies during the afternoon of July 4 by John Dunlap, a local printer. Within days the news of the declaring of independence had traveled across New England, and within a few weeks at most, public readings of the Declaration had occurred throughout the new nation.

The determination of the British Parliament to levy stiff taxes on the colonists, coupled with the fact that clashes between British troops and colonial militia had occurred, helped prompt Richard Henry Lee, delegate from Virginia, to introduce a resolution to Congress on June 7, 1776, that stated in part, "Resolved that these United Colonies are, and of right ought to be, free and independent States, that they are absolved from all allegiance to the British Crown...." Congress debated the issue and appointed a committee, whose members were Thomas Jefferson of Virginia, Benjamin Franklin of Pennsylvania, John Adams of Massachusetts, Roger Sherman of Connecticut, and Robert R. Livingston of New York, to draft a declaration of independence. On June 11 Jefferson was given the task of writing the declaration. By July 2 Congress had examined and edited the draft. On July 4 Congress ordered that the Declaration, now signed by John Hancock and Charles Thomson, secretary of Congress, be sent to the printer and that copies be distributed to the various "committees or Councils of Safety and to the several Commanding officers of the Continental Troops." Dunlap added a new heading at the top of the Declaration — "In Congress, July 4, 1776" — and that information helped establish the tradition of celebrating independence on that date.

The new nation's first newspaper to announce that the Declaration had been adopted was the *Pennsylvanischer Staatsbote* on July 5. The paper reported that "*Die Declaration in Englisch ist jetzt in der Presse: sie ist datierte, den 4ten July, 1776, und wird heut oder morgen im druck erscheinen,*" followed by a full copy printed on July 9. On July 6, the Declaration was printed in the Philadelphia *Evening Post*. On August 2 many of the fifty-six delegates were back in Philadelphia signing a copy handwritten by **Timothy Matlack**, Thomson's assistant. Thomson hid that copy for fear that the lives of the signers might be jeopardized. The original parchment is now held in the National Archives in Washington, D.C.

Although a chief reason for writing the Declaration was to sever the colonial relationship with England, it was the principles inherent in the document that became its enduring

2001

Join the Signers Celebration at the National Archives

225th Anniversary of the Declaration of Independence

Reading Ceremony at 10 a.m.

Welcome

Presentation of Colors
Performed by the Armed Forces Color Guard

"The National Anthem"
Led by Duane A. Moody

The U.S. Army 3rd Infantry "Old Guard" Fife & Drum Corps

Opening Remarks: John W. Carlin, Archivist of the United States

Reading of the Declaration of Independence by Gwen Ifill and Ray Suarez
of PBS's *The NewsHour with Jim Lehrer*, accompanied by John Adams,
Thomas Jefferson, Benjamin Franklin, and George Washington

257th Army Band, District of Columbia National Guard

Closing

The tradition of publicly reciting the Declaration of Independence on the Fourth of July was inspired by the first public readings days after independence was declared in July 1776. That tradition continues today. Shown here is the program for the National Archives celebration of 2001, when Gwen Ifill and Ray Suarez of PBS's *The NewsHour with Jim Lehrer* read the Declaration in front of a large crowd assembled on the steps to the entrance of the National Archives building in Washington, D.C. From the author's collection.

qualities and that would have the greatest impact on the generations that followed. As a guiding light for all Americans, the Declaration helped democracy to emerge in the new nation. The copies printed by Dunlap were distributed primarily as a means to communicate the news and to further unify the new states in the mission that lay ahead. The inherent value of the document as a historic icon and relic was not fully appreciated until the early nineteenth century when the Revolutionary War generation had decreased in number, and the populace had come to realize the importance of their collective experience.

Newspapers and printing houses began publishing new copies of the Declaration, some very elaborate. In July of 1816, John Binns of Philadelphia advertised a new edition of the Declaration at $13 a copy. Interest in the Declaration continued in the years that followed. As late as July 4, 1905, a 13- × 7-foot pen-and-ink copy of the Declaration was made by William V. Peacon for presentation to the Tammany Society in New York. In the twentieth century, the Coca-Cola Bottling Company issued a limited facsimile edition of the Declaration in 1942 and the Society of the Cincinnati of Maryland issued a similar but smaller edition in 1957.

One of the earliest histories of the Declaration written for popular consumption was written by William Bacon Stevens (1815–1887), author of the first scholarly history of Georgia (1847). His "History of the Declaration of Independence" was published in the *National Intelligencer* in Washington, D.C., on July 4, 1842.

Public readings

On July 8 the Declaration was publicly read twice in Philadelphia amidst numerous huzzas, firing of guns, and parading militia. Other readings that day were given in Trenton, New Jersey, and Easton, Pennsylvania. It was at these first readings that the nation's first celebrations of freedom and independence took place. Many other readings occurred in the weeks to come in the major cities and towns along the Eastern Seaboard from Boston and the New England area to as far south as Savannah, Georgia. By the early nineteenth century it had become common practice to include readings of the Declaration in ceremonies held in government buildings, churches, private residences, on public greens, and in unusual settings, such as in hotels, prisons, and boats, and to select a dignitary or town ombudsman for that honor. Some of the noteworthy settings for readings of the Declaration include that of the first recitation in Washington on July 4, 1803, at the Treasury Department by the editor of the *National Intelligencer*, Samuel Harrison Smith, and that of the first reading at Mount Vernon on July 4, 1871, by John Carroll Brent.

The Declaration was frequently translated for readings in other languages, including French, German, Finnish, Italian, Spanish, and Swedish. For example, in Columbus, Ohio, on July 4, 1889, the document was read in German, and the audience at a celebration planned for Italians, French, and Americans at Washington Square Park in New York on July 4, 1911, heard the Declaration read in both French and English. During the twentieth century public readings of the Declaration were not as common as in past times, a fact which led Martin Conboy, United States director of the selective draft during World War I, to comment in a speech he gave on July 4, 1920, at Lake Champlain, New York, that "The character of this liberty and its source and sanction are all expressed in the Declaration of Independence. It is a good thing, therefore, in celebrating the Fourth of July to revive the ancient custom of reading the Declaration of Independence, so that we may understand and imbue ourselves with the spirit of the day. Liberty is the theme of the Declaration and the spirit of this day."

Members of the U.S. Congress have publicly read the Declaration while in session in the Capitol. On July 4, 1940, although the House met mostly to enact a three-day recess for itself, the Declaration was read. The next reading occurred on July 4, 1951, for the benefit of seventy-five members and a packed gallery. The session lasted "exactly thirteen minutes." Representative John E. Rankin (Dem.–Miss.) moved that the Declaration be "re-adopted" to "affirm independence of foreign dominations." The House declined to act on his motion. On July 4, 1971, in New York, the cast of *1776*, a musical based on the Declaration of Independence, read the document in costume in Times Square.

Displays

On July 4, 1953, a draft of the Declaration of Independence was put on display as part of a "Milestones of Freedom" exhibit in the New York Public Library. On July 4, 1930, documents illustrating the development of the Declaration of Independence were put on display at the Library of Congress. On July 4,

1978, an "original second printed copy of the Declaration of Independence was donated to the city of Dallas." The copy was discovered in 1968 in a wooden crate in a Philadelphia bookstore. The copy was valued at $500,000.

PARODIES

The nineteenth century witnessed an increasing interest in creating new declarations of independence. Many were proposed as parodies on the original Declaration; others were humorous, and yet others represented political and social statements reflective of the movements in progress at that time. For example, on July 4, 1839, the *McMinnville Gazette* in Tennessee published a Declaration of Independence for an "independent Treasury" (reprinted in the Washington *Globe*). On July 4, 1849, at a ceremony at East Capitol Square in Washington, D.C., a reading of the "Teetotallers' Declaration" by A.F. Cunningham took place and was a parody on temperance issues. On July 4, 1873, the *Liberty Tribune* in Liberty, Missouri, reported that a group of farmers in Illinois issued a new declaration of independence "from the tyranny of monopoly." In Chicago on July 4, 1876, a version of the Declaration of Independence based on the perspective of the Socialists was distributed, while in Philadelphia on the same day, Susan B. Anthony and other members of the National Woman's Suffrage Association publicly read their "Declaration of Rights for Women." On July 4, 1887, the *New York Times* printed an editorial calling for a new Declaration of Independence for "commercial freedom in the world markets." In one instance, the Declaration of Independence was published in the form of poetry in the *Charleston Courier* on July 4, 1845. The newspaper explained that the rendition "furnishes a striking confirmation of the truth that the language of passion or high excitement is often that of poetry."

In the twentieth century some enthusiasts called for a completely new declaration. On July 4, 1911, at Faneuil Hall in Boston, Charles W. Eliot, president emeritus of Harvard University, called for a new Declaration of Independence "as a means of resisting the oppressive effects of industrial government." In 1925 the **Women's Peace Union** issued a "Declaration of Independence from War." On July 4, 1936, Harry W. Laidler, Socialist candidate for governor of New York, called for a new declaration of independence against "judicial tyranny and industrial autocracy."

Sources: *National Intelligencer*, 6 and 8 July 1803, 3 and 2, respectively; *Alexandria Gazette*, 9 July 1816, 4; *Globe*, 8 July 1839, 2; *National Intelligencer*, 4 July 1842, 1–4; "The Declaration of Independence in Blank Verse," *Charleston Courier*, 4 July 1845, 2; *National Intelligencer*, 4 July 1849, 3; *Liberty Tribune*, 4 July 1873, 2; *Chicago Daily Tribune*, 4 July 1876, 8; *New York Times*, 4 July 1887, 4; *Daily Ohio State Journal*, 5 July 1889, 5; *New York Times*, 5 July 1905, 14; "Celebrate in Three Tongues," *New York Times*, 5 July 1911, 5 and 16; "Conboy Sees Need to Guard Liberty," *New York Times*, 5 July 1920, 13; *New York Times*, 5 July 1936, 23; "House in Brief Session Hears Declaration Read, "*New York Times*, 5 July 1951, 8; *New York Times*, 4 July 1953, 8; *Los Angeles Times*, 5 July 1971, 7; James Munves, *Thomas Jefferson and the Declaration of Independence* (New York: Charles Scribner's Sons, 1978); *Washington Post*, 5 July 1978, B2; Karl J.R. Arndt, "First German Broadside and Newspaper Printing of the Declaration of Independence," *Pennsylvania Folklife* 35 (1986): 98–107.

"The Declaration of Independence: A Poem Commemorating the One Hundredth Anniversary of the National Birthday of the United States of America"

Published by Joseph Hamilton Martin (1825–1887) in New York in 1876.

"The Declaration of Independence of the United States of North America, July 4, 1776"

Composed (composer unnamed) as a "great National Chant" and "dedicated to the world." First line: "When in the course of human events" (Baltimore, John E. Wilson, 1861).

"The Declaration of Independence, Signed July 4th, 1776: A Song, Designed for the Public Schools and Academies"

Published as a broadside in 1858 (Pittsburgh, Pa.: Hunt and Miner, 1858). First line: "To memorize the names of those." Includes ten numbered four-line stanzas sung to the tune "Twenty Years Ago." Following the title is the following four-line verse:

> But, doubtless,
> A song which every one should know,
> Throughout our mighty nation,
> For it contains the names of those who signed the Declaration.

Declaration of War on Great Britain (1812)

An unusual event for public readings in which the Congressional act declaring war against England was read on July 4, 1812, in Petersburg, Virginia, by Benjamin Watkins Leigh. Madison's message to Congress on June 1 listed major grounds for war. On June 4 the House supported a resolution for war and the Senate voted for the declaration on June 18. On June 19 Madison issued the proclamation of war with Great Britain. On July 4, Leigh publicly read both the Declaration of War and "the President's Proclamation," as well as the Declaration of Independence. Leigh's delivery was "in his usual distinct and nervous manner" before a crowd made up of "his fellow citizens, of the military corps, and a brilliant assemblage of ladies" that had assembled in Powell's Tavern. Leigh concluded his readings "with an impressive appeal to the patriotism of his countrymen, exhorting them to unanimity, to rally around their government, to bury the little distinctions of party, and to devote their whole energies to the prosecution of the war in which we are engaged, as the surest means to bring it to a speedy and an honourable issue." His speech ended with "an instantaneous burst of applause."

Source: *The Courier*, 16 July 1812, 2.

Defense Test Day, 1925 *see* National Defense Day, 1925

Dekalb County, Alabama, School

The cornerstone of this school was laid on July 4, 1908, with over 3000 spectators in attendance. W.M. Howard presented a keynote speech.

Source: "Cornerstone is Laid," *Chattanooga Sunday Times*, 5 July 1908, 1.

"Democracy Triumphant"

A pageant presented by foreign-born citizens in Washington, D.C., at the Capitol on July 4, 1918. President Wilson and various government officials were in the audience. The event began with a parade down Pennsylvania Avenue to the Capitol. The group representing each nationality were in native costumes and carried their national flag. Included were detachments of French, British and Italian sailors. The production took place in the evening amidst "brilliant illumination of hundreds of lights." According to one newspaper report,

> The pageant depicted Humanity and her happy children meeting a sorrowful group symbolic of suffering children. Humanity summoned Justice to her aid, who in turned called upon Columbia, representing the United States. Columbia offered her entire resources — money, food armament, service, and her own sons — each represented by living characters. Then followed the heralds of the allied nations, announcing the coming of the Hope of the World, Triumphant Democracy.

Source: "President Sees a Pageant," *New York Times*, 5 July 1918, 11.

Denny Hall, University of Washington

The cornerstone for this Seattle building, named after Arthur A. Denny, was laid on July 4, 1894. The ceremony officially established the new University of Washington. Over 300 masons assisted in the event and music was provided by the First Regiment Band. Addresses were given by fifteen individuals, including Denny and Seattle mayor Byron Phelps, who said to the crowd assembled there, "The people of Seattle appreciate most highly the fact that the University of Washington is located in their midst, and I am sure every citizen of our good city will hereafter, as in the past, show to the state our gratitude for the new university here to be built."

Sources: "The New University" and "Corner-Stone Laid," *Seattle Post-Intelligencer*, 4 and 5 July 1894, 8 and 8, respectively.

Denton, Maryland, fire

On July 4, 1865, the entire business portion of the town was destroyed by fire due to "a rocket thrown in the upper story of the old E.B. Hardcastle store." Many families were left "totally destitute."

Source: "Denton, Md., Burned to Ashes," *New York Times*, 9 July 1865, 8.

Denver, Colorado, State Capitol Building

The cornerstone ceremony occurred on July 4, 1890, with Governor Job A. Cooper presiding. The event included a parade and a Masonic choir, led by John Blood, which sang "America." Items placed in the cornerstone included the Colorado and Federal constitutions, a flag, coins, and copies of newspapers. Orations were presented by Cooper, former governor Alva Adams, and two judges. A public dinner was presented at Lincoln Park.

Sources: Martin A. Wegner, "Raising the Gold-Plated Dome," Colorado State Capitol Virtual Tour Web site, 17 May 2005, <http://www.colorado.gov/dpa/doit/archives/cap/gold.htm>.

Des Moines, Iowa

The 100th anniversary of Iowa's statehood was celebrated in this city on July 4, 1946. It was President James K. Polk "who signed Iowa's bill of admittance to the Union" in 1846. Ceremonies included parades and a display representing the history of the state.

Source: "Iowa Celebrates its 100th Birthday," *New York Times*, 5 July 1946, 6.

Detroit, Michigan

The first Independence Day celebration in Detroit as reported in the city's first newspaper, the *Detroit Gazette*, occurred on July 4, 1818. The event included a military and civic parade through city streets, a ceremony consisting of an oration presented by Andrew G. Whitney, a lawyer, and a reading of the Declaration of Independence by Charles Larned. A sermon was given by John Monteith, a Presbyterian pastor who later became the first president of the University of Michigan. The day ended with a public dinner at Whipple's Hotel.

Source: Louis Rau, "First American Fourth of July in Michigan," *Michigan History Magazine* 26 (summer 1941): 292.

Dioramas

A connected series of paintings usually exhibited in a darkened location, with special effects and optical illusions. Many were displayed on special occasions. Independence Day exhibits occurred in New York City and Charleston, South Carolina, for example. The idea for a diorama was first devised in 1822 by Daguerre (chief inventor of photography) and Bouton. A popular diorama exhibit was displayed by "Hannington" on July 4, 1836, in New York. The display depicted "General Houston's glorious victory at San Jacinto and the capture of Santa Anna." On July 4, 1845, at Lege's Long Room in Charleston, there were three "performances" given by Hannington that included: an "Italian Landscape," "Bedasora in Spain," "Storm and Shipwreck," and "Fairy Grotto." The cost for viewing this exhibit was 25 cents.

Sources: *New York Herald*, 4 July 1836, 1; *Charleston Mercury*, 4 July 1845, 3.

District of Columbia, home rule

The lack of home rule in the District of Columbia has prompted a number of speeches on the Fourth. On July 5, 1926, House of Representatives Harry R. Rathbone of Illinois gave a celebration speech in which he called for home rule. Rathbone believed the residents there "are in no wise inferior to their fellow-citizens either in education, fitness for citizenship or devotion to their country," he said. "Why should the fact that they happen to live on one side of an arbitrary boundary line deprive them of the rights which they desire to possess and which are enjoyed by the people of all parts of the country?" On July 4, 1940, at a celebration of the **Oldest Inhabitants Association of Washington**, Representative Ulysses S. Guyer of Kansas called for a voting franchise in the District.

Sources: "Asks for Suffrage in Federal Capital," *New York Times*, 6 July 1926, 7; "Oldest Inhabitants Hear Guyer Urge Votes for District," *Washington Evening Star*, 4 July 1940, A2.

Douglass, Frederick (1818–1895)

One of the most influential African-American leaders of the nineteenth century, whose 1852 Independence Day oration given in Rochester, New York, on July 5, "What to the Slave is the Fourth of July?" remains the most frequently reprinted Independence Day oration in the history of the celebration. Stephen James described the address as "the consummate expression of the African American state of mind toward the hypocrisy of America's Independence celebration."

Douglass, who spent twenty years of his life as a slave, was later internationally acclaimed for his skills as a speaker and publisher. However, his legacy rests equally with his efforts as an abolitionist, and his antislavery speeches received attention across the nation. His first antislavery speech was given in 1841. His autobiography *Narrative of the Life of Frederick Douglass* (1845), which recounts his experiences as a slave, was published in 1845. Throughout his career Douglass used the Fourth of July frequently as an ideal forum for advancing his cause. He commanded substantial audiences and his speeches were articulate and influential. His landmark 1852 address was at the invitation of the Rochester Ladies' Anti-Slavery Society, and over 500 persons filled Corinthian Hall to hear his eloquent and passionate challenge to the inherent contradictions of the freedoms and equality promised by the Declaration of Independence and Constitution. "Fellow-citizens, pardon me," said Douglass, grasping the attention of his listeners,

> allow me to ask, why am I called upon to speak here today? What have I, or those I represent, to do with you national independence? Are the great principles of political freedom and of natural justice, embodied in that Declaration of Independence, extended to us? And am I, therefore, called upon to bring our humble offering to the national altar, and to confess the benefits and express devout gratitude for the blessings resulting from your independence to us?

Douglass' question posed that day, "What, to the American slave, is your 4th of July?" served as a beacon for the progress of the abolitionist movement and eventual emancipation.

Another address of equal significance he gave on the Fourth took place in 1875 in Washington, D.C., at the cornerstone ceremony for the new Israel Mission Church. Titled "The Color Question," the address focused on the new peace in the nation and its impact on African-Americans. The impact of blacks on the nation was vital, and Douglass stated that African-Americans "have had something to do with almost everything of vital importance in the life and progress of this great country." Douglass' address, according to a report in the *National Republican* (8 July) "created considerable comment and is likely to cause more."

Other Independence Day speeches by Douglass include those at the Plymouth County Anti-Slavery Society in Kingston, Massachusetts, July 4, 1843; in Anthol, Massachusetts, July 4–5, 1845; in Norfolk, Virginia, July 4, 1867, at "a large Republican meeting"; and in Frederick, Maryland, July 4, 1879.

In recent times Douglass' impact continues to be felt. On July 4, 1974, his 1852 speech was publicly read at the Kennedy Center in Washington, D.C., and there was another reading at the Smithsonian Institution on July 4, 1978. On July 4, 1993, Nelson Mandela, in an address upon receiving a Liberty Medal at Independence Hall in Philadelphia, quoted passages from Douglass' speech. On July 4, 2004, visitors to the Rochester (New York) Museum and Science Center heard six minutes of recorded excerpts of the speech as they viewed a signed copy of Douglass' address.

Sources: "Fortress Monroe and Norfolk," *New York Times*, 5 July 1867, 8; *Washington Evening Star*, 6 July 1875, 4; *American Citizen*, 19 April 1879, 4; James, "The Other Fourth of July: The Meanings of Black Identity at American Celebrations of Independence, 1770–1863," 163; Jane Rippeteau, "The Fourth Was Also a Day to Honor Frederick Douglass," *Washington Post*, 5 July 1974, B1–B2; Lynne Duke and Al Kamen, "South African Leaders Receive Liberty Medal at Independence Hall," *Washington Post*, 5 July 1993, A6; John W. Blassingame and John R. McKivigan, eds., *The Frederick Douglass Papers* (New Haven: Yale University Press, 1979–1992); Bernard W. Bell, "The African-American Jeremiad and Frederick Douglass' Fourth of July 1852 Speech," in *The Fourth of July: Political Oratory and Literary Reactions 1776–1876*, ed. Goetsch and Hurm; Benning W. De La Mater, "Douglass Heard a 'Mournful Wail,'" *Rochester Democrat and Chronicle*, 4 July 2005.

Drake, Charles Daniel (1811–1892)

U.S. senator, abolitionist, and effective orator who gave two Fourth of July orations, one in 1861 at a Union meeting held at Louisiana, Missouri, and the other in 1862 at Washington, Missouri. Drake was born in Cincinnati, Ohio, and attended schools in Cincinnati and Kentucky. He spent three years at the U.S. Naval Academy, leaving there in 1830 to study law. He became a member of the bar in 1833 and practiced law in Cincinnati and later in St. Louis. In 1862, Drake spoke out against slavery as a cause for the Civil War and was a major player in creating the Radical Union Party, whose platform called for a new constitution and immediate emancipation. Drake served for a time as a Republican in the U.S. Senate and later as chief justice of the U.S. Court of Claims, a post he held until his retirement in 1885.

Drake's Independence Day address of 1861 was titled "The Union: Its Nature and Its Assailants" and focused on support of the Constitution and how "the insurgent states asserts doctrines, and claim rights and attributes, which are without a semblance of warrant, in or out of the Constitution, and are at deadly variance with the principles on which the Union was formed, and on which its existence depends." Drake explained the nature of "state sovereignty," and why the South could never exhibit "external sovereignty, which is, by the Constitution, vested in the nation."

Drake titled his Fourth of July speech of 1862 "The Rebellion: Its Character, Motive, and Aim":

> Of the many fundamental errors of the rebellion whose deadly footsteps have marked our land with blood through the dreary twelve month past, the most incomprehensible to me is, that diversity of interest, difference of domestic institutions, and discordance of feelings and habits, justify revolution, for the sake of social separation; an error as necessarily fatal to all social unity, as in the days of our fathers, it would have been an insuperable barrier to union, if they had entertained it. For there is nothing in our history more true, than that just such diversities existed then as now; but they were not counted as a feather's weight in the scale against the benefits which union offered, and which without union were impossible of attainment.

Sources: Charles D. Drake, *Union and Anti-Slavery Speeches, Delivered During the Rebellion* (Cincinnati, 1864; reprint Miami, Fla.: Mnemosyne Publishing, 1969); William E. Parrish, "Charles Daniel Drake," *American National Biography* 6:861–62.

Droop Mountain Battlefield State Park, West Virginia

Dedicated on July 4, 1929, the site of the last significant Civil War battle, located in the Greenbrier River Valley north of Lewisburg. The battle took place on November 6, 1863. Union troops commanded by Brigadier General William W. Averell fought Confederate troops under Brigadier General John Echols for control of the Virginia-Tennessee Railroad at Salem, Virginia. The Union troops overtook the Confederate lines forcing Echols to retreat into Virginia. During the 1930s, a museum, lookout tower and other buildings were constructed in the park by the Civilian Conservation Corps.

Source: Droop Mountain Battlefield State Park, Web site, West Virginia Division of Natural Resources, 9 May 2002, <http://www.droopmountain-battlefield.com>.

Dunbarton, New Hampshire

Town with population of 2226 (in 2000) where five candidates for the 1995 presidential nomination campaigned on July 4 that year. "Patriotism, parades and politicking" was the theme of the day as Senate majority leader Bob Dole of Kansas, Senator Phil Gramm of Texas, political commentator Patrick Buchanan, Representative Bob Dornan of California, and former Reagan administration official Alan Keyes applied their speech-making skills at the festivities that included a parade and picnic "on the town's colonial-era green."

Dole, who was seriously wounded in World War II, hit upon a favorite theme when he noted that the Amherst Colonial Militia had been the first from New Hampshire to join in the American Revolution, and that 22 of the town's best died in the fighting. "I'm not here in any partisan sense," Dole said. "I'm here because I'm proud to be an American."

Gramm, who had pledged to cut taxes and government regulations, tried to appeal to all New Hampshire voters, when he said: "I can't think of a better place to celebrate the nation's birthday than a state where the motto is, 'Live free or die.'"

The town's charter is named after Dumbarton, Scotland, and was signed in 1765.

Sources: Michael Rezendes, "GOP Conservatives Celebrate in New Hampshire, Look Over Candidates," *Boston Globe*, 5 July 1995, 3; Thomas B. Edsall, "GOP Candidate Gathering Is Heavy on Collegiality," *Washington Post*, 5 July 1995, A4.

Dutch Reformed Church, Poughkeepsie, New York

This church was "nearly destroyed" on July 4, 1832, as a result of the "firing of crackers."

Source: *Niles' Weekly Register* 42/21 (21 July 1832): 373.

Eaches, Hector (1840–1875)

Artist, and son of Joseph Eaches, mayor of Alexandria, Virginia, who was one of the youngest orators to speak on the Fourth of July. On July 4, 1846, at six years of age, Eaches gave a patriotic address at the Methodist Episcopal Sunday School in Alexandria. Eaches was introduced by John McCormick, superintendent of the school, "who remarked that, although he was the last and the least of the orators, he would prove himself equal to any in giving satisfaction." According to a local newspaper, Eaches "arose with all the composure of a practiced orator, and addressed the audience with so much manliness, and to such purpose, that it was difficult to restrain the audience after the long applause." Following Hector's performance, "The School was then formed in procession, in front of the Church, from whence they were kindly escorted by the Mount Vernon Guards, to the Old Court Room, over the market house, where the whole school, and the invited guests, partook of a bountiful repast, which wound up with an abundant supply of Lemonade and Cake, until, we believe, every body was satisfied." Eaches later became an artist and, reportedly, Robert E. Lee posed for him. Ironically, Hector's mother died on the Fourth of July in 1850, at fifty-three years of age.

Sources: *Alexandria Gazette*, 10 July 1846, 2, and 6 July 1850, 2; *Out Town, 1749–1865* (Alexandria Association, 1956), 100–01.

Eads Bridge, St. Louis

This first steel bridge across the Mississippi River was dedicated on July 4, 1874. The structure, designed by James B. Eads, is one hundred feet high and spans the river with three graceful arches. Construction began in 1867 and cost $10 million. The bridge was heralded as "a symbol of progress for a city competing with Chicago to become a center of rail transportation." In 1889 the Terminal Railroad Association took charge of operating the bridge until 1989 when it was sold to the City of St. Louis. In 1998 the bridge was scheduled for an $18 million renovation funded in part by the Missouri Department of Transportation, the Illinois Department of Transportation, the Federal Highway Administration and the City of St. Louis. On July 4, 2003, the Eads Bridge reopened, "but only to pedestrians and bicyclists." The bridge opened to motorists a few days later.

Sources: Betty Magrath, "Eads Bridge Opening for Millennium," Saint Louis Front Page, Web site, 6 September 2002, <http://www.slfp.com/0105BIZp.htm>; "Landmark St. Louis Bridge Open after 11-Year Closure," *Philadelphia Inquirer*, 5 July 2003, A4.

Eagle

A symbol for the rising American republic and its power that was depicted on coins and in poetry, music, fireworks, books, toasts, oratory, and ceremonies, and was used as the name of taverns. An early use of the eagle as metaphor was written by John Quincy Adams in his diary after he heard an oration given at the Old Brick Meeting Church in Boston on July 4, 1787, by General John Brooks of the Society of the Cincinnati: "It was cautious and well guarded: but although the claws of the eagle may be concealed or withdrawn, they are always ready as a weapon to attack or to defend, whenever an opportunity shall present itself."

On July 4, 1820, in Hartfort, Connecticut, the tune "American Eagle" was performed at a dinner celebration held at the City Hotel. "The American eagle is the patriot's hope and the inspiration of the fourth of July. He soars through the realms of the poet's fancy and whets his beak on the highest peak of the orator's imagination. He is in the mouth of every politician, so to speak. He is said by them to stand on the Rocky Mountains and to dip his bill into the Atlantic, while his tail casts a shadow on the Pacific coast."

On July 4, 1846, the first newspaper started in Jasper, Indiana, was named by Henry Comingore the *Eagle*. The paper was first printed in the courthouse and ran until 1848 when Comingore moved away, leaving the town without a newspaper for ten years.

On July 4, 1876, at the Academy of Music in New York, at the back of the stage on which the ceremony took place was "a gas illuminatica of the national eagle, with the legend 1776–1876."

In 1885 in the Dakota Territory, Phineus Donan wrote an oration titled "A Scream from the American Eagle in Dakota" that was distributed to passengers on the Chicago, Milwaukee and St. Paul railway traveling west. It is an excellent example of eagleism in oratory which boasts about the physical features of America: "Do other lands boast of their great rivers? We could take up all their Niles and Thameses, their yellow Tibers, castled Rhines and beautiful blue Danubes, by their little ends, and empty them into our majestic Mississippi and Missouris, Amazons, Saskatchewans and De la Platas, without making rise enough to lift an Indiana flat-boat off a sandbar."

For at least one Independence Day occasion a live eagle was used. At the laying of the cornerstone of the Washington Monument, "a full sized American living eagle was placed on the summit of the Masonic arch" which stood in the vicinity of the ceremony.

Sources: *Times and Weekly Advertiser* (Hartford), 11 July 1820, 3; "Washington National Monument," *Niles' National Register* 74 (12 July 1848): 32; Ike Partington, "The American Eagle," *Living Age* 55/701 (31 October 1857): 282; "A Second Century Begun," *New York Times*, 5 July 1876, 1; "A Scream from the American Eagle in Dakota," *American West* 5/4 (July 1968): 45–47; *Diary of John Quincy Adams*, ed. Robert J. Taylo et al. (Cambridge, Mass.: Belknap Press of Harvard University Press, 1981), 249; DC Herald.com Web site, 5 September 2002, <http://www.dcherald.com/aboutus.html>.

East Jaffrey, New Hampshire, School House

Dedicated on July 4, 1854. A.H. Bennett presented the keynote address and a "Dedicatory Hymn" and "Celebration Hymn" by Mrs. E.K. Bailey and Rev. J.E.B. Jewett, respectively, were presented.

Source: A.H. Bennett, *An Address Delivered at the Dedication of the New School House....* (Peterborough: E.H. Cheney, 1854).

Education

An important theme on the Fourth of July for encouraging equal opportunity and improvement of education in the country. Beginning in the 1780s in New England, individuals spoke out for the advantages that education provided in society. Orators praised the progress of a free education system in American society and urged expansion of public education to all. John Gardiner of Boston, one of the first to advocate for public education on Independence Day, spoke in 1785 about the importance of education for instructing citizens in the nature of civil liberty, religion, and letters. Other orators who pursued this theme were Edward Bangs (Worcester, Massachusetts, 1791), Benjamin Silliman (Hartford, Connecticut, 1802), and Henry A.S. Dearborn (Salem, Massachusetts, 1806). More than seventy Fourth of July orations that stressed the importance of education were published in the northeastern states, but only two were issued in the South—John E. Anderson (Augusta, Georgia, 1801) and Philip Mathews (St. Helena, South Carolina, 1813).

The notion that citizens could govern themselves appropriately only if properly educated was a persistent theme. In 1789 Samuel Whitwell spoke in Boston on July 4 and remarked, "learning and education qualify a people for the noble purposes of being happily governed, while ignorance renders them inattentive to their rights and prepares them for the chains of slavery which ambition is ever read to rivet." One of the most influential speakers on the Fourth of July prior to the Civil War was **Horace Mann** of Boston. On July 4, 1842, he urged his listeners to consider public education. He admonished Boston for its lack of adequate education. Yet other orators' goals were to dismantle religious bigotry and prejudice through education (see William C. White, Worcester, Massachusetts, 1804, and William Slade, Bridport, Vermont, 1829). On July 4, 1833, Nicholas Biddle, speaking at the cornerstone ceremony at the Girard College for Orphans in Philadelphia, reminded his listeners that education was essential, especially as the population increased.

Education for women was a critical theme espoused by Fourth of July speakers. In 1810 in Salem, Massachusetts, Joseph E. Sprague said: "The education of the female sex, though it is generally considered of little consequence, is undoubtedly of the utmost importance." Women, he proposed, influence the "political points of view" expressed by men and this influence is developed at the time of childhood when mothers provide "impressions which are most deeply fixed and most difficult to eradicate." Others that called for more education for women included William P. Fessenden (Portland, Maine, 1827) and Norman Pinney (Mobile, Alabama, 1835).

Education in the South soon followed the lead of the northeastern states. A notable event was the inauguration of the public school system in Charleston, South Carolina, which took place at Institute Hall on July 5, 1856, with nearly 1800 children participating. The ceremony was "varied, and so diversified with music — social and instrumental — with speaking and reports, that the attention and interest of the vast audience were sustained throughout." During the nineteenth century, and especially due to the effects of the Civil War, the South was not able to develop a successful system of general education that provided ready access to all children. In a landmark speech titled "National Aid to Education" on July 4, 1883, ex-president Rutherford B. Hayes at Woodstock, Connecticut, emphasized "the alarming extent of illiteracy in the southern States" and therefore recommended government action. In each of eight states, the number of illiterate voters was greater than the majority of votes cast in the 1880 election. "In the history of popular education nothing is better settled than this: the only power able to establish and support an efficient system of universal education is the government," Hayes said. Major educational associations active in the 1890s included the National Council of Education, which met on July 4, 1890, in St. Paul, Minnesota, and in the early twentieth century, the **National Educational Association (NEA)**, which provided the principal leadership for the progressive movement in education during that century.

Sources: *Niles* XLIV (20 July 1833): 349–51; "The City Schools — the Pupils of Honor," *Charleston Daily Courier*, 7 July 1858, 1; "Woodstock's Jubilee" and "National Aid to Education," *New York Herald*, 5 July 1883, 3 and 4, respectively; "The National Council of Education," *Brooklyn Daily Eagle*, 5 July 1890, 4; Martin, "Orations on the Anniversary of American Independence, 1777–1876," 124–34.

Educational Alliance, New York

An association formed on East Broadway in 1889 by German Jews with the mission of providing education to European Jewish immigrants. The Alliance programs included English language training for foreigners and free lectures. The Alliance used the Fourth of July as an ideal time to introduce American customs and traditions. On July 4, 1906, for example, hundreds of immigrant children and 800 parents gathered to celebrate their new national flag. The Declaration of Independence was read in Yiddish and English. The children saluted the flag, "largely after a pattern selected by Baron de Hirsch, the founder of the Immigrant School. Everybody, immigrants and natives, shouted as the youngsters, with hands outstretched toward the colors said with solemnity 'we salute thee.'" After that the children sang "Our Own United States" and three young lads, having limited English training, attempted to read "Daniel Webster's speech at Bunker Hill." The affair ended with a rough rendition of "America." According to one reporter, "Although the words had been printed for them on their programmes, they were in English, and they floundered badly in the tune."

Sources: "Little Russans Here Celebrate the Fourth," *New York Times*, 4 July 1906, 7; Selma Berrol, "Educational Alliance," *The Encyclopedia of New York City*, 365.

Edwards, New York, fire

This town, located in St. Lawrence County, on the banks of the Oswegatchie River, was mostly destroyed by fire on July 4, 1894. "The citizens had made great preparations for one of the grandest celebrations in the history of the town. Special trains on the little railroad of which Edwards is the terminus were bringing in hundreds of people." Thirty-four buildings were burned, including the town hall; twenty-two families were left homeless. The loss was estimated at $40,000.

Source: "Nearly Swept Away," *Washington Evening Star*, 5 July 1894, 1.

1812 Overture

A spectacular standard musical work performed at Fourth of July celebrations across the country, frequently with accompaniment of artillery. Composed by Peter Ilyich Tchaikovsky in 1880, the *Ouverture Solennelle* was commissioned for the consecration of the Cathedral of Christ the Savior, a Moscow Orthodox church erected in honor of the 70th anniversary of Russia's defeat of Napoleon. The piece was first recorded by the Cleveland Orchestra in the United States in 1924 but was initially connected to the Fourth of July in 1974, when the **Boston Pops** under the direction of Arthur Fiedler gave a televised performance that year. The work, performed to the accompaniment of the sound of artillery, was considered a stunning success. After that, orchestras across the country began similarly programming the piece on their Fourth of July concerts. The idea for using artillery as an accompaniment to the work was attributed in 1940 to Eugene Ormandy of the Philadelphia Orchestra.

Sources: "Today's Radio Highlights," *Washington Post*, 4 July 1940, 22; John Petkovic, "As American as Apple Pie and a Russian Anthem," *Plain Dealer*, 3 July 2000, 1E.

Eisenhower, Dwight David (1890–1969)

Thirty-fourth president of the U.S. (1953–61). Eisenhower commanded the Allied invasion of North Africa that began on November 8, 1942. In 1943, he presided over a Fourth of July celebration held at Allied Head-quarters in North Africa with participants that included high army, navy, and air force personnel. "A red-fezzed Spahi band played 'The Stars and Stripes Forever' and a United States band followed with 'Over There.'"

On July 4, 1947, Eisenhower was in Vicksburg, where he swore in fifty-two army volunteers, spoke at a "Carnival of the Confederacy," and reviewed a two-hour parade. In his speech he told his audience of his plans to seek the office of president of Columbia University and, irregardless, that no one had as yet asked him to run for U.S. president. "I want nothing to do with politics," he said. He spoke about the Marshall Plan and warned that unless the United States built "a world structure for peace," there was the danger of a third world war.

On July 4, 1950, Eisenhower was at Valley Forge, Pennsylvania, participating in a **Boy Scouts** National Jamboree celebration. In the following year he was in London on July 4 at a service at St. Paul's Cathedral dedicating a "Roll of Honour" for the American Memorial Chapel there.

Eisenhower's most significant contribution to the heritage of the Fourth was his participation in the cornerstone laying ceremony of the east front extension of the Capitol on July 4, 1959. At the ceremony, the president, assisted by District of Columbia Masons and introduced by House Speaker Sam Rayburn, used the same silver trowel that George Washington had used in 1793 for the original cornerstone ceremony of the building. He addressed the audience and spoke about the hallmarks of freedom. "In the collision of ideas between freedom and despotism," he said, "freedom is neither won nor held in a climate of spiritual stalemate. Its preservation is a many-sided and never-ending task. Complacency today speeds the erosion of liberty tomorrow." A copy of Eisenhower's speech was added to a copper box which was placed in the cornerstone that bears the inscription "A.D. 1959." Also present at the ceremony was Senator Everett McKinley Dirksen. The east front of the Capitol was "extended thirty-two feet to align it with the Senate and House wings."

Sources: "Fourth Celebrated in Africa with

Eisenhower Presiding," *Washington Post*, 5 July 1943, 1B; John N. Popham, "General in Vicksburg Address," *New York Times*, 5 July 1947, 12; "Ike to Start Fireworks at Scout Session," *Washington Post*, 4 July 1950, 9B; *Service of Commemoration of 28,000 American Dead ...* (London: American Memorial Chapel Fund, 1951); "Capitol Fete July 4," "Eisenhower Cites Freedom's Story," and "President's Talk at Capitol Ceremony," *New York Times*, 24 June, and 4 and 5 July 1959, 22, 1 and 2, respectively.

Elizabeth Town, New Jersey

Town where an ode "composed for the occasion" to the tune of "Miriam's Song" was premiered on July 4, 1819.

Source: *Washington Whig* (Bridgeton, N.J.), 19 July 1819, 2.

Elizabethtown, Kentucky

This town, located about forty-five miles south of Louisville, in Hardin County, was officially established on July 4, 1797, and was named in honor of the wife of Andrew Hynes, an early settler in the area. The original settlement consisted of thirty acres of land divided into lots and streets.

Source: "History of Elizabethtown," city of Elizabethtown Web site, 5 September 2002, <http://www.etownky.org/etown_history.html>.

Elko County War Memorial, Nevada

This nine-ton granite monument located on the grounds of the Elko County Courthouse in Elko, Nevada, was dedicated on July 4, 1991. The memorial was placed in honor of local soldiers who died in World War II and the Korean and Vietnam wars. At the base of the monument is inscribed "Freedom is Not Free; In Memory of Our Fallen Comrades." District Judge Thomas Stringfield presided at the ceremony and Roy Heath, state VFW commander, gave an address.

Sources: *Elko Daily Free Press*, 30 May 1991 2 and 5 July 1991, as reprinted in "Elko County War Memorial, Web site, 11 September 2002, <http://www.elko-rose.com/warmemorial.html>.

Emancipation, District of Columbia

African-American residents of the District of Columbia celebrated their first Fourth of July as free people on July 4, 1862. The impetus for emancipation was first created when the House of Representatives of Congress presented a resolution on January 18, 1805, stating that "all blacks and people of color, that shall be born within the District of Columbia, or whose mother shall be the property of any person residing within said district, shall be free, the males at the age of___, and the females at the age of___" to become effective on July 4, 1805. The House as a committee of the whole voted and the motion was rejected with a vote of "31 yeas, 77 nays." In subsequent years the abolition question in the District of Columbia was brought up by a number of Congressmen, including Charles Miner (Pa.), January 6–7, 1829, and William Slade (Whig, Vermont), December 23, 1835. Under Abraham Lincoln, the institution of slavery was finally abolished in the District of Columbia on April 16, 1862, making the Fourth of July that year the first time blacks in the city celebrated as fully emancipated slaves on Independence Day. Lincoln's **Emancipation Proclamation** became effective on January 1, 1863. The Thirteenth Amendment to the Constitution, abolishing slavery in the United States, was declared in effect on December 18, 1865.

Source: *Journal of the House of Representatives*, Friday, 18 January 1805, 94 as reproduced in *American Memory: A Century of Lawmaking, 1774–1873*, Web site <http://rsb.loc.gov/ammem/amlaw/lwhj.html>.

Emancipation Proclamation

Proclaimed by President Abraham Lincoln on January 1, 1863, to extend freedom to all slaves in those states under Confederate control. Prior to the issuance of Lincoln's proclamation, Congress had enacted a number of laws to curtail slavery, including that which abolished slavery in the District of Columbia, but on the whole the laws were ineffective. Lincoln announced to his cabinet in July 1862 his plans to free slaves held by Confederates. The end of the Civil War signaled to Americans that the throes of slavery were finally finished in America, and this was later confirmed in the 13th Amendment. On July 4, 1865, there were numerous public readings of the Emancipation Proclamation, mostly throughout the North. In Washington, D.C., the reading that drew the largest crowds was that by Louis A. Bell at the **National Lincoln Monument Association** celebration. Other readings included those by the Hon. J.W. Tyler in Warren, Ohio, on July 4, 1865, with "ten to fifteen thousand persons" as spectators; J.C. Hamilton, son of Alexander Hamilton, at Saratoga Springs, New York; and E. Mercer Shreve in Trenton, New Jersey. On July 4, 1867, a reading took place in Portland, Maine, and another reading was done by D.L. Gluck at a meeting of the Enterprise Literary Association on July 4, 1869, in New York. On the occasion of the nation's Centennial, the proclamation was read by Andrew Curtis at the city park in Columbia, South Carolina.

Sources: *Washington Evening Star*, 5 July 1865, 3; *Daily State Gazette*, 7 July 1865, 3; *New York Times*, 9 July 1865, 3; *Western Reserve Chronicle*, 12 July 1865, 3; *New York Times*, 5 July 1867, 8; "Enterprise Literary Association," *New York Times*, 6 July 1869, 1; "The Glorious Fourth," *Union-Herald*, 3 July 1876, 4.

Emerson, Ralph Waldo (1803–1882)

Esteemed philosopher, essayist, lecturer, and poet who wrote "Concord Hymn," which was sung at the dedication of a battle monument located at Concord's North Bridge on July 4, 1837, and an ode sung in the Concord Town Hall on July 4, 1857. Emerson also presented sermons and orations on the Fourth of July, one with the theme "Where the Spirit of the Lord is, there is liberty" on July 5, 1829, at the Second Church, Boston; one at a meeting of the Temperance Society at Harvard University in 1843; one at an anti-slavery meeting in Dedham, Massachusetts, in 1846; and one in Oxford, Ohio, at the Miami University Literary Society meeting. In 1879, Emerson read the Declaration of Independence at the celebration held in Concord.

Emerson graduated from Harvard in 1821, where he was a class poet, and attended Harvard Divinity School. After serving as a pastor at the Second Church of Boston (1829–31), he resigned. On July 4, 1831, he was in Quincy, Massachusetts, where he heard John Quincy Adams speak.

The "Concord Hymn" was first sung at the completion of the Battle Monument, April 19, 1836. The well known first verse of the four-stanza hymn was later engraved at the base of Daniel Chester French's Minute Man statue.

> By the rude bridge that arched the flood,
> Their flag to April's breeze unfurled;
> Here once the embattled farmers stood,
> And fired the shot heard round the world

With the words "shot heard round the world" inscribed on the monument, a controversy later arose that persists today as to exactly where the first shot was fired, Concord or Lexington Green. Representatives of the Lexington Historical Society claim Lexington heard the first shot although interpreters of the North Bridge Visitor Center in Concord claim that town witnessed the first official battle. The "Concord Hymn" was sung again at the completion of the battle monument on July 4, 1837. On July 4, 1997, Poet Laureate Robert Pinsky read the "Concord Hymn" at a bridge in Concord as a "remembrance of the American past through poetry." About the poem, Pinsky said, "The poem acknowledges a tremendous of time that had already passed then between when Emerson wrote it and when farmers died painful, messy deaths here for the idea of the United States of America. I think it's a good poem, partly because it does acknowledge that long space of time, which is even longer now, between them and us."

On July 4, 1857, another ode by Emerson was sung in the town hall in Concord. E.P. Whipple thought "Emerson's poems read like oracles.... They rank with the loftiest utterances which have ever proceeded from the awakened heart and conscience and intellect of man." The opening couplet of the ode depicts "magnificent imagination, he said:

> O tenderly the haughty Day
> Fills his blue urn with fire,
> One morn is in the mighty heaven,
> And one in our desire.

In this piece, Emerson addresses the double standard he sees regarding freedom being extended to some but a "chain" given to others:

> United States! The ages plead,
> Present and Past in undersong,

Go put your creed into your deed,
Nor speak with double tongue.
For sea and land don't understand,
Nor skies without a frown
See rights for which the one hand fights
By the other cloven down.

Sources: Broadside (Concord, Mass., 1857); E.P. Whipple, "Emerson as a Poet, *North American Review* 135/308 (July 1882): 24; Ralph Waldo Emerson, *Poems* (New York: Hurst, n.d.); Albert J. von Frank, *An Emerson Chronology* (New York: G.K. Hall, 1994); *Letters of Ralph Waldo Emerson* 2: 85n, 125; *Letters of Ellen Tucker Emerson* 2:347, 348–49; Manfred Pütz, "Dissenting Voices of Consent: Margaret Fuller and Ralph Waldo Emerson on the Fourth of July," *The Fourth of July: Political Oratory and Literary Reactions 1776–1876*, 167–84; Stephanie Schorow, "Standing Their Ground Lexington and Concord Still 'Battle' Over Shot Heard 'Round the World," *Boston Herald*, 4 July 1997, Arts and Life section, 35; Jim Lehrer and Robert Pinsky, *Online News Hours: Poet Laureate Robert Pinsky*, transcript, 4 July 1997.

English, Thomas Dunn (1819–1902)

Wrote a poem "The Two Voices" (printed in 8 pages in 1860) that was read at a meeting of Phi Beta Kappa on July 4, 1860, at the College of William and Mary, Williamsburg, Virginia.

Erie Canal

On July 4, 1817, a groundbreaking ceremony occurred near Rome, New York, for the construction of the Erie Canal, referred to then as "The Grand Western Canal."

At sunrise, citizens and those associated with the canal's project gathered at a place near the arsenal and listened to an address by Judge Joshua Hathaway, who said the waterway "will unite [Lake] Erie with the Hudson, the west with the Atlantic which will scatter plenty along its boarders; carry refinement and civilization to the regions of the wilderness." The spade was passed to various officials at the ceremony. Commissioner Samuel Young then spoke:

> By this great highway, unborn millions will easily transport their surplus productions to the shores of the Atlantic, procure their supplies, and hold a useful and profitable intercourse with all the maritime nations of the earth. The expense and labor of this great undertaking bears no proportion to its utility. Nature has kindly afforded every facility; we have all the moral and physical means within our reach and control. Let us then proceed to

the work, animated by the prospect of its speedy accomplishment, and cheered by the anticipated benedictions of a grateful posterity.

Also present at the ceremony was canal commissioner Myron Holley.

The Erie Canal was 363 miles in length and was completed on October 26, 1825. It was considered the first and most successful of a group of canals that connected Eastern Seaboard cities across the western range of settlements along the Appalachian Mountains and on to the Great Lakes. The Erie Canal and others like it were considered a symbol of the development and rise of America as a strong and viable nation. The canal system brought new settlers and commerce into the backwoods of the country and promoted industrialism.

Sources: *Onondaga Register*, 23 July 1817; *Frederick-Town Herald* (Maryland), 26 July 1827, 2; David Hosack, *Memoir of De Witt Clinton* (New York: J. Seymour, 1829), 455, as printed in Noble E. Whitford, *History of the Canal System of the State of New York* (Albany: Brandow, 1906; reprint, Albany: New York State Library, 1984); "Internal Improvements in the State of New York," *Merchant's Magazine and Commercial Review* 23/4 (October 1850): 383–95.

Esmeralda

Chilean tall ship used by Gen. Augusto Pinochet as a torture chamber but which later participated in the **tall ships** parade at the Fourth of July Statue of Liberty Centennial celebration. In 1986 the U.S. House of Representatives voted by resolution (SJ 361) to exclude the ship from appearing in the Fourth of July Statue of Liberty centennial gala in New York harbor. The resolution was introduced by Michael D. Barnes (Dem. — Md.), who said, "scores of naked men and women were subjected to electric shock and mock execution" aboard the ship. Robert L. Lagomarsino (Rep. — Calif.) opposed the resolution and said, "Passing this resolution will do nothing to advance the cause of democracy in Chile." The resolution was rejected with a vote of 194 to 223.

Sources: "Roll Call: The House, Chilean Ship," *Los Angeles Times*, 3 July 1986, Metro section, part 2, 14; *Congressional Record* 132/87, 24 June 1986, 132 Cong Rec. H 4068, 99th Cong. 2nd Session.

European Conference on Troop Reductions

Took place in early July 1974 in Vienna. on July 4 conference members and North Atlantic Treaty Organization (NATO) officials and Communist diplomats drank champagne toasts in honor of the U.S. Independence Day.

Source: *Washington Post*, 5 July 1974, B1.

Everett, Edward (1794–1865)

Secretary of state, senator, governor of Massachusetts, and exemplary orator who gave no less than 81 orations and speeches during a thirty-five-year period. A considerable number of his presentations were Fourth of July orations. Most focused on the spirit of Unionism and others on historical themes. At the height of his career, by contemporary testimony, Everett's speaking abilities were considered on a par with Daniel Webster, who was thought by some to be the most highly skilled speaker in nineteenth century America.

Everett was born in Dorchester, Massachusetts, and graduated from Harvard in 1811. In 1813 he was appointed pastor of the Brattle Street Unitarian Church, and it was there that he developed his penchant for speaking. In 1814 he accepted a position as Eliot Professor of Greek at Harvard, but subsequently spent four years in Europe "pursuing a wide course of study." Everett returned in 1819 and in the following year became editor of the *North American Review*. In 1824 he was elected to Congress as a representative from the Boston area and retained that position for ten years. Two years later, Everett's first major Independence Day address was given on behalf of Phi Beta Kappa at Harvard University. It was a notable event, not only as an exceptional beginning to his career of speech-making, but also regarding the circumstances of the event itself. The speech took place in "the old church in Cambridge," which was "filled to its utmost capacity" that day. The audience included fellow students, some "elder graduates of the college," "graceful and intelligent women" in the galleries and many others. Lafayette, "who had landed in the country only about a week before" was also present, and all expected a presentation "worthy of the

opportunity." Everett spoke about the "circumstances favorable to the progress of literature in America" and he received glowing comments. A reporter for the *Christian Examiner* described the impact he had on his audience:

> The sympathies of his audience went with him in a rushing stream, as he painted in glowing hues the political, social, and literary future of our country. They drank with thirsty ears his rapid generalizations and his sparkling rhetoric. The whole assembly put on one countenance of admiration and assent. As, with skilful and flying hand, the orator ran over the chords of national pride and patriotic feeling, every bosom throbbed in unison to his touch; and when the fervid declamation of the concluding paragraph was terminated by the simple pathos of the personal address to Lafayette, his hearers were left in a state of emotion far too deep for tumultuous applause. Tears stood in old men's eyes, and unconsciously streamed down venerable cheeks, and the faces of the young and lovely, touched by light from heaven, became like the faces of angels.

On July 4, 1828, Everett delivered an oration to the citizens of Charlestown, Massachusetts, on the history of liberty in the world. On July 4, 1829, Everett, "returning from a Western tour," had a close call when the stage coach he was riding in from Frederick, Maryland, on its way to Baltimore, overturned at Poplar Spring. It happened as the stage was approaching the tavern there. "The stage was broken and several of the passengers severely scratched and bruised." On Independence Day in 1833, Everett was in Worcester speaking to an audience on why the Fourth of July should be celebrated and how the "downfall of the British empire in America" was connected to the Seven Years' War.

For the next twenty years Everett enjoyed a distinguished career. From 1835 to 1839 he served as governor of Massachusetts, then held an appointment as minister plenipotentiary at St. James. On July 4, 1835, he spoke in Beverly, Massachusetts, on the background that led up to the Revolutionary War and the life of Washington. In 1839, Everett was invited to attend the mammoth Sunday School Celebration on Staten Island on July 4, but declined, informing officials there he had executive council meetings of the city of Boston that he needed to attend. By 1845 he was back in Massachusetts serving as president of Harvard University. When secretary of state Daniel Webster died in 1852, President Fillmore asked Everett to complete Webster's term. In 1853, Everett was elected senator but left the office after one year due to declining health. On July 4, 1853, he spoke at a dinner held at Faneuil Hall. He expressed his veneration for the Fourth even though the nation's interest in it, he said, "is on the wane." Everett believed Independence Day represented the "union of the two great principles of stability and progress on which our independence was originally founded." He cautioned the new nation, eager for progress, not to move too fast: "Young America is a very honest fellow—he means well, but, like other young folks, he is sometimes a little too much in a hurry."

On July 4, 1855, Everett presented an oration, "Dorchester in 1630, 1776, and 1855," in Dorchester, Massachusetts. Other Fourth of July addresses he gave included two given in Boston in 1858 and 1860 and another in 1861 at the Academy of Music in New York. His 1858 speech was directed to the Young Men's Democratic Club. As his audience cheered, Everett encouraged the citizens of Philadelphia to "guard well Independence Hall, for it is only second to Mount Vernon, and may it stand forever the sanctuary of American patriotism. It is no irreverence to call its walls salvation and its gates praise. May the sun shine soft upon its roof and the winds of Winter knock gently at its door."

By now his speaking skills had earned him glowing critiques such as this one by a contemporary writer: "Mr. Everett is a master in what one may call literary oratory, graceful, lucid, classic, elegant, impressive." Everett was also remembered for speeches given in support of the purchase of the Mount Vernon estate by the Mount Vernon Association and at the dedication of the National Cemetery at Gettysburg on November 19, 1863. A miscellany of his speeches is found in his published 2-volume work, *Orations and Speeches on Various Occasions* (Boston: Little and Brown, 1870). Everett's preface to the book informs its readers that he revised his early speeches for this collection, "pruning" what he considered as "ambitious wordiness" reflected by his youth.

Sources: "Stage Accident," *National Intelligencer*, 8 July 1829, 3; "The Fourth of July," *Salem Gazette*, 7 July 1835, 2; *Poulson's American Daily Advertiser*, 8 July 1839, 3; "Everett's Orations and Speeches," *Christian Examiner and Religious Miscellany* 49/3 (November 1850): 396–417; *New York Herald*, 7 July 1853, 2; "Independence Day in Boston," *New York Times*, 7 July 1858, 3; "Wendell Phillips as an Orator," *Christian Examiner* 75/3 (November 1863: 396; "Edward Everett," *National Cyclopaedia of American Biography* 6:179–80; Wolfgang Hochbruck, "Edward Everett's Union Rhetoric," *The Fourth of July: Political Oratory and Literary Reactions 1776–1876*, 113–20.

Everett, John (1801–1826)

Wrote the ode "Hail to the Day," set to the tune "Wreaths to the Chieftain," that was premiered at a meeting of the Washington Society in Boston on July 4, 1825. In the previous year Everett had given an oration on Independence Day.

Source: *An Oration, Delivered July 5, 1824* (Boston: O. Everett, 1824); *Boston Courier*, 6 July 1825, 2.

Exchange Coffee House, Boston

A favorite site for Fourth of July meetings and dinners beginning on July 4, 1783, when Boston militia officers dined there. On July 4, 1825, Capt. Howe, commander of the Fusileers, and some of his men enjoyed an Independence Day breakfast there. Later that day, the Society of the Cincinnati held their meeting there. On July 4, 1828, Col. Hamilton of the Exchange prepared dinner for 600 persons attending the "friends of Gen. Jackson" celebration in **Faneuil Hall**.

Sources: *Independent Chronicle*, 10 July 1784, as reported in Travers, *Celebrating the Fourth*, 35; *Columbian Centinel*, 6 July 1825, 2; "Independence," *Boston Statesman*, 8 July 1828.

Fairbanks, Charles Warren (1852–1918)

Vice president under Theodore Roosevelt (1905–09), U.S. senator, and public official, who gave hundreds of speeches, some on the Fourth of July. Fairbanks was born in Ohio and attended Ohio Wesleyan University. He was admitted to the bar in 1874, and was an active participant in Republican politics. In 1896 he was a principal speaker at the Republican national convention for the nomination of William McKinley, followed by other important party posts. In 1897, he was elected to the U.S. Senate. His work on behalf of the party secured him the nomination for the vice presidency.

On July 4, 1905, Fairbanks attended the Centennial Celebration of Champaign County, Illinois, held in Urbana on July 4, 1905, and presented a speech in which he said, "Freedom has never come as a free-will offering. It has been purchased by the blood of those who so loved it that they were willing to die, if need be, that others might enjoy it. We have much reason to be grateful, for while there are wars and rumors of wars about the earth, while other peoples are in the throes of unrest and revolution, our people are walking the ways of peace, prepared for war, but praying that it may never again disturb our national tranquility."

On July 4, 1908, Fairbanks was in Anderson, Indiana, at Mounds Park, where he spoke out on behalf of morality in government. He said,

Where government is maintained by delegated authority as here much of politics is heard. We are a nation of politicians. Our differences are in degree and not in kind. We should seek to keep politics upon a high level. A doctrine inculcated or practiced by some, that all is fair in politics, that the end justifies the mean, is low and contemptible. It is a false doctrine and should be utterly rejected. Morality is needed in politics as well as in every other field of activity among us. In fact, the very highest code of morals should be maintained in politics, for it has to do with our liberties, our government. The government should be pure and will be pure only if we have clean politics. There should be clean politics upon the stump and in the press. The orator or the editor who will bear false witness or give currency to wicked slander in the support of a political cause should be impeached before the bar of an honest and indignant public judgment.

After Fairbanks left the vice-presidency, President **William Howard Taft** offered him the role of emissary at the Argentine centennial celebration in Buenos Aires, which he declined. Fairbanks and his wife Cornelia later visited Taft in the White House (December 1910) and on the following July 4, Taft was in Indianapolis visiting Fairbanks and his family.

Sources: "Fairbanks Praises Peace," *New York Times*, 5 July 1905, 2; "Fairbanks the Orator," *Chattanooga Times*, 5 July 1908, 3; Leslie W. Dunlap, *Our Vice-Presidents and Second Ladies* (Metuchen, N.J.: Scarecrow Press, 1988), 182–89.

Fairmount Park, Philadelphia *see* Centennial Exposition, Philadelphia

Fairmount Park Fountain, Philadelphia *see* Catholic Total Abstinence Fountain, Philadelphia

Faneuil Hall, Boston

A historic building popularly referred to as the "Cradle of Liberty," because of the town meetings that took place there prior to the Boston Tea Party in 1773. Built and given to Boston by the wealthy businessman Peter Faneuil (1700–1743) in 1742, Faneuil Hall has been a principal setting for Fourth of July celebrations and ceremonies in Boston. Public dinners were regularly held on the Fourth of July in Faneuil Hall, with one of the earliest if not largest in 1838, when 3,000 persons were present. In 1761 a fire all but destroyed the building, but it was rebuilt in its original design. Orators who presented Fourth of July addresses in Faneuil Hall include Joseph Hardy Prince (1828), Charles Francis Adams (1843), George Sumner (1859), Joseph A. Conry (1902), John A. Sullivan (1904), Robert Luce (1929), Louis J.A. Mercier (1937), John F. Kennedy (1946), James M. Gavin (1963), John Silber (1976), and Thomas M. Menino (1996).

The first female speaker at Faneuil Hall on the Fourth was Edith Nourse Rogers, Republican representative from the Fifth Massachusetts District. On that occasion in 1928, she spoke about the Republican presidential nominee Herbert Hoover and Governor Alfred E. Smith, a Democrat, of New York. Both of these men, Rogers told her audience, by "dint of hard work and with an abundance of courage" worked their way up from nothing to their present high places in government.

Sources: *Boston Evening Transcript*, 4–5 July 1838; "Edith Rogers Praises Smith with Hoover," *New York Times*, 5 July 1928, 4.

Farm Aid II *see* Nelson, Willie

Farragut, David Glasgow (1801–1870)

Naval commander whose victories in the Civil War earned him a promotion and distinction as first rear admiral of the U.S. Navy. He was subsequently given a hero's welcome on the Fourth of July in 1865 at Music Hall in Boston by officials, and thousands of children attended the event. On the 135th anniversary of Farragut's birthday (5 July), the Fourth of July in 1936 was celebrated in tandem with "Farragut Day" at Hastings, New York. The event included services at Grace Episcopal Church, which Farragut "built with personal funds," visiting privileges for the USS *Brooks*, a destroyer anchored in the Hudson River, a parade, and an address by Mayor William Steinschneider.

Sources: "In Boston," *New York Times*, 6 July 1865, 3; "Farragut is Honored by 3,500 at Hastings," *New York Times*, 5 July 1936, 23.

Faugeres, Margaretta V. (1771–1801)

Poet and daughter of poet Ann Eliza Bleecker. Faugeres wrote several poems for the Fourth of July, including "A Salute to the Fourteenth Anniversary of American Independence," in 1791; "The Birth Day of Columbia," read in New York to the members of the Cincinnati, 1793; and "An Ode for the 4th of July, 1798." This latter poem is printed on a broadside and was "Dedicated to the friends of Liberty and Independence." The poem was set to music and performed by the Uranian Musical Society in New York at a meeting of the General Society of Mechanics and Tradesmen, the Democratic Society, the Tammany Society, and the New York Cooper's Society. The work is published on the last two pages of George Clinton's, *An Oration, Delivered on the Fourth of July, 1798* (New York: M.L. and W.A. Davis, 1798).

Faugeres was born in New York City and spent her childhood in Tomhanick, New York. She married Dr. Peter Faugeres but had an unhappy life with him. After his death in 1795, Margaretta became a school teacher in New Brunswick, New Jersey, and later in Brooklyn, New York. As a poet, Mrs. Faugeres was highly regarded in her day. At the time of her death, she was described as having

a mind embellished by nature with superior endowments, and an understanding enriched with the refinements of literature, she exhibited a genius equal in fertility, correctness and energy, to the most distinguished literary characters in modern times. The effusions of her pen have often been the theme of admiration, and from persons capable of discriminating, have attracted well-merited applause.

The poems of 1791 and 1793 are published together with a group of literary works written by her mother. Margaretta Faugeres died in New York City.

A Salute to the Fourteenth Anniversary of American Independence, 1791
All hail to thy return,
O! ever blest auspicious morn,
By mercy's author giv'n:
See! To greet the happy day
Sol expands his brightest ray,
And not a cloud obscures his way,
Nor shades the face of heav'n.
More sweet this day, the cannons martial roar,
Than all the dulcet sounds which music's soul
   can pour;
For ev'ry gale that o'er Columbia flies
Bids on its balmy wings some Paean rise,
Some song of Liberty;
And ev'ry peal that mounts the skies,
In solemn tones of grandeur cries,
"America is Free!"
The Birth Day of Columbia, 1793
Come round Freedom's sacred shrine,
Flow'ry garlands let us twine,
And while we our tribute bring
Grateful paeans let us sing;
Sons of Freedom join the lay,
'Tis Columbia's natal day.

Sources: Margaretta V. Faugeres, *The Posthumous Works of Ann Eliza Bleecker in Prose and Verse to Which is Added, A Collection of Essays, Prose and Poetical* (New York: T. and J. Swords, 1793; reprint, Upper Saddle River, N.J.; Literature House, 1970); George Clinton, *An Oration Delivered on the Fourth of July, 1798* (New York: M.L. and W.A. Davis, 1798); broadside, 1798; *The Lady's Magazine and Musical Repository* (January

1801): 62–63; "Margaretta V. Faugeres," *National Cyclopaedia of American Biography* 9:366; Oscar Wegelin, *Early American Poetry* (the author, 1930; reprint: Gloucester, Mass.: Peter Smith, 1965), 32.

Federal Bridge Celebration, Washington, D.C.

One of the earliest recorded celebrations in Washington, D.C., occurred on July 4, 1792, when the Commissioners of the Federal Buildings laid the first cornerstone in Washington for a structure they called the Federal Bridge that was to span Rock Creek and to connect the capital with Georgetown. William H. Kerr presented the oration there, the first recorded Independence Day speech in Washington City.

Sources: *Georgetown Weekly Ledger*, 7 July 1792, 1; Dunlap's *American Daily Advertiser*, 21 July 1792, 14.

Federal, state, and local legislation establishing the holiday

The United States holidays are not mandated for the states by the federal government. The United States Congress or president can only legally establish an "official" holiday for the District of Columbia and federal employees. Outside of those jurisdictions, public holidays are established at the local level through enactment of a law issued by a state legislature or by an executive proclamation from a state governor. A city, town, or local municipality may also enact an ordinance regarding the celebration of the Fourth of July. As stated in the *World Almanac* (1998), however, "in practice, most states observe the federal legal public holiday."

The first official state celebration of the Fourth of July as recognized under resolve of a legislature occurred in Massachusetts in 1781. Boston was the first municipality to officially designate Independence Day as a holiday in 1783. Alexander Martin of North Carolina was the first governor to issue an executive order in 1783 for designating 4 July as Independence Day. The federal government's role in encouraging the celebration of the Fourth of July was minimal. In the private sector, suspension of work on the national anniversary was left up to individual businesses. Banks often closed on the holiday, which encouraged other businesses to close as well. However, shops that could profit by opening on Independence Day did so. These included coffee houses, restaurants, and food stands. There was typically a brisk business for fireworks, flags, ice cream, and confectionaries.

The act of Congress establishing the Fourth of July as a holiday, but without pay, for federal employees and the District of Columbia occurred in 1870. Senator Hannibal Hamlin introduced a Senate Bill (referred HR no. 2224), issued through the Committee on the District of Columbia, Forty-first Congress, Session II, on 24 June 1870, and titled "Legal Holidays in the District." Hamlin presented his rationale for the bill: "There are no legal holidays here, and this bill merely provides for what I think are the legal holidays in every state of the Union." Apparently there was no opposition to the bill which "was reported to the Senate without amendment; ordered to a third reading, read the third time, and passed." It was reported in the *Congressional Globe*, Friday, June 28, 1870, and was printed as Chapter 167:

> Be it enacted by the Senate and House of representatives of the United States of America in Congress assembled, that the following days, to wit: the first day of January, commonly called New Year's day, the fourth day of July, the twenty-fifth day of December, commonly called Christmas day, and any day appointed or recommended by the President of the United States as a day of public fast or thanksgiving, shall be holidays within the District of Columbia, and shall, for all purposes of presenting for payment or acceptance for the maturity and protest, and giving notice of the dishonor of bills of exchange, bank checks and promissory notes or other negotiable or commercial paper, be treated and considered as is the first day of the week, commonly called Sunday, and all notes, drafts, checks, or other commercial or negotiable paper falling due or maturing on either of said holidays shall be deemed as having matured on the day previous. Approved, June 28, 1870.

On June 29, 1938, by joint resolution of Congress (HJ resolution No. 551; pub. res. no. 127), the Fourth of July was legislated as a federal holiday with pay for its employees:

> Resolved by the Senate and House of representatives of the United States of America in Congress

assembled, that hereafter whenever regular employees of the Federal Government whose compensation is fixed at a rate per day, per hour, or on a piece-work basis are relieved or prevented from working solely because of the occurrence of a holiday such as New Year's Day, Washington's Birthday, Memorial Day, Fourth of July, Labor Day, Thanksgiving Day, Christmas Day, or any other day declared a holiday by Federal statute or Executive order, or any day on which the departments and establishments of the Government are closed by Executive order, they shall receive the same pay for such days as for other days on which an ordinary day's work is performed.

Section 2. The joint resolution of January 6, 1885 (U.S.C., title 5, sec. 86), and all other laws inconsistent or in conflict with the provision of this Act are hereby repealed to the extent of such inconsistency or conflict. Approved, June 29, 1938.

On January 14, 1941, it was brought to the attention of Congress by Robert Ramspeck, chairman, Committee on the Civil Service of the House of Representatives (see 77th Congress, House of Representatives Report No. 532), that the 1938 federal holiday law failed to specify that employees of the government of the District of Columbia also have the Fourth of July designated as a holiday with pay. Harry B. Mitchell, president of the United States Civil Service Commission responded back on April 7 that his office, as well as the Bureau of the Budget, had no objection to amending the 1938 law to include District of Columbia employees. On May 13, 1941, a "Holiday Leave for Per Diem Employees of the District of Columbia" amendment was enacted with the following change made to the 1938 law:

In compliance with paragraph 2a of the Rule XIII, of the Rules of the House of Representatives, changes in existing law are shown as follows (present law is in roman and new matter is in italics):

(Act of June 29, 1938, 52 Stat. 1246) That hereafter whenever regular employees of the Federal Government *or of the district of Columbia* whose compensation is fixed at a rate per day, per hour, or on a piece-work basis are relieved or prevented from working solely because of the occurrence of a holiday, such as New Year's Day, Washington's Birthday,

Memorial Day, Fourth of July, Labor Day, Armistice Day, Thanksgiving Day, Christmas Day, or any other day declared a holiday by Federal statute or Executive order, or any day on which the departments and establishments of the Government or of the District of Columbia are closed by Executive order, they shall receive the same pay for such days as for other days on which an ordinary day's work is performed.

On September 22, 1959, an act was passed by Congress (H.R. 5752, Public Law 86–362) that if the Fourth of July or any other established holiday occurs on a Saturday, "the day immediately preceding such Saturday shall be held and considered to be a legal public holiday, in lieu of such day which so occurs on such Saturday, (A) for such officers and employees whose basic workweek is Monday through Friday, and (B) for the purposes of section 205 (d) of the Annual and Sick Leave Act of 1951 (65 Stat. 681), as amended (5 U.S.C. 2064 (d))." The act also provided for a day of release for employees "whose basic workweek is other than Monday through Friday."

Occasionally, members of Congress have also either introduced bills or facilitated the passing of legislation which designated certain Fourth of July holidays with patriotic themes. In 1991, a joint resolution (H.J. Res. 278, 102nd Congress, 1st Session) was introduced June 21 by five congressmen that year as "July 4th Family Celebration Day," a bill which advocated for the importance of the family unit. On February 27, 1992, a bill (SJR 262, 102nd Congress, 2nd session) was introduced by Senator Robert W. Kasten (R.-Wisc.) that would have designated July 4, 1992, as "Buy American Day."

On February 3, 1998, Congress approved legislation (*Congressional Record*, 3 February 1998, and Public Law 105–225) that designated the 21 days between Flag Day through Independence Day as "Honor America Days." Congress declared "that there be public gatherings and activities during that period at which the people of the United States can celebrate and honor their country in an appropriate way."

See also **Fifth of July**.

Fifth of July

Throughout its history, Independence Day has been celebrated on July 5 when July 4 fell on a Sunday. Sunday events typically included religious sermons tailored especially for Independence Day themes, followed on the day after by civic celebrations. African-Americans commonly celebrated Independence Day on July 5 so as not to risk possible harassment and conflict with celebrations by whites on July 4. The ceremonies commemorated the movement for emancipation and political empowerment and served as a protest for exclusion from white celebrations. According to Matthew Dennis, "Some black leaders chose July 5 — proximate enough to Independence Day to align it with the principles of the Declaration of Independence and to draw attention to their boycott of a day steeped in hypocrisy." Sometimes referred to as "African American Freedom Day," the day was used by blacks to express their rights to use public space. Festival parades and orations were common. The New York State Abolition Day on July 5, 1827, helped to encourage other groups of African-Americans to celebrate on the day after the Fourth of July. The most celebrated oration presented on the fifth of July was that given by **Frederick Douglass** in Rochester, New York, in 1852. Titled "What to the Slave is the Fourth of July," the work brought attention to the inconsistencies and hypocrisy of freedom and equality in the nation. With the end of the Civil War and emancipation for all African-Americans, celebrations by blacks on the fifth of July declined dramatically.

Throughout the history of Independence Day, when the Fourth fell on a Sunday, some towns chose to celebrate the Fourth on July 3. For example, in 1897, the towns of Brunswick and Oakland, Maryland, celebrated on Saturday, July 3.

Sources: *Baltimore Morning Herald*, 4 July 1897; Matthew Dennis, Red, White, and Blue Letter Days: An American Calendar (Ithaca: Cornell University Press, 2002), 26; Mitch Kachun, *Festivals of Freedom: Memory and Meaning in African American Emancipation Celebrations, 1808–1915* (Amherst: University of Massachusetts Press, 2003).

Fillmore, Millard (1800–1874)

Thirteenth president of the U.S. (1850–53). Fillmore had served as vice president under Zachary Taylor and succeeded him to the presidency upon Taylor's death in July 1850. Fillmore signed the Clay Compromise of 1850 and endorsed the Fugitive Slave Act, which ultimately cost him much popularity in the North. He was president only until March 1853 and therefore enjoyed only two Fourth of July celebrations in that position. His most important contribution to the heritage of the Fourth occurred in 1851 when he presided over the cornerstone ceremony at the Capitol for the House and Senate wings. On that day he also gave a brief address welcoming the Sons of Temperance of D.C., Virginia, and Maryland, and Pennsylvania. That event took place at Monument Place (now Lafayette Square).

Sources: *National Intelligencer*, 4 and 7 July 1851, 3 and 2, respectively.

Fireworks

Fireworks are an important feature of the Fourth and satisfy the urge for individuals to experience the visual and aural elements as they celebrate this annual national ritual. Fireworks on Independence Day were first used to commemorate the celebration at Philadelphia in 1777, a year after the signing of the Declaration of Independence. "At night there was a grand exhibition of fireworks, which began and concluded with thirteen rockets on the commons." During the 18th century the use of fireworks in celebrations were confined to mostly major cities where they could be easily obtained and sold.

The first fireworks in Boston took place on July 4, 1777, followed by another display in 1779 when thirteen rockets were fired. In Philadelphia in 1783, for the Fourth, Jean Leaguay, a local merchant, advertised "a large and curious assortment of fireworks" for sale to the public. On July 4, 1799, New York citizens witnessed "the grandest fireworks ever exhibited in America" in that city.

During the nineteenth century, access to fireworks increased and the use of committees to carefully plan out town celebrations became

Fireworks at New York on the evening of the Fourth of July, as seen from Brooklyn Heights. *Harper's Weekly*, 16 July 1859. Image courtesy of HarpWeek, LLC.

common. Fireworks quickly became an important means for providing spectacular, colorful, albeit noisy, memorable endings to a day full of celebratory events. Merchants stocked their shelves and set out store-front tables with large assortments of explosives that commonly attracted long lines of customers eager to purchase everything from handfuls of small firecrackers for a penny or two to more vivid, but expensive explosives. To usher in the Fourth the sound of fireworks and the discharging of revolvers and toy cannons in the streets typically began on the evening of July 3 and in the larger cities the noise continued throughout the night and the next day.

By the 1860s the sale and distribution of fireworks had become a major business. In 1866, it was reported that two Washington, D.C., firms sold about $250,000 worth of fireworks each. In 1867, one firm "received orders for 2,000 boxes of firecrackers, 84,000 torpedoes, and 190,000 one-ball roman candles."

Along with the increased popularity of

fireworks, each year hundreds of deaths and injuries resulted from the lack of crowd control at staged exhibits, a lack of regulation in the sale of dangerous fireworks to individuals, and the use of firearms. The deaths and injuries did not go unnoticed, however. Typically following the Fourth, newspapers published long lists of casualties with descriptive comments on how the deaths and injuries occurred. For example, on July 4, 1854, in New York, "John Muller, a German, aged 19, had his left hand badly lacerated by a pistol. Dr. Derby amputated the third finger." This practice of reporting continued throughout the nineteenth century until the beginning of the **Safe and Sane Celebrations** movement in the early twentieth century.

The practice of exploding dynamite on the Fourth was an unusual tradition and mostly confined to the West during the nineteenth century. This explosive was easily accessible due to supply depots in the many mining camps. For the Fourth in 1901, J.R. Robinson, mayor of Colorado Springs, Colorado, issued a proclamation prohibiting "the explosion of all dynamite within the City limits." In Utah dynamite was used to celebrate Independence as recently as 1951, when it was reported that sticks of the explosive were still being tossed on local streets in celebration of the day. See also **Pyrotechnics and fireworks accidents** and **Pyrotechnic displays.**

Sources: *Virginia Gazette*, 18 July 1777; Boston Gazette, 7 July 1777 and 12 July 1779, the latter reported in Appelbaum, *The Glorious Fourth*, 20; *Pennsylvania Gazette*, 28 May 1783; *Daily Advertiser*, 4 July 1799, 3; "Accidents and Incidents," *New York Times*, 5 July 1854, 1; *New York Evening Post*, 3 July 1862, 2; "Facts about Fireworks," *Washington Evening Star*, 6 July 1867, 4; *Colorado Springs Gazette*, 4 July 1901, 3; *New York Times*, 5 July 1951, 8.

Fireworks by Grucci

One of the premier fireworks firms in the United States. Grucci was the "first American family to win the Gold Medal in the prestigious Monte Carlo International Fireworks Competition" in 1979. The Grucci's first major display was with the New York performance on the nation's Bicentennial. Fireworks by Grucci, located in Brookhaven, New York, traces its roots back to the Italian seaport of Bari. In 1850 there Angelo Lanzetta began making fireworks, and in 1870 he came to America. On his death in 1899, his son took over the business, which was moved to Miami during the Depression but returned to Bellport in 1929. Grucci shows have included presidential inaugurations, the Lake Placid Winter Olympics, and the World's Fair in Knoxville. The Fourth of July is their busiest time of the year with upwards of 70 displays, including the Macy's Fireworks annual show. In 1986 they provided fireworks for the centennial celebration of the Statue of Liberty and in 2001 produced their seventeenth consecutive show in Omaha, Nebraska, for World-Herald Fireworks Night, which "ranks among the largest the family produces."

Sources: Arnold Ceballos, "The Season of Light: Gruccis Brighten Holiday Weekend," *Newsday*, 3 July 1995, 7; David Hendee, "Baseball and 'World-Class' Fireworks Show's Producer Is Artist, Scientist, Politician," *Omaha World-Herald*, 4 July 2001, 13.

Fireworks catastrophes *see* Pyrotechnics and fireworks accidents

Fireworks, regulations, 19th century

Some of the earliest regulations of the use of fireworks date to 1731 when a Rhode Island law prohibited the unnecessary firing of guns and fireworks. A Pennsylvania law enacted in 1751 was similar. But when the colonies gained their independence, the use of fireworks quickly became a traditional component of celebrations and any laws that existed were mostly ignored. Early celebrations in Philadelphia (1777) and Boston (1779) featured fireworks in the form of rockets that were sent aloft. **John Adams** was aware of the significance of celebrating the Fourth of July with "illuminations" and a letter he wrote in which he mentioned that and which was reprinted numerous times in nineteenth century newspapers probably helped encourage their use. By the early 1800s merchants began dealing in fireworks and citizens had access to whatever was available for sale. Notwithstanding the physical danger in using fireworks, much of the legislation enacted had to do more with the excessive noise and the danger of setting buildings on fire than the risk to human life and limb. From the 1830s on the setting off of fireworks within city limits or close to residences was outlawed in many places. However, the laws were commonly overlooked by citizens and authorities alike.

In 1832 the editor of *Niles' Weekly Register* called for citizens to obey the laws:

> The Laws of most corporations concerning these "crackers" are grossly violated in many places — and the serious fires that have recently happened by them, we hope, will cause it to be made a criminal offence ... in any one who shall violate the laws concerning the sale of them. Children may be let-off with good scourgings; but adults, who sell them, should be taught the "art and mystery" of sawing stone, in state prisons.

Some ordinances prohibited fireworks in only specific places in town. For example, in New York in 1867, the use of fireworks by individuals was outlawed in Central Park and a local newspaper reported that the law was "strictly enforced." By 1886, the ordinance was city-wide and specified that "no person shall fire, discharge, or set off in the city of New-

York any rocket, cracker, torpedo, squib, balloon, or other firework or thing containing any substance in a state of combustion, under the penalty of $5 for each offense." Yet a reporter wrote on the Fourth of July that year that the noise from fireworks had gone on for thirty-six hours and would last for three days because the Fourth of July happened to be on a Sunday and more celebrations were scheduled for Monday. "Every adult who is able to do so flees from the city to escape them," he reported.

By 1865 Washington laws were in effect prohibiting the discharge of firearms and firecrackers, particularly after 10 P.M. Again, the laws were largely ignored. In 1869, it was reported as far away as Cincinnati that the juveniles in Washington had shot off firecrackers "in contempt of the Mayor's [Sayles J. Bowen's] proclamation" that had totally banned the firing of guns, use of gunpowder and firecrackers that year. In anticipation of the Fourth of July in 1871, the Washington law was also directed to those who sold fireworks:

> Unlawful to sell to children under the age of 17 years, firearms, gunpowder, gun caps, or other explosive substances. $5 for each offense. Unlawful to set off fireworks in any street or avenue within one hundred yards of any dwelling house.

In anticipation of the nation's centennial in 1876, Columbia, South Carolina, Mayor John Agnew issued a proclamation on July 3 prohibiting the use of "fire arms, fire crackers, sky rockets, or other explosives, or noisy substance" on Richardson Street from Elmwood Avenue to Gervais Street and the distance of "one square east and west of Richardson." This was probably the route of the parade. In Hoboken, New Jersey, Mayor August Grassman issued a proclamation for the Fourth in 1890 "prohibiting the firing of pistols, guns, and cannon within the city limits."

Ten years after the enactment of New York's ordinance, enforcement for Independence Day on 1895 was still a problem. Following the celebration, an editor of the *New York Times* wrote that the police commissioners failed to enforce the municipal ordinance prohibiting the setting off of fireworks. As a

result many persons had left town to escape the noise. "There is no more patriotism than there is sense in allowing the city to be made a pandemonium every year by a celebration which is simply barbarous, nor any excuse for converting a National holiday into a municipal nuisance," the article said.

Sources: Boston Gazette, 12 July 1779; *Niles' Weekly Register* 42/21 (21 July 1832): 373; *Cincinnati Evening Chronicle*, 6 July 1869, 1; *New York Times*, "The Central Park," 5 July 1867, 1, 5 July 1886, 4, and 6 July 1895, 4; *Washington Evening Star*, 1 July 1871; *Union-Herald* (Columbia, S.C.), 3 July 1876, 4; "City and Suburban News," *New York Times*, 3 July 1890, 2.

Fireworks, types of

Throughout the nineteenth century the public's appetite for new and more exciting fireworks continued to increase. As the Fourth of July approached, merchants made sure to stockpile all of the consumer's favorite explosives and advertised what was new that year. From the 1880s to the introduction of the Safe and Sane movement in 1903 the use and popularity of fireworks had reached unprecedented heights. A reporter writing in 1898 noted "the American Fourth of July is the greatest event the maker of firecrackers knows" and that among all countries in the world this country "spends the most upon fireworks." The new pieces introduced each year had colorful names and the public was willing to pay liberally for them. One of the favorite miniature explosives popular in Baltimore in 1880 was a little torpedo that was nicknamed "hit me hard." A local newspaper reported that "it consists of a weight, with a string attached, into which a paper cap is inserted. The weight is then dropped upon the pavement, and a considerable explosion occurs." In 1897 in Baltimore other fireworks available for purchase included "Devil among tailors," an explosive that was thrown up into the air and upon exploding threw out "a number of life-like figures, one larger than the others, supposed to represent the ruler of the infernal regions. The effect produced by this is said to be startling." Another was a large rocket that weighed eight pounds and could "ascend as high as, or higher than, the Washington Monument. A stream of sparks like the tail of a comet is thrown out behind, and when an explosion takes place balloons and golden chains are revealed." A new firework introduced in 1897, which was called a "buzz saw," was "formed of two wheels, which when the attached fuse is lighted revolve in opposite directions, the sparks resembling the jagged edges of two saws in rapid motion." Its cost was 10 cents. "Japanese day fireworks" were also available. They were described as shells that when thrown in the air, ignited and "threw off American flags, balloons and other objects." Their cost ranged from 50 to 75 cents apiece. Yet other fireworks had colorful titles: "silver maple trees," "Brazilian jugglers," and "aerolites," the latter expensive but producing "handsome fire effects."

In 1898 a "National Rocket" was introduced. It flew 1,200 feet into the air and provided a colorful meteoric shower of red, white and blue. Entirely new also was a small firecracker named "Howitzer," that was attached on a string in numbers from 1,000 to 10,000, and was intended to replicate the sounds of a "red-hot naval engagement." Water fireworks were also popular that year and were "intended to make a display on the surface of the water. The varieties are known as imps, dolphins, witches, devils, snakes, volcanoes, fountains and batteries." A "Spanish Jugglery" poured out a geyser of fire and ends with "an explosion that sends a number of flying pigeons into the air 200 feet."

Sources: *Baltimore Morning Herald*, 5 July 1880, 4, 4 July 1897, 12, and 3 July 1898, 28.

First Presbyterian Church, Atlanta, Georgia

Dedicated on July 4, 1852. John Stainback Wilson presented a discourse there for the occasion. Wilson was a surgeon at Jackson Hospital in Richmond at the time of the Civil War. He had operated on Isaac Sykes, "a musician in Stuart's Cavalry," on July 4, 1863. Sykes was wounded at Gettysburg on July 3, 1863.

Sources: *The Gospel the Charter of Liberty, a Discourse* (Atlanta: Ware's Book and Job Office, 1852); *Confederate States Medical and Surgical Journal* 1/4 (April 1964): 56.

First Presbyterian Church, Rockford, Illinois

Was dedicated on July 4, 1875. James Cruickshanks (b. 1828), pastor of the church, delivered a historical discourse for the occasion.

Source: *A Historical Discourse Delivered at the Dedication of the First Presbyterian Church of Rockford, Illinois, July 4, 1875* (Rockford: Register Company Printers, 1876).

Flag of Truce Boats

Sailed on the Fourth of July during the Civil War carrying non-combatants to safe harbors. On July 3, 1863, for example, under a flag of truce, a vessel left Philadelphia with 12–14 Secessionist women whose destination was the South. At a stopover at Annapolis, Maryland, the women were housed in the Naval School Hospital and were seen walking about the town with Union officers and soldiers, as well as assistant hospital surgeons. On July 4, the boat left with the women aboard amidst the sounds of cannon being fired for the Fourth of July from the "gun-boat" in the Severn River and from the College Green Barracks.

Another flag of truce boat, "boldly flaunting the rebel rag and cruising about the roads without molestation," was carrying "chiefly women" and was sighted in the vicinity of Fortress Monroe, Virginia, on July 3, 1861, on its way from Norfolk.

Sources: *The Press* (Philadelphia); 5 July 1861, 2; *Philadelphia Inquirer*, 7 July 1863, 2.

Flags and Banners

The flying of flags has traditionally been an important patriotic gesture by Americans on the Fourth. At the time independence was declared there was no national standard that all Americans could wave. On June 14, 1777, Congress enacted a law creating a design for a flag that would have stars, one for each state, and thirteen stripes, but the exact placement of the stars on the flag was left up to the flag maker. As a result not all American flags flown on the Fourth had identical designs. Many were quite fanciful. For example, in Williamsport, Maryland, on July 4, 1810, a U.S. flag "ornamented with appropriated devices, having this inscription: July 4, 1776" was raised in the public square. A flag raised over Fort Greene in Brooklyn, New York, on July 4, 1858, was 20 by 30 feet in size and had 33 stars on it arranged to form the letters "F.G." (Fort Greene). Moreover, as new states entered the Union, updated flags would normally have been flown on the Fourth if new flags were available but that was not always the case.

Through further legislation by Congress in 1794 and 1818, the design of the Star-Spangled Banner progressed. Information published in a popular publication, *The Port-Folio* provides facts about the 1818 legislation:

> By an act of Congress [in 1818] it has been provided, that, from and after the 4th day of July next, the flag of the United States shall be thirteen horizontal stripes, alternate red and white; and that the Union shall be 20 stars, white in a blue field. The same act also provides, that, on the admission of every new state into the Union, one star shall be added to the Union of the flag; which addition is to take effect on the 4th day of July then next preceding such addition. By this regulation the thirteen stripes will represent the number of states whose velour and resources originally effected American independence; and the additional stars (the idea of which has been borrowed from the science of astronomy) will mark the increase of the States since the adoption of the present constitution. This is the second alteration which has taken place in the flag of the United States, and we trust it will be the last.

The flag of the United States was first designated by Congress, in a resolution which was passed on the 14th of June, 1777. According to that resolution the stripes were the same as prescribed by the act of the 4th instant; and the Union was thirteen stars, white in a blue field, representing a new constellation. By act of the 13th of January, 1794, the stripes and stars were both to be fifteen in number — to take effect from the first of May, 1795. This addition of two stars and two stripes to the flag was owing to the admission of the states of Vermont and Kentucky into the Union — the former on the 4th of March, 1791 — the latter on the 1st of June, 1792. An act of April 4, 1818, established the standard of 13 stripes and one star for each state.

American flags were often flown alongside other national flags. For example, in Faneuil Hall in Boston in 1796, flags from France and Holland were flown adjacent to the American flag. During the Civil War the Confederate flag was the newest flag to achieve some prominence, and it continued to be raised in years after the war. As late as July 4, 1876, a number of them were still flown in Baltimore and other cities in the South. In 1912 President Taft issued an order that mandated a specific arrangement of the stars on the flag. One of the largest flags flown was 165 feet long and 60 feet wide and was hung from a steel wire "stretched from the Times Building to the Heidelberg Building," at Times Square in New York in 1915. On July 4, 1933, an American flag made by thirty-two mothers who referred to each other as "the Gold Star Mothers of the Melting Pot," each mother representing a different country, was displayed at Seward Park in New York and was to be presented to President Roosevelt. The most flags ever flown from a single location has occurred in Washington, D.C., when multiple flags were flown from the Capitol for sales and gifts. For example, on July 4, 1976, 10,471 flags were raised and lowered. Flying flags from the Capitol for commercial sales became an annual tradition.

Through the years other flags depicting some symbolic idea or principle were introduced. Flags representing the working classes, political factions, and houses of worship were common. In New York at the Washington Hall cornerstone celebration of the Washington Benevolent Society on July 4, 1809, a "banner of independence" was displayed and "flanked by two smaller banners with the dates of the capture of the Hessians and Burgoyne." Also in New York at a parade on July 4, 1814, two flags were displayed in tandem: one was a "banner of independence" having the date the Constitution was adopted, the other, a flag bearing the date the British evacuated the city. On July 4, 1894, a white-bordered flag denoting "universal liberty and peace" was unfurled from a liberty pole in Highlands, New Jersey.

See *Washington Evening Star*, 7 July 1856, 3 for a banner description.

Sources: *Boston Gazette*, 11 July 1796, 2; *Alexander Gazette*, 12 July 1809, 2–3; "Fourth of July," *Hagerstown Gazette*, 10 July 1810, 3; *New York Evening Post*, 2 July 1814, 2–3; *The Port-Folio* 6/1 (July 1818): 18; *New York Times*, 6 July 1859, 8; *Baltimore Bee*, 5 July 1876, 2; *New York Times*, 5 July 1894, 8; "City Waves Flag and Cheers Wilson," *New York Times*, 6 July 1915, 18; "Liberty Bell Copy Hailed on East Side; Centre of Celebration of Fourth — Flag Made by Thirty-Two Mothers is Unfurled," *New York Times*, 5 July 1933, 4.

La Flore

This French man-of-war vessel, decorated with flags and bunting, held a public reception in New York harbor on July 4, 1885. "Hundreds of persons went off to see her. A band furnished music on the upper deck while the visitors were being shown over the vessel. The main deck was finally cleared, and the sailors and many of their visitors indulged in dancing."

Source: "Like the Usual Holiday," *New York Times*, 5 July 1885, 5.

Fluegel, Herman

Composed "Another 4th of July. The Wedding-Day is Coming. Song and March" (Evansville, Ind.: Herman Fluegel, 1861), for piano, guitar, and voice. First line: "Oh my Dear your eyes look red was it weeping made them red?" The dedication reads: "This song and march is most respectfully dedicated to all true Union patriots." An 1864 edition (published by Fluegel) of "The Wedding Day is Coming" has the first line: "A welcome home to thee my boy, thy home of early youth."

Ford, Gerald R. (b. 1913)

Thirty-eighth president of the U.S. (1974–77), who presided over the nation's Bicentennial celebrations at Valley Forge, Philadelphia, and New York. Ford had spent 25 years in Congress before assuming the office of the presidency on August 9, 1974, upon the resignation of President Nixon. As vice president he attended an Independence Day event in 1975 at Fort McHenry in Baltimore, where he participated in ceremonies, and then traveled to Camp David for the remainder of the weekend. His speech at Fort McHenry focused on the importance of individual freedom. "The mass approach of the modern world places a premium on creativity and individuality," he said. "Individualism is a safeguard against the sameness of society." Ford also recalled the significance of Francis Scott Key's words as the British bombarded the fort in 1814: "The patriotism and national pride surrounding our flag, our country and their defense that night are our heritage in song and verse. The star spangled banner is an expression of love of country."

On July 3, 1976, Ford announced the start of the Bicentennial celebration through a proclamation to the nation. "In the two centuries that have passed, we have matured as a nation and as a people," he said. "We have gained the wisdom that age and experience bring, yet we have kept the strength and idealism of youth." Ford asked persons of all faiths to engage in prayer and to "give thanks for the protection of divine Providence through 200 years." He also noted the concurrent resolution of Congress adopted on June 26, 1963 (77 Stat. 944), calling for the ringing of bells throughout the nation, and he proclaimed the ringing of bells on July 4, 1976, to occur at two o'clock, Eastern Daylight Time, for two minutes "signifying our two centuries of independence." On July 4, 1976, Ford spoke in Philadelphia to a large crowd and expressed how the events of July 4, 1776, were "the beginning of a continuing adventure." He added, "The world is ever conscious of what Americans are doing, for better or for worse." See also, **Fort McHenry National Monument and Historic Shrine, Baltimore,** and **Valley Forge, Pennsylvania.**

Sources: "Individual's Role is Hailed by Ford," *New York Times*, 5 July 1975, 19; "President's Proclamation," and "President Talks," *New York Times*, 4 and 5 July 1976, 25 and 1, respectively.

Ford's Theater *see* Oldest Inhabitants Association of Washington

Forest fires

The first forest fire reported to have been started by fireworks on the Fourth of July occurred in 1913 on French Mountain near Lake George, New York. "The blaze was watched by thousands of July Fourth visitors who lounged along the shore of the lake for a mile out."

Risk of forest fires in extremely dry areas of the nation frequently resulted in the canceling of Fourth of July fireworks celebrations. In Wisconsin in 1988, numerous communities canceled fireworks due to the risk of fire, while in central California, a brush fire covering more than 2,200 acres near Yosemite National Park was fought by local firefighters. The fire was believed to be started by the use of illegal fireworks.

On July 4, 1998, many towns across Florida, as well as Disney World, canceled their fireworks due to that state's worst fire risk in over fifty years. Arizona experienced the largest wildfire in that state's history. In the communities of Linden, and Heber-Overgaard, as more than 400 homes were lost to fire, firefighters were cheered on the Fourth of July by hundreds of residents for their efforts in saving thousands more. In 2002 Colorado and other areas of the West had fire bans in effect due to unusually dry conditions.

Sources: *Washington Post*, 5 July 1998, A4; "Forest Fire by Fireworks," *New York Times*, 5 July 1913, 1; "Headline Coast to Coast, Holiday Mood" (Associated Press), *St. Louis Post Dispatch*, 5 July 1988; Alisa Blackwood, *Associated Press State and Local Wire*, 5 July 2002.

Fort Davis National Historic Site

Located in Jeff Davis County, Texas, this historic site was authorized by Congress in 1961 and became part of the national park system on July 4, 1963. There are twenty original stone and adobe buildings that date to 1880 on the 460-acre site, as well as a visitors' center with museum, lieutenant's quarters, and post hospital. Tours are available by costumed interpreters.

Sources: Robert M. Utley, *Fort Davis National Historic Site* (Washington: National Park Service, 1965); *Handbook of Texas Online*: Fort Davis National Historic Site, 5 February 2002.

Fort McHenry National Monument and Historic Shrine, Baltimore

Well-known fort that was bombarded by the British during the War of 1812, inspiring **Francis Scott Key** to write the words for "**The Star Spangled Banner.**" The British fleet's attempt to force capitulation of the fort on September 13–14, 1814, was unsuccessful. Throughout the nineteenth century, artillery salutes in commemoration of Independence Day were a common occurrence at the fort. In 1876 a salute of 13 guns signaled the beginning of the ceremony at Druid Hill Park in Baltimore, and in 1900, the annual "Salute to the Union" consisted of 45 guns. In 1975, a reenactment of the shelling of the fort in 1814 took place and 40 ships participated. President **Gerald R. Ford** gave a speech before an audience of 7000. "Let us resolve that this should be an era of hope rather than despair," he said. "Let us resolve that it shall be a time of promise rather than regret." He also viewed the raising of a replica of the flag that flew over the fort on the night it was bombarded by the British. Ford also presided over ceremonies for 41 immigrants who became American citizens by reciting their naturalization oaths. On July 4, 1959, it was at Fort McHenry that the first official raising of the 49-star flag honoring Alaska's admission to the union as a state occurred. Fred A. Seaton, secretary of the interior, and the chief administration architect for the admission of Alaska, raised the nation's icon "on a new staff, hand-hewn from Douglas fir, in duplication of the flagpole that withstood the bombardment of the British fleet." Recent Fourth celebrations have included reenactments by the Fort McHenry Guard, artillery firings, period games, bonfire lightings and readings of the Declaration of Independence.

Sources: "Municipal Celebration at Druid Hill Park," *Baltimore Bee*, 5 July 1876, 5; *Baltimore Morning Herald*, 5 July 1900, 7; "Eisenhower Cites Freedom's Story," *New York Times*, 4 July 1959, 1; "Individual's Role is Hailed by Ford," *New York Times*, 5 July 1975, 19; Bill Richards, "Area Celebrates July 4," *Washington Post*, 5 July 1975, C1–C2.

Fort Moore Memorial, Los Angeles

Also known as Fort Hill, a ceremonial flag-raising occurred there on July 4, 1847, near the Los Angeles pueblo, after a group of Mormons built a "400-foot-wide earthen-walled fort in three months." The American flag raised had 28 stars, and about 700 spectators were present. In 1897 a ceremony to

Fort Moore Memorial commemorates the site of the first Independence Day celebration in Los Angeles on July 4, 1847. Photograph courtesy of Juan Bastos.

"recall the old-time celebration" took place; it included "reminiscences of California by old-time Californians, the story of the building of the old fort on Fort Hill" and "patriotic music, and the singing of old Spanish songs." On July 4, 1997, a reenactment of the original ceremony took place with 2,500 persons in attendance. Some 100 soldiers in costume fired a 28-musket and artillery salute. The fort was named after Capt. Benjamin Moore, who was killed at the battle of San Pasqual.

Sources: "After Fifty Years: Anniversary of the First California Fourth of July," *Los Angeles Times*, 17 June 1897, 4; Bob Pool, "Reenactment of L.A.'s First July 4 a Blast from Past," *Los Angeles Times*, 5 July 1997, Metro Section, B1.

Fort Prince Charles, New York

Located on North Marble Hill at the north end of Manhattan Island in New York, this was the site for a commemorative Fourth of July celebration in 1894. Fort Prince Charles was used by General George Washington as he retreated from the Hessians in 1777. The British occupied the fort for the next seven years.

The ceremony included a history of the old fort presented by William A. Varian, a reading of the Declaration of Independence by Hugh N. Camp, and addresses by D.C. Overbaugh and I. Edgar Rich. A group of children dressed in red, white, and blue represented the forty-four states of the Union and others participated in costume with depictions of Columbia, Goddess of Liberty, Uncle Sam, and George and Martha Washington. The Old Guard Band supplied patriotic music.

Source: "King's Bridge's Celebration," *New York Times*, 5 July 1894, 8.

Fort Schuyler, Utica, New York

The dedication of the site for the fort occurred on July 4, 1883.

Source: Isaac Smithson Harley, "Fort Schuyler in History," *Transactions of the Oneida Historical Society at Utica* (Utica: the Society, 1885): 168–89.

Fort Sumter, South Carolina

The Civil War began at this site on April 12, 1861, with the firing on this federal fort by shore batteries under command of Gen. Pierre

G.T. Beauregard. Union Maj. Robert Anderson surrendered the fort on April 13 after 34 hours of relentless shelling. Three months later, on July 4, the Confederates in charge fired an Independence Day artillery salute from the Fort in response to artillery salutes by ships in the harbor.

Source: *Charleston Mercury*, 6 July 1861.

Fort Washington, New York

The first organized celebration of Independence Day at the fort took place on July 4, 1911. On November 16, 1776, British General William Howe, with 13,000 troops at his command, attacked Fort Washington, which was fortified by a garrison of Continental Army troops. Although the fort eventually capitulated, the Revolutionary forces fought gallantly. The British took over 2800 prisoners, but lost over 450 killed or wounded. The 1911 Independence Day celebration occurred under the sponsorship of the Washington Heights Men's Club. A ceremony included a procession of soldiers representing the New York Second Battery and a flag raising by Mrs. Mary A. Bordenhammer, 86 years of age, and a member of the original Daughters of the Revolution. The local Boy Scout troop assisted with the flag raising.

Source: "At Old Fort Washington," *New York Times*, 5 July 1911, 5.

Fortress Monroe, Virginia

A noteworthy site visited frequently on the Fourth of July at the time of the Civil War and after by dignitaries and statesmen, including presidents **Andrew Jackson** and **Rutherford Birchard Hayes**, in 1831 and 1879, respectively. On July 4, 1868, Gideon Welles, Commodore Jenkins and other distinguished persons arrived at the fort via the steamer *Ascutney* and witnessed a display of fireworks.

Source: "Movements of Secretary Welles and Party," *New York Times*, 6 July 1868, 5.

Foster, Stephen Collins (1826–1864)

Born on July 4, this icon of American song-writers has been honored extensively on Independence Day. My Old Kentucky Home State Park, Bardstown, Kentucky, was named in honor of the composer and has had a long tradition of Fourth of July celebrations.

Pittsburgh, where Foster was born, has had several noteworthy celebrations. On the occasion of the nation's sesquicentennial, July 5, 1926, the city honored the 100th anniversary of Foster's birth, in Schenley Park. "The Pittsburgh Symphony Orchestra, assisted by a chorus, played the better known of Foster's melodies. The program was broadcast by radio station KDKA." Several descendants of Foster were present. In New York that day a recital by Crystal Waters, with assistance by Harold Milligan, author of a biography of Foster, occurred at the headquarters of the National Music League. Before Waters sang a selection of Foster songs, Julius Hyman of "the allied Patriotic Societies" read the Declaration of Independence. Also in New York, a Foster centennial concert was presented by the Hotel Majestic String Ensemble, directed by Theodore Fishberg. There were also other occasions when Foster was commemorated. On July 4, 1906, the U.S. Marine Band performed a medley of Stephen Foster songs arranged by W. Paris Chambers at the U.S. Capitol. On July 4, 1931, a radio broadcast of Foster melodies by a group of soloists and orchestra was broadcast over radio station WEAF, New York. On July 4, 1933, 3,000 voices sang "My Old Kentucky Home" and other tunes in Bardstown, Kentucky. On July 4, 1935, a "Stephen Foster Birthday Memorial Concert" was broadcast from Greenfield Village, Michigan, over WABC, New York.

On July 4, 1958, at Bardstown the cornerstone of the Amphitheater at Federal Hill was laid and a painting of "My Old Kentucky Home" was unveiled. On July 4, 1989, a newly discovered piano work, "Autumn Waltz," by Foster was premiered by Mark Graf, pianist with the Pittsburgh Opera, and broadcast by National Public Radio.

Sources: "Pittsburgh Honors Foster" and "Stephen Foster Honored," *New York Times*, 6 July 1926, 23 and 22, respectively, and "A Glorious Fourth on the Air," *New York Times*, 28 June 1931, 29; "Music and Musicians," *Washington Post*, 8 July 1906, C5; "Concert, Recital, Pictures To-night at Majestic," *New York Herald Tribune*, 4 July 1926, 6; *Washington Post*, 5 July 1933, 5; "Today on the Radio, *New York*

Times, 4 July 1935, 28; Irvin Molotsky, "Public Radio to Play Long-Lost Foster Tune," *New York Times,* 4 July 1989, 23.

Four Mile Historic Park, Denver, Colorado

This park was founded in 1978 and has celebrated the Fourth of July annually beginning in 1980. The Denver Concert Band has entertained visitors with patriotic music for most of its celebrations. In 2001, in addition to the reading of the Declaration of Independence, a recitation of the Gettysburg Address was given, as well as a Civil War encampment reenactment, complete with artillery, with the 1st Colorado Volunteer Infantry as a highlight of the day.

Source: Ed Will, "Celebrating American History: Four Mile Park Honors Fourth of July with Lessons on United States," *Denver Post,* 29 July 2001, EE-01.

Fourth of July

The nation's most significant national holiday, marked by parades, speeches, fireworks, music, flag waving, reenactments, sporting events, picnics, patriotic ceremonies, and artillery salutes. The holiday commemorates the adoption of the Declaration of Independence by Congress on July 4, 1776. The impetus for celebrating the Fourth of July, also called Independence Day, was created in part through resolutions of Congress and the efforts of individuals such as John Adams, Francis Hopkinson, Robert Morris, and George Washington. At first the first organized celebrations were local affairs occurring in larger towns such as Philadelphia and Boston but by the early 1800s they had generally spread across the nation. At first, there was no official American flag nor was there a national anthem. In 1778 Congress officially proclaimed its support for the celebrations and in 1779 directed "the chaplains of Congress be requested to prepare sermons suitable to the occasion." Civic projects of public interest have commonly been started on the Fourth: groundbreaking of the Erie Canal, 1817; excavating the Chesapeake and Ohio Canal and commencing construction of the Baltimore and Ohio Railroad, 1828; laying the cornerstone of the Washington Monument, 1848; setting the cornerstone for the National Soldiers Monument in Gettysburg, 1865; and laying the cornerstone for the Freedom Tower in New York City, 2004.

Despite the origin of Independence Day, today Americans primarily celebrate the nation's heritage and rarely if ever are disparaging words expressed regarding anti-colonialism. The national holiday is steeped in traditions and values inherent in its long history. Although local ordinances prevent the use of fireworks in many states, access to smaller fireworks by the public continues. Celebrations are full-day affairs, with parades and speeches in the morning followed by afternoon barbecues, tailgating, and evening fireworks extravaganzas. Many Americans are seen wearing clothing in creative red, white and blue patriotic designs that express the freedoms they enjoy. Many make the most of the holiday by visiting theme parks and other popular destinations. See also **Declaration of Independence** and **"Independence Day."**

Source: Branham and Hartnett, *Sweet Freedom's Song,* 98.

Fourth of July

A play written as a radio broadcast for July 4, 1939, by Alistair Cooke (1908–2004), American journalist and broadcaster who was born in Salford, Greater Manchester, England. The play, broadcast in London, was produced by Felix Green with music arranged and conducted by Josef Honti.

Source: "Broadcasting: The Fourth of July," *London Times,* 4 July 1939, 26.

The Fourth of July: A Grand Parade March

Composed for a full military band and arranged for the piano forte by H.N. Gilles (Baltimore: John Cole, 1826).

Source: Calvin Elliker, "Early Imprints in the Thomas A. Edison Collection of American Sheet Music: Addenda to Sonneck-Upton and to Wolfe," *Notes* 57/3 (March 2001): 555–73.

"Fourth of July, a New National Song"

Written by "Miss Leslie," and "adapted to a popular military air." This work was "sung at the anniversary dinner of the Cincinnati Society of Philadelphia, July 4th 1853" (Philadelphia: Lee and Walker, 1853).

Fourth of July Canyon

Takes its name from the celebration held on July 4, 1861, by Capt. John Mullan and his men, who were building a road 624 miles in length from Fort Walla Walla, Washington, to Fort Benton, Montana. With funding of $100,000 from Congress, work on the road, which was later used by the army and the mining rush in that area, began in June 1859 and was completed in August 1862. On Independence Day in 1861 Mullan and his crew of 250 had reached the site of the canyon where they held their celebration.

Fourth of July, legislation, Boston

At a Boston town meeting in 1783, the General Court passed an act proclaiming that from then on

> The Fourth of July shall be constantly celebrated by the delivery of a Publick oration ... in which the orator shall consider the feelings, manners, and principles which led to this Great Capital event as well as the important and happy effects ... which already have and will forever continue to flow from the auspicious epoch.

Source: John Warren, *An Oration, Delivered July 4th, 1783* (Boston, 1783).

Fourth of July, legislation, Rhode Island

The Fourth of July, Christmas, Thanksgiving Day, "and Fast days, either National or State, and New Year's Day" were established as legal holidays in Rhode Island by the State legislature in 1852.

Source: *Farmer's Cabinet*, 11 March 1852, 3.

Fourth of July Mountain

Located in Southwest Nevada, just west of Lake Mohave in the Opal Mountains. About 96 percent of the Opal Mountains region is under the ownership of the Bureau of Land Management and national recreation areas. The mountains are described as "impressive as the eastern slopes of the range rise out of the Colorado River."

Source: *Opal Mountains*, Web site, <http://www.brrc.ujnr.edu/mtn/html/opal.html>.

Francis Scott Key Monument Association, Baltimore

Active in the 1880s–'90s and organized annual events that were dedicated to the memory of **Francis Scott Key**. Many of the affairs were held at Patterson Park. On the Fourth in 1892 at the park, the Hon. H.S. Cummings presented an address and a choir provided a group of patriotic pieces. On July 4, 1893, William C. Smith publicly read Washington's Farewell Address. In the following year, George R. Willis presented an oration. See also **Key, Francis Scott (1779–1843)**.

Sources: "Fun on the Fourth," *Baltimore Morning Herald*, 4 July 1892, 1; "Francis Scott Key," *Baltimore Morning Herald*, 5 July 1893, 2; "Down with Disloyalty," *Baltimore Morning Herald*, 5 July 1894, 6.

Franklin, Benjamin (1706–1790)

Statesman, author, and inventor, who was a member of the 2d Continental Congress, a signer of the Declaration of Independence and host of the first Fourth of July celebration in Europe in 1778. Born in Boston, Franklin worked as a young man in a printing shop and developed his interests in books and writing. He was editor of the *Pennsylvania Gazette* until 1748, established a circulating library in Philadelphia in 1731. His experiments regarding the nature of lightning and electricity were well known. Franklin played an important role in the repeal of the Stamp Act (1766) and after his tenure in the Continental Congress was assigned the task with John Adams of securing help from the French for the Revolutionary War efforts. While in Paris Franklin hosted Independence Day celebrations in 1778 and 1779 for the American colony there. The elaborate dinners took place in Passy. The 1778 celebration guests included French sympathizers of the cause. The 1779 celebration, of which more is known, included about forty celebrants from "Vergennes and Sartine, *premier commis* Gérard de Rayneval and Baudouin; the marquis and marquise de Lafayette; the chevalier de Laneuville and 'comte' Montfort de Prat, both officers in the American army," and a host of other dignitaries.

Among the Americans were Arthur Lee, Samuel Petrie, and Samuel Wharton. Information from Franklin's account books about what was served at the table included prices and quantities of fowl and meats, vegetables, fruit, "pintes" of wine and table settings. It is reported that the guests celebrated adjacent to a portrait of George Washington holding a copy of the Declaration of Independence. The affair included singing, a band, a ball, and the presentation to the attendees of an Independence Day poem written by the poet Feutry and printed by Franklin at his expense.

Franklin's interest in printing was honored by the establishment of the Franklin Society, an association of printers, in Boston on July 4, 1802. Another Franklin Association, active in Alexandria, Virginia, in 1818, honored the printer on Independence Day with an oration by James H. Smoot, who reminded his audience that Franklin was "firm in the cause of his native country, by his wisdom and talents determined potentates to befriend us, and the nations of Europe to become our allies." Columbia, South Carolina, had a Franklin Debating Club that had a July Fourth celebration in 1829 at the Merchant's Hotel.

On July 4, 1895, Russell Duane, supposed descendant of Franklin, read the Declaration of Independence at Independence Hall, in Philadelphia. On July 4, 1964, members of the Italian Historical Society put a wreath at the statue of Franklin at Park Row in New York.

Sources: *Independent Chronicle*, 2 and 8 July 1802, as reported in Travers, *Celebrating the Fourth*, 115; *Alexandria Gazette*, 11 July 1818, 2; *South Carolina State Gazette*, 4 July 1829, 3; "In Old Glory's Home," *Baltimore Morning Herald*, 5 July 1895, 1; *New York Times*, 5 July 1964, L45; Barbara B. Oberg, ed., *The Papers of Benjamin Franklin* (New Haven: Yale University Press, 1993) 30:44–46; *Diary and Autobiography of John Adams* 2: 317 and 4: 143–44.

Fraser, Charles (1782–1860)

Lawyer, writer, and artist who painted "South View of Fort Mechans, Charleston, July 4, 1796" and who presented an oration in Charleston's St. Michael's Church on July 4, 1808. Fraser was born in Charleston, South Carolina, attended the College of Charleston in 1792, later studied law and was admitted to the bar in 1807. According to Martha Severens, his "portraits provide a social register of Charleston during the antebellum period." Fraser was influenced or taught by Thomas Coran, a local engraver and painter, Thomas Sully, and Edward Greene Malbone, a miniaturist painter. Fraser's work caught the attention of noted artist Gilbert Stuart. From 1817 to 1860, Fraser served as a trustee of the College of Charleston. His 1808 Fourth of July oration was presented before the members of the American Revolution Society and the South Carolina State Society of the Cincinnati. It was poetic and sentimental. He discussed public virtue as it relates to liberty. "So essential is public virtue to the attainment and conservation of those privileges which are the professed object of all political reforms, that, without a regard for it, the energies of a nation must inevitably lead to its own destruction." To the members of the societies, he said, "For some of you it [the Fourth of July celebration] may perhaps be the last time. Should this solemn thought excite gloom in your minds, let it be dissipated by the assurance of that honorable remembrance in which your patriotic services shall be cherished. The unsparing hand of death has thinned your venerable ranks, but it has not extinguished your renown."

Sources: *An Oration, Delivered in St. Michael's Church* (1801); Alice R. Huger Smith and D.E. Huger Smithy, *Charles Fraser* (Charleston, S.C.: Garnier and Co. [reprint 1967]); Martha R. Severens, "Charles Fraser," *American National Biography* 8: 409–10; *Charles Fraser of Charleston: Essays on the Man, His Art and His Times*, ed. Martha R. Severens and Charles L. Wyhrick, Jr. (Charleston, S.C.: Carolina Art Association, 1983).

"Freedom Fair"

The theme for the annual Independence Day celebration (begun in the 1990s) held in Tacoma, Washington. A memorable event occurred in 1995 there when Air Force Capt. Scott O'Grady, who had been shot down in western Bosnia that year, swore in six Air Force recruits during the event at the Tacoma Waterfront.

Source: Sarah Lopez Williams, "Recruits Sworn in by Their Hero," *Seattle Times*, 5 July 1995, B1.

"Freedom Fest"

A popular theme used for Independence Day celebrations during the 1980s and after in small towns and large cities across the country. The longest running Freedom Fest celebration held was that in Tampa, Florida, which ran from 1985 to 1998. One of the most memorable events in that series was in 1990 when Santore and Sons, a fireworks display firm, celebrated its 100th anniversary year by launching the largest display of fireworks ever in that city. In 2001 the event's theme was changed to "Aquafest." In 1987, Houston, Texas, began an annual Freedom Fest celebration, which ran for several years. Other recent Freedom Fest celebrations have occurred in Kenner, Louisiana (1997); Murray, Kentucky (1998); Milwaukee (2000); Central City, Colorado (2000), San Antonio, Texas (2000), and St. Louis (2001).

Sources: Robert Keefe, "Freedom Fest Has Big Plans," *St. Petersburg Times*, 30 June 1990, 1; Steven Long, "A Festive Fourth," *Houston Chronicle*, 3 July 1992, 1; Ed Quioco and Linda Gibson, "Rain Doesn't Fizzle Fourth," *St. Petersburg Times*, 5 July 1999, 1B; Lea Iadarola, "Aquafest Is Tampa's New Fourth Fete," *St. Petersburg Times*, 28 June 2001 (Week End Online).

Freedom of Information Act (FOIA)

On July 4, 1966, the Freedom of Information Act was signed into law by President Lyndon Baines Johnson.

The act was designed to replace an earlier section of law under which government agencies considered themselves free to withhold information from the public under whatever subjective standard could be articulated for the occasion. Most importantly, the Freedom of Information Act set a standard of openness for government from which only deviations in well-defined areas would be allowed. The FOIA then went on to define those areas in a series of nine "exemptions." Finally, it provided a remedy for the wrongful withholding of information: the person requesting information from the government could take his or her case to court.

The FOIA was amended in 1974 and 1976. Through the years, "the FOIA has reflected the constant push and pull of the separation of powers between the Congress and the Executive Branch. Its enactment in 1966 culminated eleven years of investigations and deliberations in the U.S. House of Representatives and half as many years of consideration in the United States Senate."

On June 26, 1986, Senator Edward Kennedy, an original sponsor of the act, brought attention to the impending twentieth anniversary of FOIA in the Senate. He said, "because of this act, our country has become stronger, our people more knowledgeable, and our democracy more secure."

Source: *Congressional Record*, 99th Congress, Second Session, 132/11, June 26, 1986, 16015.

Freedom Park, Rosslyn, Virginia

Opened on July 4, 1996, and cited as "the only one of its kind in the country." This permanent display of eight patriotic icons on 1.6 acres located just outside Washington, D.C., depicts freedom's struggles and includes pieces of the Berlin Wall, cobblestones from a Warsaw ghetto, a bronze ballot box, a "talking circles" display representing the American Indian tradition of free speech, a display depicting the 1991 collapse of the Soviet Union, and a "Journalists Memorial" display by the organization Freedom Forum dedicated to those that gave their lives reporting the news. The cost of Freedom Park was $4 million. On July 4, 2005, the Freedom Park site was used for a citizenship ceremony (see **Naturalization**). Freedom Park is sponsored by the Freedom Forum, Westfield Realty Co., the City of Rosslyn and Arlington County, Virginia.

Source: Lan Nguyen, "New Park's Theme Is Freedom," *Washington Post*, 4 July 1996, Va1, 6.

Freedom Tower, New York City

The twenty-ton cornerstone for this memorial was laid on July 4, 2004, on the site of the World Trade Center, less than three years after the center was destroyed by terrorists. Tears and hope were shared among the officials and family members of those that lost their lives. The building that will be the world's tallest is scheduled to be completed in 2008. New York Governor George E. Pataki addressed spectators about the "resiliency of this city and the resolve of these United States." The inscription of the granite slab bears these words: "To honor and remember those who lost their lives on Sept. 11, 2001, and as a tribute to the enduring spirit of freedom.— July Fourth, 2004." The structure is expected to cost $1.3 billion.

Sources: Josh Getlin, "At Tower's Base, a Tribute," *Boston Globe*, 5 July 2004, A3; Stevenson Swanson, "At Heart of Ground Zero, a Declaration of Freedom," *Chicago Tribune*, 5 July 2004, A1.

Freedom Trail, Boston

A 2.5-mile walking trail through downtown Boston, the North End, and Charlestown that passes seventeen historic sites and landmarks, many of which were places where historic Fourth of July ceremonies were held. The sites include Boston Common, State House, Park Street Church, Granary Burying Ground, King's Chapel, King's Chapel Burying Ground, Old Corner Bookstore Building, Old South Meeting House, Old State House, Boston Massacre Site, Old North Church, Copp's Hill Burying Ground, USS *Constitution*, Faneuil Hall, Paul Revere House, USS *Constitution* Museum, and Bunker Hill Museum.

Freedom Statue, Freedom Park, Rosslyn, Virginia. The park is located outside Washington, D.C., and opened on July 4, 1996. On July 4, 2005, 41 immigrants were naturalized there. Shown here is a replica of the 19.6 foot statue of Freedom that stands atop the Capitol dome. This version, cast in bronze by Michael Maiden of Sandy, Oregon, is 7.5 feet tall. Photograph by author.

French, Benjamin Brown (1800–1870)

Clerk of the House of Representatives and commissioner of public buildings in Washington, who gave three orations, two at the Washington Monument in 1848 and 1870, and one at the Capitol in 1851. French was a popular orator who had a keen sense of history and enjoyed reminiscing about past events. He spoke at the laying of the cornerstone for the Washington Monument on July 4, 1848, and described George Washington at the cornerstone event at the Capitol in 1793. He urged his audience to think of the monument as "a mark of our affection, our veneration for the memory of the great and good man whose name it bears; and it shall hereafter be viewed by an admiring world as the evidence to all future time that this republic is not ungrateful." On July 4, 1870, French spoke again at the monument on the occasion of a presentation of a block of marble by the **Oldest Inhabitants Association of Washington.** French talked about past Fourth of July events, the death of presidents on Independence Day, and the fact that the construction of the Washington Monument had not yet been completed:

And permit me now to express the opinion — emphatically to express it — that it is not creditable to the patriotism of the American people that a national monument to Washington should be commenced here, in the city bearing his immortal name, on the banks of the broad and beautiful Potomac, which he loved so well, and after more than twenty years be left, as the Washington National Monument now stands, having the appearance of a broken shaft! If it is to remain thus, let us festoon upon its top the folded mantle, and inscribe upon the unfinished shaft the ridiculous epitaph which some fond parent caused to be engraved on the tombstone of his deceased infant:

> If I am so quickly done for,
> I wonder what I was begun for.

Posterity will surely wonder why, after so much display of intention, pride, if nothing else, should not have urged on the work to completion! Let us, then, awaken, my respected fellow-citizens, and with renewed energy "push on the column," until it reaches its intended height, and from its apex glitters the single star which is to adorn it, emblematical of that great man whose memory stands preeminently above all others in the hearts of the American people.

French also composed a national hymn that was sung on November 19, 1863, at the consecration event of the Gettysburg Battlefield and again on July 4, 1865, at the cornerstone laying event for the Gettysburg National Soldier's Monument.

Sources: *National Intelligencer*, 6 July 1848, 3; *Washington Evening Star*, 5 July 1870, 4; "Gettysburgh," *New York Times*, 6 July 1865, 8; Benjamin Brown French, *Witness to the Young Republic: A Yankee's Journal, 1828–1870*, ed. Donald B. Cole and John J. McDonough (Hanover: University Press of New England, 1989), 620.

French Monument, Providence, Rhode Island

Referred to also as the "French Memorial," the monument was dedicated on July 4, 1882, and was inscribed "to the citizens of Providence" who were "our allies in the Revolution." The "double-based ledger monument constructed of granite, with legends and symbols in relief," and conceived by Rev. Frederic Denison, was dedicated to French soldiers who were buried in the "North Burying Ground" in Providence. The soldiers were part of Rochambeau's army that consisted of "between 6000 and 7000 men" who marched in Rhode Island in 1782. Many of the soldiers who became sick due to disease died in Providence.

The ceremony for the monument included a military procession, the flying of French flags, music by the Boston City Band, including renditions of the "Marseilles" and "Star-Spangled Banner," and an oration by Denison.

Sources: *Dedication of the French Monument by the City of Providence, R.I....* (Providence: Providence Press Company, 1882); "The French Memorial," *Providence Daily Journal*, 5 July 1882, 1.

Fritchie, Barbara

The restored home of Barbara Fritchie (also Frietchie) in Frederick, Maryland, was dedicated on July 4, 1927. Fritchie was remembered for supposedly flying an American flag from her window when "Stonewall Jackson led his Confederated troops through Frederick in 1862." For the ceremony, Mayor Lloyd C. Culler of Frederick welcomed the spectators, and Miss Eleanor Abbott, great-grandniece of Mrs. Fritchie, recited John Greenleaf Whittier's poem "Barbara Fritchie." A portrait of Whittier was presented by Baltimore Mayor William F. Broening to the Barbara Fritchie Memorial Association and was to be displayed in the home. Music was provided by the First Regiment Band.

Sources: "Barbara Fritchie's Home Is Dedicated," *Baltimore Sun*, 5 July 1927, 4; "Barbara Fritchie Home Dedicated," *Washington Evening Star*, 5 July 1927, 12.

Fuller, Margaret (1810–1850)

Transcendentalist who contributed an article to the *New York Daily Tribune* on July 4, 1845, with commentary on the ironies of the Fourth of July as an America "soiled" and steeped in the tradition of slavery.

Source: *New York Daily Tribune*, 4 July 1845, 2, as quoted in Dennis, *Red, White, and Blue Letter Days*, 24; *Margaret Fuller: Essays on American Life and Letters*, ed. Joel Myerson (Schenectady, N.Y.: 1978), 297–300.

Fuller, Melville Weston (1833–1910)

The only chief justice of the U.S. (1888–1910) who died on the Fourth of July.

Barbara Fritchie House and Museum, Frederick, Maryland. This restored home was dedicated on July 4, 1927. Photograph by author.

According to an article published in the *Boston Evening Transcript*, "Judge Fuller of Maine" read an original poem in the Town Hall in Concord, New Hampshire, on 4 July 1876. He was born in Augusta, Maine, held a degree from Bowdoin College (1853) and later moved to Chicago where he was active in politics, serving as a member of the Illinois Constitutional Convention (1862) and the Illinois House of Representatives (1863–65). Fuller died at his summer home in Sorrento, Maine.

Source: "Fourth of July Celebrations," *Boston Evening Transcript*, 5 July 1876, 8.

Fulton, Robert (1765–1815)

Inventor, artist, and engineer who was presented posthumously with a gold medal on July 4, 1826, by the Common Council of New York City for his work in establishing and developing steamboat service in America. Born in Little Britain, Pennsylvania, Fulton engaged himself in internal improvements, such as canal development and the application of steam power to boats. His first vessel, *Clermont*, began regular commercial service between New York City and Albany in 1807. Fulton's accomplishment in this area led to the building of hundreds of steamboats that served as the primary mode of transportation on the nation's interior waterways. Many of these boats provided excursions on Independence Days, and these holiday trips became a national pastime that lasted until the Civil War. Fulton's work led to other related developments, such as the use of steam to power a warship.

Fulton's gold medal was one of four awarded that day, the other three being intended for the three living signers of the Declaration of Independence (Adams, Carroll, and Jefferson). Robert Fulton's son received the medal in honor of his father, who was described as a "genius in the application of steam."

The steamship *Fulton* was named after the inventor, and the testing of this large vessel took place on July 4, 1815, leaving from the wharf known as Corlear's Hook in New York City. The trip lasted over 6 hours with a distance of forty-five miles covered. The vessel also participated in Fourth of July celebrations, such as the one in New York City in 1841. Anchored off the Battery, fireworks were set off from her decks.

Sources: *National Intelligencer*, 10 and 12 July 1815, 3 and 2, respectively; *Richmond Enquirer*, 14 July 1826, 4; *New York American*, 7 July 1841, 1.

Gage, Lyman J. (1836–1927)

Banker and secretary of the treasury under Presidents William McKinley and Theodore Roosevelt who, on July 4, 1900, at the auditorium in Atlantic City, New Jersey, gave an unusual speech in which he attacked the press, a symbol of America's freedom. Born in Deruyter, New York, Gage was president of the American Banker's Association in 1883 and president of the Chicago Board of Directors of the World's Columbian Exposition in 1890. Gage was highly regarded for helping to get the Gold Standard Act passed in Congress in 1900. His Independence Day address questioned "the methods of sensational newspapers which, he said, by their lurid and often untruthful description of happenings, do a great deal of harm, disturbing the peace of mind of the people and the commercial interests of the nation." Gage also mentioned the prosperity of the country "and the outlook for the territory which has recently come under the Nation's flag."

Sources: "Mr. Gage on the Press," *New York Times*, 5 July 1900, 7; Leslie F. Tischauser, "Lyman Jackson Gage," *American National Biography* 8:606–07.

Gardiner, John (1733?–1793)

Attorney and political activist who, according to Stephen Elliot James, presented the first Independence Day oration styled as a literary piece and as a model for proper public orator skills. Born in Boston, Gardiner studied locally in Boston, then left for Great Britain where he pursued advance studies at the University of Glasgow in 1752. Upon graduation, Gardiner practiced law in Wales and London. He later traveled to the Caribbean as attorney general for St. Christopher's Island and there began his activities as a political radicalist. After the Revolutionary War in 1783, he returned to the United States where in Boston he set up a law practice and was appointed justice of the peace. On July 4, 1785, he presented an oration that included a twenty-page addendum that served as a statement of instruction in the art of elocution and a model for other orators.

Gardiner continued efforts at reform. His election to the Massachusetts House of Representatives in 1789 provided him the opportunity to help repeal the state's anti-theater laws. Gardiner died on his way to Boston aboard the ship *Londoner* when the vessel sank during a storm.

Sources: *An Oration, Delivered July 4, 1785* (Boston: 1785); James, "The Other Fourth of July, 63–66; Peter R. Virgadamo, "John Gardiner," *American National Biography* 8:696–97.

Garfield, James Abram (1831–1881)

Twentieth president of the U.S. (1881), who was assassinated while in office. His shooting on July 2, 1881, resulted nationally in the most subdued Fourth of July in the nineteenth century. Garfield was president for only six months so had no opportunity to celebrate the Fourth during his tenure. Garfield was born in Cuyahoga County, Ohio, and was elected to the Ohio senate in 1859. He served in the Civil War, distinguishing himself in engagements at Shiloh and Chickamauga.

On July 4, 1881, much of the country came together to pray for Garfield's life and to pay special tribute to his presidency. The New York Board of Aldermen adopted resolutions expressing sympathy for the dying president. The editor of the *Baltimore Morning Herald* expressed: "The anniversary of the republic's birth yesterday was a sad and gloomy one. Instead of witnessing fifty millions of people rejoice at the event which gave them life and freedom over one hundred and five years ago, we beheld a nation plunged in mourning and bewildered with grief." The *New York Times* reported that "the day, altogether, was perhaps the quietest Fourth of July New York has ever seen. It seemed as if representatives of all the other nations of the earth were celebrating the anniversary of American independence, while America herself looked on and wrung her hands. Americans seemed to consider the Nation in too desperate a strait to indulge in any merry-making." In Washington, as Garfield lay gravely ill at the White House, the city's chief of police issued an order banning all fireworks so the president would not be disturbed by the noise.

On Independence Day in the following year, eulogies and statements were presented in many locales in memory of the president. An oration in the form of a eulogy that brought attention was given by Rev. Mark Hopkins, president of Garfields College, at Williams College in Williamstown, Massachusetts. The address was a lengthy account of Garfield's life and was mentioned in New York, Chicago and Providence, Rhode Island, newspapers. About Garfield's early life and struggles, Hopkins said how Garfield "resembled President Lincoln, but his struggles were more steady in their aim and more diversified in their means, and so were adapted to awaken a wide sympathy." Unveiled that day at Williams was a "Garfield Memorial window."

The year before his fatal shooting, Garfield had been a guest speaker at the dedication of the **Soldiers' Monument** in Painesville, Ohio, on July 4, 1880. He spoke about the symbolism the statue represented and prophetically asked his audience if any were willing to give their lives for their country. "Let me put the question to you for a moment. Suppose your country, in the awfully embodied form of majestic law, should stand above you and say, 'I want your life, come up here on the platform and offer it,' how many would walk up before that majestic presence and say, 'Here I am; take this life and use it for your great needs?'"

Sources: "A Speech by Gen. Garfield," *New York Times*, 5 July 1880, 1, and 5 July 1881, 1; *Baltimore Morning Herald*, 5 July 1881, 2 and 4; "A Quiet Fourth of July," *New York Times*, 5 July 1881, 3; "A Mournful Meeting," *Chicago Daily Times*, 5 July 1882, 6; "President Garfield," *Providence Daily Journal*, 5 July 1882, 1; "A Tribute to Garfield," *New York Times*, 5 July 1882, 1.

Garfield Monument, San Francisco

Was unveiled in Golden Gate Park, San Francisco, California, on July 4, 1885, with thousands of spectators present. Horace Davis delivered an address.

Source: "California Celebrations," *Los Angeles Times*, 5 July 1885, 1.

Garibaldi, Giuseppe (1807–1882)

Born on July 4, this political leader and soldier fought for the Roman republic in 1849 and then came to New York, where he stayed until 1853. Italian-Americans thought highly of Garibaldi and erected a statue of him in Washington Square Park in 1888. On July 4, 1907, 10,000 Italian-Americans celebrated a new Garibaldi Memorial in honor of the Italian patriot's birthday.

Each year Italian residents from all over New York assembled to celebrate the Fourth of July and Garibaldi's birthday at the memorial. At times the political perspectives of those gathered there were different and the risk of fights prevailed. On July 4, 1925, for example, 350 Fascist marchers, the "black shirts," marched to the memorial and nearly 1000 anti-Fascists, "the red shirts," were already there. Two riots had already occurred causing injuries and a heavy presence of police using "night sticks" averted a much larger riot at the memorial. "After paying tribute to the memory of the great Italian liberator the crowd began to return to Manhattan. Small groups of the opposing factions met frequently aboard Staten Island trains and ferries. But they were so scattered among other passengers that they made little trouble."

Through the years individuals continued to visit the monument on the Fourth of July but their numbers dwindled. On July 4, 1964, members of the Italian Historical Society placed a wreath at the monument, while about sixty spectators watched.

Sources: *New York Times*, 5 July 1907, 6; "Fascists and Red in Two Riots Here over Garibaldi Fete," *New York Times*, 5 July 1925, 1 and 3; Philip Benjamin, "Nation Observes a Quiet Holiday," *New York Times*, 5 July 1964, 45; Mary Elizabeth Brown, "Giuseppe Garibaldi," in *The Encyclopedia of New York City*, 451.

Garnet, Horatio

Musician who composed "Ode for American Independence, July 4th, 1789," with words by Daniel George (1759?–1804). First line: "'Tis done! the edict past, by heav'n decreed."

Sources: *Massachusetts Magazine* 1/7 (July 1789): 453–54; *American Musical Miscellany* (Northampton, 1798), 142–47; Henry M. Brooks, *Olden Time Music* (Boston, 1888), 155–56; Carolyn Rabson, *Songbook of the American Revolution* (Peaks Island, Maine: Neo Press, 1974).

Garrett Park, Baltimore

This park was dedicated on July 4, 1877. This first annual celebration held there included the

raising of a large silk American flag, during which the band played "The Star-Spangled Banner"; reading of the Declaration of Independence by Prof. E. Burnett; musical selections sung by the West End Glee Club; recitation, by Mr. Wm Roche; oration on the "Triumphs of right in the Formation of the American Government," by Prof. Burnett; Poe's "Raven" read by Mr. Roche; and a selection of "Love" by Miss Pennington. The assemblage, about four hundred in number, were then invited to ice cream and cake, after which the exercises closed.

Source: "Dedication of Garrett Park," *Baltimore Bee*, 5 July 1877, 4.

Garrison, William Lloyd (1805–1879)

Newspaper editor and one of the most significant abolitionists of the nineteenth century, who gave a number of anti-slavery orations on the Fourth of July. His first oration, presented on July 4, 1829, at the Park Street Church in Boston, is credited by some as "marking the beginning of the American abolitionist crusade."

Garrison was born in Newburyport, Massachusetts, and was raised in poverty. After leaving home in the 1820s he tried his hand at editing a number of newspapers in Massachusetts and Vermont, but these endeavors failed as a result of his "censorious" temperance and antislavery stance. His association with Benjamin Lundy as coeditor of *The Genius of Universal Emancipation* in Baltimore led to a libel suit that landed him in

jail. Garrison had accused a merchant in Massachusetts of involvement in the slave trade. In 1829 twenty-three-year-old Garrison gave his Independence Day address on slavery to members of the American Colonization Society. His words greatly surprised his audience. Expecting a typical patriotic presentation, his listeners were told of his shame for the country that hypocritically touted the rights of men while the "national sin" of slavery existed:

I speak not as a partisan or an opponent of any man or measures, when I say, that our politics are rotten to the core. We boast of our freedom, who go shackled to the polls, year after year, by tens, and hundreds, and thousands! ... I stand up here in a more solemn court ... to obtain the liberation of two millions of wretched, degraded beings, who are pining in hopeless bondage — over whose sufferings scarcely an eye weeps, or a heart melts, or a tongue pleads either to God or man.

William E. Cain has noted comments by Garrison's biographer, John L. Thomas, that this speech "contained the germ of almost every argument Garrison ever used." Garrison based that argument on four propositions: (1) that slaves are entitled to redress, (2) that "non-slave-holding states" are still responsible because they support a national government that condones slavery, (3) "that no justificative plea for the perpetuity of slavery can be found in the condition of its victims, and (4) that education and freedom "will elevate our colored population to a rank with the white." In this speech Garrison supported the movement for colonization in Liberia. Later he would reject that notion, arguing against its racist undertones.

In the 1830s, Garrison extended his anti-slavery influence through his editorship of the *Liberator*, a widely circulated newspaper that advocated for immediate emancipation. He also was instrumental in the establishment of the New England Anti-Slavery Society in Boston in 1832 and in the following year the Philadelphia-based American Anti-Slavery Society. It was for this latter organization that he formalized the principles and ideals of his anti-slavery stance with the writing of the society's *Declaration of Sentiments*. This work encouraged others to actively work towards abolition through campaigning, speaking out, and launching additional anti-slavery newspapers and societies.

Garrison's abolitionist role as a spokesperson for the movement became more pronounced. His alignment with outspoken supporters in the woman's rights movement, as well as African-American abolitionists and religious figures, helped to stem strong criticism directed at him from popular opposition across the country. Garrison took advantage of the patriotic national holiday to bring additional attention to his cause. On July 4, 1838, he delivered an address in Marlboro Chapel in Boston. He was forthright and poignant:

> Fellow Citizens; what a glorious day is this! What a glorious people are we! This is the time-honored, winehoned, toast-drinking, powder-wasting, tyrant-killing fourth of July — consecrated, for the last sixty years, to bombast, to falsehood, to impudence, to hypocrisy. It is the great carnival of republican despotism, and of Christian impiety, famous the world over.

On Independence Day in the following year he was in South Scituate, Massachusetts, where he addressed the Old Colony Anti-Slavery Society. On July 4, 1850, in Abington, Massachusetts, his views were presented to an anti-slavery celebration in the form of a hymn titled "American Hypocrisy."

Perhaps his most far-reaching and remarkable Fourth of July event was that of July 4, 1854, in Framingham, Massachusetts, when he burned copies of the Fugitive Slave Law (1793) and the U.S. Constitution. On July 4, 1860, Garrison was back in Framingham again speaking out for the complete "abolition of slavery throughout the land." He stressed that the Republican Party had more friends for the anti-slavery cause than the Democratic party, but that the Republican party had no power or encouragement to abolish slavery in slaveholding states. He mentioned Senator Henry Wilson (Massachusetts) and Abraham Lincoln and their views on slavery.

On July 4, 1893, the town of Newburyport, Massachusetts, unveiled a monument to Garrison.

Sources: *Selections from the Writings and Speeches of William Lloyd Garrison* (1852; reprint, Negro Universities Press, 1968); "'Independence Day': Anti-Slavery Celebration at Framingham," *Liberator*, 20 July 1860, 1; "A Statue to Garrison," *Baltimore Morning Herald*, 5 July 1893, 2; *William Lloyd Garrison and the Fight Against Slavery: Selections from* The Liberator, ed. William E. Cain (Boston: Bedford Books of St. Martin's Press, 1995); James Brewer Stewart, "William Lloyd Garrison," *American National Biography* 8: 761–65; James, "The Other Fourth of July, 135–41.

Garvey, Marcus Mosiah (1887–1940)

Black nationalist leader who established the Universal Negro Improvement Association (UNIA) in 1914 and spoke at Liberty Hall in New York on July 4, 1922, to members of the association calling for a new government "for a great people and promulgating the doctrines of the emancipation of 400 million negroes." His philosophy emphasized pride of race and separatism.

Garvey was born in St. Ann's Bay, Jamaica, and lived for a time in London. In 1916 he moved the UNIA headquarters from Jamaica to Harlem in New York in 1916. He published a weekly newspaper, *Negro World*, and in 1919 created the Black Star Line, a steamship company that catered to African-Americans. In 1923, he landed in prison as a result of a fraudulent stock scheme, but was later released and deported back to Jamaica.

The significant part of Garvey's Independence Day speech in 1922 was the laying of his plan and philosophy for the UNIA and what the organization's effect on the country would be. He explained to his audience, "I want you to realize that the Universal Negro Improvement Association has made a wonderful impression on the entire country, and we have changed the attitude and the feeling and the sentiment of a large number of people toward the organization — not only people of our own race, but people of the other race. I want to say that this organization has made a large number of friends through the visit that I have carried out through the Western States, and especially the Southern States."

Sources: *The Marcus Garvey and Universal Negro Improvement Association Papers*, ed. Robert A. Hill

(Berkeley: University of California Press, 1985), 4:690–99; E. David Cronon, "Marcus Mosiah Garvey," *Encyclopedia* Americana 12:316.

Gates, Horatio (1727–1806)

American Revolutionary War general who celebrated the Fourth of July in 1778 by giving a dinner. Born in Essex, England, Gates began his military career in the British army and after retiring moved to Virginia. At the onset of the Revolutionary War, Gates was named commander of the northern army in 1777.

Sources: *Connecticut Courant*, 14 July 1778; Edward P. Hamilton, "Horatio Gates," *Encyclopedia Americana* 12:343.

Gehrig, Lou (1903–1941)

Remarkable baseball player for the New York Yankees who was stricken with the fatal illness that bears his name, Lous Gehrig's disease, or amyotrophic lateral sclerosis, causing him to announce his retirement before 60,000 fans in Yankee Stadium on July 4, 1939. The Yankees organization designated Independence Day that year as "Lou Gehrig Appreciation Day." A newspaper reporter described the moment Gehrig stepped onto the field: "There stood the still burly and hearty Babe Ruth alongside of Gehrig, their arms about each other's shoulders, facing a battery of camera men." Gehrig "spoke of the men with whom he had been associated in his long career with the Yankees," and said these now famous words, "You've been reading about my bad break for weeks now, but today I think I'm the luckiest man alive." He was then given gifts of silver and paper scrolls by his admirers.

On July 4, 1989, the 50th anniversary of Gehrig's retirement, the Yankees honored him. At the ceremony in Yankee Stadium, a videotaped message from President George Bush was conveyed to the baseball fans and others there. "Today, in the House that Ruth built," he said, "we pause to salute another great Yankee, Lou Gehrig. Lou was one of my childhood heroes and one of the greatest baseball players in history. For those of us who remember Lou's grace and ability and steadiness, we also remember that dreadful disease taking

him away so quickly." Gehrig was elected to the Baseball Hall of Fame, Cooperstown, New York, in 1939.

Sources: John Drebinger, "61,808 Fans Roar Tribute to Gehrig," *New York Times*, 5 July 1939, 1, 21; "Bush Salutes Lou Gehrig," *New York Times*, 5 July 1989, D11.

Geib, George (1782–1842?)

Pianist, organist, and "professor of music" who composed "God Save America: A Patriotic Song," which was performed at the City Theatre in New York by "Mr. Lamb" on July 4, 1822. Geib dedicated the piece "to the people of the United States." Geib was born in London and brought to America in 1797 by his father. As a pianist, he began giving concerts in New York in 1811. In 1823–24 he was employed as an organist at St. Matthew's Church. For years Geib was listed in the city directories as a "professor of music" and he owned a piano forte and a music store on Broadway. "God Save America" was published by Geib at his New York store in 1822, with a re-issue in the following year.

Sources: *New-York Advertiser*, 6 July 1822, 2; Wolfe, *Secular Music in America 1801–1825: A Bibliography* 1:290; Clark, *The Dawning of American Keyboard Music*, 84, 131.

George III, King of Great Britain and Ireland (1738–1820)

Reigning English monarch at the time of the start of the Revolutionary War, who opposed the American colonies' bid for independence. Much of the Declaration of Independence was directed to the king. "The history of the present King of Great Britain is a history of repeated injuries and usurpations, all having in direct object the establishment of an absolute tyranny over these States." Although the king was not directly responsible for the Stamp Act of 1765 and the Townshend duties of 1767, the colonists nonetheless expressed anger at the throne. Thomas Paine through his tract *Common Sense* published in January 1776 helped to foment this discontent.

At the start of the Revolutionary War, throughout the thirteen colonies all emblems of the king were torn from buildings, and portraits and effigies were burned. When New

Yorkers heard news of the declaring of independence, the equestrian statue of George III was torn down and the lead was melted down for use as bullets. The unkindly sentiments about King George surfaced again on July 4, 1807, when citizens of Petersburg, Virginia, marched with an effigy of George III on a pole after they had learned of the shelling of the USS *Chesapeake* by the British warship *Leopard* a few days earlier (see **USS *Chesapeake* and *Leopard* battle**).

Sources: *Virginia Gazette*, 26 July 1776; *Enquirer*, 11 July 1807, 2.

Georgia State Capitol Building, Atlanta

This Atlanta landmark was dedicated on July 4, 1889. Similar in style to the U.S. Capitol, the building, constructed of Indiana limestone, "was designed by architects Willoughby J. Edbrooke and Franklin P. Burnham of Chicago, Illinois and constructed by Miles and Horne of Toledo, Ohio." The front of the structure has a four-story portico with stone pediment, with six Corinthian columns. Adorning the top of the dome is the fifteen-foot "Miss Freedom" statue. The Georgia State Legislature, which met for the first time in Atlanta on July 4, 1868, now had a permanent home with the completion of this building.

Source: Secretary of State, State of Georgia Web site, <http://www.sos.state.ga.us/museum/html/capitol_facts.html>.

German-Americans

One of the largest immigrant groups speaking a foreign language in America that actively celebrated the Fourth of July. In the eighteenth century, the principal Independence Day celebrations by Germans occurred in the Moravian settlement in **Salem, North Carolina**, with the first event taking place on July 4, 1783. A combination of religious and cultural practices served as a basis for that celebration and those that followed. About thirty years later the Pennsylvania Moravian community in Lititz had also become an active contributor to the tradition of celebrating Independence Day, beginning with its first Independence Day celebration in 1811. On July 4, 1843, the practice of illuminating the town's

Spring Park with candles was begun, and the tradition has continued every year to the present. The 1843 celebration also had a public supper, a reading of the Declaration of Independence in German, and an evening concert conducted by Rev. Peter Wolle that included a performance of the conductor's composition *Come Joyful Halleluyahs*.

In the nineteenth century, immigration of Germans to America increased considerably. Voluntary associations reflecting the different areas of Germany were formed and were an important means for retaining traditions, regional culture and loyalties. German-Americans often read the Declaration of Independence and presented orations and toasts in their native language. In Reading, Pennsylvania, on July 4, 1805, at a celebration of Republicans there, toasts to the nation were presented in German. In the following year, on July 1, the Declaration of Independence was published in the *Readinger Adler* in German. On July 4, 1831, in York, Pennsylvania, an oration was presented in both German and English. On July 4, 1848, in Charleston, "the German Volunteer Corps, German Fire Company, and German Friendly and Fusilier Societies moved in procession to the German Lutheran Church, where an oration in German was delivered by the Rev. Mr. Muller." Muller spoke about the strong ties those in Charleston had to their homeland, Germany. "No Germany, the true sons and daughters cannot forget thee, and if their fortunes led them unto the remotest regions, and if they resided amidst a people, where even thy name was unknown, yet would a thought often fly to the, O, fatherland, and memory bring blessed forms unto their souls," he said. After the ceremony, Charleston citizens presented flags to the "masters of Germans vessels now in port." Public readings in German of the Declaration took place on Independence Day in Pittsburgh at Diamond Square (1869), Chicago at Wright's Grove (1876), New York City at Jones' Woods Colosseum (1876), and Columbus, Ohio (1889), the latter at a ceremony in which a monument to the German poet **Johann Christoph Friedrich von Schiller** was dedicated.

In St. Louis and Watertown, Wisconsin, Germans, not followers of the more austere Puritan beliefs, elected to celebrate the Fourth on Sunday when it fell on that day, rather than waiting until Monday. In Watertown in 1852, Independence Day programs on Sunday were in German and ceremonies on Monday were in both English and German.

Among the most active and visible German associations were the singing societies that held concerts, choral festivals, and vocal competitions on the Fourth of July. The German choral festivals were some of the largest celebrations of their kind and were unique to the Independence Day traditions in America. Typically at the larger festivals, associations from many cities assembled in a host location. The festivals often lasted several days and much of the music they performed was of German or European origin. In New York, on July 4, 1870, the New York Turnverein, 10,000 strong, under Conrad Kuhn, president, met at Jones' Woods with other German singing societies. The festival consisted of gymnastics, dancing, singing, target shooting and the flying of American and German flags. An 1876 celebration at Jones' Woods included a fifty-piece orchestra, directed by Reinhold Schmeiz, that played mostly German works but ended with the "Star Spangled Banner."

On July 4, 1891, in Newark, New Jersey, a grand Sängerfest of the Northeastern Sängerbund took place in Caledonian Park with 147 societies, representing Baltimore, New York, Philadelphia, and Trenton, New Jersey, among others. The performances scheduled were numerous and took place in a "vast auditorium." A combined choir of 5,000 Sängerbunders was expected to sing the "Star-Spangled Banner," assisted by an orchestra of 200 instruments. Each society had its own "tent headquarters" which freely "dispensed hospitality" in the form of "foaming lager beer." There were also restaurants and food booths set up on the grounds. Just prior to the opening concert, Carl Lentz of the Northeastern Sängerbund and a veteran Union soldier gave a speech, following by another from Gov. Leon Abbett. Two concerts took place that day and included works by Beethoven, Gounod,

Strauss, and others. Works reminiscent of Independence Day included C. Attenhofer's *Freedom of Nations* and Max Spicker's *American Fantasy*.

It was not uncommon for works composed specifically for the Fourth of July to appear on these programs. In Chicago on July 4, 1876, a "Hymn to Liberty," by Emil Dietzsch, was premiered by a grand chorus of the German singing societies of that city.

Sources: *Readinger Adler*, 9 July 1805 and 1 July 1806; *York Gazette*, 12 July 1831; "The Fourth of July," *Charleston Courier*, 6 July 1848, 2; *Daily Missouri Republican*, 3 July 1852; *Pittsburgh Commercial*, 3 July 1869, 2 and 4; "The Day Among the Germans," *New York Times*, 5 July 1870, 8; "The Germans," *Chicago Tribune*, 5 July 1876, 3; "Centennial Saenger Verband," *New York Times*, 5 July 1876, 7; *Daily Ohio State Journal*, 5 July 1889, 5; "Patriotism and Music," *New York Times*, 5 July 1891, 2; William F. Whyte, "Chronicles of Early Watertown," *Wisconsin Magazine of History* 4 (1920–21): 289–90; R. Ronald Reedy, *Celebration in Lititz Pennsylvania: The 175th Anniversary History of Independence Day Observances with a Narrative of the Lititz Springs Park, 1818–1992* (Lititz, Pa.: 175th Lititz Fourth-of-July Anniversary Celebration General Committee, 1992).

German Singing Society Hall, Union Hill, New Jersey

The cornerstone of this building in Hudson County was laid on July 4, 1890. Located at New York Avenue and Lewis Street, the proposal for the building was brick, three stories high, at a cost of $50,000.

Source: "New Jersey," *New York Times*, 5 July 1890, 3.

Gerry, Elbridge (1744–1814)

Vice president of the U.S. (1813–14) under President James Madison and the only signer of the Declaration of Independence buried in Washington, D.C. Gerry's grave located in Congressional Cemetery is visited regularly on the Fourth by admirers. On Independence Day in 1962, for example, over 200 persons gathered at the site. On July 4, 1876, at Meacham's Grove, Dupage County, Illinois, "Miss Ada Gerry, a descendant" of Elbridge publicly read the Declaration of Independence. Gerry was born in Marblehead, Massachusetts, and was a member of the Continental Congress, 1776–80 and 1783–85.

Sources: "Meacham," *Chicago Tribune*, 6 July

1876, 8; *Washington Post*, 5 July 1962, B1; George Billias, *Elbridge Gerry, Founding Father and Republican Statesman* (New York: McGraw-Hill, 1976).

Gettysburg National Cemetery, Pennsylvania

Dedicated on November 19, 1863, when President Lincoln gave his timeless Gettysburg Address, Gettysburg is the site of the deadliest single battle of the Civil War, with over 51,000 soldiers killed or wounded. The battle took place July 1–3, 1863, with the Union Army of the Potomac forcing Gen. Robert E. Lee's Army of Northern Virginia to retreat on July 4. The battle was a significant turning point of the war. On February 11, 1895, Gettysburg National Military Park was established to preserve and memorialize the armies that fought there. Through the years over 1,400 monuments were dedicated on the site, many on the Fourth of July. **Battle reenactments** of those three fateful days were popular beginning in the early 1900s and served to educate the generations that followed on the significance of what happened there.

On the first anniversary of the battle, four to five thousand persons were there. A procession included discharged soldiers from various Pennsylvania Reserves, faculty and students of the "Pennsylvania College, other military units and local citizens. Music was provided by the Chambersburg Brass Band. The ceremony was held on Culp's Hill. The Rev. John R. Warner presented an oration in which he described the "great battle of one year ago." The Declaration of Independence was read by Charles R. Horner of Gettysburg.

National Soldier's Monument in the Soldiers' National Cemetery at Gettysburg, Pennsylvania. The cornerstone was laid on July 4, 1865. The monument was carved by noted sculptor Randolph Rogers. Shown here are the marble figures of Plenty and History, two of four depictions representing history, war, peace, and plenty. Photograph by Terry Heintze.

On July 4, 1865, the cornerstone ceremony for the National Soldier's Monument took place and included a civic and military procession, an oration by Gen. Oliver O. Howard and a poem by Col. Charles G. Halpine. Music was provided by the Ninth Veteran Reserve Corps Band "and proved a most acceptable and popular feature of the occasion." The Baltimore Musical Association sang "French's Hymn," composed by **Benjamin Brown French**. President Andrew Johnson could not attend because of illness. Members of the Grand Lodge of Masons of Pennsylvania laid the cornerstone, which contained documents from each state and a number of coins.

In the years that followed the Civil War,

Monument of the 54th Regiment, New York Infantry, Gettysburg National Historical Military Park, dedicated on July 4, 1890, is located on Wainwright Avenue, East Cemetery Hill. This rear image shows the plaque that describes the regiment's battle and casualties. Listed also are other Civil War battles in which the New York troops fought. Photograph by Terry Heintze.

the Gettysburg battle fields were visited annually by veterans of the war and those who fought there. For example, on July 4, 1886, 100 carloads of excursionists arrived for a ceremony there with Chaplain J.W. Sayres, who preached a sermon. In the evening there was a dress parade "reviewed by Gen. Sickles and the officers of Battery C, third United States Artillery." Also present was the Grand Army of the Republic Cavalry Post of Philadelphia. The dedication of other monuments and other ceremonies typically took place on the third through the fifth of July.

SELECTED FOURTH OF JULY
DEDICATIONS, CORNERSTONE
CEREMONIES, AND REENACTMENTS

July 5, 1886: The Philadelphia Corn Exchange Regiment dedicated a 3½-foot-high granite tablet at the first position of the regiment and the spot where Capt. Richard W. Davis fell. Joseph Tomas, surgeon of the regiment, delivered an oration and William Brice of Philadelphia gave an address. The tablet was presented to the Battlefield Memorial Association by S. Crossley, president of the Survivors' Association.

July 4, 1890: The Fifty-Fourth Regiment New-York Volunteers unveiled a monument to their comrades, particularly the color bearer, who was shot defending the flag from an attack by the Louisiana Tigers. Capt. F. J. Werneck made an address that delivered the monument to the Gettysburg Association and the Hon. Calvin Hamilton, president of the association, accepted it. George F. Roesch delivered an oration and Charles G.F. Wahle, Jr., gave an address.

July 4, 1890: A monument, a bronze figure set on a low granite tower, was dedicated to the 54th New York Infantry Regiment.

July 4, 1891: The Seventy-Second Regiment Pennsylvania Volunteers from Philadelphia dedicated a bronze monument.

July 4, 1897: A monument to the First Minnesota Infantry regiment was dedicated.

July 4, 1914: Veterans of the battle of Gettysburg met.

July 4, 1938: The 12th Infantry of the

U.S. Army rededicates Round Top on the 75th anniversary of the battle.

July 4, 1922: A reenactment of Pickett's Charge took place by the Fourth Brigade of the U.S. Marines using modern armaments.

The battle reenactment on July 4, 1922, was an unusual event. Two reenactments of the same battle served as a comparison of 1863 and 1922 armaments. Many of the portrayers were troops who had served in World War I. "The battle opened at the exact time of Longstreet's assault made in 1863, by the Tenth Marine Artillery which boomed forth from Seminary Ridge an attack on the Union Heights on Cemetery Ridge." Muskets and period artillery were used. On the following day the Marines again enacted the battle, this time "using tanks, airplanes, balloons, trench mortars, and many other modern devices."

Sources: "Gettysburg," *Philadelphia Inquirer*, 5 July 1864, 8; "Gettysburgh," *New York Times*, 6 July 1865, 8; *New York Times*, 5–6 July 1886, 1 and 1 respectively, 5 July 1891, 8, and 4–5 July 1922, 4 and 7, respectively; "Their Comrades Remembered," *New York Times*, 5 July 1890, 1; A.H. Opsahl, *1st Minn Monu[ment] Dedication* (Minnesota, 1897); *Washington Evening Star*, 5 July 1913, part 1:5; Gettysburg National Military Park Web site, <http://www.nps.gov/gett/>.

Giant Buckeroo Street Parade, Molalla, Oregon

Site for the annual Giant Buckeroo Street Parade. On July 4, 1990, Senator Bob Packwood (R.— Ore.) and others were there wearing yellow ribbons as a demonstration of their support for the timber industry's need to cut down trees versus those who supported the preservation of spotted owls who needed the trees for habitation.

Source: *The Oregonian*, 5 July 1990, B2.

Gilles, Peter, Sr. (fl. 1817)

Teacher and composer, who wrote *President Monroe's March*, which was performed in New York in honor of the president on July 4, 1817. The work had earlier been "dedicated and presented to the president on his late visit to this city, and accepted by his excellency as his adopted march." For the Independence Day performance, Gilles had arranged the work "with accompaniments for a completely full Military Band, in the style of the imperial music of France." Gilles came to America around 1815 and settled in New York. He played oboe and English horn in concerts there. His march was likely published in 1817, and re-issued that same year with slightly different imprint data.

Sources: *New-York Evening Post*, 2 July 1817; Wolfe, *Secular Music in America*, 1:314–15.

Gilman, Samuel Foster (1791–1858)

Clergyman and writer who wrote a "Union Ode" composed for the Union Party of South Carolina and sung on July 4, 1831, to the tune of "Scots wha has wi' Wallace bled." Gilman was born in Gloucester, Massachusetts. When his father died, young Samuel came under the care of Stephen Peabody, a Congregational clergyman who prepared him for studies at Harvard College where he graduated in 1811. For the next few years he engaged in various pursuits, taught at Harvard, worked in a bank, and wrote articles for the *North American Review*. In 1819 he married another writer, Caroline Howard, and moved to Charleston, South Carolina, where he served as minister to the Second Independent Church, a Unitarian congregation. For the next forty years, Gilman "sought to re-create something like the moral and cultural leadership that Unitarian clergy practiced in his New England home." During that time he published a number of writings that included poetry and literary pieces, including "Fair Harvard," a poem written in 1836 at Harvard's bicentennial (and now the university alma mater), *Memoirs of a New England Village Choir* (1829), and an ode performed in 1850 at the funeral of **John C. Calhoun**. According to Daniel Howe, Samuel and Caroline Gilman "were respected as the leading literary lights of Charleston."

Gilman's "Union Ode" was composed in response to the nullification controversy regarding the imposition of tariffs by the federal government. The work was reprinted thirty-three years later during the Civil War by *Harper's Weekly* as an example of a South Carolinian whose leanings favored the Union.

Hail, our Country's natal morn,
Hail, our spreading kindred-born,

Hail, thou banner, not yet torn,
Waving o'er the free!
While this day in festal throng
Millions swell the Patriot song,
Shall not we thy notes prolong,
Hallowed Jubilee?
Who would sever Freedom's shrine?
Who would draw the hateful line?
Though by birth one spot be mine,
Dear is all the rest.
Dear to me the South's fair land;
Dear the Central mountain-land;
Dear New England's rocky strand;
Dear the prairied West.
By our altars, pure and free;
By our laws' deep-rooted tree;
By the Past's dread memory;
By our Washington;
By our common kindred tongue,
By our hopes — bright, buoyant, young;
By the tie of country strong,
We will still be one!
Fathers! — have ye bled in vain?
Ages! — must ye droop again?
Maker! — shall we rashly stain
Blessings sent by thee?
No! Receive our solemn vow,
While before thy throne we bow,
Ever to maintain, as now,
Union, Liberty!

Sources: "A South Carolina Ode for the Fourth of July," *Harper's Weekly*, 9 July 1864; Daniel Walker Howe, "Samuel Foster Gilman," in *American National Biography* 9:63–64.

Girard College for Orphans, Philadelphia

The cornerstone of this school for "poor male white orphan children" and named after Stephen Girard, merchant and mariner of Philadelphia, was laid on July 4, 1833. The mission of this undertaking was to the "cause of education, morals, and the country." The college was located on a tract of forty-five acres, situated on the "Ridge Road." Girard purchased the land from William Parker for the purpose of establishing the school. The ceremony included an address by Nicholas Biddle, chairman of the trustees of the college, who said,

It is not unreasonable to conjecture that in all future times, there will probably be in existence many thousand men who will owe to Girard the greatest of all blessings, a virtuous education; men who will have been rescued from

want, and perhaps from vice, and armed with power to rise to wealth and distinction. Among them will be found some of the best educated citizens, accomplished scholars, intelligent mechanics, distinguished artists, and the most prominent statesmen.

Source: *National Intelligencer*, 10 July 1833, 2.

"Glorious Fourth"

One of the most frequently used phrases throughout the history of the Fourth of July in celebrations to honor and herald the day. The first recorded use of "Glorious Fourth" was on July 4, 1777, in Philadelphia among a large number of celebrants at a dinner, and news about the "glorious Fourth" there was reprinted in Williamsburg. "The glorious Fourth of July was reiterated three times accompanied with triple discharges of cannon and small arms, and loud huzzas that resounded from street to street through the city," so reported the newspaper. The "glorious fourth" was set in perpetuity. The phrase has been used in orations and speeches, in song and book titles, in poetry and newspaper reports, and wherever the holiday has been celebrated. On July 5, 1870, the leading headline for news of the holiday was titled "The Glorious Fourth." On July 2, 1905, a poem titled "Glorious Fourth" by Nixon Waterman was published in the *Washington Sunday Star*.

Source: *Virginia Gazette*, 18 July 1777.

"Goddess of Liberty"

A mythical and significant Revolutionary War and Fourth of July icon that symbolizes the American freedoms that reign triumphant over the broken symbols of despotism. The Goddess of Liberty, sometimes referred to as "Lady Liberty," was depicted in parades, orations, toasts, and pyrotechnical displays and frequently provided opportunities for women to participate directly in Independence Day ceremonies.

On July 4, 1852, the Goddess of Liberty was represented in an epic "National Tableau" billed as the "largest pyrotechnical structure ever fired in the United States," in Boston. A Goddess of Liberty was decorated with thirty-one stars, elaborate scrolls and "Liberty" spelled out. Columns and urns bore the names of heroes and battles from the American Revolution. Emerging from each column were "immense jets of flame," and 500 rockets provided a grand finale. On July 4, 1855, in New Haven, Connecticut, as part of a parade of hundreds of girls and boys, a young lady portrayed the Goddess of Liberty "riding in a fanciful chariot, drawn by a Shetland pony." On the Fourth in 1868, a parade in Newark, New Jersey, featured a "wagon drawn by eight horses, containing [the] Goddess of Liberty, surrounded by thirteen young ladies, representing the original Federal Union." On July 4, 1890, the Goddess of Liberty was portrayed by Miss Blanche Bennett at the ceremony in Ocean Grove, New Jersey.

Sources: "Independence Day," *Liberator*, 2 July 1851, 106; "In New-Haven," *New York Times*, 7 July 1855, 3; "Newark," *New York Times*, 5 July 1868, 8, and 5 July 1890, 2; Branham and Hartnett, *Sweet Freedom's Song*, 98–99.

Gomes, (Antônio) Carlos (1836–1896)

Brazilian composer who wrote a musical tribute to the United States on the occasion of the American Centennial. The title page reads: "To the American people. Hymn for the first Centennial of the American Independence, celebrated at Philadelphia. Composed by command of his Majesty, Dom Pedro II, emperor of the Brazil, by A. Carlos Gomes." The work was performed at Independence Square by Gilmore's Orchestra.

Gomes began composing early in his life and studied at the Imperial Conservatory of Music in Rio de Janeiro. His predilection for opera led him to study in Italy where he wrote several successful operas and lived for most of his life. Gomes was in Milan at the time he composed *Hymn for the Centennial*.

Sources: "Home and Foreign Gossip," *Harper's Weekly*, 15 July 1876; "City of the Declaration," *New York Times*, 5 July 1876, 3; Gerard Béhague, "Carlos Gomes," *New Grove Dictionary of Music* (New York: Groves Dictionaries, Inc., 2000).

Goodwin, William (1790 or 1791–1872)

Wrote the "patriotic song" "Union Forever! & the Birth-day of Freedom! Or, the Fourth of July." This poem appeared on an "advertisement for his business of tracing American heirs of unclaimed estates in Great Britain." On the song sheet is written: "A patriotic song written as an expression of respect and good will for his adopted country."

Source: Broadside (New Haven, Conn.: W. Goodwin, 18 — —).

Gordon, William (1728–1807)

This author and clergyman is credited with giving the first sermon on Independence Day, on July 4, 1777, "preached before the General Court," under the title "The Separation of the Jewish Tribes, After the Death of Solomon." After the sermon, based on I Kings 12:15, the Massachusetts House of Representatives enacted legislation that "Mr. Greenleaf and Col. Porter, with such as the honorable Board may join," delivered to Gordon "the thanks of the General Assembly."

Gordon was born at Hitchin, Hertfordshire, England, was trained as a clergyman and began his ministry in 1752 in an Independent Church in Ipswich. He sympathized with the movement for American independence and left England for America in 1770. In 1772, he was ordained the pastor of the Third Congregational Church in Roxbury, Massachusetts. In part due to his ardent support for independence he was made chaplain of the Provincial Congress. He later took on the task of writing a history of the Revolution (*The History of the Rise, Progress, and Establishment of the Independence of the United States of America*, 1788). According to Howard H. Martin, "Gordon's sermon compared the separation of the Jewish tribes after the death of Solomon to the American revolt in order to show how the Bible had been used in the past to instruct in civil liberty." His 1777 Fourth of July sermon was also published and widely circulated.

Sources: *Boston Gazette*, 7 July 1777; Martin, "Orations on the Anniversary of American Independence, 1777–1876," 19–20; "William Gordon," *Dictionary of American Biography* (New York: Charles Scribner's Sons, 1931), 7:426.

Gould, Hannah Flagg (1789–1865)

Composed "Columbia's Birth-day: An Ode for the Fourth of July," in *Poems* (Boston: Hilliard, Gray, 1839), 3 vols.

(First stanza)
We hail Columbia's Natal Day,
And see its glories shine,
To light the votive gifts we lay
At Freedom's holy shrine!

Hannah Gould was cited by one of her contemporaries as "one of the most popular of our poets. Short as her pieces are, their grace, fancy, and sprightliness have rendered them familiar to the lovers of piquant varieties in the poetical banquet, and endeared her name as that of a lively household friend, whose delicate wit and benevolent cheerfulness can enliven dullness or despondency."

Source: "The Female Poets of America," *North American Review* 68/143 (April 1849): 422.

Gow, John L. (1797–1866)

Attorney, educator, and amateur musician who wrote the song "The Birth-Day of Freedom," a four-stanza poem which was first sung on July 4, 1823, in Alexandria, Virginia, at a dinner for a large party of individuals who had returned from a ceremony held at Mount Vernon. Born in Hallowell, Maine, Gow studied law in Fredericksburg, Virginia, and later moved to Washington, D.C., where he was assistant editor of the *National Journal*. In 1824 Gow moved to Washington, Pennsylvania, where he worked diligently, furthering the cause of education. "In 1831 Mr. Gow was appointed visitor and examiner to West Point by President Jackson, and again in 1849 by President Tyler."

In attendance at the celebration of the Fourth were Vice President Daniel D. Tompkins, Col. Archibald Henderson, director of the U.S. Marine Band, and Commodore John Rodgers.

(First stanza)
Shall the genius that dawn'd upon tyranny's
    night,
And now swells to the blaze of meridian glory;
Shall the luster of arms, in the perilous fight,
And the heroes, whose names are recorded in
    story—
Shall the victor's renown
And the patriot's crown,
By his country bestow'd, to oblivion go down?
No! the birth-day of Freedom awakens the
    song
Of her sons who to ages her fame shall prolong.

Sources: *National Intelligence*, 8 July 1823, 3; J.H. Beers and Co., *Commemorative Biographical Record of Washington County, Pennsylvania* (Chicago: J. H. Beers and Co., 1893), 36.

Graf Zeppelin

A German airship that was used on July 4, 1930, for an Independence Day celebration by forty-four Americans "and persons connected to American enterprises." The cruise left from Friedrichshafen and lasted about one hour.

Source: "Americans in Germany Honor U.S. Anniversary," *Washington Evening Star*, 4 July 1930, A2.

"Grand Federal Procession," Philadelphia

Popular name for the largest and most spectacular parade in the eighteenth century, which took place on July 4, 1788. The event was planned by Francis Hopkinson, signer of the Declaration of Independence, poet, and musician who was an ardent support of the Constitution. The parade signified the successful ratification of the Constitution by ten states, encouraged the remaining three to join the others, and assured the future of a government established for and by the people. The mile-long parade made up primarily of the working classes and militia of Philadelphia, accompanied by an assemblage of dignitaries, was a precursor of the type of parades that would be common in many cities and towns beginning in the early nineteenth century.

The day began with the ringing of bells of Christ Church and an artillery salute from the vessel *Rising Sun* in the harbor. Other ships were dressed up for the occasion. The parade had 87 divisions made up of 5000 costumed individuals representing every trade imaginable. No less than 17,000 spectators were on Union Green to view the event. The procession began with twelve "axe men dressed in white frocks" followed by various individuals representing the declaring of independence and the stages of the war. An "ornamented car in the form of a large eagle" representing the Constitution was pulled by six horses. Ten individuals representing the ten states that ratified the Constitution marched as a group. A 36-foot-high building with 13 Corinthian columns depicting the strength of the Union was drawn along the streets by 10 white horses. Another float drawn by four horses was a 9-foot-square stage with a fully operating printing press issuing copies of the ode "Oh for a muse of fire!" composed for the occasion by Hopkinson. Proceeding along was a band of musicians performing "a grand March" composed for this particular Fourth by the noted Philadelphia composer Alexander Reinagle. The carvers and gilders displayed an ornamented car complete with 13 ornamented pilasters and a ten-foot-high center column with "a bust of General Washington, crowned with a wreath of laurel and dressed in the American uniform." Many of the tradesmen carried colorful banners emblazoned with mottos such as "May our Country never want Bread" (the Bread and Biscuit Bakers) and "Venerate the Plough" (the Agricultural Society). Following the parade an oration was given by James Wilson, followed by a dinner complemented by ten toasts.

See also **Colleges and universities**, **John Nixon**, *Union*.

Sources: "Grand Federal Procession," *Pennsylvania Gazette*, 9 July 1788; "Observations on the Federal Procession ... ," *American Museum* 4 (July 1788): 75; Appelbaum, *The Glorious Fourth*, 29–30; Travers, *Celebrating the Fourth*, 70–88.

"Grand National Jubilee"

The theme for a concert presented on July 4, 1822, at Chatham Garden in New York City. Among the many works performed was a "Grand Symphony" by Haydn and a song, "'Huzza! Here's Columbia for ever,' composed by [A.] Clifton, of Baltimore."

Source: *New York-Advertiser*, 6 July 1822, 3.

Grandstands and platforms

These structures were commonly built in preparation for Fourth of July celebrations during the nineteenth and twentieth centuries to accommodate large crowds, but due to either poor or hasty construction many of them collapsed. On July 4, 1840, in Portsmouth, New Hampshire, at a "Friends of the Administration" celebration, a large pavilion erected in the form of an amphitheatre collapsed, throwing nearly a thousand persons to the

ground. There were broken bones, but no one was killed. In Georgetown on July 4, 1842, at the military companies' celebration held at Parrott's Woods, immediately after Congressman Joseph R. Underwood from Kentucky delivered his oration, the speaker's platform collapsed throwing Underwood, District of Columbia mayor William W. Seaton, **George Washington Parke Custis** "and several other gentlemen" to the ground. "Fortunately, no lives were lost, no limbs broken," although one person suffered a bloody nose.

A number of Independence Day grandstand collapses occurred in circuses, including one in Rochester, New York, in 1852, at a performance of the Raymond and Co.'s Circus and Menagerie, when hundreds of persons were asked to leave the show due to the seats collapsing, which caused several injuries. In the following year in Columbus, Ohio, during a performance of a circus there, forty seats "gave way" injuring three persons.

On July 4, 1855, in Taunton, Massachusetts, after a day's celebration of speech making, music, and march steps, just prior to the fireworks display, a whole range of seats in the grandstand collapsed, spilling some 800 persons to the ground. Injuries and deaths were reported. On July 4, 1888, residents of Water Valley, Mississippi, experienced a frightful day when fifty people were injured when a building over a grandstand collapsed.

On July 4, 1908, in New Bedford, Massachusetts, one of the largest disasters of its kind occurred when 1,500 persons fell to the ground as the bleachers on the "local ball grounds of the New England league" gave way. About 200 persons were injured. On Independence Day in 1926, near Chatham, New Jersey, on the banks of the Passaic River, a grandstand collapsed throwing people off, as a pageant depicting colonial life and the birth of a new nation was being presented. On July 4, 1947, in Wildwood, New Jersey, a section of the boardwalk collapsed, injuring forty. On July 4, 1967, in Atlanta, Georgia, moments after a policeman warned spectators to get off a scaffold at a "Salute to America" parade, the structure collapsed, throwing 30 persons eight feet to the ground. Twenty-five persons were injured although not seriously. "Some kids started jumping up and down on it when the parade started and it caved in," said a spectator.

Sources: *Baltimore Sun*, 9 July 1840, 2; *National Intelligencer*, 6 July 1842, 3; *Rochester Daily Advertiser*, 7 July 1852, 3; "Accident at a Circus," *New York Times*, 9 July 1853, 8; "In Taunton," *Boston Daily Journal*, 5 July 1855, 1–2; "Fifty Persons Injured," *New York Times*, 6 July 1888, 1; "Two Hundred Injured," *Chattanooga Sunday Times*, 5 July 1908, 1; *New York Times*, 6 July 1926, 5, 5 July 1947, 1, and 5 July 1967, 33.

Grant, Ulysses Simpson (1822–1885)

Eighteenth president of the U.S. (1869–77) and soldier who was honored numerous times in Independence Day celebrations for his gallantry and heroisms. Grant was born in Point Pleasant, Ohio, and graduated from the U.S. Military Academy in 1843. He served under Zachary Taylor and Winfield Scott during the war with Mexico (1845–48) and received accolades for his actions at Chapultepec. He later tried his hand at a number of ventures, including farming, real estate, and business, but at the onset of the Civil War was commissioned with the Illinois Volunteer Infantry. He was instrumental in the winning of several battles, most notably Shiloh (April 1862) and the Battle of Chattanooga (November 1863). Grant's capture of Vicksburg on July 4, 1863, was an important turning point in the war and provided confidence to Lincoln that an end of the conflict was possible. In 1866, Grant received a commission as full general, served as secretary of war for a brief period, and was elected president on a Republican ticket. Although his administration was plagued with some serious scandals, forcing resignations of some cabinet members, as well as public reaction regarding the financial panic of 1873, Grant was revered and hailed annually as a popular figure in events on Independence Day.

On July 4, 1870, Grant was in Hartford, Connecticut, and spent the morning traveling by train to Woodstock, stopping at a number of towns along the way to receive cheering crowds and generally enjoying the day. In Plainfield he addressed an audience following a speech given in his honor. At Woodstock he joined other dignitaries on a platform and listened to an array of addresses, after which he assisted in the planting of an elm tree, near the Elwood Hall Female Seminary.

In 1876 President Grant participated in opening and closing ceremonies, May 10 and November 10, respectively, of the **Centennial Exhibition** in Philadelphia, but was in the White House on July 4 receiving tributes on the **Centennial** from around the world.

On July 5, 1880, Grant received a hero's welcome in Emporia, Kansas. Fifteen thousand people were present to see the general pass under an "immense arch of evergreens, bearing a banner with the words, 'Welcome to Grant,' across Commercial Street." The town was beautifully decorated with flags, bunting, and "an immense car filled with school-children attracted the General's attention." At the Grove, Grant gave a very brief address.

After his death, it was common for individuals to assemble at Grant's tomb at Riverside Park in New York on the Fourth of July for ceremonies. On July 4, 1914, for example, 5,000 persons "gathered for a band and choral concert and patriotic addresses. From the front of the Tomb to the south end of the plaza in Riverside Park red, white, and blue electric lights were stretched." Henry Clews, the principal speaker, paid tributes to Lincoln, Grant, Sherman, and Sheridan, "all of whom were friends of his." Borough president Marcus M. Marks spoke on "Our Flag," and Judge John Jerome Rooney provided "a historical survey of the battle of the Revolution fought in and around New York."

Sources: *New York Times*, 4 and 5 July 1870, 1 and 8, respectively; "Gen. Grant in Kansas," *New York Times*, 6 July 1880, 1; "Brilliant at Grant's Tomb," *New York Times*, 5 July 1914, 3.

Gray's Gardens, Philadelphia

A popular location during the 1790s for celebrating the Fourth of July. The Gardens provided food and entertainment in a "banqueting house built of stone" with a "spacious hall." Other features included gravel walkways that led through flurries of exotic plants, flowers, and rows of fruit trees, a summer house where transparencies were displayed, a greenhouse and the "Grove." Tuesday and Saturday evening the gardens were illuminated with about 2500 lamps. "The lamps, among the trees, are so artfully disposed, as to render a discovery by what means they are suspended impossible, and we are almost ready to conclude the whole the effect of magick." Entertainment included concerts, dinners, displays of paintings and **transparencies**. On July 5, 1790, an ode, "Amidst the Joys of This Auspicious Day," was sung:

> Amidst the joys of this auspicious day,
> Our allied Gallia claims a grateful lay.
> Gallia great and good,
> By her treasure and blood,
> Columbia's friend in fiery trial stood.
> Gallia great and good, &c.
> Her valiant sons travers'd the main,
> For freedom fought, nor fought in vain.
> And now the firm intrepid band
> For freedom combat in their native land.
> Propitious heaven our prayer grant!
> May virtuous Gallia never want
> A blessing in true freedom's ample store.
> May Gallia's and Columbia's hands
> Be join'd by freedom's sacred bands,
> Till time shall be no more.

On July 4, 1791, a concert of vocal and instrumental music was provided, beginning at 6 A.M. and concluding at 10 P.M. A miniature ship *Union* was "dressed with the colours of the different nations in alliance with the United States and elegantly lighted at night. Three tables, with 100 covers each, furnished with roast beef, rounds, hams, &c. &c. ready to cut-and-come-again, from morning until night."

On July 4, 1792, guests were treated to a variety of food such as "roast beef, rounds, hams, tongues, &c. &c. from morning until night." A liquor bar was available, with wine "kept in reservoirs of water and ice." Deserts were available, including "iced creams of a great variety, fine cakes, &c."

Sources: *Universal Asylum and Columbia Magazine* 5/1 (July 1790): 57; "Gray's Gardens," *Massachusetts Magazine* 3/7 (July 1791): 413–17; *Pennsylvania Gazette*, 29 June 1791, and 4 July 1792.

Grow, Galusha A. (1823–1907)

U.S. congressman from Pennsylvania who in 1861 was the only person ever to be elected as U.S. Speaker of the House of Representatives on the Fourth of July. Grow was born in Ashford, Connecticut, but spent considerable childhood years at Glenwood, Pennsylvania. He graduated from Amherst in 1844, was elected to Congress as its youngest member in 1850 and served until 1863. In the early 1870s Grow lived in Texas in order to fulfill responsibilities as president of the Houston and Great Northern Railway. In 1894 he was again elected to Congress and served until 1903. Grow was best known for authorship of the Homestead Act of 1862 which opened Western lands to free settlement and as a strong supporter of the Union during the Civil War.

Grow faced two opponents for the election as Speaker: Frank P. Blair and John J. Crittenden. Grow was elected Speaker after multiple ballots, shortly after he gave a speech that included a tribute to the signers of the Declaration of Independence followed by a plea to his constituents that the nation be preserved even though several states had seceded from the Union. "Not one foot of American soil can ever be wrenched from the jurisdiction of the Constitution of the United States until it is baptized in fire and blood," he said. Grow received tremendous applause from the floor and public galleries.

On July 4, 1877, Grow spoke at the Susquehanna County (Pa.) soldiers' monument dedication ceremony in Montrose, Pennsylvania. On July 4, 1894, he addressed a crowd at the celebration at Roseland Park, in Woodstock, Connecticut. See also **Soldiers Monument, Montrose, Pennsylvania**.

Sources: *National Reporter*, 6 July 1861, 2; "The Celebration at Woodstock," *New York Times*, 5 July 1894, 8.

Guilford Courthouse National Military Park, North Carolina

A significant Revolutionary War battle that took place at Guilford Courthouse (now Martinsville) in North Carolina on March 15, 1781, when Continental forces under the command of Generals Daniel Morgan and Nathanael Greene inflicted heavy casualties on British troops, forcing British Gen. Charles

Cornwallis to retreat to Wilmington to receive reinforcements by sea.

Through the years numerous Fourth of July celebrations and ceremonies at the site have taken place. The first significant celebration occurred there on July 4, 1891, when Kemp P. Battle, professor of history at the University of North Carolina, presented an address. On Independence Day in the following year Walter Clark, associate justice of the Supreme Court of North Carolina, spoke about Col. William R. Davie, a participant in the Guilford battle.

On July 4, 1893, thousands of spectators assembled on the battlefield to witness the dedication of the monument to the North Carolina troops under Major Joseph Winston, erected by Gov. Thomas M. Holt. One of the grandest celebrations to take place there, the event included a parade, music by the Lexington Silver Cornet Band, a poem by Henry J. Stockard, and numerous speeches, the most eloquent speech one given by George T. Winston, president of the University of North Carolina. "There are moments in human history when time pauses in her flight and hovers doubtful which way to turn, until human courage and human genius direct her course," he said. "Such a moment was the battle of Guilford."

On July 4, 1894, a ceremony of commemoration for that battle took place and Vice President Adlai E. Stevenson (under Grover Cleveland) presented a speech. On July 4, 1901, a "Colonial Column" and monument to Captain James Morehead (1750–1815) was unveiled. Addresses were given by Charles B. Aycock (1859–1912) and R.F. Beasley. On July 4, 1904, a monument to the memory of Judge David Schenck (1835–1902) was unveiled. James E. Shepard (1847–1910) gave an address on the occasion. On July 4, 1906, a monument to Gen. Francis Nash (1720–1777) was unveiled. An address by Alfred Moore Waddell (1834–1912) was presented at the ceremony. On July 4, 1931, the sesquicentennial celebration of that battle was observed.

Sources: *A Memorial Volume of the Guilford Battle Ground Company* (Greensboro, N.C.: Reece and Elam, 1893); *Rocky Mountain News* (Denver), 5 July 1894; "Mr. Stevenson in North Carolina," *Washington Evening Star*, 4 July 1894, 1; *Addresses of Hon. Chas. B. Aycock and R.F. Beasley* ... (Greensboro, N.C., 1901); *An Address by Hon. James E. Shepard on the Life and Character of the Late Judge David Schenck* (Greensboro: Guilford Battle Ground Co., 1904); *Gen Francis Nash: An Address by A. M. Waddell* ... (Greensboro, N.C.: Guilford Battle Ground Co., 1906); *Washington Post*, 5 July 1931, M3.

Gwinnett Justice and Administration Center, Atlanta, Georgia

On July 4, 1990, a time capsule was placed there to be opened on July 4, 2040. Organizers chose a varied selection of items that were placed in the stainless steel box, including histories of cities, newsletters, newspaper articles, a bumper sticker, a Boy Scouts of America handbook, and a videotape.

Source: Larry Hartstein, "Gwinnett History," *Atlanta Constitution*, 9 August, 1998, 03JJ.

Hagerstown Daily News

This Maryland newspaper began publishing on July 4, 1879, and ceased December 19, 1887. It was published daily, except Sunday.

Haggenmacher, J.H.

Composed "The 4th of July. Grand Chorus," written "expressly for the celebration of that day; for voice and piano." First line: "Exalted day! Exalted day! We greet with music thy return" (New York: Firth & Hall, n.d.)

"Hail Columbia"

Popular national song sung frequently on the Fourth of July that was published in May 1798 by Joseph Hopkinson (son of Francis Hopkinson) and competed with "The Star-Spangled Banner" for the place of national anthem during the nineteenth century. Hopkinson wrote the words to be sung to the popular tune of "The President's March" (Philadelphia: B. Carr, 1793) by Philip Phile (d. 1793), who may have composed it after George Washington's inaugural as president in 1789.

From the time of its first publication, "Hail! Columbia" was printed in numerous editions, some for voice and piano, others for a combination of instruments. It is difficult to know exactly what musical arrangements and editions might have been used for its numerous performances on the Fourth of July. Many of the renditions, however, are found in Richard Wolfe's compilation cited below. Although most of these arrangements were published in major cities, such as New York, Philadelphia, and Baltimore, it was not long before the song was sung in many other large and small cities across the nation. Frequently when "The President's March" was performed as an instrumental, it was done so under the alternate title of "Hail! Columbia."

The first likely vocal performance of "Hail! Columbia" on Independence Day occurred in 1798, by a "Mr. Williamson," at the Ranelagh Garden in New York City. Little is known about Williamson other than his popularity as a vocalist and that he performed at least one other patriotic song in that city, "The Federal Constitution & Liberty Forever" (1798). On July 4, 1801, the "President's March" was performed at the **White House** by the **United States Marine Band** under the command of William Farr, and "Hail Columbia! Happy Land" was sung by Captain Thomas Tingey, commandant of the Washington Navy Yard that same day at a dinner celebration attended by the "heads of departments" and civil and military officials.

That the tune enjoyed immense popularity is supported by the frequency of times the melody was set to new lyrics. For example, the words for the White House performance in 1801 were written by Thomas Law. But only a few years later on July 4, 1807, at Stelle's Hotel in Washington City, a "Mr. Cutting" sung "Columbia, Hail," which a local newspaper reported had originally been sung "by a party of Americans" at a Fourth of July celebration in London. On July 4, 1811, also in Washington, a new version of "Hail Columbia" appeared, this one billed as "an original song" by J.J. Moore. For the Fourth of July in Worcester, Massachusetts, in 1817, Edward D. Bangs wrote an ode that was set to the tune.

By the 1820s, "Hail! Columbia" had become a standard tune performed on Independence Day in celebrations across the nation. On July 4, 1827, it was played in Frederick, Maryland, by the Frederick Blues Band as they marched in the parade along Market and Patrick streets. On July 4, 1831, the tune was played in both Charleston, South Carolina, and Richmond, Virginia. In 1851 Dodworth's Band played the tune at the Tammany Hall Fourth of July celebration in New York. By the 1850s the increasing popularity of the "Star-Spangled Banner" challenged the status of "Hail! Columbia" as the only national anthem. On July 4, 1876, both songs were sung by a chorus in Montrose, Pennsylvania, at a cornerstone-laying ceremony for a soldier's monument. After the Centennial, performances of "Hail! Columbia" greatly diminished.

Sources: *National Intelligencer*, 6 July 1801, 2, 8 July 1807, 1, and "Fourth of July," 6 July 1811, 2; Edward D. Bangs, "Ode for the Anniversary of American Independence, July 4th, 1817," broadside, 1817; *Frederick-Town Herald*, 30 June 1827, 3; *Richmond Enquirer*, 8 July 1831, 3; *New York Herald*, 6 July 1851, 1; *The Republican*, 10 July 1876; Oscar G.T. Sonneck, *A Bibliography of Early Secular American Music* (Washington, D.C.: Library of Congress, 1945), 171–74; Wolfe, *Secular Music in America.*

"Hail! Sons of Freedom! Hail the Day"

Patriotic song composed by a citizen of Lancaster, Pennsylvania, on July 4, 1794. Sung to the tune "Marseilles Hymn."

Sources: *American Daily Advertiser*, 2 August, 1794; Oscar G.T. Sonneck, *A Bibliography of Early Secular American Music* (Washington, D.C.: Library of Congress, 1945), 176.

"Hail to the Chief"

A popular tune performed on the Fourth of July as well as other occasions and one that is officially associated with the president of the United States. The tune is typically played to announce the Chief Executive's arrival. The melody of "Hail to the Chief" is derived from an old Gaelic air and was first used in a dramatic version of Sir Walter Scott's *The Lady of the Lake* by James Sanderson, an English composer, and first performed in 1812 in New York. In Sanderson's setting, the tune is played as an announcement of Highland Chieftain Sir Roderick Dhu:

Hail to the chief, who in triumph advances
Honor'd and blessed be the evergreen pine!

Although it has been suggested in recent years that John Quincy Adams was the first president to hear the tune performed in his honor, at the groundbreaking ceremony of the **Chesapeake and Ohio Canal** on July 4, 1828, there is no conclusive proof to substantiate that. A close examination of the *National Intelligencer* for July 1828, the source of the claim, reveals only that the U.S. Marine Band performed during the morning that day, playing various airs from a barge on its way to the groundbreaking site. No mention was made of the specific tunes. However, "Hail to the Chief" was performed in Washington later that day by an "excellent band" at a celebration of the city's printers. Evidence points to May 29, 1829, as the date the tune was first played for a sitting president — President Jackson. Jackson had attended a cornerstone-laying ceremony for the first lock of the C & O Canal, had dinner in Georgetown, and was "entering his carriage" to return to the White House when the Marine Band "struck up the air of 'Hail to the Chief.'"

The tune was first associated with a president on February 22, 1815, to commemorate the life of George Washington and the end of the War of 1812. During the first half of the nineteenth century "Hail to the Chief" was commonly performed on the Fourth of July to honor individuals such as Lafayette, Samuel Sprigg, John Randolph of Roanoke, Winfield Scott, and Andrew Jackson, as well as other heroes that fought in the Revolutionary War and War of 1812. Not long after, the tune was being played elsewhere as a separate piece to highlight special occasions and individuals. The Harmonic Society of Georgetown played the tune on July 4, 1820. In Washington, on July 4, 1824, the tune was used for a new "original ode" titled "Blest Be the Day," by S.R. Kramer, performed at the Columbia Typographical Society celebration. In 1826 on the 50th anniversary of American independence, "Hail to the Chief" was played in the Dutch Stone Church in Fishkill, New York, by a band of musicians that heralded the arrival of a procession of citizens and cavalry there. On July 4, 1827, at a celebration in Fleet's Spring, Virginia, the tune was played following a toast to "John Randolph of Roanoke." On July 4, 1830, at a celebration

held at St. Michael's Church by the '76 Association of Charleston, South Carolina, the tune was played after a toast to John C. Calhoun. In 1831, a band performed "Hail to the Chief" at Gaetano Carusi's Saloon at an Independence Day dinner event for the participants of the ceremony held earlier that day at the Capitol. In 1833, the tune was played in Charleston, South Carolina, at an Independence Day dinner following a toast to Andrew Jackson. The first performances of "Hail to the Chief" in the White House were likely during the administration of Martin Van Buren (inaugurated 1841) and were rendered by the Marine Band. During the administration of President John Tyler (inaugurated 1841), his wife Julia Gardiner, a woman with "regal attitudes" ordered the band to play "Hail to the Chief" on the occasions of official presidential appearances, and by the time of Abraham Lincoln's administration (1861–65), the tune's official association with the president had been firmly established.

As the tune continued to be played more frequently as an acknowledgment of the president's presence or arrival, it continued to be played on the Fourth of July as a patriotic gesture to other important figures as well. For example, on July 4, 1855, at a celebration held in Grahamville, South Carolina, a band struck up the tune after a toast was given to Governor James H. Adams of South Carolina.

Sources: *Metropolitan*, 6 July 1820, 2; *National Intelligencer*, 7 July 1824, 3, and 4 July 1831, 3; *Richmond Enquirer*, 10 July 1827, 2; "Chesapeake and Ohio Canal," *Baltimore Patriot*, 1 June 1829, 2; "'76 Association," *Charleston Mercury*, 7 July 1830, 2; *Charleston Courier*, 6 July 1833, 2; *Charleston Mercury*, 19 July 1855, 2; Elise K. Kirk, "Hail to the Chief," *American Music* 15 (summer 1997): 123–36 and *Musical Highlights from the White House* (Malabar, Fla.: Krieger Publishing Co., 1992, 21; Philip Henry Smith, *General History of Duchess County from 1609 to 1876, Inclusive* (Paling, N.Y.: the author, 1877).

Hale, Nathan (1755–1776)

Was hanged as an American spy by the British in September 1776. The town of Huntington on Long Island, New York, unveiled a monument to Hale on July 5, 1894. Hale lived for a time in Huntington, and it was on the shores of Huntington Bay that Hale was captured by the British. In attendance at the ceremony was a detachment of the First Artillery, U.S. Army of Fort Hamilton, under the command of Sergeant John H. Finnegan. The unveiling ceremonies on Main Street included a prayer by the Rev. H.Q. Judd, pastor of the Huntington Methodist Church, music by a local band, followed by "a historical sketch of Capt. Nathan Hale by Robert Lenox Belknap, chairman of the exercises. It was a complete review of the life of the gallant patriot." In the audience were a number of prominent persons, including ex-governor Richard C. McCormick. The band played "Hail, Columbia," and the entire assemblage arose and sang "America." Thirteen volleys were fired by artillerymen. General Stewart L. Woodford, 127th Union Regiment, also gave a brief speech. He said, "Today, you are adding this monument to the memory of the patriot who, arrested upon your shore, paid the penalty of life for the service he had sought to render his country."

A newspaper report described the monument:

> The monument stands at the head of Main Street. It is a cylindrical shaft of polished granite surmounted by a stone sphere. The base is of solid stone, and is about six feet square, and in the form of a basin. Water will be supplied through the mouth of a dolphin. The monument is about fifteen feet high, and its location is at a point where several important roads converge.

Hale's name has been remembered occasionally on Independence Day. On July 5, 1926, the American Legion parade in Huntington featured Alvah M. Floyd, who won "a prize for the correctness of his appearance impersonating Nathan Hale," and on July 4, 1933, the daring exploits of Nathan Hale were depicted through a radio program titled "Lives at Stake" over radio station WRC in Washington, D.C.

Sources: "In Memory of Nathan Hale," *New York Times*, 5 July 1894, 4; "Nathan Hale Represented," *New York Times*, 6 July 1926, 10; "Radio Dial Flashes," *Washington Post*, 4 July 1933, 10.

Hamburgh, South Carolina, massacre

A Centennial Fourth of July Democratic celebration on July 4, 1876, in Hamburgh, South Carolina, resulted in seven deaths, including six African-American soldiers of the Hamburgh militia and one white individual. The event was reported in numerous newspapers across the country and shortly after, a debate about the massacre took place in Congress. Although slightly differing versions of the story were printed, what likely happened is that on Independence Day a group of black military companies unintentionally blocked a road, not allowing two whites returning to their homes in Edgefield, South Carolina, to pass by. On the following day the whites lodged a complaint with Prince Rivers, the black magistrate and chief of the state militia. A trial was scheduled, but the black soldiers swore that they would submit to no punishment "inflicted" by the magistrate should an unfavorable ruling be issued. The magistrate ordered the soldiers to give up their muskets and pistols but the soldiers refused and about fifty of them fortified themselves in an old brick house. Rivers summoned a group of 200 individuals "to uphold the law." A piece of artillery with blank cartridges was discharged three times to "scare" the soldiers out. When they emerged and fled, the shootings took place. One of those killed was Jim Cook, the Hamburgh city marshal. It was reported as well that a drunken mob "gutted several small shops" after the fight was concluded. Due to the killings and, to some degree because the event occurred on the nation's Centennial, a national uproar ensued.

Sources: "Row in Hamburg" and "The Hamburg Riot," *Augusta Constitutionalist*, 9 and 11 July 1876, 4 and 4, respectively; Philip S. Foner, "Black Participation in the Centennial of 1876," *Negro History Bulletin* 39 (February 1976): 532–38; debate on the Hamburgh massacre in the U. S. House of Representatives, July 15 and 18, 1876: House of Representatives (44th, 1st session); *Washington Evening Star*, 18 July 1876, 1, 4.

Hamilton Literary and Theological Institution, New York

The Hamilton Institution was later renamed Madison University in 1846 and again renamed Colgate University in 1890. Two noteworthy Fourth of July celebrations occurred there in 1838–39 in which two odes and one hymn were premiered. On July 4, 1838, an "original hymn" of five stanzas by Benjamin F. Taylor was sung to the tune "America."

> (First stanza)
> Break forth, ye hills, in song,
> Your green old heights along,
> From clime to clime!
> And you, ye stars, sing forth,
> Who charmed the cradl'd earth,
> When light sprang into birth,
> In youthful time!

A five-stanza ode by William Carey Richards was also sung by the choir to the tune "Parma."

> (First stanza)
> Loud swell the Pean to the skies,
> Join the triumphal lay;
> Let grateful praise to heaven arise
> On Freedom's natal day!
> Praise for our country's weal,
> Praise for a free and Christian birth,
> Praise for the joys we feel!

As part of the ceremonies William W. Everts, Baptist pastor of the Walnut Street Church in Louisville, Kentucky, presented an oration, and E.E.L. Taylor recited the Declaration of Independence.

On July 4, 1839, an anonymous six-stanza ode was sung by a choir to the tune "Herald."

> (First stanza)
> Lo! The day, the East adorning
> Hastens onward to its birth;
> And the pearly light of morning
> Flashes o'er the expectant earth.
> Zion's Watchmen!
> Lift your songs of sacred mirth.

C.J. Radford gave a public reading of the Declaration of Independence that day, and J.F. Jones presented an oration.

Sources: "Order of Exercises on the Sixty-Second Anniversary of American Independence, Wednesday, July 4, 1838," broadside; "Order of Exercises on the Sixty-Third Anniversary of American Independence, Thursday, July 4th, 1839," broadside, as reprinted in *An American Time Capsule* (Library of Congress), Web site, 12 September 2002.

Hamlin, Hannibal (1809–1891)

The only vice president of the United States to die on July 4. Hamlin was an active participant in Independence Day celebrations, and he introduced a bill in Congress in 1870 making the Fourth of July a holiday for federal employees. (See **Federal, state, and local legislation establishing the holiday**.)

Hamlin was born at Paris Hill, Maine, studied law in Portland and later practiced law in Hampden. He served in the Maine legislature from 1836 to 1841 and in 1847. In the following year he was elected to Congress, where he served for five years. In 1857 he was governor of Maine. He later served as port collector in Boston but returned to the Senate in 1869, where he served until 1881. In Bangor, Maine, on July 4, 1865, before a crowd of 30,000, Hamlin delivered an oration, described as "most able and eloquent." On July 3, 1890, Hamlin was at a meeting of the **Army of the Potomac Society** in Portland, Maine. He spoke briefly to the crowd and received "three hearty cheers." Hamlin died while playing cards at the Tarnatine Club in Bangor, Maine. An article in the *Bar Harbor Record* highlighted the significance of Hamlin:

> His death deprives the country of one of its most honorable men, Maine of one of her distinguished sons and Bangor of her most prominent and beloved citizen. His career has covered a period of the greatest importance in American history. With nearly every great and good movement of this period his name has been connected.

Sources: *Buffalo Express*, 6 July 1865, 1; *New York Times*, 6 July 1865, 5; "A Comparison of Armies," *New York Times*, 4 July 1890, 1; "Ashes to Ashes," *Bar Harbor Record*, 9 July 1891, 4; "Hannibal Hamlin," *Houston Daily Post*, 5 July 1891, 3.

Hampton, Iowa, courthouse

The first courthouse built in Hampton was dedicated on July 4, 1857. It was built by F.A. Denton and "resembled a one-room school house of that era." It was in use by Franklin County until 1866, when it was removed to a new location. Franklin County was created on August 5, 1855, and took its name in honor of Benjamin Franklin.

Source: Iowa's Fifth District, Web site, 5 September 2002, <http://www.house.gov/latham/COH-ISFRANK.htm>.

Hancock, John (1737–1793)

Merchant and president of the Second Continental Congress (May 1775–October

1777), who was the first signer of the Declaration of Independence printed on July 4, 1776, and encouraged celebrating the Fourth of July. Due to a resolution passed by the Continental Congress on July 4, 1776, it was Hancock who sent George Washington a printed copy of the Declaration of Independence on July 6 so that Washington could read the document to his troops in New York on July 9.

Hancock was born in North Braintree (now Quincy, Mass.) and graduated from Harvard in 1754. In 1763 he was a partner of the Thomas Hancock and Co. mercantile firm. He was a leading participant in the Revolutionary cause, first as president of the Massachusetts Provincial Congress in 1774 and as a delegate to the 2d Continental Congress. He and Charles Thomson, secretary of the Congress, were the first to sign the printed broadside copy of the Declaration of Independence on July 4. Later he became the first governor of Massachusetts, a position he held for nine terms (1780–93). Although re-elected president of the Continental Congress in 1785, he was not able to serve very long due to illness.

A study of newspaper reports indicate that Hancock's name was only occasionally mentioned in Fourth of July celebrations following the war, notwithstanding his role in achieving independence. He was an ardent supporter of the importance of celebrating the day. He said it was "the birthday of a nation; it was a day pregnant with greater events in a political view of freedom that the world had ever seen; not only the nation of which we are a part, but all the Nations of the World will probably derive great & lasting blessings from it." On 10 June 1790, Hancock had petitioned the General Court asking that artillery be fired on the forthcoming Fourth of July and that a "frugal collation in the Senate Chamber at twelve o'clock" take place, but on 23 June the court declined the recommendation, due to the "great debt under which the people were laboring."

Some years after his death his name took on increased meaning and deference. On July 4, 1853, for example, in Philadelphia, at least 10,000 persons visited Independence Hall and according to a newspaper account, each attempted to sit in the chair that Hancock used during the sessions of the Continental Congress. Also, occasionally ceremonies were held at the gravesite of Hancock at the Granary Burial Ground in Boston. On July 4, 1929, William H. McMasters, vice president of the Thomas Jefferson League of Massachusetts, delivered an address there. He said, "I bespeak for our people a willingness to follow in the footsteps of Hancock, if the time shall ever come when a new declaration of independence must be written for the people of the Republic."

Sources: "For Jeffersonian Revival," *New York Times*, 5 July 1929, 5; *Daily News*, 6 July 1853, 2; *Encyclopedia of American History*, 1049; Paul D. Brandes, *John Hancock's Life and Speeches: A Personalized Vision of the American Revolution, 1763–1793* (Lanham, Md.: Scarecrow Press, 1996), 173–74; Gerard W. Gawalt, "Words and Deeds in American History: Selected Documents Celebrating the Manuscript Division's First 100 Years," *American Memory*, Web site, 5 April 2002.

Hanoi, Vietnam

The capital of the Socialist Republic of Vietnam, which was extensively bombed by U.S. forces in 1965–68 and 1972 and the site for the first Fourth of July celebration given there in 1995 by 500 Americans since the end of the Vietnam War. The celebration took place where the former American consulate stood, and the "Star-Spangled Banner" was played over loudspeakers.

Source: Tim Larimer, "'Oh, Say Can You See...?' You Can, in Vietnam!" *New York Times*, 5 July 1995, A4.

Harding, Warren Gamaliel (1865–1923)

Twenty-ninth president of the U.S. (1921–23). Harding was Ohio state senator (1899–1903) and U.S. senator (1915–21).

As a nominee for president, on July 4, 1920, Harding and his wife traveling by automobile to Marion, Ohio, from Washington, had arrived in Cumberland, Maryland, and there received an "impromptu reception at his hotel."

His first Fourth of July as president, in 1921, was spent as a guest of Senator Joseph S.

Frelinghuysen in Raritan, New Jersey. There he attended a service at the Third Dutch Reformed Church, held a public reception, and played a round of golf. A few days previous Harding had sent a Fourth of July message to the Hebrew Sheltering and Immigrant Aid Society in New York commending the association for its "Americanization work." "I hope you may have all success in your laudable efforts for the propagation of true Americanism," he wrote.

On July 4, 1922, Harding and the First Lady were in his hometown of Marion, Ohio, with family. He participated in the town's centennial exercises held at the fairgrounds. His speech focused on the goal of the labor unions to dominate the manufacturing sector of the country. "A free American has the right to labor without any other's leave," he said. "It would be no less an abridgment to deny men to bargain collectively. Governments cannot tolerate any class or grouped domination through force. It will be a sorry day when group domination is reflected in our laws."

On July 4, 1923, Harding was in Meacham, Oregon, continuing on his "Voyage of Understanding" that began in June. He took part in the Oregon Trail Celebration that heralded the eightieth anniversary of the arrival of the first immigrant wagon there. He rode in a Concord stage coach drawn by six horses and was symbolically initiated into the Cayuse Tribe. On August 2, 1923, Harding died from a reaction to tainted food.

Sources: "Harding Reaches Zanesville, Ohio," *New York Times*, 5 July 1920, 3; "Harding to Rest July 4," "Harding Extols Jews' Works," and "President Ends Holiday," *New York Times*, 24 June, 3 July and 6 July 1921, 12, 26, and 9, respectively; "Brave Honest Words," *Los Angeles Times*, 7 July 1922, II4; *New York Times*, 5 July 1923, 5.

Hardin-Simmons University, Abilene, Texas

The cornerstone of this university's first building, the Old Main Building, was laid on July 4, 1891. Hardin-Simmons was chartered under the name Abilene Baptist College, and later changed to Simmons College (1891) after James B. Simmons, its principal donor. Simmons, originally from New York, had drawn

attention for his assistance in establishing seven schools for the education of freed African-Americans in the South following the Civil War. He also had donated funds to avert a financial crisis of Columbian University (now George Washington University) in 1874.

Simmons wrote on April 4, 1891, that the first building on the campus should be "a durable and handsome structure. An inviting college building will add greatly to the attractiveness of the school and will help not a little to improve the patronage and the moneyed contributions." Old Main Building was completed in February 1892 and was made of brick, "three stories high, and containing ten rooms and a chapel well arranged." It stood on an elevation overlooking the town toward the south and having a delightful view of the surrounding country in all directions.

The first session of school began in September 1892 with a faculty of not more than five or six. In 1941, Hardin-Simmons University became affiliated with the Baptist General Convention of Texas. Today Hardin-Simmons has some 2,300 students representing 36 states and 13 countries.

Source: Thomas B. Prescott, "The History of Simmons University" (M.A. thesis, University of Texas, 1930).

Harford County, Maryland, Court House

On July 4, 1900, a memorial tablet was unveiled at the site of the old court house. A number of speeches were given, including one by Thomas R. Clendinen of the Baltimore City Bar.

Source: "Harford Celebrations," *Baltimore Morning Herald*, 4 July 1900, 5.

Harford County, Maryland, Declaration of Independence

The signing of America's first declaration of independence in 1775 by thirty-four Marylanders took place near old Harford Town, Maryland, at a little hamlet known as Bush, adjacent to the Bush River. On July 4, 1900, a granite monument was unveiled to the memory of that signing. At the ceremony, Col. Herman Stump, president of the Revolutionary Association of Harford County, addressed the audience about the men who signed the document, and Thomas R. Clendinen of Baltimore presented an oration also on the history of the contributions of Harford's men, but emphasized the importance of women at the time of the Revolutionary War. He said, "Valiant and good as the men of Harford have been, their mothers, wives, and sweethearts were better — they showed in no uncertain way their position, but they encouraged the case of the men; and it is not difficult to believe that but for the approval of the women the men would not have been so brave."

Source: "First Declaration," *Baltimore Morning Herald*, 5 July 1900, 5.

Harlem, New York, Fire of 1886

One of the largest Fourth of July fires in Harlem, which was caused by a lighted cigar tossed into a pile of fireworks; it occurred on July 5, 1886. Four buildings were destroyed and serious damage to several others resulted. The damage was estimated at $200,000. The fireworks were located in Morris Strausky's "fancy goods store" at 125th Street. According to a reporter,

the entire show window and front of the store were filled with the dangerous goods and for days the sidewalk before the store has been incumbered with tables, loaded down with fireworks, so that it has been almost impossible for pedestrians to pass. Shortly after 6 o'clock four half-drunken men came up the avenue and stopped in front of Strausky's store. They were all smoking, and one of them, Strausky says, either dropped or threw a burning cigar into a basket filled with fireworks and ran away.... When the firemen arrived the building was ablaze from end to end, and the stock of fireworks made it dangerous to approach it. There were loud explosions every instant, and skyrockets came flying out of the windows and shot across the avenue, striking the buildings on the opposite side.

Other buildings destroyed or badly damaged included the auction rooms of Justus Cooke, which contained 25 pianos, clothing and furs, a restaurant owned by J.J. Cohrs, a market owned by the Nauss Brothers, a chop house owned by Kelley and Hoff, a delicatessen owned by George Ruppell, and the Glenwood apartment house.

Source: "Four Buildings Burned," *New York Times*, 6 July 1886, 1.

Harrison, Benjamin (1833–1901)

Twenty-third president of the U.S. (1889–93). Grandson of William Henry Harrison, 9th president. Harrison, a lawyer, held a number of significant positions prior to his presidency. He was a reporter for the Indiana Supreme Court during the 1860s, served in the Civil War, and was elected to the U.S. Senate (1881–87). As president, Harrison participated in a number of Independence Day celebrations. On July 4, 1889, he was in Woodstock, Connecticut, where he spoke to a large crowd. "I am sure I look into the faces this morning of a body of citizens filled with honest pride in the story of their country and full of serious purpose to maintain those institutions from all taint of corruption or decay," he said. "I think such meetings as these, the old-fashioned Fourth of July celebration, have in them very elevating and instructive power." On Independence Day in 1890, Harrison was at his favorite summer retreat, Cape May, New Jersey. Typically his July 4 holiday there included entertainment and "patriotic instruction for both young and old." Several speeches were given on that day, one titled "The Day We Celebrate," by Senator Hawley, and another, "Duties in 1876 and 1890," by the Rev. Henry L. Wayland. Poems were recited, including one titled "The Ghost of an Old Continental," read by Frederick Emerson Brooks. Harrison had also sent a special American flag to the American Art Students' Association in Paris to be displayed at their celebration, which included 650 guests. On July 4, 1892, Harrison visited the monument grounds behind the White House to see the celebration there, but later he and Mrs. Harrison drove out of the city to escape the noise. On July 4, 1893, Harrison was back in Cape May, New Jersey, where he gave an address on the "rights and duties of citizenship" before a large audience. He was "loudly applauded when he concluded."

Sources: "Gen. Harrison Did Speak," *New York Times*, 5 July 1889, 1; *National Leader*, 11 July 1889, 4; "A Flag for the Students," and "At the Harrison Cottage," *Washington Post*, 5 July 1890, 1; "The President's

Holiday," *New York Times*, 5 July 1892, 1; "Ex-President Harrison Spoke," *New York Times*, 5 July 1893, 9.

Harrison, William Henry (1773–1841)

Ninth president of the U.S. (1841). Although Harrison was not in office as president long enough to celebrate a Fourth of July, he was occasionally honored in name. On July 4, 1843, he was toasted at a Whig celebration in Philadelphia, with a toast to "The memory of Harrison: illustrious in life, faithful even unto death."

Source: "Celebration of the Fourth: At Philadelphia," *National Intelligencer*, 8 July 1843, 3.

Hart, John (1711–1779)

Signer of the Declaration of Independence and a delegate to Congress from New Jersey, a monument to whose memory was dedicated on July 4, 1865, in Hopewell, New Jersey. Hart was born in Stonington, Connecticut, and later moved with his parents to a farm in the vicinity of Hopewell. He lived his entire life there, married in 1740, and became a well-respected civic leader, holding such posts as justice of the peace, county judge, and judge of the court of common pleas. At the onset of the war, Hart was driven off his land by the British and was forced to hide in nearby mountains. On returning after the victorious battles at Princeton and Trenton, he learned of the death of his wife and that his family had fled the area. Regrettably, Hart did not live long enough to see the American victory in 1781.

On the occasion of the dedication of a monument to Hart in 1865, Joel Parker (1816–1888), governor of New Jersey, presented an oration in which he provided a summary of the events that led to the signing of the Declaration of Independence and John Hart's participation in the Revolutionary War effort. Speaking to descendants of the Hart family, Parker described John Hart as a "man, of humble origin, modest and unassuming, without advantages of early education, a plain farmer, [who] had, by his integrity of character, his wisdom, his practical sense, and his patriotic zeal, acquired such an influence among his colleagues as to be esteemed worthy to stand side by side with Jefferson and Adams, Franklin and Rush, Stockton and Witherspoon, the most eloquent, the most learned, the most distinguished statesmen of the land." Another speech was given by Jacob Weart, chairman of the commission for the monument.

The monument was reported to be "a plain shaft of Quincy granite, not lofty but appropriate and tasteful in design and execution" and part of its inscription read "Erected by the state of New Jersey by act approved April 5th, 1865." The ceremony to Hart's memory included Carpenter's Brass Band of Lambertville, which performed sixteen tunes, a reading of the Declaration of Independence by the Rev. J. Romeyn Berry, and a dinner that included members of the Hart family and invited guests. "The dinner was very fine, and reflected great credit both to the hearts and hands of the ladies: nothing was wanting to make the occasion most agreeable."

Sources: Joel Parker, *Oration at the Dedication of a Monument to the Memory of John Hart ...* ([1865]; Trenton, N.J.: Pamphlets in American History, Revolutionary War, RW 380); "Dedication of the Hart Monument," *Daily State Gazette*, 7 and 8 July 1865, 3 and 2 respectively; Robert G. Ferris, ed., *Signers of the Declaration* (Washington, D.C.: United States Department of the Interior, 1975), 71–72; Cleon E. Hammond, *John Hart: The Biography of a Signer of the Declaration of Independence* (Newfane, Vermont: Pioneer Press, 1977).

Harvey Cedars Life Saving Station, Toms River, New Jersey

On July 4, 1894, gold medals were presented to the captain and crew of the station for the rescue of the crew of the schooner *A.F. Crockett*, which went aground during a storm in the previous month.

Source: "Brave Men Rewarded," *Washington Evening Star*, 4 July 1894, 2.

Haswell, Anthony (1756–1816)

Newspaper editor and author who wrote six songs for the Fourth of July in 1807 in Vermont. Haswell was born in Portsmouth, England, and immigrated to America in 1769. He worked for a time as an apprentice to printer Isaiah Thomas in Boston, but later moved to Vermont. In 1783 he began publishing the *Vermont Gazette* at Bennington and was later appointed postmaster general. He served in that post until 1784. Haswell's political views leaned towards republicanism. When he opposed the "prosecution of Matthew Lyon and John Adams' election to the presidency," he was charged and sentenced for sedition. His fine was $200 and imprisonment for two months. "The people of Vermont sympathized with him so strongly that they postponed the Fourth of July celebration [in 1791] until the expiration of his term of imprisonment on July 9th and then received him with the greatest enthusiasm. The fine exacted from him was repaid by the state fifty years later to his descendants." Haswell's set of Fourth of July songs included "A Slight View of the World, Taken July 4th, 1807"; "Liberty Universal"; "A Review of Past Scenes"; "Independence, July 4, 1807"; "The Triumph of Principle"; "Anniversary of the Declaration of Independence of the United States of America by a Citizen of the United States," and information about these songs exists in an 1807 broadside that may have been published in Bennington.

Source: *The National Cyclopaedia of American Biography* 8:261.

Hawaii

Fiftieth and final state to be admitted to the union, on July 4, 1960. The law for Hawaii's statehood was signed by President Eisenhower in August 1959.

The first reported Fourth of July celebration in Hawaii occurred in Honolulu in 1814 when Americans there gave a dinner for King Kamehameha and ships in the harbor fired artillery salutes. In the years that followed, annual celebrations by the American community were common. On July 4, 1894, the Republic of Hawaii was proclaimed after a revolution of sugar planters in 1887 that resulted in "a liberal constitution and a government under their influence."

Sources: Harold Whitman Bradley, *The American Frontier in Hawaii: The Pioneers, 1789–1843* (Stanford University Press, 1942); Appelbaum, *The Glorious Fourth*, 46; "Hawaii Will Join the Union Friday," *New York Times*, 19 August 1959, 14.

Hayes, Rutherford Birchard (1822–1893)

Nineteenth president of the U.S. (1877–81). On July 4, 1876, Hayes was at Independence Hall in Philadelphia sitting on a grandstand with other dignitaries reviewing a parade. When he arrived he "was loudly cheered as he took his seat." On July 4, 1877, Hayes spent a few hours in the White House receiving guests that included Attorney General Bishop Simpson and various U.S. congressmen. On July 4, 1878, Hayes was on his way back from the **Wyoming Valley Massacre** centennial celebration in Pennsylvania, where he spoke to a crowd of 60,000. Then the president held a reception on the grounds of the residence of William Conyingham and before a crowd of 10,000, he spoke, "concluding with the remark that, 'If unlike his predecessor in officer, Gen. Grant, he did know enough to not say anything, he hoped he did know when to stop.'" Hayes returned to the White House in the late afternoon of July 5.

On July 4, 1879, President Hayes was at Fortress Monroe in Virginia with the First Lady, "Messrs. Webb C. and Burchard [sic] Hayes, Secretaries Sherman and McCrary, Attorney General Devens and Secretary Thompson, with other ladies and gentlemen." The party arrived on the *Tallapoosa* on July 4 where they were met by

> General Getty and staff, and the command, headed by the band, paraded on the wharf to receive the distinguished visitors. They proceeded to General Getty's quarters, where the officers were presented, after which they repaired to the ramparts and witnessed some target practice with fifteen inch guns. At one o'clock the party re-embarked on the Tallapoosa and sailed for the capes, returning at 8 P.M. to witness the fireworks.

President Hayes returned to Washington on the following morning. On July 4, 1880, Hayes was in the White House receiving guests. On July 4, 1883, he gave a speech titled "National Aid to Education" at Woodstock, Connecticut.

Sources: "General View of the Day," *New York Times*, 5 July 1876, 4; *Evening Star*, 5 July 1877, 1; "The President in Pennsylvania," *Evening Star*, 5 July 1878, 1; "The Presidential Party at Fortress Monroe,"

Baltimore Morning Herald, 7 July 1879, 1; *Evening Star*, 6 July 1880, 1; "Henry C. Bowen's Fourth," *New York Times*, 5 July 1883, 5.

Haynes, Lemuel (1753–1833)

Revolutionary War veteran and pastor who was the first African-American to give an Independence Day address, on July 4, 1801, at Rutland, Vermont. Haynes was born in Hartford, Connecticut, and was given up for indentured servitude as a child. In 1774 he joined the Connecticut Minutemen and in the following year the Continental Army. After the war, Haynes studied theology at Middlebury College in Vermont, and was "the first African American with an advanced degree from a white college."

Haynes' 1801 oration was titled "The Nature and Importance of True Republicanism, with a Few Suggestions, Favorable to Independence" (printed by William Fay, 1801). Although much of his address echoed traditional themes of Fourth of July oratory, such as commending the Declaration, American society, and the unity of the nation, he suggested the inherent republican opportunity to extend freedom to all African-Americans. "A free republican government has the preference to all others in that it tends to destroy those distinctions among men that ought never to exist," Haynes said. "All men are born equally free and independent."

Source: James, "The Other Fourth of July," 93–109.

Heck Hall, Northwestern University

Dedicated on July 4, 1867, in Evanston, Illinois. Built by the Methodist Episcopal Church "under the auspices of the American Methodist Ladies' Centenary Association and the Garrett Biblical Institute," the building was described as standing "on the edge of a primeval grove near Evanston, which is also occupied as the campus of the Northwestern University. The upper windows overlook the blue waters of Lake Michigan on the east, and prairie and forest landscapes of great beauty are visible in every other direction." The structure was named after Mrs. Barbara Heck, "who, in 1766, aided Philip Embury in the organization of the original and memorable John Street Church in the city of New York."

Source: *Harper's Weekly*, 13 July 1867, 436.

Hero of the North; or, The Deliverer of His Country

This three-act play, interspersed with songs, was performed on July 4, 1815, at the Washington Theatre in the District of Columbia. Tickets were for sale at W. Cooper's Music and Book Store on Pennsylvania Avenue and at Joseph Milligan's in Georgetown.

Source: *National Intelligencer*, 3 July 1815, 3.

Hessian Band

Musicians assigned with the Hessian mercenaries, hired by the British to fight in the Revolutionary War. They had the distinction of providing music for the first Fourth of July celebration in Philadelphia in 1777. The Hessian musicians were captured by George Washington and the Continental Army at the battle of Trenton on December 26, 1776. They were taken back to Pennsylvania and impressed into service by Washington. The musicians performed for Congress at a dinner event on Independence Day in 1777. One newspaper account reported that the band "heightened the festivity with some fine performances suited to the joyous occasion."

Source: *Virginia Gazette*, 18 July 1777, 2–3.

Hewes, George Robert T. (1742–1840)

Touted as "the last survivor of the [Boston] tea party," Hewes, a shoemaker, was toasted at a dinner party in Boston on July 4, 1835.

Source: Alfred F. Young, "George Robert Twelves Hughes (1742–1840): A Boston Shoemaker and the Memory of the American Revolution," *William and Mary Quarterly*, 3rd ser. 38/4 (October 1981): 561–623.

Hewitt, James (1770–1827)

Violinist, music teacher, conductor, music publisher, and composer, who wrote *The 4th of July, a Grand Military Sonata for the Piano Forte* (1801) and other works on Revolutionary War era subjects. Hewitt was one of the best-known composers in New York and Boston. He was born in Dartmoor, England, and came to New York in 1792. In 1798 he purchased a music store from Benjamin Carr and began publishing music, including many of his own compositions. In 1811 he was in Boston, where he became music director of the Federal Street Theatre and organist at Trinity Church. Later he spent time again in New York but moved back to Boston, where he died. Prints of his work *The 4th of July* were available for sale at his New York store and also at D. Bowen's Columbian Museum in Boston. The music is adorned with "an eagle poised on a globe, with a scroll reading 'Excelsior' in its talons. Flags, a rifle and a bayonet appear to either side and a cannon, a drum and a mortar at its base." Other similar works Hewitt composed include *The Battle of Trenton: A Favorite Historical Military Sonata* (1812–14) and *The Boston Brigade March* (1824?), both for piano.

Hewitt's "Live Triumphant or Contending Die, an Ode" (New York: J. Hewitt's Musical Repository, n.d.) for voice and piano, was sung by "Mr. Caulfield at the celebration of the Fourth of July 1809 by the Washington Benevolent Society." First line: "Auspicious day the annual rite we bring while gratefull offrings on thine."

Sources: Wolfe, *Secular Music in America* 1:371–74; Clark, *American Keyboard Music through 1865*, 51–65.

Hewitt, John Hill (1801–1890)

Noted composer of Civil War songs including his best known "All Quiet on the Potomac To-Night" (1863). Hewitt composed an ode that was first sung by a choir representing the Apollo Association "and other distinguished amateurs from the several choirs of the city" on July 4, 1843, at the **Temperance Hall** celebration in Washington, D.C.

Source: *National Intelligencer*, 4 and 6 July 1843, 3 and 3, respectively.

Hibernian Societies riot

Took place on July 4, 1853, in the Ninth Ward of New York City, with several injured and 37 rioters arrested. The riot occurred as a result of the Ancient Order of Hibernians parade being disturbed by a passing stage driver. The police arrived and the Hibernians engaged in fights with them.

Source: *New York Herald*, 5 July 1853, 1.

Hoban, James (1808–1846)

Attorney, son of James Hoban, noted architect, who gave no less than ten Fourth of July orations during the years 1833–45, with three of them at Georgetown College. On July 4, 1838, he presented two addresses, one in the morning in Washington for the Union and Literary Debating Society at Brown's Church on 10th Street and the other at the dinner ceremony in Georgetown for the Philodemic Society at Georgetown College. A reporter noted that at Brown's Church, "Mr. Hoban delivered the Oration in a most effective and eloquent manner. Never, we are told by the most competent judges, did the orator go beyond his masterly effort pronounced on the late Anniversary. The Oration gratified all who heard it, and Mr. Hoban has been since unanimously called upon to furnish a copy for publication." Other speeches included those at the Jefferson Library Association meeting at City Hall (1833), Potomac Pavilion at Piney Point, Maryland (1839), Metropolitan Lyceum of Washington (1840), Democratic ceremony at Shuter's Hill in Maryland (1844), and a temperance societies celebration "on grounds west of the President's House" (1845).

Source: Heintze, "Orations, Speeches, and Readings of the Declaration of Independence in Washington, D.C. and Surrounding Towns on the Fourth of July: 1801–1876."

Holmes, Andrew Hunter (1789–1814)

On July 4, 1827, a sword was presented to Virginia governor David Holmes on behalf of "distinguished services of Gen. [Andrew Hunter] Holmes." Addresses by Governor William Branch Giles (1762–1830) and Philip Norborne Nicholas (1775?–1849) were presented on the occasion.

Source: *Martinsburg Gazette and Public Advertiser*, 19 July 1827.

Holmes, Oliver Wendell (1809–1894)

Wrote the hymn "Welcome to All Nations" (Boston: Oliver Ditson; New York: Charles H. Ditson; Chicago: Lyon and Healy, 1876) for chorus and orchestra, which was premiered on May 10, 1876, at the opening exercises of the **Centennial Exhibition** in Philadelphia, and again on July 4, 1876, at Independence Square, Philadelphia. The text was set to music ("American Hymn") by Matthias Keller (1813–1875). Holmes also gave a speech on July 4, 1858, in Boston.

Sources: *Harper's Weekly*, 17 July 1858; Thomas Franklin Currier, *A Bibliography of Oliver Wendell Holmes*, ed. Eleanor M. Tilton (New York: Russell and Russell, 1971), 157; Edith L. Markham, "Poetry Written for the Opening Exercises and the Fourth of July Celebration at the 1876 Centennial Exhibition in Philadelphia" (M.A. thesis, University of North Carolina, 1950).

"Honor America Day"

The theme for a celebration that took place in Washington, D.C., in 1970. The event was launched in reaction to previous Fourth of July celebrations whose participants had voiced protests against the government and the Vietnam War. The purpose of this celebration was "to rekindle the American spirit of patriotism and respect for individual liberties that made America great and to demonstrate to the world that, while we face problems as individuals and as a nation, we are proud of our country and welcome this opportunity to honor America." The Honor America Day Committee consisted of honorary chairmen Harry S. Truman and Lyndon B. Johnson, Mrs. Dwight D. Eisenhower, Bob Hope, the Rev. Billy Graham, and Hobart Lewis of *Reader's Digest*. A memorial service was held at the Lincoln Memorial, with music by the U.S. Army Band. A choir of 500 voices, "a procession of flags," and a parade along Constitution Avenue highlighted the day.

Sources: "A Different Kind of Rally," *U.S. News and World Report*, 6 July 1970, 10; *Los Angeles Times*, 5 July 1970; *Washington Post*, 5 July 1970, A1.

Hoover, Herbert Clark (1874–1964)

Thirty-first president of the U.S. (1929–33). He graduated from Stanford University in 1895 with a degree in mining engineering. During World War I he served as U.S. Food Administrator for rationing and conserving food during the war years. From 1921 to 1928 Hoover served as secretary of commerce. As a Republican his goal as president was to create an efficient government based on sound eco-

nomic measures, but unfortunately the onset of the Great Depression in 1929 dampened any possibility of that. His dedication to humanitarian matters through his work in directing agencies for relief in Europe after both world wars remains his legacy. He was honored on the Fourth of July for those efforts.

Hoover generally tried to stay out of the public eye on the Fourth of July. On July 4, 1929, he issued an announcement that Independence Day would be the last time that he would shake hands with the public until September when the weather was cooler. A newspaper reporter stated that he shook 774 hands, including all the members of the Philadelphia Harmonica Band, that day. The remainder of the day for the president was spent in the White House and later that evening watching fireworks from the south portico. Hoover had been asked by three cities to give addresses on the Fourth that year: in Asheville, North Carolina, to the Southern Publishers Association; in New York before 20,000 naturalized citizens; and at Philadelphia at Independence Hall. Meanwhile in Warsaw, Poland, where Hoover was extremely popular, an unusually large Fourth of July celebration was held in Hoover Square in front of the American memorial there. This tribute to Hoover's work in heading the relief mission in Europe after the war and to his first year as president included the flying of American and Polish flags and the playing of band music.

On Independence Day in 1930, Hoover issued a proclamation for a special session of the Senate to take place after the holiday to consider his London naval treaty. Before leaving the White House for his Rapidan fishing camp in the Virginia mountains, he signed a rivers and harbors bill and issued a statement in which he said, "It was with particular satisfaction that I signed the rivers and harbors bill, as it represents the final authorization of the engineering work by which we construct and coordinate our great systems of waterways and harbors, which I have advocated for over five years; it was promised in the last campaign and in my recommendations to Congress." At his mountain lodge, Hoover worked on a message to the Senate regarding the treaty to be delivered when he returned. Among his guests at the mountain lodge were Assistant Secretary of War David S. Ingalls and newspaper editor Mark Sullivan.

On July 4, 1931, it was announced by Edouard Renard, prefect of the Department of the Seine in Paris, at the closing ceremonies of the "week of American nations" convention, that a street there was to be named after Herbert Hoover for his efforts in aiding France and other countries after the war. Renard told the representatives of 22 American republics gathered there that "Our Belgian friends remember with us all that the Belgians and French owe to the great animator of the allies supply system, who has been raised to the highest post by his fellow countrymen and has not ceased to concern himself with compassionate heart over the misery and suffering born of war — I name President Hoover." In attendance at the ceremony was Gen. **John J. Pershing**, who also had a street named after him that day. Meanwhile Hoover was in the White House having a telephone conference with Secretary of the Treasury Andrew W. Mellon, who was in Paris handling negotiations over Hoover's war debt plan. Later that day Hoover, accompanied by a number of guests that included Senator Reed of Pennsylvania, left for his Rapidan camp.

On July 4, 1932, Hoover was at his Rapidan camp working on his acceptance speech for the Republican convention. With him were various government advisers, including Representative Bertrand H. Snell of New York, the Republican convention chairman. Meanwhile in Washington, "thousands of bonus marchers" gathered at the Capitol and marched up Pennsylvania Avenue to the White House as a symbolic "demand for cash payments of their compensation certificates."

As ex-president, on July 4, 1935, Hoover gave a speech before 6000 persons at Grass Valley, California, on the preservation of individual liberty. He recalled his days as a student mining engineer and how he often walked from Nevada City "in the mud, to save stage fare." About liberty, Hoover said, "In this crisis of liberty and this darkening eclipse of human freedom through the world, America

has today a transcendent mission to civilization far beyond our own safety. It is our duty to hold bright the light of individual liberty."

In 1958 President Eisenhower sent Hoover to Brussels on the presidential plane *Columbine* to deliver the Independence Day address at the Brussels Worlds Fair. The 84-year-old ex-president spoke about American accomplishments, world aid, and the "misrepresentations and vicious propaganda" regarding so-called American imperialism. "Probably the greatest misrepresentation of our ideals," he said, "is that we are imperialistically minded and that we daily practice imperialism. We have no desire to impose our formula of life or method of government upon other nations. We make no claim that our system or our people are perfect." On July 5, which the Belgian government had designated "Hoover Day," Hoover spoke again. Both speeches were translated into several languages and heard throughout the world.

In recent years Hoover continues to be honored on the Fourth. In 2003 a celebration was held at the Herbert Hoover Presidential Library Museum in West Branch, Iowa, with public readings from the nation's charters and music provided by a Civil War reenactment band.

Sources: "3 Cities Ask Hoover for July 4 Speech" and "Hoover Stops Handshaking with the Public Until Fall," *New York Times*, 13 June and 4 July 1929, 3 and 1, respectively; "President to Spend the 4th at Rapidan" and "Hoover Summons Senate for Monday to Act on Treaty," *New York Times*, 4 and 5 July 1930, 3 and 1, respectively; "Poles Celebrate Fourth," *New York Times*, 5 July 1929, 7; "Hoover Will Rest After Hard Week" and "France Honors President Hoover," *Washington Evening Star*, 4 July 1931, 1, and 5 July 1931, A2; "Honored at Paris," *Washington Post*, 5 July 1931, M1; "Hoover Reads Roosevelt's Acceptance Speech; Is Working on His Own at Rapidan Camp" and "President to Spend Fourth at His Camp," *New York Times*, 4 July 1932, 1 and 12, respectively; "Hoover Back in Gold Country Warns of Attack on Liberty," *Christian Science Monitor*, 5 July 1935, 5; David Willey, "Hoover Decries Anti-U.S. Mood," *Washington Post*, 5 July 1958, A2.

Howard's Park, Baltimore

Located in Baltimore, Maryland, Howard's Park (now known as Mount Vernon Place) was an important site for significant Baltimore City celebrations during the nineteenth century.

On July 4, 1812, at Howard's Park, Lieut. Col. William H. Winder presented the oration of the day and replaced William Pinkney, attorney general of the United States, who was supposed to address the crowd, but, due to an "unexpected absence from the city," did not. Winder, born in Somerset County, Maryland, was a state's attorney and in March 1812 was appointed by President Madison as lieutenant colonel of the Fourteenth U.S. Infantry. Two days after giving his Independence Day oration he was "promoted to full colonel and ordered north to join American forces on the Niagara frontier." Later assigned by President Madison to defend Washington as head of the Tenth Military District, his military record was tarnished when the British routed his troops at the Battle of Bladensburg.

Winder's oration was an exquisite impromptu piece written over the course of "but a few days" that were wrought with "pressing avocations." Winder encouraged his listeners to remember the "band of heroes" who fought for liberty, to put political partisanship aside, and not let the "national honor" fade. Regarding the outbreak of war with England, he proclaimed, "Let every one devote himself zealously to discharge his duty, and we shall terminate the conflict triumphantly; but if we come to the contest with distracted wills and divided power, we shall certainly prolong and increase its evils, and may even render the issue doubtful." Winder proclaimed George Washington as a man "transcendent among heroes and patriots" who helped save the country after the Revolutionary War when "discontents, jealousies, resentment for the supposed ingratitude of their country had begun to swell the breast of many of those gallant heroes." See also **Washington Monument, Baltimore**.

Sources: "Oration Delivered on the 4th of July, 1812...," *Weekly Register* 2/45 (11 July 1812), 306–08; John C. Fredriksen, "William Henry Winder," in *American National Biography* 23:629–30.

Howe, Julia Ward (1819–1910)

Poet, author, and abolitionist who wrote the words of "The Battle Hymn of the Republic," which was first published in the *Atlantic Monthly* (February 1862) and quickly became the unofficial Civil War hymn of the Union Army. Howe worked on behalf of women's rights and was married to Samuel Gridley Howe, himself an abolitionist. Together with Lucy Stone, Mrs. Howe established the New England Woman Suffrage Association. She also had close ties with other similar organizations. The first recorded performance of the "Battle Hymn" on the Fourth of July was given by a group of church choirs in Newton, Massachusetts, in 1862. Her penchant for writing poetry resulted in a number of collections, including *Passion Flowers* (1854) and *Words for the Hour* (1857), and she was invited to recite her favorite verse publicly. On July 4, 1893, in Woodstock, Connecticut, at H.C. Bowen's residence, Roseland Park, she read poetry to a distinguished audience which included Seth Low, president of Columbia College, David J. Brewer, justice of the U.S. Supreme Court and A.R. Spofford, librarian of Congress.

Howe's poem, "Hymn for the Fourth of July," appeared in *At Sunset* (1910).

(First stanza)
Our fathers built the house of God;
Rough-hewn, with haste its slabs they laid,
The savage man in ambush trod,
And still they worshiped undismayed.

Sources: Broadside, "Grand National Union Concert" (Newton, Mass., 1862); "Mr. Bowen's Celebration," *New York Times*, 5 July 1893, 9; Kenneth A. Spaulding, "Julia Ward Howe," *Encyclopedia Americana* 14: 510.

Hubball, Eletia (fl. 1820s)

The first published Independence Day address by a woman in the Washington, D.C., area occurred on July 4, 1821, at Market Square in Alexandria, Virginia. Hubball spoke on the occasion of a flag presentation to the Alexandria Company of Light Infantry, commanded by Capt. Nicholas Blasdell. Hubball, a young lady who had been elected by her friends to present the standard, made her appearance, accompanied by six other females, "bearing the most beautiful flag we have seen for many days." She "was received with 'present arms,' and an enlivening air from the band." She spoke about the responsibilities of the "citizen soldier," to uphold freedom and honor and never to be "tarnished with vice or immorality":

> The songs of freedom assuming the manly and dignified attitude of Citizen Soldiers, and emulating each other in the acquirements of military discipline, to enable them in the hour of danger to defend their country, maintain their liberty and protect us from licentious and daring invaders, must ever possess in our hearts an influence superior to the ordinary impressions created by social intercourse. Receive then your flag, and defend it worthy of yourselves and fathers, and we fervently trust that in your pursuit of discipline and military glory, it will never by tarnished with vice or immorality prove to the world that morality and virtue are the concomitants of the citizen soldier.

Source: *Alexandria Gazette*, 7 July 1821, 2.

Hudson, Massachusetts

The most serious fire in the history of that town occurred on July 4, 1894. According to a newspaper report, "it originated about 3 P.M. in a small building near F.H. Chamberlin's Shoe Factory, and, fanned by a strong breeze, spread very rapidly in an easterly direction." Many stores, homes, civic buildings, including the site of the town's newspaper *The Enterprise*, were destroyed. The estimated loss was $500,000. It was believed that the cause was lit firecrackers. Hudson is located 28 miles west of Boston and has a population of just over 17,000.

Sources: "The Dangerous Firecracker," *New York Times*, 5 July 1894, 1; "Hudson's Ruins Smoking," *Washington Evening Star*, 5 July 1894, 3.

Hungary

Exemplary Fourth of July celebrations occurred in this country during the 1920s under the auspices of the Hungary-America Society. In Budapest on July 4, 1922, Count Albert Apponyi, Hungarian statesman and other dignitaries heard addresses from Eugene Pivany of Cleveland and Theodore Brentano, American minister. On July 4, 1926, Apponyi gave a speech in gratitude to the United States and hoped that "America might long remain the leading nation of the world." Theodore Brentano replied that "the friendly feeling of Hungarians was reciprocated in America." Guests at the celebration included Archduke and Archduchess Franz Joseph. Throughout

the city, church bells tolled and thousands listened to speeches in the park at the site where the Washington Monument was erected. A celebration for the 25th anniversary of the unveiling of the Washington Monument took place in the park on July 4, 1931. Nicholas Roosevelt, American minister at Budapest, spoke to the crowd: "Like yourselves, the American people have transformed a wilderness into a great farming community and created in this farming community great cities and finally great industrial centres."

Sources: "Magyars Observe Our Holiday" and "Hungary Observes Fourth," *New York Times*, 4 July 1922, 15, and 5 July 1926, 5, respectively; "Washington Honored in Budapest Exercises," *New York Times*, 5 July 1931, 19.

Ice Cream

One of the popular refreshments eaten on the Fourth of July during the nineteenth century and after. Ice cream was commonly hawked by vendors in booths set up on the Fourth and also sold in ice cream and confectionary stores that were open for business on the holiday. As a special treat fresh fruits of the season were added to the ice cream.

Ice cream was also occasionally given to children without charge. In Charleston, South Carolina, on July 4, 1831, ice cream was distributed free to everyone. On July 4, 1898, ice cream was given out to the women and children at the Willow Tree Alley celebration in Washington, D.C. In Boston, on July 4, 1910, the city had its first "safe and sane" holiday and because of the "limitation put upon the use of explosives and noise-creating instruments, the youth of the city" were treated to free ice cream on the common.

The pleasure of eating ice cream on a hot and sunny July day was not without its risks, however. In Coulterville, Illinois, on July 4, 1886, a large group of farmers and guests who had assembled at the spring there to celebrate the Fourth of July ate ice cream that "was made in copper kettles, and stood for several hours in the vessels before being served" to nearly 100 persons. A few hours later the majority of them took suddenly ill "with all the symptoms of corrosive poisoning." Two young children died and two others were not expected to live. Others were in danger of dying. "An examination of the vessels showed that the ice cream absorbed a great quantity of the copper."

Sources: *Charleston Courier*, 6 July 1831, 2; "Poisoned by Ice Cream," *New York Times*, 7 July 1886, 3; *Washington Evening Star*, 4 July 1898, 12; "Free Ice Cream in Boston," *Washington Post*, 4 July 1910, 5.

Illinois State Fair

The cornerstone of the exposition building of the State Fair was laid on Independence Day in 1894.

Source: George Franklin Seymour, *Oration Delivered on the Occasion of the Laying of the Corner Stone of the Exposition Building of the State Fair of Illinois, July 4th 1894* (Boston: G.R. Willis, 1894).

Immigrants

The Fourth of July served as an ideal time to officially welcome new immigrants into the country, to engender pride and patriotism, and to urge them to celebrate their newly adopted land. According to Roy Rosenzweig, immigrants celebrated the Fourth "to reassert ethnic ties and customs" and "to affirm and reinforce their own distinctive values and priorities." On Independence Day in New York City in 1850, a newspaper reported that "the glorious demonstrations of the memorable 4th had such effect upon the unnaturalized inhabitants of New York, that they thronged the respective offices in the City Hall yesterday [July 5] in vast numbers, anxious to declare their intentions of becoming citizens of the great republic of freedom." However, occasionally new immigrants were involved in public socializing that led to fights. Much of that was caused by drunkenness and general rowdiness. In Worcester, Massachusetts, on July 4, 1902 and 1903, immigrants were either blamed or arrested for causing disorderliness on city streets; some were thought to have hurled "dynamite crackers at motormen and defenseless women." Acculturating immigrants was a concern of town officials there.

Before the Civil War there were already attempts at finding ways to help adapt immigrants to their new society. Public readings of the Declaration of Independence on Independence Day were one method. On July 4, 1857,

in New York City, the document was read "to the immigrants on Ward's Island, and explained by one of the commissioners of emigration. Some extraordinary provender was also furnished them which made them of course feel that they lived in the promised land."

Encouraging immigrants to vote was another way. On July 4, 1927, in New York City, 20,000 native and naturalized citizens eligible to vote attended a reception at City Hall as guests of the Mayor's Committee on Independence Day Reception to First Voters.

In addition, a myriad of organizations were established to assist those new to America, and the Fourth of July was an important day for planned activities. On July 4, 1916, in Trenton, New Jersey, at Cadwalader Park, "New Citizens' Day" was proclaimed and celebrated. Trenton Mayor Donnelly gave an address and several medals were handed out.

One of the largest national celebrations whose purpose it was to demonstrate immigrants' loyalty to America and to pledge their patriotism to this country occurred on July 4, 1918. Referred to as "Loyalty Day," a group of foreign-language bureaus for immigrants under the auspices of a Committee on Public Information petitioned President Wilson in May 1918 for his support and to issue an official loyalty proclamation.

On July 4, 1922, the New York League of Foreign-born Citizens provided a musical program and copies of the *New York Times* that included a facsimile of the Declaration of Independence to everyone in the audience.

See also "**Americanization Day**," **Naturalization on the Fourth**, and "**Parade of Nations**."

Sources: *New York Herald*, 6 July 1850, 1; *New York Times*, 6 July 1857, 2; "Big Day at Trenton," *Philadelphia Inquirer*, 5 July 1916, 3; "Foreign-Born Celebrate," *New York Times*, 5 July 1922, 4; *New York Times*, 5 July 1927, 5; Roy Rosenzweig, *Eight Hours for What We Will: Workers and Leisure in an Industrial City, 1870–1920* (Cambridge: Cambridge University Press, 1983), 156.

Independence Creek, Missouri

Named by Meriwether Lewis and William Clark, leaders of an expedition to explore the

Louisiana Territory, on July 4, 1804, near today's Atchison, Kansas. It was President Thomas Jefferson who sent out the expedition, from St. Louis in May 1804. Lewis and Clark traveled up the Missouri and eventually landed at the site which they named after Independence Day. According to their account, the boat's small brass cannon was fired and the forty-six men that celebrated that day were given an extra rationing of whiskey. A year prior, Thomas Jefferson had written a letter to Lewis on July 4, 1803, in which he "solemnly pledged the faith of the United States" to pay the debts incurred by Lewis and Clark. In 2003 at Monticello the four-year Lewis and Clark Bicentennial (1803–06) was begun and included a mobile commemorative exhibit, "Corps of Discovery II: 200 Years to the Future," led by the National Park Service. On July 4, 2004, the exhibit was located at Kaw Point at the mouth of the Kansas and Missouri rivers in Kansas City, Kansas. When the Bicentennial is completed, Corps II will have visited over 100 communities from coast to coast. Other Lewis and Clark commemorative events in 2004 included a program sponsored by the National Park Service at Fair St. Louis titled "On the Trail with Lewis and Clark."

Sources: James D. Harlan and James M. Denny, *Atlas of Lewis and Clark in Missouri* (Columbia: University of Missouri Press, 2003); Elin Woodger and Brandon Toropov, *Encyclopedia of the Lewis and Clark Expedition* (New York: Facts on File, 2004); "Thomas Jefferson to Meriwether Lewis, July 4, 1803," Web site, *American Memory Project*, Library of Congress <http://memory.loc.gov/ammem/collections/jefferson_papers>.

"Independence Day"

The anniversary of the adoption of the Declaration of Independence on July 4, 1776. The term has been used in some state legislation regarding the holiday. For example, in the Connecticut General Statues, title 1, chapter, 2, "Legal Holidays and Standard of Time," the holiday is referred to as "the fourth day of July (known as Independence Day)." Early in the history of the celebration, the use of "Independence Day" was in some places more popular than "Fourth of July," but the latter phrase gradually increased in popularity dur-

ing the nineteenth century. Edward E. Hale, reminiscing about how the Fourth of July was celebrated in the past in Boston, for example, recalled in 1890 that "in my boyhood [the event] was called 'Independence Day' much more than it is now."

Source: Edward E. Hale, "The Fourth of July," *New England Magazine* 8/6 (August 1890): 698–99.

Independence Day Rock, Wyoming

Named after the Fourth of July and located on the Sweetwater River about midway between the towns of Rawlins and Casper. The rock is granite, measures 1,900 feet long and 700 feet wide, and rises 128 feet tall. Although the origin of its name is uncertain, historian Aubrey L. Haines believes it occurred as a result of mountain men Thomas Fitzpatrick and his friends, who arrived at its base on July 4, 1824. Independence Rock was a stopover destination for travelers on the overland trail. Once there it was common to carve or write personal names with chalk or tar on the rock, also known as "The Register of the Plains," as a testimony of accomplishment for the journeys undertaken. Hundreds of names with dates are inscribed and that information confirms a number of Independence Day celebrations as likely having taken place there.

Celebrations of the Fourth of July at Independence Rock and in the vicinity are noted in a number of diaries and journals. For example, Nathaniel J. Wyeth, a fur trader from New England, after having visited "Rock Independence," celebrated the Fourth of July a number of miles distant near the Green River. On July 4, 1852, after passing by Independence Rock, Enoch Conyers and his group held a grand celebration in a valley near the site. They dined on potatoes, baked beans, rice, pickles, freshly baked breads, rolls, and "Sweetwater Mountain cake."

Sources: *The Journals of Captain Nathaniel J. Wyeth's Expeditions to the Oregon Country 1831–1836*, ed. Don Johnson (Fairfield, Wash.: Ye Galleon Press, 1984); Enoch W. Conyers, "The Diary of E. W. Conyers, a Pioneer of 1852," *Transactions of the Thirty-third Annual Reunion of the Oregon Pioneer Association* (Portland, Ore.: 1905), 456–58; Robert Spurrier Ellison, *Independence Rock, the Great Record of the Desert* (Casper, Wyo.: Natrona County Historical Society,

1930); Richard Reeves, "Fourth of July on the Oregon Trail a Century Ago," *Buffalo News*, 4 July 1995, 38; Weldon Willis Rau, *Surviving the Oregon Trail 1852* (Pullman, Wash.: Washington State University Press, 2001), 103–06.

Independence Hall, Philadelphia

The Pennsylvania State House, referred to as Independence Hall after 1824 when Marquis de Lafayette visited the building, was the site of the assembly house for the Pennsylvania government, the Second Continental Congress (1775–1776), under which the signing of the Declaration of Independence took place, and the Constitutional Convention (1787). It was the east room on the first floor that was first referred to as the "Hall of Independence," but later the entire structure took the name.

The construction of the building began in 1732. After 1800 Charles Willson Peale rented the premises and established a museum of arts and sciences. Later Independence Hall provided a meeting place for the government of the town of Philadelphia until 1901, when a new city hall was built. In 1876 part of Independence Hall served as an exhibit area for the centennial celebration. It was in that year on July 4 that Susan B. Anthony spoke on women's rights. It was the most notable speech given there during the nineteenth century. In 1948 the building and immediate grounds were designated as the Independence National Historical Park. Throughout the nineteenth century the patriotic aura of Independence Hall continued to grow. Its public space provided opportunities on the Fourth for individuals and groups to voice concerns on women's rights, temperance and ethnic acculturation. During the 1960s it was civil rights issues and the Vietnam War that came to the fore.

During the Civil War, Independence Hall was open to the public on the Fourth as a place where persons could reflect on the founding of the country. In 1862, "a constant influx of country people, contemplating the pictures and the immortal old liberty bell" was reported. Following the Civil War, each year a large wooded grandstand was built to provide a place for the presentation of speeches and ceremonies. For example, on Independence Day in 1897, Philadelphia Mayor War-

wick and ex-ambassador to England Thomas F. Bayard presented speeches to a crowd of 5,000. Bayard mentioned the Liberty Bell and said it "seemed to him to be the real orator of the day." The celebration was sponsored by the Society of the War of 1812, and German singing societies provided much of the music.

Events were often varied and interesting. On July 4, 1870, a temperance mass meeting was held there with music provided by Hassler's Band. There were several addresses and "an original and lengthy poem" by John Hickey was recited.

On July 4, 1893, hundreds of persons representing patriotic societies and various European nationalities assembled there. Dignitaries assembled on a grandstand to give addresses. Historic American flags were flown as well as the "French Bourbon flag." On July 4, 1912, Congressman J. Hampton Moore presented an oration there. He "impressed on his hearers a sense of reverence for the Constitution." Moore mentioned the admission of Arizona and New Mexico to the union: "These are the last territories in Continental United States that can be admitted to the Union. There is now no more territory to be taken into the Union unless we shall consider the admission of our colonial possessions. We have increased the number of Uncle Sam's partners from 13 to 48."

The first president who participated in an event at Independence Hall on July 4 was George Washington in 1795. Presidents who gave speeches at Independence Hall included Woodrow Wilson (1914), John F. Kennedy (1962), Gerald R. Ford (1976), William Clinton (1993), and George W. Bush (2001). Other noteworthy speakers included Patrick J. Hurley, secretary of war, on July 4, 1931. On July 4, 1966, an exact replica of Independence Hall was opened to the public at Knott's Berry Farm in Buena Park, California. The opening was announced in the U.S. Congress on June 21.

Sources: "The Fourth of July, *Philadelphia Inquirer*, 5 July 1862, 8; "Temperance Meeting in Independence Square," *Philadelphia Inquirer*, 6 July 1870, 2; "On Hallowed Ground," *Philadelphia Inquirer*, 5 July 1893, 1; "A Glorious Day It Was, Indeed," *Philadelphia Inquirer*, 6 July 1897, 1; "Moore's Oration on Historic Site Stirs Big Crowd," *Philadelphia*

Inquirer, 5 July 1912, 1; Charlene Mires, "Independence Hall," *Encyclopedia of American Studies* (New York: Grolier Educational, 2001), 2:344–45.

Independence, or the Fourth of July, 1799

This drama ("Interlude") in one act was premiered on July 4, 1799, at the Hay-Market Theatre in Boston.

Source: *Independent Chronicle,* 1–4 July 1799, 3.

Indiana Territory

This parcel of land was formed on July 4, 1800, from the western part of the Northwest Territory. Vincennes was selected as the seat of government and President John Adams named **William Henry Harrison**, later the 9th president of the U.S., as the first territorial governor. Harrison convened his judges and enacted a code of seven laws for the territory and various resolutions.

Sources: *Executive Journal of Indiana Territory, 1800–1816,* Indiana Historical Society publications, vol. 3; "The Indiana Daughters of the American Revolution Commemorates the 200th Anniversary of the Indiana Territory," Web site, 5 September 2002, <http://www.ipfw.edu/ipfwhist/historgs/dar/plate.htm>.

Indians (American) *see* Native Americans

International Freedom Festival, Detroit, Michigan

This event occurred on July 4, 1959, in Detroit's Civic Center and was a joint celebration of United States Independence Day and Canada's Dominion Day, July 1 (later, Canada Day). Highlights included the presentation of a new flag bearing the star of the new state of Alaska, a flag raising with children representing every state and Canada's 10 provinces, and fireworks launched off three barges by Toshio Ogatsu, pyrotechnician and president of Japan's largest fireworks factory.

The presentation opened with a 21-gun salute, and continued 1,500 feet above the river. Two 25-foot by 40-foot "spectaculars" were rigged on the end barges: "Salute to the queen" had a fiery outline of the North American Continent flanked by a symbol of the American Eagle and Queen Elizabeth's royal insignia. The second was "'Independence Day Then and Now,' portraying three figures of the spirit of '76 bear-

ing a flag of the period of the 13 colonies, which would change to the 49-star flag, with a 50th star representing Hawaii circling in the background."

Source: Jenny Nolan, "The Bloody Fourth That Ended Do-It-Yourself Fireworks in Detroit." *Detroit News* Web site, <http://detnews.com/history/fireworks/fireworks.htm>.

International Peace Jubilee

A series of concerts organized by musician and band leader Patrick S. Gilmore (1829–1892) in Boston to commemorate the end of the Franco-Prussian war. The event began on June 17, 1872, and ended on July 4 of that year. **William Lloyd Garrison**, who professed to have attended every day, commented in a letter he wrote on July 4, 1872, that "It has been an occasion of indescribable enjoyment to me. Nothing approaching such an exhibition has the world ever witnessed."

Source: *The Letters of William Lloyd Garrison,* 6 vols., ed. Walter M. Merrill and Louis Ruchames (Cambridge, Mass.: Belknap Press of Harvard University Press, 1981), 6:232–33.

Irish-Americans

By the early 1850s a considerable portion of the growing unskilled labor immigrant population in Eastern Seaboard cities was Irish, and this precipitated a greater Irish presence on the Fourth of July. Nowhere was the impact of this ethnic group more prevalent than New York, where by 1855, most of the 20,000 unskilled laborers were Irish. To accommodate the needs of this working class, mutual aid organizations were formed, and many took advantage of the Fourth of July holiday as a means of raising their visibility. On July 4, 1852, for example, a New York City parade boasted the Shamrock Benevolent Society, Erin Paternal Benevolent Society of Brooklyn, and the Irish American Society, among others. Not unlike other ethnic groups, the Irish frequently held their own celebrations, many of which emphasized the exploits of Irish homeland heroes. In Newark, New Jersey, for example, the Irish celebration on Independence Day in 1886 included two parades,

a big mass meeting, and many speeches. Many homes had green flags with harps of gold displayed from windows and citizens wore green ribbons. An Irish military regiments processed to City Hall, one from Caledonian Park and another from Military Park. At City Hall they met and paraded back to Caledonian Park where speeches were given by Governor [Leon] Abbett and other dignitaries. Hon. Samuel J. Randall spoke stressing the importance of what Gladstone was attempting to do for Ireland.

He said, "If modern civilization meant anything it meant the right of local self-government."

It was not uncommon for tension to arise between different ethnic groups. As early as July 4, 1838, fights broke out in the Sixth Ward in New York when American-born youths clashed with Irish immigrants in the streets there.

The Irish played a significant role for the North in the Civil War. The well-known New York "Irish Brigade" led by General Thomas Francis Meagher participated in some significant battle engagements. Following the war, Meagher was appointed secretary of the Territory of Montana and acting governor from 1865 to 1867. On July 4, 1905, an equestrian bronze statue of Meagher was unveiled on the Capitol Grounds in Helena, Montana.

Another noteworthy event occurred on July 4, 1880, when the United Irishmen of Philadelphia celebrated at South Broad Street Park in that city. On July 4, 1921, members of the American Association for the Recognition of the Irish Republic (AARIA) paraded up Fifth Avenue in New York. "There were fifty bands in the procession, and, on an order from Major Michael A. Kelley, Secretary of the association, British and jazz music were tabooed. Patriotic airs and Irish melodies predominated." Judge Alfred J. Talley of General Sessions presented a speech in which he said, "There is no nation that has contributed so much in blood, in brain and in constructive power generally to this country of ours as the Irish People have. There is no sentiment or process of reasoning expressed in the Declaration of Independence that does not apply to Ireland today with force equal to that which made it the property of the colonies in 1776." In Chicago that day, 25,000 Irish-Americans adopted a resolution condemning Charles W. Hutchinson, vice president of the Corn Ex-

change National Bank, for blocking the AARIR from meeting in the South Park. The Irish paraded and celebrated in Normal Park.

Sources: *Philadelphia Inquirer*, 6 July 1880, 2; "Newark's Irish Celebration," *New York Times*, 6 July 1886, 8; *Washington Evening Star*, 5 July 1905, 1; "Multitude Parades for Irish Republic" and "Irish Barred from Park," *New York Times*, 5 July 1921, 3; Appelbaum, *The Glorious Fourth*, 81–84.

Ives, Charles Edward (1874–1954)

Remarkable American composer who wrote "The Fourth of July" (movement 3 of *A Symphony: New England Holidays*), whose musical idea is novel, if not unique. The work depicts the sounds of fireworks explosions and clouds of smoke. The piece is based on Ives' boyhood years growing up in Danbury, Connecticut, and his experiences on the Fourth of July. Ives writes, "It's a boy's 4th. His festivities start in the quiet of the midnight before, and grow raucous with the sun. Everybody knows what it's like — if everybody doesn't — Cannon on the Green, Village Band on Main Street, fire crackers, shanks mixed on cornets, strings around big toes, torpedoes, church bells..." The work was composed in 1912–13 and its first known performance was in Paris on February 21, 1932. Ives is considered the most important composer of art music in twentieth century America. He was an accomplished organist and, ironically, he worked in the insurance business for over thirty years.

Sources: Charles E. Ives, *Memos*, ed. John Kirkpatrick (New York: W.W. Norton, 1972), 104; J. Peter Burkholder, "Charles Ives," *Grove Music Online*, 2005.

Jackson, Andrew (1767–1845)

Seventh president of the U.S. (1829–37), whose popularity resulting from his successful military ventures and his less popular political stances were reflected in Fourth of July celebrations in many cities and towns across the United States. Jackson served briefly in the American Revolution, later practiced law, and was a congressman from Tennessee (1796–97). Jackson was an ardent participant in Fourth of July events during the 1820s. On each subsequent Fourth of July, he was in a different Tennessee city either celebrating or being honored. On July 4, 1822, he received a sword as voted by the Tennessee legislature in 1819 to honor his War of 1812 service. In 1824 he attended an Independence Day celebration on July 3 in Nashville and on July 6 celebrated again at the Fountain of Health near the Hermitage, his home. In 1825–28 he attended celebrations in Franklin, Pulaski, and Nashville, respectively. On July 4, 1828, he was present at the celebration in Carthage and later that afternoon joined a dinner celebration in Lebanon. On the following day he was in Hartsville attending a public dinner there.

Jackson's attempt at the presidency in 1825 failed, but he was elected four years later. His popularity grew out of his military feats, first defeating the Creeks in 1813–14 and the British at New Orleans in 1815. In 1818 Jackson commanded an invasion of Florida at the same time Secretary of State John Quincy Adams was having discussions with Luis de Onis, the Spanish minister, regarding a settlement. Jackson captured Pensacola and executed two British subjects who had been accused of aiding the enemy. Although Jackson's Florida campaign received popular approval, it was the manner in which the campaign was conducted which caused the disdain of most of the president's cabinet members. The division in support of Jackson was particularly evident in the nation's capital during the first few months of his presidency.

On the eve of the Fourth of July in 1828, a "Declaration of Objections" to the election of Jackson for president was published in the *Political Arena* (Fredericksburg, Virginia) and reprinted in the *Frederick-Town Herald* (Maryland) "as a parody on the Declaration of Independence" and presented "in a condensed form, most of the charges and objections against General Jackson, which so decidedly unfit him for the elevated and responsible station of the chief magistracy of this country." The opening lines provide an interesting comparison of this "Declaration" with Jefferson's document.

When in the course of public events, it becomes necessary for one party to oppose the political Chief, who, to the surprise of the nations of the earth is supported by another, for a dignified and lofty station, for which the fiat of nature's God disqualifies him — a decent respect for the advancement of their cause requires that they should declare the reasons which impel them to the opposition.

We hold these truths to be self-evident, that certain requisites are necessary in a Chief Magistrate; that amongst these, are respect for the laws, knowledge of the constitution, experience in public affairs, and acquaintance with the political and diplomatic history of the country. That the generous and enlightened support of his fellow citizens, is the highest incentive of the Patriot; and that capricious distrust of public servants is as conducive to despotism, as unsuspecting confidence.

Meanwhile Jackson was in Carthage, Tennessee, celebrating Independence Day and on July 5 was honored at a public dinner in Hartsville.

On July 4, 1829, in Washington, a written statement of confidence to President Jackson was presented by General Van Ness on behalf of the Board of Aldermen and Common Council to assuage the unpopularity the president was experiencing in the city. On that day, Jackson was supposed to appear at a ceremony for laying the cornerstone block of lock number 2 on the **Chesapeake and Ohio Canal**, but due to severe rain, that event was postponed and Jackson remained in the Executive Mansion. He held a reception with refreshments at 1 P.M. for public officers, foreign ministers, and private citizens, who "paid their respects to the Chief Magistrate" and enjoyed music provided by the U.S. Marine Band.

Jackson's popularity was evident in many other cities such as Charleston, South Carolina, and Norfolk, Virginia. He was invited to attend the Union Party in Charleston on July 4, 1831, but could not due to other commitments. A letter he wrote on June 14 in responding to the invitation advised the celebrants to consider "the immense value of your national Union to your collective and individual happiness; to cherish a cordial, habitual, and immoveable attachment to it." Jackson's letter was read aloud at the celebration that day. On that same day he had been invited to join the Volunteer Corps of Norfolk in celebration of the Fourth but also declined. He wrote back, "My soul will be with you in the commemoration of an event that has afforded the first proof that man is capable of self-government." In fact, Jackson, at about the time of the Fourth, was at Fortress Monroe, near Norfolk.

During his presidency Jackson remained in Washington in July, at times only long enough to attend to his duties, such as reviewing military troops and to leave immediately after for rest and recreation. On July 4, 1832, Jackson was at the Executive Mansion working on a bill to extend and modify the Charter of the Bank of the U.S. It was a task "peculiarly suitable to the day, and [ ] he had come to the conclusion that it ought not to become a law," and so he vetoed it and returned it to the Senate.

Occasionally Jackson was honored in song and verse. The following "Ode for a Jackson Celebration, July 4th 1834" was printed in the *Boston Mercantile Journal* and reprinted in the *Frederick-Town Herald* (16 August 1834, 2). Sung to the tune of "Hail to the Chief," the poem has three stanzas of which below is the first:

> Ninety-nine cheers for the hot-headed hero!
> Ninety-nine more for Van Buren his squire!
> Who sit at their leisure and fiddle like Nero,
> Enjoying the frolic, while Rome is on fire.
> Hurray for Hickory!
> None but old nick, or he
> Could help us poor fellows to dine!
> We are all collar men;
> Anarchy come again!
> Hurray for Jackson! Blanks, paper, paper and twine!

On July 4, 1836, at the Boston Democratic Celebration in Boston, *Jackson's Grand March* (Boston: Parker and Ditson, 1836), written in honor of Gen. Jackson by S. Knaebel, was performed by the Boston Brass Band.

Jackson's popularity lasted for most of the century. On July 4, 1893, the Andrew Jackson Democratic Club in New York held its celebration. Under Jackson, Arkansas (July 4, 1836) and Michigan (July 4, 1837) first celebrated Independence Day as the 25th and 26th states. Today Jackson continues to be remembered through the activities held annually on the Fourth at his home, Hermitage. In 2004 a celebration called "Relive Independence Day 1815!" was held on the grounds that

included authentic military encampment and drills, political speeches from the era, cannon and musket demonstrations and a reenactor playing the part of Jackson.

Sources: *The Papers of Andrew Jackson*, 6 vols., ed. Harold D. Moser (Knoxville: University Tennessee Press, 1980–2002); "*Frederick-Town Herald*, 5 July 1828, 2; *Daily Cincinnati Gazette*, 15 July 1829, 2; "The Fourth of July," *National Intelligencer*, 7 July 1829, 3; *Connecticut Mirror*, 16 July 1831, 2; *The Globe* (Washington City), 9 July 1831, 3, and *National Intelligencer*, 8 July 1831, 3; *National Intelligencer*, 11 July 1832, 2; *New York Times*, 5 July 1893, 9.

Jackson Hall, Washington, D.C.

The cornerstone for this Washington, D.C., building on Pennsylvania Avenue was laid on July 4, 1845. The same hand trowel "with which General Washington officiated at the foundation of the Capitol" was used. A local newspaper described the event:

> A numerous procession marched along Pennsylvania Avenue, from the Union printing office to the site of Messrs. Blair & Rives's building, which they call Jackson Hall, on Pennsylvania Avenue, where the procession halted, for the purpose of laying the cornerstone of the intended edifice. The procession, which consisted of the several Democratic Associations of this city and other democratic citizens, was headed by the ancient and respectable brotherhood of Free and Accepted Masons. The latter, with their Grand Master, Dr. Magruder, and other officers in their insignia of office made an imposing display.

Amidst music provided by the German Band, "the Honorable Mr. Shields, Commissioner of the General Land Office," presented an oration which was considered "eloquent and appropriate to the occasion."

Jackson Hall, completed in the following year, was dedicated on July 4, 1846. The building served as a meeting place for the city's Democratic associations.

Sources: *National Intelligencer*, 7 July 1845, 3; "Local News," *National Intelligencer*, 8 July 1846, 4.

Jefferson Library Association

The first meeting of this Washington City organization took place on July 4, 1833. The association was established "for the benefit of apprentices, mechanics and other working men of Washington City" and included

100 members. The library consisted of 1,500 volumes. The group's meeting took place at the City Hall and an oration was presented there by the popular speaker James Hoban.

Source: "Jefferson Library Association," *National Intelligencer*, 4 July 1833, 3.

Jefferson Memorial, Louisville, Kentucky

A Jefferson memorial was presented to the people of Kentucky in this town by the brothers Isaac W. and Bernard Bernheim and was dedicated on July 4, 1900.

Source: A plaque on the sculpture, located on Main Street, Louisville, Kentucky.

Jefferson Monument, University of Missouri at Columbia

The six-foot granite obelisk that served as a marker for 50 years at the gravesite of Thomas Jefferson at Monticello was presented as a gift to the University of Missouri and unveiled there on July 4, 1885. The monument was put in place at the president's residence about seven years after Jefferson's death in 1826. In the decades that followed, the grave site was left to deteriorate. In 1883 a new monument was erected there with funds provided by Congress. Prior to the placement of the new memorial, plans by the descendants were underway to move the original obelisk to the campus of the University of Missouri. It was "the first state university in the Louisiana Purchase Territory" and Jefferson had facilitated its purchase during his administration as president. It was Alexander Frederick Fleet, a University of Virginia graduate, whose idea it was to move the monument to Missouri. The monument was placed adjacent to Academic Hall on the campus and unveiled amidst addresses by Missouri senator George E. Vest, United States secretary of state Thomas F. Bayard and Captain James B. Eads, noted Missouri engineer. Through the years the monument was moved to different settings on the campus and finally to its present location on Francis Quadrangle, next to the chancellor's residence. The marble plaque which was attached to the monument when it sat at Monticello is maintained in a university vault. The plaque bears the words that Jefferson himself requested:

> Here was buried Thomas Jefferson[,] Author of the Declaration of American Independence of the Statute of Virginia for religious freedom & Father of the University of Virginia

Source: William Peden, *The Jefferson Monument at the University of Missouri* (Columbia: University of Missouri — Columbia Development Fund, 1977).

Jefferson statue, Avondale, Ohio

Unveiled on July 4, 1897, on the lawn of the residence of Thomas J. McGrath. The bronze statue was carved by August Mundenk. A "brief speech" was made by Cincinnati mayor Gustav Tafel and an oration was given by Col. George Washington of Newport, Kentucky. The base of the monument is inscribed: "All men were born free and equal."

Source: "Bust of Jefferson Unveiled," *Washington Post*, 6 July 1897, 1.

Jefferson, Thomas (1743–1826)

Third president of the U.S. (1801–09) and author of the Declaration of Independence, Virginia legislator and governor (1779–81), first U.S. secretary of state (1790–93), second vice president (1797–1801), and third president of the United States (1801–09). Together with John Adams and George Washington, he shares the greatest attention as the most revered and distinguished politician honored in Independence Day celebrations in the history of the country. Jefferson hosted the first Fourth of July celebration and reception in the President's House on July 4, 1801. The occasion established a tradition of similar celebrations throughout his presidency and for other presidents that followed. According to newspaper reports, from 1803 to 1808, many of those attending Jefferson's receptions assembled for dinner at Stelle's Hotel each year. It is not known if Jefferson was among the group. Jefferson was not only instrumental in recruiting some of the finest musicians for the U.S. **Marine Band**, but also in bringing the ensemble to Washington City and having them first perform at the White House.

Following his death, Jefferson continued to be praised and celebrated on Independence Day. In Petersburg, Virginia, on July 4, 1827,

R.R. Collier gave an impressive speech about Jefferson and his writing of the Declaration of Independence. Collier asked his audience how they felt about the statesman: "Can a life, fellow-citizens, thus spent in the service of his country, fail to excite your admiration, and to enlist your gratitude?" See also **White House**.

Sources: *National Intelligencer*, 6 July 1801 and 1803, 2 and 3 respectively; "Celebrations," *Richmond Enquirer*, 13 July 1827, 2.

Jerusalem

The first Fourth of July celebration headed by Paul Knabenshue, the new American general consulate, took place on July 4, 1929. As a newspaper reported, "Americans in Palestine have been celebrating the Fourth of July for many years, but this year, for the first time, the festivities have been headed by a Consul general." Knabenshue made an address in which he lauded all of the nations in the Middle East. He described Jerusalem as "a strong attraction for Americans as evinced by the great number of tourists visiting Palestine annually and by the important contributions made by Americans of the various religious, educational and charitable institutions established here." The day's events included a reception and a "solemn service" at St. George's Cathedral.

Source: "4th in Jerusalem Brings Out Throngs," *New York Times*, 5 July 1929, 7.

John, Pilgrim (fl. 1860s)

Composed "Pro Patria! A National Song for the Fourth of July, 1862." This work, for voice and piano, was dedicated to Abraham Lincoln. First line: "Our country's glorious birth, Glory of all the earth, July, July the Fourth!" (Brooklyn: D.S. Holmes, 1862).

Johnson, Andrew (1808–1875)

Seventeenth president of the U.S. (1865–69). On July 4, 1866, the veterans of the War of 1812 visited Johnson in the White House and gave brief addresses, to which the president responded in kind. On July 4, 1868, Johnson issued a Third Amnesty Proclamation in Washington, D.C., and it was printed in the *Washington Evening Star*, 4 July 1868, 1.

Source: "The Fourth of July," *Washington Evening Star*, 5 July 1866, 1.

Johnson, James (1811–1891)

Lawyer, politician and governor of Georgia (June to December, 1861), James Johnson addressed citizens of Savannah on July 4, 1865, telling them that slavery was dead and they needed to renew their allegiance to the Union. Johnson, born in Robinson County, North Carolina, graduated from the Georgia State University at Athens in 1832. He practiced law in Columbus, Georgia, and was elected to the U.S. Congress in 1851. President Andrew Johnson appointed him as provisional governor of Georgia for his abilities in the reconstruction of that state following the Civil War. He was described as highly devoted to his work in restoring Georgia to the Union. "He was firm, just and conservative, and it was fortunate for the state that so grave a task fell into the hands of man so fair, honest and able." In his later years he held a number of positions in the state, including judge on the state bench.

Sources: "From Savannah," *Indianapolis Daily Journal*, 13 July 1865, 1; "James Johnson," *The National Cyclopaedia of American Biography*, 1:227–28.

Johnson, Lyndon Baines (1908–1973)

Thirty-sixth president of the U.S. (1963–69), who is principally remembered on Independence Day as having signed the **Freedom of Information Act (FOIA)**, July 4, 1966. The law assures the public increased access to federal records through judicial review of government decisions to withhold records. Regarding the bill, Johnson said: "Democracy works best when the people have all the information that the security of the nation permits. No one should be able to pull curtains of secrecy around decisions which can be revealed without injury to the public interest."

Johnson's celebration of the Fourth was marred somewhat that year due to the protests lodged worldwide against the **Vietnam War**. While citizens protested in France, England, Italy, Denmark, Norway, Sweden and West Germany, letters of congratulations on the nation's birthday were received by Johnson from West Germany's President Heinrich Luebke, the Philippines' President Ferdinand Marcos, and Emperor Hirohito of Japan.

On July 4, 1963, Vice President Johnson was at Independence Hall making a speech, advocating "for less talk and more action to obtain civil rights for all Americans."

Frequently, Johnson preferred celebrating the Fourth in privacy at his LBJ ranch in Texas, enjoying various recreations such as boating in Granite Shoals Lake and reading congratulatory letters from around the world, while devoting some portion of the day to official business. On July 4, 1966, he discussed "the supplemental appropriations necessary to carry out the new civil rights law" with his staff in Texas and in Washington.

On July 4, 1968, President Johnson was in Texas, accompanied by forty foreign diplomats for a celebration of the Hemis-Fair in San Antonio.

Sources: Murray Illson, "Nation Marks 4th in Ideal Weather," *New York Times*, 5 July 1963, 1; John W. Finney, "Johnson Relaxes with Friends on Texas Ranch and Goes Boating," *New York Times*, 5 July 1964, 1; "Americans Mark 4th as Critics Jeer" and John D. Pomfret, "Johnson Supports Greater Access to U. S. Data," *New York Times*, 5 July 1966, A1 and 25, respectively; "Johnson and Diplomats to Visit the HemisFair," *New York Times*, 4 July 1968, 10.

Jones, Skelton (d. 1812)

Publisher, lawyer, and orator who delivered a funeral oration in Richmond on July 4, 1807, in response to the battering of the American frigate *Chesapeake* by the British warship *Leopard* on June 22 off the coast of Norfolk, Virginia, and another address on July 4, 1812, in Petersburg, Virginia, following President's Madison proclamation of war against Great Britain on June 19. Jones' 1812 oration was one of the most impassioned Independence Day orations of the early nineteenth century.

The Richmond celebration in 1807 was laden with heavy hearts and anger due to the **USS *Chesapeake* and *Leopard* battle.** The British had boarded the *Chesapeake* demanding that commander Captain James Barron hand over a group of British deserters. Barron refused and the *Leopard* began firing broadsides into the *Chesapeake*. Within twenty minutes, three American sailors had been killed and eighteen others wounded, including Barron. The badly damaged *Chesapeake* made its way back to Norfolk. The public was aroused and incensed. Skelton Jones was called upon to speak at the July 4 celebration in Richmond. It was reported that the event was particularly fraught with "enthusiasm and fervour" and that "Richmond was on that day the miniature of the nation." Skelton spoke in the Hall of the House of Delegates following a reading of the Declaration of Independence at 2 P.M. His oration was considered "impressive and affecting."

Jones was invited by the citizens of Petersburg, Virginia, on Independence Day in 1812 to address "this momentous crisis" and that "old and haughty nation," England. Jones' address included what he called a "tale of truth," that "right [is] on our side," and that "one word in their own language, which we do not understand, and that is the word *fear*." His scathing attack on British history was characterized as one of atrocities and subjugations of others, and he carefully presented numerous details to support his claim. Jones specifically addressed the British practice of impressing American merchant seamen into the British navy:

The free-born, the independent, the proud and dignified citizen of the great American Republic, inoffensively pursuing his honest avocation, is captured, enslaved and condemned, upon the giddy round-top, or the blood-stained deck, in one of those inventions of man, called a ship of war, to fight against his countrymen — perhaps his brother. We see him next upon the gangway for the expression of a noble hatred against those principles which reduced him to slavery. Divested even of the habiliments with which his oppressors had found it in their interest to cover him: his reverend locks streaming to the "viewless wind," — receiving, upon his bare back from the hands of a stripling midshipman, the rope's end, or the cat-o-nine-tails, until "that spirit is broken which can never be bent," — lacerated beyond endurance and beyond the vigor of human life to bear — dead — he is sewn in a hammock, and the surge receives him — released from the society of slaves — and thought fit food for the monsters of the deep: — More monstrous they that float upon its surface.

In 1816, together with John Burk, Jones participated in the compiling of a history of Virginia.

Sources: *The Enquirer*, 7 July 1807, 2; *The [Washington?] Courier*, 16 July 1812, 2–3; John Burk, *The History of Virginia: From Its First Settlement to the Present Day* (Petersburg, Va.: Dickson and Pescud, 1804–1816).

"Jubilee"

Term used to represent the Fourth of July as a "great national festival" throughout the nineteenth century, but remembered chiefly for its use as the theme of the 1826 fiftieth anniversary celebration. An early use of the term occurred in the oration (Dunham and True, 1795) delivered by Samuel Worcester, Hanover, New Hampshire, in 1795 at Dartmouth: "Hail the auspicious day! Well may it be celebrated as the festival of man, as the jubilee of nations." Independence Day in 1798 in Philadelphia was described in the *General Advertiser* as the day of the "Great Jubilee of Americans." The first use of the term in Washington City occurred on July 4, 1801, when the celebration there was referred to as "first year of the Republican Jubilee." On July 4, 1816, in Fredericksburg, Virginia, the day was considered a "jubilee for us not merely as Americans, but as [free] men," while in Versailles, France, on that day the event was cited as a "jubilee of freedom" and one "to be hailed with joyful acclamations." In Worcester, Massachusetts, Independence Day in 1820 was referred to by a local newspaper as a "National Jubilee." In New York on July 4, 1822, a concert took place at Chatham Garden and was billed as a **"Grand National Jubilee."** In both South Carolina and Georgia in 1823, the day was referred to in the "Minutes of the Synod" of those states as a "national jubilee." In Carlisle, Pennsylvania, on July 4, 1826, the ceremony there was described as the "First jubilee of American Independence" and in Greenville, South Carolina, William B. Johnson delivered a "jubilee" Independence Day address (Republican Office, 1826). On July 4, 1840, in Harrisburg, Pennsylvania, an editorial published in *The Magician* was titled "The National Jubilee" and the author extolled the virtues of "national freedom." The term was used in Baltimore in 1842 to describe Independence Day and in Portsmouth, New Hampshire, on July 4, 1853.

Sources: *General Advertiser*, 4 July 1798, 2; "Fourth of July, 1801," *National Intelligencer*, 3 July 1801, 3; *Virginia Herald*, 19 June 1816; *Kentucky Palladium*, 19 July 1816, 3; *National Aegis*, 12 July 1820, 2; *New York Advertiser*, 6 July 1822, 3; *Pittsburgh Recorder* 2/48 (25 December 1823): 759; *Democratic Republican and Agricultural Register*, 5 July 1826, 2–3; *The Magician*, 4 July 1840, 2; *Niles' National Register*, 9 July 1842, 1; *The Portsmouth Jubilee: The Reception of the Sons of Portsmouth Resident Abroad, July 4, 1853* (Portsmouth: C.W. Brewster and Son, 1853).

Jubilee, or the Triumph of Freedom

"A new patriot piece" first performed at the Theatre in New York on the evening of July 4, 1826. One of the play's characters was the Goddess of Liberty, portrayed by "Mrs. Stickney."

Source: *New York Evening Post*, 3 July 1826, 2

Kansas-Nebraska Act of 1854

The passage of this bill on May 30, 1854, which repealed the Missouri Compromise that had supposedly settled the slavery issue in the Louisiana Purchase territories, was reflected in Independence Day observances across the country. The bill had been introduced in Congress by Senator Stephen A. Douglas. The result was that slavery could now be introduced in the new territories. The passage of this bill only weeks before the symbolic national holiday resulted in persons throughout the North expressing dissention and anger on Independence Day. From Ontario, Indiana, to New York City, people assembled on the Fourth of July to offer resistance to the expansion of slave territory. In Pepperell, Massachusetts, effigies of President Pierce were burned. In Boston the Rev. A.L. Stone exclaimed in his oration, "we must admit no more slave states." In Providence, Rhode Island, Jerome B. Kimball, the town's key orator that day, said, "The Rights of a portion of the free citizens of a newly organized Territory have been grossly outraged and their just privileges ruthlessly trampled in the dust.... Let the free States of the North and West put themselves under the contribution to secure to her the enjoyment of those rights, to the full extent of the constitutional guaranties." Other opponents who spoke on the Fourth of July regarding the act of 1854 included **William Lloyd Garrison** and Henry David Thoreau.

Sources: *Oration Delivered Before the Municipal Authorities of the City of Providence by Jerome B. Kimball ...* (Providence: Knowles, Anthony Co., 1856); Cora Dolbee, "Fourth of July in Early Kansas, 1854–1857," *Kansas Historical Quarterly* 10 (February 1941): 34–78 (see also 8 [1939]: 115–39); Hennig Cohen and Tristram Potter Coffin, eds., *The Folklore of American Holidays*, 3rd ed. (Detroit: Gale, 1999), 277–78.

Kaskaskia Island, Illinois, Bell

Eleven years older than the Liberty Bell in Philadelphia, the Kaskaskia Bell was rung on July 4, 1778, on the occasion when George Rogers Clark and a group of soldiers drove the British off the island. The bell was cast in La Rochelle, France, in 1741, and presented to the church of Illinois as a gift from King Louis XV. The bell was used until 1874 when a hairline crack was found. In 1948 the State of Illinois provided a new structure for the bell and in 1999 Kaskaskia Island celebrated the 50th anniversary of the building and the 30th anniversary of the annual Independence Day program. Kaskaskia Island is located six miles north of Chester, Illinois.

Source: "30th Annual Independence Day Program and 50th Anniversary of Shrine Building July 4 at Kaskaskia Bell," Illinois Historic Preservation Agency, *News*, 14 June 1999.

Kennedy, John Fitzgerald (1917–1963)

Thirty-fifth president of the U.S. (1961–63). Kennedy was born in Brookline, Massachusetts, and attended Harvard University. He served in the navy during World War II. He was elected to the U.S. Congress in 1946 and served two terms. In 1960 Kennedy ran for the presidency against Republican Richard Nixon and won. Kennedy's first major Fourth of July event was in 1946 when he gave a speech titled "Some Elements of the American Character" at Faneuil Hall in Boston.

In 1961, President Kennedy was at his retreat at Hyannis Port on the Fourth. The Kennedy Administration had issued a directive in April 1961 "restricting the use of Federal funds for the holiday celebrations at embassies." The party given in London at Winfield House, the U.S. ambassador's residence, was sharply curtailed and limited only to foreign diplomats stationed there. On July 4, 1962, Kennedy spoke before 100,000 persons at Independence Hall in Philadelphia and proposed a "Declaration of Interdependence." He called for a mutual European-American partnership "in trade, aid, and common defense." "I will say here now, on this Day of Independence, that the United States will be ready for a Declaration of Interdependence." He said "that we will be prepared to discuss with a united Europe the ways and means of forming a concrete Atlantic partnership, a mutually beneficial partnership between the new union now emerging in Europe and the old American Union founded here." After giving his speech, Kennedy went to Camp David in Maryland.

In Jerusalem on July 4, 1966, a memorial to President Kennedy was dedicated by Chief Justice Earl Warren amidst a crowd of 5000 Israelis and Americans.

Sources: "Kennedy Curb on Funds Reduces Scale of Envoys' July 4 Parties," *New York Times*, 5 July 1961, 1, 3; William H. Stringer, "Kennedy Asks 'Declaration of Interdependence,'" *Christian Science Monitor*, 5 July 1962, 1; "Americans Mark 4th as Critics Jeer," *Washington Post*, 5 July 1966, A1, 16.

Key, Francis Scott (1779–1843)

Key was born in Frederick, Maryland, attended St. John's College in Annapolis, and became a lawyer. He is remembered chiefly on the Fourth of July for composing the nation's national anthem, "The Star-Spangled Banner." But Key was also an excellent speaker. On July 4, 1831, he spoke in the Rotunda of the Capitol and addressed supporters of President Andrew Jackson. In an attempt to moderate opposing sentiments in a politically divided city, Key asked those assembled to simply share with him, in his words,

> What the blessing in which calls forth, on this day, a nation's gratitude and joy. What it is which, throughout the limits of our spreading country, calls together countless multitudes, assemble, like ourselves, to testify their reverence for the day. What it is that raised their song of triumph, as if one heart animated all the mass, and beat in every pulse of our population.

A reporter writing for *The Globe* stated, "Mr. Key's oration was eloquent, and seemed to have been inspired by the grand memorials with which he was surrounded." Just prior to his oration, the "Star-Spangled Banner was played."

Another poem by Key associated with Independence Day is "For the Fourth of July, 1832," published in *Poems* (1857). Key's verse reflects both his patriotism and spirituality:

Before the Lord we bow —
The God who reigns above,
And rules the world below,
Boundless in power and love.
Our thanks we bring,
In joy and praise,
Our hearts we raise
To heaven's high King.

On July 4, 1888, Key was commemorated in San Francisco with the unveiling of a monument to his honor. On July 4, 1900, at a celebration held at Glyndon Park in Baltimore and sponsored by the Temperance Camp Association and Glyndon Cornet Band, Edwin Higgins delivered an address upon "the Life and Times of Francis Scott Key." He spoke about Baltimorean James Lick who built the Key Monument in Golden Gate Park in San Francisco. "Lick honored Key and his song because they helped to make his own achievements and benefactions possible." See also **"Star-Spangled Banner"** and **Francis Scott Key Monument Association, Baltimore**.

Sources: *The Globe*, 6 July 1831, 2; *National Intelligencer*, 15 July 1831, 2; *San Francisco Chronicle*, 5 July 1888, 8; *Baltimore Morning Herald*, 5 July 1900, 10.

Key West, Florida, City Hall

This Florida landmark was dedicated on July 4, 1876. Included in the ceremony was an address presented by Walter C. Maloney.

Source: *A Sketch of the History of Key West, by Walter C. Maloney: An Address Delivered at the Dedication of the New City Hall, July 4, 1876, at the Request of the Common Council of the City* (Newark, N.J.: Advertiser Printing House, 1876).

Kidd, William (ca. 1645–1701)

A monument to Captain Kidd was "unveiled" at Pleasure Beach, opposite Bridgeport, Connecticut, on July 4, 1894, at the spot where the pirate was supposed to have buried treasure in 1696. The monument reportedly stood 25 feet tall. Kidd was hanged for murder and piracy on May 23, 1701.

Source: "Monument to Capt. Kidd," *New York Times*, 3 July 1894, 9.

King, John Alsop (1788–1867)

Governor (1857–59) of New York who suffered a probable heart attack while giving a Fourth of July oration in 1867 at a meeting of the Jamaica Literary Union in Jamaica, Long Island, and died three days later on July 7. King was the son of Rufus King and served in the War of 1812. He was elected to the New York legislature in 1819, and to the U.S. Congress from 1849 to 1851, and was elected governor of New York. According to a newspaper account, "his death was sudden and unexpected.... While in the act of addressing the audience he was observed to exhibit evidence of sudden illness, and to lean on the table for support. He was conveyed from the stand fainting, and was shortly after taken to his home by his son, Mr. Richard King." At the funeral service, the Rev. W.J. Johnson relayed to those present part of King's words that seemed to prophesize his impending death:

I rejoice to meet you on this day; I rejoice to see your young hearts kindling with the hour; I rejoice to see with what enthusiastic fervor you have hailed the unfolding of the Star Spangled Banner, which on this day ninety-one years ago, first greeted our eyes. Never forget that upon you will devolve the important duty of maintaining and strengthening the Government of your country. Your country expects it of you, God requires it; those, who, like me, have nearly finished their work, now look to you to carry forward your country in the great future that awaits her. Cultivate always a respect for religion and virtue. No people or country can prosper or become great without this. Let your aim be ever the service of your country and your God. Be ever ready to yield your lives, your fortunes and your sacred honor at her call.

Source: "Death of Ex-Gov. John A. King," *New York Times*, 8 July 1867, 5, and 11 July 1867, 8; "John Alsop King," *The National Cyclopaedia of American Biography*, 3:50–51.

King, Thomas Starr (1824–1864)

Universalist minister and orator who gave Fourth of July orations in Boston, Fulton,

New York, and Sacramento, California. King was born in New York City but spent time growing up in Portsmouth, New Hampshire, and Charlestown, Massachusetts, due to the itinerant travels of his father, Thomas Farrington King, a Universalist minister. With only a little formal training, Thomas entered the trades during the early 1840s but increased his knowledge through reading and attending lectures in Cambridge and Boston. His penchant for learning led him to theological study under the tutelage of Hosea Ballou, a local Universalist orator. In 1845 King gave his first sermon and a year later was ordained and became pastor of the Universalist Church of Charlestown, a post he held for two years. In 1848 King, then pastor of the Hollis Street Unitarian Church in Boston, began drawing large crowds who wanted to hear him speak. His popularity also gave him numerous opportunities to lecture. His patriotic sentiments led to invitations to speak on Independence Day. On July 5, 1852, he delivered an oration titled "The Organization of Liberty on the Western Continent" (Boston: Rockwell and Churchill, 1892) and on July 4, 1855, he was in Fulton, New York, where he gave an oration (Fulton, N.Y.: T.S. Brigham, 1855).

By 1860 King had moved to California, where he became a prominent figure in the establishment of Unitarianism there. On July 4 of that year he was invited to speak at the Episcopal Sunday School Mission celebration in San Francisco. With the onset of the Civil War in 1861 and the fate of California in crisis, King lectured and spoke for the advantages for the state to throw its allegiance to the Union rather than remaining neutral or seceding to become a separate republic. On July 4, 1861, he gave an oration titled "Two Declaration of Independence: 1776 and 1861" in Sacramento (San Francisco: J.G. Coggins, 1862). King also helped to raise money for the U.S. Sanitary Commission, which provided medicines to Union field hospitals. He died in San Francisco of pneumonia, caused from a bout of diphtheria. King was posthumously honored with a statue in San Francisco's Golden Gate Park and one in the U.S. Capitol.

Source: Henry W. Bowden, "Thomas Starr King," *American National Biography*, 12: 718–19.

Kings Mountain, Battle of

On July 4, 1927, a bronze and granite marker was dedicated on Kings Mountain in North Carolina to commemorate the battle that took place there on October 7, 1780, between 900 American frontiersmen under Col. Isaac Shelby and Col. William Campbell and a British Loyalist force of 1,100 under Maj. Patrick Ferguson. The ceremony was sponsored by the North Carolina Historical Commission and a number of guest speakers were present, including former governor Cameron Morrison. The victory in the battle by the Americans was due to their keen marksmanship and forced a retreat by Cornwallis's army. Twenty-eight Americans were killed and others wounded.

Source: "Kings Mountain Shaft Dedicated," *Washington Evening Star*, 4 July 1927, 19.

Kingsville, Texas

This town was established on July 4, 1904, when the first train of the St. Louis, Brownsville and Mexico Railroad came into town. The land for the site was given by Mrs. Henrietta King, of the King Ranch dynasty, who also funded the building of the First Presbyterian Church and donated land for other churches. In 1913, the Kleberg County seat was established at Kingsville. In 1966 the last passenger train left the Kingsville station. On July 4, 2004, Kingsville celebrated its centennial celebration.

Source: Quincy C. Collins, "Crossing 100 Years: Kingsville, Born Along the Rails, Revamps Depot for Centennial," *Corpus Christi Caller-Times*, 20 May 2004, B1.

Kinney Hotel, East Saginaw, Michigan

This two-story brick structure on Washington Avenue was set on fire "by a firecracker that was set off in a bedroom." One man was killed and three others injured, including Archie Kinney, the proprietor. The building was heavily damaged.

Source: "Terrible Result of a Fire," *New York Times*, 5 July 1890, 2.

Knight, Mrs. Helen Cross (1814–1906)

Wrote "Cold Water Pledge," a song for the Fourth of July that was sung at a temperance convention, July 4, 1844, on Boar's Head, Hampton Beach, New Hampshire.

Source: broadside (New Hampshire: Samuel Fabyan, Jr., 1844).

Kregg's store fire, Cleveland

The S.S. Kregg five and dime store caught fire on July 3, 1908, due to an explosion of fireworks on display in the store. At least seven shoppers were killed and thirty others injured. The explosion, which may have been caused "by sparks from a device which was being demonstrated," caused panic among the hundreds of clerks and shoppers. "While the panic upon the main floor was in progress the flames from the fireworks counter rapidly advanced to other parts of the store. The smoke and flames were whirled up the stairways to the second and third floors." Many individuals jumped from the second and third floor windows. Others were "crowded in the windows and upon the ledges" until the firemen arrived with ladders and a net.

Source: "Fireworks Blaze Kills 7 in Store," *New York Times*, 4 July 1908, 12.

Krimmel, John Lewis (1786–1821)

Philadelphia artist who painted "Fourth of July in Centre Square" around 1812 as his rendition of a typical Philadelphia Independence Day setting, and created another painting of the same subject in 1819 that demonstrated the changes in society that had taken place since the first painting. Krimmel was born in Ebingen, Germany, and upon the deaths of his parents was raised by his sister and brother. After studying art with the court painter Johann Baptist Seele, Krimmel left Germany for Philadelphia in 1809. After a brief attempt as a merchant's assistant, he pursued a career as an artist and achieved considerable success, emphasizing paintings depicting common scenes in life. According to Milo Naeve, "Krimmel earned a place in Philadelphia and in the history of American painting as the first artist basing his reputation on con-temporary genre subjects." Krimmel's works were exhibited at the Pennsylvania Academy of the Fine Arts (Philadelphia) and the American Academy of the Fine Arts (New York).

The 1812 painting depicts an assemblage of a group of citizens conversing with each other. Only young boys and dogs are shown as moving about. The 1819 painting illustrates a larger crowd in a more festive atmosphere. The celebrants in military uniforms seem to dominate the festivities. Fashions have changed. There are pictures of George Washington and a war scene is prominently displayed. Military personnel from the navy and the army symbolize national unity. The paintings are held in the Museum of American Art of the Pennsylvania Academy of Fine Arts and the Historical Society of Pennsylvania.

Sources: Anneliese Harding, *John Lewis Krimmel: Genre Artist of the Early Republic* (Winterthur, Del.: Winterthur, 1994), 166–70; Milo M. Naeve, "John Lewis Krimmel," *American National Biography*, 12:921–22.

Ku Klux Klan

A secret society that was organized in the South after the Civil War to thwart African-American equality by frequently inflicting terror against blacks and white sympathizers. The Klan reached its peak of activity during the 1920s. They frequently used the Fourth of July as an opportunity to hold rallies, which in turn resulted in protests and conflicts with anti–Klan groups.

On Independence Day in 1926, the state "Klorero" of the realm of New York met at Mineola, Long Island, with some 3,000 men and women who participated in a parade. The women marched in specially made costumes but other events were cancelled due to a less than expected turnout.

Near Babylon, New Jersey, on July 4, 1927, about 5,000 Klan members assembled and charged Al Smith, governor of New York, with interfering with their meeting and "throttling free speech." According to D.L. Van Ober, a Klan member from Jamaica, New York, "The Klan is not anti–Jew, anti–Catholic, anti-negro, nor anti-anything; and if those who oppose it want to demonstrate their Americanism they will cease their attack on peaceful assemblage and put an end to the violation of the principle of free speech in the state of New York."

More recently, on July 4, 1977, the Klan held a rally in Columbus, Ohio. About 100 anti–Klan protestors carrying banners — "Organizing Committee for a National Workers Organization," "Friends Against Racism," and "Kent State University Revolutionary Student Brigade" — provided their own counter demonstration.

Sources: "Klan Celebrates on Merrick Road," "Klan Meeting Fails to Draw Throngs" and "Women and Girls Parade with Klan," *New York Times*, 5 and 6 July 1926, 13 and 8, respectively; *New York Times*, 5 July 1927, 4; "Klansmen and Demonstrators Battle in Ohio," *Washington Post*, 5 July 1977, A3.

Lafayette, Marquis de (Du Motier, Marie Joseph Paul Yves Roch Gilbert) (1757–1834)

French general who fought in the American Continental Army during the Revolutionary War as a volunteer. He was commissioned major general and was wounded during the war. Americans were forever after indebted to Lafayette for his service. The country's endearment for the patriot became an annual expression of affection on the Fourth of July. Around the country hundreds of toasts and tributes were offered him. After the war he returned to his homeland. When Lafayette came back to America in 1824–25 as an elderly man to tour the country, he was once again heralded everywhere he went. A tune, "Lafayette's March," was written in his honor and had several performances on the Fourth, including Washington (1828), Natchez, Mississippi (1836), and Piney Point, Maryland (1839). On July 4, 1825, Lafayette was in New York participating in the cornerstone-laying ceremony for the Apprentices' Library, the first free library to be established in Brooklyn. He assisted "the free-masons of Long Island," and following the ceremony he and all of the journeymen processed to the church "where he attended divine worship." Later, Lafayette reviewed the local militia and was honored in the city council chamber, followed by dinner.

On July 4, 1830, in Paris, Lafayette attended a celebration held by Americans at

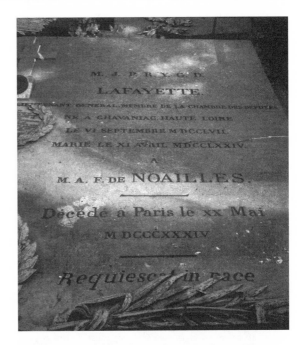

The Marquis de Lafayette's gravesite at Picpus Cemetery, Paris, popular for wreath laying ceremonies on the Fourth of July. Lafayette fought alongside Americans during the Revolutionary War and was considered a hero. Photograph courtesy of George Arnold.

"Leintier's, rue Richelieu," where a "sumptuous dinner" was served. After the customary toasts, Lafayette was asked to address the group. He spoke, paying homage to Washington, Jefferson, and Adams in his comments. He mentioned the good will afforded him on his recent trip through the states. Lafayette offered a toast to his companions there: "The constitution of the United States — the price of blood — the work of wisdom — the happy republican compound of state rights and federal energy — may it ever stand far above party collisions, under the sole patronage of national good sense and self-government."

On July 4, 1832, Lafayette attended another celebration in Paris at Leintiers amidst celebrated company, including Samuel F.B. Morse and James Fenimore Cooper. Included among the guests were Lafayette's son and grandson, G.W. Lafayette and Oscar Lafayette. Morse presented a brief address extolling the virtues of Lafayette. His speech "was interrupted with applause at almost every sentence, and the sentiments greeted by 9 cheers." After the band played the "Pairsienne," General Lafayette arose and spoke:

> While, on this happy day, my 55th commemoration of our great Fourth of July, I am delighted to breathe among you, an American atmosphere; it retraces at once to my mind the youthful recollection of a first, patriotic love, the filial and fraternal emission of friendships formed in times of trial and danger. It also retraces the subsequent forty years of unshaken affection, confidence and solicitude, bestowed by the American people upon an absent, adopted son, and more lately, an unparalleled, daily, hourly welcome of more than thirteen months through the twenty-four states of the union, which in a continued series, have come to this very moment, to cheer a grateful heart. And, while I most feelingly enjoy the marks of your approbation, expressed in so flattering terms by our honorable president, I am happy to acknowledge, that the proudest day of my life has been that day of my solemn reception in the bosom of congress, when their president, in the name of the people of the United States, did officially declare, that every sentiment, every act of my long eventful life, has proved worthy of a disciple of the American school.

Lafayette died on May 20, 1834. A few days later, American citizens at Paris assembled at the Hotel of the American Legation to pay their respects to the general. Through the efforts of Thomas B. Barton, charge d'affaires of the United States, and Dunscomb Bradford, American consul, and others, resolutions were adopted honoring Lafayette and they were delivered to the general's family. The group also agreed to "wear crape on the left arm for three months." The funeral ceremony for the interment of Lafayette on May 22 was also of keen interest to Americans and a detailed description was published on July 8 in the *Richmond Enquirer*. Meanwhile, on July 4, special honors were presented as a tribute to the patriot and his "deep attachments for, and sincere admiration of, our institutions and laws" at a celebration in Columbia, Virginia. At the church, by resolutions adopted, Lafayette was placed in the "highest rank among the citizens of this country" and that all participants agreed to "wear crape on the left arm for thirty days."

After the Civil War the memory of Lafayette was rekindled. On the occasion of an 1876 Centennial parade in Indianapolis, a "handsomely-decorated wagon" representing "Lafayette and his staff" progressed through city streets while abroad, annual gatherings by both Americans and French on the Fourth at Lafayette's tomb at Picpus Cemetery near Paris became an annual event. On July 4, 1886, at Woodstock, Connecticut, Levi P. Morton, U.S. vice president (1889–93), spoke on the life of Lafayette. In 1889, Lafayette's grandson was present when a wreath was laid on the patriot's tomb. On July 4, 1894, in Washington, D.C., as part of a parade of several Revolutionary War societies, the U.S. Marine Band played the "Marseillaise" and saluted as the group passed a statue of Lafayette.

On July 4, 1900, a statue in honor of Lafayette, a gift of American school children to France, was presented by Ferdinand W. Peck, president of the Lafayette Memorial Commission, to President Emile Loubet, in Paris. For the ceremony the American flag flown from the Eiffel Tower and numerous buildings. The monument was located in Lafayette Square. Within an amphitheatre were 2,000 invited guests, including many French and American officials. Sousa's Band provided the music. American ambassador Horace Porter read aloud a letter from President McKinley and then spoke to the assemblage:

> That love for freedom, that friendship, that sacrifice, that patience, that heroism which brought Gen. Lafayette to the shores of the new continent to stand side by side with our Washington when a nation was in the throes of its birth, when our forefathers saw no light through an almost hopeless gloom, will give an undying incentive to patriotism, and live in grateful memory so long as our institutions shall endure.

Following Porter, President Loubet spoke:

> When Lafayette crossed the ocean to help a distant people win its independence, he was not the plaything of heroic folly. He served a deep political object. He was about to found the friendship of two peoples on the common worship of their motherland and liberty. This friendship, born in the brotherhood of arms,

has developed and strengthened through the century which is ending. The generations which follow us will not let it become enfeebled. They will strive to multiply the amicable relations and exchanges of sympathy between the two shores of the Atlantic, and will thus give a precious pledge to the peace of the world and to progress and humanity.

After a third speech given by John Ireland, archbishop of St. Paul, Minnesota, the statue was unveiled by two young boys, "Gustave Hennocque, great grandson of the Marquis de Lafayette, and Paul Thompson, son of the projector of the monument," while Sousa's Band "played a new specially composed march — 'Hail to the Spirit of Liberty.'"

Lafayette continued to be honored in the twentieth century. On July 4, 1914, Hanson Cleveland Coxe, U.S. deputy consul general in Paris, laid a wreath at Lafayette's gravesite. A large assemblage of dignitaries representing both countries were present, including Ambassador Myron T. Herrick. On July 4, 1951, "France's contribution to American independence was dramatized" with a parade that reproduced "a scene in April, 1790 when Lafayette, newly returned from America, reviewed the French National Guard on the Champs-Elysées." Lafayette was played by actor Jean Dehelly and the French Guards were dressed in the uniforms of the time.

Sources: A. Levasseur, *Lafayette in America in 1824 and 1825* (Philadelphia: Carey and Lea, 1829; reprint, New York: Research Reprints, 1970), 2:217–20; "Celebration in Paris, of the Fourth of July," *Niles' Weekly Register* 39/2 (4 September 1830), 23–24; *Niles' Weekly Register* 43/1 (1 September 1832): 6; "Funeral of Lafayette, May 22," *Richmond Enquirer*, 8 July 1834, 2 and 15 July 1834, 3; "Independence Day Elsewhere," *New York Times*, 5 July 1876, 5; "In a Patriotic Manner," *Washington Post*, 6 July 1886, 1; "The Fourth of July," *London Times*, 5 July 1889, 5 and 5 July 1900, 6; *Washington Evening Star*, 4 July 1894, 2; "Lafayette Statue Unveiled in Paris," *New York Times*, 5 July 1900, 7; "Lafayette Monument Accepted by President," *New York Herald*, 5 July 1900, 10; "Decorate Lafayette Tomb," *New York Times*, 5 July 1914, 3; "Lafayette's Aid Dramatized," *New York Times*, 5 July 1951, 6.

Lagoon of Nations

A spectacular, first-of-its-kind, synchronized water, light, and sound show that took place at the World's Fair in New York on the evening of July 4, 1939. In a pool of water 400 feet wide and 800 feet long, "the Spirit of George Washington" was depicted by a 150-foot-high burst of water, and with music composed by Robert Russell Bennett and played by a forty-four-piece orchestra. A newspaper described how

gradually, the fountain patterns depict the growth of the country, George Washington dies, and the central white jet falls, but comes back in blue to represent his spirit towering over the nation he founded. The spectacle proceeds to a dramatic climax with the building of the flag — massed red, white and blue effects — with a final shower of fireworks — bombs, mines, comets, saucissons [flying fish] and candle batteries.

The display was the design of Jean Labatut, professor of architecture at Princeton, and a staff of 113 men were employed to produce the show.

Source: "Spectacle of Fire to Thrill Crowds," *New York Times*, 4 July 1939, 3.

Lake Independence

Located in Hennepin County near Maxwell Bay and Independence, Minnesota. Lake Independence "derived its name from a party of Fourth of July excursionists" who discovered the body of water likely on July 4, 1854. Kelsey Hinman was the individual who "named it Lake Independence, in honor of the national holiday."

Source: Edward Duffield Neill, *History of Hennepin County and the City of Minneapolis* (Minneapolis: North Star Publishing Co., 1881), 263.

Las Vegas, Nevada

On July 4, 1879, two locomotives bearing Mexican and U.S. flags arrived there, initiating rail service for the largest town in the New Mexico territory at that time.

Source: *New Mexico Magazine*, Web site, 20 September 2002, <http://www.nmmagazine.com/features/memories3.html>.

Latrobe Gate, Washington Navy Yard, District of Columbia

Referred to as "the oldest, continuously-manned Marine sentry post in the nation," Latrobe Gate was designed by architect Benjamin Latrobe and built in 1805–06. On July

4, 1807, the eagle which crowned the Latrobe Gate was unveiled to the sound of a federal salute and the tune "Yankee Doodle." The eagle was carved by Giuseppi Franzoni of Pisa, Italy. A local newspaper described the eagle as "colossal" and "sculptured in one block of free stone. It is independently of its pedestal 5 feet 6 inches high. The eagle is represented at the moment of preparation for flight. His right foot is elevated and rests on the shank of an anchor."

Sources: "Washington City," *National Intelligencer*, 8 July 1807, 1; "Latrobe Gate," *Naval District Washington*, Web site, <http://www.ndw.navy.mil/NavyYard/LatrobeGate.htm>.

Lawrence Academy, Groton, Massachusetts

This school was destroyed by fire on July 4, 1868. Books and equipment were saved. According to a newspaper report, "The fire is supposed to have caught from Chinese crackers thrown on the piazza by a boy. The loss on the building is $4,000, and is covered by insurance."

Source: "The Burning of an Academy in Massachusetts," *New York Times*, 7 July 1868, 5.

Lee, Richard Henry (1732–1794)

Member of the Second Continental Congress who introduced on 7 June 1776 the resolution that called for a declaration of independence. It was for his part in securing that independence that Lee was honored occasionally on the Fourth of July. On July 4, 1842, at a temperance celebration in Centreville, Virginia, James M.P. Newby, the orator that day, commemorated Lee by reciting the resolution to his audience.

Source: "Temperance Celebration in Centreville, Va.," *Alexandria Gazette*, 12 July 1842, 2.

Lehigh Canal, Pennsylvania

Seven barges of coal arrived in Philadelphia from Mauch Chunk on July 4, 1829, and were the first coal transport vessels to pass through the newly opened Lehigh Canal. "A large supply of Lehigh coal may now be expected to arrive regularly during the remainder of the season," a newspaper reported.

Source: *National Intelligencer*, 8 July 1829, 3.

Leicester Academy, Worcester, Massachusetts

Leicester Academy opened a new building on July 4, 1806, and Aaron Bancroft (1755–1839) presented an oration on education for the occasion.

Source: *Importance of Education, Illustrated in an Oration Delivered before the Trustees, Preceptors & Students of Leicester Academy...* (Worcester: Thomas and Sturtevant, 1806).

Lemonade

A popular drink on the Fourth of July from the early 1800s until the present. In the nineteenth century lemonade was served in tin or wooden pails and sold from booths and tables set up on Independence Day in towns across the country. The drink cost about a penny a glass in New York in 1855, and was made typically from either fresh lemons and limes when available or from sweetened lemon syrup that was mixed with water. In Washington City, for example, "fresh limes" were available for sale for the Fourth of July in 1815 at George Kneller on Pennsylvania Avenue and in Frederick, Maryland, on July 4, 1826, individuals could buy both lemons and lemon syrup at W. Fischer's shop. Not every one was satisfied with the product, however. On July 4, 1854, people enjoying the day in New York's Central Park were disappointed in the "iced-lemonade, which, sadly deficient in sugar, floated small sliced lemons upon its surface, in dingy brown pails."

Drinking lemonade made from lemon syrup could be hazardous to one's health, as it was not always made from natural ingredients. An article in a New Orleans newspaper in 1875 brought attention to the sort of lemon syrup that was typically tainted, made of "tartaric acid, and even if oil of lemon is used it is the cheapest and most impure, being strongly adulterated with oil of turpentine; the sweetening is supplemented with glucose, the manufactured grape sugar from rotton [sic] starch." On July 4, 1881, 500 persons celebrating Independence Day in Harrisonville, Missouri, were poisoned by drinking lemonade made of acid. A newspaper reported that six persons died and "one hundred more are dangerously ill and expected to die. The affair has cast a gloom over the whole surrounding country."

Sources: *National Intelligencer*, 4 July 1815, 2; *Frederick-Town Herald*, 4 July 1826, 1; *New York Times*, 6 July 1854, 2; "Nasty Summer Drinks," *New Orleans Republican*, 18 July 1875, 6; "A Wholesale Poisoning," *Baltimore Morning Herald*, 6 July 1881, 1.

Lenox, Massachusetts

On July 4, 1922, citizens of this town presented a historic pageant in a parade that depicted life during the 1790s and 1800s. Characters included the duke and duchess of Richmond. The American Legion Band of Pittsfield led the parade, which included a 1500-pound liberty bell and a Lenox stage coach built in 1820.

Source: "Lenox Colonists in Historic Pageant," *New York Times*, 5 July 1922, 19.

"Let Freedom Ring"

An annual tradition begun on July 4, 1963, whereby houses of worship and buildings in every American community across the country simultaneously rang their bells thirteen times, exactly at 1 P.M. and for 4 minutes. President Kennedy had endorsed the start of this tradition. On July 4, 1998, four children who were descendants of signers of the Declaration of Independence tapped the **Liberty Bell** 13 times, signaling the start of that year's "Let Freedom Ring" tradition.

Sources: Murray Illson, "Nation Marks 4th in Ideal Weather," *New York Times*, 5 July 1963, 1; *Philadelphia Inquirer*, 4 July 1998, A12.

Lewis, Ida (1842–1911)

America's first female lighthouse keeper who was presented with a "beautiful and costly" lifesaving boat on Independence Day, July 5, 1869, by the inhabitants of Newport, Rhode Island, for her lifesaving acts of courage. Ida Lewis was born in Newport as Idawalley Zoradia and at the age of fifteen began assisting her father, Captain Hosea Lewis, as keeper of the Newport Harbor lighthouse on Lime Rock. When her father was left partially paralyzed with a stroke three years later, "Ida," as she was affectionately known among the community, took over as keeper of the lighthouse. She was officially appointed light

keeper in 1879 after having demonstrated her abilities in numerous daring rescues that occurred in the later 1850s and thereafter. One event in March 1869 brought Lewis national attention. During a blizzard, she and her brother Hosea had managed to rescue two soldiers whose boat had overturned and brought them to shore. This exploit was reported in *Harper's Weekly* (July 1869), and Susan B. Anthony herself heralded the event in her own journal, the *Revolution* (July and September 1869). Lewis spent the remainder of her life on the island, first raising her children from an ill-fated marriage and later spending time with her other brother Rudolph there. She continued to receive accolades and awards for additional lifesaving activities, with the most important honors being gold medals from Congress, the state of Rhode Island, and American Cross of Honor Society. She also received a number of silver medals. On the fiftieth anniversary of her service in 1906, a pension for life of $30 a month was awarded to her by the Carnegie Hero Fund. The lifeboat *Rescue* and Lewis's medals are preserved in The Newport Historical Society.

Sources: Rosanna Ledbetter, "Ida Lewis," *American National Biography*, 13:580–82; "Ida Lewis, the Newport Heroine," *Harper's Weekly* (31 July 1869); "The Passing of Ida Lewis, the Heroine of Newport," *New York Times*, 29 October 1911, 9.

Lewisohn Stadium of the College of the City of New York

Popular New York site for Fourth of July concerts, ceremonies, and other events, beginning in 1915. The stadium was named after Adolph Lewisohn (1849–1938), financier and philanthropist, who gave the structure to the college. The first Fourth of July event staged there in 1915 was billed as "American Day." "The speakers' stand was on the field, and over the 12,000 auditors played the rays of Edison's new 2,000,000 candle power searchlight, shown to the public for the first time. A searchlight played on a big American flag at each end of the structure." (See also **New York Edison Company**.) The audience sang a new work composed by the Rev. O.W. Peterson, "a Methodist clergyman in a small Maine college," titled "God Save the President."

On July 4, 1916, 15,000 persons were in the stadium to witness "an elaborate program of tableaux, music, and oratory." Johanna Gadski sang the "Star-Spangled Banner," and the Halevy Chorus and Serbian Chorus, "assisted by a double band," provided additional music.

On Independence Day in 1918, the Mayor's Committee of Women on National Defense hosted the celebration there which included a speech by Secretary of the Navy Josephus Daniels, essentially the same one he had presented at Tammany Hall in the morning. Regarding America's entry into World War I, Daniels remarked, "We shall pay a heavy toll before victory comes, but all is not staked on a single battle and neither reverses on land nor sinkings of merchant vessels (a species of piracy on a par with that which Jefferson stamped out when he was President) will avail, because the Americans and their brave associates with 'immortal hate' of 'despicable deeds' have the 'unconquerable will' and 'courage never to submit or yield.'" Included among the dignitaries was Mrs. William Randolph Hearst, chairperson of the Mayor's Committee. As a crowd of 8,000 persons looked on, "a giant electric American flag glittered, while scores of searchlights from the roof of the stadium made the arena almost as light as day." Music was supplied by the naval band from the USS *Recruit*.

On July 4, 1942, 5,500 persons gathered at the stadium to hear Jacques Abrams perform the Edward MacDowell Piano Concerto No. 2 with the New York Philharmonic Orchestra, under director Alexander Smallens. On July 4, 1961, the Lewisohn Stadium Orchestra performed works by American composers Paul Creston and William Schuman before an audience of 8,000.

Sources: "City Waves Flag and Cheers Wilson," *New York Times*, 6 July 1915, 18; "15,000 Gather in Stadium," *New York Times*, 5 July 1916, 12; "U.S. Marines Thrill Throng in Stadium," *New York Times*, 5 July 1918, 11; "American Works Heard at Stadium," *New York Times*, 5 July 1942, 28; "Music: Elman at Stadium," *New York Times*, 5 July 1961, 28.

Liberty Bell

A symbol of American independence and freedom, located at Independence National Historical Park in Philadelphia. This 12-foot iron bell was cast in 1751 in London by Thomas Lester's foundry and bears an inscription taken from Leviticus 25:10: "Proclaim Liberty throughout all the land unto all the inhabitants thereof." The bell was originally placed in the Pennsylvania State House (later Independence Hall) in Philadelphia in March 1753 and began her illustrious history by ringing for such events as the coronation of King George III in 1761, then Continental Congress in 1774, and the battles of Lexington and Concord in the following year. In 1776 the bell was rung on July 8 on the occasion of the first public reading of the Declaration of Independence in that city, but there is no evidence that it was rung on July 4 upon the signing of the historic document. During the Revolutionary War, the bell was taken to Allentown, Pennsylvania, and placed in a church there to keep it out of the hands of the British, but after the War it was returned to Philadelphia. During those early years the Liberty Bell was tolled frequently, calling politicians to meetings, announcing deaths of significant persons, and heralding special days and events, such as the Fourth of July.

The Liberty Bell did not receive its name until 1839, when it became associated with the antislavery movement. A pictorial representation of the bell first appeared in a pamphlet titled *The Liberty Bell, by Friends of Freedom*, distributed to the public at the Massachusetts Anti-Slavery Fair in Boston. The bell's connection to the Fourth of July may have been the result of George Lippard's story, *Fourth of July 1776*, published in the *Saturday Courier* (1847), in which the bell is rung on that day. For the next forty years it was generally believed that the bell had been rung on the first July 4, but that story was finally put to rest by Herbert Friedenwald in his book *The Declaration of Independence, an Interpretation and an Analysis* (New York, 1904) in which he states that there is no evidence to believe that the Liberty Bell was rung on Independence Day in 1776. The Liberty Bell's last ringing was in 1846 on George Washington's birthday.

Through the years it was traditional that

the bell was tapped each year, announcing the age of the nation's declaring of independence in 1776. On July 4, 1894, for example, the bell was tapped 118 times. "Many thousands of people gathered in the streets surrounding the historic building and a continuous cheer was kept up until the echo of the last stroke of the bell had died away."

In 1893 a "new liberty bell" known as the Columbian Liberty Bell was cast at the Clinton H. Meneely Bell Foundry in Troy, New York. The first ringing of the bell was set for July 4 and was "controlled by electrical communication with Chicago." According to the Chicago program, "a button will be touched at noon in Chicago and electricity will put the speakers at the World's Fair and the bell at Troy into communication."

On July 5, 1915, the Liberty Bell was placed on a specially constructed railroad car and began a six-month tour with its final destination scheduled at the Panama-Pacific Exposition. Two years prior the Society of the Descendants of the Signers of the Declaration of Independence had met in Philadelphia on July 4, 1913, for their annual meeting and passed resolutions recommending against the removal of the Liberty Bell to San Francisco. Nonetheless the bell was exhibited first in a number of Pennsylvania towns, then in the Midwest towns of Ohio, Indiana, and Iowa.

On July 4, 1934, the Liberty Bell was rung by a hammer "guided by an electrical impulse transmitted from Rear Admiral Richard E. Byrd's base in Antarctica." The sounds were transmitted by radio to around the world. The event was sponsored by CBS and Philadelphia Mayor J. Hampton Moore spoke.

An important symbol for Fourth of July celebrations everywhere, the Liberty Bell has been often depicted in fireworks displays and parades. In Dubuque, Iowa, in 1916, for example, "two great illuminated emblems of draped flags appeared beside the representation of the Liberty Bell. The word 'Liberty' stood out above the bell. As the red, white and blue lights were manipulated to show the flags waving the bell was shown swinging back and forth." In Ridgewood, New Jersey, on July 4, 1926, a liberty bell made from paper pulp

molded from copies of the *New York Times* was featured in a parade there. The large bell was painted to resemble bronze and was displayed on a float that depicted a Colonial blacksmith shop. On the Fourth in 1933, a copy of the Liberty Bell was displayed in an automobile in a parade at Seward Park and other streets in New York City, and passed by thirty-two "patriotic demonstrations." In 1976 a new Liberty Bell Pavilion was built for the American Bicentennial. The tradition of gently tapping the bell continues today. See also **"Let Freedom Ring."**

Sources: "Display Well Liked," *Dubuque Daily Times-Journal*, 5 July 1916, 7; *New York Times*, 5 July 1894, 8; "The New Liberty Bell," *New York Times*, 4 July 1893, 8; "Would Keep Liberty Bell," *New York Times*, 5 July 1913, 2; "Liberty Bell Starts West," *New York Times*, 6 July 1915, 18; "Papers Form Liberty Bell," *New York Times*, 6 July 1926, 7; "Liberty Bell Copy Hailed on East Side," *New York Times*, 5 July 1933, 4; "Byrd Rings Liberty Bell by Electrical Impulse," *New York Times*, 5 July 1934, 10; Elizabeth Schafer, "Liberty Bell," in *Encyclopedia of American Studies* (New York: Grolier Educational, 2001), 3:1–2.

Liberty Fanfare

Composed by John Williams and performed by the Cleveland Orchestra at its eleventh annual July 4th concert on Public Square in Cleveland in 2000.

Source: John Petkovic, "As American As Apple Pie and a Russian Anthem," *Plain Dealer*, 3 July 2000, 1E.

"Liberty Pole"

Similar to a **liberty tree**, a symbol for the Revolutionary War depicted in Fourth of July celebrations. Liberty poles were erected in a number of towns prior to the American Revolution. They served as meeting places where colonials openly expressed their dissatisfaction with the British as well as to mark significant events. In 1766 a liberty pole was raised in New York City in celebration of the repeal of the Stamp Act. As an American icon, the idea of the liberty pole and its tradition was carried through the nineteenth century and was endeared in the nation's collective memory through raisings, song and word, the naming of towns, and as part of Independence Day celebrations. On July 4, 1838, a local newspaper printed a toast to a liberty pole that had been raised in Sparta, New York: "The Liberty Pole erected in honor of this day by the patriotic citizens of Sparta, near the spot where the first Standard of Liberty was reared in this town under the authority of the Continental Congress. May it ever continue to be the rallying point and the pride of freemen. In Jackson, Mississippi, a liberty pole was erected on the eve of the Fourth of July in 1837 and in Rochester, N.Y., a liberty pole was erected in 1846, and a second pole was raised and stood from 1861 to 1889."

Frequently liberty poles were designated as "political poles" and were raised on Independence Day during election years. At Georgetown in Washington on July 4, 1856, a group of "young Democrats" raised an 87-foot-high hickory pole near the corner of Fourth and Market Streets. At the top an American flag floated along with "a streamer bearing the names of the Democratic nominees." Not to be outdone, the Know Nothings, another political party, also "raised quite a handsome one at the foot of Potomac street, near the wharf, which was inaugurated last night."

On Independence Day in 1858 in San Francisco, someone forgot to raise the American flag up the liberty pole in the plaza and a scathing editorial was published the following day in the *Daily Alta California* that urged citizens to chop the pole down and use it as firewood to benefit the poor. "When this city cannot afford to hoist the flag of our country upon that pole, on each recurring Fourth of July, it should be at once removed from the public square; for as long as it remains, it is a standing reproach upon our patriotism and veneration for the fathers of the country."

On July 4, 1859, a liberty pole 136 feet high was dedicated at Fort Greene, Brooklyn, New York, while the Navy Yard Band played the "Star-Spangled Banner."

During the Civil War, pole raisings in the North remained popular on the Fourth of July but the events typically reflected war interests. On July 4, 1861, a pole raising took place by the "friends of the Union" at the residence of R.L. Waters "on the Baltimore turnpike, three miles E. Frederick City [Mary-

land]," with "distinguished speakers" addressing the crowd.

After the Civil War other notable liberty pole ceremonies occurred. On July 3, 1876, Mayor Charles Siedler presided over the dedication of a new pole in Jersey City, New Jersey, to the sounds of a 38-gun salute by the Hudson County Artillery. On July 4, 1895, a new 175-foot-high liberty pole was dedicated in Buffalo, New York, following a parade there. Nearly 50,000 spectators attended the event to see what was described as the tallest such pole in the world. On July 4, 1939, it was announced in the *New York Times* that the pole was to be taken down. It "recently developed a bend and investigation revealed that the interior was rusted." In Wisconsin, a small town, located near the city of Viroqua, is named Liberty Pole.

Sources: *Hudson River Chronicle*, 10 July 1838, 2; *The Mississippian*, 7 July 1837, 3; "Georgetown Correspondence," *Washington Evening Star*, 5 July 1856, 2; *Daily Alta California*, 5 July 1858, 2; *New York Times*, 6 July 1859, 8; *Frederick Examiner*, 3 July 1861, 3; "In Jersey City," New York Herald, 3 July 1876, 3; "Big Celebration in Buffalo," *New York Times*, 5 July 1895, 3; "Buffalo to Lose 175-Foot Pole," *New York Times*, 4 July 1939, 3.

"Liberty Ships"

New United States Navy vessels that were launched beginning in 1942 as part of a massive build up of armaments to defeat enemy forces during World War II. On the Fourth of July in 1942 the first triple launching of liberty ships occurred at the Bethlehem-Fairfield shipyard in Baltimore. The vessels included the *Joseph Stanton*, *William Wirt* and *Luther Martin*. Thomas M. Woodward of the United States Maritime Commission spoke to those assembled there: "The war news of the last few weeks, makes us the more determined to produce materials which the United Nations need to win this war, and, above all, the ships to carry these war materials to our men on the fighting fronts," he said.

On July 4, 1943, the *George Cohan*, a boat named for the American song writer, was launched in Baltimore before a crowd of 20,000. It was the 161st liberty ship launched at the Bethlehem-Fairfield shipyard. A band played "Yankee Doodle Dandy" and Eddie Cantor sang the Cohan songs "Harrigan," "Give My Regards to Broadway," "It's a Grand Old Flag" and "Over There." Cantor spoke to the spectators, saying, "If there ever was one man who was a symbol of our great nation, that man was George M. Cohan. He always tried to project the spirit of America. His songs came from the pen and the heart. He waved the flag because he loved it."

Other launchings on Independence Day that year included the two destroyers *Hickox* and *Healy* at the Kearny, New Jersey, yards of the Federal Shipbuilding and Dry Dock Company, as well as a number of other vessels in other shipyards.

Sources: "Triple Launching on 4th Is Set for Liberty Ships," *New York Times*, 3 July 1942, 8; "Three Ships Leave One Yard in a Day," *New York Times*, 5 July 1942, S6; *Washington Evening Star*, 5 July 1942, A13; "Launch Ship Named for George Cohan," *New York Times*, 5 July 1943, 7.

"Liberty Tree"

An American icon and living emblem where colonials assembled to pledge their loyalty and honor for the cause of liberty. The liberty tree, frequently referred to as the "tree of liberty," became a national icon and was often referred to as a living symbol of the rise and growth of the American republic. The seeds given forth from the tree carried great distances by the winds of time resulted in the germination of freedom in other countries. The first liberty tree, an elm, was located in Boston and served as a rallying place for the Sons of Liberty. It was located at the intersection of Essex Street and Washington Street (previously Orange Street). In 1775 the British felled the tree, cutting it into fourteen cords of firewood.

Liberty trees were planted in a number of towns and they later served as a living memory of the events before and during the Revolutionary War. References to the "Liberty Tree" were especially evident on the Fourth of July, in poetry, music, toasts, and orations. One of the significant instances which helped to immortalize the symbol was Thomas Paine's poem "Liberty Tree," written early in the American Revolution:

In a chariot of light, from the regions of day,
The Goddess of Liberty came,
Ten thousand celestials directed her way,
And hither conducted the dame.
A fair budding branch from the gardens above,
Where millions with millions agree,
She brought in her hand as a pledge of her
    love.
And the plant she named Liberty Tree.

Paine's "Liberty Tree" was set to music for two voices in 1803, and again in 1813, with melody and bass.

On July 4, 1838, at a celebration held on Circus Hill in Sing Sing, New York, a toast was presented to "The Liberty Tree: Reared by our Fathers in the days of their peril, and freely nourished with their blood. May it extend over the nations, and flourish forever."

The first Boston orator, John Warren,

The oldest surviving liberty tree located on the grounds of St. John's College, Annapolis, Maryland, was cut down in fall 1999 because of decay caused by insects and severe damage from Hurricane Floyd in September of that year. This photograph, by the author, was taken shortly before the tree was destroyed.

made reference to the "stately Tree of Liberty" on July 4, 1783. On Independence Day in 1787 in Philadelphia, James Campbell said, "The tree of liberty shall yet grow and flourish among us." On July 4, 1848, Robert Winthrop, Speaker of the House of Representatives, mentioned the liberty tree in the context of movements for liberty in European nations, at the ceremony honoring the laying of the cornerstone of the Washington Monument: "We see in them the influence of our own institutions. We behold in them the result of our own example. We recognize them as the spontaneous germination and growth of seeds which have been wafted over the ocean, for half a century past, from our own original Liberty Tree!" Howard H. Martin lists other orators who referenced the "liberty tree," including James Campbell (Philadelphia 1787), Jonathan Maxcy (Providence, Rhode Island, 1795), James Burnet (Weston, Connecticut, 1799), and John L. Scott (Mayslick, Kentucky, 1857).

The oldest surviving liberty tree was located on the grounds of St. John's College in Annapolis, Maryland. This majestic 400-year-old poplar tree had an illustrious history. It was under its canopy of splendid branches that Maryland's Sons of Liberty met to reflect and discuss resolutions of revolution. The numerous ceremonies held through the years following the Revolution were a testimony to the tree's symbolism. For example, on July 4, 1827, the Fifth Light Infantry from Baltimore, troops from Fort Severn, the Annapolis Volunteers and St. John's College Cadets gathered to honor the day. Present were Governor Joseph Kent and Mayor Richard Harwood of Annapolis. It was reported that "a handsome cold collation was set out under the ancient Liberty Tree."

In 1907, the Liberty Tree's health was in danger due to decay caused by insects within her trunk. A hollow area in the tree that extended 56 feet above the ground was filled with 55 tons of concrete. In 1975, the tree suffered wind damage resulting in an extensive crack in the trunk. Repairs were made using bolts and filler material. In September 1999, Hurricane Floyd did additional damage with another five-inch-wide crack in one of the principal branches. Upon the advice of qualified arborists that the tree was in danger of toppling due to a lack of structural strength, the decision was made by St. John's College officials to cut it down. That event took place on October 25, 1999. Christopher Nelson, president of St. John's, issued this statement to the public and nation: "We at St. John's and across the land will mourn the loss of this tree. The Liberty Tree carries so much meaning to all of us as a symbol of our nation's identity; it was already a bulwark in the early days of our struggle for independence. We are also losing an old friend, one that has stood by generations of students in their years of study and play, one that has spread its protective boughs over generations of graduating seniors, celebrating countless new beginnings in the college's annual commencement ceremonies." A descendant of the tree that was planted in 1889 on the St. John's College campus stands in front of the Greenfield Library. On July 4, 2001, a Bible box made from remnants of the tree was presented by Philadelphia mayor John F. Street to President Bush at Bryn Mawr, Pennsylvania.

During the latter half of the twentieth century, the planting of trees on the Fourth of July took on additional meaning and significance. For example, on July 4, 1951, Senator James H. Duff (R. — Pa.) announced a plan to Congress for distributing oak seedlings to representatives of the then forty-eight states, and on July 4, 1980, people in Cleveland planted fifty-three trees in memory of the American hostages that were held in Iran.

Sources: "Celebrations," *Richmond Enquirer*, 13 July 1827, 2; *Hudson River Chronicle*, 10 July 1838, 2; *Songster's Museum* (Northampton, 1803), 95–97; *The American Patriotic Song Book* (Philadelphia, 1813), 22–24; "The Fourth of July in Washington — Mr. Winthrop's Oration," *National Era*, 13 July 1848, 110; *New York Times*, 5 July 1951, 8; *Washington Post*, 4 July 1980, A25 and 5 July 1980, A8; Jefferson Morley, "Revered Tree's "Historic Vigil About to End," *Washington Post*, 19 October 1999, B1; "Liberty Tree Work Completed," news release, 27 October 1999, St. John's College; "Liberty Tree," Maryland State History Web site, <http:www.sos.state.md.us/sos/kids/html/liberty tree2.html>, 2 February 2002; Arthur Schlesinger,

"Liberty Tree: A Genealogy," *New England Quarterly* 25 (1952): 435–58; Robert P. Hay, "The Liberty Tree: A Symbol for American Patriots," *Quarterly Journal of Speech* 55 (1969): 414–24; Martin, "Orations on the Anniversary of American Independence, 1777–1876," 311–312.

Library of Congress

For many years the Library of Congress was the repository for the nation's charters. The library provided for the public viewing of the documents. On July 4, 1930, eleven documents illustrating the development of the Declaration of Independence were put on display. On July 4, 1939, the library's copy of the Declaration of Independence was put on display for the first time in fifteen years. In 1952 the Declaration and Constitution were transferred to the **National Archives and Records Administration (NARA)**. On July 4, 1988, Librarian of Congress James Billington hosted a Soviet delegation, headed by Nikolai Sernenovich Kartashov, director of the Lenin State Library, at a gathering to watch the Fourth of July fireworks from the top of one of the Library of Congress buildings.

Sources: "Documents Reveal Declaration Origin," *Washington Post*, 5 July 1930, 2; *Washington Post*, 4 July 1988, D7.

Lieber, Francis (fl. 1861)

His eight-stanza poem titled "Our Country and Her Flag" was published in Washington in the *National Intelligencer* on July 4, 1861.

> We do not hate our enemy —
> May God deal gently with us all!
> We love our Land; we fight her foe;
> We hate his cause, and that must fall.

Source: *National Intelligencer*, 4 July 1861, 2.

Lillari Railroad Park, Sparks, Nevada

The James C. Lillari Railroad Park was dedicated on July 4, 1976, in commemoration of the Bicentennial and as "a memorial dedicated to the thousands of Chinese who played a major role in the history of Nevada." Sparks, Nevada, is located east of Reno, was established in 1904, and was named after Governor John Sparks (1903–08).

Source: Sparks, Nevada, Web site, 1 January 2004, <http://m1.aol.com/casinonews/sp-area.htm>.

Lincoln, Abraham (1809–1865)

Sixteenth president of the U.S. (1861–65). Lincoln's Fourth of July legacy centered on his convening of Congress for the first time ever on Independence Day in 1861 and the impact of his **Emancipation Proclamation** on the celebration of the holiday. Lincoln was born in Hardin County, Kentucky, of humble beginnings. He worked on a farm and later fought in the Black Hawk War. He was elected to the Illinois legislature and served for nearly eight years. He gained a national reputation in the late 1850s running against Stephen A. Douglas for senator and challenging him in debates. He was elected president in 1860 and immediately set about rallying the Union cause.

On July 4, 1861, Lincoln sent an address to Congress but a reading of it was postponed until the next day. Meanwhile he attended a flag raising at the south front of the Treasury Department. He raised the national standard, a gift to the city by the Union Committee of New York, up a new 100-foot pole as a band played the "Star-Spangled Banner." In 1862 on the Fourth, Lincoln entertained an association of soldiers of the War of 1812 in his White House office. Each soldier was introduced to the president, who exchanged greetings.

Through the years Lincoln has been commemorated on the Fourth through the unveiling of statues, meetings of associations named after him, and in speeches and reenactments. On July 4, 1914, a bust of him was unveiled in Christiania, Norway, and Smith Stimmel presented an address in his honor. On July 4, 2004, "President and Mrs. Abraham Lincoln" were portrayed by actors at the Old Court House in St. Louis.

Sources: *Washington Evening Star*, 5 July 1861 and 1862, 3 and 3 respectively; Smith Stimmel, *Address at the Unveiling of Bust of Abraham Lincoln, July 4th, 1914* (1914?).

Lincoln Pioneer Village, Rockport, Indiana

This site was dedicated on July 4, 1935. Philip Lutz, Jr. (b. 1888), attorney general of Indiana, presented a speech titled "The Fourth of July in Lincoln's Time and Today."

Source: *New York Times*, 5 July 1935, 15.

Program

ONE HUNDRED FORTY-SECOND ANNIVERSARY
of
LINCOLN'S GETTYSBURG ADDRESS

"Four score and seven years ago--"
1863

Soldiers' National Cemetery
Gettysburg, Pennsylvania

November 19, 2005

Rain location: Christ Chapel, Gettysburg College
(Corner of North Washington and Stevens Streets)

Lincoln Statues, Racine, Wisconsin

The city of Racine has the only statue representing both Abraham Lincoln and Mary Todd Lincoln in the country. It was unveiled on July 4, 1943. Mary Todd Lincoln was in Racine from June to August, 1867, visiting Racine College with her son Tad. Lena Rosewall, who died in 1935, bequeathed funds for the statue, which was sculpted by Frederick C. Hibbard. In July 1997, a patriotic ceremony commemorating Mary Todd Lincoln and the installation of lights was presented.

In downtown Racine, on July 4, 1884, on the 50th anniversary of the town, Haymarket Square was renamed Monument Square and on that day, a marble memorial in honor of Civil War soldiers from Racine was dedicated.

Sources: Terry Flores, "City Dedicates Rare Statue of Lincoln's Wife," *Racine Journal Times*, 4 July 1997; Web site, Racine County, Wisconsin, <http://www.VisitRacine.org/history/monument_memorial.html>.

Lindbergh Park, New York City

Dedicated on July 4, 1927, in celebration of the first New-York-to-Paris aviator, Charles Augustus Lindbergh. About 3500 spectators were present and they sang the "Star-Spangled Banner." Speakers included George V. McLaughlin, former police commissioner, and Philip I. Nash of the Coney Island Chamber of Commerce. The park is located at Norton's Point, "on the tip of Sea Gate." A newspaper reported that "Letters five feet high will proclaim the name to every ship entering the harbor."

Source: "New York Enjoys Dignified Fourth," *New York Times*, 5 July 1927, 5.

Littlefield, Texas

This town was formally established on July 4, 1913. Located 35 miles from Lubbock, the population of Littlefield is currently close to 7,000. The town was established as a result of the Littlefield Lands Company, which was organized in August 1912 by Maj. George Washington Littlefield, who was selling over 79,000 acres of his Yellow House Ranch. The town of Littlefield served as the center of the operation. The site for Littlefield was chosen conveniently on the Santa Fe Railroad line under construction from Lubbock to Texico, New Mexico. Settlers in Littlefield included Mennonites, with some lot buyers coming from East Texas and some northern states, and others from the states of the Great Plains area.

Sources: David B. Gracy II, *Littlefield Lands* (Austin: University of Texas Press, 1968); *Handbook of Texas Online*: Littlefield Lands Company, 5 February 2002.

Locomotive collisions

An entertainment in which a head-on collision between two full-sized railroad locomotives takes place as a demonstration of the power of the engines and for the amusement for the spectators. On July 4, 1900, at the Fair Grounds in Indianapolis, a large crowd witnessed two locomotives collide at twenty-five miles per hour. Another similar event took place at Brighton Beach race track, Coney Island, New York, on July 4, 1906, before 40,000 spectators. On the Fourth in 1911, President **William Howard Taft** witnessed a similar event in Indianapolis.

Sources: *Harper's Weekly*, 21 July 1900 and 21 July 1906.

London, England

Celebrations in London by the American colony there have occurred over the last century. On July 4, 1885, Americans attended a celebration at the Buckingham Palace Hotel. U.S. financier Cyrus W. Field gave a speech on the history of the United States and told his audience that "the work of freedom which had been begun by Washington had been completed by Lincoln."

Opposite: **Program for the reenactment of the 142nd anniversary of Abraham Lincoln's Gettysburg Address, November 19, 2005, Soldiers' National Cemetery, Gettysburg, Pennsylvania. Lincoln's address of November 19, 1863, may have been inspired in part by his Independence Day speech of July 7 of that year when he noted "eighty odd years ago, upon the Fourth day of July, for the first time in the world, a union body of representatives was assembled to declare as a self-evident truth that all men were created equal." From the author's collection.**

The Engines at the Moment of Collision

How the Interlocked Locomotives looked a few Moments after the Crash

A RAILROAD COLLISION MADE TO ORDER

On the Fourth of July 40,000 spectators gathered at the Brighton Beach race-track to witness the edifying spectacle of a pre-arranged railroad wreck and the incidental destruction of two costly and able-bodied locomotives. The engines were started from opposite ends of a track seven-eighths of a mile long by their respective crews, who jumped as soon as they had got the engines well under way. The locomotives met near the centre of the track, while moving at a high rate of speed. Both were badly wrecked by the crash, although not completely demolished.

Photograph by Joles

1034

On July 4, 1913, an editorial printed in the London *Times* mentioned that the Fourth of July had become an "Anglo-American festivity":

> It has become one of the established functions of British life, and we who rarely commemorate the triumphs of our history make an annual point of joining with America in celebrating its greatest disaster. Such a spectacle as is seen twice a year in London of Englishmen eulogizing Washington's memory and honoring Independence Day, would be wellnigh unimaginable anywhere else.... It means in the first instance that they are celebrating the most tragic blunder in British history, and in the second that they are paying tribute to the memory of the man who brought Britain to her lowest depth of humiliation and impotence. It has come to be a sort of annual penance.

On July 4, 1969, President Nixon's daughter, Patricia, helped Ambassador Walter H. Annenberg and 200 British and foreign officials celebrate the Fourth.

Sources: "In Foreign Lands," *Philadelphia Inquirer*, 6 July 1885, 2; "Fourth a Function of British Life," *New York Times*, 5 July 1913, 3; "Patricia Nixon Celebrates at London Embassy Party," *New York Times*, 5 July 1969, 2.

Los Angeles Memorial Sports Arena

Dedicated on July 4, 1959, with Vice President **Richard Milhous Nixon** presiding. The arena is located in Exposition Park and is home to the USC men's and women's basketball teams. The building was dedicated to the "recognition of all who served their country in all wars."

Source: "Eisenhower Bids Americans Tell Freedom Story," *New York Times*, 4 July 1959, 1.

Low, Samuel (b. 1765)

Composed an "Ode for the Federal Procession" (broadside, New York, 1788?) and

Above: Los Angeles Memorial Sports Arena, dedicated on July 4, 1959, with Vice President Richard M. Nixon presiding. Photograph courtesy of Juan Bastos.

Opposite: Staged locomotive collision at Brighton Beach, Coney Island, July 4, 1906. The engines at the moment of collision (top) and how the locomotives appeared moments after the crash. *Harper's Weekly*, 21 July 1906. Image courtesy of HarpWeek, LLC.

"Ode for the Fourth of July, 1800," the latter read in St. Paul's Church, "before the General Society of Mechanics & Tradesmen, Tammany Society ... and other associations and citizens," and another ode read in 1801 in New York before the Mechanic, Tammany, and Coopers' Societies.

Sources: Matthew L. Davis, *An Oration, Delivered ...* (New York: W.A. Davis, 1800); George I. Eacker, *An Oration Delivered ...* (New York: William Durell, 1801).

Lowell, James Russell (1819–1891)

Author, poet, and diplomat who wrote "An Ode for the Fourth of July, 1876," intended for delivery by invitation at the Taunton, Massachusetts, Fourth of July celebration in 1876, but declined by the author because he was "unable to finish it to his satisfaction." The work was later published in the *Atlantic Monthly* in December 1876, "urged by a natural desire not to defer its publication till our Centenary year had closed."

Lowell was born in Cambridge, Massachusetts, son of Charles Lowell, a Congregational clergyman. He began a course of study at Harvard in 1834, but due to a lack of attention to his work and to not following regulations, was suspended several months before graduation. He later completed his studies in Concord under the tutelage of a local minister. During this time, however, his talents as a writer were acknowledged. He published several essays and poems in *Harvardiana*, the college magazine, and a *Class Poem* (1838), the latter a work in honor of being selected class poet by his fellow students. During the 1840s, Lowell's poems were published in a number of leading literary journals, including *Southern Literary Messenger* and *United States Magazine and Democratic Review*. His first volume of verse was *A Year's Life* (1841) followed by *Poems* (1844). "The critical response to Lowell's verse was unusually favorable." His published verse in the 1860s and '70s is considered "distinguished poetry in a philosophical, public vein." His distinguished literary career provided opportunities for editorships of leading journals, including *Atlantic Monthly* (1857) and *North American Review* (1864). In his later years, his interest in politics afforded him a position as Massachusetts delegate to the Republican convention in 1876 and in the following year an appointment under Rutherford B. Hayes as U.S. minister to Spain. It was during this period of political interest that Lowell composed his "Ode for the Fourth of July, 1876." The work was well received. F.H. Underwood characterized the poem as containing "a lofty tone of sentiment and grand poetic diction." D.H. Chamberlain considered Lowell's ode as "a splendid and earnest tribute to the founders of New England and of America."

(First stanza)
Entranced I saw a vision in the cloud
That loitered dreaming in yon sunset sky,
Full of fair shapes, half creatures of the eye,
Half chance-evoked by the wind's phantasy
In golden mist, an ever-shifting crowd:
There, 'mid unreal forms that came and went
In robes air-spun, of evanescent dye,
A woman's semblance shone preeminent,
Not armed like Pallas, not like Hera proud,
But, as on household diligence intent,
Beside her visionary wheel she bent
Like Arete or Bertha, nor than they.

Sources: *Atlantic Monthly* 38/230 (December 1876): 740–47; D.H. Chamberlain, "James Russell Lowell," *New England and Yale Review* 55/261 (December 1891): 496; F.H. Underwood, "James Russell Lowell," *Harper's New Monthly Magazine* 62/368 (January 1881): 270; Thomas Wortham, "James Russell Lowell," *American National Biography*, 14:40–43.

Lynch, Anne Charlotte (1815–1891)

Teacher, author and poet, who wrote "Ode for the Fourth of July." She was born in Bennington, Vermont, in 1820 and was educated in Albany, New York. Her father, Patrick Lynch, was an Irish patriot who studied at Dublin University and was later captured during the Irish Rebellion of 1798, spent time in prison, and was subsequently banished. He immigrated to America in 1812.

Lynch had a keen interest in writing, which resulted in "innumerable stories, essays, and criticisms." While living in Providence, Rhode Island, she edited the *Rhode Island Book* (Providence, 1841) that contained "selections from authors of that state." Her early years were spent teaching as well, first at the Albany Female Academy and later in Providence. She then moved to New York, and it was there that her first collection was published in 1848. She also compiled a *Handbook of Universal Literature* (New York, 1860), "containing concise accounts of great authors of all ages and their works." In 1855 she married Vincenzo Botta, a teacher of Italian language and literature. The two settled in New York where he worked at the University of the City of New York and she held literary salons for both well and lesser known literary figures, politicians and artists.

Out of a modest literary output of poetry and articles, Anne Lynch Botta wrote only one Independence Day piece: her four-stanza "Ode for the Fourth of July" was patriotic and considered a bright homage to American pride and honor.

A glorious vision burst
On Europe's dazzled sight,
Upon that day when first
Columbia sprang to light;—
When our New World, till then concealed,
In virgin beauty stood revealed.
But more sublime that day
When the young nation rose,
And cast her chains away,
And dared her tyrant foes:
Thrones quaked, and despots trembled then,
For bonds were rent and slaves were men.
The torch of Liberty,
Relighted on that day,
Streamed over land and sea
With brighter, holier ray.
Hail to our Country! Hail to thee,
Auspicious day that saw her free!
Let the star-spangled flag
Upon the free air float;
Let hill, and vale, and crag,
Prolong the cannon's note:
"Live the Republic!" let this be
The watch-word of our liberty.

Source: *Appleton's Cyclopaedia of American Biography*, ed. James Grant Wilson and John Fiske (New York: Appleton, 1887).

Madison, Dolley (1768–1849)

First Lady to James Madison, fourth president of the U.S., and the first woman to give an Independence Day address in Washington City on July 4, 1808. Dolley, as she preferred to be called, was the acknowledged hostess of Washington, giving tea parties, receptions, and visiting with others in and about town, first in her role as wife of the secretary of state (1801–09) and later as First Lady (1809–17). As one of the last surviving widows of the framers of the Constitution, she was given an open and lifetime invitation to the floor of the House of Representatives by Congress and was frequently there for important events. Each year on Independence Day, as well as on other special occasions, she was acknowledged and honored by ordinary citizens and dignitaries alike who called on her at her residence at Lafayette Square and at Montpelier, the Madison plantation in Virginia.

On Independence Day in 1808 Dolley spoke to the local militia after having presented them with a flag: "In the morning Capt. Brent's troop of cavalry paraded before the house of Mr. Madison, when Mrs. Madison presented them with an elegant standard, accompanied by a patriotic address, to which Capt. Brent made an appropriate reply." Of Dolley's Fourth of July celebrations participated in, it was her last one in 1848 at the cornerstone ceremony of the Washington Monument that was the most memorable. She, together with other dignitaries, was afforded a special carriage for the procession to the Capitol, as well as a "conspicuous" seat close to the ceremony.

Sources: *Universal Gazette*, 7 July 1808, 2; *Daily Union*, 5 July 1845, 3; "The Anniversary," *National Intelligencer*, 6 July 1848, 4; Paul Zall, *Dolley Madison* (Huntington, N.Y.: Nova History Publications, 2001); Dolley Madison, *Memoirs and Letters of Dolly Madison* (Port Washington: Kennikat Press, 1971).

Madison, James (1751–1836)

Fourth president of the U.S. (1809–17) who helped draft the Virginia state constitution (1776), served in the Continental Congress (1780–83) and proposed the Bill of Rights of the Constitution. Madison was honored in song and praise annually on Independence Day for his role in getting the Constitution adopted and as president even though his popularity had somewhat diminished as a result of his less than stellar leadership of the **War of 1812**. In keeping with the tradition started by Jefferson, Madison opened the Executive Mansion for receptions on the Fourth of July, except for July 4, 1813, when he was ill that day. In 1810, he attended a Baptist Meeting

House service in Washington and heard Robert Polk's oration there. In the following year he reviewed troops in front of the White House and heard an oration presented by Samuel Sprigg in the church on F Street. Later that afternoon, at a dinner celebration on the banks of the Tiber River for a group of citizens numbering 200 to 300, the U.S. Marine Band performed *Madison's March* "following a toast to The President of the U. States." This tune, first appearing in print in 1809 (with one variant by Alexander Reinagle of Philadelphia and another by Philip Mauro of Washington), became one of the most popular in its day and was played frequently on Independence Day in cities and towns across the country.

On July 4, 1814, Madison issued a presidential order to the states, "directing them to detach and hold for instant service their quotas of a national force of 93,000." On July 4, 1827, Madison was at the Orange, Virginia, Court House Celebration, and according to the *Richmond Enquirer*, addressed an audience assembled there. In 1834, Madison was invited to attend the Democratic Festival in Philadelphia on the Fourth but declined in a letter in which he wrote, "But the gratification I might feel in being present on an occasion cherishing the constitutional doctrines maintained by Virginia in 1798–9, as an authentic view of the relations between the Government of the Union and the governments of the States, is denied to me by the debility and indisposition under which I continue to labour." Madison encouraged the Democrats to remember to "offer the memory" of Thomas Jefferson.

Sources: *National Intelligencer*, 6 July 1810 and 1811, 2 and 2, respectively, and 5 July 1813, 3; *Richmond Enquirer*, 13 July 1827, 2; "The 4th of July," *Los Angeles Times*, 4 July 1889, 7; *James Madison Letters* (New York: Townsend, 1884), 4:344.

Madison's Proclamation of War *see* Declaration of War on Great Britain

Magayohi (Chief Star)

A chief in the Sioux nation who gave a speech on July 4, 1888, in Lidgerwood, Dakota (now North Dakota).

This land which lies about us was once the property of my people; you have now possession of it and have made yourselves homes and are rearing your families on the land which formerly belonged to my forefathers. I have no complaint to make of this fact, for it is perhaps better as it is. Our desire is to become like the white man; to learn to cultivate the land and to make a living from it; to learn to read and to write and to transact business; to learn the principles of government and become citizens; to acquire title to 160 acres for each member of our tribe. We have faith in the Great Spirit and in the Great Father at Washington, and believe that in time your people will teach my people to be like you; the negro's skin is darker than ours, and you have made a man of him; we ask the government to do us the same justice.

Source: "Speech of an Indian Chief," in *American Missionary* 42/9 (September 1888): 255.

Maloney, American Centenniel

The name of a baby born on July 3, 1876, and named by his or her Irish parents in New York City in commemoration of the nation's centennial celebration.

Source: *Boston Daily Globe*, 4 July 1876.

Mammarello explosion, Philadelphia

A tragic loss of life of children due to a single explosion of fireworks occurred in Philadelphia on July 4, 1900, in front of the bakeshop of Antonio Mammarello. Seven children, ages five to eleven, were killed when a young child fired a blank cartridge at close range in a collection of fireworks sitting on a stand. The fireworks included "giant firecrackers, torpedoes, rockets and chasers." The windows of many stores and residences in the area were shattered.

When the smoke lifted, "More than a score of children were found lying on the street, burned and bleeding. Trolley cars and wagons were pressed into service, and they were taken to the hospitals, where the four children died."

Source: "Fatal Fireworks," *Baltimore Morning Herald*, 5 July 1900, 11.

Mann, Horace (1796–1859)

This educator and statesman played a significant role in the educational reform movement in America and presented a memorable oration on education on July 4, 1842, in Boston. Mann was born in Franklin, Massachusetts, and studied at Brown University. After attending the Litchfield Law School in Connecticut, he practiced law in Massachusetts (Dedham and Boston) until 1837. He was elected to the Massachusetts house (1827–33), then to the office of president of the state senate (1836–37). Under his influence a state board of education was established through an education bill of 1837 which called for extensive reforms including the proposing of nonsectarian education. He established the first state public school in 1839 at Lexington, Massachusetts.

In 1842 the city council of Boston invited Mann to speak on the Fourth of July. He gave a lengthy presentation that broke with traditional oratory expectations. Instead of "glorifications of our great country and our great people," Mann's theme centered on the notion that "our existing means for the promotion of intelligence and virtue are wholly inadequate to the support of a Republican government." He carefully set out his argument that effective self-government depended wholly on a well-educated populace and that "the first great principle of a republican government" is that schools should be open to all and all the masses educated. However, Mann stated, "There is not a single State in this whole Union, which is doing any thing at all proportionate to the exigency of the case."

On July 4, 1865, in Boston, a statue of Horace Mann was unveiled.

Sources: *An Oration Delivered before the Authorities of the City of Boston* (Boston: J.H. Eastburn, 1842); *Norwich Weekly Courier*, 13 July 1865, 3.

Mansfield, Ohio, Electric Street Railway

The opening of the electric railway system in this town was celebrated on July 4, 1887, with a "Mardigras and industrial parade." The system included four and a half miles of track and five cars, and was created by an ordinance passed by the city council on March 30, 1887, that gave the authority to operate it to S.T. Dunham of New York. The first electric cars used were "horse-drawn cars with fifteen horsepower motors installed" and the fare was five cents. The celebration that day included "Professor Leon," who gave a rope-walking exhibition, followed by a fireworks display later that evening.

Source: *Ages Past: A Short Pictorial History of Mansfield, Ohio*, Web site, 4 October 2002, <http://Mansfield.w8jaz.com/index.html>.

Marcy, William Learned (1786–1857)

Governor of New York, U.S. secretary of war and secretary of state, who died on July 4 while vacationing at Ballston Spa, New York. Marcy was born in Southbridge, Massachusetts, and graduated from Brown University in 1808. He served in the War of 1812 and then went to Troy, New York, where he practiced law. Marcy gradually rose through the ranks of civic responsibilities first as state comptroller (1823), then as a judge on the state Supreme Court (1829), a member of the U.S. Senate (1831) and governor of New York (1833–1838). As governor Marcy increased the New York canal system and improved education and libraries. In 1844, he was appointed secretary of war by President James Polk. Marcy devoted much of his tenure to pensions and Indian treaties. In 1853 he was appointed secretary of state under President Franklin Pierce, a post he held until his death. During that time Marcy was responsible for twenty-four treaties, one of which was the Gadsden Purchase, which added a considerable amount of land to the United States so that a transcontinental railroad could be constructed. According to Phyllis F. Field, Marcy was "exhausted by his labors" and may have died as a result of that.

On July 4 Marcy was at the Sans Souci Hotel in Ballston. He had breakfast and shortly after complained of a pain in his side. He left the hotel, and walked to the office of Dr. Moore. "Not finding the latter therein, he returned to his room in the hotel. The doctor came in a few minutes, and on going to the room found Mr. Marcy lying dead upon a couch, with an open book on his breast. He had just written a letter to Hon. J.M. Botts."

Marcy's death greatly affected New Yorkers who remembered him principally for his work as governor. According to a New York correspondent, the news was "received by all classes of people with a deep feeling of regret; for, however politicians might differ with him on matters of Governmental policy, all must agree that he was one of the eminent men of the times, whose name and who labors in diplomacy and statesmanship justly entitle him to a bright page in the country's annals."

Sources: "From Our New York Correspondent," *National Intelligencer*, 6 July 1857, 3; "Particulars of Gov. Marcy's Death, &c," *National Intelligencer*, 7 July 1857, 3; "The Late Wm. L. Marcy," *National Intelligencer*, 8 July 1857, 3; Phyllis F. Field, "William Learned Marcy," *American National Biography*, 14:496–98.

Marietta, Ohio

Site of the first Fourth of July celebration and oration in 1788 west of the Alleghany Mountains in the Northwestern territory. In that year the Ohio Company of Associates established this town at the confluence of the Muskingum and Ohio rivers. The settlement took its name in honor of Marie Antoinette, the queen of France, who had aided the young country in its battle for independence from Great Britain. On the other side of the Muskingum river, opposite the town, Fort Harmer was erected. Independence Day in 1788 was announced by a federal salute from the fort, and the American flag was hoisted. At 12:30 P.M., "Gen. Harmar, with the ladies, officers, and other gentlemen of the garrison, arrived at the city." James Mitchell Varnum, one of the judges of the Western Territory, gave an oration in which he extolled the day, promised that all citizens would be equally protected under the laws, and advised the crowd that they must treat the Native Americans "with humanity and kindness and should meet the challenges of living in this new territory." His statement that "every class of citizens will be equally protected by the laws" provided a prophetic perspective of how the Declaration of Independence would ultimately socially shape the destiny of the new nation.

Following the oration, at 2 P.M. the ladies and gentlemen partook of "an entertainment, prepared for the occasion." After dinner the company drank 14 toasts. "The greatest order, propriety and harmony prevailed through the day, which was closed by a beautiful illumination of Fort Harmar."

Source: *An oration, Delivered at Marietta, July 4, 1788, by the Hon., James M. Varnum, Esq.* (Newport, R.I.: Peter Edes, 1788).

Marysville, Pennsylvania, riot

On July 4, 1870, a riot broke out at a picnic held by black military companies, resulting in several persons shot.

Source: *Washington Evening Star*, 8 July 1870, 4.

Mason, Lowell (1792–1872)

Wrote the music for "With Thy Pure Dews and Rains" (words by John Pierpont; published, Boston: Mason Bros., 1829), which was performed at the Park Street Church in Boston on July 4, 1829, on the same program as the **William Lloyd Garrison** speech. Mason also directed the first performance of **"America," or "My Country 'Tis of Thee,"** which took place at the Park Street Church on July 4, 1831. On the Fourth in 1843, Mason conducted a "select choir of Pupils of the public schools" in performing an ode in Boston's Faneuil Hall.

Source: *Memoirs of John Quincy Adams*, 11:389.

Masonic Hall, Hudson, New York

This building at Hudson, New York, was "nearly destroyed" on July 4, 1832, as a result of the "firing of crackers."

Source: *Niles' Weekly Register* 42/21 (21 July 1832): 373.

Masonic Hall, Zanesville, Ohio

The cornerstone of this building was laid on July 4, 1857.

Source: *Daily Ohio State Journal*, 7 July 1857, 2.

Massachusetts State House

The cornerstone of the Massachusetts State House was laid on July 4, 1795, with Paul Revere and Governor Samuel Adams in attendance. The building was designed by Charles Bullfinch.

Source: *Independent Chronicle*, 6 July 1795.

Matlack, Timothy (1736–1829)

Merchant, brewer, and inscriber of the Declaration of Independence in 1776 who, at age 90, publicly read the Declaration of Independence in Philadelphia on July 4, 1821.

Matlack was born in Haddonfield, New Jersey, the son of Quakers. His family moved to Philadelphia in 1746. By the 1760s he had established himself in business as a brewer and later merchant although much of his time was spent pursuing frivolous pastimes, such as horse racing and cockfighting, while neglecting his business. His activities eventually landed him in debtors' prison. He obtained his release, however, through the help of other Quakers, but also lost his privilege of Quaker membership.

With the outbreak of war in 1775, Matlack got involved in politics. He developed a set of radical yet simple principles which linked him with other independence-seeking leaders, such as Thomas Paine and James Cannon. He became one of Pennsylvania's influential leaders and held numerous posts beginning in 1775 when he was named clerk for assisting Charles Thomson, secretary of the Second Continental Congress. On July 19 of that year he was asked to inscribe the Declaration of Independence, a task he completed by August 2 in time for the fifty-six signers who had returned to Philadelphia to affix their names to the document.

In 1780 he became a Pennsylvania delegate to the Second Continental Congress and was elected to the esteemed American Philosophical Society. In 1781 and 1782, he was a director of the Bank of North America, but Republicans later lodged charges against him regarding his alleged mismanagement of funds. The case was later dropped. During the remainder of his life, Matlack held a variety of other positions, including a commissioner for the Delaware River (1789), clerk of the state senate (1790–1800) and state master of the rolls (1800). For several years he lived in Lancaster and later moved to Holmesburg, Pennsylvania, where he died.

Sources: *New York American*, 7 July 1821, 2; James Munves, *Thomas Jefferson and the Declaration of Independence* (New York: Charles Scribner's Sons,

1978), 124; Gaspare J. Saladino, "Timothy Matlack," *American National Biography*, 14:707–08.

Mattoon, Illinois

City where a Nurses Monument was dedicated on July 4, 1987.

Source: "Dedication: Nurses Monument, July 4, 1987" (videorecording, 1987; copy in Mattoon Public Library).

McAllen International Museum

This museum, located in McAllen, Texas, was founded by the town's Junior League in 1967 and its newest building was dedicated on July 4, 1976. The museum collections include Latin American folk art, contemporary prints, paintings from the 16th to 20th centuries, and other collections that represent the local area. The building includes a Discovery Center principally for children, the Spectrum Theatre (opened in 1991) and the Meteorology Exhibit (completed in 1993).

Source: "History," McAllen International Museum Web site, 11 September 2002, <http://www.hi-line.net/~mim/enhanced/history.html>.

McKinley Monument, Atlanta

On July 4, 1922, the city of Atlanta unveiled a bronze memorial tablet to the memory of President McKinley near the Peace Monument in Piedmont Park. The monument was placed in Stone Mountain granite. At the ceremony, messages from President Harding and Gov. Harry L. Davis of Ohio were read.

Source: "Atlanta Unveils McKinley Memorial," *New York Times*, 5 July 1922, 4.

McKinley Statue, Chicago

On July 4, 1905, a statue of President William McKinley in McKinley Park, Chicago, was unveiled and Judge Peter Stenger Grosscup (1852–1921) presented an address for the occasion.

Source: *Address Delivered by Judge Grosscup on the Occasion of the Unveiling of the McKinley Statue in McKinley Park, Chicago, July 4, 1905* (Chicago: Chicago Legal News Co., 1905).

McKinley, William (1843–1901)

Twenty-fifth president of the U.S. (1897–1901). McKinley preferred spending quiet Fourths at the White House or at his summer home in Canton, Ohio. McKinley was born in Niles, Ohio, and served in the Union Army during the Civil War. He was admitted to the Ohio bar in 1867 and practiced law in Canton. After serving as a Republican congressman (1876–90), he was elected governor of Ohio in 1891 and 1893, and president in 1896. During his tenure of governor, McKinley gave addresses in several Independence Day celebrations. One took place at the Lakeside, a "Chautauqua of the Great Lakes" event of 1892. Lakeside, located near Lake Erie in Danbury Township, was established in 1873. The event that day included music and fireworks.

Another occurred in Cleveland in 1894, when McKinley spoke at the dedication of the **Soldiers and Sailors Monument**. A third took place in the following year when he spoke in Chicago at one of the largest patriotic demonstrations of organized labor held in that city. He said to a large audience that day, "The American laborer not only does more and better work, but there are more skilled, intelligent, and capable artisans here now in proportion to the population than in any other nation of the world."

Another significant event occurred at the White House in 1898, when he received a "memorial" on behalf of the Empire State Society and Sons of the American Revolution lauding him for his management of the war with Spain. McKinley received hundreds of telegrams that day congratulating him on the nation's victory at Santiago, Cuba, on July 3. Other events included that of July 4, 1900, when McKinley was in Canton, Ohio, reviewing a parade of "industries" there. McKinley was assassinated on September 6, 1901.

Sources: Lakeside Camp Meeting Program Bulletin, July 2–4, 1892; "Stevenson and McKinley Speak," *New York Times*, 5 July 1895, 5; "President McKinley's Fourth," *Baltimore Morning Herald*, 6 July 1897, 2; "At the White House," *Washington Evening Star*, 4 July 1898, 3; "President Reviews a Parade," *New York Times*, 5 July 1900, 7.

McPherson, James Birdseye

McPherson, Kansas, and McPherson county are named after James B. McPherson, the highest ranking Union officer to die in battle during the Civil War, and a statue was

dedicated in his honor there on July 4, 1917. The statue is located in the town's Memorial Park.

Source: *McPherson When It Matters* Web site, 11 September 2002, <http://www.mcphersonks.org/local.html>.

Mecklenburg Declaration

Supposedly adopted by a convention held in Charlotte, Mecklenburg County, North Carolina, and delivered to the North Carolina delegation at Philadelphia for presentation to the Continental Congress. The twenty resolutions adopted on May 20, 1775, annulled all laws and commissions mandated by the British crown, and it was believed consequently by some that these resolutions might have been the germ of Jefferson's immortal Declaration of 1776. Reference to the Mecklenburg resolutions were printed in the *South Carolina Gazette* (13 June 1775) and a number of northern newspapers. Interest in the document surfaced occasionally at annual Fourth of July events. On July 5, 1894, for example, the *Seattle-Post Intelligencer* (p. 4) printed the story behind the resolutions. No original copy of the Mecklenburg Declaration has ever been found. While some believe the document to be a hoax, the tradition within the state is genuine. The date of the resolutions is on the state seal and May 20 is a legal North Carolina holiday.

Source: Daniel J. Boorstin, *The Americans: The National Experience* (New York: Random House, 1965), 385–86.

Meek, Alexander Beaufort (1814–1865)

Poet and prose writer. Composed "The Day of Freedom," a celebrated poem that was read before the Ciceronian Club and other citizens of Tuscaloosa, Alabama, on July 4, 1838, and presented an oration on July 4, 1848, in Mobile, Alabama, to the soldiers returning from the war with Mexico. Meek was born in Columbia, South Carolina, and graduated from the University of Alabama in 1833. His classmates chose him to give the Fourth of July oration. Meek spent his life both as an attorney and pursuing literary endeavors which resulted in a significant reputation as one of the "young state's cultural, intellectual, and political leaders." His poems were widely disseminated throughout the South, mostly through southern periodicals.

His "The Day of Freedom," a poem being one of the "longest and most elaborated" of this genre, was highly regarded by contemporary reviewers, one of whom remarked: "We have read it with much gratification, not only because its thought is warmly and rightly patriotic, but because it has a fair proportion of good poetry — and this, we take it, is no small matter, in times like these, when the land is smitten, as it were, with a plague-irruption of jingling and unjingling, measured and unmeasured trash." Another said, "It is instinct with the truest patriotism, and abounds in beautiful passages." Following are selected opening stanzas:

> If it be good to think on virtues past, —
> If many a noble secret, rich and true,
> On history's pictur'd page, neglected lies,
> From which the heart might sage instruction
>   glean,
> And a sweet moral learn, to guide its path,
> Thro' time's bewildering labyrinths aright,
> If the brave deeds by patriot sires achieved,
> When view'd again, their children haply
>   prompt
> To a pure emulation, and inspire
> A kindred spirit, and a genial love,
> A gratitude ennobling to the heart,
> Oh, sure it must be good and right always,
> To nurse the memories of this sacred day!

Meek's oration was a tribute to the soldiers who fought in the war with Mexico, as well as a brief history of the major battles and their heroes:

> Soldiers of Mexico, we give you here, the first greetings of the American people. Everywhere in your progress through the land, you will be met by the cheers and admiration of one sex, and the smiles and the love of the other. While we will drop with you the tears of profoundest and tenderest sorrow for the loss of those who now sleep in soldiers' graves, upon the mountain slopes and battle plains of Mexico, while we shall long keep bright their memories in the sanctuaries of the heart, we will yet extend to the survivors, our warmest gratitude, our most imperishable admiration.

Sources: "Meek's Fourth-of-July Poem," *The Hesperian* 1/6 (October 1838): 493; "Notices of New Works," *Southern Literary Messenger* 25/6 (December 1857): 476; A.B. Meek, *Songs and Poems of the South*, 3rd ed. (Mobile: S.H. Goetzel, 1857); A.B. Meek, *Romantic Passages in Southwestern History* (New York: S.H. Goetzel, 1857).

Meineke, Christopher (1782–1850)

Composer, organist, and choirmaster who wrote two works that were performed on the Fourth of July. *Jubilee March, and Quick Step* (Baltimore: John Cole, 1820) for piano was performed (perhaps in Baltimore) on July 4, 1826. *Rail Road March for the Fourth of July* (Baltimore: Geo. Willig, 1828) was dedicated to the directors of the **Baltimore and Ohio Railroad**, whose construction was inaugurated on July 4, 1828.

Meineke was born in Germany, came to the United States in 1800 and settled in Baltimore where he served as choirmaster at St. Paul's Episcopal Church.

Source: Clark, *The Dawning of American Keyboard Music*, 143.

Mexican War (1846–48)

War between Mexico and the United States as a result of the U.S. annexation of Texas, and which led to the acquisition of a large territory of land in the Southwest. Notably Texas and California entered the union on July 4, 1846 and 1851, respectively. Other events on the Fourth included July 4, 1848, in New York, when "bodies of soldiers recently fallen on the battlefields of Mexico were escorted through the city by the Baxter Blues, accompanied by Dodworth's Brass Band." In 1876, veterans of the war marched on July 4 down Main Street in Los Angeles amidst "statues of national heroes and pictures of Washington" placed in key areas. On July 4, 1916, 85-year-old Charles J. Murphy, "said to be the sole survivor of the Mexican War," was honored at City Hall, New York City.

Sources: *New York Weekly Herald*, 8 July 1848, 15; "Celebrations of Old-Time Days Recited," *Los Angeles Times*, 3 July 1927, G1; "2,000,000 Here Salute the Flag," *New York Times*, 5 July 1916, 12.

Middle Dutch Church, New York

Site for a sermon titled "The Blessings of America" preached by William Linn (1752–1808) and an ode "composed for the occasion" by William Pitt Smith and set to music by "Mr. Van Hagen on July 4, 1791" in New York City. This event was sponsored by the Tammany Society, or Columbia Order.

Source: *The Blessings of America* (New York: Thomas Greanleaf, 1791).

Middlebury, Vermont, Centennial

On July 4, 1866, Middlebury, Vermont, celebrated its centennial at the farm once owned by Mr. Seely, the "first pioneer" who made the first clearing of the land. The event was sponsored by the Middlebury Historical Society. Rev. Cephas H. Kent read from the family Bible of the original pioneer. Brainerd Kellogg presented an oration, providing information on Middlebury's early settlers. Mrs. Julia C.R. Dorr's poem "O Mighty Present! From Our Souls Today" was read.

Source: *Oration by Prof. Brainerd Kellogg* (Middlebury, Vt.: Register Book and Job Printing Establishment, 1866).

Mill Prison, Plymouth, England

The site for the first Independence Day celebration on foreign soil, on July 4, 1778. American prisoners of war celebrated the Fourth of July in the early morning in 1778 by wearing hand-made cockades made of paper and decorated with 13 stripes and 13 stars. At 1 P.M., according to Charles Herbert's diary, we "drew up in thirteen divisions, and each division gave three cheers, till it came to the last, when we all cheered together, all of which was conducted with the greatest regularity. We kept our colors hoisted till sunset, and then took them down." See also **Prisons**.

Source: Francis D. Cogliano, "'We All Hoisted the American Flag:' National Identity among American Prisoners in Britain during the American Revolution," *Journal of American Studies* 32/1 (April 1998): 27.

Mississippi Insurrection of 1835

An insurrection by slaves planned for July 4, 1835, was thwarted by a "faithful Negro man, who was in all the secrets, and was to have been high in command, and who revealed to his master the whole plan" a few days before the Fourth of July. The affair had been planned over a six month period and was "headed by white men.... A great many Ne-

groes were in consequence taken up in Madison County, from whom the committee found out who the white leaders were. About ten Negroes and five or six white men have been hung, without any form of law or trial except an examination before the Examining Committee. They are still going on trying and hanging."

Sources: *Maine Farmer and Journal of the Useful Arts* 3/27 (7 August 1835): 215; *Nashville Banner*, 15 July 1835.

Missouri Pacific Railroad

Began operation as the Pacific Railroad on July 4, 1851, in St. Louis. Chartered by the State of Missouri on March 12, 1849, the proposal for the new railroad was to have the line extend to western Missouri and on to the Pacific Ocean. The first section of the railroad opened for service on December 9, 1852.

Source: *Brief History of the Missouri Pacific*, Web site, 24 September 2002, <http://skyways.lib.ks.us/history/mp/mphist.html>.

Monroe, James (1758–1831)

Fifth president of the U.S. (1817–25) and 3rd president to die on the Fourth of July. A popular president whose first term was dubbed the "era of good feeling." All but one of the 232 electors voted for him. Monroe was the second president to close the Executive Mansion on the Fourth so he could travel to other states to speak about the importance of individual rights and principles of free government. During the first week of July in 1817 he was in New England, eventually arriving in Boston to celebrate the Fourth there.

In early July 1819, Monroe was in Lexington, Kentucky, being entertained by the citizens and town officials. He was supposed to join with Andrew Jackson in attending services at the Chapel of Transylvania University on Sunday, July 4, but "in consequence of fatigue and a slight indisposition, declined being present." A "Committee of Arrangements" visited him at his lodgings. Its chairman delivered the official welcoming speech and the president responded in kind. Monroe thanked the group. "In visiting our maritime and inland frontiers, with the interior, I have been prompted by a strong sense of duty to my county," he said. "A free intercourse between the Chief Magistrate of this Union and his fellow citizens, is not only in strict accord with the principles of the Constitution, but it is a duty enjoined on him by these principles."

Although not the first to close the Executive Mansion to the public on the Fourth (see **James Madison**), Monroe's absence from the city on July 4, 1820, disappointed some residents of Washington. The editor of Georgetown's newspaper *The Metropolitan* printed a scathing criticism of the president in its Independence Day issue:

> We know not how this gentleman stands with his spiritual confessor, indeed that is none of our business; but this we will undertake to say, that he has been a greater political Sabbath-breaker than any other who preceded him in the high and responsible situation of chief magistrate of this nation. When almost all the individuals in the nation, are indulging in emotions of gratitude towards the authors of their liberty, the mansion of the people, the residence of the President is shut up and made to present an aspect, disconsolate, gloomy, and joyless as the very grave.

Monroe died at the residence of his son-in-law Samuel Gouverneur in New York. The editor of the *Connecticut Mirror* thought, as did many others at the time, that it was destiny that accounted for Monroe's death on the Fourth. Around midnight on July 3, "when the noise of firing began," Monroe, who was gravely ill, "opening his eyes inquiringly and when the cause was communicated to him," it was immediately indicated that "he understood what the occasion was." When the public heard the news numerous tributes were offered. The Superior Court and Court of General Sessions of the Peace adjourned as a mark of respect. The members of the New York State Society of the Cincinnati agreed to wear badges of mourning for thirty day, and in many cities artillery fired salutes as an announcement of the news.

About 70,000 persons attended Monroe's funeral, "with a line of march, which extended nearly two miles." His body was in view on a platform in front of City Hall. President Duer of Columbia College address the crowd, opening his eulogy with these words:

Another anniversary of our national independence has been consecrated by the death of another of those patriots who assisted to achieve it — of another of those statesmen, who, after a long course of public service, attained the highest office in the Government; to the foundation of which he had contributed by an early devotion of life and fortune to his country.

From there Monroe's body was taken to St. Paul's Church for the service presided over by the Rev. Bishop Onderdonk and the Rev. Wainright. Monroe was interred at the cemetery located at Bleecker and Second Streets. His mahogany coffin bore the following inscription on a silver plate:

JAMES MONROE,
Of Virginia,
Died 4th July, 1831,
Aged 74 Years.

In early July 1858 the remains of Monroe were brought from New York on the boat *Jamestown* to Richmond for permanent internment in Hollywood Cemetery. Accompany the boat, which arrived on July 4, was the steamer *Glen Cove*, with the New York 7th Regiment, "the chivalrous guard of honor." Accompanying the remains was John Cochrane, U.S. representative from New York. A procession to the cemetery included a "hearse drawn by six white horses." That evening all of the participants celebrated the Fourth of July with a dinner and appropriate toasts.

On the centennial of Monroe's death, July 4, 1931, a celebration was broadcast by WJZ from the University of Virginia campus, and William R. Castle, under-secretary of state, gave an address titled "Aspects of the Monroe Doctrine." Also the Washington *Evening Star* published a commemorative article on the life and death of the president.

Sources: "The President's Tour, *National Intelligencer*, 8 July 1817, 2; "President Monroe and the 4th of July," *The Metropolitan*, 4 July 1820, 2; "Death of James Monroe," *Connecticut Mirror*, 9 July 1831, 2–3; "Funeral of James Monroe," *National Intelligencer*, 11 July 1831, 3; *Richmond Enquirer*, 9 July 1858, 1; *New York Times*, 4 July 1931, 3; James Waldo Fawcett, "Monroe—100 Years After," *Washington Evening Star*, 5 July 1931, A5; *Papers of James Monroe: A Documentary History of the Presidential Tours of James Monroe, 1817, 1818, 1819*, ed. Daniel Preston (Westport, Conn.: Greenwood Press, 2003).

Montana State Capitol, Helena

The cornerstone of the state capitol building in Helena, Montana, was laid on July 4, 1899. The event included a parade of military units and addresses by Governor Robert B. Smith, ex-governor Joseph K. Toole, and ex-senator Wilbur F. Sanders. Toole, who was the first governor of Montana through appointment by President Cleveland, spoke about the early history of the state, his views about the state motto, and the rebellion in the Philippines. For the laying of the cornerstone, the gavel used "was made of wood from the estate of George Washington, at Mount Vernon." The plan for the building called for a large dome, "a balustraded terrace, from which rises the main story, having on each face a projecting pavilion with columns, pilasters, and pediment in the Corinthian style, and supported at each angle by a square pavilion with half-spherical crown."

Source: "Montana's New Capitol," *New York Times*, 5 July 1899, 1.

Monticello, home of Thomas Jefferson

Located near Charlottesville, Virginia, this home was designed by Jefferson and built in 1768–1809 in a neo-classical style. Together with the White House and Mount Vernon, Monticello has the distinction of being the most important residence intertwined with the celebration of the Fourth in the history of the country. But it was only after the death of Jefferson in 1826 and a period of decline in the estate that long overdue attention was finally given to the home and Americans came to realize the true significance of this American icon. In the early years only a few events of significance occurred in Charlottesville that were directly connected to Jefferson. For example, on July 4, 1838, a newspaper reported the Declaration was publicly read from an "original draft, in the handwriting of Mr. Jefferson."

In 1879 Jefferson Monroe Levy, a member of Congress from the state of New York, purchased Monticello and began hosting annual Fourth of July celebrations there. Typically his events included ceremonies at the grave of the president, a reading of the Declaration of Independence and fireworks in the evening. In 1888, his guests assembled "in the main hall of the mansion." In 1900 Levy himself read the Declaration before a number of "distinguished guests."

In 1924, delegates of the National Educational Association (NEA), which was holding its convention in Washington, traveled to Charlottesville to visit the University of Virginia and Monticello. William Jennings Bryan and Frank Cody, superintendent of schools in Detroit, gave speeches in the university's stadium and the reception after was held at Monticello.

On July 4, 1926, a religious freedom service was held at the base of Jefferson's tomb with Gov. Harry Flood Byrd of Virginia presiding. Addresses were presented by the Rev. William T. Manning, bishop of New York, Samuel H. Goldenson, rabbi of Rodef Shalom Temple, Pittsburgh, and the Rev. Charles W. Lyons, president of Georgetown University.

On July 5, 1926, Monticello was formally dedicated as the home "given to the nation." It had been purchased from Jefferson Levy for $500,000 raised by national subscriptions. At the ceremony a speech was given by George Gordon Battle, sesquicentennial commissioner of New York, who said, "Our leaders must still stand by the truth and hold fast to that which is good. There can be no true liberty without enlightenment." Another address was presented by Secretary of State Frank B. Kellogg. A special feature of the event was the awarding of a "Jefferson medal" to Claude G. Bowers (1879–1958) of New York for his book *Jefferson and Hamilton: The Struggle for Democracy in America* (1925).

On July 4, 1931, "the original desk on which was signed the treaty of peace between the United States and Mexico" was placed on permanent exhibition at Monticello. Concurrently a reception was held in honor of the 100th anniversary of Monroe's death. Various officials representing the Monroe Centennial Memorial Commission, Virginia Institute of Public Affairs, and the Jefferson Memorial Foundation were present. Acting Secretary of State Richard Castle, Jr., officially accepted the desk which was donated to Monticello by Miss Fanny M. Burke of Alexandria, Virginia, and who was a great-great-granddaughter of Thomas Jefferson.

On July 4, 1936, President Franklin D. Roosevelt visited Monticello and presented a eulogy to Thomas Jefferson and placed a wreath on his tomb. On July 4, 1947, President Truman gave a speech there denouncing the Soviet stand against a joint European recovery project.

In 1963, the tradition of naturalizing citizens at Monticello began. The first event was presided over by Thomas J. Michie, judge of the U.S. District Court of Western Virginia and a member of the Foundation Board of Trustees. A typical ceremony includes "a concert of American patriotic music; the petitioners for naturalization, their family, friends and guests" and an "invited guest who reads the preamble to the Declaration of Independence; and a guest speaker delivers remarks before the new citizens take the oath of citizenship. After the formal proceedings, the day ends with a true Fourth of July picnic." On July 4, 1975, fifty persons received their citizenship and in 1996, sixty-six individuals representing thirty-three countries were naturalized. In 2003 the naturalization ceremony was presided over by Senior U.S. District Court Judge James H. Michael, Jr. Immigrants represented 35 countries.

Speakers at Monticello, 1963–2006

1963	Sir Robert Menzies, prime minister of Australia
1964	Henry J. Taylor, former U.S. ambassador to Switzerland
1965	Monsieur Helde Alphaud, French ambassador
1966	Torben Ronne, Danish ambassador
1967	Henry H. Fowler, secretary of the treasury
1968	Eugene V. Rostow, undersecretary for political affairs, Department of State
1969	U. Alexis Johnson, undersecretary for political affairs, Department of State
1970	J. Sergeant Reynolds, lieutenant governor of Virginia
1971	Mills E. Godwin, Jr., former governor of Virginia
1972	Harry Flood Byrd, Jr., U.S. senator from Virginia
1973	Albertis S. Harrison, Jr., justice, Supreme Court of Virginia and former governor of Virginia
1974	Louis B. Wright, director emeritus, Folger Shakespeare Library
1975	Dumas Malone, Thomas Jefferson Memorial Foundation professor of history emeritus, University of Virginia
1976	Gerald R. Ford, president of the United States
1977	Caryl Parker Haskins, Thomas Jefferson Memorial Foundation trustee
1978	John N. Dalton, governor of Virginia
1979	Clifton Waller Barrett, Thomas Jefferson Memorial Foundation trustee
1980	Charles F. Baldwin, ambassador in residence, University of Virginia
1981	Merrill D. Peterson, Thomas Jefferson Memorial Foundation professor of history, University of Virginia
1982	Charles S. Robb, governor of Virginia
1983	J. Kenneth Robinson, U.S. representative, Seventh Virginia Congressional District
1984	John O. Marsh, Jr., secretary of the army
1985	John W. Warner, U.S. senator from Virginia
1986	Kenneth W. Thompson, director, White Burkett Miller Center for Public Affairs, University of Virginia
1987	Gerald L. Baliles, governor of Virginia
1988	John Charles Thomas, justice of the Supreme Court of Virginia
1989	Henry J. Abraham, James Hart Professor of Government and Foreign Affairs, University of Virginia
1990	L. Douglas Wilder, governor of Virginia
1991	Jacques Andreani, ambassador of France to the United States
1992	Carl Sagan, David Duncan Professor of Astronomy and space Sciences, Cornell University
1993	John T. Casteen III, president, University of Virginia
1994	David McCullough, Pulitzer Prize–winning biographer and historian
1995	Roberto C. Goizueta, chairman and CEO, the Coca-Cola Company
1996	Richard Moe, president, National Trust for Historic Preservation
1997	General Colin L. Powell, former chairman of the Joint Chiefs of Staff, Department of Defense
1998	Andrew Young, former United States ambassador to the United Nations
1999	James S. Gilmore III, governor of the Virginia
2000	Madeline Albright, secretary of state

2001	Vartan D. Gregorian, president of the Carnegie Corporation
2002	Frank McCourt, author
2003	Allen H. Neuharth, founder of the Freedom Forum and *USA Today*
2004	W. Richard West, Jr., director of the National Museum of the American Indian, Washington, D.C.
2005	I.M. Pei, architect, native of China and U.S. citizen
2006	Christo and Jeanne-Claude, environmental artists

See also **Jefferson Monument, University of Missouri at Columbia.**

Sources: *Alexandria Gazette*, 12 July 1838, 2; "The Fourth at Monticello," *Washington Post*, 7 July 1888, 1; "Where Jefferson Died," *Baltimore Morning Herald*, 5 July 1900, 3; "Educators to Visit Monticello July 4," *New York Times*, 1 July 1924, 21; *New York Times*, 5 July 1926, 11, "Jefferson's Home Given to Nation as People's Shrine," *Washington Post*, 6 July 1926, 1, 9, and 5 July 1936, 22; "Two-Day Exercises at Monticello Attract Distinguished Speakers," *Washington Sunday Star*, 4 July 1926, 6; "Desk Used in Pact with Mexico Given," *Washington Post*, 3 July 1931, 2; *Washington Evening Star*, 5 July 1947, A1; *Washington Post*, 5 July 1963, C1; Henry Mitchell, "Citizens on Patriotism's Land," *Washington Post*, 5 July 1975, B1, B3; Marc Leepson, *Saving Monticello* (New York: Free Press, 2001); Adrienne Schwisow, "Virginians Celebrate the Nation's 227th Birthday," *Virginian-Pilot*, 5 July 2003, B2; *The Great Birthday of Our Republic: Celebrating Independence Day at Monticello* (Charlottesville, Virginia: Thomas Jefferson Foundation, 2003); *The Great Birthday of Our Republic* Web site, "Independence Day Celebration and Naturalization Ceremony at Thomas Jefferson's Monticello, <http://lcweb.loc.gov/bicentennial/propage/VA/va-5_h_goode1.html>.

Morford, Henry (1823–1881)

Author, journalist, and poet who wrote a "patriotic poem" titled "Tammany and Union," read at the New York Tammany Society celebration on July 4, 1861. Morford was born in Monmouth, New Jersey, and published poems in the *New Yorker* and *Saturday Evening Post*. His collections included *Rhymes of Twenty Years* (1859) and *Rhymes of an Editor* (1873). In 1852, he began the weekly newspaper *New Jersey Standard*, but sold it in 1855. He later moved to New York City where he continued his journalism activities, as well as writing novels. According to Daniel Webster Hollis, "his verses were not widely known or respected by contemporary critics."

Sources: "Celebration of the Tammany Society," *New York Times*, 6 July 1861, 2; Daniel Webster Hollis, III, "Henry Morford," *American National Biography*, 15:814–15.

Morning Post, London

This newspaper printed the Declaration of Independence on August 17, 1776, and on July 4, 1926, reprinted a miniature reproduction of that page.

Source: *New York Times*, 5 July 1926, 5.

Morris, George Pope (1802–1864)

On July 4, 1853, at the municipal celebration held in the First Baptist Church in Providence, Rhode Island, Morris's "Anthem" (first line: "Freedom spreads her downy wings") and a poem "The Flag of Our Union" (first line: "A song for our banner") were sung by a youth choir whose members were drawn from the city's public schools.

Sources: *Municipal Celebration of the Seventy-Seventh Anniversary of American Independence ...* (Providence, R.I.: Knowles, Anthony and Co., 1853); "Fourth of July in Providence," *New York Daily Tribune*, 6 July 1853, 6.

Morris, Gouverneur (1752–1816)

Framer of the Constitution, diplomat, and businessman who was honored posthumously with a marble monument that was unveiled in the Bronx, New York, at St. Ann's Protestant Episcopal Church on July 4, 1932. Morris was born in the Bronx and attended the Academy of Philadelphia and King's College, New York. In May 1775 he was elected a member of the New York Provincial Congress and assisted in the framing of the New York State constitution. In October 1777 he was elected a delegate to the Continental Congress where he was an active participant. During the 1780s, in addition to helping frame the U.S. Constitution, he spent time investing in a number of business ventures, and spent time in both London and Paris serving as emissary and plenipotentiary, respectively, by request of President Washington.

On July 5, 1813, Morris delivered an "American Independence" oration at the request of the Washington Benevolent Society in New York. Morris died three years later and was buried at St. Ann's Protestant Episcopal

Church. The monument of 1932 was appropriately erected there. Mrs. Edward W. Curley, "a direct descendant of Paul Revere," unveiled the tablet with the assistance of Mildred J. and G. Parsons Morris, family descendants. "Mrs. Roberta Keene Tubman, a descendant of William Hooper, a signer of the Declaration of Independence, sang 'The Star-Spangled Banner.'"

Sources: "Monument to Gouverneur Morris Unveiled at Church Where He and Brother Are Buried," *New York Times*, 5 July 1932, 3; Max M. Mintz, "Gouverneur Morris," *American National Biography*, 15:896–99.

Morris, Lewis (1726–1798)

Signer of the Declaration of Independence whose honor was celebrated at St. Ann's Episcopal Church of Morrisania in New York. On July 4, 1926, the 200th anniversary of the birth of Morris was celebrated in tandem with Independence Day festivities that included a parade of various army and navy organizations and patriotic societies that marched from the town's Soldiers' Monument to the church. The principal speaker was Congressman Anthony J. Griffin, who in his address titled "The Bronx in the Revolution" urged that the town's historic monuments be conserved. About Lewis he said, "Because he was modest, honest and sincere and never blew his own horn he has been neglected by historians. His younger brother, Gouverneur, had the gift of oratory, as well as a talent for writing, and it is for this reason that the elder brother gave way to the younger and sank into comparative obscurity."

Source: "Historic Church Has Patriotic Service," *New York Times*, 6 July 1926, 7.

Morris, Robert (1734–1806)

Financier of the American Revolution who, appointed by Congress as superintendent of finance on February 20, 1781, was one of the first "federal" administrators to give his employees the day off on the Fourth of July. Morris was born near Liverpool, England, and received some schooling in Philadelphia. His financial experience stems for his work with the shipping and mercantile house of Charles Willing. Morris took up the Patriot cause in 1775 when the Pennsylvania assembly made him a member of its council of safety. A number of important associations followed: he was a member of the committee of correspondence, a delegate to the Continental Congress to 1778, and a member of a secret committee for obtaining munitions. Morris's work in procuring supplies for the army after the start of the Revolutionary War was critical, and Congress acknowledged that by appointing him superintendent of finance (20 February 1781).

On the morning of July 4, 1782, Morris was in his office receiving requests from Colonel John Patton, Captain Allibone and Colonel Guerney for money to fit out ships "employed in Defence of Delaware." Once the details were worked out and the party had left, Morris in remembering the day was the Fourth of July,

> directed the Office to be shut and dismissed all persons employed in it that they might be at leisure to indulge those pleasing reflections which every true American must feel on the recollection that Six Years are now Completed since that decisive Step was taken in favor of the Freedom of their Country, and that they might each partake of the Festivity usual on Holydays.

On July 4, 1783, again, Morris "dismissed the Clerks from Service that they might enjoy the Day in the manner most agreeable to themselves." That day Morris celebrated the Fourth by inviting "a company of forty Gentlemen, consisting of Foreigners, Military and Civil Officers, and Citizens, and spent the afternoon and Evening in great Festivety and Mirth."

Morris's financial efforts during the war were instrumental in the ultimate victory. Morris resigned his position as superintendent in January 1783. Although after the war he was invited by Washington to serve as secretary of the treasury, he declined, preferring to be elected U.S. senator from Pennsylvania (1789–95). In his later years a number of land speculations brought him financial ruin, which landed him in debtor's prison (1798–1801).

Sources: *Encyclopedia of American History*, 1108; "Diary: July 4, 1782" and "July 4, 1783," in *Papers of*

Robert Morris, 1781–1784 (Pittsburgh: University of Pittsburgh Press, 1995), 5 and 8:529–30 and 244, respectively.

Morristown National Historical Park

This New Jersey park was dedicated on July 4, 1933. The event included a parade, music by the American Legion Bugle and Drum Corps, and members of the Daughters of the American Revolution in Colonial costumes. Speeches were given by New Jersey governor A. Harry Moore and Secretary of the Interior Harold L. Ickes. Due to its strategic location, George Washington chose Morristown for his headquarters during the winters of 1777 and 1779–80. On the site is the Ford Mansion, where Washington wrote "letters of appeal for his ragged and starving Revolutionary army." About Washington, Ickes said, "For his steadfastness, which was greater than courage; for his clear vision, which transcended brilliance, Washington has had few, if any, equals in history."

Sources: "Ickes Dedicates Morristown Park," *New York Times*, 5 July 1933, 3; Morristown National Historical Park Web site, <http://www.nps.gov/morr/>.

Morrow, Dwight W. (1873–1931)

Envoy extraordinary and minister plenipotentiary to Mexico (1927–30), who was honored posthumously on July 4, 1932, in Mexico City when a bas-relief tablet was unveiled in the chancellery of the United States Embassy by Javier Sanchez Mejorada, managing director of the National Railways of Mexico. In comparing Morrow with "the illustrious sons of your country," Mejorada said, "It was he who with President Calles gave new life and warmth to a cold friendship between our two peoples; who was desirous of understanding and loving Mexico and who made us better understand your country and love it. He honored his country and at the same time served humanity." U.S. Ambassador J. Reuben Clark acknowledged the gift and said, "Ambassador Morrow had changed the course of two great streams of people which were flowing turbulently to a threatening collision and which he had succeeded in causing to flow peacefully side by side toward an ever-

increasing friendliness, mutual growth and development for the common welfare and cultural achievement of the two nations."

Sources: "Mexicans Unveil Tablet to Morrow," *New York Times*, 5 July 1932, 2; *Washington Post*, 5 July 1932, 3.

Mount Beacon Monument, New York

A monument to commemorate the top of the mountain that was used by Washington's army for beacon lights was dedicated at Mount Beacon, near Fishkill Landing, New York, on July 4, 1900. Attendees included the local Melzingah Chapter of the Daughters of the American Revolution (DAR) and other similar chapters from across the state. An address was made by Samuel Verplanck, state regent of the DAR. After the statue was unveiled by Emily De Windt Seaman, regent of Melzingah Chapter, "beacon fires were started" with "responsive fires from the Military Academy at West Point, from the home of Gen. Daniel Butterfield," and other locations.

Source: "Monument on Mount Beacon," *New York Times*, 5 July 1900, 9.

Mount Rushmore National Memorial, North Dakota

On July 4, 1991, fifty years after its completion in 1941, the stone-carved granite faces of Presidents George Washington, Thomas Jefferson, Abraham Lincoln and Theodore Roosevelt on Mount Rushmore in South Dakota were dedicated by President George H.W. Bush. Through the years, as the Mount Rushmore project progressed, an annual Fourth of July celebration had taken place there and many of the 400 persons who had worked on the faces returned each year.

This enormous project was undertaken in 1924 by sculptor Gutzon Borglum upon an invitation from Doane Robinson, a state historian. Borgium was no stranger to participating in Fourth of July ceremonies. On July 4, 1916, he presented a speech titled "The Americanism of Lincoln," in the Great Hall of the College of the City of New York. Through the years some 450,000 tons of granite were blasted from the face of the mountain, which stands 5,725 feet high. Mount Rushmore was named in 1885 for Charles E. Rushmore, a New York lawyer.

On July 4, 1930, Borglum's 60-foot face of George Washington was unveiled before 2,500 spectators. Cleophas Cisney O'Harra (1866–1935) gave an address titled "The Black Hills, the Birthplace of the Americas," and Borgium described his achievement as "a monument to the aspirations of a great people, not to individual men." Joseph S. Cullinan, chairman of the federal commission in charge of the project, called the monument "America's shrine for political democracy."

In October 1941 the monument was completed but because of events related to World War II, it was never officially dedicated until 1991 when President Bush presided over the two-day event. Although Bush referred to the dedication as "an extraordinary Independence Day," the event had some dissention expressed by members of the Sioux tribe who were there. In 1868 the Black Hills were granted to the Sioux in perpetuity but the treaty was later abrogated. A member of the tribe "whose ancestors were killed at the 1890 massacre at Wounded Knee," believed the carved faces "ruin the looks of the Black Hills" and the four presidents represented on these "sacred hills" were not "favorable to the indigenous people."

In 1980 a commemoration of the fiftieth anniversary of the unveiling took place. At the ceremony the Strategic Air Command Band from Offutt Air Force base in Omaha performed, and some of Borgium's original crew were there as well.

In more recent times annual celebrations have drawn large crowds to witness fireworks, music by military bands, and airplanes commemorating the day with flyovers.

Sources: "15,000 Gather in Stadium," *New York Times*, 5 July 1916, 12; "Washington's Face Unveiled on Mt. Rushmore," *New York Times*, 5 July 1930, 1; "Big Statue of Washington Is Unveiled at Rapid City," *Washington Post*, 5 July 1930, 2; Robert J. Dunphy, "Notes: A Fiftieth Anniversary for the Mount Rushmore Monument," *New York Times*, 29 June 1980, 27; *50th Anniversary Commemoration of the George Washington Dedication, Mount Rushmore National Memorial, July 4, 1930–1980* (Rapid City, S.D.: Mount Rush-

more National Memorial Society of Black Hills, 1980); Martin Walker, "Sioux Angered by Monumental Crime," *The Guardian* (London), 4 July 1991; Maureen Dowd, "For Bush, a Special Day at Rushmore," *New York Times*, 4 July 1991, A8; *Milwaukee Journal Sentinel*, 26 March 1998, 7.

Mount Theodore Roosevelt

This mountain, the highest peak in the Black Hills, located near Deadwood, South Dakota, was renamed in honor of former President Roosevelt on July 4, 1919. "An immense crowd" heard Maj. Gen. Leonard Wood present the keynote speech.

Sources: "6,000-Foot Peak Named for T.R.," *Cleveland Plain Dealer*, 5 July 1919, 5; *New York Times*, 5 July 1919, 8.

Mount Vernon, home of George Washington

The importance of Mount Vernon as a symbol for Washington following his death in 1799 was often reflected in orations, ceremonies, and entertainments. The estate was one of the most popular historic sites for visitors in the nineteenth and twentieth centuries. For example, in New York City on July 4, 1800, a garden, named after Mount Vernon, had a model of the house, "20 feet long by 24 feet high, illuminated by several hundred lamps," on display for the public to see. During the 1820s through 1850s it was a popular entertainment for groups of individuals to travel down the Potomac on steamers for a visit to Mount Vernon, to have dinner on the grounds there, pay their respects at the tomb, and to enjoy a panoramic view of the Potomac River. So many visitors took advantage of this entertainment that Bushrod Washington announced on July 4, 1822, that the unruliness of the crowds prompted him to issue a notice that large groups arriving by steam boat and engaging in "eating, drinking, and dancing parties" on the grounds would be prohibited. Agreements for improvements were likely made by the steamboat captains because the excursions continued. On July 4, 1839, the steamboat *Phoenix* left Bradley's Wharf in Washington at noon taking a "numerous company with a band of music" down the Potomac to Mount Vernon. As reported in a local newspaper, "the company was gratified with a sight of Mount Vernon and returned home late in the evening, much delighted with their pleasure excursion." On that same day, the steamboat *Sydney* took members of the **Native American Association** to the estate. During this period, the reading of Washington's Farewell Address was preferred in public ceremonies. The first reported reading of the Declaration of Independence occurred on July 4, 1871, and was by John Carroll Brent, member of the Oldest Inhabitants Association of Washington.

One of the outstanding celebrations at Mount Vernon in its history was that of July 4, 1918, when Woodrow Wilson was there to speak on behalf of international independence from tyranny. On the grounds were no less than 1,000 American soldiers, numerous troops representing thirty other nations, and an assemblage of dignitaries. The other principal speaker was Felix J. Stryckmans of Chicago, who represented a group of Belgian-Americans. He elaborated on the renewed vows of loyalty foreign-born citizens shared with all Americans. Noted singer John Mc-Cormack presented a rendition of the "Star-Spangled Banner."

Sources: *National Intelligencer*, 4 July 1822 and 8 July 1839, 3 and 3, respectively; *New York Times*, 4 July 1872, 5; "War Cannot End with Compromise, Wilson Declares," *New York Times*, 5 July 1918, 1; Heintze, "Orations, Speeches, and Readings of the Declaration of Independence," 2.

Mount Vernon

This steamboat, one of the largest and "best fitted vessels" of her class to navigate the Potomac River prior to the Civil War, was damaged due to a brawl that broke out on July 4, 1859, between residents of Alexandria and Washington. The *Mount Vernon* was built in Philadelphia in 1846 and was 200 feet in length. At the time of her launching, a reporter provided this description: "The arrangement of the cabins, both of that for the gentlemen and those for the ladies, is not only comfortable in the fittings, but altogether in good taste. The adornments are not only very rich in their quality but are tasteful throughout." On Independence Day in 1859, the boat left Washington for Glymont, a "most beau-

tiful and agreeable spot on the Potomac," stopping at Alexandria to take on additional passengers. On the return trip, residents from both towns exchanged words and a fight broke out at the dock in Alexandria, which resulted in damage to the vessel:

> Upon the arrival of the "Mount Vernon" at the Alexandria wharf yesterday, on a return excursion trip, a fierce stone battle was entered upon between Alexandrians and Washingtonians, or rather the Alexandrians of the excursions commenced such an assault upon the boat. Our informant, who was on board and behind the smoke-stack, says the stones came like hail, and was varied with an occasional crack of a pistol. The order was given to cast off the ropes for the boat, then came a shower of stones that smashed the glass and thin wood work of the steamer. A lady was struck upon the head with a large stone, inflicting a very ugly wound. It was surprising that amid such a storm of missiles, so few persons were hit at all, and but a single one seriously injured.

Sources: *Alexandria Gazette*, 9 July 1846, 3 and 6 July 1859, 3; *Washington Evening Star*, 2 and 5 July, 1859, 2 and 3, respectively.

Muncy/Loyalsock, Pennsylvania, Canal

The first passage of a boat on the newly completed run of the West Branch of the Pennsylvania Canal stretching from Muncy to Loyalsock, Pennsylvania, took place on July 4, 1834. Citizens from Sunbury, Northumberland, Milton, and Muncy gathered to witness the packet *James Madison* arrive from Northumberland at the lock at Loyalsock. A number of military groups were there to fire salutes in honor of the occasion. Then the entire party processed into Williamsport in over twenty carriages and shared in a "sumptuous feast, prepared in Mr. Hall's best style." Following the dinner the group processed through the town to the edge of the river bank, "where the whole party united in the unreserved expression of their admiration of the surrounding country."

Source: Reprinted from the *Williamsport Chronicle* under the title "The Celebration — Fourth of July — Opening of a New Section of the W.B. Canal," *Hazard's Register of Pennsylvania* 14/341 (19 July 1834): 43.

Music

An important entertainment for expressing patriotism, nationalism, and freedom on the Fourth of July. A precedent for music and verse was established prior to the declaring of independence when John Dickinson's "Liberty Song" (1768) was written in protest to the British Stamp Act of 1765 and became a rallying cry for independence. During the Revolutionary War a number of songs gained popularity and helped foster a tradition of heralding the struggles and similar heroic efforts of the patriots. Some of these songs represented local areas while others were topical, some focusing on specific battles. An example titled "Siege of Savannah" told how the Americans were held off the coast of Georgia by the British and another song, "On Christmas day in seventy-six"(first line), described the battle of Trenton. Ironically in 1777 in Philadelphia it was the German soldiers who were captured by Washington's troops that provided the first musical reported performance at a Fourth of July celebration. The members of the **Hessian Band** were apparently skilled enough to learn and play the popular tunes requested by members of Congress.

Following the war, celebrations helped to encourage the writing of many new songs that lauded the victory and the new freedoms. Music quickly became an integral part of the ritual. On Independence Day in 1783, the Moravians in **Salem, North Carolina**, premiered a *Psalm of Joy* or *Freudenpsalm*, a set of anthems with newly composed text that commemorated the end of the war. On the same day, William Billings's "The States, O Lord with Songs of Praise," an anthem, was first heard at the Brattle Square Church in Boston. In the following years numerous other pieces were either premiered on the Fourth or performed annually. Some tunes such as "Hail Columbia!," "Star-Spangled Banner," and "My Country 'Tis of Thee" were universally acknowledged as national anthems prior to the Civil War. Later Katherine Lee Bates' "America the Beautiful" also quickly achieved the status of a national icon, as did "Columbia, the Gem of the Ocean." Other songs on the Fourth in the nineteenth century were used to highlight an occasion or symbolically to commemorate a notable figure or special group. For example, the popular song "America, Commerce, and Freedom" was performed to honor America's endeavors in developing commercial sectors whereas "Roslin Castle," a dirge, represented the death and memory of George Washington. The tune "Yankee Doodle" was often chosen on the Fourth by musicians to acknowledge military units, the people of the United States, or the country itself. Among the most frequently performed songs and tunes on the Fourth in the early decades of the nineteenth century were "Auld Lang Syne," "Come Haste to the Wedding," "Hail to the Chief," "Jackson's March," and "Marseilles Hymn." In 1801 James Hewitt published his *4th of July: A Grand Military Sonata* for the piano.

Musicians and singers were honored when asked to provide appropriate music and to perform for civic affairs. Music was used to accompany toasts at dinners, in parades, and at special ceremonies. Ensembles were generally small and frequently consisted of woodwinds, strings, and drums. A notable highlight for the history of bands was the establishment of the United States Marine Band in 1798. Starting with its first Independence Day performance in Philadelphia in 1800 and due to the high level of musical skills shared by its musicians as well as its extensive repertoire, the ensemble quickly became the single most important band that performed on the Fourth of July during the nineteenth century. The band helped to elevate the importance of music on the holiday by its varied performances. As the years passed, many brass and cornet bands were established and larger ensembles were created to meet the demand of celebrants on the Fourth. In the 1840s, Flagg's Brass Band and Dodworth's Band were active in Boston and New York, respectively. Groups that performed after the Civil War included the Grafulla and Gilmore bands and the Theodore Thomas Orchestra in New York, the Seventh Regiment Band and Blanchard-Fitzgerald Band in Los Angeles, and the Union Cornet Band in Buffalo, New York. On July 4, 1870, the Queen City Cornet Band of "19 pieces" paraded in Burlington, Vermont. By the 1890s Sousa's Band emerged as an important ensemble that would influence the music performed at celebrations throughout the twentieth century.

Following the Centennial, women were invited to take part in musical programs, particularly as soloists for patriotic songs. A favorite solo was "The Star Spangled Banner." Some of the performances on the Fourth included Clara Louisa Kellogg in Hartford, Connecticut (1876); Miss Anna L. Fuller in Philadelphia (1880); Miss Agnes B. Huntington in London (1882); Miss Lida Clinch in Sacramento, California (1885); Miss Josie Welden in Downey, California (1890), and Mrs. Thomas C. Noyes in Washington, D.C. (1905). Also during this period the German Männerchor and Sängerbunders hosted large musical events in Chicago, New York, Washington, D.C., and cities in New Jersey, Ohio, and Pennsylvania on the Fourth. For example, at the sixteenth annual festival of the Northeastern Sängerbund held in Caledonia Park, Newark, New Jersey, on July 4, 1891, there were 5,000 singers accompanied by an orchestra of 200 pieces.

Since the early nineteenth century, music was also used as an accompaniment to fireworks. One of the earliest events occurred in New York on July 4, 1822, when musical interludes were provided during the fireworks spectacle. In Boston in 1849, there were twenty-one pyrotechnic displays on the Common and they were complemented by performing bands. On July 4, 1852, in New York, Adkins Brass Band performed "Hail! Columbia" and "The Star-Spangled Banner" at City Hall in accompaniment to the fireworks there. By the 1860s, many of the fireworks displays at New York's numerous parks and gathering places had musical accompaniment by popular bands. For example, on July 4, 1868, at Madison Square, a newspaper reported that Schineller's Band provided "a delightful aid to their enjoyment." At Tompkins Square, on the same day, Wannemacher's Band accompanied fireworks there.

By the 1920s large symphony orchestras and newly formed bands such as the Boston Symphony, the New York Philharmonic, the Lewisohn Stadium Orchestra, and the Goldman Band began providing musical programs on the Fourth, and classical composers turned to the holiday as a way of getting new works heard. On July 4, 1934, for example, composer Robert Russell Bennett conducted his *Concerto Grosso for Small Dance Band and Symphony Orchestra* in its New York premiere at the Lewisohn Stadium. Also on the program was composer Deems Taylor, who conducted "the first stadium performance of his *Circus Day.*" By the latter part of the twentieth century, musical extravaganzas with popular headliners were common.

Sources: *New York Advertiser,* 6 July 1822, 3; *Boston Daily Times,* 4 July 1849, 2; "The Fireworks," *New York Times,* 7 July 1852, 2; "The Celebration of the Fourth," *Buffalo Express,* 6 July 1863, 3; "The Fireworks," *New York Times,* 5 July 1868, 8; "The Celebrations of the Fourth," *St. Albans Daily Messenger,* 5 July 1870, 3; *New York Times,* 4 July 1891, 2; "1776: Songs Sung in the Revolutionary War," *Los Angeles Times,* 2 July 1893, 22; "Activities of Musicians," *New York Times,* 1 July 1934, X4; Simon V. Anderson, "American Music during the War for Independence, 1775–1783" (Ph.D. dissertation, University of Michigan, 1965); David McKay, "William Selby, Musical Emigré in Colonial Boston," *Musical Quarterly* 57/4 (October 1971): 609–27; Heintze, "Music Sung and Played on the Fourth of July in the Nineteenth Century," *Fourth of July Celebrations Database.*

Music Teachers National Association (MTNA)

Organized in 1876 in Delaware, Ohio, by Theodore Presser and a group of teachers. Meetings of the association were typically three days in length and were scheduled to occur over the Fourth of July, likely as a way to promote American music. The association's mission was directed to "mutual improvement by interchange of ideas, to broaden the culture of music, and to cultivate fraternal feeling." The July 5, 1887, meeting featured the first concert for the Fourth whose program consisted entirely of American works. The event took place in Tomlinson Hall in Indianapolis, Indiana, and the composers performed included Arthur Foote, F.Q. Dulcken, Frank V. Van der Stucken, Henry Holden Huss, John Knowles Paine, Otto Singer, and Dudley Buck, whose piece, *Festival Overture, "The*

Star-Spangled Banner, was a fitting conclusion to the concert. The July 4, 1888, meeting took place in Chicago in the Exposition Building. During the concert that day, reporters noted that the firecrackers and pistol shots taking place outside the hall made it difficult to hear the music. Other Fourth of July meetings took place in the Academy of Music in Philadelphia (1889), Detroit (1890), and Saratoga Springs, N.Y. (1894).

Sources: *Grove's Dictionary of Music and Musicians: American Supplement*, ed. Waldo Selden Pratt (New York: Macmillan Co., 1928), 302–03; E. Douglas Bomberger, *"A Tidal Wave of Encouragement": American Composers' Concerts in the Gilded Age* (Westport, Conn.: Praeger, 2002), 18–19.

"My Country 'Tis of Thee," *see* "America"

My Old Kentucky Home State Park, Bardstown, Kentucky *see* Foster, Stephen Collins

Natchez Institute

This institute in Natchez, Mississippi, was dedicated on July 4, 1845. Addresses (Natchez: Free Trader Office, 1845) were delivered by A.P. Merrill and J.S.B. Thacher.

National Aeronautics and Space Administration (NASA)

NASA has a unique and colorful history of celebrating the Fourth of July from outer space. Many flights were conveniently launched to coincide with the nation's birthday.

The spacecraft *Columbia* has an illustrious history. After seven days in space in July 1982, *Columbia* landed at Edwards Air Force Base in California on Independence Day. President Ronald Reagan was there and gave a ten-minute welcoming speech for astronauts Thomas K. Mattingly and Henry W. Hartsfield. "They reaffirmed to all of us that as long as there are frontiers to be explored and conquered, Americans will lead the way," Reagan said.

The astronauts gave the president and first lady "a tour of the nose of the spacecraft." Meanwhile a celebration and reunion that included retired astronaut Alan B. Shepard, Jr., and various flight directors took place in the mission operations control room upon the completion of the STS-4 mission.

The rebuilt space shuttle *Discovery* was taken to its launch pad on July 4, 1988, in a ceremony attended by 2,000 Kennedy Space Center workers. At the end of the event a recording of the "Star-Spangled Banner" was heard over loudspeakers. The shuttle program had been grounded since January 28, 1986.

On July 4, 1992, *Columbia* was again a center of attention as seven astronauts aboard the vessel unfurled the Stars and Stripes and chanted "Happy Birthday, America" from space. "As the song 'God Bless the U.S.A.' played, scenes of Earth, 184 miles below, filled huge television screens at mission control." On Independence Day in 1995 a "flawless" undocking of the American shuttle *Atlantis* and the Russian space station *Mir* took place after a five-day East-West linkup.

On July 4, 1996, *Columbia* was again in orbit around the earth as Independence Day greetings were sent by astronauts. The *Pathfinder* spacecraft landed on Mars on July 4, 1997. President Clinton hailed the day: "On this important day, the American people celebrate another exciting milestone in our nation's long heritage of progress, discovery, and exploration."

On July 4, 2001, astronauts Susan Helms and Jim Voss gave a birthday greeting via large screens during a performance by the National Symphony Orchestra of "2001, A Space Odyssey" at the Fourth of July Capitol Fourth concert held on the west lawn of the U.S. Capitol in Washington, D.C. The event was broadcast live on PBS.

On July 4, 2005, NASA's spacecraft *Deep Impact* was slammed into the comet Tempel 1 at 23,000 mph, creating the greatest blast on the Fourth in the history of the celebration.

Sources: Thomas O'Toole, "Pinpoint Landing for Shuttle," *Washington Post*, 5 July 1982, 1; "Rebuilt Shuttle Crawls to Pad," *Washington Post*, 5 July 1988, A3; "Astronauts Celebrate the Fourth," *New York Times*, 5 July 1992, 17; *New York Times*, 5 July 1995, A10; Washington *Post*, 5 July 1997, 1; NASA "News Release" (release 01–134), 2 July 2001 on NASA Web

site <http://www.nasa.gov/audience/forresearchers/
features/index.html>; Guy Gugliotta, "NASA Succeeds in Crashing Craft Into Comet," Washington
Post, 5 July 2005, A1, A5.

National Amateur Press Association

The oldest amateur press organization in
the world, founded on July 4, 1876, in
Philadelphia. On July 4, 1926, this association celebrated its 50th anniversary. Each year
awards are presented in the areas of poetry,
fiction, history of amateur journalism, editorial comment, miscellaneous prose, art, editing, and printing.

Sources: *Washington Evening Star*, 6 July 1926,
17; National Amateur Press Association Web site,
<http://amateurpress.org>.

National Archives and Records Administration (NARA)

NARA is an independent federal agency
(established by act of Congress in 1934) that
helps preserve the nation's history by oversee-
ing the management of all federal records.
NARA's mission is to ensure ready access to
the essential evidence that documents the
rights of American citizens, the actions of federal officials, and the national experience.
NARA manages the Presidential Libraries system. It holds the treasured cornerstone documents of the nation, including the Declaration
of Independence, the Constitution of the
United States, and the Bill of Rights. It also
holds the Deed of Gift of the Statue of Liberty, July 4, 1884. The current archivist of the

The National Archives, Washington, D.C., July 4, 2000. An annual Independence Day celebration is held here with reenactors, patriotic music, addresses, and a public reading of the
Declaration of Independence. Photograph by author.

United States is John W. Carlin, former Kansas governor.

In addition to administering records and documenting federal activities, NARA provides public awareness programs that herald the nation's most important documents. Each year on the Fourth of July, citizens across the nation come to the National Archives to see the Declaration of Independence and experience the aura of these charters of freedom, the nation's most sacred documents. On the Fourth of July NARA provides a public reading of the Declaration of Independence on the steps of its Washington building. Crowds gather to hear patriotic music, performances by the U.S. Army "Old Guard" Fife and Drum Corps, and Revolutionary War reenactments.

In 2002–2003 the National Archives was closed to the public on Independence Day while the building underwent a major renovation and provisions were made for implementing environmental enhancements for the preservation of the documents. On the evening of July 4, 2001, a rotunda ceremony that marked the final lowering of the charters of freedom took place. The 2003 event was held at Washington's Union Station in association with National History Day. The theme was "Freedom's Journey," which helped to promote a national road trip for an original 1776 Dunlap Broadside of the Declaration of Independence. By July 4, 2004, the rotunda was reopened to the public.

Sources: *Washington Post*, 5 July 1990, C1, 4; *The United States Government Manual 2005/2006* (Washington, D.C.: Office of the Federal Register, National Archives and Records Administration).

National Civil Rights Museum (NCRM)

Dedicated on July 4, 1991, the National Civil Rights Museum is located in Memphis, Tennessee, and was created to assist the public in understanding the lessons of the Civil Rights Movement and its impact and influence on the human rights movement worldwide, through its collections, exhibitions, research and educational programs. On September 28, 1991, the museum opened in what was once the Lorraine Motel. The facility includes a museum shop, gallery, auditorium, 19 exhibit halls, 2 multi-purpose rooms, an archives and library.

Source: *Washington Post*, 5 July 1991, A10.

National Constitution Center, Philadelphia

Opened on July 4, 2003, with U.S. Supreme Court justice Sandra Day O'Connor and Philadelphia mayor John Street presiding. The $185 million structure was designed by New York architect Henry N. Cobb. A notable feature is its exposition hall with its statues of the forty-two delegates "present for the signing of the Constitution on September 17, 1787. Displayed also are the first printings of the Constitution, an inkwell Abraham Lincoln used in signing the Emancipation Proclamation and exhibits recalling the many controversies that have tested the Constitution in its history." At the start of the ceremony a large piece of stage apparatus fell over, "slightly injuring the center's president Joseph M. Torsello and Mayor Street." On July 4, 2005, the Normandy Liberty Bell, a copy of the Philadelphia Liberty Bell, was on display from Normandy, France, and was rung by acting secretary of the air force, Michael Dominguez.

Sources: David B. Caruso, "Cities Celebrate Independence Day with Multitude of Events," *Virginian-Pilot*, 5 July 2003, A7; Benjamin Forgey, "A More Perfect Union," *Washington Post*, 4 July 2003, C1; "Frame's Fall Mars Opening," *Philadelphia Inquirer*, 5 July 2003, A1; Sandy Bauers, "Celebrations Big and Small, All Lively," *Philadelphia Inquirer*, 5 July 2005, A6.

National Convention of Colored Men

First met on July 4, 1892, at the Zion Baptist Church in Cincinnati, Ohio, "to consider the interests of the race." Daniel A. Rudd was elected chairman and J.F.T. Carr, vice chairman, from among the one hundred men and women present. A number of speeches were given. The following resolution was agreed upon:

We ask nothing of you in behalf of colored people, except the right to eat the bread our own hands have earned, to dwell safely in our own homes, to pursue our vocations in peace, to be granted a fair and equal opportunity in the race of life, to be protected under the law, and to be judged according to the law. We appeal to you against murder and violence, against robbery and extortion, against hasty and cruel judgments, against fierce mobs that outrage our people and desolate their homes.

Source: "Colored Men in Convention," *New York Times*, 5 July 1892, 4.

National Defense Day, 1925

Cities across the country named July 4, 1925, as National Defense Day (also "Defense Test Day") with appropriate exercises to test the nation's readiness in case of war, to bring attention to the issue, and to see how fast volunteers could be mustered for war duties. In New York City, fifty U.S. military planes flew over the city and the Declaration of Independence was publicly read from one of the planes and transmitted by radio and broadcast over radio station WOR, and members of the **Women's Peace Union of the Western Hemisphere** held an antiwar demonstration at Battery Park. At Fort Wadsworth Reservation in New York, planes dropped flour bombs on tanks with 5000 spectators looking on. A total of twenty-two cities and towns presented reports on their success and activities of the day. In every state, except Wisconsin, the National Guard and army reserves were mustered. In Philadelphia, a two-hour demonstration attended by 4,500 citizens also heard speeches by Mayor Kendricks and songs by a chorus of school children. Pittsburgh and Erie, Pennsylvania, also had events. In Richmond, 3,000 persons watched an air show. In Des Moines, Iowa, Senator Albert B. Cummins spoke out against pacifists who would have Americans "stand helpless before an armed world." In Los Angeles, more than 15,000 persons participated in peace-time exercises on the campus of the University of Southern California. "Airplane mechanics reported, offering their services to the flying corps. Cobblers reported to volunteer their talents in keeping a war-time army shod. Horseshoers were there to pledge themselves to keep the hoofs of the mounted squadrons

fit for duty." Twenty-nine radio stations from around the country were "hooked up" for broadcast simultaneously a radio program from the War Department in Washington, D.C. The broadcast featured a number of speakers and a conversation between Vice President Charles G. Dawes and General John J. Pershing. Total number of participants across the country was estimated at 6 million.

Sources: "Defense Muster Pleases Officials," *Baltimore Sun*, 5 July 1925, 1, 10, and "Maryland Is Reported Apathetic to Test Day," *Baltimore Sun*, 5 July 1925, 10; "City Joins for Test," *Los Angeles Times*, 5 July 1925, 1, 12; "Big Radio Program for Defense Day," *New York Times*, 24 June 1925, 31; "Cummins Scores Pacifists" and "Planes and Tanks Operate," *New York Times*, 5 July 1925, 18.

National Educational Association (NEA)

For many years this organization held its annual meeting to coincide with the Fourth of July and a number of notable speeches were given at the events. The importance, if not power, of the NEA drew significant speakers to the podium on Independence Day. On July 4, 1910, the meeting was held at the Harvard Stadium in Boston and President **William Howard Taft,** Governor William Walton Kitchin of North Carolina, and prominent representatives of local universities were the invited speakers.

On July 4, 1905, the annual meeting was at Asbury Park, New Jersey, and music was provided by the Ocean Grove Festival Orchestra. On July 4, 1914, the NEA met in St. Paul, Minnesota, and several speeches were presented, one by Lloyd E. Wolfe, who advocated for the promotion of teachers based on merit.

One of the notable meetings occurred in New York on Independence Day in 1916. William Jennings Bryan spoke at Madison Square Garden and endorsed the NEA's pacifist position that military training in schools was not appropriate. On July 4, 1921, the association met in Des Moines, Iowa, in the city auditorium, and members heard a speech by Nathan E. Kendall, governor of Iowa. On July 4, 1930, at the 68th annual convention, held in Columbus, Ohio, John H. Finley, associate editor of the *New York Times*, presented a speech on interdependence among nations. On July 4, 1951, the NEA met in San Francisco, and the keynote speaker was Frank W. Weil, New York social welfare expert. He warned his audience that the United States was "in danger of committing suicide through apathy toward the threat of world communism."

Sources: *New York Times*, 5 July 1905, 4; "Taft on the Philippines," *New York Times*, 5 July 1910, 13; "Nation's Educators Meet," *Baltimore Sun*, 5 July 1914, 2; "Teachers Cheer Bryan Pacifism," *New York Times*, 5 July 1916, 4; "Educators of Nation Gather at Des Moines," *San Francisco Chronicle*, 5 July 1921, 11; "Nation's Educators Hear Finley Speech," *Washington Post*, 5 July 1930, 3; "Educators Told National Suicide Threatens U.S.," *Boston Globe*, 5 July 1951, 13.

National Lincoln Monument Association, Washington, D.C.

An African-American organization created in May 1865 to raise funds to build a National Lincoln Monument Institute, to honor Lincoln's memory. The purpose of the school was to educate the "children of the freemen and their descendants." The first meeting of the association was held on July 4, 1865, making it the first national African-American Fourth of July celebration. From eight to ten thousand persons gathered on the public grounds south of the White House to hear J.F. Cook, a local D.C. teacher, read the Declaration of Independence, L.A. Bell read the Emancipation Proclamation, and a number of speeches, one by Senator Henry Wilson of Massachusetts, who was the author of the bill to abolish slavery in the District of Columbia. "I came here to meet free men," Wilson said, "and listen to the words of humanity, of justice, and of liberty.... slavery is dead and buried forever." There was also a reading of a "spirited" poem by the Rev. John Pierpont titled "Let There Be Light." Also read were letters of congratulations from several dignitaries, including Governor John A. Andrew of Massachusetts, Frederick Douglass, and Salmon P. Chase, chief justice of the Supreme Court. A procession included nearly 1,500 children and 400 teachers representing the Washington City Sunday School Union. Music was provided by the Union Cornet Band. The gath-

ering received national attention with accounts published in a number of newspapers, including the *Norwich Weekly Courier* and *Indianapolis Daily Journal*.

Sources: *Celebration by the Colored People's Educational Monument Association in Memory of Abraham Lincoln on the Fourth of July, 1865* (Washington, D.C.: Mcgill and Witherow, 1865); *Daily National Republican*, 5 July 1865, 1–2; *Evening Star*, 5 July 1865, 3.

National Museum of American History, Washington, D.C.

Part of the Smithsonian Institution complex, this site has sponsored some historic Fourth of July celebrations and ceremonies. For example, on the Fourth of July in 1978, an event there included more than 200 musicians, artists, and craftspersons performing and demonstrating old-fashioned traditions. Reenactments of Patrick Henry's "Liberty or Death" address and an oration by Frederick Douglass were given. In 1981 twenty-eight immigrants took the oath of citizenship.

Sources: "Historic Fourth at the Museum," *Washington Post*, 8 June 1978, B5; "A Safe and Sane (but Glorious!) Fourth," *Washington Post*, 3 July 1981, W3.

Native American Association

Active in the 1830s–1840s in New York, Baltimore, New Orleans, Philadelphia, and Washington. The members consisted primarily of native-born Protestant Americans who rallied to restrict immigration and stem the growth of Catholicism in America. The movement was commonly referred to as nativism, and members used the Fourth of July to make known their views. On July 4, 1838, for example, one hundred members of the Native American Association of the Washington area met at the grounds of Daniel Carroll and engaged in speechmaking, music, and a dinner prepared by Isaac Beers, of the Native American Hotel. In the following year on the Fourth, nativists of Washington and Alexandria, Virginia, cruised down the Potomac River aboard the *Sydney*, and when the steamer came to opposite of Mount Vernon, Joseph H. Bradley read the Declaration of Independence.

On July 4, 1844, in Philadelphia, nativists paraded carrying banners that depicted

Washington and the Goddess of Liberty as icons of their beliefs. At their ceremony they read the Declaration of Independence and Washington's Farewell Address. In commemoration of the day a *Native American Grand March* (1844), composed for piano and "published in honor of the Native American Association" was printed in Philadelphia by Osbourn's American Music Saloon. Sentiments regarding the restrictions against immigrants lasted throughout the remainder of the century. On July 5, 1886, at a Fourth celebration in San Francisco, Frank M. Pixley "caused a sensation" when he spoke out in favor of naturalized citizens as long as they restrained from entering politics. "I am not in favor of a native American party, of an organization that would exclude from its lines men who have been born abroad, who have come voluntarily to the country, and who since they have become citizens have not obtruded themselves into our political affairs," he said.

Sources: "Fourth of July Celebrations," *National Intelligencer*, 9 July 1838, 3, and 8 July 1839, 3; John Hancock Lee, *Origin and Progress of the American Party in Politics* (Philadelphia: Elliott and Gihon, 1855); "Pixley's Ple [sic]," *Los Angeles Times*, 7 July 1886, 1.

Native Americans

Share a proud and significant tradition of participation in Fourth of July events as both spectators and participants that spans almost 200 years. Ironically, as the nation was faced with addressing equitably the plight of Native Americans and with extending the promises and principles of the Declaration of Independence to them in a similar fashion as to African Americans, as espoused by the abolition movement, Native Americans were actively utilizing the Fourth as a means for increasing their understanding of a culture frequently hostile to theirs. One of the early events that speaks to this notion occurred on July 4, 1820, at a ceremony held in the House of Representatives in Washington City. On that occasion a number of "Indian chiefs," including Chief Big Bear, as well as members of the Osage tribe, witnessed an oration presented by Thomas Randall, an attorney, and a reading of the Declaration of Independence by John H. Henshaw. Some of the Native

American guests stayed at the Davis's Hotel. Another early event occurred on July 4, 1831, when a tribe of Pequoad Indians celebrated the day with a war dance at their wigwam, south of Alexandria, Virginia.

Orators on the Fourth have included **John Wannuaucon Quinney**, credited with presenting in 1854 the first recorded Fourth of July oration by a Native American, in Reidsville, New York. Quinney, a Muh-he-connew, was chief of the Stockbridge band, which consisted of various tribes which had been relocated. Others included Allen Wright, governor of the Choctaw Nation, who spoke at the Fort Scott, Kansas, celebration on July 4, 1878, and G.W. Grayson, who addressed the Cherokee Nation on July 4, 1881. After the Civil War, reports of Native American celebrations increased in the press. In 1875 at Atoka, Indian territory, one of the largest Fourth of July celebrations took place and included 3000 Native Americans sharing "a bountiful dinner," with speeches by Governor Allen Wright, "an educated Choctaw," and Chief Col. Coleman, "who spoke in the Choctaw language. His address was particularly interesting and progressive. The Hon. M.W. Reynolds of Kansas was orator of the day and his subject, 'American Manhood,' was well handled." Other dignitaries in attendance and who spoke included the Hon. B.W. Perkins, judge of the Labette District, Kansas, Mayor Weight, and Col. Kelso. In 1883, in Yankton, S.D., seven hundred Yankton and Sautee Sioux participated in the celebration there. Chief Justice Edgerton was the selected orator. On that same day in Santa Fe, New Mexico, members of the Zuni tribe held a ten-mile foot race for the benefit of eastern whites, and members of the Apache tribe raced on their ponies, held a sham battle, and presented tribal medicine demonstrations.

A tradition of annual Fourth of July pow-wows began in the twentieth century and has included celebrations in numerous states across the nation, including Northern Cheyenne, near Lame Deer, Montana, the annual Ute celebration at Fort Duchesne, Utah, and the Sisseton-Wahpeton Sioux event at Agency Village near Sisseton, South Dakota.

Other events have included a Spokane Reservation pow-wow in Washington in 1923, a 3-day Fourth of July pow-wow in which the amusements included horse racing, bucking contests, ball games, foot racing, and wrestling. In 1931 Native Americans from several western states took part in the Osage pow-wow July 2–5 in which there were roping contests, dances, and a reenactment of a traditional buffalo hunt. See also **Black Hawk** and **Magayohi (Chief Star)**.

Sources: *National Intelligencer*, 4 and 10 July 1820, 3 and 2, respectively; *National Messenger*, 7 July 1820, 3; *Washington Gazette*, 5 July 1820; *Alexandria Gazette*, 7 July 1831, 2; *Cincinnati Daily Gazette*, 6 July 1875, 5; *Daily Argus*, 5 July 1883, 2; "The Santa Fe Celebration," *New York Times*, 5 July 1883, 5; "Indians Plan Celebration," *Spokesman-Review*, 2 July 1923; "Osage Indians, Legion Join in Fourth of July Powwow," *Oklahoman*, 24 June 1931, 11; Wolfgang Hochbruck, "'I Ask for Justice': Native American Fourth of July Orations," *The Fourth of July: Political Oratory and Literary Reactions 1776–1876* (Tübingen: G. Narr, 1992), 155–65.

Natural Bridge, Virginia

On July 5, 1926, a bronze and granite marker commemorating the granting of Natural Bridge, a natural earthen structure over Cedar Creek in western Virginia, by George III to Thomas Jefferson on July 5, 1774, was unveiled. "The tablet commemorates the fact that the Natural Bridge patent was surveyed by George Washington about 1750 and was granted to Jefferson just two years prior to the Declaration of Independence." The event was sponsored by the Daughters of the American Revolution, and 2000 spectators, including tourists from 38 states, were present. Churchill J. Gibson, rector of Robert E. Lee Memorial Church at Lexington, Virginia, delivered an address.

Source: "Unveil Jefferson Marker," *New York Times*, 6 July 1926, 14.

Naturalization on the Fourth

A popular tradition in which large numbers of immigrants are sworn in as new citizens of the United States. The impetus for these mass citizenship oaths on Independence Day began in the early twentieth century and were a result of changing unfavorable political conditions in various parts of the world that brought individuals to the United States, as well as an emergence of a new awareness of the important contributions immigrants make to the fabric of the nation. At the end of World War I, newly formed organizations such as the League of Foreign-Born Citizens, which in 1921 established a program of consecration on Independence Day for new citizens, helped to encourage Americans to express a sense of "warmth and friendliness" towards immigrants. Most major cities having federal judges that can conduct the swearings have provided special naturalization ceremonies on the Fourth. One of the first and most important of these events occurred in Washington, D.C., on July 4, 1919, when at the "presidential stand at the north side of the Washington Monument," 51 men and 51 women, "representing the States and territories of the union" were given the oath of citizenship by Secretary of the Interior Franklin K. Lane. On the eve of the Fourth in 1933, 200 men and women representing 24 countries were sworn in at the naturalization court in San Francisco.

More recently naturalization ceremonies have occurred in historic settings such as **Monticello**, whose tradition of such ceremonies began in 1963. In 1976, 7,230 persons were sworn in at the Miami Beach Convention Center, and the event was cited as "the greatest mass swearing in of new citizens in the country's history. Most were Cuban exiles though there were others from many countries." The "Star-Spangled Banner" was sung. On July 4, 1981, 28 individuals were sworn in at a special ceremony held at the "We the People" Hall at the National Museum of American History in Washington, D.C. U.S. District Court judge Thomas A. Flannery presided and informed the group that they now had "freedom to speak your mind on any issue, without fear of being put before a firing squad if you happen to disagree with the government." On the Fourth in 1988, 200 immigrants took the citizenship oath under the Gateway Arch in St. Louis. On July 4, 1998, the Immigration and Naturalization Service scheduled oath-taking for 18,500 immigrants in 27 ceremonies, with the largest in Los Angeles. In 2005 a group of new U.S. citizens recited the

Pledge of Allegiance on board the USS *Constitution* and affirmed their fidelity in the presence of U.S. District Court judge Rya W. Zobel, herself a German immigrant, and in Rosslyn, Virginia, at **Freedom Park**, 41 men and women representing 27 countries took the oath of allegiance.

Sources: "World's 4th Today," *Washington Post*, 4 July 1919, 1; Nathaniel Phillips, "The Day for Immigrants," *New York Times*, 22 July 1923, 28; "Group Naturalized on Eve of Fourth," *Los Angeles Times*, 4 July 1933, 3; "28 Take Oath as Citizens in Special Ceremony," *Washington Post*, 5 July 1981, B5; Patrice Gaines-Carter and Rene M. Lynch, "Bang-Up Fourth Gushes with Patriotism, Revelry," *Washington Post*, 5 July 1988, D1; *Washington Post*, 5 July 1998, A3; Liz Cho, Harry Reasoner, Derek McGinty, "Fourth of July Celebrations from July 4, 1976," *World News Now* (ABC), Burrelle's Information Services, 4 July 2001; Michael Levenson, "A Welcome Pledge," *Boston Globe*, 5 July 2005, B1, B5; Ruben Castaneda, "New Citizens Await Fresh Opportunities," *Washington Post*, 5 July 2005, B7.

Naumburg, Elkan (1834–1924)

Merchant, banker, and patron of music who built "the beautiful stone bandstand, often called the 'Temple of Music,'" on the mall in Central Park, New York City. Naumburg arrived from Europe in 1850 and first settled in Baltimore. After making considerable money as a banker, he became one of New York's major donors as a contributor to the Bohemian Music Fund and the first patron of music to give free concerts in the parks. Those that were "given on holidays attracted audiences of as many as 20,000 persons."

On July 4, 1925, in the bandstand in Central Park, an Independence Day concert honoring Naumburg was given by Hugo Riesenfeld, renowned motion picture music composer and arranger, and his orchestra. Naumburg's sons, Walter W. and George W., sponsored the event. "The shell was decorated with flags and a large colored portrait of George Washington. An elaborate program bore the likeness of Elkan Naumburg." The orchestra played "The Star-Spangled Banner" and a number of works by Mendelssohn, Schubert, Chopin, Liszt, and Wagner.

Sources: "Elkan Naumburg dies in 90th Year," *New York Times*, 1 August 1924, 11; "Concert in Memory of Elkan Naumburg," *New York Times*, 5 July 1925, 21.

Neal, John (1793–1876)

Novelist, proponent for gymnastic studies, and activist for women's rights who was the first to advocate for women's suffrage in an oration delivered on July 4, 1838. Neal was born in Portland, Maine, the son of a Quaker schoolmaster. He attended Portland Academy and various Quaker schools, the one at Windham representing the most "miserable" period of his life. Neal later spent time as a shopkeeper's apprentice and later in Baltimore as a partner in a business venture with John Pierpont and Joseph Lord. After the business failed, Neal pursued the study of law, languages, and literature.

By 1823 Neal had become an accomplished writer, and had achieved some notoriety through his literary endeavors. He wrote several novels, such as *Keep Cool* (1817), *Logan* (1822), *Seventy-Six* (1823), a play, *Otho* (1819), a book of poetry, *The Battle of Niagara* (1818), and numerous magazine and newspaper articles. Despite his success, Neal decided to leave Baltimore, mainly as a result of a life-threatening situation that arose due to an unfortunate story he wrote that apparently involved Pierpont's young sister-in-law, as well as critical attacks against William Pinkney, Baltimore lawyer and statesman.

Neal traveled to England and there undertook literary pursuits writing articles about American authors for British magazines. In 1827, Neal was back in the United States, settling in Portland, practicing law, writing additional novels, and turning his attention to health reform and women's rights. In 1828 he was instrumental in establishing Bowdoin College's first gymnasium but faced opposition for his efforts to have blacks accepted into Portland's classes. Neal favored the colonization movement over abolitionism. Also, in 1824, while in England, Neal publicly voiced his views for the equality of the sexes in an article he wrote for *Blackwood's*, "Men and Women," and later took up the cause in America. His oration (Portland: Arthur Shirley, 1838) on women's rights was delivered on July 4, 1838, in Portland before the Whigs of that town.

Sources: "John Neal," *Continental Monthly* 2/3

(September 1862): 275–81; Benjamin Lease, "John Neal," *American National Biography* 16: 258–59

Negro Slave Monument, Ocala, Florida

This monument, located in Dr. Martin Luther King Jr. Park in Ocala, Florida, was dedicated on July 4, 2002, and was funded by the Ocala City Council. According to a local resident, the memorial "represents the prayers of black people who prayed to be delivered from slavery."

Source: Susan Latham Carr, "Monument Seen As Symbol of Honor, Healing," *Ocala Star-Banner* Web site, 11 September 2002, <http://www.starbanner.com?News/prayersheard703.shtml>.

Nelson, Willie (b. 1933)

Popular singer-musician, song writer, and actor who started a series of Fourth of July picnics in 1971 that drew thousands of music lovers that "cut across the traditional categories of pop, country and rock." The original picnic was held in Dripping Springs, Texas, and included a crowd of 50,000. Nelson's goal of showcasing the talent of such non-Nashville musicians as Merle Haggard, Tex Ritter, and Roy Acuff at the first picnic earned him the title of "country music renegade" and garnered considerable press attention for his musician-friends and him. In 1976, the picnic was held near Gonzales, Texas, with Nelson and singer Kris Kristofferson drawing a crowd of 150,000. Two years later, the site was moved to the Cotton Bowl in Dallas and was promoted as the Texas World Music Festival. Nelson expressed his displeasure in this urban setting: "I liked it better when it was out in the pasture — there's no lake to run and jump into." In 1981 his picnic was held on his own Pedernales golf course and country club located near Austin, Texas. In 1983 the setting was the Giants Stadium in the Meadowlands, East Rutherford, New Jersey. This 10-hour marathon featured seven acts, including Merle Haggard, Waylon Jennings, Linda Ronstadt, Emmylou Harris, and the Stray Cats. Ronstadt and Harris were noted for creating connections between country music and the Los Angeles popular music mainstream by including the works of coun-

try music songwriters on their albums. In 1984 Nelson's picnic was held at South Park Meadows near Austin, Texas, amidst a crowd of 20,000. Performers included Kris Kristofferson, Waylon Jennings, Jerry Jeff Walker, and others. In 1995 and 1998–99 Nelson's picnics were held in Luckenbach, Texas; the 1998 event again featured Emmylou Harris, along with Ray Price, Leon Russell, and others, and the 1999 event there included 38 musical groups that performed over a twelve-hour period. On July 4, 2000, Nelson's picnic was held at Southpark Meadows, in Austin, Texas, with forty acts including headliners Rodney Hayden and Doc Mason. In 2003 the event took place at the new Two River Canyon Amphitheatre in Spicewood, Texas (see **Radio broadcasts**) and in 2004 at the Fort Worth Stockyards.

In 1985, Nelson, together with Neil Young and John Mellencamp, founded Farm Aid, an annual concert whose goal was to bring attention to the problems facing family farmers and to help those that are in financial crisis. In the following year Farm Aid II was held in Manor, Texas, on July 4 and was the only one in the series to take place Independence Day. Even though there were some 75 music acts, including Waylon Jennings, the Beach Boys, Rita Coolidge, Dave Mason, and others, and the holiday drew thousands to the concert, the event raised far less money than Farm Aid I. The less than expected attendance was thought to be a result of having the concert opposite major coverage of the Statue of Liberty 100th anniversary event.

Sources: *Wall Street Journal*, 1 July 1976, 1; Stephen Holden, "Willie Nelson Festival Rolls Into Meadowlands," *New York Times*, 1 July 1983, C6; Bill Curry, "Tame Picnic," *Washington Post*, 4 July 1978, B1; "Liberty Centennial Suspected as Competitor: Farm Aid II Gifts Far Less Than Hoped," *Los Angeles Times*, 6 July 1986, 25; Jon Bream, "Pop Music Review: Politics Provide the Spark at Farm Aid VI Benefit," *Los Angeles Times*, 26 April 1993, F4; "Parades, Patriotism and Pyrotechnics," *New York Times*, 5 July 1984, B16; *Houston Chronicle*, 4 July 1998, 5; "Hot List: Fourth of July," *Houston Chronicle*, 2 July 1999, 2 (Technology); Dan Willging, "Concerts: Willie Nelson's Fourth of July Picnic," *Dirty Linen* 90 (October–November 2000): 30.

New Brunswick, New Jersey

The home of poet Joyce Kilmer, who was born in this town, was dedicated as a national shrine on July 4, 1930. The event was attended by 700 citizens, including Mrs. Fred B. Kilmer, the poet's mother, who recited the poem "Trees," one of the poet's most celebrated pieces. Other speakers included Gen. Henry J. Reilly, a commander under whom Kilmer served in World War I, and Captain Prospar Cholet, representing the French Army. Another ceremony occurred at Court House Square, where a memorial tablet with flagpole was presented in Kilmer's memory. Kilmer was a sergeant in the U.S. Army and was killed in action in July 1918. His residence was located at 17 Codwise Avenue.

Source: "Kilmer Birthplace Becomes a Shrine," *New York Times*, 5 July 1930, 18.

New Canaan, Connecticut

Celebrated its 150th year as an incorporated town (1801) and 300 years of settlement on July 4, 1951. The event included a band concert and parade that featured floats, one carrying a model for an 1801 church and another carrying a cobbler and his family making shoes, the craft reflecting the shoe industry of New Canaan.

Source: Laurie Johnston, "New Canaan Marks Its 150th Year As a Town but It's Really Over 300," *New York Times*, 5 July 1951, 27.

New German Club, Stapleton, New York

The cornerstone for this association's Richmond Road building on Staten Island was laid on July 4, 1874.

Source: "Staten Island," *New York Times*, 6 July 1874, 8.

New Hartford, Connecticut, Town Hall

Dedicated on July 4, 1876. The ceremony included addresses by J.B. Foster, J.B. Betts, and Nathaniel Morse. The Declaration of Independence was read by Capt. Henry R. Jones, and Clara Louisa Kellogg sang the "Star-Spangled Banner." Additional music was provided by the Nepang Band, and a dance followed later that evening.

Source: "Observances in Other Parts of the State," *Hartford Courant*, 6 July 1876, 1.

New Haven, Connecticut, Centennial

Reached this anniversary on January 8, 1884, but its celebration took place on July 4 that year. With 50,000 visitors and residents in town, the events included the ringing of bells, "day fireworks on the green," firing of 100 guns from the summit of East Rock, and a parade consisting of "military, firemen, and civic societies," reviewed by Connecticut governor Thomas M. Waller. The ceremony took place in Center Church and included a historical address by the Rev. T.R. Bacon.

Source: "New Haven's Centennial," *New York Herald*, 5 July 1884, 10.

New Haven Opera House

This Connecticut landmark, owned by Paul C. Skiff, was severely damaged by fire on July 4, 1893. A Russian amateur company was thought to blame, by leaving a lighted candle or cigar "so placed as to form a nucleus of a large fire that would develop six or seven hours later." The entire back part of the theatre, whose value was estimated at $100,000, was destroyed.

Source: "The New-Haven Opera House Burned," *New York Times*, 6 July 1893, 3.

New York Edison Company and electric light displays

Provided some of the largest electric light shows in the nation on the Fourth of July beginning in 1910. In New York on July 4, 1914, an impressive 26,000 incandescent bulbs hung "through the trees of the parks, and on some of the notable public buildings and monuments." Many of the parks were lit with bulbs and special colored illuminations were lit in De Witt Clinton Park, Seward Park, Grant's Tomb, Sailors and Soldiers' Monument, and other sites. A local paper mentioned that "in those places where folk-dancing and other programmes for entertainment have been scheduled there will be a special splurge of 2,000 to 5,000 candle-power bulbs — the largest ever manufactured." (See also **Lewisohn Stadium**.)

Electric lights were used as a feature of Fourth of July celebrations as early as 1876 when at Omaha the celebration included "a grand electric display" with lights placed "on the steeple of the High School building and the other on the Southwest corner of the roof of the U.P. company's office, throwing the light up Farman Street." In 1882 in Providence, Rhode Island, a minute after midnight on July 3, Tenro Park had four large lights turned on and other parks were also illuminated.

Electric lights were also frequently used for different effects. On July 4, 1916, in New York City, City Hall, the Borough Halls, and the Washington Arch at the foot of Fifth Avenue had "huge American flags traced in electric lights."

Before the Civil War novel lighting devices included Professor Grant's Calcium Light, which was "exhibited from the west front of the Capitol," on July 4, 1850, illuminating Pennsylvania Avenue. At 9 P.M. that evening, the light shone "from the Capitol gate to the grounds surrounding the President's house, more than a mile in extent." A newspaper reported that the light "is far more intense and brilliant than the Drummond light; and, unlike that system of illumination, we are informed that this is available for all purposes of practical lighting, being easily managed, and far cheaper than oil or coal gaslight."

After the Civil War, new forms of lighting apparatus were introduced. On July 4, 1869, at Madison Square in New York City, the Oxyhydrogen Heat and Light Company displayed a new device that according to a local newspaper report was quite effective: "The square and vicinity was brilliant with steady rays of vivid and almost blinding intensity, which greatly surpassed the refractive power of the ordinary gas lamp. The exhibition attracted great attention." Another example occurred again in New York on July 4, 1876, when at the Union Square celebration the plaza at both ends of the square was lit up with gas jets, and at the Democratic Building at Fourteenth Street and Broadway, each story of the structure had "gas jets closely placed,

and shining through small colored globes, while a bright circle of colored gas lights crowned the top of the lofty tower."

Sources: "Incidents and Accidents on the Fourth," *National Intelligencer*, 6 July 1850, 4; *New York Times*, 6 July 1869, 1; "Centennial Day," *Omaha Republican*, 4 July 1876, 4; "Scenes at Union Square," *New York Times*, 5 July 1876, 12; "Newport: The Electric Light," *Providence Daily Journal*, 4 July 1882, 8; "Blaze of Electric Lights," *New York Times*, 4 July 1914, 16; "2,000, 000 Here Salute the Flag," *New York Times*, 5 July 1816, 12.

New York Freeman's Journal

Began publication on July 4, 1840, by editor William E. Fitzgibbon. In 1841, the newspaper merged with the *New York Catholic Register*.

New York Riots of 1857

On July 4, 1857, a group of drunken men and women from Cow Bay quarter in New York City started a fight with the "Bowery crowd" resulting in a riot that lasted for two days. Small arms fire caused the deaths of 6 men, and over 100 others were wounded. According to one eye-witness,

About 1 o'clock on the morning of the 4th of July, a party of the Dead Rabbits, whose object, so I understood, was to beat all the new policemen they could find, in coming through the Bowery, between Bayard and Walker streets, espied two Metropolitans. They rushed for them, when the policemen sought refuge in No. 40 Bowery. The Dead Rabbits immediately commenced an attack with stones and other missiles on No. 40 Bowery, when those inside, armed with tumblers, &c., rushed out, and succeeded, with the aid of a few others, in driving them to their own haunts, the Five Points.

Sources: "Rioting and Bloodshed" and "A Version of the Dead Rabbit Riot," *New York Times*, 6 July 1857, 1, and 13 July 1857, 1, respectively.

New York Typographical Society

Celebrated its 50th anniversary on July 4, 1859, at its meeting place, "No. 3 Chambers Street." Three members of the society who assisted in its establishment in 1809 were present: George Mather, David H. Reins, and Daniel Fanshaw. Speeches were presented and a number of letters of congratulations were read. John W. Francis spoke on the significance of

Benjamin Franklin, George Washington, and Patrick Henry.

Source: "Semi-Centennial Anniversary of the New-York Typographical Society," *New York Times*, 6 July 1859, 1.

Niagara Falls Hydraulic Canal

On July 4, 1857, navigation on the canal from Lake Erie to Niagara Falls was opened and Stephen M. Allen (1819–1894), president of the Niagara Falls Water Power Co., presented an address for the occasion before "a great crowd of people." Three steamers passed through the canal that day: the *Signet*, with Allen on board; the *Swallow*; and the *Alliance*, commanded by John Christian. "They were received by the immense concourse of people present with loud huzzas and the roaring of cannon."

On Independence Day in the following year, at the celebration of the opening of the hydraulic canal, a crowd gathered expecting to hear an address by Allen, but the dam gave way, "carrying off about 15 feet of the embankment." No one was injured. That day the local fire department and citizens mounted a parade and an oration was presented by F.J. Fithian of Buffalo.

Sources: "Opening of Navigation between Lake Erie and the Great Hydraulic Canal," *New York Times*, 7 July 1857, 4; *Address on Occasion of the Opening of Navigation to Niagara Falls* (Niagara Falls: Pool and Sleeper, 1857); *Washington Evening Star*, 8 July 1858, 2.

Niagara Falls, New York

A traditional spectators' and daredevil's attraction on Independence Day. The first time a person rode a vessel over the Niagara Falls rapids was on July 4, 1888. Robert William Flack had constructed a 15-foot container named "Phantom." It was 5 feet wide and 34 inches deep and was made of white

Ford Tri-Motor Airplane "Miss Niagara." On July 4, 1928, Sky View Lines inaugurated sightseeing flights at night over Niagara Falls. Photograph D 12361, Local History Collection, courtesy of Niagara Falls (Ontario) Public Library.

pine with a liner of white oak. The space between the pine and oak was filled with "an unknown material lighter and more buoyant than cork." A propeller wheel operated by hand furnished the power. Before attempting his feat, Flack handed a program to a *New York Times* reporter that read:

> I am going through to Lewiston. I shall start just as soon as the crowd gets on the bridge where they can see me. I shall stop 20 minutes in the whirlpool for the reporters to see me, and then I shall go on through Foster's flats to Lewiston. Nobody has ever been through Foster's flats yet, and I'll be the first one. I hope I'll turn 20 somersaults to prevent anybody else from trying it.

Flack strapped himself to the seat, floated out into the rapids and was killed five minutes later. Other daredevils who challenged the falls included George Stathakis on July 4, 1930, and Jean Lussier, the "conqueror of Niagara," on July 4, 1928.

Another noteworthy event was the inauguration of sightseeing flights at night over Niagara Falls on July 4, 1928, by Sky View Lines.

Sources: "Swallowed by the Rapids," *New York Times*, 5 July 1888, 1; *Historic Niagara Digital Collections*, Niagara Falls Public Library, <http://www.nfpl.library>.

Nixon, John (1733?–1808?)

Presented the first public reading of the Declaration of Independence in Philadelphia at the State House (later Independence Hall) on July 8, 1776. "A very large number" of citizens received the reading with "general applause and heartfelt satisfaction." On July 4, 1788, on the occasion of the Grand Federal Procession in Philadelphia, Nixon led the portion of the parade, whose theme was "Independence," on horseback. Nixon wore a cap of liberty. The pendant that flew from the staff he held bore the words "4th July, 1776."

Sources: *New York Times*, 4 July 1871, 2; "Order of Procession" (Historical Society of Pennsylvania).

Nixon, Richard Milhous (1913–1994)

Thirty-seventh president of the U.S. (1969–74). Nixon was an active participant in Fourth celebrations at the Western White House in San Clemente, California, Camp David, and Key Biscayne, Florida. Born in California, Nixon attended Whittier College and served in World War II. He was elected to the U.S. Congress (1947–50) and the Senate (1951–53) and served as vice president (1953–61). He was nominated for president in 1960 and elected president in 1968 and 1972.

On July 4, 1959, he was in Los Angeles participating in dedication ceremonies for the new Memorial Sports Arena. On July 4, 1962, former vice president Nixon gave an anticommunist address at a ceremony in Aalborg, Denmark. On July 4, 1969, President Nixon was in Key Biscayne, Florida, serving as grand marshal for a parade there. Forty members of the U.S. Marine Band were flown to Biscayne to play "Hail to the Chief" and other patriotic music. On Independence Day in 1971, Nixon was at Camp David and flew back to the White House on July 5 to preside over the certification ceremonies in the East Room establishing "the 18-year-old vote as the law of the land" — the 26th amendment to the Constitution. On July 4, 1972, Nixon presented a radio address from San Clemente, California, in which he unveiled plans to issue an invitation to people around the world to visit the United States during its Bicentennial celebration. "As we look forward to America's bicentennial, just four years from today," he said, "we also have a feeling of healthy impatience for change — a determination to make this good land even better."

In the following year at San Clemente, Nixon held a staff conference and celebrated the Fourth at a party at the San Clemente Inn, "a large motel near the Nixon residence." He spent his final Fourth of July as president at Key Biscayne. He had recently returned from a trip to Moscow where he and Soviet leader Leonid I. Brezhnev exchanged gifts.

Sources: *Washington Post*, 5 July 1962, A2; "Nixon Greets Young Fans While Taking Break in Leading July 4 Parade in Key Biscayne," *New York Times*, 5 July 1969, 1; "Nixon to Attend Rite Today Certifying 18-Year-Old Vote," *New York Times*, 5 July 1971, 26; "Nixon Invites World to Visit U.S. for Bicentennial," *New York Times*, 5 July 1972, 18; "Nixon, in Quiet Holiday, Holds Staff Conference," *New York Times*, 5 July 1973, 17; "A Painting for Nixon, a Car for Brezhnev," *New York Times*, 5 July 1974, 8.

Nootka Sound, Pacific Coast

Site for the first Fourth of July celebration in 1789 by a group of Boston mariners on the North American Pacific Coast, on the west shore of what is now Vancouver Island, British Columbia. The celebration took place on the American ship *Columbia*, under the command of John Kendrick, after 13 rounds of cannon fire. A festive dinner included guests from Spanish and English ships present in the sound. The Spanish ship San Carlos fired off a thirteen-gun salute that day. American sources for this event are not extant but both Spanish and English documents corroborate its occurrence.

Sources: "The Proud Pageant," *Life*, 2 July 1951, 36–37, 39–44; Dagny B. Hansen, "July Fourth, 1789," *American West* 13/4 (July/August 1976).

Northridge earthquake

One of the briefest, yet most meaningful, parades in California during the 1990s took place on July 4, 1994, in Sylmar, California, following the Northridge earthquake that occurred on January 17 of that year when 57 of the 600 residences there were destroyed. With their homes and personal belongings gone, the people of Sylmar nonetheless expressed national sentiment and community pride as they mounted a 45-minute parade through the streets of the Oakridge Mobile Home Park by a "homey line-up of vans and pickup trucks, decked out with red, white, and blue streamers, balloons and pinwheels. It wasn't much to look at, but the caravan summed up the community spirit."

Source: Richard Lee Colvin and Jennifer Oldham, "Variations on a Theme," *Los Angeles Times*, 5 July 1994, B1, 3.

Norwich, Connecticut, anniversary *see* Taft, William Howard (1857–1930)

"Ode for the Fourth of July"

Published in *The American Musical Miscellany* (Northampton, 1798). First line: "Come all ye sons of song." Sung to the tune: "God Save the King." Facsimile in Louis C. Elson, *History of American Music* (New York: Macmillan, 1904), 145–46.

"Ode, for the Fourth of July, 1800"

This anonymous four-stanza piece was published expressly for the *Baltimore Weekly Magazine*.

Swift strike the lyre and sweep the sounding
   string,
Let Heav'n and earth with *Io Paeans* ring,
To Hail the day — the ever glorious Day,
That freed *Columbia* from tyrannic sway;
Lo! On the plain
A martial train —
Shout forth triumphant-rend the vaulted sky,
"Free let us live, or else resolve to die."
Each youthful breast beats high with patriot
   flame,
To emulate the virtues of that name,
That erst with warrior arm detraction hurl'd,
And broke the slavish chains of half a world:
'Twas Washington,
Freedom's great Son,
Who gave the Western World the power *to be*
Great, Independent — void of tyranny.
And now behold the warlike toil is o'er,
The drum and martial fife are hard no more;
Each youth returning piles his burnish'd arms,
And joins the festive Board where *Beauty*
   charms:
Drinks to the Day,
When Freedom's sway,
First made *Columbia* own her glorious power,
And feel the influence of her mighty Dower.
The virgin train shall chaunt the song of
   praise,
And in harmonious notes their voices raise;
To him the father of the just and brave
(Whose mighty word's omnipotent to save):
For all the good
On us bestow'd,
Since first he gave unto our shores a name,
Or bade our deeds be registered by Fame.

Source: *Baltimore Weekly Magazine*, 5 July 1800, 88.

"Ode for the Fourth of July, 1847"

A ten-stanza piece published in *The American Whig* 6/1 (July 1847): 55–59.

First stanza
Forth from the willows, where the wind
Hath sighed its saddest note to thee,
Where breathings of a mournful mind
Have made thy chords in unison to be,
Come. O my harp! And wake thy cheerful
   strings,
Make of thy gladdest song a joyous birth.
'Tis thine to listen while the spirit sings,
And echo forth the notes to all the earth

'Tis thine the music of the soul to hear,
The heaven-sent music in the poet's heart,
And by the wondrous magic of thine art
To make the strain be heard by every human
    ear.
Come from the willows, harp!— a new, new
    song
Waits on the wings of poesy to fly—
A new, new song, both loud and long,
Its theme, among the highest, high!
Breathe out the notes the sighing wind hath
    taught,
No longer with the waving willows mourn;
For lo! A joy to all the land is brought,
Th' expected beams the waiting hills adorn.
Rejoice, rejoice!— make every heart rejoice!
The sun has given the glittering hills a voice.
From east to west the glory flies away,
Till all the land is glowing in the day.

"Ode: Nations Rejoice, Jehovah Reigns"

This ode was sung at Christ Church, New York City, on July 4, 1796.

Nations rejoice, Jehovah reigns,
Tyrannic pow'r slav'ry's chains,
And *Freedom's* banner raise;
The human race their rights avow,
All nations catch the sound;
See crowns and scepters tumbling low,
And kings appear confound.
Columbia first the voice obey'd,
Of the celestial word,
Each haughty foe appear'd dismay'd,
And drew the murd'rous sword.
Her vengeful foes their strength unite,
To blast the precious seed;
But he, who all creation rules,
Pronounc'd our country — Freed.

Source: *Rural Magazine; or, Vermont Repository* 2/8 (August 1796): 415.

Odes: *"We Will Gather in Pride to the Glorious Rite"* and *"Hail, Our Country's Natal Morn!"*

On July 4, 1831, these four-stanza odes were "sung by the choir" in the First Presbyterian Church at Charleston, South Carolina, at a celebration of the "Union and States Rights" party. The first "original" ode has four stanzas and was accompanied by Jacob Eckhard, Sr., on the organ. It was sung to the "air" for "The Star-Spangled Banner." A reporter described this ode in this way: "The language

of the Ode itself is to our taste perfect, every line conveys an idea appropriate and comprehensive, and expressed in chaste and ennobling terms. The chorus of both odes were joined in by the audience."

"Original Ode"

We will gather in pride to the glorious rite,
In the faith of the free from our sires that descended;
And who shall resist us, when thus we unite,
For the Union they fought for and nobly defended,
To hallow the hour
When freed from the pow'r
Of Britain, our eagle first taught her to
    cower —
We will gather in triumph, in gladness and
    mirth,
And bless our free nation — free'st nation of
    earth.

"Second Original Ode"

Hail, our country's Natal morn!
Hail, our spreading kindred born!
Hail thou banner not yet torn,
Waving o'er the free!
While, this day, in festal throng,
Millions swell the patriot song,
Shall not we thy notes prolong,
Hallow'd jubilee?

The second ode was sung again on July 6 at a soiree of the Union and States Rights Party with 4,000 persons in attendance. The accompanist this time was Eckhard's son, Jacob Eckhard, Junior. A local newspaper reported:

At about half past 9 o'clock [P.M.], upwards of 1000 printed copies of the two Odes, written for the occasion, and sung in the church at the celebration of the 4th by the Union Party, were distributed among the Company, when they were sung with great effect by the amateur choir, accompanied by Mr. Jacob Eckhard, Jun. on the Piano, in which more than a thousand ladies mingled their sweet voices. The enthusiasm excited by these Odes was so great, that they were called for and repeated several times.

Sources: *Charleston Courier*, 6 and 8 July 1831, 2 and 2, respectively; *Niles' Register*, 16 July 1831, 346.

"Offering of Peace" Parade and Pageant

Took place in Washington, D.C., on July 4, 1919. The parade celebrated the return of world peace, and participants included embassies and legations of all allied and associated governments. "The newly formed nations of Czechoslovakia, Poland, Lithuania and of the Serbs, Croats, and Slovenes were presented for the first time in a parade held in the nation's capital." The pageantry included industry, returning soldiers, calls of art, the land, children, labor, and liberty. At the steps of the Capitol, a crowd of thousands heard a chorus of several thousand sing patriotic songs, accompanied by the U.S. Marine Band. "Scenes of the return of peace were portrayed in pantomime."

Source: "Capitol Marks Return of Peace," *Cleveland Plain Dealer*, 5 July 1919, 4.

Ohio Canal

The ground breaking for the Ohio Canal took place in Lancaster, Ohio, on July 4, 1825, with 8,000 spectators present. This inland waterway was to connect the Ohio River with Lake Erie. "On the day previous, all the roads leading to the point selected for the celebrations were crowded with people on foot, on horseback, and in every description of vehicle, hastening to witness the scene." Speeches were given by Governor **De Witt Clinton** of New York, Governor Jeremiah Morrow of Ohio, and Thomas Ewing, the orator of the day, "who occupied the attention of the audience with an address of half an hour. The concourse of people was very large. Two spades were delivered by the canal commissioners, one into the hands of Governor Morrow, of Ohio, and the other into those of Governor Clinton of New York, who standing opposite to each other, went stoutly to work and threw the first shovels full of earth, amidst the plaudits of thousands and the roar of artillery." Clinton addressed his audience in a "manner in the highest degree impressive":

It will unite the East and the West, the North and the South, by identity of interest, by frequency of communication, and by all the ties which can connect human beings in the bonds friendship and social intercourse.... This great work will also confirm your patriotism, and make you proud of your country. You will now have not only the markets of New Orleans and New York, but of Philadelphia, Baltimore and Montreal.

After the ceremony a large assemblage of persons enjoyed dinner. "There were four parallel lines of tables one within another, and occupying three sides of a square, covered with the greatest profusion of excellent fare, and calculated for the accommodation of one thousand persons."

By 1827, eighty-four miles of the Ohio Canal had been completed and were navigable. On July 4 of that year, on the Portage Summit of the canal, the day was celebrated by "letting in the water and navigating the first boats." The summit was located about thirty-three miles from Lake Erie,

and the most elevated point between it and the Ohio River being nearly 400 feet above the Lake, with which it is connected by 42 locks. The boats reached Cleveland, the outlet of the Canal in the lake, at an early hour, when the passengers, among whom were the Governor, the Canal Commissioners, and other leading personages, landed; and a procession being formed, marched to the public square, where the declaration of independence was read, and an oration pronounced. A public dinner and ball concluded the festivities of the day.

The Ohio Canal opened in Cleveland with Governor Allen Trimble arriving there on the first boat, *State of Ohio*.

Sources: *Frederick-Town Herald*, 21, 23, and 30 July 1825, 3, 3, and 2 respectively; "Ohio Canal Celebration," 13 August 1825, 2; *Cleveland Herald*, 6 July 1827.

Ohio State Capitol, Columbus

The cornerstone of the new Capitol was laid on July 4, 1839, with appropriate ceremonies. Ex-governor Jeremiah Morrow addressed the crowd as a block that included a copy of the Declaration of Independence, the Constitution of the U.S. and constitutions of 27 states, the Ordinance of 1787, the statues of Ohio, and other items, was set in place. Rev. (R.?) Cressy provided an invocation in which he said that "The corner stone of the capitol of Ohio has not been intended for an ephemeral existence. The edifice that will rest upon it is destined to an immortality equal to the pyramids of Egypt."

Source: "Capitol of Ohio," *Alexandria Gazette*, 12 July 1839, 3.

Oklahoma City Bombing

City for the most poignant Fourth of July celebration in Oklahoma in 1995, if not the nation, following the bombing of the Federal Building on April 19 that year in which 168 people were killed and more than 500 injured. A crowd of thousands including volunteer aid workers, families of those that lost loved ones, and others gathered to witness American flags that had been previously lowered to half-staff in remembrance be raised to full staff. Oklahoma governor Frank Keating said that the "U.S. flag had a special meaning for Oklahomans" and that "the pessimism and despair of April 19 are over." Keating added, "It flew from the damaged building, it shone proudly from the uniforms of the rescue workers and it draped the caskets of the victims." He said, "It was stained and it was torn, but it was beautiful."

At 9:02 A.M., the time of the explosion, members of military and law enforcement and relief groups raised new flags up 14 poles on the south steps of the state Capitol, accompanied by a drum roll and the roar of four F-16 fighters overhead.

Volunteers, and rescue workers from Virginia, California, Maryland, Florida, Arizona and other states joined in the ceremonies.

Source: Libby Quaid, "A Special Fourth in Oklahoma," *Philadelphia Inquirer*, 5 July 1995, A4.

Old Capitol, University of Iowa

The oldest building on the campus of the University of Iowa (founded 25 February 1847) and originally the seat of government for the Territory of Iowa, whose cornerstone was laid on July 4, 1840. Robert Lucas, territorial governor, presided at the ceremony which was witnessed by a few "pioneer residents of Iowa City," as well as some Native Americans. The building's architect was John F. Rague, who also designed the Illinois State Capitol in 1834. There was a parade, dinner, and oration presented that day. Supposedly deposited in the cornerstone was a copper box containing copies of the Declaration of Independence, the United States Constitution, the Organic Law of the Territory of Iowa, laws enacted by the First Legislative Assembly, the Journal of the House of Representatives, and various newspapers; but when the cornerstone was removed in 1970 "in hopes of finding the valuable artifacts," the copper box was not there. It is believed that the documents may have been removed during a 1920–22 restoration of the building.

The completion of the building took fifteen years at a cost of $125,000. It was constructed of limestone cut from quarries along the Iowa River with a supporting structure made from hand-hewn native oak. In 1857 when the capital was removed to Des Moines, Old Capitol was given to the University of Iowa. "In the first years after its donation to the University, the building served as the main classroom area." Old Capitol is now a museum with a gift shop.

Sources: "Old Capitol: SUI's Oldest, Most Historical Building," *Daily Iowan*, 9 June 1960, 6; "Old Capitol Cornerstone Yields — Nothing," *Iowa City Press-Citizen*, 18 December 1970, 1A.

Oldest Inhabitants Association of Washington (D.C.)

The oldest association in Washington that continues to meet and celebrate on the Fourth of July. Their founding mission was "to cultivate social intercourse and unite ourselves more closely as original settlers of the District of Columbia." The organization was established in December 1865 and their annual meetings were held on Independence Day. Meetings were generally held in the city court room in City Hall and later at the Old Engine House at 19th and H streets. Other celebrations were held at Analoston Island, at Carusi's Saloon, on the grounds at Washington Monument, at Epiphany Church Parish House (1926), at Corcoran Building, at Mount Vernon, at Masonic Temple (1882), and at Alton Farm (1904–05). A number of their meetings were significant. On July 4, 1876, for example, on the occasion of the nation's centennial, the association met at Ford's Theater with thirteen members of Congress in attendance. It was the first organized Independence Day celebration to take place in the theater and the first time in the history of the country that the United States Congress enacted legislation directing its members to attend a Fourth of July celebration. L.A. Gobright, who gave the oration that day, acknowledged their guests from Congress: "In the name of the entire people of the United States, we thank them for their presence, and wish them many returns of this happy occasion!"

Activities at the meetings varied but usually included music and recitations. For example, on July 4, 1886, Robert Ball was elected vice president of the organization and responded with singing "The Star Spangled Banner." On July 4, 1905, Mrs. Thomas C. Noyes became the first woman member in the association's history. At the ceremony, she gave a brief speech and sang a number of songs, including "The Star-Spangled Banner" and "Annie Laurie." A Sängerbund chorus added to merriment by singing "Dixie." Another significant occasion was on July 4, 1930, when Edward F. Colladay, as principal orator, urged voting rights be extended to the residents of the District of Columbia and John Clagett Proctor, a local historian, read an original poem. On July 4, 1943, Proctor again read another poem he wrote to the association. Another significant celebration occurred on July 4, 1937, when Cloyd H. Marvin, president of the association, gave an address on "righteous citizenship." He too called for full voting rights for the citizens of the District of Columbia. John Clagett Proctor read another original poem titled "Independence Day."

On July 4, 1956, the association had its final Fourth of July celebration at the Old Union Engine House, which had served as its meeting place since 1909.

Sources: *Washington Evening Star*, 8 December, 30 June, and 5 July 1876, 1, 1 and 4, respectively; "The Fourth in the City," *Washington Post*, 6 July 1886, 2; "Gala Fourth at Alton Farm," *Washington Post*, 5 July 1905, 2; "Oldest Inhabitants Urge District Vote," *Washington Post*, 5 July 1930, 14; "Violent Trend in Strikes Hit by Dr. Marvin," *Washington Post*, 6 July 1937, 16; *Washington Evening Star*, 5 July 1943, A7; *Washington Post*, 5 July 1956, 13.

"On Independence Day: Give Three Cheers for the Fourth of July"

Words by Earle C. Jones; music by Tom Kelley (New York: Joseph W. Stern, 1907). For voice and piano. First line: "Hark! Awake! Ye freemen rally."

Operation Desert Storm, 1991

Frequently referred to as Gulf War I, this war was waged between the United States and Iraq beginning on January 17, 1991, in order to liberate Kuwait, which had been seized by the Iraqi Republican Guard. By late February Kuwait City had been freed and the war was brought to a successful conclusion. The Fourth of July that year was marked by patriotism and pride by Americans across the nation. President Bush was in Marshfield, Missouri, watching a parade of military units from Fort Leonard Wood and addressing a crowd of spectators: "Desert Storm has at last brought the recognition and honor to our sons and daughters who served in Vietnam," he said. As reported at the White House, Bush awarded medals of freedom to Gen. Colin L. Powell, Gen. H. Norman Schwarzkopf, Secretary of State James A. Baker, Secretary of Defense Dick Cheney, and National Security Advisor Brent Scowcroft. In New York, over 30 planes from World War II and the Gulf War flew over the harbor.

Sources: *New York Times*, 4 July 1991, A8; Maureen Dowd, "An Old-Fashioned Day of Patriotism," *New York Times*, 5 July 1991, A1.

Operation Iraqi Freedom, 2003–

Combat operations began on March 17, 2003, to depose Saddam Hussein and the Ba'athist regime from power in Iraq. The reasons for the campaign included the United States' stance on regional security and U.S. interests and the ongoing global war on terrorism. On July 4, U.S. troops celebrated the Fourth at Hussein's Baghdad palace. Meanwhile at Forbes Field in Topeka, Kansas, while returning troops and families celebrated in Philadelphia, 5000 anti-war demonstrators protested the nation's presence in Iraq. In 2004–2006 uncertainties regarding the outcome of the war became widespread and a headline—"Patriotism Mixes with Reflection" in the *Miami Herald* seemed to mirror the American mood. The Iraqi War dominated the national consciousness and full support of the service men and women was unquestioned.

During this time naturalization ceremonies for foreign-born military serving in the war were highlights of the holiday celebrations. President Bush urged patience and courage as combat continued and Americans honored its fallen soldiers.

Sources: "Bush: Freedom Is for All," *Miami Herald*, 5 July 2005, 3A; Rebecca Dellagloria and Nikki Waller, "Patriotism Mixes with Reflection," *Miami Herald*, 5 July 2004, B1, B6; "Cities Celebrate Independence Day with a Multitude of Events" and "U.S. Troops Celebrate Fourth with Cookout at Saddam's," *Virginian-Pilot*, 5 July 2003, A7 and A13, respectively; "Thousands Protest Near Center Dedication," *Philadelphia Inquirer*, 5 July 2003, B1.

"Operation Sail" *see* Bicentennial

Our Own United States

This outdoor pageant was presented by the Bureau for American Ideals at Columbus Circle in New York City on July 4, 1924. Irish baritone Thomas Hannon directed the play and was the principal vocalist. Principal characters included John Hancock, Patrick Henry, Betsy Ross, George Washington, Thomas Jefferson, and Abraham Lincoln. "The most impressive scene was the reading and signing of the Declaration of Independence. It was presented with faithful accuracy, minute men, soldiers of Washington's armies, and citizens of that time serving as a background for the momentous scene in the Independence Hall."

Source: "Pageant Held in Street," *New York Times*, 5 July 1924, 13.

Pacific Cable *see* Theodore Roosevelt

Paige, Robert George (fl. 1830s–40s)

Singer, musician, and instructor who sang a newly written ode (author unnamed), "Hurrah for the Fourth of July!" to the tune "Hurrah for the Bonnets of Blue," on July 4, 1838, at the Presbyterian Church in Sing Sing, New York. "At the close of the song, we are sorry to say, a portion of sealing [sic] in the right wing of the church gave way, and, falling upon the people below, for a moment created considerable alarm. It being ascertained that no material injury was done, the audience be-

came composed, and listened to a national air from the Band, and the parting benediction."

The ode was sung again at dinner and "hundreds of voices joined in the chorus." Walter M. Smith proposed a toast to "Professor Paige": "His exquisite voice and polished musical talents, which have delighted us repeatedly this day, are happily blended with his urbanity and science as a gentleman and instructor. Here's a cheer for the land of the birth, and a heart-warm welcome to all who are dear to him." Paige was the author of *Hymns and Canticles of the Church* (N.Y., 1844) and arranged a number of songs, including "I Hear Thee Speak of a Better Land" (music by Mrs. Hemans, 1836) and "They Have Given Thee to Another" (music by Henry R. Bishop, 1830s).

Source: *Hudson River Chronicle*, 10 July 1838, 2.

Paige, Timothy (1788–1822)

Composed an "Ode for the Fourth of July, 1821" that was read at the Baptist Meeting House in Southbridge, Massachusetts, on July 4, 1821. On that occasion John Bisbe (1793–1829) presented an oration.

Source: John Bisbe, *An Oration, Pronounced July 4, 1821 ...* (Worcester, Mass.: Henry Rogers, 1821).

Paine, Robert Treat, Jr. (1773–1811)

Poet, lawyer, orator, and son of Robert Treat Paine, signer of the Declaration of Independence. Robert Jr. was possibly the author of a poem titled "Ode for the Fourth of July, 1811" that was printed as a broadside under the name Robert Treat Paine. He was born in Taunton, Massachusetts, and entered Harvard in 1788, where he generally excelled in his studies but due to a student scuffle in his senior year was publicly censured. During this time, Paine had developed a penchant for poetry and composed "Nature and Progress of Liberty," which was read as a valedictory poem. He also wrote poetry for the *Massachusetts Magazine* and won a gold medal during the early 1790s for a "prologue in verse" he submitted for a premiere performance held in the Boston Theatre in Federal Street. In 1795 Paine received attention by writing a poem titled "The Invention of Letters: A Poem ... on the Day of Annual Commencement" for Harvard's commencement and in 1797 a Harvard Phi Beta Kappa poem titled "The Ruling Passion." In 1798 the crisis with France inspired Paine to write more songs that received national attention: "Adams and Liberty" (published in eleven editions before 1800) and "Adams and Washington." Paine enjoyed acclaim also by receiving invitations to present commemorative speeches. In 1799 he presented "an oration Written at the request of the Young Men of Boston," which focused on the end of the Franco-American Alliance, and a eulogy on the death of Washington. Paine was admitted to the Massachusetts bar in 1802 and practiced law for only a brief period before devoting the remainder of his life to his literary endeavors. The "Ode for the Fourth of July, 1811" was one of the last works he wrote, having died in November of that year.

Sources: Oscar Wegelin, *Early American Poetry* (the author, 1930; reprint, Gloucester, Mass.: Peter Smith, 1965), 192; Winfred E.A. Bernhard, "Robert Treat Paine, Jr.," *American National Biography*, 16:923–25.

Paine, Thomas (1737–1809)

Paine came to America in 1774 and became highly influential in advocating for independence from England. His popular anonymous pamphlet *Common Sense* (1776) was an important document in fostering colonial support for the effort. His series of *Crisis* papers (1776–83) helped create the solidarity needed to declare independence and to follow through with a strong federal union. Paine's positions included secretary to the committee on foreign affairs of the Continental Congress (1777–79) and clerk of the Pennsylvania assembly (1779). After the war he went abroad, where in England and France his seditious and unfavorable political views landed him in a French jail. When he was released in 1794 through the efforts of U.S. minister James Monroe, he returned to America and lived his final years in obscurity in New Jersey and New York. Following his death, a six-stanza poem supposedly by him titled "The Fourth of July," sung to the tune "Rule Britannia," was published in *Lady's Weekly Miscellany* in 1810.

(First stanza)
Hail great Republic of the world!
The rising empire of the west,
Where famed Columbus, of mighty mind inspir'd!
Gave tortur'd Europe scenes of rest.
Chorus
Be thou for ever, for ever, great and free,
The land of love and liberty.

On July 4, 1950, a monument to Thomas Paine was dedicated at Burnham Park in Morristown, New Jersey. The piece was sculpted by George Lober and was presented to the city by the Thomas Paine Memorial Committee. For the occasion Carl John Bostelmann wrote a five-stanza poem.

He is no stranger, here in Morristown,
Who sits with quill in hand astride a drum,
To write historic words of courage down
For men to read, whatever crisis come.

Sources: *Lady's Weekly Miscellany* 10/18 (24 February 1810): 288; "Tom Paine Returns to Morristown," *New York Herald Tribune*, 5 July 1950, 22.

Palo Duro Canyon State Park, Texas

Scenic park, located in the Texas Panhandle in Armstrong and Randall counties, that was formally dedicated on July 4, 1934. More than 7,000 persons attended the affair, which featured a cornerstone ceremony, ribbon cutting, and a performance by the Leonard Stroud Rodeo, sponsored by the Texas State Park Board. The acquisition of the park was begun on January 6, 1908, when Congressman John H. Stephens of Wichita Falls introduced a bill for the purchase of the land, but it took many years to achieve the objective. Finally, on May 17, 1931, "Palo Duro Park" had its grand opening with 25,000 persons from 14 states attending the ceremonies.

Sources: Heather Lanman, Park Interpreter, Palo Duro Canyon State Park; Peter L. Petersen, "A Park for the Panhandle: The Acquisition and Development of Palo Duro Canyon State Park," in *The Story of Palo Duro Canyon*, ed. Duane F. Guy (Lubock: Texas Tech University Press, 1979).

Panama

This Latin-American country celebrated its first official Fourth of July event on July 4, 1919. "The schools of Panama yesterday, on the eve of the holiday, held exercises in celebration of the occasion, the program comprising songs and addresses of an appropriate nature."

Source: "Fourth, a Panama Holiday Now," *New York Times*, 5 July 1919, 7.

Pan-American Exposition

Held at Buffalo, New York, in 1901 to highlight the progress of a century and to encourage social and commercial endeavors. On July 4 "Independence Day Music" was presented at the East Esplanade Bandstand by the Havana, Cuba, Municipal Police Band, conducted by Capt. Guillermo M. Tomas. The band was sent to the exposition "as a special compliment to the people of the United States." A number of pieces by both American and Cuban composers were performed. One Cuban work written for the exposition and premiered that day was a march, "To Buffalo," by D. Lopez.

Source: *Official Daily Program of the Pan-American Exposition* (Buffalo, N.Y.: The Exposition Company, 1901), 4.

"Parade of Nations"

The theme of the New York Fourth of July celebration in 1911 consisted of a parade of immigrants representing various countries, including China, Germany, Switzerland, Italy, Japan, Norway, Greece, Finland, Hungary, and Ireland, and a gathering on the grounds adjacent to City Hall, which was under restoration. The United States was represented by a group of North American Indians which led the parade. Most groups were dressed in representative costumes. For example, the Greeks were dressed in classical garb and costumes representing modern times. "Athens passed in shining helmet with spear and target, and she was attended by men in the flowing white robes of antiquity, their arms laden with flowers." Modern Greeks were dressed in "curious white kilts" and cadets dressed in khaki uniforms. Arthur Farwell's *Hymn to Liberty* was performed by the United German Singers and Stretz's Military Band played the "Star-Spangled Banner." Giacomo Quintano's new arrangement of "America" was sung and Edward Markham read his original

poem "Let there be prayer and praise."

Source: "City Hall Centenary," *New York Times*, 5 July 1911, 4.

Paris, France

One of the most important cities in the world to celebrate the American Fourth of July holiday. The French regularly paid homage to America's sacred holiday by draping American flags on buildings and having orchestras play patriotic American tunes. Banquets were common with invited guests, including heads of state, French and American journalists, and others.

The first Fourth of July celebration on foreign soil to include dignitaries and heads of state occurred in 1778 at Passy. **Benjamin Franklin** and John Adams hosted a dinner for "the American Gentlemen and ladies, in and about Paris." Many of the Paris events were reported in newspapers from the 1890s to 1930s. For example, a celebration of the American colony on July 4, 1893, featured a dinner hosted by General Meredith Read. Guests included Prince Roland Bonaparte, the Marquis of Bersano, and J.F. Loubet, "who recently founded a prize in the French Institute for the best work in American history."

On July 4, 1900, on the occasion of the unveiling of the **Lafayette** statue, a flag hung "from the pinnacle of the Eiffel Tower, thus dominating the whole city." Hotels provided appropriate menus for the many "intimate dinners" enjoyed there. Speeches given expressed sentiments about the "enormous community of interests" shared between the two peoples. On Independence Day in 1913, banquets were held in the Latin Quarter and at the leading hotels, while orchestras played patriotic tunes. At the American Chamber of Commerce dinner event, "the French Government honored the occasion by sending a detachment of Republican Guards, who, in their picturesque uniforms, were disposed at intervals behind the long guest table." On July 4, 1915, for the first time in the history of the celebration of the American Chamber of Commerce there, nine members of the French Cabinet attended the Independence Day banquet. Another noteworthy celebration of the

American Chamber of Commerce occurred on July 4, 1921, before 1,500 Americans and 120 "distinguished French guests," when retiring American ambassador Hugh C. Wallace urged the United States to join the League of Nations, and Germany to pay reparations to France for that country's losses during World War I. "I shall never give up my faith that the League of Nations was born to live and the hope that America will join it in due season."

The Fourth of July in 1925 included the dedication of the new American Embassy, visits to the "perpetual flame" above the tomb of the Unknown Poilu in the Arc de Triomphe, and "exercises were conducted in most of the schools and other institutions having American connections."

On July 4, 1935, plaques in honor of John Paul Jones were unveiled at the Rue des Ecluses, the site where the admiral was buried until 1905, and in honor of Benjamin Franklin and King Louis XVI of France, both of whom signed the treaty of friendship on February 6, 1778, at the building which now is the Hotel de Coislin.

Sources: *New York Times*, 5 July 1893, 9, 5 July 1913, 3, 6 July 1915, 18, and 5 July 1935, 3; "League Born to Live, Wallace Declares," *New York Times*, 5 July 1921, 1–2; "American Embassy in Paris Dedicated," *Los Angeles Times*, 5 July 1925, 2.

Parker Opera House, Hinton, West Virginia

On July 4, 1894, the balcony of this building collapsed, burying many persons thirty feet below. At the time of the accident a Fourth of July dance was being held inside the opera house and the dancers crowded out upon the balcony to witness the town's parade "when the whole structure fell with a crash carrying those upon it down with it into the street below, mashing and bruising those upon the sidewalk watching the procession." At least 2 persons were killed, and many others injured.

Source: "Crushed Under a Balcony," *Washington Evening Star*, 5 July 1894, 1.

Paterson, New Jersey, Centennial

Celebrated the 100th anniversary of its founding on July 4, 1892. The entire town was festooned with American flags. All the mills blew their whistles and 100 artillery salutes were fired from Garret Rock and from the Soldiers Monument. "Nearly every business house in the city, many of the mills, and most of the private dwellings are adorned with flags and streamers, mingling the sunset dyes with the starry blue of the heavens. Everybody wears a badge or a button." Included also was a parade having 14 divisions of "French, Italian, Polish, Bavarian, Holland, Swiss, and other societies, with their national banners and colors and a goodly number of Highlanders with kilts and bare limbs." Patterson's mill workers "wore handsome silk scarves, of their own weaving; others, from the ribbon mills, carried blocks of ribbons partly unwound, which they held up on canes, as the sign of their handicraft." That evening "jubilee exercises" were held in "a huge tent on Carroll Street." An address was given by Parke Godwin.

On July 4, 1792, on the occasion of the town's establishment, a meeting was held at the Passaic Falls, and Major Pierre Charles L'Enfant, who designed the nation's capital, was selected as the "engineer to layout the town." Also present at the meeting was Alexander Hamilton, who a year earlier had prepared the act for incorporating the town.

Source: "Founded by Hamilton" and "Great Day for Paterson," *New York Times*, 4 July 1892, 1, and 5 July 1892, 8, respectively.

"Patriotic Volunteer"

This ballet was presented at the new theater at Chatham Garden in New York City on July 4, 1824.

Source: *New York Daily Advertiser*, 5 July 1824, 2.

Peace Monument, Washington, D.C.

Located at the entrance to the Capitol grounds in Washington, D.C., that was a popular and symbolic place to gather for Independence Day events. The monument commemorates the deaths of naval personnel during the Civil War. The monument was the initiative of Admiral David D. Porter and was sculpted by Franklin Simmons. The monument, erected

Peace Monument with the U.S. Capitol in the background, constructed in 1877–1878 in commemoration of naval personnel who lost their lives during the Civil War. At the top of the monument, the figure "Grief" weeps as "History" holds a tablet inscribed, "They died that their country might live." The site has been a popular gathering place for both celebrators and protest marchers on Independence Day. Photograph by author.

in 1877–1878, has served as a site for both celebrators and protest marchers. On July 4, 1894, a group of Coxeyites led by Carl Browne met at the base of the monument and attempted to enter the grounds but were turned back by Capitol police reinforced by fifty officers of the District force fearing trouble from the group. Browne

> wearing a wig of long, yellow hair, impersonated the Goddess of Liberty. He rode a small horse, from the back of which he addressed a crowd of some two or three hundred. He spoke of the present depression throughout the country, the needless expense of paying interest on bond issues, and the need of good roads.

On July 4, 1915, a ceremony was held at the monument to honor Abram Springsteen, the youngest veteran of the Union armies, who had enlisted at the age of eleven. Springsteen, attired in his original uniform and with his Civil War era drum in hand, stood at the monument while "Taps" was sounded.

Sources: "Exercises at the Washington Monument — Parade by Coxeyites," *New York Times*, 5 July 1894, 8; "Runs His Own Parade," *Washington Post*, 4 July 1915, 11; *Architect of the Capitol* Web site <http://www.acc.gov/cc/grounds/art_arch/peace.cfm>.

Pearl Harbor, attack by Japanese

On Sunday, 7 December 1941, Japanese naval and air forces attacked the United States fleet stationed at the Pearl Harbor naval base in Hawaii, resulting in great loss of life and a U.S. declaration of war on Japan the following day. This event and the subsequent war greatly changed the tenor of Independence Day celebrations in 1942 and in years following. Not since the war of 1812 had direct attacks on U.S. territory occurred, and the nation's assurance of its isolation and defense was greatly questioned.

Across the nation the 1942 Independence Day celebrations were reported as mostly "quiet" affairs. City wide parades and jubilant festivities were "given up as inappropriate in wartime." Fireworks displays were generally cancelled due to blackouts. Some ceremonies held in Philadelphia, for example, were military related. At the base of the Liberty Bell, 200 young men were inducted into the armed forces as Frank Smith, presiding judge of the

Number 5 Court of Common Pleas said to the group, "We vow that the foes of freedom shall be destroyed, so that peace may again prevail throughout this world." His sentiment was a common theme expressed elsewhere. In Washington President Roosevelt urged citizens to work on the holiday in order to help the war effort. That day he conducted business and received numerous Independence Day congratulatory messages from world leaders, as well as purchasing the first of the 3-cent "Win the War" postage stamps which went on sale that day. He also issued a Fourth of July statement, proclaiming the holiday as a beacon for the world in the fight for freedom. Meanwhile, on the streets of Washington, "civilian protective forces" were in place and under instruction to be available in case of emergency. Although there were no parades, public gatherings or displays of fireworks, a stage revue titled *Three Cheers*, which featured a new song, "Wave that Flag, America," by Howard Acton and Phelps Adams of the National Press Club, was performed at Loew's Capitol Theater.

In New York City, residents heard 408 air raid sirens wail during its normal noontime test. Business was off due to a slump in visitors. Perhaps the prominent event of the day was the service of the eternal light as flags of the allied nations were colorfully displayed in a "V" for victory. In Los Angeles, a group of army engineers built a 740-foot pontoon bridge in a park lake in only 14 minutes as a demonstration of military readiness. The city also held a military parade of 33,000 soldiers in an eight-mile column, was reported as the longest parade in Los Angeles' history. In Riverside, California, citizens honored Capt. Travis Hoover, "who flew one of Gen. Doolittle's Tokyo raiders on April 18."

Sources: "Army Engineers Bridge Park Lake in Period of 14 Minutes," "Parade of U.S. Might Cheered," and "Riverside Gives Ovation to Tokyo Raider," *Los Angeles Times*, 5 July 1942, A1, A14; "Philadelphia 4th Quiet," *New York Times*, 5 July 1942, 23 and 25; "President Buys War Stamps," *New York Times*, 5 July 1942, 35; *Washington Post*, 4 July 1941, 5.

Peekskill, New York, Centennial

This city celebrated its centennial anniversary during the first week of July 1916, and "in conjunction with the Fourth of July festivities." A ceremony included a speech by ex–secretary of state **William Jennings Bryan**, a short history of Peekskill read by Leverett F. Crumb, president of the village, and William J. Charlton, village treasurer, a luncheon, and military review.

Source: "Bryan at Peekskill Praises Soldiers," *New York Times*, 5 July 1916, 18.

"Pegasus of Apollo!"

A series of three poems under that title published in the *Worcester Magazine* in 1786–87.

The first work was printed under the heading "Columbia" and titled "A Cantata for the Fourth of July," written in New York, June 3, 1786, by an anonymous writer. The piece includes a recitative and 6 airs. First line: "Where Alleghany rears her lofty Brow."

The second was titled an "Anniversary Ode" and written "in commemoration of American independence," New York, July 4, 1786, again by an anonymous writer. The piece included 13 stanzas.

(first stanza)
As time rolls ceaseless round the sphere,
And brings in peace another year,
We greet the annual morn,
From which we date our country's rise,
When nature taught us to be wise,
Nor live on hope forlorn.

The third was titled "A new song, sung on the 4th of July, 1787," and first appeared in the Petersburg, Virginia, *Intelligencer*.

(first stanza)
In a chariot of light, from the regions above,
The goddess of freedom appear'd;
The sun beams of day, emblazon'd her way,
And empire America rear'd;
To sustain the vast fabrick her offspring were taught,
She smill'd on each patriot birth;
But shielded her charms, secure in the arms
Of her chieftain celestial on earth.

Sources: *Worcester Magazine* 1/17 (22 July 1786): 204, 1/19 (8 August 1786): 228 and 3/21 (15 August 1787): 275.

Pelissier, Victor (ca. 1745–ca. 1820)

Composer and instrumentalist who wrote the music for the "musical drama" *The Fourth of July; or, Temple of American Independence*, which was premiered on July 4, 1799, at the "Theatre" in New York City. Pelissier came to Philadelphia in 1791 and was likely of French background. He was a French horn player and arranged music for the stage. No published copy of *The Fourth of July* has been located.

Sources: *Daily Advertiser*, 4 July 1799, 3; Clark, *The Dawning of American Keyboard Music*, 43.

Pennsylvania State House *see* Independence Hall

Pentalpha Lodge, Gaithersburg, Maryland

A ceremony for the completion of this building took place on July 4, 1900, at noon, in Gaithersburg, a town a few miles north of Washington, D.C. J.B. Adams publicly read the Declaration of Independence and the Germantown Brass Band provided music. "A mammoth flag was raised over the building and the service concluded by firing a salute of 13 guns."

Source: *Baltimore Morning Herald*, 5 July 1900, 5.

Perry, Oliver Hazard (1785–1819)

American naval officer who in the War of 1812 defeated the British fleet at the Battle of Lake Erie. At Put-in-Bay, Ohio, on July 4, 1913, the cornerstone of the Oliver Hazard Perry victory monument was laid by members of the Ohio Grand Lodge of Masons. Part of the event included a banquet at the Hotel Commodore with guests that included Ohio commissioners of the Perry's Victory Centennial, Governor Judson Harmon of Ohio, members of the General Assembly, the Supreme Court, and state officers of Ohio. The event celebrated not only Perry's victory, but also the campaign of Gen. William Henry Harrison. A reporter described the design of the finished monument: "A Doric column of granite 330 feet high and 45 feet in diameter, surmounted by a spectators' gallery reached by elevators above which will tower a tripod holding a beacon light, which will be visible for miles over Lake Erie." An address was presented by Col. Henry Watterson, vice president general of the

Interstate Board, who "compared Perry with John Paul Jones, the two, he said standing on one pedestal." Watterson also spoke about how "overlegislated the republic is." Perry's victory made him a national hero and his report on the battle contained his famous words "We have met the enemy and they are ours."

Source: *Washington Evening* Star, 5 July 1913, part 2:8.

Pershing, John J. (1860–1948)

General John J. Pershing, an active participant on the Fourth of July, was the commander in chief of the American Expeditionary Forces in Europe during World War I. On July 4, 1917, in Paris, Pershing helped celebrate the allied heroism of World War I, and he reviewed the American 16th Infantry. That was followed by a trip to the French cemetery where he spoke briefly, after remarks by U.S. Colonel C.E. Stanton. As the course of the war bore on, Pershing was again in Paris on July 4, 1918, where he joined celebrations at Chaumont's Hôtel de Ville. He was greeted as a hero and French school children flocked to him; flowers were presented, with congratulations from "the mayor of Chaumont and high civil and military officials." Pershing responded with this reflection: "Today constitutes a new Declaration of Independence, a solemn oath that the liberty for which France has long been fighting will be attained."

On July 4, 1919, Paris celebrated again. Pershing was at the Hôtel de Ville on the evening of July 3 and received a plaque from the city of Paris. On the following day he reviewed American troops with President Raymond Poincaré, went to "Picpus cemetery and Lafayette's tomb for a wreath laying," made a visit to Pershing Stadium where he viewed Inter-Allied games featuring military drills, and spent an evening at the opera, viewing a performance of *Faust*.

Following the war, on July 4, 1920, Pershing sent a message to members of the American Legion and other former service men. He said,

To the men of the Legion whose blood and sacrifices have proved their devotion we owe the deepest debt of gratitude, and it is to them

that we look for constant inspiration that our efforts to maintain forever a country where all men shall be free and equal may be supported by the same patriotism that gave them the victory in the great war.

On that day Pershing was at the British Embassy in Washington, where he received an engraved sword from the City of London in commemoration of his military achievements in Europe.

On July 4, 1924, Pershing was back in Paris at a luncheon at the "American Village," as a guest of the American Olympic team. On July 4, 1927, Pershing was in Indianapolis assisting in cornerstone ceremony for the **War Memorial** there. On July 4, 1931, it was announced by Francois Latour, president of the Municipal Council, that streets in Paris would be named after Pershing and former president **Herbert Clark Hoover**. See also **National Defense Day, 1925**.

Sources: *New York Times*, 5 July 1917, 1 and 6 July 1920, 17; "Pershing Message to American Legion," *New York Times*, 5 July 1920, 13; *New York Times*, 5 July 1924, 10; *New York Times*, 5 July 1927, 14; "France Honors President Hoover," *Washington Evening Star*, 5 July 1931, A2; Frank E. Vandiver, *Black Jack: The Life and Times of John J. Pershing*, 2 vols. (College Station: Texas A and M University Press, 1977).

Philadelphia City Hall

The cornerstone for this public building, located at Penn Square (Broad and Market Streets), was laid on July 4, 1874. Philadelphia mayor William S. Stokley presided over the ceremony and Benjamin Harris Brewster was the orator. He spoke about the importance of the city of Philadelphia and noted, "We are erecting a structure that will in ages to come speak for us with the tongues of men and angels." The Declaration of Independence was read by William H. Maurice and a band provided music. Deposited in the cornerstone were numerous documents, including the U.S. Constitution, the Constitution of Pennsylvania, the charter of the city of Philadelphia, elevation and plans for the building, and various medals.

At the same time of this event, the cornerstone of the new armory of the First City Troop was also being laid, and the Girard

Avenue bridge, touted as the widest bridge in the world, was being opened for the first time.

Sources: "The New Public Buildings" and "The Glorious Fourth," *Philadelphia Inquirer*, 2 and 6 July 1874, 2 and 2, respectively.

Philadelphia Liberty Medal

The Philadelphia Liberty Medal and a $100,000 award are presented annually on July 4 at Independence Hall in Philadelphia to honor "an individual or organization from anywhere in the world that has demonstrated leadership and vision in the pursuit of liberty or conscience or freedom from oppression, ignorance or deprivation." In 2001 the Verizon Foundation was the chief underwriter of the award.

The medal was established in 1988 by We the People 2000, made up of Philadelphia business and civic leaders who were involved in the commemoration of the bicentennial of the Constitution. Recipients of the medal are selected by the International Selection Commission, a group of significant persons from government, education, world affairs, culture and business.

WINNERS

1989   Polish president Lech Walesa
1990   Former U.S. president Jimmy Carter
1991   Nobel laureate and former Costa Rican president Oscar Arias and the French medical and human rights organization *Medicins sans Frontieres* (joint prize)
1992   U.S. Supreme Court justice Thurgood Marshall
1993   South African leaders F.W. de Klerk and Nelson Mandela (joint prize)
1994   Czech president Vaclav Havel
1995   U.N. high commissioner for refugees Sadako Ogata
1996   Jordan's King Hussein I and former Israeli prime minister Shimon Peres (joint prize)
1997   CNN International
1998   Former U.S. senator George J. Mitchell, chairman of the 1998 Northern Ireland peace talks
1999   South Korean president Kim Dae Jung
2000   Scientists Dr. James Watson and Dr. Francis Crick (joint prize)
2001   United Nations secretary-general Kofi Annan
2002   U.S. secretary of state Colin L. Powell
2003   Sandra Day O'Connor, Supreme Court justice

2004   Hamid Karzai, president of Afghanistan
2005   Viktor Yushchenko, president of Ukraine; event was postponed to September 17, 2005.

Source: *Philadelphia Inquirer*, 5 July 2001, A6

Philippine Islands

The Philippines were occupied by the U.S. at the conclusion of the Spanish-American War in 1898. Not long after, an insurrection for independence, led by Emilio Aguinaldo, was suppressed. Aguinaldo was captured on March 23, 1901. On July 4, 1902, President Roosevelt issued an amnesty proclamation for all prisoners, estimated to number 600, and the insurrection was declared officially over. On that day in Manila the proclamation was publicly read in both English and Spanish following a parade of 6,000 Americans and Filipinos. "Acting Gov. Wright and Gen. Chaffee reviewed the procession, and Capt. Crossfield delivered an oration. He defended the American policy in the Philippines, predicted the ultimate complete acceptance of American institutions by the Filipinos, and denounced the critics of the Philippine policy."

It was not long after that a movement for Philippine independence was begun. On July 4, 1904, Jacob G. Schurman, president of Cornell University, spoke in Montclair, New Jersey, at a celebration there recommending that the Philippine people were ready for independence. "Success and greatness" of a nation "are not a function of bigness of empire," he said, and asserted that maintaining the Philippines was not in the best interest of the United States. "It must be admitted that our present relation to the Philippine Islands is, in a measure, abnormal and jarring to our principles," he said. "I have always believed that the American people would treat the Filipinos as they have already treated the Cubans: help them to establish a Government which shall derive its powers from the consent of the governed, help them, in the majestic language of Jefferson, to assume among the powers of the earth the separate and equal station to which the laws of nature and nature's God entitle them."

President William Taft continued the

conversations about the Philippines on the Fourth of July when in 1910, he spoke in Boston at the Harvard Stadium before the **National Education Association**. He described the extension of the American form of government to the Philippines: "When the time shall arrive in which the Filipinos can be safely trusted to organize and maintain permanently their own Government, and this Government shall withdraw from the islands or offer to do so, the proposition of the Declaration of Independence will then have been fulfilled and the Government will be a just one, for it will rest on the consent of the governed."

On July 4, 1911, Manuel L. Quezon, resident commissioner of the Philippines, spoke on behalf of independence at the annual meeting of the Tammany Society in New York. "No nation can long endure having at the same time two opposite governmental institutions — one at home and another abroad," he said. "You cannot, without being untrue to yourselves, continue to celebrate, year after year, the Declaration of Independence, thus reaffirming its doctrines, and at the same time pursue a policy in the Philippines which is in flagrant contradiction with these doctrines."

Annually on the Fourth of July, Filipino veterans paid tribute to the United States. A 1927 event included fourteen thousand veterans led by General Emilio Aguinaldo.

Finally, on July 4, 1946, through executive proclamation (printed in the *New York Times*) by President Harry S Truman, the United States gave independence to the Philippines and the Republic of the Philippines was established. In the years that followed, the Philippines held several significant celebrations. On July 4, 1961, Manila staged one of its grandest Independence Day celebrations in honor of Gen. Douglas MacArthur. On July 4, 1971, Ambassador Henry A. Byroade unveiled a monument there that commemorated the destruction of American flags by U.S. personnel there twenty-nine years earlier so as to prevent the Japanese from finding them.

Sources: "Filipinos Listen to Amnesty Proclamation," *New York Times*, 5 July 1902, 7; "Schurman Urges Early Action on the Philippines," *New York Times*, 5 July 1904, 16; "Taft on the Philippines," *New York Times*, 5 July 1910, 13; "Democracy's Hopes Greet Tammany," *New York Times*, 5 July 1911, 5; "Filipino Rebels of 1899 Pay Tribute to U.S. Flag," *New York Herald Tribune*, 5 July 1927, 8; "Philippines Proclamation," *New York Times*, 5 July 1946, 5; *New York Times*, 5 July 1961, 1; *Los Angeles Times*, 5 July 1971, 1.

Phoenix, Arizona, fireworks explosion

Occurred on July 4, 1890, at the start of the fireworks when the first rocket set off the entire display "comprising some large and costly pieces." A general stampede took place and two persons were injured.

Source: "How Phoenix Celebrated," *Los Angeles Times*, 5 July 1890, 5.

"Photo of the Century"

On July 4, 1999, 112 people all born on the Fourth of July gathered in front of Independence Hall in Philadelphia for a "Photo of the Century," co-sponsored by Kodak.

Source: *Chicago Tribune*, 5 July 1999, 3.

Pickwick Club disaster, Boston

Cited as one of the worst disasters in Boston history, the building, the old five-story Hotel Drefus, in which the Pickwick Club was celebrating the nation's independence on July 4, 1925, collapsed. "Probably 100 to 200 persons were dancing in the club at the time of the collapse, which came just before 3 A.M." At least twelve persons died. The building was located in the China Town resort at 12 Beach Street.

Sources: "12 Known Dead, Others Trapped in Dance Hall Ruins," *New York Times*, 5 July 1925, 1–2; "12 Known Dead Found in Ruins of Boston Hotel," *Baltimore Sun*, 5 July 1925, 1, 12.

Pierce, Franklin (1804–1869)

Fourteenth president of the United States (1853–57). Pierce graduated from Bowdoin College in 1824, studied law, and rose through the political ranks first as a congressman (1833–37), then as a U.S. senator (1837–42). He served in the war with Mexico under Winfield Scott. Pierce was elected president in 1852, led a pro-slavery administration, and signed the **Kansas-Nebraska Act of 1854**, an action which resulted in negative reactions to him on Independence Day that year.

Pierce's contributions to the heritage of the Fourth were varied. On July 4, 1852, prior to his presidency, Pierce was in Boston with the Massachusetts Society of the Cincinnati drafting a resolution which honored the statesman **Henry Clay**, who had died a few days previous. On July 4, 1853, Pierce was in the White House writing a letter of acceptance for an invitation to attend the grand opening of the Crystal Palace in New York on July 15. On Independence Day in 1854, he entertained guests that included students of the Western Presbyterian Sabbath School. Later that evening he walked across Pennsylvania Avenue to Monument Square and viewed the fireworks there. Effigies of Pierce were burned in New England that day because of his signing of the Kansas-Nebraska Act. But in New York at a dinner ceremony held by the Tammany Society, John Cochrane, surveyor of the Port of New York, lauded Pierce. "Here, on this anniversary, amid the trophies of its past triumphs, and surrounded by the traditions of its ancient democratic days," Cochrane said, "the Society of Tammany takes him in her arms, and will bear him aloft in all his future career. He deserves well of his country, for the constancy and success with which he has advanced her true interests."

In 1855, Pierce and the first lady vacationed in Cape May, New Jersey, on the Fourth. After his presidency he was invited to attend the unveiling of a monument to Revolutionary War heroes in Chelmsford, Massachusetts, on July 4, 1859, but the event was postponed to September 22 of that year due to "unforeseen obstacles." Pierce was in Europe in July and forwarded his regrets in an eloquent letter in which he expressed his concerns for the future of the country. The "gallant, self-sacrificing men who achieved Independence," he said, were no longer living. He also wrote about the achievements of George Washington and his impact on his country. In addition, Pierce fondly recalled how "some eighteen officers and soldiers who served in the Revolution" sat assembled one day in 1824 "around my father's table" in his house.

On July 4, 1863, Pierce was in Concord, New Hampshire, where he addressed a crowd of 25,000 persons at a meeting of Democrats.

"He spoke warmly in favor of a restoration of the Union, and of peace, and against all ultra and arbitrary proceedings."

Sources: "The Massachusetts Society of Cincinnati and Henry Clay," *New York Times*, 7 July 1852, 1; *New York Times*, 7 July 1853, 4; "Independence Day," *New York Times*, 5 July 1854, 1; "Letter from Ex-President Pierce," *New York Times*, 9 July 1859, 8; *Alexandria Gazette*, 7 July 1863, 1.

Pierpont, John (1785–1866)

Popular poet whose work "Independence" (first line: "Day of Glory! Welcome Day!"), cited in the *North American Review* in 1829 as a "specimen of American poetry," was sung in Providence, Rhode Island, at the First Baptist Meeting House, on July 4, 1856.

Sources: "Specimens of American Poetry," *North American Review* 29/40 (October 1829): 495; *Oration Delivered Before the Municipal Authorities of the City of Providence by Jerome B. Kimball ...* (Providence: Knowles, Anthony Co., 1856).

Pike's Peak, Colorado

(Official spelling is Pikes Peak.) Popular site for spectacular and unusual Fourth of July events. One of the first was by George W. Altemus of Camden, New Jersey, who created a volcano-like effect by utilizing rockets and kerosene on the top of the mountain on July 4, 1890. A local newspaper reported that "the mountain has the appearance of an enormous volcano, vomiting forth an immense volume of fire, and rockets shooting in every direction, and the illumination can be seen for 100 miles in every direction when not cut off by clouds." A similar and much larger explosion was conducted on July 4, 1901, when fifteen barrels of oil and numerous containers of gasoline was ignited resulting in a "a fiery beacon, 500 feet long and blazing for hundreds of feet in the air." Part of the celebration that day was the unfurling of an American flag strung together by a set of kites, set aloft at an estimated altitude at 18,000 feet.

The idea for setting off explosives on the tops of mountains may have first been introduced on the nation's centennial in 1876. On July 4, explosions and rockets were set off simultaneously on Sugar Loaf Mountain and Mount Davidson, near Virginia City, Nevada. At Mount Davidson, five cords of firewood soaked in coal oil produced sixteen-foot flames. "The whole top of the mountain seemed on fire," one reporter noted. Another event took place on top of Mount Hood near Portland, Oregon, on July 4, 1885. A group attempted to set off an explosive device but failed when an avalanche took place and put out the fire. "If the party had remained half an hour longer, everyone must have been killed," said a reporter for a California newspaper.

Pike's Peak is also the site of the second-oldest automobile race in the U.S. held on the Fourth of July, with the first race occurring in 1916. "The 12.4-mile drive on dirt roads took them about a half-hour." The first time that an automobile was driven to the top of the mountain was on September 8, 1900, when Brisben Walker of New York performed the feat. On July 4, 1995, on the 73rd running, 149 entrants raced to beat the record of 10:04:06. In 1995, racing legend Bobby Unser believed the Pike's Peak race was more highly regarded than the Indianapolis 500.

Sources: "Bonfires and Fireworks," *Daily Territorial Enterprise*, 6 July 1876, 3; "An Avalanch on Mt. Hood," *Los Angeles Times*, 7 July 1885, 1; "On Pike's Peak," *Los Angeles Times*, 5 July 1890, 5; "John Brisben Walker's Feat," *New York Times*, 10 September 1900, 3; *Colorado Springs Gazette*, 3 July 1901, 8; "Pike's Peak Fiery Beacon," *New York Times*, 5 July 1901, 1; Marco R. della Cava, "Pikes, the Racer's Peak," *USA Today*, 3 July 1995, 1D.

Pittsburgh Pirates Baseball Park (Forbes Field)

The park opened on June 30, 1909, and the first Independence Day game was played a few days later. Located in the Schenley district, the park, owned by the Pittsburg Athletic Co., was designed by Charles W. Leavitt, Jr., of New York. The grandstand, cited as the largest in the world, seated thirty thousand persons and was 896 feet long and 95 feet deep. There were three tiers, "the two upper ones being reached by elevators," and all entrances and exits were accessed using inclines instead of steps. Twenty-eight rows of seats stretched along the first and third base sides.

Source: http://www.baseballalmanac.com/stadium/st_forbes2.shtml.

"Pledge of Allegiance"

First recited by children in public schools in 1892 and published that year in a children's magazine, *Youth's Companion*, the pledge was subsequently publicly recited on a number of Fourth of July celebrations. Some of the recitations included large audiences. On July 4, 1921, for example, everyone present at the Tammany Society meeting in New York recited the pledge. On July 4, 1927, at the Sylvan Theater on the Monument grounds in Washington, Judge Mary O'Toole led a large crowd in reciting the pledge. Some recitations were unusual, such at that on July 4, 1941, when the Pledge of Allegiance was spoken by Harland Fiske Stone, 11th Chief Justice of the U.S., from Estes Park, Colorado, by radio broadcast to millions of Americans. Standing with four World War veterans before a large American flag in front of the Stanley Hotel, Stone pledged his "allegiance to the flag of the United States of America" before several hundred persons. "It was a pulse-quickening moment. A vast unseen audience repeated the words pledging fealty to their flag. Afterward the Chief Justice repeated the pledge, with his immediate audience joining in."

The wording was expanded by the National Flag Conference, American Legion, in 1923–24 and Congress incorporated the pledge in the legislative code for the flag in 1942. In 1954, Congress added the words "under God." In 2002 atheist Michael Newdow, believing that the phrase "under God" violated the doctrine of "separation of church and state," attempted to have the courts declare the Pledge of Allegiance unconstitutional. What resulted was a renewed interest in and attention to the importance of the pledge. Many urged retention of the text as is. On July 4 of that year, in response to Newdow, President George W. Bush publicly recited the pledge in front of the Jackson County Courthouse in Ripley, West Virginia. His speech there also included a reference to the pledge. He said, "The people, when we pledge our allegiance to the flag, feel renewed respect and love it represents. And no authority of government can ever prevent an American from allegiance to this one nation under

God." And on that day at the Esplanade in Boston, with the accompaniment of the Boston Pops Esplanade Orchestra, Keith Lockhart conducting, eight-year-old Laurie Angela Hochman sang a musical arrangement she wrote of "The Pledge of Allegiance."

The text of the pledge: "I pledge allegiance to the flag of the United States of America and to the Republic for which it stands, one Nation under God, indivisible, with liberty and justice for all." See also **Sylvan Theater, Washington, D.C.**

Sources: "Tammany Observes Day with Oratory," *New York Times*, 5 July 1921, 2; "Program of Independence Day Celebration at Sylvan Theater," *Washington Post*, 4 July 1927, 2; *New York Times*, 5 July 1941, 6; Jeff Jacoby, "The Founders and God," *Boston Globe*, 4 July 2002, A11; "President Honors Veterans at Fourth of July Celebration," White House Web site, 5 July 2002; *Boston Herald*, 6 July 2002, 025.

Poetry

The tradition of celebrating Independence Day with poetry was established during the early republic. Verse was used to represent specific events, topics, and themes. Poems were often incorporated into Fourth of July oratory or presented as stand-alone pieces. Orators that inserted poetry in their addresses displayed their prowess as poets and created variety in their deliveries. When **George Washington Parke Custis** presented his Independence Day oration in 1825 at his Virginia mansion, "Arlington House," he reminded his audience that Lafayette's return to America (in 1824–25) finally brought attention and recognition to this patriot, a "beacon fire" whose glare "helped light the world to freedom":

Still in the paths of virtue to persevere,
From past or present it's despair,
For blessings ever wait on virtuous deeds,
And tho' a late, a sure reward succeeds.

Newspapers were a popular medium for publication and provided dissemination to larger audiences. Some poems were published anonymously. Typically some were described as "original" and composed specifically as a premiere reading for the Fourth. Much of the verse was written to glorify the rise of the republic, to exalt national patriotic sentiments, and to celebrate political achievements of national heroes.

Poetry of the late eighteenth century frequently reflected partisan political or simply personal views that exemplified mythical ideals, whereas throughout the nineteenth century, verse gradually reflected more nationalistic perspectives. One of the notable pieces of the period was Francis Hopkinson's "Ode for the 4th of July 1788" that heralded the rise of Columbia as America's muse and the importance of good government for a successful nation. Occasionally commemorative anthologies of Independence Day poetry were issued to aid those planning future celebrations. One of the first was *Patriotic Vocalist, or Fourth of July Pocket Companion: A Selection of Approved Songs, on National Subjects, for the Use of Public Assemblies, Celebrating the Anniversaries of American Independence, and Washington's Birth Day* (Salem, Massachusetts: 1812).

Common themes included American nationalism, divine providence of independence and freedom, national heroes, and the personification of mythical characters, such as the goddess Columbia. Wartime verse provided opportunities for poets to express their favor or rejection of war. Whereas a call "To fight, to die, but not to yield" published as an anonymous "Ode for the Fourth of July — 1812," which urged a call to arms against English atrocities, noted poet William Cullen Bryant in his Fourth of July *Odes* of 1814 and 1815 openly rejected the War of 1812. Social issues such as abolition, temperance, education, and unionism sparked new themes for aspiring poets. On July 4, 1831, the Rev. **Samuel Foster Gilman** of Charleston, South Carolina, had presented his "Union Ode" for the Union Party of South Carolina, which was reintroduced in 1864 as a piece representing "the civil war of secession."

A number of Independence Day poems were set to favorite tunes, such as "Anacreon in Heaven," "The President's March," and "Marseillaise," that in turn helped to popularize the verse. Among the most favorite and enduring poetry written included "Hail, Columbia" (Joseph Hopkinson), "The Star-Spangled Banner" (Francis Scott Key in 1814), and

"America" ("My country, 'Tis of Thee," S.F. Smith in 1832).

The last great body of poetry written for the Fourth was generated on the occasion of the 1876 **Centennial** celebration, when poets across America submitted numerous hymns, odes, and other verse for publication and recitation.

The latter twentieth century signaled a decline in popularity for poetry written expressly for the Fourth. According to Bernd Engler, poets frowned upon American nationalism and "expansionist interests that dominated the political agenda." Engler cites two examples of poems that express this disenchantment: E.E. Cummings' "next to of course god America i" (1968) and Robert Lowell's "Fourth of July in Maine" (1968).

Sources: *Maryland Gazette*, 28 July 1825, 2; *Harper's Weekly*, 9 July 1864; Bernd Engler, "Fourth of July Poetry, 1776–1876," in *The Fourth of July: Political Oratory and Literary Reactions 1776–1876*, 111.

Polk, James Knox (1795–1849)

Eleventh president of the U.S. (1845–49), who continued the tradition of opening the White House to the public on the Fourth of July and whose presence at the ceremony for the laying of the cornerstone of the Washington Monument on July 4, 1848, helped bring attention to the significance of creating this national icon. Polk was born in Mecklenburg County, North Carolina, and graduated from the University of North Carolina in 1818. He was a state legislator (1823–25), congressman (1825–39) and governor of Tennessee (1839–41). It was during Polk's administration that the Texas boundary dispute led to war with Mexico.

In 1845, Polk's first Fourth of July as president was spent in the Executive Mansion receiving guests, including a group of students from the Fourth Presbyterian Church. On July 4, 1846, he entertained over 400 Sabbath-school children, 250 boys and girls in the East Room and another 200 in the circular parlor. The latter group sang a hymn for the president. On Sunday, July 5, Polk attended divine worship in the Hall of the House of Representatives where he heard the Rev. Mr. Baker preach.

In June and July of 1847, Polk was touring in the northeastern states garnering support for the war. The most important event for Polk was his presence at the July 4, 1848, cornerstone ceremony for the **Washington Monument** in Washington, D.C.

Sources: "Fourth of July Celebrations in the City of Washington," *National Intelligencer*, 7 July 1845, 3; *Diary of James K. Polk*, ed. Milo Milton Quaife (Chicago: A.C. McClurg, 1910; reprint, New York: Kraus Reprint Co., 1970), 2:12.

Pontiac, Illinois fire

On July 4, 1874, a massive fire caused by a firecracker destroyed a major part of the town including the Phoenix Hotel, the Courthouse, "with all the records of the county, and the Union block, the finest in the town, containing seven large stores," consisting of several law firms, a furniture store, and hardware, grocery and clothing stores, at a total loss of $200,000.

Sources: "A Hotel, Court-House, and Business Burned by a Firecracker," *New York Times*, 6 July 1874, 1; "Illinois: Disastrous Fire at Pontiac," *Philadelphia Inquirer*, 6 July 1874, 1.

Port Jervis Soldiers' Monument, New York

This Civil War monument was unveiled at Orange Square in Port Jervis, New York, on July 5, 1886, with an audience of 15,000 in attendance. The monument, "constructed of Quincy granite, is 45 feet in height, contains 60 pieces, and weighs 60 tons." The firm of Frederick and Field of Quincy, Massachusetts, designed the monument, which is topped off by a statue of a soldier, sculpted by Edward King. "The statue represents a color bearer, holding in his left hand the American flag, while his right hand rests on his sword, which he is in the act of drawing from the scabbard." The celebration included an artillery salute, a parade of 3,000 men, and "ten or twelve brass bands and several drum corps." Lewis E. Carr of Albany presented an oration followed by the unveiling that was signaled by the tolling of the bell of Drew Methodist Episcopal Church. Another oration was presented by Gen. Stewart L. Woodford of Brooklyn and a poem read by Lieut. E.G. Fowler, editor of the *Orange County Farmer.* The celebration ended with military drills and fireworks.

Source: "In Honor of Her Soldiers," *New York Times,* 6 July 1886, 3.

Porter, David (1780–1843)

Naval officer and the first American minister to Turkey (1831–43), who had a monument to his honor unveiled in Constantinople on July 4, 1922. Porter was born in Boston, served as a midshipman on the USS *Constellation* in 1798, and was promoted to lieutenant in the following year. By 1812 he had been promoted to captain and had participated in the war with Tripoli (1803–05) and War of 1812. Porter was later appointed to the Navy Board in Washington, D.C., subsequently resumed active service in the navy, and was court-martialed for taking unauthorized military action in Puerto Rico. His suspension from duty prompted him to resign in 1826. Porter died in Constantinople.

The tablet noted that Mr. Porter was the first American representative to Turkey, and that he "carried out the negotiations leading to the ratification of the first treaty between the United States and Turkey." For the occasion Rear Admiral Bristol, commander of the U.S. naval forces in Turkish waters, and Gabriel Rayndal, American consul general at Constantinople, presented speeches.

Source: "Porter Tablet Unveiled," *New York Times,* 5 July 1922, 4.

Portland, Maine, fire

One of the worst fires ever to occur on Independence Day took place on July 4, 1866, in Portland. Almost half of this town of 30,000 was destroyed. Reports placed the blame on an errant firecracker or sparks from a locomotive in a pile of wood shavings in Deguio and Dyer's boat shop "between Commercial and Fore Streets." According to one report, the shop caught fire and very quickly "spread to Upham's flouring Mill, and thence to the sugar-house of John B. Brown & Sons. Then the flames were caught by some Irish huts at Graham's corner. Short work was made of these; and the fire, fed by a gale from the south, marched on, fighting its way through the principal retail business houses of the town

to the new City Hall. Every thing in its path was reduced to a smoking ruin." When it was over, the fire had consumed some 320 acres and destroyed 1500 structures, including the Athenaeum Library, the natural history museum, city hall, eight churches and many hotels. As many as 13,000 persons were left homeless. Ironically, the morning papers of July 4 had announced "that the pyrotechnic display of that evening would be of unusual magnificence, they did not foresee in what direful sense their prediction would be fulfilled before the day closed." In the following year on the Fourth of July, "being the first anniversary of the great fire," the day "passed very quietly," the use of fireworks being "almost totally dispensed with." An oration was presented at Congress-Square Church by the Rev. E.C. Bolles, and readings of the Declaration of Independence and the Emancipation Proclamation were given.

The 1866 fire in Portland was following by one near the city in 1893 when the Hotel Waldo, on Little Chebeague Island, was burned to the ground. The fire was believed to have been caused by a firecracker. All of the guests escaped without injury, although many lost all their clothes and other belongings.

By July 4, 1886, Portland was rebuilt and residents held a grand celebration on the 100th anniversary of its incorporation.

Sources: "The Portland Fire," *Harper's Weekly,* 28 July 1866, 465–66; "Portland," *Harper's Weekly,* 21 July 1866, 451; "Celebration at Portland, Me.," *New York Times,* 5 July 1867, 8; *The Daily Pioneer Press* (Saint Paul and Minneapolis), 5 July 1886, 1; Richard C. Ryder, "Portland's Fiery Fourth," in *American History Illustrated* 18/6 (October 1983): 10–19; *New York Times,* 5 July 1893, 9.

Portsmouth

A 20-gun sloop of war whose keel was laid on July 4, 1798, "a happy presage of supporting that independence on ocean," in Portsmouth, New Hampshire. "The *Portsmouth* was built of the best seasoned timber, under the direction of Colonel James Hacket, United States Naval Director and beneath the superintendance of Col. Thomas Thompson, agent of supplies." This copper bottomed vessel's dimensions were 93 feet keel and 31 feet beam. She was launched on October 11, 1798, and was placed under the command of Daniel McNeil from Boston, with Captain Richard Tibbets as first lieutenant. "John Adams, esq. of the *Revenue Cutter*, bade her welcome to old ocean by a federal discharge of sixteen guns; John Wardrobe, esq. of the private armed ship *Cato* returned the salute; and an immense concourse of attendant citizens manifested their pleasure by repeated huzzas." One of the important missions of the *Portsmouth* was that of bringing back to the United States the Treaty of Amity and Commerce with France in December 1800.

Sources: "Naval Architecture," *Porcupine's Gazette*, 24 October 1798; *Pennsylvania Gazette*, 17 December 1800.

Poughkeepsie, New York

A church in this town burned to the ground as a result of a firecracker "carelessly thrown by a boy."

Source: *Baltimore Sun*, 8 July 1843, 2.

"Power of Freedom"

The theme for the Houston, Texas, Independence Day celebrations in 2000 and 2001. The 2000 fireworks event, which drew an estimated 1 million spectators, was sponsored in part by Reliant Energy and was billed as "the last Independence day of the millennium." Included was a concert by the **Beach Boys**. Power of Freedom 2001 was sponsored by British Petroleum, and the Beach Boys returned in concert.

Sources: *Houston Chronicle*, 6 July 2000, A19, and 9 June 2001, A30.

Presidente Sarmiento

The training ship of the Argentine navy that fired a national salute on July 4, 1900, on the Hudson River near Grant's Tomb. The ship then steered up the Hudson River and anchored off Ardsley, where the officers of the vessel were entertained at dinner provided by Charles R. Flint at the Ardsley Club. Many distinguished officials attended, including the Argentine and Uruguay ministers to the United States, Charles S. Fairchild, ex-secretary of the U.S. Treasury, Gen. Griffin of West Point, and Gen. Benjamin F. Tracy, ex-secretary of the navy.

Source: "Notable Company at Dinner," *New York Times*, 5 July 1900, 9.

President's March see "Hail! Columbia"

Price, William (1755–1808)

In 1794 William Price hosted the first Fourth of July celebration southwest of the Alleghenies for forty Revolutionary soldiers at his home, five miles west of Nicholasville, Jessamine County, Kentucky. Price served in the Continental Army, first as a private; he later was promoted through the ranks to major. He took part in the battles of Brandywine, Germantown, Monmouth, and Princeton, and was at the surrender of Lord Cornwallis at Yorktown on October 19, 1781. The celebration included a dinner and general merriment. On the following day, in a letter Price had written to his friend Isaac Shelby, governor of Kentucky, he commented: "Throughout the limits of our country — from Massachusetts to Georgia — the hearts of a free and happy people have been dedicated on yesterday to the contemplation of the great blessings achieved and bequeathed to us by such heroic leaders as George Washington, Israel Putnam, and Nathaniel Green." On July 4, 1941, a marker was placed at the burial site of Price by the Trabue Chapter of the Daughters of the American Revolution.

A reenactment of the 1794 celebration was done by members of the Jessamine County Historical and Genealogical Society and descendants of Col. Price on July 4, 2002. According to Kathy Hall, a direct descendant of Col. Price, a bag-piper played "Amazing Grace" and a ceremony occurred at the Price marker. Revolutionary War re-enactors appeared in period dress, and a speech by Ron Bryant of the Kentucky State Historical Society brought attention to the patriotism of Price and the forty soldiers.

Sources: Sarah Johnston Price, "July 4th, 1794 in Jessamine County, Ky.," *Journal of American Antiques* (July 1949); Greg Kocher, "'We are Reminded': 1700's Jessamine Independence Gathering Re-Enacted," *Lexington Herald-Leader*, 5 July 2002, B1–B2.

Wreath laying ceremony, William Price gravesite, July 4, 2002. Col. Price held the first Independence Day celebration southwest of the Alleghenies on his farm near Clear Creek, five miles west of Nicholasville, Kentucky, in 1794. Photograph courtesy of Kathy W. Hall.

Princeton, New Jersey, centennial

This town celebrated the centennial anniversary of its incorporation on July 4, 1913, with a ceremony "in front of old Nassau Hall and an elaborate display of fireworks in Brokaw Field." The presiding officer for the day was Bayard Stockton, "a direct descendant of a signer of the Declaration of Independence." Major Gen. Alfred A. Woodhull read the Declaration of Independence and R.M. McElroy, professor of American history at Princeton University, presented the address. President Woodrow Wilson, who was invited to the affair but declined, sent a letter of regret with these words: "The stout little borough is to be congratulated upon its history of slow and peaceful development, and of growing distinction. Will you not convey to my friends and neighbors there greetings that come direct from my heart?"

Occasionally celebrations with fireworks and band concerts occurred on the grounds at Princeton such as that at Palmer Memorial Stadium on July 4, 1927.

Sources: "Princeton's Centenary," *New York Times*, 5 July 1913, 8; "Fireworks at Princeton," *New York Times*, 5 July 1927, 5.

Prisons

In the nineteenth and early twentieth centuries illustrious and unusual Fourth of July celebrations took place in penal institutions. The affairs were typically designed to help re-establish a sense of civility and function for an individual for his or her eventual return to society. Fostering national pride was also important in rehabilitating individuals into law-abiding citizens.

At the California State Penitentiary, on Independence Day in 1858, prisoners were permitted to run the grounds and the "ordinary labors of the day were suspended." They were treated as well to a "sumptuous repast" in a large room decorated with wreaths and garlands by the convicts. California governor John B. Weller presided over the affair and the Declaration of Independence was publicly read.

On July 4, 1859, a group of convicts and visitors at the District of Columbia penitentiary assembled in the prison's chapel for a celebration. The room was decorated with flowers and evergreens. A newspaper reported that in front of the audience

> [a]ppeared in handsome letters on a blue ground the motto: "We Still Love Our Country." In the rear of the visitors were the male convicts in their prison uniform of parti-colored white and blue clothes, and separated from them by a screen (punctured, however, with numerous "peepholes," showing the strength of feminine curiosity,) were the female convicts. Copies of a written programme with colored embellishments on the margin, bearing the names of "Washington," "Lafayette," "Montgomery," "Koscinsko," were distributed among the audience, and were carefully preserved and taken away by the recipients.

A group of five convicts sang the "Star-Spangled Banner" and convicted murderer C.H. Barrett read the Declaration of Independence. R. Smith, serving a conviction for forgery, gave an oration in which "he felt keenly the degradation which attached to him, but his fixed resolve was to hereafter redeem his good name." He ended "with an appeal to his fellow prisoners to aspire to a higher position, and urging upon them that to this end there was no surer means than the cultivation of true patriotism."

In Baltimore in 1876 the inmates of the penitentiary were treated to a "Centennial dinner." On Independence Day in 1882, an operatic company of forty performers calling themselves the "Summer Garden Concert Company" of the Academy of Music gave a concert there. Before an audience of 534 convicts and 250 invited guests, Lisetta Eilani sang the "Star-Spangled Banner." She "brought down the house" and "her powerful voice nearly took the roof off," one reporter noted. "She has made a hit in Baltimore, and everybody should go to the Academy and hear her."

In that same year at the Ohio state penitentiary in Juliet, Illinois, 1,500 convicts enjoyed performances by the Blaney Quartett Club of Chicago and the Braidwood Band. The Rev. James McLeod read the Declaration of Independence to the inmates and Mrs. H.S. Smith read a patriotic selection titled "The Rising of 1776," followed by a violin solo performed by William Lewis of the Chicago Musical College.

On July 4, 1920, Sing Sing penal institution in New York provided music by the Aurora band and chicken dinners to all of the inmates, including James O'Dell, "Bull" Casidy and twenty-one other men in the "death house."

On Independence Day in 1921 prisoners of the State Reformatory for Women in Bedford, New York, presented a patriotic play, "The Golden Star," for "residents of the countryside for miles around. The setting and the costumes were unique and pretty." Included was music by the Mount Kisco Band and "dancing for the prisoners."

In rare instances, prisoners were pardoned on Independence Day. On July 4, 1922, Governor John J. Blaine of Wisconsin announced in an address that he intended to "extend executive clemency to every man in Wisconsin prisons" who were incarcerated due "directly or indirectly" to causes borne out of service to the nation. "When I can take these boys out of prison and put them into colleges, I will be satisfied," he said. In the following year on the Fourth of July, Governor James C. Walton of Oklahoma awarded clemency to a number of convicts in his state and used the occasion to express his dislike for capital punishment.

Sources: "Holiday at the Penitentiary," *Daily Alta California*, 7 July 1858, 2; *Washington Evening Star*, 5

July 1859, 3; *Baltimore Bee*, 5 July 1876, 5; *Chicago Tribune*, 5 July 1876, 7; Parker LaMoore, "Band Plays As Walton Fires Defense Guns," *The Oklahoman*, 5 July 1923; "Gala Day at the Penitentiary," *Baltimore Morning Herald*, 5 July 1882, 4; "Prisoners Observe 4th," *New York Times*, 6 July 1920, 17; "Bedford Prisoners in Play," *New York Times*, 5 July 1921, 2; *New York Times*, 5 July 1922, 16.

Proctor, Thomas (fl. 1766–1778)

Director of the Regimental Band of Philadelphia, Colonel Proctor is believed to have supplied the music for the July 4, 1778, celebration held in the City Tavern for members of Congress and other dignitaries. Proctor was born in Ireland, and settled in Philadelphia not long before his marriage to Mary Fox in December 1766. Proctor was a house carpenter by trade and might have been the builder of the tavern. Among the eight guests entertained at the celebration were Samuel Holten, a delegate of Congress from Massachusetts, and Chief Justice Thomas McKean. By all accounts the band, which included "clarinets, haut-boys, French horns, violins and bass viols," was considered excellent.

Source: Sterling E. Murray, "Music and Dance in Philadelphia's City Tavern, 1773–1790," in *American Musical Life in Context and Practice to 1865* (New York: Garland Publishing, 1994), 10–11.

Prohibition

The period between 1920 and 1933 in which the Eighteenth Amendment (ratified January 29, 1919) of the Constitution banned the manufacture and sale of alcohol in the United States. The prohibition movement was an extension of nineteenth century temperance activities, as well as legislation adopted by states beginning in the 1850s that prohibited the sale of alcohol. During the 1890s, sites such as Prohibition Park on Staten Island, New York, gained renown for prohibition activities held there. Attendance of officials and other dignitaries, especially on the Fourth of July, was common. On July 4, 1893, for example, meetings of the National Prohibition Association were held in the auditorium there. Ex-governor John P. St. John of Kansas gave an oration that "combined patriotism and prohibition," as well as his sentiments regarding the national financial crisis.

A number of other organizations were instrumental in passing state laws and ultimately the constitutional amendment. Most of these associations were active on the Fourth of July. The Prohibition Party was organized in 1869 as a pro-temperance party with campaigns in national politics beginning in 1872. Candidates for president appeared in every campaign during the party's existence but never won any electoral votes. The Fourth of July was a popular occasion for speech-making by the party, sometimes drawing thousands. On July 4, 1894, over 5000 persons were present at Prohibition Park to hear ten speeches, in addition to a key-note oration by the Rev. Louis A. Banks of the Hanson Place Methodist Episcopal Church of Brooklyn. "He declared that the duty of the patriotic American was the destruction of the saloon. Saloons were the hotbeds of anarchy, and the government, in licensing saloons, was festering that which would overthrow Government." What is perhaps most noteworthy of this event is that two of the speeches were given by women — Mrs. Ella A. Boole and Mrs. Sarah A. Morris — which signaled the importance of women's involvement in the movement. Another significant organization was the Anti-Saloon League of America, founded by Howard Hyde Russell (1855–1946) and organized nationally in 1895.

In response to the passing of the Eighteenth Amendment, "anti-dry" associations were quickly organized to work towards a repeal of the legislation. For example, on July 4, 1921, the American Liberties League sponsored a demonstration and parade on Fifth Avenue in New York that included close to 15,000 marchers. "Slogans and mottoes, derisive of prohibition and calling for the restoration of wine and beer, were scattered in profusion all through the procession." One of the banners displayed "the Anti-Saloon League is getting groggy. Hand it the punch." There were also bands totaling 922 musicians that played such tunes as "How Dry I am," and "Hail, Hail, the Gang's All Here."

Enforcing Prohibition was difficult at best and on December 5, 1933, Congress passed the Twenty-first Amendment, repealing the

Eighteenth Amendment. See also **Temperance movement.**

Sources: "Prohibition Park Opening," *New York Times*, 5 July 1893, 4; "Prohibitionists Hear Speeches and Celebrate on Staten Island," *New York Times*, 5 July 1894, 8; "Fewer than 20,000 in Anti-Dry Parade," *New York Times*, 5 July 1921, 1–2.

"Psalm of Joy" *see* Salem, North Carolina

Puerto Rico

On July 4, 1927, the first Fourth of July celebration by Spanish veterans of 1898 in Puerto Rico occurred with a parade "headed by Capt. Angel Rivero, the last Spanish military governor of Porto Rico." Many of the Spanish veterans that fought in the war were reported to have become American citizens. "Capt. Rivero directed the firing of the last cannon of the San Juan batteries at American vessels."

On July 4, 1985, supported by the Puerto Rican Independence Party, large numbers of citizens demonstrated in San Juan for independence from the United States. Included in a parade of floats were pall-bearers marching with coffins representing those who had died in various wars. An envoy of President Reagan read a statement in the official San Juan parade: "Puerto Ricans, both on your beautiful island and on the mainland, continue to add special meaning to our way of life." See also **Winthrop, Beckman.**

Sources: *Washington Evening Star*, 5 July 1927, 9; "Puerto Ricans Demonstrate for Independence from U.S.," *New York Times*, 5 July 1985, A6.

Pullman Strike, Chicago

Occurred in early July 1894 in Chicago and eventually spread to 27 states as a boycott on Pullman cars by railroad workers. George Pullman, owner of the factory that produced the cars, had laid off workers and cut wages for others. Railroad traffic was greatly curtailed by the strike and when violence broke out, President Grover Cleveland selected July 4 to activate federal troops to counteract the railroad strikers, who were led by Eugene V. Debs, president of the American Railway Union. According to a newspaper report on Indepen-

dence Day, "With rifles leveled and revolvers drawn, half of the Second Battalion Fifteenth Regiment, United States Infantry, proceeded through a dense mob of more than 5000 men, boys, women, and children to their camp in the stock yards today." Debs responded to a United Press reporter regarding Cleveland's actions: "The first shot fired by the regular soldiers at the mobs here will be the signal for a civil war. Bloodshed will follow, and 90 percent of the people of the United States will be arrayed against the other 10 percent. I would not care to be arrayed against the laboring people in the contest, or find myself out of the ranks of labor when the struggle ended. I do not say this as an alarmist, but calmly and thoughtfully." The strike was over when Debs was jailed for contempt.

Sources: "Bayonets Subdue Strikers" and "Debs Wildly Talks Civil War," *New York Times*, 5 July 1894, 1–2; "The Fourth since 1776," *Life*, 7 July 1947, 14–16.

Pyro Spectaculars

One of the largest fireworks display companies in America, founded in Oakland, California, 100 years ago by the Souza family, whose founding patriarch, Manuel de Sousa, lost an arm to exploding fireworks. Sousa, who later changed his name to Souza, left the Azores in 1879 and for a time worked in the cane fields of Hawaii before coming to California to establish his fireworks company. In 1933 he mistakenly picked up a live shell, which exploded, and later lost his arm as a result of blood poisoning. Pyro Spectaculars is responsible for hundreds of shows each year. The San Francisco display is one of the largest shows they manage. In 1995 they first provided pyrotechnics for the Capitol Fourth show in Washington, D.C. In 1996, for the first time in the history of fireworks in that city, Pyro's fireworks were choreographed to "accent a medley of patriotic tunes played through loudspeakers and broadcast on radio." The 25-minute show concluded with a 5-minute arrangement of the "Star Spangled Banner."

Sources: Philip P. Pan, "Fireworks Show to Burst with Patriotic Song," *Washington Post*, 4 July 1996, B3; Kenneth Howe, "Firework's Firms Family Affair," *San Francisco Chronicle*, 4 July 1997, C1.

Pyrotechnic displays

Official fireworks sponsored by local towns and municipalities required the services of pyrotechnics experts to plan and mount unusual displays to satisfy the need for Americans to enjoy an audio-visual experience on the Fourth. By the late nineteenth century these displays were common in most communities. They helped to provide an alternative for those who had the urge to set off noisy and dangerous explosives on city streets. According to newspaper descriptions of events, it was the set pieces that drew the most appeal to spectators. These displays, carefully mounted on wooden stands and platforms, ranged from petite exhibits to large displays hundreds of feet in length. Popular visual elements included images of heroic figures and popular phrases and mottoes spelled out in various patriotic colors. Typically each display was given a descriptive name by the pyrotechnist to reflect the intention of the exhibit. Toward the end of the nineteenth century, set pieces for displays were gradually replaced by sky fireworks.

Nineteenth century displays were colorful and exciting to watch. In Charleston, South Carolina, on July 4, 1828, fireworks, exhibited at the Tivoli Garden, included "rockets and shells, ornamented with stars." There were "mosaic roses" concluding with "a grand transparency of Gen. Andrew Jackson, surrounded with brilliant suns, stars, etc." On July 4, 1865, in Washington, D.C., three hundred rockets were set off on the grounds south of the White House, and colorful set displays included "Pyramid of Serpents," "Cross of Honor," "National Coat of Arms," and other displays named after Lincoln and Washington. On July 4, 1853, at the White Point Garden in Charleston, South Carolina, the fireworks "consisted of flights of rockets, shells ornamented with colored stars and serpents, wheel-rockets, sun pieces, pyramids of roman candles, brilliant stars, fly wheels, mosaic roses ... [and] the temple of liberty 35 feet high arched with stars supported with handsome columns, surmounted by the American Eagle and United States coat of Arms."

New York and Boston had some of the best and most exciting and elaborate pyrotechnic displays. In New York the city's Common Council annually allotted a sum of money to be distributed for the displays presented in the various city parks. Pyrotechnic firms submitted their bids to a Committee of Arrangements that selected the firms based on the best programs. For example, for the 1862 celebration, the Common Council provided $6000 to fund 18 separate fireworks displays. The City Hall display was considered the most important and had the most money provided, at $950. Joseph G. Edge and Isaac A. Edge's "Programme of Arrangements," advertised by the brothers, which promised that the fireworks would "equal, if it does not surpass anything of the kind ever attempted in this City." To add to the evening festivities, Connell's Band was engaged to play favorite melodies as an accompaniment to the fireworks. Although sky displays were as popular as they are today, it was the set pieces placed on specially made platforms and stands that highlighted the pyrotechnist's skill and drew the largest crowds of spectators.

On July 4, 1852, one of the largest displays prior to the Civil War occurred in Boston on the Common when a "National Tableau," 275 feet long and 80 feet tall, was ignited. Depicted was a statue of the Goddess of Liberty, the word "liberty," the seal of the United States, thirty-one stars, "names of battles and Revolutionary War heroes," with 500 rockets exploding.

For the Fourth in 1854 in New York a display of "the Goddess of Liberty crowning George Washington, with a Mosaic Battery on each side" was considered a chef-d'oeuvre of pyrotechnic skill. In 1858 also in New York "standing pieces" included a "piece consisting of two wheels, revolving in contrary directions" which in the center "was suddenly filled with globes of colored fires," and a piece titled "The Shield of the Union," which was described as "a brilliant wheel of various fires, with crimson and yellow rosettes" with a center piece having the word "'Union' each letter enclosed by a shield." The most "superb" piece exhibited was "The Triumph of America," described as "sixty feet and one hundred feet in length":

It commenced with a wheel of Maltese rayounaut and jessamine fires, with centre of colored lancework, the whole being encircled by an arc composed of shields, eagles, stars, and other emblems of the Union, and surrounded by the coat of arms of the United States. On each side of this centre were kaleidoscopes with revolving centres, the whole terminating with a grand flight of rockets, bombs, mines, Roman candles, etc.

For the Fourth in 1886 in Los Angeles, the municipal fireworks' main attractions were the set pieces. One was a "July 4th" with adjacent "exploding batteries." Another was "the national emblem, in the form of a shield, in red, white and blue, flanked on the left by the emblematic scales of Justice" and the final piece was twenty feet long and twelve feet high and depicted a

> life-size bear with open mouth; on the left the Goddess of Liberty; an honest miner swinging a pick next on the right, which was also flanked on the right by the American eagle, with spread wings; over the eagle appeared in large figures, "1886," and extended beneath the whole appeared the words "Good Night."

From the twentieth century to the present, pyrotechnic displays became highly organized extravaganzas utilizing developing technology to introduce new and more elaborate effects. Today fireworks firms such as Firepower Displays Unlimited, **Pyro Spectaculars**, **Fireworks by Grucci**, and **Zambelli Fireworks Internationale** use laptop computers to set off displays, and computer chips embedded in shells help time the explosions in milliseconds. Shows can be previewed on computers using special software, and fireworks can be precisely timed to the accompaniment of music. Firms have also introduced new color combinations in addition to the more traditional red, white, and blue. It is little wonder that these shows continue to draw tens of thousands each year and that this spectacular entertainment is likely to continue for years to come.

Sources: *Charleston Courier*, 4 July 1828, 3; *Daily Morning Chronicle*, 6 July 1865, 4; "Independence Day," *Liberator*, 2 July 1852, 106, as reported in Branham and Hartnett, *Sweet Freedom's Song*, 98–99; *Charleston Mercury*, 6 July 1853, 2; "The Fire Works," *New York Times*, 5 July 1854, 1, and 6 July 1858, 1; *New York Times*, 4 July 1862, 6; "The Fourth," *Los Angeles Times*, 6 July 1886, 4; David Ovalle, "Fireworks Become More High-Tech to Spark Crowds," *Miami Herald*, 4 July 2005, B1–B2.

Pyrotechnics and fireworks accidents

The manufacture, transportation, and sale of fireworks have always posed a serious threat to communities across the nation. Not only has the careless use of explosives caused innumerable deaths and injuries, but there has also been extensive destruction of property due to fires ignited by fireworks. The laws enacted during the nineteenth century to curb the use of dangerous fireworks were largely ignored. An editorial in a New York newspaper in 1850 reflected the seriousness of the matter:

> During the 4th the little boys seems to feel that they had an unlimited license to do just whatever they pleased and many of them took particular pleasure in exploding fire crackers and pistols in the faces of ladies, by way of startling them. This practice ought to be suppressed.

In Geneva, New York, on July 4, 1842, an unfortunate accident occurred after the usual ceremonies of the day were over. A large group of persons had assembled "at the head of Seneca street, and in front of the bank" to witness the fireworks. "Rockets had been provided, some of them of a very large kind; weighing as was said, six pounds." After four or five had been discharged, a spark of fire ignited the box containing the other rockets and fireworks. "The rockets lying in a horizontal position, flew of course in the same direction; and the staging was of such a height as gave them a direction the most destructive to human life. At least one individual was killed and eight others seriously wounded."

The first major Independence Day accident in Washington, D.C., occurred in 1845 when two persons were killed when a stand of rockets fell over after they had been ignited. Another serious explosion took place on the Boston Common on July 4, 1857, when a mortar used for throwing shell rockets exploded, killing four persons and wounding several others. Among the dead was 49-year-old George P. Tewksbury, harbor master for the port of

Fireworks on the night of the Fourth of July, drawn by Winslow Homer. Shown is an errant rocket landing on the head of a spectator, an acknowledgment of the danger of pyrotechnic displays at that time. *Harper's Weekly*, 11 July 1868. Image courtesy of HarpWeek, LLC.

Boston "and most estimable and worthy citizen." Tewksbury left a wife, three sons, and four daughters. It was reported that a young man named Patrick Cook, employed by Hovey and Co., lit the fuse causing the explosion.

The igniting of fires from lit firecrackers was another serious concern. In some localities ordinances were enacted to deal with this problem. For Independence Day in 1868, Brooklyn, New York, outlawed the use of all explosives "within the fire district" except for authorized fireworks displays and artillery salutes in military parades. Notwithstanding laws such as this, each year numerous fires resulted from the use of fireworks near buildings. In 1893 it was reported that "The greatest danger with firecrackers in the tenement house neighborhoods is at night, when the boys explode them from the windows or drop them into the street from the roof."

After the Civil War concerns about the deaths and injuries inflicted through the use of fireworks continued. An editorial in the *Baltimore Morning Herald* on July 4, 1879, summarized the problem and issued this warning:

> This day will be fraught with danger to life and property from fire, and it is to be hoped that each individual in the city will make it a point, as far as in his power, to restrain the use of firearms and fire-crackers, that the loss of life and property may as far as possible be averted. The "boys" are prepared to shoot off their own fingers and hands, and to put all other people in danger as part of their way of celebrating the "Glorious Fourth." Last year's stock of pistols have again found their way into juvenile pockets, and before the week is out the news columns of the various papers will show the usual number of mutilated limbs, blinded eyes and probable loss of lives.

An article titled "The Dark Side of the Day," published in the *New York Times* in 1882, indicated by the fatalities and injuries listed that most of the casualties were youths.

On July 4, 1910, at West Side Park in Newark, New Jersey, about 10,000 persons were "watching a city fireworks display when an iron mortar which was being used for the firing of bombs burst, sending pieces of iron hurling through the crowd. Several persons were injured."

On July 4, 1951, in Cheviot, Ohio, an aerial bomb exploded among spectators injuring fifteen persons. "The bomb was described as a triple-exploding type and witnesses said it broke apart in the air and the largest charge fell or was blown into part of the crowd sitting on a hillside." On Independence Day in 1974 at the popular Wolf Trap Farm Park just outside Washington and near Reston, Virginia, a box of fireworks exploded, injuring three persons.

Sources: "The Fourth—Melancholy Casualty," *Alexandria Gazette*, 12 July 1842, 3; *National Intelligencer*, 9 July 1845, 3; *New York Herald*, 6 July 1850, 1; *New York Times*, 7 July 1857, 5; "The Preparations in Brooklyn," *New York Times*, 4 July 1868, 8; *Baltimore Morning Herald*, 4 July 1879, 2; "The Dark Side of the Day," *New York Times*, 5 July 1882, 5; *New York Times*, 5 July 1893, 4, and 5 July 1910, 8; "15 Hurt at Public Fireworks," *New York Times*, 5 July 1951, 25; "Wolf Trap Farm Fireworks Hurt 3," *Washington Post*, 5 July 1974, A1, A9.

Quakers

The first group to express their dissent on the Fourth of July. During the first organized celebration of the Fourth of July in Philadelphia in 1777, the Quakers generally expressed their opposition to the celebration of the event by not illuminating their windows, a popular aspect of ritual that year.

An unusual ceremony that took place by Quakers on the Fourth of July occurred on July 4, 1917, on the meeting house grounds at Tower Hill, South Kingstown, Rhode Island, when a "tablet to the memory of Friends" was unveiled. Caroline Hazard (1856–1945) presented an address at the ceremony.

Sources: "Address at the Unveiling of a Tablet to the Memory of Friends on the Meeting House Grounds on Tower Hill, July 4, 1917" (unpublished manuscript; copy in Rhode Island Historical Society Library); Travers, *Celebrating the Fourth*, 23.

Quincy, Illinois, Court House

On July 4, 1876, the cornerstone of the New Court House was laid with "Masonic ceremonies, conducted by grand master Loundsburg." The event included a parade with three military companies, followed that evening by fireworks.

Sources: "Quincy," *Chicago Tribune*, 5 July 1876, 7; "At Quincy, Ill," *St. Louis Globe-Democrat*, 5 July 1876, 8; *Washington Evening Star*, 5 July 1876, 7.

Quinney, John Wannuaucon (1797–1855)

Stockbridge Mohican tribal leader who presented an Independence Day address in Reidsville, New York, in 1854. Quinney was born on the New Stockbridge reservation near Oneida, New York. He attended the English school of Caleb Underhill at Yorktown, New York (1810–13) under the sponsorship of the U.S. government. His leadership abilities propelled him to overseer of the tribe. When the tribe decided to migrate west before the War of 1812, Quinney handled all the business, first by working towards obtaining land in Wisconsin, near Green Bay, and negotiating land rights and values with the New York legislature in 1825 and the federal government in Washington. For thirty years, he fought on behalf of his tribe to obtain a permanent home for them and to secure tribal ownership of the land in Wisconsin. Finally in 1856, after his death, federal officials through "deception" and the "crude use of whiskey" designated a tribal home near Bowler.

In 1854 Quinney became a U.S. citizen, nevertheless still declaring himself a "Native American," the first such use of the phrase to represent North American Indians. His Fourth of July speech that year described the history of the Muh-he-con-new nation and its decline and claimed that it had been mistreated by the government:

What are the treaties of the general Government? How often and when has its plighted faith been kept? Indian occupation forever is next year, or by the next Commissioner, more wise than his predecessor, re-purchased. One removal follows another, and thus your sympathies and justice are evinced in speedily fulfilling the terrible destinies of our race.... These events are above our comprehension, and for a wise purpose. For myself and for my tribe I ask for justice—I believe it will sooner or later occur—and may the Great and Good Spirit enable me to die in hope.

Sources: John W. Quinney, "Celebration of the Fourth of July, 1854, at Reidsville, New York ... ," State Historical Society of Wisconsin *Report and Collections* 4 (1859): 313–20; David R. Wrone, "John Waun-Nau-Con Quinney," *American National Biography*, 18:45–46; "Independence Day Speech (1854)," *The American Studies Anthology*, ed. Richard P. Horwitz (Wilmington, Del.: Scholarly Resources, 2001), 77–82.

Quincy, Josiah (1772–1864)

Congressman, mayor of Boston, and president of Harvard who had the distinction of presenting two Fourth of July orations in Boston exactly fifty years apart: in 1798 and in 1848. Quincy was born in Boston, graduated from Harvard in 1790, briefly practiced law, and was elected to Congress in 1804, where he served until 1813. In 1823, he was elected mayor of Boston and devoted the next five years to improving all aspects of the city, including fire safety, garbage removal, and urban renewal. According to Robert A. Mc-Caughey, Quincy "left Boston the cleanest, most orderly and best governed city in the United States." From 1829 to 1845, Quincy was president of Harvard University and was successful in his efforts towards improving the curriculum and faculty. Quincy died on July 1 and, fittingly, the *New York Daily Tribune* published his obituary on the front page of its Independence Day issue.

Sources: *Boston Daily Advertiser*, 6 July 1848, 2; Robert A. McCaughey, *Josiah Quincy (1772–1864): The Last Federalist* (Cambridge, Mass., Harvard University Press, 1974), and "Josiah Quincy," *American National Biography*, 18:37–39.

Quincy, Massachusetts, centennial

Celebrated its 100th anniversary on July 4, 1892. Large crowds gathered to witness a parade of local organizations and associations. **Charles Francis Adams, Jr.** delivered the oration in the First Church. Later that day a banquet took place in the Robertson House and 100-gun salutes were fired at sunrise and sunset.

Source: "Quincy's Centenary," *New York Times*, 5 July 1892, 1.

Radio broadcasts

With the advent of radio, politicians, presidents, and others recognized this medium as a significant venue for reaching a mass pop-ulation across a wide geographical area on the Fourth of July. Radio provided the opportunity for many to share the moment together and to hear programs that were produced especially for the occasion. By the early 1920s many stations in a number of cities were programming a wide variety of shows. On July 4, 1923, from New York, WEAF broadcast the entire New York Tammany celebration, which included speeches and music. WJZ, also in New York, had a "Patriotic program by Sons of the American Revolution." Springfield, Massachusetts, residents heard a "Patriotic Address" on WBZ and a similar address was broadcast over KDKA in Pittsburgh. In the following year on the Fourth, KFI in Los Angeles broadcast a "Patriotic Concert" and WMC Memphis and WSQJ in Chicago both provided Independence Day programs. On July 4, 1926, station WGN in Chicago broadcast the voices of four presidents — Theodore Roosevelt, Warren G. Harding, Woodrow Wilson and William Howard Taft — from recordings made of "important speeches." The addresses focused on labor, farming, and the death of American soldiers in World War I. On July 4, 1927, a "radio concert," the first of its kind, took place in Baltimore. Broadcast over WBAL, the Baltimore Parks Symphony Orchestra and the Municipal Band performed popular patriotic works to a crowd of 8,500 at Patterson Park.

The 1930s and '40s also witnessed significant broadcasts. On July 4, 1931, on the 100th anniversary of the death of President James Monroe, the centennial celebration was broadcast over station WJZ from the University of Virginia. Other events broadcast that day included the dedication of Fort Nonsense Park in Jockey Hollow, near Morristown, New Jersey, over WOR; "a dramatic narrative by Edgar White Burrill," with patriotic music, over WEAF; an address by Assistant Secretary of State James Grafton Rogers over WABC; the ceremony at Tammany Hall over WOR, WABC, and WNYC; and the event at Independence Hall over WABC.

In 1941 Wendell L. Willkie, presidential candidate of the Republican Party in 1940, broadcast an Independence Day address over NBC. He described the national sentiment:

All over America people are gathered in city, in village and in town, celebrating the Fourth of July, which is America's patriotic holiday. Speakers are telling of our heroic past, reciting the deeds, the gallant deeds, of our soldiers, recalling to our people our long struggle for liberty and the developments of our free system. Songs are being sung, songs that move the hearts of men. Prayers are being offered all over America.

Franklin Roosevelt was the first president to reach a national audience by way of radio on the Fourth of July. In 1936, he broadcast his Independence Day address over WABC radio from Monticello, Thomas Jefferson's estate. He explained to all Americans who heard him that day how the courage and vision that Jefferson and the other founders of the republic had still held true in the modern age of the twentieth century. On July 4, 1941, he broadcast another address from the Roosevelt Library at Hyde Park, New York. Another radio address in that decade included one titled "Oh! Say, Can You See ..." by Frank Kingdon, educator and author, over WOR in New York on July 4, 1943. Throughout the years patriotic music was a popular feature of these broadcasts. For example, on July 4, 1952, New York radio station WQXR broadcast music by American composers throughout the day.

With the introduction of television during the late 1940s, radio began sharing the airwaves for the distribution of both live and recorded broadcasts of Fourth events. On July 5–6, 1975, an "American Profile" series of 30 broadcast spots on the nation's history was sponsored by WTOP radio in Washington, D.C. Each spot was 4–10 minutes in length and focused on a range of individuals such as Thomas Jefferson, James Howe, a Tory spy, and Elizabeth Loring, supposed mistress of the British general William Howe.

In 2003 XM Satellite Radio provided the first exclusive national broadcast through this medium on the Fourth of July. Listeners throughout the nation, if not the world, heard Willie Nelson's 30th anniversary Fourth of July family picnic weekend concert. See also "Salute to America."

Sources: "Today's Radio Program," *New York Times*, 4 July 1923 and 1924, 23 and 23, respectively;

"Voices of Four Ex-Presidents to Go on the Radio Tonight," *New York Times*, 4 July 1926, 1; "8,500 at First Radio Concert of Kind in Baltimore Park," *Baltimore Sun*, 4 July 1927, 16; "A Glorious Fourth on the Air," *New York Times*, 28 June 1931, 29; *New York Times*, 4 July 1931, 3; Wendell L. Willkie, "The Significance of Independence Day: The Meaning of American Liberty," *Vital Speeches of the Day* 7/20 (1 August 1941): 617–18; Frank Kingdon, "Oh! Say, Can You See...," *Vital Speeches of the Day* 9/21 (15 August 1943): 654–55; *New York Times*, 4 July 1952, L15; Jean M. White, "American History 'Updated,'" *Washington Post*, 5 July 1975, B8; "XM to Air First Ever National Radio Broadcast of Willie Nelson's July 4th Picnic Concert," press release, XM Radio, 20 December 2003.

Raleigh, North Carolina, State Capitol

The cornerstone of the "new State Capitol" was laid on July 4, 1833, "on the ruins" of the building that had been destroyed by fire two years prior. The ceremony included a parade from the Government House to Capitol Square, an artillery salute, a reception, and addresses by S.J. Baker, grand master of the Grand Lodge of the State, Judge Seawell, and Governor David L. Swain, who said to his audience,

What an incentive to the Statesmen of our Country in all future times, do such memorials afford, to attempt something worthy of themselves and their Sires! Their fathers secured for them the enjoyment of rational liberty. Will they not transmit their privileges unimpaired to posterity? Their fathers laid the foundation of future greatness, and will not their children enlarge, improve, complete the noble structure? I trust, we do not assume too much, when we answer, confidently and proudly, that they will — when we proclaim that North Carolina is true to herself, and her sons emulous of their ancestral glory; that the listlessness with which she seems for a season to have been surrounded is dispelled, and that her citizens will make a strenuous, a united, a successful effort to develop her resources, and promote her prosperity.

Source: "Fourth of July Incidents: At Raleigh, N.C.," *National Intelligencer*, 13 July 1833, 3.

Ramsay, David (1749–1815)

Historian and politician who was the first to give a Fourth of July oration, on July 4, 1778, in Charleston, South Carolina. Ramsay was born in Lancaster County, Pennsylvania, and graduated from the College of New Jersey (now Princeton University). In 1773 he moved to Charleston, where he established a medical practice and was involved in political activities that supported the anti-British movement. His views about independence were shaped through his vision of a nation having a unique cultural identity and political framework. His Fourth of July oration served as a summation of his thoughts on the future of the United States and was one of the first works to encourage a national consciousness.

A local newspaper summarized Ramsay's oration and noted "the many advantages resulting from Independence, the superiority the citizens of a free republick enjoy over the subjects of a despotick monarchy, and the prospects of the arts and sciences being soon cultivated with unexampled ardour in this western world." Ramsay's piece expanded on the rationale for independence spelled out in the Declaration of Independence by the founding fathers and prophetically, if not brilliantly, proclaimed the possibilities and dreams of the new nation. With patriotic fervor, he predicted correctly that the independence of the new nation would encourage immigration: "Where life, liberty, and property are well secured, and where land is easily and cheaply obtained, the natural increase of people will much exceed all European calculations." He correctly predicted the growth of the arts in America; with the encouragement of "the free governments of America," "there will be poets, orators, criticks, and historians, equal to the most celebrated of the ancient commonwealths of Greece and Italy." Moreover, "the arts and sciences ... will spread far and wide, till they have reached the remotest parts of this untutored continent." He correctly understood how the international stature of the new nation would be achieved. International commerce would be promoted, Ramsay said, and our ships would "ride triumphant on the ocean, and to carry American thunder around the world." Equally important about this oration was that it was delivered in the South, providing a key patriotic statement from this region of the country.

Ramsay's role as a historian and supporter of American nationalism was reflected in his monumental *History of the American Revolution* (1789), published in six editions, and his *History of South Carolina* (1809). According to Arthur Shaffer, "these two works stood as prototypes for Ramsay's generation, and he became the nation's most respected historian and one of its premier literary figures."

Ramsay delivered another oration in St. Michael's Church in 1794 for the citizens of Charleston and members of the American Revolution Society of which he was a member, and the State Society of Cincinnati. In this address, Ramsay told how he delivered the first oration in the United States sixteen years before. He laid out in some detail how successful the country had been thus far as independence unveiled itself and also urged its citizens that there was still much to be done. "Industry, frugality and temperance, are virtues which we should eminently cultivate." Of significance also about this oration is that Ramsay sensed the events of the Revolutionary War period as becoming distant in time and memory. The older generation was dying off and it was now up to the next generation to carry forth the spirit and strength. "Many of those tried friends, who bravely fought our battles, or who wisely conducted our civil affairs, through the late revolution, have taken their leave of this earthly stage, and a new generation has nearly grown up in their places. On them it depends to finish what their fathers have begun."

Sources: *South Carolina and American Gazette*, 9 July 1778; David Ramsay, *An Oration on the Advantages of American Independence* (Charlestown: John Wells, Jr., 1778); *An Oration Delivered in St. Michael's Church ...* (Charleston: W.P. Young, 1794); "Cincinnati," *Columbian Herald*, 2 July 1794, 4; Robert L. Brunhouse, ed., "David Ramsay, 1749–1815: Selections from His Writings," *Transactions of the American Philosophical Society* 55/4 (1965): 1–250; Arthur H. Shaffer, *To Be an American: David Ramsay and the Making of the American Consciousness* (Columbia: University of South Carolina Press, 1991); Arthur Shaffer, "David Ramsay," *American National Biography*, 18:93–94.

Randalls Island, New York

Named for its owner Jonathan Randall after the Revolutionary War, the island is part of Manhattan and consists of 195 acres. After Randall's death in 1830, the city purchased the land and used it for a children's reformatory called the House of Refuge and the Idiots' and Children's Hospital. Annually, Fourth of July celebrations were held there as a means for developing a sense of patriotism and civic responsibility in the young children. Many celebrations were sponsored by various groups and associations from New York and elsewhere. On July 4, 1853, the Mechanical Fire Company of Baltimore participated in the celebration and presented a silk American flag to the children. "The ceremony took place on a platform, erected in a shady grove on the northwest point of the Island." Ralph Trembly, representing the Columbia Engine Co. of New York, spoke to the boys and girls about the flag and encouraged them, "when occasion required, be found ready to rally round and defend it."

At the 1858 Fourth of July celebration, "350 children were plentifully fed with roast beef and its necessary concomitants, and then regaled with the allowance of oranges, candies, and the indispensable peanuts usual on this festive anniversary." One of the young students was "dressed in full military costume" and he "delivered a patriotic speech commendable for its brevity."

Sources: "The Boys of Randall's Island — Banner Presentation," *New York Times*, 6 July 1853, 2; "The Fourth at the Institutions," *New York Times*, 6 July 1858, 1; Gerard R. Wolfe, "Randalls Island," in *The Encyclopedia of New York City*, 985.

Randolph-Macon Academy

Formally dedicated on July 4, 1890, at Bedford City, Virginia. This school served as a preparatory academy to Randolph-Macon College and was the initiative of W.W. Smith, president of the college. "The buildings are conceded by experts to be the most perfectly equipped schools in the United States, the design being the result of a prize contest between six Northern architects. They are fitted with the most perfect sanitary arrangements, lighted with Edison electric light throughout, and contains a large gymnasium with Sargent apparatus." Eighty newspaper reporters were at the ceremony, as were many distinguished persons, including "Govs. [E. E.] Jackson, Gordon," and Philip W. McKinney (Virginia), and ex-governor Fitzhugh Lee (Virginia). United States senators Alfred H. Colquitt (Georgia) and John W. Daniel (Virginia) "were on the programme, but were unavoidably kept away by pressing business of State." Also present were representatives from Johns Hopkins University, Washington and Lee, Emory and Henry College, Richmond College, the University of Virginia, and Vanderbilt University. "Dr. Moses D. Hoge of Richmond, in the absence of Bishop Wilson, delivered the dedication address, which was strong and eloquent."

Source: "Randolph-Macon Academy," *New York Times*, 5 July 1890, 2.

Reagan, Ronald (1911–2004)

Fortieth president of the U.S., who participated in various noteworthy Fourth of July events. Reagan was born in Tampico, Illinois. His early career years were spent as a radio sports announcer and then Hollywood actor. He starred in numerous films and was elected president of the Screen Actors Guild. He was elected governor of California and served from 1967 to 1975, followed by two terms as U.S. president, 1981–89. On July 4, 1982, the president was at Edwards Air Force Base in California, where he welcomed astronauts Thomas K. Mattingly and Henry W. Hartsfield, who had returned from space that day aboard the shuttle *Columbia*. "They reaffirmed to all of us that as long as there are frontiers to be explored and conquered, American will lead the way," he said during a ten-minute address.

In 1983, President Reagan issued an Independence Day statement in which he said, "It's always been my belief that by a divine plan this nation was placed between the two oceans to be sought out, and found by those with a special brand of courage and love of freedom. America is still a land of heroes with all the courage and love of freedom there ever was before. And that's our best hope for the future."

On July 4, 1984, Reagan was in Daytona Beach, Florida, at the Firecracker 400 stock car race. It was at this event that Richard Petty won his 200th Cup victory. Reagan also attended a "Spirit of America" picnic that day in Dacatur, Alabama, where he spoke to campaign workers.

Sources: *Washington Post*, 5 July 1981, 1; "Pinpoint Landing for Shuttle," *Washington Post*, 5 July 1982, A1; "Answers About U.S. for This Fourth Day of July," *Washington Post*, 4 July 1983, A6; "The Firecracker 400 Message," *Washington Post*, 4 July 1984, A18; "Reagan to Visit Picnic and Race on July 4," *New York Times*, 30 June 1984, 6; Ed Hinton, "Fantastic Fourth: Petty's 200th and Final Victory Remains His Most Memorable," *Orlando Sentinel*, 3 July 2004.

Rebild National Park, Denmark

Located near Jutland, Denmark, this park began an annual celebration of the Fourth of July in 1912 and was interrupted only by the German occupation during World War II. The Danish American Association had purchased the land in 1911 and presented it to Denmark as a gift from Americans. The park was dedicated on August 5, 1912, and by stipulation, the park would forever be reserved for Americans "on the Fourth of July and such other days that are nationally celebrated throughout the United States." The Fourth of July celebrations at Rebild were spectacular events typically drawing thousands of revelers to hear speeches by distinguished celebrants. A luncheon was also traditional. On July 4, 1935, a crowd of 2000, including 700 Danish-born Americans, celebrated there.

Due to the German occupation in Denmark during World War II the Rebild celebration tradition was kept alive through celebrations in the United States. In 1942 the Danes in America celebrated on behalf of their homeland when 2000 of them gathered in Metuchen, New Jersey, to mark the 30th anniversary of the July 4 festival in Denmark.

On July 4, 1946, in celebration of the end of the war, the event at Rebild was remarkable and included two U.S. destroyers, *Perry* and *Warrington*, that were there to represent America. Speeches by Premier Knud Kristensen and U.S. minister Josiah Marvel, Jr., were given. Marvel presented a Delaware flag as a gift to the Danes who reciprocated with a welcome home lunch for 500 Americans of Danish descent.

Sources: "Denmark Accepts a Park," *New York Times*, 4 July 1912, 16; "2000 Celebrate 4th at American Park in Denmark," *Chicago Daily Tribune*, 5 July 1935, 3; "2000 Danes Celebrate," *New York Times*, 5 July 1942, 28; "Danes Celebrate Day," *New York Times*, 5 July 1946, 6.

Regimental Band of Philadelphia *see* Proctor, Thomas

Revolutionary War Monument, Charlotte, Tennessee

This monument honors the Revolutionary War soldiers buried in Dickson County, Tennessee, and was dedicated on July 4, 1976.

Source: "Revolutionary War Soldiers Buried in Dickson County, TN," Dickson County, Tennessee, Web site, 11 September 2002, <http://www.dctn.com/revsol.html>.

Richmond, Kentucky

This city was founded in 1798 on land owned by Colonel John Miller, a soldier in the Revolutionary War. In that year the Kentucky legislature approved the relocation of the Madison County seat from Milford to a site owned by Colonel Miller. Miller's land was purchased by the county and the new town was officially named Richmond in honor of Miller's birthplace, Richmond, Virginia, on July 4, 1798.

Source: "The History of Richmond" Web site, <http://www.richmond-ky.com/richmondfacts.htm>.

Rio de Janeiro, Brazil

In this city the "Amizade," or friendship monument, presented by the people of the United States through the auspices of the American Chamber of Commerce to Brazil, was dedicated on July 4, 1931. With a Brazilian army battalion in full dress, U.S. representative Richard P. Momsen gave an address and Emundo de Miranda Jordao replied on behalf of the Centro Curioca. The marble statue was presented to Brazil at the time of its centennial in 1922 by Charles Evans Hughes but it went into storage until a site could be decided. The monument depicts a woman, twenty-six feet in height. "In one hand she holds an olive branch and in the other clasps the entwined flags of the U.S. and Brazil." At the base are busts of Washington and Nose Bonifacio, considered the father of Brazil.

One of the earliest acknowledgements of the Fourth of July in Rio occurred on July 4, 1833, when the Brazilian Marine Bugle Corps sounded reveille in front of the U.S. embassy.

Sources: *New York Times*, 5 July 1931, 19, and 5 July 1933, 6; *Washington Evening Star*, 5 July 1931, B2.

"River Carnival," Cranford, New Jersey

A water pageant tradition "reminiscent of old Venice" that began in the late 1800s. The event on July 4, 1927, had thousands of spectators on the banks of the Rahway River. They watched a flotilla of boats and barges all decorated. A committee of New Jersey mayors acted as judges.

Source: "20,000 at River Pageant," *New York Times*, 5 July 1927, 17.

Rochambeau, Jean-Baptiste-Donatien de Vimeur, comte de (1725–1807)

French officer who had a monument to his memory dedicated in Newport, Rhode Island, on July 4, 1940. Edgar Erskine Hume (b. 1889) presented an address on the occasion. Rochambeau and his forces fought along side of Washington and the Continental Army and helped force the surrender of Cornwallis at Yorktown, Virginia.

Source: *Rochambeau; Marshal of France, Friend of America: Address at the Dedication* (Newport, R.I.: 1940).

Rodney, Caesar Augustus (1772–1824)

The only signer of the Declaration of Independence who wrote a letter on July 4, 1776, that refers specifically to the Declaration of Independence and the events that took place on that occasion. Rodney describes to his brother Thomas in Dover, Delaware, how he traveled by thunder and rain to arrive in time "to give my voice in the matter of independence." The letter passed through the hands of various individuals until it was auctioned off at Christie's in New York in 1989 to Albert H. Small of Washington, D.C., who in turn promised to donate the letter to the University of Virginia. On July 5, 1926, the letter was printed in the *New York Times* (p. 15) and

on June 27, 1940, in the *Garfield County News* (Utah). Rodney was toasted as "the sincere defender of the people's rights" in a New York Independence Day celebration in 1805.

Sources: *American Citizen*, 11 July 1805, 2; Jack Jurden, "At Long Last, See Caesar Rodney's Historic Words," *Delaware News Journal*, 26 October 2003, <www:delawareonline.com>.

Roosevelt, Franklin Delano (1882–1945)

Thirty-second president of the U. S. (1933–45), who presented significant and candid Fourth of July addresses, both as governor of New York and as president of the nation. Roosevelt graduated from Harvard in 1904, and was elected governor of New York in 1928, serving two terms. Running on the Democratic ticket in 1932, he was elected president, defeating Herbert Hoover. Roosevelt highlighted his term of office by enacting economic and social legislation in answer to the depression that plagued the nation. Elected to a second term, he led the country during World War II by helping to establish a strong inter-Allied war machine. He was elected to an unprecedented third term (1940), followed by a fourth (1944), but died three months later on April 12.

On July 4, 1929, Roosevelt, on his way to Albany, stopped in Spring Valley, New York, located in Rockland County, to address an audience of 2000. He spoke about the "inefficiency" and "backwardness" of local government, but applauded Independence Day. "The Fourth is becoming saner, both in the way it is being celebrated and in the thoughts which it summons. Speakers no longer spend their time denouncing England for its treatment of the colonies," he said. "No one in the United States wishes any harm to George V for what George III did." Roosevelt also visited the State Orthopedic Hospital for Children at West Haverstraw, Bear Mountain Park, and Camp Smith, near Peekskill, where he reviewed the troops.

On Independence Day in 1936, Roosevelt was at Monticello, where he presented a eulogy on Jefferson. About the third president, he said, "He applied the culture of the past to the needs and the life of the America of his day. His knowledge of history spurred him to inquire into the reason and justice of laws, habits and institutions. His passion for liberty led him to interpret and adapt them in order to better the lot of mankind."

On July 4, 1939, Roosevelt and the first lady entertained almost eighty persons at their Hyde Park, New York, home, including Wilhelm Munthe de Morgenstierne, Norwegian minister to the United States, and Henry Noble MacCracken, president of Vassar College. After his lawn party, Roosevelt held a press conference in which he called on the Senate "to reverse the House action to forbid shipments of arms and munitions to nations at war."

On July 4, 1940, Roosevelt donated a library to house his papers. That repository is now the Franklin D. Roosevelt Presidential Library and Museum, administered by the National Archives and Records Administration.

His Independence Day address in 1941 called for America's pledge to fight for freedom. He compared the U.S. entry into World War II with the colonists' declaring independence in 1776. Whereas in 1776 Americans sought to protect their own freedoms, in 1941 Americans needed to protect the freedoms of other nations. "We know too that we cannot save freedom in our own midst, in our own land, if all around us — our neighbor Nations — have lost their freedom."

Sources: "Roosevelt Assails Rural Government," *New York Times*, 5 July 1929, 5; "Roosevelt Speech at Jefferson Home," *New York Times*, 5 July 1936, 3; "Task Likened to Jefferson's by Roosevelt," *Washington Post*, 5 July 1936, A1, A6; "Roosevelt Urges Senate to Reverse the Arms Embargo" and "President Coatless at Picnic," *New York Times*, 5 July 1939, 1 and 5, respectively; *The Public Papers and Addresses of Franklin D. Roosevelt*, comp. Samuel I. Rosenman (New York: Russell and Russell, 1941), 10:254–55; Franklin D. Roosevelt, "A Pledge to Country and to Flag," *Vital Speeches of the Day* 7/19 (15 July 1941): 588–89; "Franklin Delano Roosevelt," *Encyclopedia of American History*, 1141.

Roosevelt, Theodore (1858–1919)

Twenty-sixth president of the U.S. (1901–09) and active participant on the Fourth

of July before and during his presidency. Roosevelt was born in New York City and served as lieutenant colonel of the Rough Rider Regiment in the **Spanish-American War** and was awarded posthumously the Congressional Medal of Honor. After the war Roosevelt was elected governor of New York and then vice president under William McKinley. Roosevelt assumed the presidency upon the latter's assassination.

On July 4, 1899, Governor Roosevelt gave a speech at his hometown of Oyster Bay, New York. The event took place in Audrey Park, "opposite the railroad station." At that event other speakers predicted that Roosevelt would be the next president.

On July 4, 1902, Roosevelt was in Pittsburgh, where he gave a speech at Schenley Park, before an assemblage of 200,000 persons. He arrived early in the morning and took part in a four-mile parade that included prominent congressmen and Pennsylvania governor William Alexis Stone. When the president reached the speaker's stand, the band played "Hail to the Chief," and 600 members of the United German Societies of Allegheny sang "The Star-Spangled Banner." Brig.-Gen. Willis J. Hulings read the Declaration of Independence. This was followed by Roosevelt's speech, in which he discussed the importance of the Declaration of Independence and the two great epochs of the nation: those of Washington and Lincoln. He mentioned the proclamation for peace in the Philippines and acknowledged the American troops that fought there. Cuba was also on the president's mind, as he explained prophetically, "Cuba must occupy a peculiar relation to us in the field of international politics. She must in a larger sense be a part of the general political system in international affairs of which this Republic stands as the head."

On Independence Day in 1903, Roosevelt gave a speech in Huntington, New York, on the occasion of that town's 250th anniversary. That day he also inaugurated the new MacKay or Pacific Cable to the Philippines by sending a message to Governor Taft with a reply received in thirty minutes. Roosevelt also sent a message from Oyster Bay around the world to Clarence Mackay at Roslyn, Long Island, with the message received in sixty-one minutes.

When Roosevelt was at Sagamore Hill, his summer home in Oyster Bay on Long Island, New York, on Independence Day, he enjoyed going for long horseback rides, setting off fireworks "from the bottom of the hill in front of the house," and sitting on the veranda with his family, relatives, and house guests. On July 4, 1904, he had a picnic celebration with his extended family at Cove Neck, "about six miles from Sagamore Hill," concluding with evening fireworks and dancing "on the big veranda, which was gaily decorated with Chinese lanterns."

On the Fourth in 1906, Roosevelt was in Oyster Bay presenting a sermon-like speech in a pouring rain that was based on an address by Abraham Lincoln "which he [Lincoln] spoke in a remarkable little address delivered to a band of people who were serenading him at the White House just after his reelection to the Presidency. He said [Roosevelt's words], 'In any great national trial hereafter the men of that day, as compared with those of this, will be as weak and as strong, as silly and as wise, as bad and as good. Let us therefore, study the incidents of this as philosophy from which to learn wisdom and not as wrongs to be avenged.'" Roosevelt encouraged his listeners to be good citizens, to address the maladies of society but do so "without either hatred or exultation over those at whose expense it has been necessary that it should be cut out."

On July 4, 1916, Roosevelt presented a stirring speech before 5,000 persons. At Oyster Bay he spoke of "his intention to organize a force for service in Mexico in the event of war." He said, "No nation is either fit to be free, or will permanently be permitted to be free, unless it is able to protect all of its own rights with all of its own power. It is with a nation as with an individual." Roosevelt also described to his audience how to be "pleasant" and "decent" citizens. He also reviewed a number of troops and sailors from the USS *Baltimore* who paraded that day.

After Roosevelt died, persons continued to pay homage to him on the Fourth of July. In 1920, for example, "a steady stream of tourists from all over the country" stopped at his gravesite at Oyster Bay to leave flowers in his memory.

Sources: "Gov. Roosevelt Will Speak," *New York Times*, 4 July 1899, 10; *New York Times*, 5 July 1899, 2; "Crowds in Pittsburg Cheer the President," *New York Times*, 5 July 1902, 1–2 and 5 July 1903, 1; "President Roosevelt Writing the Message Which Opened the New Pacific Cable," *Harper's Weekly*, 18 July 1903, 1183; "President and Party Celebrate the Fourth," *New York Times*, 5 July 1904, 16; "President Spoke On in Drenching Rain," *New York Times*, 5 July 1906, 1–2; "The President's Fourth," *New York Times*, 5 July 1908, 12; "Roosevelt Assails the Militia Muster," *New York Times*, 5 July 1916, 3; "Homage at Oyster Bay," *New York Times*, 6 July 1920, 4.

Ross, Betsy (1752–1836)

This American patriot who is credited by some with making the first American flag was honored occasionally on the Fourth of July through reenactments and other tributes. On July 4, 1926, for example, in Lenox, Massachusetts, Eleanor Davis was dressed as Betsy Ross, sewing the flag as she sat on a float that was drawn through city streets before numerous visitors from all the Berkshire Hills. On July 4, 1961, the flag that flew continuously over her grave in Philadelphia was stolen.

Sources: "Show Betsy Ross in Lenox Parade," *New York Times*, 6 July 1926, 24; *New York Times*, 5 July 1961, 25.

Russell, John Miller (1768–1840)

Presented an oration in Charlestown on July 4, 1797 (Charlestown: J. Lamson, 1797), and wrote "A Poem on the Fourth of July, 1798" that was published in Boston by Manning and Loring, 1798.

Source: Oscar Wegelin, *Early American Poetry* (the author, 1930; reprint, Gloucester, Mass.: Peter Smith, 1965), 67.

Ryland Chapel, Washington

The cornerstone for this church at Maryland Avenue and 10th Street was laid on July 4, 1844. At the ceremony, "an excellent prayer was offered up by the Rev. Mr. Phelps, and an appropriate and impressive sermon was delivered by the Rev. N[orvel] Wilson, from the text 'How goodly are thy tents, O Jacob, and thy tabernacles, O Israel.'" The Rev. William

Ryland, navy chaplain, and the Rev. Wilson presented addresses.

Source: *National Intelligencer*, 3 and 8 July 1844, 3 and 3, respectively.

Sabbath Day and the Fourth of July

Throughout the history of Independence Day, when July 4 fell on a Sunday, in most places the civic ceremonies were celebrated on the following Monday. Church services continued as planned on the Sabbath with sermons and other sacred exercises frequently focused on the spiritual meaning of the Fourth of July. References and comparisons of the Declaration with scripture from the **Bible** were common. In Philadelphia in 1790, it was reported that "the 4th of July, being Sunday, was recognized by our citizens' assembling at their respective places of public worship, where they heard discourses suitable to the happy occasion. There more public rejoicings were reserved till the following day." At Christ Church on Sunday, the Rev. Dr. Smith gave "an excellent and most animated discourse" to parishioners made up of "the officers of government, the Cincinnati, the militia in uniform, and a numerous audience of respectable citizens.

Source: *Universal Asylum and Columbian Magazine* 5/1 (July 1790): 58.

Sabbath-School Movement

Began in the 1790s and continued throughout the 19th century. Also referred to as the Sunday School Movement, their celebrations were very popular and were frequently held on the Fourth of July in cities across the country. The events provided opportunities for children to present brief addresses and prepared recitations, such as readings of the Declaration of Independence and what they had learned about the nation's history, and simply have fun. The schools' primary mission was to control children's activities, to get youngsters off the streets, and to teach "proper behavior" and "cleanliness." According to Franklin Eddy, these Independence Day events helped the young to be "instructed in the principles of civil and religious freedom, which were attended with most gratifying results, and continued to be practiced for

many years. Sometimes that day was made the occasion of a general canvass of the town or parish, to secure new scholars for the Sabbath-school." The Bible was the principal source of instruction.

The first Sabbath-school society organized in the country was the First-Day or Sunday-School Society of Philadelphia in 1791. In 1792 the first Sabbath school established in the state of New York was started in Stockbridge. Within a few years, schools were opened in various other places, including New York City (1803), Hudson, N.Y. (1803), Patterson, N.J. (1794), Kent, Md. (1806), Beverly, Mass. (1809–10), Boston (1812), and Pittsburgh (1809). Some of the societies formed attracted thousands of children, such as the New York Female Sunday School Union, established in 1816, and the New York Sunday-School Union of the same year. By the 1820s, there were several hundred Sunday schools in the nation, and the ideas and principles elicited from the movement had widespread impact on individual churches, most of which typically held events on the Fourth of July. Another important association was the District of Columbia Sabbath School Union, active in the 1830s and after. Numerous churches participated in the movement; and at least one Sabbath school, that of Mr. Post's Church near City Hall, was fully integrated; both white and black children were encouraged to attend. The success of Washington's Sabbath school efforts prompted the editor of *The National Intelligencer* to comment on it in 1833:

The value of this institution is becoming daily more apparent; thousands and tens of thousands are thus rescued from ignorance, profligacy, and crime, and made capable of becoming useful members of society.... It is to the young mind that his salutary instruction is calculated to be communicated with the greatest and best effect. It is then that impressions are more easily and more lastingly made, and the amount of good resulting from the united cooperation of thousands thus engaged, Sabbath after Sabbath, throughout the country, in communicating instruction, cannot be estimated.

One of the largest celebrations of the Sabbath school movement occurred in New

York City on July 4, 1839, when "twelve or fourteen thousand children were conveyed in a fleet of steamboats to Staten Island, where they were entertained at a place called Pine Grove." The celebrations began on the boats as they converged on the harbor. Each boat had a clergyman who gave "brief but appropriate prayers to the great Ruler of nations, mingled with thanksgivings for the return of the jubilee of civil and religious freedom, and for the blessings which the nation so richly enjoys." Meanwhile there was much singing going on. "A number of animating and patriotic odes, adapted to the occasion, set to music and taught to the children, were sung in full chorus. The effect of these exercises was very pleasing. Of course they were not simultaneously sung; so that when the children of one boat were silent, the music of more than a thousand infant voices would steal sweetly across the water from another." On Pine Grove a large tent, one hundred feet in diameter, was set up, along with many other tents for the "headquarters of different schools." New York governor **William Henry Seward** addressed the crowd and there was additional singing and many patriotic recitations.

Sabbath school celebrations were frequently held in tandem with Temperance events because of the mutual interest of dissuading children from using alcohol. On July 4, 1841, in Westfield, Massachusetts, seven hundred Westfield Sabbath School children sang temperance songs and pledged "perpetual hate, to all that can intoxicate."

The White House was also instrumental in fostering interest and support for the movement. During the tenures of presidents Martin Van Buren, John Tyler, James K. Polk, Zachary Taylor, and Franklin Pierce, Sabbath school children were welcomed into the White House on the Fourth of July, where they gave brief speeches and sang songs.

Sources: *National Intelligencer*, 6 July 1833 and 9 July 1839, 2 and 2, respectively; *Sabbath School Celebration in Norwich, July Fourth, 1839* (Norwich, 1839?); *Westfield Newsletter*, 7 July 1841, 2, as reported in Anne Marie Hickey, "The Celebration of the Fourth of July in Westfield, 1826–1853," *Historical Journal of Massachusetts* 9/2 (1981), 44; Franklin Eddy, *The Sabbath-School Century* (Hamilton, Ohio: J.H. Long,

1882); Anne M. Boylan, "Sunday Schools and Changing Evangelical Views of Children in the 1820s," *Church History* 48 (September 1979): 320–33; Anne M. Boylan, "Presbyterians and Sunday Schools in Philadelphia, 1800–1824," *Journal of Presbyterian History* 76/1 (Spring 1998): 37–44.

Safe and Sane Celebrations

Represent a reform movement active from about 1903 to 1916 to curb the injuries and deaths due to the use of guns and fireworks on the Fourth of July. Cities and towns passed new legislation to ban the use of fireworks and created new ways to celebrate patriotism and national pride. It was the press that first brought attention to the large numbers of deaths and injuries occurring each year. Although newspapers had reported Independence Day accidents caused by fireworks from the early 1800s, after the Civil War the number of occurrences printed grew in number and more ghastly details of the injuries were provided. By 1900 the number of deaths across the country each year from the careless use of explosives and toy pistols numbered in the hundreds with many more injuries reported. The *Chicago Tribune* listed numerous deaths caused by tetanus infections caused by fireworks in 1901 and more than 1000 injured children. In 1903 the American Medical Association (AMA) in Chicago began tracking fireworks casualties. Because of the high numbers the AMA encouraged legislation to ban the manufacture and sale of fireworks. Organizations such as the Department of Child Hygiene of the Russell Sage Foundation, as well as various municipal authorities, were active in recommending alternative ways to celebrate so that working class and immigrant citizens could be more enticed to participate. The Sage Foundation's Division of Recreation issued a guide, *The Celebration of the Fourth of July by Means of Pageantry*, to provide ideas for plays and musical events. Noted American composer Arthur Farwell, supervisor of municipal concerts in New York City in 1910–12, contributed the musical notes for this publication. He also composed a new national anthem, "Hymn to Liberty," that was premiered in New York City on July 4, 1911.

In 1906 San Francisco and Portland,

Oregon, were among the first cities to either ban the sale of fireworks or to offer alternative activities. By 1909–10 the movement had gained momentum. "Safe and sane" celebrations were provided in many major cities and towns across the country. There were historical pageants, parades with patriotic floats with individuals dressed to represent their countries of origin (see, for example, **"Parade of Nations"**), sporting events, and numerous officially sponsored events in public parks that included concerts and daylight municipal fireworks.

Washington's first safe and sane celebration occurred in 1909. There were two daylight fireworks displays and a third "elaborate display of fireworks in the evening on the White Lot" directly behind the White House. Boston had its first event in 1910 and the day was uncharacteristically quiet. The city gave away free ice cream to the youngsters on the common and President **William Howard Taft**, who was in Boston that day speaking to an audience, remarked how he hoped the safe and sane movement "would spread throughout the Union."

Cleveland had its first celebration in 1909 without any accidents reported. In the previous year, eleven persons had lost their lives and scores were injured. In 1910 the city enjoyed several athletic events and a parade of 10,000 school children. New York celebrated its first sane holiday in 1910. Officials encouraged participation in "exercises and games in 250 city schools by the children."

In 1911 celebrations of Independence Day across the country reflected the popularity, growth, and achievements of the movement. Injuries and deaths were reduced. Chicago, celebrating its second sane Fourth of July, had "a parade, historical tableaux, patriotic exercises, play festivals, and band concerts." The parade was three miles in length and included 5,000 participants with seventeen nationalities represented. There were twenty floats "depicting events in the city's history," which progressed through city streets to the delight of 300,000 onlookers. Kansas City, Missouri, had water sports and other athletics, as well as thirteen bands of music performing in city parks. In Milwaukee "dangerous fireworks and explosives were banned" by city officials but identical programs of activities in six city parks were provided as entertainment. In St. Paul, Minnesota, Governor Adolph O. Eberhart and Mayor Herbert P. Keller led a parade of "5,000 gayly dressed boys and girls" after which athletic contests and races took place. In Denver 100,000 persons gathered and sang "My Country 'Tis of Thee" and watched a military and "industrial parade." Santa Fe, New Mexico, celebrated with a historic pageant.

During the 1930s due to unacceptable levels of casualties, the movement had a resurgence. New anti-fireworks ordinances were enacted. In 1937 a model state fireworks law was created by the National Fire Protection Association encouraging the prohibiting of selling fireworks for retail use, but permitting public displays "authorized by a state fire marshal or local fire chief." In 1939 four states adopted variations of the model law and in following years other states did the same. That year John L. Rice, New York commissioner of health, in tandem with the Greater New York Safety Council issued a list of rules for assuring a safe Fourth of July. By 1953 twenty-eight states had fireworks laws in place and fourteen other states and the District of Columbia limited the sale of fireworks to those considered as "safe" with proper supervision. However, as in the past, enforcement proved to be problematic, especially with clandestine sales and individuals who transported purchased fireworks across state lines. Injuries from fireworks were decreased but not eliminated. In 2003, an Associated Press report noted 100 injuries on the Fourth each year. In Nebraska, for example, in 2003, Omaha was the only city in that state to prohibit the use of fireworks.

See also **Pyrotechnics and fireworks accidents.**

Sources: *Evening Star*, 5 July 1909, 1; "Day Pleases Official," *Washington Post*, 6 July 1909, 2; "Safe and Sane Day the Country Over" and "Chinese Join Celebration," *New York Times*, 5 July 1910, 18; "Free Ice Cream in Boston" and "New York Safe and Sane," *Washington Post*, 4 July 1910, 5; "New National Hymn to Be Sung Here on the Fourth," "Safe and Sane the

Nation Over," and "Fourth Quiet Also in Other Cities," *New York Times*, 2 July 1911, SM4, and 5 July 1911, 4 and 6, respectively; William Chauncy Langdon, *The Celebration of the Fourth of July by Means of Pageantry* (Division of Recreation, Russell Sage Foundation, 1912); "Rules for Safe Fourth Offered to Public," *New York Times*, 4 July 1939, L3; "Lingering Glory," *Life*, 4 July 1955, 53; Joe Ruff, "Omaha Still Has State's Only Fireworks Ban," *Associated Press State and Local Wire*, 26 June 2003.

"St. Domingo" Riot, Philadelphia

Occurred in Philadelphia on July 4, 1804, when about one hundred blacks assembled and took over the southwest part of the city for several hours and fought a group of whites. The group threatened the whites with a "West Indian–type rebellion saying they would shew them St. Domingo." A year later on July 4, 1805, Philadelphia whites in fear of a similar event prevented the African-Americans from assembling on the public square.

Sources: *Philadelphia Freeman's Journal*, reprinted in *Albany Centinel*, 20 July 1804; Shane White, "'It Was a Proud Day': African Americans, Festivals, and Parades in the North, 1741–1834," *Journal of American History* 81/1 (June 1994): 34.

St. John's College, Annapolis, Maryland *see* "Liberty Tree"

St. John's Episcopal Church, Buffalo, New York

This church was destroyed by fire on July 4, 1868, when a rocket exploded in the church spire. The fire was "out of reach of the engines," and because the superintendent of the Fire Department was absent from the city, the fire was badly managed, and the costly edifice, with its fine organ and library, was totally destroyed. A reporter noted that "nothing is now left but the massive stone walls."

Source: "St. John's Episcopal Church in Buffalo Destroyed by Fire," *New York Times*, 6 July 1868, 5.

St. Mary's College Alumni Lodge

Overlooking the St. Mary's River, near St. Mary's City, Maryland, the lodge was dedicated on July 4, 1924. The building was originally a college seminary stable made from bricks taken from the 1676 Maryland State House. The lodge has three bedrooms and serves as a guest house for visitors and college alumni.

Source: St. Mary's College of Maryland, Web site, 9 May 2002, <*http://www.smcm.edu/map/alumni.htm*>.

St. Paul's Parish Schoolhouse, New York

The cornerstone of the schoolhouse was laid on July 4, 1891.

Source: *New York Times*, 5 July 1891, 9.

Salem, Massachusetts, bonfires

A tradition that dates to 1814 in celebration of the treaty of the War of 1812, and carried through the 1920s, in which large stacks of wood piled high were lit before large crowds. On July 4, 1927, on historic Gallows Hill, a 110-foot-tall, carefully constructed stack with the Star-Spangled Banner at the top waving in the wind was lit with over 60,000 spectators in attendance. The base of the structure consisted of 1000 railroad ties discarded by the Boston and Maine Railroad. The cost of this event was $2000.

Source: "110-Foot Bonfire Opens Fourth in Historic Salem," *New York Herald Tribune*, 4 July 1927, 6.

Salem, North Carolina

The first official celebration of the Fourth of July in the state of North Carolina took place in Old Salem on July 4, 1783. The inducement to celebrate was not only a result of the end of the Revolutionary War but was also encouraged by a proclamation issued by North Carolina governor Alexander Martin (ca. 1740–1807) in which he directed on June 18, 1783, that Independence Day be annually celebrated as a "Day of Solemn Thanksgiving to Almighty God" for establishing the United States as an independent nation. His was the first such proclamation by a state governor regarding the celebration of the holiday on July 4. Heeding the governor's proclamation, it was the Moravians of Salem that presented the most significant event. There were "devout and religious exercises," that included an outdoor procession and a typical Moravian Love Feast. Music was an important part of the celebration and musical director Friedrich Peter premiered his new choral work *Freudenpsalm*. According to the Salem Diary, "At eight in the evening, the congregation assembled in the Gemein Haus Saal, where the choir sang 'Praise Be to Thee, Who Sittest Above the Cherubim,'" followed by a procession through the town streets. The diary lists annual Independence Day ceremonies to the Civil War. Typically there were speeches, readings of scripture, and recitations of the Declaration of Independence.

On July 4, 1966, the first reenactment of the historic 1783 celebration began with a torchlight procession through Old Salem. Since then annual celebrations have occurred and have included public readings of the Declaration of Independence and reenactment ceremonies.

Sources: *Winston-Salem Journal*, 5 July 1966; Marilyn Gombosi, *A Day of Solemn Thanksgiving: Moravian Music for the Fourth of July, 1783, in Salem, North Carolina* (Chapel Hill: University of North Carolina Press, 1977); Vincent A. Cannino, "Celebrating the Fourth in Salem" (M.A. thesis, University of North Carolina at Greensboro, 1998); Adelaide Fries, ed., *Records of the Moravians in North Carolina* (Raleigh: State Department of Archives and History, 1968), 1841.

"Salute to America"

This radio program sponsored by the U.S. Department of the Interior began in 1989 as a one-hour Independence Day show and continued for twelve years with over eighty country stars volunteering their time and talents. Both LP and compact disc recordings were issued with the help of producer and host Steve Brooks. Brooks reported that some 457 stations broadcast the show. Public service announcements during the show helped bring attention to lesser known national parks; U.S. Fish and Wildlife Service wildlife refuges; the Bureau of Reclamation's water management and conservations efforts; the Minerals Management Service's Land and Water Conservation Fund; the U.S. Geological Survey's topographical maps; the Bureau of Land Management and the use and protection of our public lands; the Office of Surface Mining, Reclamation and Enforcement and its efforts to stop acid mine drainage.

In 2001, Interior Secretary Gale Norton was featured on the program, which also included country artists Rascal Flatts, Tracy Lawrence, the Bellamy Brothers, Montgomery Gentry, and Tim Rushlow, among others.

Source: "Secretary Norton Joins Country Music Stars for July 4th Salute," *News*, U.S. Department of the Interior, 18 June 2001, <http://www.doi.gov/news/010618.html>.

Samnorwood, Texas

Located in north central Collingsworth County, this town was formally established on July 4, 1931, when the Fort Worth and Denver Northern Railway completed its line from Childress to Pampa. Samnorwood sits in an "agricultural and ranching area," serves as the area's shipping center, and has maintained a population of slightly over 100 since its founding. The 1931 Fourth of July included a picnic and "typical fanfare."

Sources: Clyde Chestnut Brown, *A Survey History of Collingsworth County, Texas* (M.A. thesis, University of Colorado, 1934); Fred Tarpley, *1001 Texas Place Names* (Austin: University of Texas Press, 1980); "Samnorwood, TX," *Handbook of Texas Online* <http://tsha.utexas.edu/handbook/online>.

San Francisco, California

The first Fourth of July celebration in what is now San Francisco occurred in 1836 as the first houses there were being built. Jacob P. Leese had finished building his house by July 4 of that year and had a glorious celebration made up of officers and families from the Presidio, and "officers from ships in the harbor and families from the Mission." Festivities included a dinner, music and dancing. "It was the occasion of the first raising of the American flag on the site of the future San Francisco, ten years before the official flag-raising in Portsmouth Square."

Source: Hennig Cohen and Tristram Potter Coffin, eds., *The Folklore of American Holidays*, 3rd ed. (Detroit: Gale, 1999).

San Francisco de los Tejas Mission Park

This 363.5-acre park, located in Grapeland, Texas, in Houston County, 22 miles northeast of Crockett, was dedicated on July 4, 1935. It was built in 1934 in commemoration of Mission San Francisco de los Tejas, the first Spanish mission established in the province of Texas, in 1690. Within the grounds is the Joseph Redmund Rice Log House, built in 1928, and one of the oldest structures in the area. About 5000 persons attended the Fourth of July ceremony in 1935. It was hosted by Texas judge and historian Armistead Albert Aldrich (1858–1945). Aldrich, who was a popular orator, served as a county judge, 1892–96, and was a representative to the 27th Texas Legislature.

Source: Mary Ann Edwards, "Armistead Albert Aldrich," *Handbook of Texas Online*, <http://www.tsha.utexas.edu/handbook/online/articles/view>.

Sänger Hall, Toledo, Ohio

This new hall was dedicated on July 4, 1871.

Source: *Toledo Blade*, 3 July 1871, 2.

Sängerbund societies *see* German Americans

Santleman, William H.

Director (1898–1927) of the U.S. Marine Band, who composed *Our Glorious Banner: A Fourth of July Patriotic March*, printed for piano as a music supplement of the *San Francisco Examiner*, 30 June 1901.

Saratoga, Battle of

Significant Revolutionary War battle in which American forces, under Gen. Horatio Gates, defeated the British under Gen. John Burgoyne. Greatly outnumbered, Burgoyne surrendered on October 17, 1777. The American victory was a turning point in the war. As a result the French were persuaded to support the American cause. On July 4, 1782, Saratoga celebrated its first Independence Day celebration when "officers of the Regement" of the Continental Army drank toasts with a "volley of Musquets at the end of each." Another noteworthy celebration "in the field on which the formidable army of Burgoyne surrendered" took place on July 4, 1828, when 5000 persons assembled there for a ceremony that included "52 soldiers of the Revolution."

Gen. Gates himself was occasionally heralded on the Fourth for his victory at Saratoga. For example, when Gulian C. Verplanck, a member of the New York state constitutional convention in 1867, spoke at the dedication of the **Tammany Hall Building** on July 4 that year, he honored Gates as a "distinguished" member of "its old-time organization." The battlefield, located forty miles north of Albany, New York, was designated as a National Historical Park in 1938 by the U.S. Congress. Throughout the years, ceremonies at the park have been highlighted with readings of the Declaration of Independence, eighteenth century toasts, musket firings, and drinking of **lemonade**, a popular nineteenth century beverage. On July 4, 2004, a special citizenship ceremony was held when twenty individuals were naturalized to the sounds of a fife and drums band and musket firings.

Sources: *National Intelligencer*, 28 July 1822, 3; "Corner-Stone of Tammany Hall," *New York Times*, 5 July 1867, 1; Jeremiah Greenman, *Diary of a Common Soldier in the American Revolution, 1775–1783*, ed. Robert C. Bray and Paul E. Bushnell (DeKalb, Ill.: Northern Illinois University Press, 1978).

Schiller, Johann Christoph Friedrich von (1759–1805)

A monument to this German poet was dedicated in Schiller Park in Columbus, Ohio, on July 4, 1889.

Source: *Daily Ohio State Journal*, 5 July 1889, 5.

Schurz, Carl (1829–1906)

German-American statesman and writer the monument in whose honor was unveiled in Oshkosh, Wisconsin, on July 4, 1914. Emil Baensch (b. 1857) of Manitowoc, Wisconsin, presented the key address at the ceremony. Schurz was an ardent supporter of Abraham Lincoln, and worked on behalf of the Union during the Civil War. He also was secretary of the interior under President Hayes, as well as Washington correspondent for the *New York Tribune*.

Source: "Dedicatory Address Delivered in Oshkosh, Wis., July 4, 1914" (1914; copy in Auburn University Library and other repositories).

Scott, Winfield (1786–1866)

Soldier who was a hero of the War of 1812 and the Mexican War, and was honored during his lifetime in numerous Fourth of July celebrations. Scott was born in Laurel Branch, Virginia, and attended the College of William and Mary. His notoriety was secured with his gallant performance at the battles of Chippewa and Lundy's Lane in 1814. He also participated in the Black Hawk War and in campaigns against Seminole and Creek Indians. From 1841 to 1861 he was general commander of the army. In 1852 he settled in New York and in that year was a Whig candidate for the presidency, but was decisively defeated by Franklin Pierce.

Scott often received invitations to attend Independence Day ceremonies. In June of 1849 he was asked to join a celebration of Whigs at the Chinese Museum in Philadelphia but declined, informing them that he had a previous engagement. His letter to them was read aloud at that event. The Whigs responded with a toast to "General Winfield Scott—the skilful commander, the gallant soldier, the accomplished gentleman; his laurels are green and glorious, and his fame is immortal."

On July 4, 1850, General Scott attended the consecration ceremony at **Washington's Revolutionary War Headquarters, Newburgh, New York**, memorializing the headquarters there of Washington during the Revolutionary War.

On July 4, 1861, Scott was in Washington participating in a military review with Abraham Lincoln. It was a significant event for Scott. The crowd that had assembled there cheered him repeatedly. The Garibaldi Guard filed passed the wooden platform on which the general was seated with the other dignitaries, and "each man of the whole thousand drew from his hat or breast the green sprig which so strikingly ornamented them, and threw it towards and in many instances upon the person of the veteran hero of Lundy's Land and Cerro Gordo, while from the head of each company there was a beautiful bouquet of natural flowers thrown into his lap in the same manner." Scott died on May 29, 1866, and on the following Fourth was honored in Brooklyn, New York, by not having a military parade.

Sources: "Anniversary Festivities," *National Intelligencer*, 10 July 1849, 2; *Washington Evening Star*, 5 July 1861; *Brooklyn Daily Eagle*, 3 July 1866, 2; *Encyclopedia of American History*, 1148; *The Encyclopedia of New York City*, 1053.

Seawell, Benjamin (1743–1821)

A monument to this general's memory was unveiled by the Lebanon, Tennessee, chapter of the Daughters of the American Revolution, on July 4, 1927. Seawell had commanded a regiment from Pitt County, North Carolina, during the Revolutionary War.

Source: Nannie Seawell Boyd, *A Brief Sketch of the Life of Col. Benjamin Seawell, Jr.* (1927?; copy in library at the University of North Carolina Chapel Hill).

Second Church of the Evangelical Association

The cornerstone for this German church located on 53rd Street near 9th Avenue in New York City was laid on July 4, 1869. The church's design was one of all brick, 34 feet wide by 65 feet long. "It is intended first to erect only the basement story, which will be used only as a place of worship until the congregation gets money enough to enable it to build the superstructure." The pastor was the Rev. R. Deisher and parishioners numbered about fifty members.

Source: *New York Times*, 5 July 1869, 8.

Seneca Falls, New York

The site for the first convention devoted to women's rights in July 1848. Lucretia Mott and Elizabeth Cady Stanton organized the meeting and drafted the Declaration of Sentiments that focused on women's grievances. Closely modeled after the Declaration of Independence, the document proclaimed the equality of men and women and the oppression of women. The convention adopted resolutions calling for legal equality, educational and professional opportunities for women, the right to control their own property, and the right to vote.

Sources: Milton J. Klein, ed., *The Empire State: A History of New York* (Ithaca: Cornell University Press, 2001), 337–38; "Declaration of Sentiments (1848)," in the *American Studies Anthology*, ed. Richard P. Horwitz (Wilmington, Del.: Scholarly Resources, 2001), 70–76.

Sentinel

The office of the *Sentinel*, a newspaper in Stamford, Connecticut, was destroyed on July 4, 1832, as a result of the careless use of firecrackers.

Source: *Niles' Weekly Register* 42/21 (21 July 1832): 373.

Sesquicentennial Exposition, Philadelphia

A world's fair held in Philadelphia, Pennsylvania, in 1926 to celebrate the 150th anniversary of the signing of the Declaration of Independence. The Liberty Bell served as a symbol of the fair and an 80-foot replica of the bell lighted with 26,000 bulbs "in amber, ivory and rose colorings" adorned the entrance to the exposition grounds. The light from the bell could be seen as far away as New York. City Hall was also illuminated with 860 flood lights and a 200-foot-tall "Tower of Light" had the most powerful searchlight ever built mounted on top of the building. The whole resulted in the grandest light show ever seen in the nation.

Over 30 countries participated in the exposition. The fair, not considered a success due to an attendance of only 6 million persons, ran from June 1 to November 30, with the official ceremonies and exhibits occurring on July 4. President Calvin Coolidge presided over the event and spoke to a crowd of 35,000 at the stadium located on the exposition grounds. His speech was broadcast over radio stations WJZ and WRC. Celebrations of the Fourth are not held to introduce new tenets of government but rather to "reaffirm and reestablish those old theories and principles which time and the unerring logic of events have demonstrated to be sound," he said. Coolidge credited the original pronouncements of liberty not to Jefferson, but to the "preachers of Colonial New England, such as Thomas Hooker and John Wise." Philadelphia Mayor W. Freeland Kendrick also spoke.

Sesquicentennial events were celebrated in other cities. In Washington 25,000 persons gathered at the Capitol to hear the United States Marine and Army bands and a pageant presented by 35 "leading patriotic and civic organizations," with a cast of 1000. The story was written by Marie Moore Forrest and consisted of three grand episodes: "The Foundation of America," "The Progress of America," and "The Strength and Hope of America."

The work depicted numerous figures in American history with portrayers in full costume. The pageant was broadcast over radio station WCAP.

In Annapolis the dedication of a bronze tablet commemorating Maryland's four signers of the Declaration took place with speeches by Maryland governor Albert C. Ritchie and Annapolis mayor Allen Bowie Howard. In Charlottesville, Virginia, Jefferson Levy, owner of **Monticello**, formally presented the Jefferson estate to the nation in a ceremony held in Cabel Hall at the University of Virginia.

Sources: "District Unites Tomorrow to Observe Independence Day," *Washington Evening Star*, 4 July 1926, 8; "District Ready for Gala Independence Day Fete," *Washington Post*, 4 July 1926, 1; "President's Speech Will Be Broadcast" and "Sesquicentennial World's Greatest Light Spectacle," *New York Times*, 4 July 1926, F6; "Independence Signers Honored in Annapolis," *Washington Post*, 5 July 1926, 3; "Coolidge Invokes Founders' Ideals As Guide to Nation," *New York Times*, 6 July 1926, 1.

Seton Hall College, South Orange, New Jersey

Site for a simultaneous "Slovak Day" and "Independence day" celebration on July 4, 1929, with 20,000 Slovaks in attendance. In keeping with a tradition started "many years ago" by the Rev. Stephen Furdek of Wilkes-Barre, Pennsylvania, "numerous societies and parishes in New York, New Jersey and Pennsylvania" assembled to witness a "field mass celebrated by the Rev. A. Adzima of Bayonne," a parade through South Orange, a musical concert at the college, and speeches by former governor A. Harry Moore of New Jersey and others.

Source: "20,000 Slovaks Celebrate," *New York Times*, 5 July 1929, 21.

Sewanee: University of the South

A convention of dioceses of the Protestant Episcopal Church in the southern states met on July 4, 1857, at Look-Out Mountain, near Chattanooga, Tennessee, to establish a "University for the Southern States." Twenty trustees and bishops representing seven states began the ceremony in a procession that included Rezin Rawlins, a Revolutionary War soldier carrying a flag, and a brass band from

Chattanooga that played the "Star-Spangled Banner." They marched to the spot chosen for the "exercises" that included singing of the 100th psalm, readings from the Bible by the Right Rev. Bishop Green of Mississippi, a reading of the Declaration of Independence by G.B. Duncan, and an oration by the Right Rev. James H. Otey, bishop of Tennessee. Otey spoke about the "distinguished privileges" the people of this new nation possessed and said that intelligence and virtue "are the chief supports of our civil institutions," but that the "state does not and cannot make provision for that teaching which underlies all virtue." With an absence of religious training in public schools, Otey proposed that "the prime end aimed at in our projected University, is, then, to make the Bible the ultimate and sufficient rule and standard for the regulation of man's conduct as a rational and accountable being." Otey then offered a strategy for raising the funds necessary to establish the school and answered the "suspicion" by some that the school was sectional rather than national: "The name is one of convenient description: it is no party war-cry, no sectional pass-word: all such interpretation we utterly disclaim." A "Declaration of Principles" set forth by the trustees for the establishment of the school was signed on July 6.

Source: *Proceedings of a Convention of the Trustees of a Proposed University for the Southern States* (Atlanta: C.R. Hanleiter, 1857).

Seward, William Henry (1801–1872)

Statesman, attorney, and active participant on the Fourth of July. Seward was born in Florida, Orange County, New York, and graduated from Union College in 1820. He was admitted to the bar in 1822 and was elected to the state senate in 1830 as a member of the Anti-Masonic Party. In 1838 he was elected governor of New York and served two terms. Subsequently he served two terms in the U.S. Senate (1848 and 1854) where he expressed his opposition to slavery. In 1861 he was appointed secretary of state under Lincoln and later after Lincoln's assassination, under President Andrew Johnson. Seward is popularly remembered for his expansionist views, the acquisition of Alaska from Russia in 1867, and for advocating for the annexation of Hawaii.

Seward delivered one of his early Independence Day orations (published, Auburn: W. Lindsly, 1825) on July 4, 1825, at Auburn, New York. On July 4, 1831, he was in Syracuse, where he delivered an oration (Syracuse: Campbell and Newton, 1831) at the anti-Masonic celebration there. Seward spoke about the importance of freedom. He said, "Another land may be dear to him, because it contains the spot where he was born, the home of his childhood, the haunts of his youth, the field of his manly labors, the graves of those whose memory he loves and venerates; but that land which man most loves, is the land where his limbs are unshackled and his soul is free."

One of the most colorful events Seward attended was the Sabbath School and Temperance Celebration in New York on July 4, 1839. "Twelve or fourteen thousand children were conveyed in a fleet of steamboats to Staten Island, where they were entertained at a place called Pine Grove." This was one of the first flotilla events commemorating the Fourth of July in New York harbor and would be followed by similar events in years to come. It was estimated that 1000 ships were in the harbor, "all gaily dressed in honor of the day." The "flag-ship" of the flotilla was the *Sandusky*, and Seward was on board with "several officers of his suit" and other distinguished gentlemen. After disembarking the ship, Seward and his party proceeded to a grove of cedars, where a stage had been erected for the invited guests, members of the Academy of Sacred Music, and President Van Buren. Following a reading of scripture and singing of an ode, Seward addressed the crowd expressing his commendations to the organizers of the event. "Sunday schools and common schools are the great leveling institutions of this age. What is the secret of aristocracy? It is that knowledge is power," he said. With the completion of the ceremony, the official party retired to the *Sandusky* for dinner.

Seward was also invited to attend the Whig celebration that day but sent a letter explaining his previous engagement in New

York. His letter, read aloud to the Philadelphia group, included the following sentiment: "The Hall of Independence — a sacred monument of the revolution. The patriotism of Philadelphia is a guaranty for its preservation."

As governor of New York, Seward attended the 100th anniversary celebration of Cherry Valley, N.Y., on July 4, 1840, and gave a speech before a crowd estimated at 25,000. On July 4, 1861, Seward was with Lincoln in Washington, first at a flag raising ceremony at the front of the Treasury Department and later seated alongside the president on a wooden platform on Pennsylvania Avenue directly in front of the White House. There they and other members of the Cabinet reviewed thousands of parading troops. After the parade a large cheering crowd surged forward to the platform and "called loudly for Secretary Seward, who finally came forward, and after an eloquent allusion to the imposing military display just witnessed, said, in conclusion, that the people had decided by their votes the questions which had so long agitated the nation, but that a few discontented ones had not been satisfied with such decision, and had appealed to the bullet, and now the bullet must decide it — and God is on the side of liberty."

On July 4, 1864, Seward was in Washington riding about in a carriage and narrowly avoided serious injury when a rocket set off by a young boy struck him above his eye. On July 4, 1869, he was in San Francisco, where he and the town's mayor participated in a parade.

Sources: "Remarks of Governor Seward" and "Whig Celebration — Windmill Island," *Poulson's American Daily Advertiser*, 10 and 12 July 1839, 2 and 3, respectively; *Encyclopedia of American History*, 1149; John Sawyer, *History of Cherry Valley from 1740 to 1898* (Cherry Valley, N.Y.: Gazette Printing, 1898); *Sabbath School Celebration in Norwich, July Fourth, 1839* (Norwich, 1839?); *National Republican*, 8 July 1861, 3; Alexandria *Gazette*, 7 July 1864, 4; "The Fourth on the Pacific Coast," *Washington Evening Star*, 6 July 1869, 1.

Seymour, George Franklin (1829–1906)

Bishop of the American episcopate who delivered an oration on July 4, 1894, on the occasion of the laying of the cornerstone of the exposition building of the state fair of Illinois. Seymour was born in New York City, and graduated from Columbia College in 1850 and General Theological Seminary in 1854. After a number of parish appointments he wound up back at the seminary, where he was elected professor of ecclesiastical history in 1865 and dean of the institution in 1875. In 1878 he was elected bishop of Springfield, Illinois, where he took up residence. In his 1894 oration Seymour outlined the history and growth of the country and the purpose of the Illinois State Fair. "Thus it will be seen that our State Fair is an institution designed to promote directly the solid prosperity of our country, and so add to the greatness of our Fourth of July." Seymour ended his presentation with a look at the future. "When the orator of that distant day, the Fourth of July, 1994," Seymour said, "sums up the grand account of what a century has produced for our nation, he will justly claim for our Empire State, then embracing full twenty millions of happy people within its borders, no inconsiderable portion of what a hundred years have wrought for our mighty Republic."

Sources: George Seymour, *Oration Delivered on the Occasion* (Boston: G.R. Willis, 1894); "George Franklin Seymour," *The National Enclopaedia of American Biography* (New York: James T. White, 1900), 10: 357–58.

Seymour, Horatio (1810–1886)

Governor of New York and candidate for president whose speech on July 4, 1863, at Tammany Hall was said to have incited the New York City draft riots that took place a few days later. Seymour was born in Pompey Hill, near Syracuse, N.Y., and after studying law in Utica received his license in 1832. He was an ardent Democrat and was elected a member of the state assembly in 1841 and mayor of Utica in the following year. Seymour was governor of New York in 1853–54 and 1863–64. In 1856 he was a New York delegate to the Democratic National Convention and was a supporter of Stephen A. Douglas for the presidency. On July 4, 1856, Seymour spoke in Springfield, Mass. His speech was based on one he had made in New York at Tammany Hall nine months previous. When Lincoln was elected and the Civil War broke out, Seymour cautiously supported the war effort but was apprehensive about Lincoln's growing powers and "war-induced limitations on press freedoms and civil liberties." In 1862 as newly elected governor of New York, Seymour opposed Lincoln's efforts to initiate a military draft. With stiff resistance in some quarters of New York, Seymour spoke out about the draft on Independence Day in 1863, and his words likely precipitated the civil disturbance that followed. His popularity as governor was expressed on July 4, 1854, when a "Governor's March" was played in his honor by Shelton's Brass Band following a toast to the "chief magistrate" of the state at a dinner at Tammany Hall.

Seymour was considered well-read and an above average orator. His speech on July 4, 1863, took place at the Brooklyn Academy of Music. He spoke about the importance of the government respecting citizens' civil rights during wartime and that questionable, "treasonable" doctrine could be undertaken "by a mob as well as by a government." Within days a riot broke out and although Seymour was not present at the time, his speech was cited as the cause of the disturbance.

Other Fourth of July orations by Seymour included one given at the Democratic Convention at Tammany Hall on July 4, 1868. He was chosen president of the convention and his speech was described as "a tirade against the Republican policy of reconstruction." Another speech titled "The Future of the Human Race" was given on July 4, 1876, at Rome, New York. According to a report in the *Springfield Daily Republican*, Seymour was too sick to attend and had someone else read the address. On July 4, 1879, he was at Auburn Prison addressing the prisoners there.

Sources: "Independence Day," *New York Times*, 5 July 1854, 1; *New York Herald*, 6 July 1863; "The Governor and the Police," *Harper's Weekly*, 16 January 1864; "Domestic Intelligence: The Democratic Convention," *Harper's Weekly*, 18 September 1968, 451; "Other Celebrations," *Springfield Daily Republican*, 5 July 1876, 6; Stewart Mitchell, *Horatio Seymour of New York* (Cambridge, Mass.: Harvard University Press, 1938; reprint, New York: Da Capo Press, 1970); Joel H. Silbey, "Horatio Seymour," *American National Biography*, 19:687–88.

Shasta, California

Cited as the first town in northern California to celebrate the Fourth of July. The 1850 affair was held in a log house for boarders by a man named Johnson. Food included "roast beef, boiled ham, light bread, and pies made from dried Chile peaches." An American flag was tied to the branches of an oak tree. Participants from many of the original thirteen states were there as well as several Europeans. Royal T. Sprague, a chief justice of the Supreme Court of California, who recorded the event in his diary, read the Declaration of Independence and several short speeches were given by others.

Source: Benjamin Shurtliff, "Shasta," *Overland Monthly and Out West Magazine* 36/212 (August 1900): 157–58.

Shays' Rebellion

On July 4, 1927, a tablet was dedicated at Petersham, Massachusetts, "to mark the surprise and capture in that town of the insurgents under Daniel Shays" on February 4, 1787. The monument was presented to the Petersham Historical Society by the New England Society of Brooklyn. Harrington Putnam gave the "presentation address." Shays, a captain during the Revolutionary War, was a debt-ridden farmer who led 1,200 insurgents against the Massachusetts militia in Springfield as a result of mounting farm and home foreclosures and the high cost of court fees. The ensuing fight drove Shays from Springfield to Petersham, where his forces were eventually routed. Shays escaped to Vermont but was later pardoned (13 June 1788). The monument was placed on the grounds of the Petersham Historical Society by the New England Society of Brooklyn, New York.

Sources: "Tablet Marks End of Shays Rebellion," *New York Times*, 5 July 1927, 11; *Proceedings at the Dedication of a Tablet at Petersham, Massachusetts, July 4, 1927* (Brooklyn, New York: New England Society of Brooklyn, 1927?); *Encyclopedia of American History*, 137–38.

Shelby's Fort, Tennessee

Located near Beaver Creek in Tennessee in what is now the town of Bristol. This was the site for the first Fourth of July celebration in 1777 in Tennessee (which became a state in

1796). The fort was named after Evan Shelby (1720–1794), a Marylander and notorious Indian fighter. The fort was a well-known resting place for travelers, including, for example, Daniel Boone, George Rogers Clark, and other pioneers on their way west. Included in the celebration were militia formations, shooting contests and the firing of the fort's artillery. There was also a reading of the Declaration of Independence and an explanation of the commemoration to members of the Cherokee nation.

Sources: James B. Jones, Jr., *Every Day in Tennessee History* (Winston-Salem, N.C.: John F. Blair, 1996), 131–32; Carole Hammett and Fred Smoot, "Shelby's Forth and Squabble State," *The Land of Our Ancestors* (TNGen Web Project History Presentation), <http://www.tngenweb.org/tnland/squabble>.

Shelbyville, Tennessee, Centennial Celebration

Occurred on July 4, 1876, with addresses by T.H. Caldwell, E. Cooper, and H.L. Davidson. A poem by G.N. Tillman was read as well.

Source: *Centennial Celebration 4 July 1876* (Chattanooga: 1877).

Sherman, Roger (1721–1793)

Merchant, statesman, and signer of the Declaration of Independence. Born in Newton, Massachusetts, Sherman studied law, was a justice of the peace in Litchfield County (1755–61) and a judge of the superior court (1766–67). He was a delegate to both Continental Congresses (1774–81 and 1783–84) and was on the committee which drafted the Declaration of Independence and Articles of Confederation. After the Revolutionary War, Sherman lobbied on behalf of the Constitution and was elected to the U.S. House of Representatives (1789–91), followed by the U.S. Senate (1791–93).

History places Sherman at the Fourth of July celebration in 1788 held in the Brick Meeting House in New Haven, Connecticut. There he heard Josiah Meigs, publisher of the *New Haven Gazette and Connecticut Magazine*, read the Declaration of Independence and heard a performance of a federal hymn composed by Barna Bidwell, a tutor at Yale College. Following the official exercises, Sherman joined the others for a dinner at the State House. See also USS *Constitution*.

Source: "New Haven," *Connecticut Courant*, 14 July 1788, 2.

Sherman, William Tecumseh (1820–1891)

Soldier who graduated from West Point (1840), served remarkably during the Civil War, and after remained in the limelight, frequently participating in Fourth of July celebrations. Sherman was born in Lancaster, Ohio, served in the War with Mexico (1846–47) and fought in several major Civil War battles, including 1st Bull Run (1861), Shiloh (April 1862), after which he was promoted to major general, and the Battle of Chattanooga. He is perhaps best remember for his invasion of Georgia when he captured Atlanta (September 1864) and commenced his "March to the Sea," finally taking Savannah (December). Sherman's army of 60,000 men pillaged and destroyed everything within a 60-mile wide swath of land, 300 miles in length. Although the march was largely unopposed and helped bring the war to a close, the general's tactics were loathed by many.

After the war, Sherman enjoyed a wave of popularity in the North, but nonetheless felt compelled to explain why he believed himself justified for the manner in which he conducted the Georgia campaign. On July 3–4, 1865, Sherman was in Louisville, Kentucky, where he heard a welcoming address by Senator James Guthrie of Kentucky and responded to it, participated in a reception and civic celebration, and witnessed a balloon ascension (this information is taken from a plaque at the Louisville city wharf). In the following year, he was in Salem, Illinois, on July 4, giving a speech in which he defended his military decisions made in Georgia to a mostly friendly crowd of 25,000. Against a backdrop decorated with "tattered battle-flags of various Illinois regiments," Sherman said,

Now you all remember when we took Atlanta it looked as though with our army strung along a line of six or seven hundred miles the head of the column would be crushed. If I had gone on stringing out my forces would there not have been a time when the head of that column would have been crushed in? You soldiers are general enough to see that.... Some of your Illinois regiments would not have come home. Therefore I resolved in my mind to stop the game of guarding their cities, and destroy their cities.

Now, my friends, I know there are parties who denounce me as inhuman.... I care not what they say. I say that it ceased to be our duty to guard their cities any longer. I determined to go through their country, and so I took one army myself and gave my friend [Gen.] George Thomas [1816–1870] the other, and we whaled away with both. Therefore we destroyed Atlanta, and if we had destroyed all the cities of the South in order to bring about the result in view it would have been right.

Ironically, following his speech, a glee club of "young ladies and gentlemen" sang the popular song "Sherman's March to the Sea."

At least three additional noteworthy events occurred. On July 4, 1872, Sherman was in Madison, Wisconsin, where he was elected president of the Army of the Tennessee Society. At that celebration he assisted in the presentation of "a handsome badge of the society" to Ella Wheeler, a poet. Later they all dined at the Park Hotel. On July 4, 1876, Sherman was in Philadelphia at Independence Hall reviewing troops parading. On July 3–4, 1890, Sherman celebrated his final Fourth in Portland, Maine, at a celebration of the **Army of the Potomac Society**, where he praised the troops that fought in the Civil War.

Sources: "Items," *Weekly Missouri Democrat*, 18 July 1865, 2; "Our National Anniversary: Speech of Gen. Sherman," *Weekly Missouri Democrat*, 10 July 1866, 1; *New York Times*, 10 July 1865, 1, 6 July 1872, 1, 7 July 1876, 2, 4 July 1890, 1, and 5 July 1890, 2.

Ship parades

Spectacular events featuring ships began in the eighteenth century and were re-introduced in recent times as "tall ships" parades on the occasion of the **Bicentennial**. Other major tall ships parades on Independence Day included the 100th anniversary of the Statue of Liberty parade in New York Harbor in 1986 and the Millennium parade event in 2000.

Parades of boats and individual ships, both military and merchant, participating in

the Fourth of July were first popularized in Philadelphia harbor one year following the signing of the Declaration of Independence. On July 4, 1777, "all the armed ships and gallies in the river were drawn up before the city, dressed in the gayest manner, with the colours of the United States and streamers displayed." All of the ships fired artillery salutes.

A few years later on July 4, 1788, on the occasion of the ratification of the Constitution by ten states, again in Philadelphia, "ten vessels, in honor of the ten states of the union, were dressed, and arranged through the whole length of the harbour, each bearing a broad white flag at the mast-head, inscribed with the names of the states respectively, in broad gold letters. The ships at the wharves were also dressed on the occasion."

In the nineteenth and early twentieth centuries, events in which boats of varying size gathered on the Fourth helped to keep the tradition alive. For example, on July 4, 1828, a flotilla of steam boats and barges processed up the Potomac River to the site selected for the groundbreaking ceremony of the C and O Canal. Newspaper reports frequently commented on the visual effects of boats on parade and the popularity of excursionists to use boats to travel to places of recreation on the Fourth. An interest in boats was also popularized due to the many sailing regattas that were held on the holiday and to the tradition that boats were decorated on the Fourth. On July 4, 1860, a regatta featuring numerous vessels of all sizes gathered off the Battery in New York Harbor. In Boston on July 4, 1876, "the harbor was filled with excursion boats of all classes" and the sailing regatta "attracted thousands." In New London, Connecticut, a regatta was held in the harbor and the shipping displayed flags of all nations.

Other ships parades included one in Atlantic City, New Jersey, on July 4, 1900, that featured 100 parading sailboats. On July 4, 1933, 150 United States warships, decorated in multicolor signal bunting, gave a simultaneous 21-gun salute at 30 ports along the Pacific coast.

In 1976 on the occasion of the Bicentennial the first of a number of modern tall ships parades were started. "Operation Sail 1976" took place on the occasion of the 200th anniversary of the founding of the nation in New York Harbor and brought together an assemblage of the remaining square-riggers over 200 feet in length, as well as other sailing vessels (see **Bicentennial**). The 1986 "Salute to the Statue of Liberty" tall ships parade in New York Harbor was 18 miles in length and included 250 colorful vessels representing 30 nations (see **Statue of Liberty**). The 270-foot *Simon Bolivar* from Venezuela flew sails having the image of Lady Liberty and the accolade "Signs of Liberty" while the *Gloria* from Columbia also attended, sporting three masts, and its sailors singing an anthem representing their country. Daytime fireworks highlighted colors representing the countries of the ships as they passed by the statue. Earlier that day 21-gun salutes could be heard as an International Naval Review took place that included 31 military vessels representing the United States and 14 other countries.

On July 4, 1992, another tall ships parade took place in New York Harbor on the occasion of the 500th anniversary of Christopher Columbus's voyage to the New World. The 11-mile parade up the Hudson River included 270 ships from 37 nations. After the terrorist attack on September 11, 2001, tall ships parades were no longer planned. An exception occurred, however, on July 4, 2004, when the Brazilian tall ship *Cisne Branco* visited Baltimore Inner Harbor for the 150th anniversary of the USS *Constellation*.

Sources: *Virginia Gazette*, 18 July 1777; "Grand Federal Procession," *Pennsylvania Gazette*, 9 July 1788; "Independence Day Elsewhere," *New York Times*, 5 July 1876, 5; Margot Hornblower, "Millions View Colorful Shower in Honor of Refurbished Statue," *Washington Post*, 5 July 1986, A1, A11; "In Atlantic City," *Baltimore Morning Herald*, 5 July 1900, 1; *New York Times*, 5 July 1900, 7; *Washington Post*, 5 July 1933, 2; Robert D. McFadden, " A Quiet Majesty Sails the Hudson with Tall Ships," *New York Times*, 5 July 1992, 1; "A July Fourth Celebration," *Baltimore Sun*, 5 July 2004, A1.

Shires' National Theater, Cincinnati

The site for a "grand Fourth & Fifth of July Celebration" in 1862, at which a number of premiere performances took place. In the afternoon of July 4 a "patriotic drama" titled *Fourth of July in the Morning* was presented, with a "National Dance, by Miss Rosa Hill." In the evening a play titled *Young America* was presented as was a recitation of "Our Flag Forever" by Alice Hogan. On July 5 the plays *Cherry & Fair Star* and *Uncle Tom's Cabin* were performed. Other holiday events at the theater included music by the Mammoth Minstrel Band, a "Corps de Ballet of 50 young ladies and an army of supernumeraries," and "Rainford's Empire Minstrels."

Source: *Cincinnati Daily Gazette*, 4 July 1862, 4.

Signers Monument, Augusta, Georgia

This 50-foot monument on Greene Street was dedicated on July 4, 1848, and honors signers of the Declaration of Independence, including George Walton, twice governor of Georgia and Georgia chief judge, and Button Gwinnett, a Savannah merchant who was born in Connecticut.

Source: Bill Varian, "Monument Recalls Signers of the Declaration," *Augusta Chronicle Online*, 21 June 1996.

The Signing of the Declaration

A historical pageant produced by the Congress of the Bronx Open Forum, at City Hall, New York City, on July 4, 1916. Students of the Forum impersonated the principal characters.

Source: "2,000,000 Here Salute the Flag," *New York Times*, 5 July 1916, 12.

Sigourney, Mrs. Lydia Howard (1791–1865)

The first person to present an ode in Boston's Faneuil Hall on Independence Day, July 4, 1843.

The work was a three-stanza ode:
Clime! Beneath whose genial sun
Kings were quell'd, and freedom won:
Where the dust of Washington
Sleeps in glory's bed,—
Heroes from thy Sylvan shade
Chang'd the plough for battle-blade,—
Holy men for thee have pray'd,—
Patriot martyrs bled.
Crownless Judah mourns in gloom —
Greece lies slumbering in the tomb —
Rome hath shorn her eagle-plume,—

Smith Tower, Seattle, Washington, named after Lyman Cornelius Smith and the highest skyscraper outside New York at the time it was opened to the public on July 4, 1914. Item 3587, Photograph Collection, courtesy of the Seattle Municipal Archives.

Lost her conquering name,—
Youthful Nation of the west,
Rise! With truer greatness blest,
Sainted bands from realms of rest,—
Watch thy brightening fame.
Empire of the brave and free!
Stretch thy sway from sea to sea,—
Who shall bid thee bend the knee
To a tyrant's throne?—
Knowledge is thine armor bright,—
Liberty thy beacon-light,
God himself thy shield of might,—
Bow to Him alone.

Another Sigourney poem titled "Fourth of July" (first line: "We have a goodly clime"), with music by George W. Clark, was published in the latter's *The Liberty Minstrel* (New York: Leavitt and Alden, 1845). On July 4, 1853, in Providence, Rhode Island, at the First Baptist Church, Mrs. Sigourney's poem "Song" (first line: "Clime! Beneath whose genial sun") was presented.

Sources: Broadside, "Order of Performances at the Sixty-Seventh Anniversary of American Independence" (Boston: John H. Eastburn, 1843), in *An American Time Capsule*, Web site, <http://www.smithtower.com/History.html>. 12 September, 2002; *Municipal Celebration of the Seventy-Seventh Anniversary of American Independence* ... (Providence, R.I.: Knowles, Anthony and Co., 1853).

Smallwood, William (1732–1792)

In Mattawoman, Maryland, on July 4, 1876, the cornerstone to a monument in memory of Major General Smallwood, a Revolutionary War hero, was laid. Smallwood was once governor of the state. The stone was set near the mouth of Mattawoman Creek by "a delegation of the Masonic Lodge at Port Tobacco" and the Declaration of Independence was read by Simon Joseph and an oration delivered by A.K. Browne. In attendance was "a delegation of patriotic ladies and gentlemen" from Washington who arrived on the steamer *Harbinger*.

Source: "Celebration at Mattawoman, Md.," *Washington Evening Star*, 5 July 1876, 4.

Smith Tower, Seattle

Opened to the public on July 4, 1914. At the time of its construction, this skyscraper was the tallest building in the country outside of New York. Located on 2nd Avenue, the 465-foot-high structure had 42 stories and was first owned by business tycoon Lyman Cornelius Smith. On that first day, 4,400 persons ventured to the top of the building.

Sources: "New Smith Tower Receives Thousands," *Seattle Post-Intelligencer*, 5 July 1914, 2; Smith Tower Web site, April 2004.

Society of the Descendants of the Signers of the Declaration of Independence, Philadelphia

This association was established in 1908 and met annually on the Fourth of July. Perhaps the most newsworthy meeting occurred on July 4, 1913, when the society had their congress in the Continental Hotel. It was discovered that more than 200 persons had become members under "false pretenses" and their names were "stricken from the rolls." It was reported also that "some cases have been discovered where family trees were manufactured" and that "the investigation has been made quietly in order that there will be no scandal."

Source: "Not Signers' Descendants," *New York Times*, 4 July 1913, 4.

Soldiers and Devens Monuments, Worcester, Massachusetts

Two monuments were dedicated on July 4, 1906, in Worcester, Massachusetts: one to the soldiers of Worcester County who fought in the Civil War and the other, an equestrian statue, to Major-General Charles Devens (1820–1891), soldier, orator and jurist. Devens was born in Charlestown, Massachusetts, studied at Harvard, and served in the state senate (1848–49). At the start of the Civil War, he volunteered for service, participated in numerous battles, and eventually rose to the level of brevet major general. He was wounded several times and during the Battle of Cold Harbor (June 1864) he commanded his troops from a stretcher due to a severe bout of rheumatism.

The Devens ceremony included a parade of 1300 war veterans, the playing of the "Star-Spangled Banner" by a local band, and speeches by several officials, including Warren Goodale of the county commissioners and Massachusetts governor Curtin Guild, Jr. Guild told the story of how Devens worked to free runaway slave Thomas Sims, who had been returned to his owner. After Sims was granted freedom during the Civil War, Devens "secured him employment in the Department of Justice." The principal orator for the event was Gen. Stewart L. Woodford of New York, who spoke about Devens' life.

Sources: *Dedication of the Equestrian Statue of Major-General Charles Devens* (Worcester, Mass.: Commonwealth Press, 1907); Michael A. Cavanaugh, "Charles Devens, Jr.," *American National Biography*, 6:498–99.

Soldiers and Sailors Memorial Building, Zanesville, Ohio

The Muskingum County Soldiers and Sailors Monumental Association dedicated this building on July 4, 1889.

Source: *Dedication of the Soldiers' and Sailors Memorial Building* (Zanesville: The Association, 1889).

Soldiers and Sailors Monument, Buffalo, New York

At the celebration of Buffalo's semi-centennial anniversary of the incorporation of the city on July 4, 1882, the cornerstone of a soldiers and sailors' monument was laid in a driving rainstorm. The day's event included a "monster" parade, eight miles in length. Ironically, when the monument was unveiled on July 4, 1884, the ceremony had to be moved indoors due to a driving rain. See also **Connecticut Street Armory.**

Sources: "A Double Anniversary," *Baltimore Morning Herald*, 5 July 1882, 1; "A Gala Day at Buffalo," *New York Times*, 5 July 1884, 2.

Soldiers and Sailors Monument, Cleveland, Ohio

This monument for Cuyahoga County was dedicated on July 4, 1894, in Public Square in Cleveland. The celebration included "a 100-gun salute at sunrise, a reading of the Declaration of Independence, oratory by Gov. William McKinley and a 44-gun salute at noon followed by the 'Grand Process' of every military and civic organization in Cuyahoga County." According to Lou Mio, the monument was not a popular undertaking and a number of political battles ensued regarding its construction and maintenance over the years. At the ceremony Joseph Benson Foraker (1846–1917) presented a speech. A description of the monument in 1894 stated that "it is strictly American in design, commemorative of American deeds and triumphs in the war of the rebellion." In 1992 Levi Scofield described the monument in this way: "Around the exterior of the base are four bronze sculpture groupings depicting various battle scenes. Inside the monument's base, a tablet room lists names of the area's 10,000 Civil War veterans, including Scofield. Four bronze-relief sculptures depict war-related scenes."

On July 4, 1994, a one-hundred-year celebration for the monument took place that included a performance by the "Singing Angels, Civil War reenactments, a reading of the Gettysburg Address, and plenty of speakers, including Gov. George V. Voinovich and James McPherson, Princeton history professor and author of nine books on the Civil War."

Sources: *Official Program Dedication Soldiers and Sailors Monument* (Cleveland: Whitworth Bros., 1894); *Seattle Post-Intelligencer*, 5 July 1894, 1; Levi Scofield, "Monumental Decisions," *Cleveland Plain Dealer*, 15 November 1992, 12; Lou Mio, "100 Years and Still a Landmark: Public Square Monument Dedicated July 4, 1894," *Cleveland Plain Dealer*, 1 July 1994, 1B; Wendy Scott, "Monument Work Brings Rewards," *Cleveland Plain Dealer*, 3 July 1998, 6B.

Soldiers and Sailors Monument, Detroit, Michigan

A 3½-ton cornerstone was laid for this monument on July 4, 1867, under the auspices of the Michigan Soldiers' Monument Association. The monument was officially dedicated on April 9, 1872. In 2003, the monument underwent a restoration and moving of the structure to the city's new Campus Martius Park. In the process a large copper box that was stashed in the cornerstone area in 1867 was

retrieved. All of its contents had been destroyed by water, except for a silver dollar with the inscription "J.H. Morrison, jeweler, Detroit, Mich., July 4th, 1867" and a silver medallion that depicts Michigan's coat of arms and a tribute in words to the "gallant soldiers and sailors of the State who fought and fell on the war of 1861–65, for the preservation of the Union and Freedom."

Sources: "Letter from Gen. Sheridan," *New York Times*, 8 July 1867, 7; M.L. Elrick, "Civil War Memorabilia: Two 1860s-Era Silver Pieces Shine from the Muck Found Inside a Detroit Monument," *Detroit Free Press*, 11 October 2003.

Soldiers' and Sailors' Monument, White Plains, New York

Site for a Civil War monument unveiled on July 4, 1872. The monument was described as a "bronze figure of an infantry soldier, resting on his musket" and eight feet tall, rested on a "granite pedestal of equal height." On that day a procession marched to the monument on the "public green, opposite railroad Avenue," and the Rev. Mr. Wheatley, pastor of the Methodist Episcopal Memorial Church, delivered a brief speech. Other patriotic speeches and remarks were provided by Clarkson N. Potter, ex-judge Robert S. Hart of Mount Kisco, "Mr. Morse and Gen. Hamilton, grandson of Alexander Hamilton."

Source: "Unveiling a Soldiers' and Sailors' Monument at White Plains," *New York Times*, 5 July 1872, 5.

Soldiers' Memorial Building, Lebanon, New Hampshire

Was dedicated by the Soldiers' Memorial Building Association on July 4, 1890.

Source: *Services at the Dedication of Soldiers' Memorial Building, Lebanon, N.H., Friday, July 4, 1890* (Lebanon, N.H.: A.B. Freeman, 1890).

Soldiers Monument, Cabot, Vermont

This monument was dedicated on July 4, 1876, "to the memory of Cabot soldiers who fell in the great war of the Rebellion 1861–1865" (inscription). The memorial is dedicated to thirty-seven men and is twenty-one feet high. Its location is on the grounds near the Cabot United Church.

Source: Jane Brown, *Cabot, Vermont: A Collection of Memories from the Century Past* (Cabot, Vt.: Cabot Oral History Committee, 1999).

Soldiers Monument, Centre Sandwich, New Hampshire

The dedication of this memorial tablet occurred on July 4, 1894. The ceremony was at the Town Hall and included an oration by George H. Marston of Lowell, Massachusetts.

Source: *Exercises at Dedication of Memorial Tablet* (Sandwich, N.H.: Sandwich Reporter job print, 1894).

Soldiers' Monument, Lancaster, Pennsylvania. Dedicated on July 4, 1874. The plaque for the "Goddess of Liberty" reads, "Erected by the people of Lancaster County, to the memory of their fellow citizens who fell in defense of the union in the war of the rebellion 1861–1865." Photograph by author.

Soldiers Monument, Cherryfield, Maine

Was dedicated on July 4, 1874, and an address by Israel Washburn (1813–1883) was presented on the occasion.

Source: *Dedication of the Soldiers Monument at Cherryfield, Maine, July 4, 1874* (Portland: Bailey and Noyes, 1874).

Soldiers Monument, Cheshire, Connecticut

Dedicated on July 4, 1866. Speeches by "Colonel Wooster" and the "Rev. Professor Hoppin" were given at the ceremony.

Source: *Dedication of the Soldiers Monument at Cheshire, Conn.* (New York: W.W. Rose, 1866).

Soldiers' Monument, East Windsor, New Jersey

In this town on Independence Day in 1875, the East Windsor Soldiers' Monument Association dedicated a monument at the corner of Rogers and Stockton Streets in memory of the men from East Windsor and Hightstown who fought and died in the Civil War. Edward T. Green delivered the oration.

Source: Edward T. Green, *Oration Delivered Before the East Windsor Soldiers' Monument Association, at Hightstown, N.J., July 5th, 1875* (Trenton, N.J.: Murphy and Bechtel, 1875).

Soldiers Monument, Flushing, New York

A cornerstone was dedicated on July 4, 1866, with a ceremony and an oration by the Rev. George R. Crooks and "remarks" by Morris Franklin. A local newspaper reported the monument to be made of granite, "9 feet at the base, and 37 feet in length."

Source: "The Day at Flushing," *Brooklyn Daily Eagle*, 5 July 1866, 2.

Soldiers Monument, Haverhill, Massachusetts

Dedicated on July 5, 1869. Byron DeWolfe (1835–1873) wrote a poem for the occasion (first line: "Brave comrades, we remember yet").

Source: Broadside (Lawrence, Mass.: R. Bower, 1869).

Soldiers' Monument, Holyoke, Massachusetts

Dedicated on July 4, 1876. C.W. Slack of Boston was the orator, and he stated that the sculptor of the monument was an officer in the Confederate Army. Present at the ceremony was the Holyoke mayor.

Source:"The Brilliant Dedication of the Soldiers' Monument," *Springfield Daily Republican*, 5 July 1876, 5.

Soldiers Monument, Jersey City, New Jersey

On July 4, 1922, a monument to 147 soldiers who were killed during World War II was unveiled. It was described as "a life-size bronze figure of a woman, her arms filled with laurels. It is called 'Triumphant America.'" As part of the ceremony, 147 roses were dropped during a two-hour period from an airplane flying above the site.

Source: "Roses Fall on Monument," *New York Times*, 5 July 1922, 21.

Soldiers' Monument, Lancaster, Pennsylvania

This monument was unveiled and dedicated on July 4, 1874, in the town's Centre Square. Included in the ceremony were military units comprising the Grand Army of the Republic, and several patriotic societies. Music was provided by a band and choral society. Ex-governor Andrew G. Curtin was the orator. He discussed the significance of Pennsylvania in the Civil War and the "conciliation" of the national government and society. At the close of his address, four young girls, orphans of soldiers killed in the war, unveiled the statue, described as a "Goddess of Liberty" with "four statues at the base."

Source: "Soldiers' Memorial," *Philadelphia Inquirer*, 6 July 1874, 8.

Soldiers Monument, Marblehead, Massachusetts

Dedicated on July 4, 1876. The event included a "procession in four divisions," and the monument was unveiled by the president of the monument association.

Source: "Other Places," *Boston Evening Transcript*, 5 July 1876, 6.

Soldiers Monument, Montrose, Pennsylvania

Dedicated on July 4, 1877, at Monument Square in memory of the soldiers of Susquehanna County "who gave their lives for the preservation of the Union in the war of 1861–65." The event included military and civic parades, music by the Brooklyn Cornet Band and the 44th Regiment Band of Binghamton, and an oration by **Galusha A. Grow**, congressman from Pennsylvania and ex-Speaker of the House of Representatives. He spoke on the history of the country, the Civil War, and the significance of the monument and the soldiers that fought for their nation. "The night of our first great disaster is passed, and the foundations of our national greatness still stand strong," he said. "Turning from the shades of a sorrowful past, let us hail the sunlit dawn of a glorious future."

The monument was designed by Capt. J.R. Lyons of Montrose and stands 30 feet in height. The piece is articulated with words by Andrew Jackson and a carved crown reflecting "a halo of glory terminating in the apex of the arch, on the two sides of which are inscribed, in large raised letters, 'Give, then, the dead their due.'" An "earth-work, or miniature fort" that surrounds the base was considered by one reporter as "novel" and the "most interesting feature of the monument."

Sources: "Oration Delivered by Hon. G.A. Grow" and "The Fourth of July," *Republican*, 16 July 1877, 1 and 4, respectively.

Soldiers' Monument, New Hartford, Connecticut

New Hartford dedicated a Soldiers' Monument on July 4, 1893. The memorial was built by the Temple Brothers of Rutland, Vermont. At the ceremony Judge Fenn of the "supreme bench" delivered the address. *New Haven Evening Register*, 5 July 1893, 2; Civil War Monuments of Connecticut Web site, <http://www.chs.org/ransom/073.htm>.

Soldiers Monument, North Weymouth, Massachusetts

This monument was dedicated on July 4, 1868. At the ceremony George Bailey Loring (1817–1891) presented an oration.

Source: *An Oration Delivered at the Dedication of the Soldiers' Monument in North Weymouth, Mass.* (Weymouth, Mass.: C.G. Easterbrook, 1869).

Soldiers' Monument, Owego, New York

A monument to soldiers of past wars was unveiled in this Tioga County town on July 4, 1891, and Secretary of the Navy Benjamin F. Tracy gave a speech in honor of the day. He spoke about the restoration of the union. "In spite of their defeat the Southern people discovered in the results of the war the foundation of a new prosperity," he said.

Source: "Tioga's Soldier's Monument," *New York Times*, 5 July 1891, 1.

Soldiers' Monument, Painesville, Ohio

This monument was dedicated on July 4, 1880. **James Abram Garfield** was the principal speaker.

Source: "A Speech by Gen. Garfield," *New York Times*, 5 July 1880, 1.

Soldiers Monument, Point Pleasant, New Jersey

On July 4, 1925, a bronze tablet with the names of 170 veterans of World War I from the vicinity was unveiled. The monument was located at Richmond and River Avenues and "is encased in the base of a naval gun." The dedication address was given by the Rev. Isaac Whitaker, pastor of the Central Methodist Episcopal Church. Included in the event was a parade made of "civic and patriotic organizations," and soldiers.

Source: "Soldiers' Tablet Unveiled," *New York Times*, 5 July 1925, 18.

Soldiers Monument, Poughkeepsie, New York

On July 4, 1867, extensive preparations for a celebration to benefit a fund for erecting a soldiers monument were "only partially car-

ried out, owing to a severe thunderstorm." It was reported that "thousands of people had assembled from the surrounding country, and were greatly disappointed. There was to have been a large procession composed of military companies, civic societies, trades unions, etc., a balloon ascension and fireworks in the evening. The rain, however, prevented the fulfillment of the promises held out."

Source: "Disappointment at Poughkeepsie," *New York Times*, 5 July 1867, 8.

Soldiers' Monument, Rensselaerville, New York

Was dedicated on July 4, 1867, and Lyman Tremain (1819–1878) presented an oration for the occasion.

Source: *Oration Delivered at the Dedication of the Soldier's Monument at Rensselaerville, July 4, 1867* (Albany, N.Y.: Van Benthuysen Print. House, 1867).

Soldiers Monument, Sing Sing, New York

A cornerstone was laid for this monument on July 4, 1872. B.A. Willis presented an oration on the occasion of the event.

Source: *Oration Delivered by Colonel B.A. Willis at Sing Sing, N.Y....* (Sing Sing: Democratic Register Print, 1872).

Soldiers' Monument, Tarrytown, New York

The cornerstone of a monument in sleepy Hollow Cemetery near Tarrytown was laid on July 4, 1870, "to the memory of the brave soldiers who lost their lives during the late war." Many citizens of Brooklyn, Newburg, Nyack, Sing Sing, Spring Valley, Tarrytown, and other places were present. "The procession formed in the public square, opposite the railroad depot, in Tarrytown, and marched to the cemetery where the corner-stone was laid by Hon. Moses H. Grinnell, after which Col. Lansing delivered an eloquent oration appropriate to the occasion."

Source: "A Soldiers' Monument," *New York Times*, 5 July 1870, 4.

Soldiers Monument, Willoughby, Ohio

This 14-foot-tall monument was dedicated on July 4, 1885, in memory of those who served in the Civil War. The structure was designed by Joseph Carabelli of East Cleveland, and the names of soldiers are inscribed on the monument as well as the names of battles. Eight hundred veterans attended the celebration.

Source: Faith Corrigan, "Northern Ohio's Civil War Heritage" (typescript held by the Willoughby Historical Society).

Soldiers Monument, Woodlawn Heights, Bronx, New York

Unveiled on July 4, 1925, with 1000 spectators present. The memorial shaft commemorates World War I veterans from the area and was located at East 238th Street and Van Cortlandt Park. "Sailors, marines, Boy Scouts and veterans' organizations also participated." An artillery salute was fired and "Alford J. Williams Jr., son of Alderman Alford J. Williams and holder of the American aviation speed record of 266 miles an hour, flew over the crowd in a navy airplane and entertained onlookers with spirals and tail spins, nose dives and loop-the-loops, almost directly over their heads. Later he landed and made a short speech calling for a stronger air service." The memorial shaft bore the names of Woodlawn men who enlisted in the war, including eight who died in service, and at the top was a globe of polished granite. "The work was designed by Jule Holland."

Source: "Monument Unveiled to Woodlawn's Dead," *New York Times*, 5 July 1925, 18.

Sons of Ham, Memphis, Tennessee

Formed prior to the Civil War, this "mutual aid" organization, made up of African-American tradesmen, is credited with conducting the first organized black post–Civil War Fourth of July celebration in Memphis, in 1866. The event included a picnic and parade. A local newspaper reported substantial crowds were present and dressed in "holiday attire." For the next twenty years, the Sons of Ham, along with other black benevolent organizations such as the Independent Pole-Bearers, Daughters of Ham, Daughters of Zion, Sisters of Zion, Sons of Zion, the Mechanics Benevolent Association and the St. Johns Relief Society planned and led large Fourth of July celebratory events in

Memphis, often drawing as many as 5,000 persons from the surrounding area. During the mid-1870s there began a gradual assimilation of blacks into a reinvigorated white political movement whose goal it was to "gain command of local events." Also, "disfranchisement and Jim Crow segregation helped to pave the way for a rapid embrace of Independence Day by Memphis whites."

Source: Brian D. Page, "'Stand by the Flag': Nationalism and African-American Celebrations of the Fourth of July in Memphis, 1866–1887," *Tennessee Historical Quarterly* 58/4 (1999): 284–301.

Sons of the American Revolution

Founded in California on July 4, 1876, by 50 descendants of veterans of the Revolutionary War. Charters for forming branches of the society were sent to twenty states. In 1883, a society for the Sons was started in New York City. In 1889 a number of societies were formed in several states. On July 4, 1890, a Washington, D.C., branch of the society with 120 members (men and women) met for the first time. The meeting took place at the Norwood Institute. A reception committee consisted of Rep. William C.P. Breckinridge (Dem.— Ky.), Gen. H.V. Boynton, J.N. Toner, and Senator James S. Sherman (Rep.— N.Y.). Speeches were given by Rep. (Clifton Rodes?) Breckinridge, Rep. Joseph Wheeler (Dem.— Ala.), Rep. Charles H. Grosvenor (Rep.— Ohio), Rep. Benjamin Butterworth (Rep.— Ohio), who spoke about the men at Valley Forge, and Rep. John J. Hemphill (Dem.— S.C.), who "cited the men that the South had contributed to positions high in national affairs to show that it had performed its share to make this the greatest country the world had ever seen."

Another interesting meeting of the Washington-based society took place on July 4, 1899, at the Columbia Theater. Music was provided by the U.S. Marine Band and an oration was presented by Henry E. Davis.

Sources: "With the Spirit of '76," *Washington Post*, 5 July 1890, 7; "Will Observe the Fourth" and "No Exercises at Monument," *Washington Post*, 1 and 3 July 1899, 2 and 7, respectively.

Sousa, John Philip (1854–1932)

The composer and bandmaster who quickly became an American musical icon due to the patriotic music he first composed and performed in the 1890s. Sousa was born in Washington, D.C., and enlisted in the U.S. Marine Band in 1868, where he developed his musical skills for the next seven years. In 1876 he was a member of an orchestra conducted by the French composer Jacques Offenbach at the Centennial Exposition. In 1880 Sousa was appointed director of the Marine Band, a post he held until 1892, after which he formed his own Sousa Band. Sousa's renown as a musician and conductor was unprecedented. His bands toured throughout the United States and Europe and the marches he composed established him as the "March King" in households everywhere. A number of his marches were chosen for performance annually on the Fourth of July and to this day they continue to be patriotic crowd pleasers. These include *Semper Fidelis* (1888), *The Washington Post* (1889), *The Liberty Bell* (1893), and the best known *The Stars and Stripes Forever!* premiered in Philadelphia on May 14, 1897.

On July 4, 1894 and 1895, Sousa's Concert Band performed at Manhattan Beach on Coney Island. His *Manhattan Beach* (1893) march was composed in recognition of his concerts he gave there each summer. On July 3–4, 1900, Sousa provided the music for the unveiling of the Washington and Lafayette statues in Paris, France. The band performed *The Stars and Stripes Forever!* and helped to introduce this important work to European audiences. The popularity of this particular march prompted other bands to perform the work; for example, Fanciulli's Seventy-First Regiment Band performed a rendition at Central Park in New York on July 4, 1902, and the well-known Goldman Band broadcast a rendition on July 4, 1927, on New York radio station WEAF. After World War II the tune was used by bands and orchestras across the country in accompaniment of pubic fireworks displays. See also **Lafayette, Marquis de.**

Sources: *New York Times*, 1 and 5 July 1894, 12 and 9, respectively; "France Accepts America's Gift," *Washington Post*, 4 July 1900, 7; "Concert in Central Park," *New York Times*, 4 July 1902, 2; Stuart Hawkins, "On the Radio," *New York Herald Tribune*, 4 July 1927, 10; Paul E. Bierley, "John Philip Sousa," *Grove Music Online* (Oxford University Press, 2005).

Soviet-American Peace Walk

About 220 Soviets and 100 Americans left Washington, D.C., on June 17, 1988, to walk across the country on behalf of peace. On July 4 they reached Coralville, Iowa, where they participated in the town's parade of "fire trucks, marching bands, floats, clowns and politicians" and were applauded by hundreds of residents there.

Source: "Headline: Coast to Coast, Holiday Mood" (Associated Press), *St. Louis Post Dispatch*, 5 July 1988.

Space flights *see* National Aeronautics and Space Administration (NASA)

Spanish-American War

Cuban insurrection against Spanish rule in 1895 helped to foster sympathy by Americans for the Cuban struggle for independence. President Cleveland declined to intervene but after the destruction of the USS *Maine* in Havana Harbor on February 15, 1898, President McKinley was authorized by Congress to wage war. In less than four months the Americans had successfully forced the Spanish to surrender. The war had provided a resurgence of patriotism and pride by all Americans and helped to diminish disconsolate feelings about the American Civil War that had carried on for over thirty years.

During the Spanish-American War, the opposing navies engaged in battle in Cuban waters on July 3, 1898. With an American blockade in place outside Santiago Harbor, the Spanish fleet attempted to escape to open sea. The Spanish were defeated in a four-hour battle which signaled the end of the war. The news that reached the United States on July 4 resulted in one of the greatest national occasions for celebrating the Fourth of July since the Civil War era.

In the following year the Fourth of July was designated as "Santiago Day." In New York, Custom House workers petitioned the

Treasury Department to declare Santiago Day an official holiday. The city celebrated for two straight days as most persons celebrated the double holiday. Of significance, many stores and "mercantile organizations, including the Wholesale Jewelers' League, Dry Goods Association, and the Board of Trade and Transportation suspended business for two days. The stock exchanges were also closed, although the banks and public offices remained open.

In Newport, Rhode Island, Santiago Day was celebrated by "the dressing of the warships" and most other vessels in the harbor. "At noon the vessels of the squadron fired a National salute of twenty-one guns" and the rest of the day was celebrated with sports, races and dinners. In Omaha at the Greater American Exposition, Santiago Day included a speech by Postmaster-General Charles Emory Smith, who commented on the events at Santiago "and endorsed the attitude of the administration in the Philippines." Also present was a Spanish-American War veteran, Major-General Joseph Wheeler, who received "a great reception from the crowd" assembled there.

On July 4, 1901, Spanish-American War veterans marched in a parade in Nome, Alaska. On July 4, 1907, in Guthrio, Oklahoma, a group of veterans assembled for their annual reunion with a celebration and sham battle. As recent as July 4, 1951, Spanish-American War veterans celebrated in Boston, where they commemorated the sinking of the Spanish fleet in Santiago Harbor.

Sources: "Exposition Celebrates," *Los Angeles Times*, 4 July 1899, 2; "Santiago Day Celebrated" and "Santiago Day at Newport," *New York Times*, 4 July 1899, 10; *Nome News*, 6 July 1901, 1; "Rough Riders in Annual Reunion," *The Oklahoman*, 5 July 1907, 5; "The Fourth since 1776," *Life*, 7 July 1947, 14–16; *Boston Globe*, 5 July 1951, 3.

"Spirit of America"

The theme for a Fourth of July celebration in Decatur, Alabama, in 1973 at which Senator Edward M. Kennedy gave an address and Alabama governor George C. Wallace, having almost lost his life from an assassin's bullet, received the Audie Murphy Patriotism Award. In his speech, Kennedy admonished Nixon and the abuses inherent in the Water-gate scandal. He also cautioned his listeners that freedom "must be everlastingly guarded" by all generations.

Sources: *New York Times*, 5 July 1973, 1; Jules Witcover, "Kennedy Blasts Nixon, Hails Wallace 'Spirit,'" *Washington Post*, 5 July 1973, A1.

"Spirit of '76"

A common phrase used in parades, post-cards, and revelry throughout the history of the Fourth of July to represent the efforts of the founders, the war, and the great principles. At a celebration of the '76 Association in Charleston, South Carolina, on July 4, 1848, a toast was presented to "The Spirit of '76: It still lives and burns — may it live and burn forever." In 1858 in Chicago a balloon was named the "Spirit of '76." See **Balloon ascensions**.

Source: "'76 Association," *Charleston Courier*, 8 July 1848, 2.

Sports and games

Throughout the history of Fourth of July celebrations, sports and games have provided a popular means for participation in the nation's birthday. Spectator sports helped strengthen an awareness of community and national pride. Sports frequently mirrored the social and geographical interests of local communities. For example, on July 4, 1810, farmers of New Haven, Connecticut, held a plowing match, and on that same day in Bangor, Maine, an "Indian regatta in birch canoes with paddles" featured races having three heats. On the Fourth in the following year, games in Utica, New York, included wheelbarrow races, a "grand Pig Chase," and pole climbing. In New York on Independence Day in 1857, peddlers of all kinds sent up improvised stands in which they drew in crowds willing to try their hand at shooting at targets "at a cent a shot." Another popular game was ring toss at "heads of nails stuck upright in a board on the ground." Games were also popular for outside celebrations on lawns and in parks. For example, on James Draper's estate in Worcester on July 4, 1884, his 200 guests, who were members of the Massachusetts Grange, enjoyed playing croquet, quoits, swings, baseball, tenpins, and target practice.

As the popularity of sports continued to grow during the nineteenth century, clubs devoted specifically to such leisure activities were established. In New York on July 4, 1860, the city's Common Council allotted extra funds to support a five-race rowing regatta for boats of all sizes. On July 4, 1870, another Independence Day rowing regatta took place in New York with the Argonauta Club, the Larchmont and National Yacht Clubs, and the Piermont Rowing Association participating. Other popular sports included cricket, which was played in New York at Prospect Park, and bicycle races at Pomona, California, in 1894. In Los Angeles, on July 4, 1891, a tennis tournament was held. In Santa Barbara, California, on the Fourth in 1894, field and track events and boating races were held.

In the early twentieth century automobile races were introduced and boxing firemen contests were also popular. One of the significant fights in the history of the sport occurred on July 4, 1910, when African-American Jack Johnson knocked out white boxer Jim Jeffries, causing race riots across the nation. Another national boxing spectacle took place on July 4, 1919, in Toledo, Ohio, when Jack Dempsey and Jess Willard fought for the heavy-weight crown. Dempsey defeated Willard decisively in the third round. In the West rodeo events were scheduled to coincide with the Fourth such as, for example, the St. Paul Rodeo (Oregon), whose first rodeo on July 4, 1936, quickly became an annual tradition. However, the Prescott, Arizona, rodeo is touted as the oldest "cowboy tournament" in the West with its first event held on July 4, 1888. In Corona, California, on July 4, 1902, a fireman's hose contest was reported as "consisting of a 450-foot run with cart, lay 150 feet of hose, and coupling and procuring stream [and] was won by the Riverside Company."

The most important sport introduced in the nineteenth century and firmly associated with the Fourth was baseball. In the 1840s and 1850s, the first organized baseball club, the Olympic Ball Club of Philadelphia, played ballgames on the Fourth, and the sport was quickly popularized with games occurring in both large and small towns. In Portland, Maine, on July 4, 1864, organized baseball was premiered when Harvard College beat Bowdoin College. On July 5, 1885, a doubleheader was played between the towns of Portland and Biddeford, Maine, and baseball caught on as a popular pastime in the West. On July 4, 1918, baseball was introduced as America's national pastime to English spectators when 40,000 onlookers including the king and queen enjoyed a game between army and navy teams at London's Chelsea Football Grounds.

Also in the twentieth century the "Safe and Sane Movement" helped to promote the lowering of fireworks casualties with the creation of public playgrounds and established sports to offer alternative forms of enjoyment on the Fourth. On the Fourth in 1913 in New York, for example, safe and sane athletic events were held on all public parks throughout the day. Athletic associations were established, including Public Schools Athletic League, Military Amateur Athletic League and the Amateur Athletic Union.

Currently auto racing dominates the national sporting scene with the annual Pepsi 400 (previously named the Firecracker 400) held in Daytona, Florida, and the Pike's Peak International Hill Climb.

Sources: *Salem Gazette*, 24 July 1810, 2; *New York Times*, 6 July 1857, 2; "The Corporation Regatta," *New York Times*, 6 July 1860, 4; *Buffalo Express*, 6 July 1865, 1; *Utica Daily Observer*, 5 July 1866, 1, 3; "In Boston," *New York Times*, 5 July 1870, 5; "A Quiet Fourth of July," *New York Times*, 5 July 1881, 3; *Worcester Evening Gazette*, 5 July 1884; "At the Tennis Court," *Los Angeles Times*, 5 July 1891, 7; "Pomono," *Los Angeles Times*, 22 May 1894, 9; "Tuesday's Letter," *Los Angeles Times*, 4 July 1895, 13; "Corona," *Los Angeles Times*, 6 July 1902, 8; John Donovan, "Sports and the Fourth," *Sports Illustrated.com* Web site <http://sportsillustrated.cnn.com/inside_game/archives/john_donovan/>, 4 July 2003; S. W. Pope, *Patriotic Games: Sporting Traditions in the American Imagination, 1876–1926* (New York: Oxford University Press, 1997).

Springfield, Illinois, State Capitol building

The "Old State Capitol" served as the fifth Illinois statehouse from 1839 to 1876. Its cornerstone was laid on July 4, 1837. The building was the site for key events, ceremonies, and speeches. Abraham Lincoln presented some notable addresses there, such as his 1858 "House Divided" speech during his campaign to be elected Illinois state senator. On July 4, 1839, Springfield officially became the third capital of Illinois. In 1860, Lincoln used the "Governor's Room" as a base for his presidential election campaign. When Lincoln was assassinated in 1865, the Representatives' Hall was used as a place of remembrance for the president before gravesite services at Oak Ridge Cemetery. The Old State Capitol was renovated in 1969 and was designated as a state historic site.

Source: "Old State Capitol," Illinois State Historical Markers Web site, 12 September 2002, <http://www.historyillinois.org/frames/markers/241.htm>.

"Star Spangled Banner"

The U.S. national anthem and the most important song sung and played on the Fourth of July. The words were written by Francis Scott Key, who was on board a British ship on September 14, 1814, when it unleashed a twenty-five hour bombardment of Baltimore's **Fort McHenry**. Key's text was set to the tune "To Anacreon in Heaven," attributed to John Stafford Smith for the Anacreontic Society of London about 1775. Within a year the song, which had been published in the Baltimore *Patriot*, had immediate popularity and was permanently etched into the nation's heritage. On March 3, 1931, an act of Congress legally established the song as the nation's national anthem. The song has had an illustrious history in its use and the numerous variant texts set to it. Early performances occurred on July 4, 1815, when it was sung at the Washington Theatre by "Mr. Steward" and sung at another celebration at Bellevue, near Baltimore. On July 4, 1826, on the fiftieth anniversary of the signing of the Declaration of Independence, the tune was sung or played at celebrations in New York, Annapolis, Pittsburgh, and Petersburg, Virginia. The first performance by the U.S. Marine Band occurred on July 4, 1817, at Vauxhall Garden in Philadelphia.

Other performances of the tune on the Fourth during the 1820s–1830s occurred in St. Louis (1822), the District of Columbia (1828), Charleston, South Carolina (1828), New York (1831), Natchez, Mississippi (1836), and Elizabethtown, New Jersey (1838).

The tune of the 'Star-Spangled Banner" was frequently used as a setting for newly composed words for performances specifically on the Fourth of July. In celebration of the Fourth in 1833, a new text under the title "The Triumph of Union" was sent to the tune and printed in the Washington *Globe*. On July 4, 1835, for example, an ode (first line "Proud day for Columbia, we hail thee with song!") written for the tune was published in St. Louis. The ode was sung by the Franklin Society and was written by "a Lady of well known literary acquirements." The tune was often used for political texts, some of which were written to bring attention to a particular cause or issue. In Philadelphia, a four-stanza "Whig Patriotic Song," composed for July 4, 1837, was set to the tune and published in *Poulson's American Daily Advertiser*. The first line, "Midst the turmoil of party and anarchy's strife," reflects the tenor of the text.

Occasionally the words to the tune were not sung but simply read. Charles Hanford recited the "Star-Spangled Banner" just outside Washington, D.C., at Glen Echo Park, Maryland, on July 4, 1892.

Through the years critics have argued for adopting a new anthem. On July 4, 1922, the Rev. Robert Watson, pastor of the Second Presbyterian Church in New York, gave a sermon in which he explained why the national anthem needed to be replaced with another, one whose music is "simple, within a reasonable range, with plenty of melody, yet dignified." Watson said, "It should be proclaim the ideals of a true democracy" and "be constructed with a broad historic basis." On July 4, 1997, media mogul Ted Turner brought attention to the "militaristic" and "warlike" words. But as Columbus, Ohio, journalist Barbara Zuck responded in 2002, and as most Americans would likely agree, "The words, notably the famous first verse, were written by a concerned American anxiously watching a war, worried that the flag was gone, that the country was no longer safe and secure."

Sources: *Baltimore Patriot & Evening Advertiser,*

"Star Spangled Banner" (1854), for piano, by Charles Grobe. This set of "brilliant variations" was one of numerous renditions of the national anthem that were popular in the 19th century and typically performed on the Fourth of July. Grobe's use of the phrase "The Stars and Stripes Forever" predates John Philip Sousa's popular march of the same title by forty years. From the author's collection.

7 July 1815, 2; *National Intelligencer*, 3 July 1815, 3; *Richmond Enquirer*, 15 July 1817, 1; *Globe*, 6 July 1833, 2; *The Western Examiner*, 9 July 1835, 206; *Poulson's American Daily Advertiser*, 4 July 1837, 2; "Celebration at Glen Echo," *Washington Post*, 4 July 1892, 5; "Nation Needs New Song, Says Pastor," *New York Times*, 5 July 1922, 16; George J. Svejda, *History of the Star-Spangled Banner from 1814 to the Present* (Washington, D.C.: Division of History, Office of Archeology and Historic Preservation, 1969); William Lichtenwanger, "The Music of the Star-Spangled Banner: From Ludgate Hill to Capitol Hill," *Quarterly Journal of the Library of Congress*, July 1977; Barbara Zuck, "Oh! Say, Can You Sing?," *Columbus Dispatch*, 4 July 2002, 01B.

States Entering the Union

By an act of Congress in 1818, a state entering the Union was officially recognized as such on the first July 4 following the date of the enacted legislation.

States entering the Union	Date
Vermont, Kentucky	May 1, 1795
Tennessee, Ohio, Louisiana, Indiana, Mississippi	April 13, 1818
Illinois	July 4, 1819
Alabama, Maine	July 4, 1820
Missouri	July 4, 1822
Arkansas	July 4, 1836
Michigan	July 4, 1837
Florida	July 4, 1845
Texas	July 4, 1846
Iowa	July 4, 1847
Wisconsin	July 4, 1848
California	July 4, 1851
Minnesota	July 4, 1858
Oregon	July 4, 1861
Kansas, West Virginia	July 4, 1863
Nevada	July 4, 1865
Nebraska	July 4, 1867
Colorado	July 4, 1877
North Dakota, South Dakota, Montana, Washington, Idaho	July 4, 1890
Wyoming	July 4, 1891
Utah	July 4, 1896
Oklahoma	July 4, 1908
New Mexico, Arizona	July 4, 1912
Alaska	July 4, 1959
Hawaii	July 4, 1960

The number of states in the Union changed every few years and that resulted in occasional inaccurate ceremonial acknowledgments and outdated flags flown. On July 4, 1892, flags with forty-four stars were supposed to be flown across the nation, but in New

Title page of an oration presented by Charles Theodore Russell at the municipal celebration in Boston, July 4, 1851. Russell, an attorney, was among those in the 19th century who extolled the virtues "elasticity and adaptation" of the U.S. Constitution, as the territory of the country was expanded and new states were added. From the author's collection.

York, "an old flag with thirty-five stars was floating" above the Federal Building and the flags flown over City Hall had only forty-two stars each. There was one flag with 44 stars seen; it was arranged in four rows of seven stars each and two rows of eight stars each. "It was said that four parallel rows, with eleven stars in each, had been suggested, but the suggestion was not adopted, as it was feared that colored voters would become utterly demoralized by seeing 'fo,' 'leven , fo'ty-fo' on their country's ensign."

On July 4, 1906, many parts of the country, believing that Oklahoma was already a state, fired 46-gun artillery salutes. "The error traveled as far as Manila.... What is more astonishing is that at some forts in this country, some as near to Washington as Forts Howard and McHenry, Md., salutes of forty-six guns were fired."

Sources: "Old-Style Flags Flying," *New York Times*, 5 July 1892, 8; "Salute to Oklahoma," *New York Times*, 4 July 1906, 7; "Oklahoma Not a State," *New York Times*, 5 July 1906, 1.

Statue of Liberty (New York)

Located on Liberty Island in New York Harbor, this 151-foot-high copper statue is a universal symbol of liberty and political freedom. It was presented to the American people as a gift from France on July 4, 1886, and dedicated on October 28 that year. The statue was designated as a national monument on October 15, 1924.

The unveiling of the statue, which was conceived as "Liberty Enlightening the World" by French politician Edouard Rene Lefebvre de Laboulaye and sculptor Frédéric Auguste Bartholdi, was originally intended for the Centennial Exposition in Philadelphia in 1876, but although the monument was not finished in time for the event, the raised arm and torch were sent to Philadelphia for display. The 1886 presentation took place in Paris. Levi Parsons Morton, U.S. minister to France and later vice president under Benjamin Harrison, officially received the statue and "thanked France in the name of President Arthur and the American people." The statue is an emblem of liberty, the torch is freedom's light to the nations of the world and the Roman numerals on the tablet in her left hand spell the date — July 4, 1776.

On July 4, 1889, a replica of the Statue of Liberty was unveiled on the Isle de Cygnes. Present was Whitelaw Reid, U.S. minister to France, who acknowledged "the two great republics in their generous efforts to broaden the foundations of liberty, equality, and fraternity."

From 1984 to 1986, the statue underwent extensive renovation but was completed in time for its extraordinary centennial in July 1986. On June 26, 1986, the House of Representatives passed two joint resolutions for commemorating the event. House Joint Resolution 664 requested a proclamation be issued by the president that "individuals and groups across the United States ring bells on July 3, 1986, immediately following the relighting of the torch of the Statue of Liberty in New York City" and that July 3 be designated as "Let Freedom Ring Day." Another was a concurrent resolution (362) that on July 4 during the lighting of the torch, "a moment of silence be held and that the light of hope for the return of the Americans held captive in Lebanon be rekindled." The event was broadcast around the globe and included ten tons of fireworks set to music and a tall ships parade of hundreds of vessels. A ceremony with French president François Mitterrand and 3000 dignitaries was addressed by President Reagan. There were military bands jubilantly performing, as American and French postage stamps in honor of the statue were handed to Mitterrand and Reagan. Chrysler Chairman Lee A. Iacocca, principal fund-raiser for the renovation of the statue, hosted 800 Chrysler dealer families aboard the *Queen Elizabeth 2*.

Through the years, the Statue of Liberty has been the site for significant Fourth of July events, from a suffragists' demonstration of 1915 sponsored by the Empire State Campaign Committee in which an **"Appeal for Liberty"** was read, to fireworks displays including that of July 4, 1934, when an army warehouse near the base of the statue was burned down startling Fourth of July sightseers. After 9/11, the statue was closed to the public, but was reopened on August 3, 2004.

Sources: "Bartholdi's Statue," *New York Herald*, 5 July 1884, 5; "Bartholdi's Statue Presented," *New York Times*, 5 July 1884, 1; "France's Liberty Statue," *New York Times*, 5 July 1889, 5; "Fire Near Statue of Liberty Spoils a Quiet Anniversary on Bedloe's," *New York Times*, 5 July 1934, 19; *Washington Post*, 5 July 1934, 1; *Congressional Record*, 99th Congress, second session 132/11 (26 June 1986): 15662; Margot Hornblower, "Millions View Colorful Shower in Honor of Refurbished Statue," *Washington Post*, 5 July 1986, A1, A11.

Stevenson, Adlai E. (1835–1914)

Vice president (1893–97) under Grover Cleveland, who gave an "eloquent and patriotic" speech on July 4, 1892, in Peoria, Illinois, while running for office on the Democratic ticket. Refraining from commenting on politics, Stevenson "sketched the history of the Nation since the Declaration of independence," and directed his thoughts to the struggle in Ireland.

Today, fellow-citizens, enjoying liberty in the largest degree in this favored land, our thoughts turn to unfortunate Ireland, the ancestral home of so many of our countrymen. Oppressed by merciless exactions, with cruel landlordism, the heritage of each succeeding generation, yet struggling against odds for a larger measure of freedom, Ireland challenges at once our sympathy and admiration. May we not believe that the morning of a brighter day is soon to dawn on that gallant people, and that the fruits of centuries of suffering will be to them individual freedom of home rule.

Source: "Mr. Stevenson's Oration," *New York Times*, 5 July 1892, 2.

Stone, Harland Fiske (1872–1946) see "Pledge of Allegiance"

Stone, Thomas (1743–1787)

Maryland delegate to the Continental Congress and signer of the Declaration of Independence. On July 4, 1978, the Maryland Society of the Daughters of the American Revolution placed a memorial plaque in his honor at the foot of his memorial at Port Tobacco, Maryland. The Thomas Stone National Historic Site preserves his residence and gravesite.

Stone was born in Frederick, Maryland, but lived most of his life in Charles County, in southern Maryland. His home, Haberdeventure, was built in 1771, and he had two daughters and one son. Stone was one of the few delegates that preferred reconciliation with England, rather than conflict.

Source: Della Gray Barthelmas, *The Signers of the Declaration of Independence: A Biographical and Genealogical Reference* (Jefferson, N.C.: McFarland, 1997), 254–55.

Story, Isaac (1774–1803)

Wrote "Liberty, a Poem," which was delivered on the Fourth of July, probably in 1795, in Newburyport, Massachusetts. On July 4, 1801, he presented an oration in Worcester.

Sources: *Liberty, a Poem* (Newburyport, Mass.: William Barrett, 1795); *An Oration, on the Anniversary of the Independence of the United States of America* (Worcester, Mass.: Isaiah Thomas, Jr., 1801).

Story, Joseph (1779–1845)

Active on the Fourth of July as a poet and orator. On July 4, 1804, he delivered an oration and wrote a song for the ceremony at Salem. Wrote an ode for July 4, 1811, that was printed in the *National Intelligencer*, 30 July 1811, 3.

Source: Joseph Story, *An Oration, Pronounced at Salem* (Salem: Carlton, 1804).

"The Story of America" see Sesquicentennial Exposition, Philadelphia

Stratford Hall, Stratford, Virginia

Site for a commemorative ceremony on July 4, 1931, where two signers of the Declaration of Independence, Richard Henry Lee and Francis Lightfoot Lee, were honored by the Society of Colonial Dames of Virginia and the Lee Foundation. Another similar event took place in 1937. Stratford Hall in Stratford, Virginia, is the birthplace of Robert E. Lee.

Source: *New York Times*, 5 July 1931, 19.

"Strike! Strike! The Chord, Raise! Raise the Strain"

Composed for the celebration on July 4, 1815, in Lexington, Massachusetts, by "Mrs. Rowson." The "national song" has four stanzas and was first sung by "Mr. Rowson."

Strike! Strike! The chord, raise! Raise! The strain,
Let joy re-echo round each plain,
Your banners be unfurl'd;
Hail! Hail! The day when deathless Fame
Gave to Columbia rank and name,
Amid the astonish'd world.
The Muses snatch their harps sublime,
To publish Jove's decree,
Columbia to the end of time
Shall flourish great and free.

Source: *National Intelligencer*, 14 July 1815, 3.

Sturbridge Village, Massachusetts

Old Sturbridge Village is a re-created community where the daily life, work, and community celebrations of a rural New England town of the 1830s are portrayed by reenactors. The village is situated on 200 acres and over 40 exhibits include restored houses, farms, gardens, meeting houses, water-powered mills, tin, blacksmith and pottery shops, a district school, and a bookbinding office. Each year the settlement celebrates the Fourth through special ceremonies and events. Typical events on Independence Day at Old Sturbridge have included cannon demonstrations, nineteenth-century dancing, and dramatic readings of the Declaration of Independence.

An unusual event occurred on July 4, 1951, when an army artillery detachment fired a thirteen-gun salute using a 105-mm. gun. The resulting reverberations caused the glass in the historic buildings to break. Only a week prior, a hailstorm had cracked nearly 100 windows, which had been quickly repaired. Other Fourth events have included raising and lowering of a 26-star American flag, patriotic songs, 1830s baseball games, an old-fashioned tug of war, and music from the Old Sturbridge Village Junior Fife and Drum.

Sources: *New York Times*, 5 July 1951, 27; Jennifer A. Clark, "Fourth of July Sparks Cannon at Sturbridge," *Boston Herald*, 29 July 1997, 050; "Old Sturbridge Boasts 'Best' Fourth of July," *News-Times* online edition, <*http://archives.newstimes.com/leisure/20030sv.htm*>, 16 July 2004.

Sully, Sally (fl. 1817–1856)

Wrote "Patriotic Song Commemorative of Opening the Union Hotel in the City of Richmond, Virg, on the Fourth of July, 1817." Music by Leroy Anderson. (Printed, New York: J.A. and W. Geib, [1818–1821]). First line: "Down the stream of time have glided." Sally Sully was listed as a "professor of music" in the Richmond, Virginia, directory for 1856.

Source: Wolfe, *Secular Music in America, 1801–1825: A Bibliography*, 2:890.

Sumner, Charles (1811–1874)

Distinguished statesman, lawyer, and activist in the peace movement who frequently spoke recommending the outlawing of war.

His best known address was titled "The True Grandeur of Nations" (published by the American Peace Society) presented in Boston on July 4, 1845. His address represents an important document of the pacifist movement during the mid-nineteenth century. Sumner condemned war suggesting military forces cost more money than the commerce they were to protect. Further, Christianity outlawed war and conflict precipitated the downfall of morality. In some corners his speech provoked hostile criticism. In the following year, **Fletcher Webster** delivered an address in Boston advocating on behalf of war when all efforts for peace have failed.

Sumner was an opponent of the Mexican War and helped establish the Free-Soil party in 1848. He opposed the Kansas-Nebraska Bill of 1854 and as a result of a speech he gave concerning Kansas on May 22, 1856, he was physically attacked by Rep. Preston Brooks (S.C.). Due to the injuries he sustained, Sumner was forced to leave the Senate. He recuperated at Falkland, the summer estate of his friend **Montgomery Blair**, the manor located in Silver Spring, Maryland, a few miles outside of Washington. A few weeks later, in anticipation of the Fourth of July ceremony held in Springfield, Massachusetts, officials there invited Sumner to the event. Sumner, who was still at Falkland, declined the offer and in a letter he wrote on July 2, made a poignant expression of his dislike of slavery and admonished others on the nation's natal day to "dedicate the anniversary of our Independence to generous efforts, by which our country may be emancipated from a tyranny far worse than that against which our Fathers rose. I trust that you will all, without regard to old party distinctions, declare your independence of the Slave Oligarchy, and pledge yourselves to maintain your declaration honestly and firmly by your votes."

Sumner's interest assuring that the Declaration's principle — "all men are created equal" — was equally afforded to all immigrants was evident on July 4, 1870, when Congress was considering a naturalization bill. Sumner offered an amendment, striking the word "white" from the naturalization laws, "making them apply equally to all foreigners." Upon pressure to withdraw the amendment, Sumner refused, arguing "that the restriction of the privilege of naturalization to white men was in derogation of the principles of the Declaration of Independence, that all men are created equal."

Sources: "Latest Intelligence" and "The Fourth in Other Cities," *New York Times*, 4 July 1856, 1, 8 July 1856, 3, respectively, and 5 July 1870, 5.

Sunoco Welcome America!

The theme for Philadelphia's Independence Day celebrations that began in 1993 by Welcome America, Inc., a non-profit organization. The first event was created to herald the opening of the Pennsylvania Convention Center. All of the events have been free due to the generosity of over 170 sponsors. Highlights in 2001 included "Go 4th and Learn" which featured "the artistic and creative talents" of Philadelphia's youth, the Philadelphia Liberty Medal award presentations, the Let Freedom Ring Ceremony, the Pennsylvania Memories Last a Lifetime Parade, and the Sweet Sounds of Liberty Concert and Fireworks Spectacular. On July 6, 2002, Philadelphia Mayor John Street gave a radio address that commended Sunoco for its support. "Our annual celebration of July 4th must be commensurate with the prominent role our city played in our nation's history," he said. "How fortunate we are in Philadelphia to have a corporation like Sunoco that understands the importance of the holiday to our great city and has demonstrated its love of Philadelphia through its continuing and critical support of our Welcome America celebration."

Sources: Sunoco Welcome America! Web site, <http://www.americasbirthday.com>, 8 April 2002; "Radio Addresses: Sunoco and the Meaning of Commitment," Web site, 6 July 2002, <http://www.phila.gov/radio>.

Susquehanna Museum, Havre de Grace, Maryland

At this museum, on July 4, 1999, town officials dedicated a memorial exhibit in commemoration of 232 Harford County residents who died in World Wars I and II and the Korean and Vietnam Wars.

Source: *Baltimore Sun*, 5 July 1999, B2.

Swan City, Colorado, Post Office

The "most notable" Fourth of July event in the state of Colorado in 1884 was reported in this mining town, when the miners blew up the post office there as a result of the group not being supplied fireworks to celebrate the holiday. No one was injured in the event.

Source: "A Post Office Blown Up," *New York Times*, 5 July 1884, 2.

Sylvan Theater, Washington, D.C.

An outdoor amphitheater located on the Washington Mall and a traditional site for Independence Day concerts, ceremonies, and speeches during the last eighty-five years. The city's "first celebration of Independence Day by pageantry and song in a government-owned theater" took place there on July 4, 1917, before an audience of 15,000. The production, titled "The Call of the Allies," and written by Mrs. Christian Hammick, included allegorical figures of Joy, Peace, Liberty and Freedom, fleeing from the stage and pursued by War. "As each character appeared the Marine Band played the national anthem of the nation represented." A chorus was directed by William Stansfield, with solos by Miss Edna Thomas, Mrs. Anna Brett Summy and Lewis Thompson.

On July 4, 1926, the U.S. Navy Band provided the first night time musical performance as an accompaniment to the fireworks display on the Mall. On Independence Day in 1927, with music provided by the U.S. Marine Band, Charles F. Carusi, president of the D.C. Board of Education and grandson of Nathaniel Carusi, a musician who performed on the Fourth of July in Annapolis in 1816, read portions of the Declaration of Independence. Judge Mary O'Toole also recited the "Pledge of Allegiance." On July 4, 1929, Senator Pat Harrison of Mississippi gave an address. On July 4, 1930, a speech by Senator Simeon D. Fess of Ohio at the Sylvan was broadcast over radio station WRC. On July 4, 1931, Assistant Secretary of State James Grafton Rogers gave a "debt moratorium" speech there and on July 4, 1950, John Foster Dulles spoke about the North Korean invasion of South Korea. On July 4, 1952, the program

"Salute to the Armed Services," was postponed until July 5 due to rain.

Sources: "Give 'Call of the Allies' at the Sylvan Theater," *Washington Evening Star*, 5 July 1917, 12; *Washington Evening Star*, 5 July 1926, 1; "Capital Observes Nation's Birthday in Patriotic Fetes," *Washington Evening Star*, 4 July 1927, 1; *New York Times*, 4 July 1929, 7; *Washington Post*, 5 July 1931, 2; *Washington Star*, 4 July 1933; "July 4 Crowd Told Strife Will Be Costly," *Washington Post*, 5 July 1950, 1, 7; "Fourth of July Show Tonight at Monument," *Washington Post*, 5 July 1952, A1.

Tacoma, Washington, Trolley Accident

The 1900 Fourth of July celebration held in Tacoma, Washington, was abruptly halted when a trolley car carrying revelers on their way into Tacoma to watch the parade left the track and crashed, killing 40 persons and injuring 65 others. The train had left Edison, a suburb, and had 104 passengers aboard. As the car approached a bridge it jumped the track and "turned and fell seventy-five feet through the air, when it struck the side of a gulch, where the framework was smashed." According to a newspaper reporter, the wreck was the worst in that state's history.

Sources: "Excursionists Die," *Baltimore Morning Herald*, 5 July 1900, 11; "Forty Killed in Trolley Accident," *New York Herald*, 5 July 1900, 10.

Taft, William Howard (1857–1930)

Twenty-seventh president of the U.S. (1909–13). The only man to have served both as president and chief justice of the U.S. Supreme Court (1921–30). Taft made several appearances on the Fourth of July during his presidency and it was under his tenure that the "safe and sane" movement for ridding the Fourth of unofficial fireworks was begun. On Saturday, July 3, 1909, before leaving for Paramatta, his summer White House in Beverley, Massachusetts, Taft issued a letter to the district commissioner expressing his content and encouragement of the safe and sane idea. "I am heartily in sympathy with the movement to rid the celebration of our country's natal day of these distressing accidents that might be avoided and are merely due to a recklessness against which the public protest cannot be too emphatic." On Monday, July 5, Taft was in Norwich, Connecticut, assisting in that town's celebration of the 250th anniversary of its founding and the 150th anniversary of its incorporation. He reviewed a military parade from Buckingham Memorial, gave a speech, and held a public reception.

On July 4, 1910, Taft was at Harvard Stadium where he addressed the **National Education Association (NEA)**. He discussed the Constitution "at some length and spoke of the extension of the American form of government to the Philippines" (see also **Philippine Islands**). Taft commented on the significance that the NEA meeting was held on the Fourth of July. "The presence in this audience of thousands of those engaged in the education of the youth of the country on this natal day of the republic," he said, "suggests the discussing of the relation of education to democratic government." On that day Taft also visited several nearby cities. In Everett, he was delighted with a large parade of school children. In Somerville, he saw a characteristic Independence Day parade. In Boston he presented a speech about that town's effort in the "safe and sane" movement.

On July 4, 1911, Taft was in Indianapolis where he reviewed "a sane Fourth of July parade," and witnessed a staged train locomotive wreck. He presented a speech on reciprocity that evening at a banquet ceremony at the Claypool Hotel, sponsored by the Marion Club, a Republican organization. A reporter noted that in his address "the President dwelt upon the advantages to the agricultural interest of the removal of Canadian duties, and declared that the measure, while Republican in spirit, was non-partisan." Earlier that day Taft had visited Washington Park, where he awarded prizes for a pageant presented there, followed by a "long ride to the Fair Grounds" to see the two locomotives collide. A reporter noted,

The President was particularly interested in the collision. The two locomotives, starting under full steam on the same track, came together at high speed two hundred yards from where the President sat. Neither one left the track, but both were reduced to scrap iron.

In 1912, Taft was at Paramatta. There he presented a brief speech before the Taft Club of Beverly, followed by a visit to the Myopia Hunt Club where he played a round of golf.

Sources: "Norwich Celebration Begun," *New York Times*, 5 July 1909, 7; "Taft for a Sane Fourth," *New York Times*, 6 July 1909, 3; "Taft on the Philippines" and "Safe and Sane Day the Country Over," *New York Times*, 5 July 1910, 13 and 18, respectively; "President Defends Reciprocity Plan," *New York Times*, 5 July 1911, 11; "Taft Welcomed Back to Beverly," *Philadelphia Inquirer*, 5 July 1912, 10.

Tall ships *see* Ship parades

Tammany Hall, New York

Popular name of the political organization in New York that dominated Democratic Party matters there from its founding in the 1780s to the mid-20th century. The Society of St. Tammany worked towards influencing city and state elections in their favor, while expanding their political base through assisting the working class and new immigrants. For over 100 years Tammany met regularly on the Fourth of July in an effort to mix party politics with patriotism, and their efforts were largely successful. The society consistently produced some of the grand and memorable highly ritualized celebrations in New York. Numerous speakers of national repute gave addresses there. Musical works were premiered and the events commonly included poetry recitations and readings of the Declaration of Independence. On July 5, 1893, an editorial in the *New York Times* best described Tammany's traditions:

> The Tammany Society has at least the distinction of keeping up from year to year a more fervid celebration of the anniversary of our national independence than any other organization in the country. If in that celebration there is fully as strong a flavor of partisanship as of patriotism, it is to be excused on the ground that Tammany is a partisan organization and makes little pretense to being anything else. The practice of getting Democratic speakers or eliciting letters from Democratic leaders from all parts of the country gives the Fourth of July celebration in Tammany Hall its chief interest.

Throughout the years, their meetings were held in different buildings, known as wigwams, first on Spruce Street (1798–1812), the second at Nassau and Frankfort Streets (1812–68), another on 14th Street (1868–1929), and the last at Union Square (1929).

Tammany leaders, referred to as "sachems," were held in great esteem by society members, and they courted political patronage by inviting well-known Democratic congressmen and other political leaders to speak on Independence Day. Members of the wigwam, referred to as braves and squaws, frequently dressed in colorful costumes and sporting regalia, with the most important ceremonial headdress being the "Cap of Liberty," a symbol of bravery and freedom. At the ceremony in 1858, a new liberty cap was presented to replace the previous one. The "semi-oval part" of the hat was of "rich red silk, the base of blue velvet, from the top is suspended a golden tassel, and on the border are thirteen stars in silver, designating the old confederation of states." The events included much pomp and ceremony and the buildings were typically gaily decorated with flags, banners, and pictures.

One of the earliest reported celebrations occurred on July 4, 1791, when the society marched up Broad Street to the New Dutch Church where they heard the Declaration of Independence read and an address. From there they processed to the Battery, where they enjoyed an artillery salute.

At the Fourth of July celebration in 1858, amidst numerous flags and banners of the thirteen States suspended on the walls, Caleb Cushing gave an oration and ex-senator of New York State William McMurray presented a red and blue "Cap of Liberty" to the society. On July 4, 1877, for example, the grand hall featured a plaster bust of Washington with a "background of white muslin dotted with golden stars." A "blue silk banneret, inscribed in gold letters, 'The Brave, the Wise, and the Good'" was displayed in front. There were additional Tammany banners and "gaudy full length lithographs of the Goddess of Liberty and of Washington. In all the doors and windows, on the front of the gallery, beneath it, and at intervals among the painted State shields on the walls, were draped in fan shapes American flags."

Through the years, Tammany provided an ideal setting for the premiere of new musical works, poetry, and performances by a wide variety of ensembles. One of the regular groups that appeared there was the "Tammany Glee Club." On July 4, 1861, the group sang "The Standard of the Free" by John Mahon. On July 4, 1864, a number of public school children premiered a work by Charles F. Alney titled "The Voice of '76." On July 4, 1870, a song, "The Standard of Freedom," was sung by William H. Davis and a poem titled "Old Tammany," by John G. Saxe, was read. A Tammany event on July 4, 1921, combined several patriotic attractions, including singing by the Tammany Glee Club and music by Ward's Band, a reading of "An American's Creed" by Abraham Kaplan, president of the Municipal Civil Service Commission, and a "Pledge to the Flag" by Tammany members and the audience.

Readings of the Declaration of Independence were a popular feature of the celebrations, with at least one of them a memorable occasion. On July 4, 1870, Edward Randolph Robinson, a descendant of Thomas Jefferson, recited the sacred document before a large crowd assembled there.

On July 4, 1919, Miss Elizabeth McCrystal was the first female in the history of the society to give a speech at its annual Fourth gathering. Her "short talk" followed a reading of the Declaration of Independence by Gov. Alfred E. Smith. On the occasion of the 150th anniversary of Tammany Hall on July 4, 1936, speeches by Attorney General Homer Cummings and Senators Robert F. Wagner and Royal S. Copeland were presented. Prior to the ceremonies at the hall, "a parade was headed by thirteen Grand Sachems in full regalia, to Union Square for a patriotic demonstration around the Liberty Pole."

On July 4, 1928, the last society celebration in its 14th Street hall was held. Supreme Court Justice Alfred H. Townley read the Declaration of Independence and Governor Alfred E. Smith addressed Tammany members. Smith's speech was broadcast over local radio station WNYC. "The down-trodden, the poor, the oppressed of every country have looked to America and America has cared for them," he said. "The children of today can say

that they lived in the period of American history, when divine Providence used the power, the wealth and the strength of this country for the preservation of the peace of civilization."

Sources: *Federal Gazette and Daily Advertiser*, 6 July 1791; "The Celebration in Tammany," *New York Times*, 6 July 1858, 1; "Celebration of the Tammany Society," *New York Times*, 6 July 1861, 2; *New York Daily News*, 6 July 1864, 2; "Things in New York," *Philadelphia Inquirer*, 6 July 1870, 2; "The Celebration at Tammany Hall," *New York Times*, 5 July 1870, 1; "Tammany's Celebration," *New York Times*, 5 July 1877, 6; "Talks in Tammany Hall," *New York Times*, 5 July 1893, 4; "Wigwam to Hear Woman," *New York Times*, 30 June 1919, 12; "Tammany Observes Day with Oratory," *New York Times*, 5 July 1921, 2; "Smith Defends Tammany as Braves Roar Welcome," *New York Times*, 5 July 1928, 1; "Tammany Hall 150 Years Old: Hails Roosevelt," *Washington Post*, 5 July 1936, A2.

Tammany Hall Building (1867), New York

This was the third building, its "wigwam," used by the Tammany Hall political organization. It was located at East 14th Street near 3rd Avenue. The cornerstone of the new Tammany Hall was laid on July 4, 1867, with the sounds of Grafulla's Band playing at the exercise. The ceremony was held in Irving Hall. Exactly a year later on July 4, the building was dedicated. Speaking at the ceremony was politician Gulian C. Verplanck in his last public appearance. On July 4, 1928, the last celebration of the Tammany Society took place there. Governor Alfred E. Smith addressed its members. On July 4, 1929, a new building was dedicated at Fourth Avenue and Seventeenth Street. Speakers included Governor Franklin D. Roosevelt and former governor Alfred E. Smith, and Mayor James J. Walker. A special tribute was paid to John R. Vooris, grand sachem, who was nearing 100 years of age.

Sources: *New York Citizen*, 29 June 1867, 8; "Corner-Stone of Tammany Hall," *New York Times*, 5 July 1867, 1; *Harper's Weekly*, 9 April 1870; *New York Times*, 5 July 1928, 1–2, and 4 July 1929, 7.

Tammany Society, Philadelphia

Active from the late 1780s with numerous members and guests who celebrated the Fourth of July. On July 4, 1814, the Society assembled with great pomp at "brother Trotter's, at Richmond, on the Delaware." Artillery was discharged, the Declaration of Independence read, and members "sat down to two tables, of 160 feet each in length, well and plentifully supplied with the best products of the season." After the dinner 18 toasts were drunk, with one offered to "Peace — The end of war is peace, and an end to the present war, so soon as our enemy shall be restored to reason."

Source: "Anniversary of American Independence," *Philadelphia Aurora General Advertiser*, 6 July 1814, 2.

Taylor, Bayard (1825–1878)

Writer and poet who was highly regarded in his day and who composed noteworthy poetry for the 1876 Centennial celebrations of the Fourth of July held in Philadelphia, New York, and Washington, D.C. He publicly recited his "National Ode" (first line, "Sun of the stately day") from memory "amidst thunders of applause" at Independence Square in Philadelphia on July 4. Published in Boston, the work received considerable attention in a number of cities across the country, including, for example, Omaha, Nebraska. In London, parts of his poem were publicly read at the Centennial Fourth celebration held by the American Legation at the Westminster Palace Hotel. His "Song of 1876" ("Waken, voice of the land's devotion!") was written for the New York celebration and reprinted in newspapers across the country. In Washington, D.C., his "Centennial Bells" was read by John Tweedale at the First Congregational Church. Taylor was born in Kennett Square, Pennsylvania, and early began a long distinguished career writing poems and articles, many of which were based on extended tours he took in Europe, Egypt, India, and China. Among his most popular volumes of verse were *A Book of Romances, Lyrics, and Songs* (1851) and *Poems of the Orient* (1854).

Sources: *Chicago Tribune*, 5 July 1876, 2; "Celebration at the Congregational Church," *Washington Evening Star*, 5 July 1876, 4; "Editor's Easy Chair," *Harper's New Monthly Magazine* 53/316 (September 1876): 621–22; *The National Ode* (Boston: James R. Osgood, 1876); "City of the Declaration" and "Greetings from Abroad," *New York Times*, 5 July 1876, 3 and 7, respectively; *Omaha Republican*, 6 July 1876, 2.

Taylor, Joash Rice

Wrote an ode on the occasion of the "national anniversary" celebrated at Kenyon College, Gambier, Ohio, on July 4, 1839.

Source: J. Rice Taylor, *Ode Written for the Celebration....* (Gambier: G.W. Myers, 1839).

Taylor, Zachary (1784–1850)

Twelfth president of the U.S. (1849–50), who was inaugurated on March 4, 1849, but served only until his death on July 9, 1850, caused by food poisoning during the Fourth of July celebration in the nation's capital. Taylor was born in Montebello, Virginia, and served for 40 years in the U.S. Army. He fought in several wars, most notably in the War with Mexico, where he defeated Santa Anna at Buena Vista in February 1847, an engagement that made him a national hero. On July 4, 1849, Taylor went over to the East Park near the Capitol to hear P.R. Fendall present an oration and later received the children of the E Street Baptist Church in the East Room of the White House. He listened to an address by Master R.W. Wilcox and two hymns ("Auspicious morning hail!" and "Loud raise the peal of gladness") sung by the children. Taylor thanked the group for their visit and "wished for them all long lives of happiness and prosperity." Meanwhile in New York, Taylor's letter of acceptance, written December 13, 1848, for the invitation to be an honorary member of the New York State Society of the Cincinnati, was read aloud at the latter's meeting that day. At Wilmington Delaware, at Central Hall, the following toast was offered to the president: "President Taylor: The regenerator and restorer of the policy of Washington and the earlier Presidents — A policy opposed to war, conquest, and territorial aggrandizement, which preserves us from the entanglements of foreign diplomacy and ambition, and gives us in exchange the blessings of peace, commerce, and national prosperity."

On July 4, 1850, Taylor, along with members of his cabinet, attended the celebration held in front of the Washington Monument where he observed the ceremonial reception of a block of marble from the Corporation of Washington. On the following day he became ill with what was diagnosed as cholera. During the next several days his condition worsened, and on July 9 he died surrounded by members of his family.

Sources: "Sabbath School Visit to the President," and "New York Correspondence," *National Intelligencer* 6 July 1849, 1 and 3, respectively; "Anniversary Festivities," *National Intelligencer*, 10 July 1849, 2.

"Teachers and Scholars Parade," Charleston College

On July 4, 1844, a city-wide festival of teachers and students of Charleston College took place. A highlight of the day was a parade made up of members of the faculty, trustees of the college, and students. The procession wound its way through city streets and ended at a refreshment area that provided "ice lemonade, cakes, [and] fruit." Ceremonial exercises took place on the college campus and consisted of a prayer and three student addresses.

Source: *Charleston Mercury*, 4 July 1844, 2.

Temperance Hall, Washington

The cornerstone for this building was laid on July 4, 1843. The ceremony was attended by the Sons of Temperance, Total Abstinence Society, and Washington Light Infantry and Union Guards. **A.F. Cunningham**, clerk of the Treasury Department, read the Declaration of Independence, and the Reverend French S. Evans gave the oration. "The orator of the day delivered an excellent and animated address, which riveted [sic] the attention of the company for upwards of an hour and afforded them high gratification." An original ode by **John Hill Hewitt** was also sung.

Source: *National Intelligencer*, 6 and 10 July 1843, 3 and 3, respectively.

Temperance movement

Started in the early 1800s by physicians and clergymen and others who viewed the consumption of alcohol as a physical and moral issue. The use of alcohol on the Fourth of July was a common practice brought about principally by the drinking of toasts at the celebration dinners, as well as the revelry in the streets. The abundance of alcoholic beverages frequently resulted in undignified behavior and drunkenness that spilled out onto town streets as participants made their way home after hours of indulgence. In some towns general rowdiness, a common expectation on the Fourth of July, was increased due to the use of intoxicating drinks. Frequently fistfights and brawls resulting from opinionated discussions regarding politics and other social issues broke out. That drinking alcohol was prevalent on Independence Day as early as the 1790s is evident from the commentary published in local newspapers. In Philadelphia *Porcupine's Gazette* thought the Fourth of July in 1798 celebration there was "more peaceable" probably because "there were less toasts drunk than usual; that there was more public spirit and less Jamaica spirit afloat, than has been usual on like occasions for some years past." From the 1820s to the Civil War, in cities large and small, the temperance movement had an impact on how the Fourth of July was celebrated, in parades, speeches, and ceremonies. Moreover, with the establishment of national associations dedicated to the cause, momentum was increased. In 1826 the American Temperance Society was founded and was followed in 1874 by the Women's Christian Temperance Union (WCTU), which by the turn of the century had become the largest women's association in the country.

These teetotaling festivals stressed the sobriety of all those participating and toasts were drunk using cold water, lemonade, or other non-alcoholic drinks. Orations frequently quoted scripture and warning that this malaise threatened America with downfall and doom. Signs and banners were a common feature of these celebrations. In Concord, New Hampshire, on July 4, 1843, the anniversary of independence was celebrated "generally on temperance principles."

Many cities had temperance societies and groups that met to address common concerns. In Washington on July 4, 1842, a "Grand Total Abstinence Celebration" made up of several area temperance societies took place. On July 4, 1845, in Washington, D.C., for example, "The temperance associations of Washington dedicated the day to a combined effort for the furtherance of the great moral and public-spirited cause in behalf of which their exertions are directed." Sometimes these meetings were directed specifically to children. For example, on July 4, 1838, a "juvenile temperance celebration" was held in Litchfield, Connecticut. In Jonesborough, Tennessee, on July 4, 1842, a boy carried a sign that read "All's right when Daddy's sober!" See also **Prohibition**.

Sources: *Porcupine's Gazette*, 5 July 1798, 3; *National Intelligencer*, 4 July 1842; *Hill's New-Hampshire Patriot*, 6 July 1843, 1; *The Whig and Independent Journal* (Jonesborough, Tenn.), 13 July 1842; *Daily Union*, 5 July 1845, 219 (3); Litchfield broadside, 1838, Connecticut Historical Society; Hay, "'Freedom's Jubilee': One Hundred Years of the Fourth of July, 1776–1876," 136–41.

Tennessee State House, Nashville

The cornerstone for the Tennessee State House in Nashville was laid on July 4, 1845. The celebration began with the students of the Nashville University marching to the First Baptist Church early in the morning and listening to an address by W.N. Bilbo, which was described as "gorgeous luxuriance of expression and vigor of style, which, telling on the sympathies of his excited auditory, gave infinite effect to his originality." A large procession of individuals then marched shortly after 11:00 A.M. from the town square to the grounds in front of the residence of Judge Campbell. In addition to the "state officers" and other dignitaries in the group, were the Free Masons, who were responsible for laying the cornerstone. "Decked in their habiliments, and bearing the insignia of their order, they did indeed exhibit a majestically imposing appearance. They were preceded by their band, and displayed three banners, on each of which was depicted a column, with a motto superscribed; on the first 'Beauty,' on the second 'Strength' and on the last 'Wisdom.'" Edwin H. Ewing, the orator for the occasion, spoke about the history of Tennessee, the importance of universal suffrage and the significance of the day. "We are met to lay the corner-stone of a people's State House, to give expression to a people's will, and a people's pride, not by commencing that which is to end in an empty display of mere architectural beauty, or the perpetuity of a vain and sentimental ostentation, but to end in that whose uses shall be our pride, our glory and our safety."

In the cornerstone were deposited a scroll highlighting the important events of the history of Tennessee, copies of newspapers of Nashville, a copy of the Declaration of Independence and various other documents, some American coins, "from the eagle down to the cent," a copy of the Constitution and By-Laws of the Independent Order of Odd-Fellows, and a silver plate engraved with the names of the "steamboats in the New Orleans and Nashville trade."

Sources: *Nashville Daily Republican Banner*, 7 July 1845; *Description of the State Capitol of Tennessee* (Nashville: Cameron and Co., 1859).

"Tennessee Valley Appreciation Day"

Held in the Muscle Shoals area of Tennessee, on July 4, 1935, this celebration took place in recognition of the work of the Tennessee Valley Authority (TVA). About 30,000 spectators were present to view a mile-long parade consisting of 57 floats that traveled along a 25-mile-long route, ending at Big Springs Park. Governors Hill McAlister of Tennessee and Bibb Graves of Alabama reviewed the parade. President Franklin D. Roosevelt signed the TVA Act on May 18, 1933. The act's goals included the development of electric power through the control of the federal government, flood control, and relief of unemployed persons.

Source: "30,000 See Pageant in Tennessee Valley," *New York Times*, 5 July 1935, 14.

Texas, annexation to the Union

Members of the Convention of Texas with Thomas J. Rusk, president, signed an "Ordinance" on July 4, 1845, establishing Texas as a state of the Union, as based on a U.S. Congressional resolution of March 1, 1845. The convention took place in Austin, Texas. The consent of Congress was based upon three conditions: (1) that the Constitution adopted by the people of Texas be submitted to the president of the United States, to be laid before Congress no later that January 1, 1846; (2) that all public "edeficies, fortifications, barracks, ports and harbors, navy and navy yards, docks, magazines, arms and armaments pertaining to the public defense" of Texas be ceded to the United States and that any debts and liabilities in these matters will not "become a charge upon the Government of the United States"; (3) that in new states carved out of the western territory shall be entitled to admission to the Union with the provision that states north of the Missouri Compromise line, "slavery or involuntary servitude (except for crime) shall be prohibited."

Source: "Documents 80–121: 1836–1846," in *Treaties and Other International Acts of the United States of America*, ed. Hunter Miller (Washington: Government Printing Office, 1934), vol. 4.

Third Presbyterian Church, Trenton, New Jersey

On July 4, 1879, the church with its 180-foot steeple was destroyed by fire when a "falling sky-rocket" landed on its shingle roof. Four firemen were injured when the roof caved in on them. A newspaper reported that "had not the rain fallen in torrents, there would have been a terrible conflagration, as the church was surrounded by frame buildings."

Source: "Other Losses by Fire," *New York Times*, 5 July 1879, 5.

Thomas, Isaiah (1749–1831)

The Declaration of Independence was first publicly read in Worcester, Massachusetts, in 1776 by Thomas. The reading took place from the roof of the porch of the Meeting-House "and [was] received with loud cheers and congratulations." On July 4, 1826, Thomas stood on the identical spot at the Meeting House where he originally read the Declaration.

Sources: "Revolutionary Reminescence," *Mobile Argus*, 19 August, 1823, 1; *National Intelligencer*, 12 July 1826, 3.

Thompson, Amira (Carpenter), Mrs.

This New York state poet wrote "A Pastoral Play, in One Act, Designed for the Fourth of July," published in a volume of poetry titled *The Lyre of Tioga* (Geneva, N.Y.: J.

Rogert, 1829). This book focuses on scenes of life in Tioga County. Mrs. Thompson published the work under her married name. She lived near the present city of Elmira, N.Y. Her Fourth of July play takes place on Clinton Island, near Elmira, and includes a group of young ladies and gentlemen representing labor, temperance, frugality, justice, and liberty, each of whom is accountable to the "Genius of America." Included is a supporting chorus of Greek gods and goddesses, two of whom prepare a feast that ends the play.

Ting-Fang, Wu

Chinese minister to the United States who gave an Independence Day speech at Independence Square in Philadelphia in 1901 predicting the United States "will become the greatest power upon the earth."

Source: *New York Times*, 5 July 1901, 5.

Toasts

The drinking of patriotic toasts on the Fourth was an important celebratory function that occurred at Independence Day dinners. This ritual was a male affair. Only very rarely did females initiate their own celebrations that included alcoholic toasts. An exception occurred on July 4, 1798, in Middletown, Connecticut, in a grove belonging to Capt. G. Starr. A group of women drank six toasts — to the United States, Mrs. Adams, Mrs. Washington, valor and patriotism, volunteers of America, and Daughters of America. After the ceremony the group walked (accompanied by a few men) to a liberty tree where the celebration ended. An editor of a local newspaper was shocked at the "ridiculous behavior" of the women who downed "six glasses of good Madeira." He believed "that neither Mrs. Adams nor Mrs. Washington will feel themselves much honoured by the clumsy compliments of these toping dames."

Typically the ritual included "regular" and "volunteer" toasts. The regular toasts often numbered thirteen, representing either the new states in the Union or the original colonies. Toasts were carefully prepared beforehand by a designated group, set to paper, and copies were submitted both to the celebration committee for its approval and a representative of the local newspaper for public dissemination. The readings were usually brief and some were set in verse. According to a newspaper editor writing in 1839, "a toast, to be good, should be brief, pointed, pithy, and classic."

Each reading was followed by an outburst of cheering, often in multiples of three, as well as the firing of muskets and artillery, and the singing of a patriotic air associated in some way with the text of the toast. Some toasts were drunk standing and in silence, such as those to George Washington following his death in 1799. Toasts were presented in a prescribed order; for example, toasts "to the day" of Independence, the country, the "heroes of '76," and so forth. The final toast was almost always dedicated to females, who were referred to as the "American fair." The range of topics for toasts was extensive and included symbolic metaphors, such as the Goddess of Liberty and the eagle, national and local dignitaries, patriots, the nation's charters, other countries, the military, agriculture and commerce, and partisan political perspectives. Volunteer toasts were usually unspecified in number and were offered by others at the celebration.

Examples of regular toasts include "Our country — The land of the free, and the home of the brave" read in 1828 in Washington City to the tune "Hail Columbia"; "Washington — May his name be forgotten when his principles shall cease to be considered the political creed of his countrymen," offered in Charleston, South Carolina, in 1828 at a celebration of the "Irish Volunteers"; "The American Fair — The world was sad, the garden was a wild, and man the hermit, sigh'd 'till woman smil'd," at Richmond, July 4, 1830.

Sources: "Female Toasting," *Porcupine's Gazette*, 14 July 1798, 2; *Charleston Courier*, 6 July 1808 and 7 July 1828, 3 and 2, respectively; "Fourth of July, 1828," *National Intelligencer*, 7 July 1828, 3; "Fourth of July Toasts," *Alexandria Gazette*, 16 July 1839, 2; Hay, "Freedom's Jubilee: One Hundred Years of the Fourth of July, 1776–1876," 102–16.

Todd, Timothy (1758–1806)

Revolutionary War soldier and later physician in Arlington, Vermont, who wrote

the words for "Ode for the Fourth of July, 1799" (Hudson, N.Y.: G. Fairman, 1799), which was set to music by the Rev. Chauncey Lee. Todd "was a man of considerable literary taste and talent, and wrote many medical and other articles for the journals of the day, and on various occasions pronounced popular orations." On July 4, 1808, for example, he delivered an oration at East Guilford, Connecticut. For five years Todd represented Arlington in the General Assembly and for three years in the Governor's Council.

Sources: Timothy Todd, *An Oration Delivered at East Guilford, in Connecticut the Fourth Day of July, 1801* (Rutland, Vt.: William Fay, 1801); John Edwards Todd, *The Todd Family in America or the Descendants of Christopher Todd, 1637–1919* (Northampton, Mass.: Press of Gazette Printing Co., 1920), 73–75; Oscar G.T. Sonneck, *A Bibliography of Early Secular American Music* (Library of Congress, 1945), 310.

Toledo, Ohio, strike

City where Fourth of July parades and other celebrations scheduled for July 4, 1979, were postponed to Labor Day due to an unsettled labor situation regarding city police and fire fighters. By July 5, Toledo's 200 bus drivers returned to work. A back-to-work order for 3,700 municipal employees was issued with heavy fines if disobeyed.

Sources: *Los Angeles Times*, 5 July 1979, 17; *New York Times*, 5 July 1979, 12.

Tompkins, Daniel D. (1774–1825)

Attorney, governor of New York (1807–17), and vice president under President James Monroe, who was an active participant in Fourth of July ceremonies both as a speaker and spectator. In 1820, Tompkins was in New York at City Hall on the Fourth with other dignitaries reviewing parading military brigades. On July 4, 1823, he gave an address in Alexandria, Virginia, at a dinner for a group that had visited Mount Vernon earlier that day. In 1838, in Peekskilll, New York, at an Independence Day dinner, Tompkins was toasted along with De Witt Clinton: "Their heads were sound, their hearts were pure."

Sources: *New York Gazette and General Advertiser*, 6 July 1820, 2; *Washington Gazette*, 9 July 1823, 2; *Hudson River Chronicle*, 17 July 1838, 3.

Topeka, Kansas

The first Independence Day celebration in this town occurred on July 4, 1855, and is remembered by two significant events: E.C.K. Garvey published the first issue of the town's first newspaper, *The Kansas Freeman*, and a whisky riot occurred when some citizens of Topeka who had a dislike for the sale and use of whisky demanded of the one liquor dealer in town that he forfeit his stock. When he did not comply, the mob took possession of the whisky barrels and set them on fire. A newspaper later reported: "Without one dissenting voice let the decree go forth from our midst that the demon intemperance shall be forever banished from among us."

Source: *The Folklore of American Holidays*, 279.

Toronto, Canada

The first official Fourth of July celebrated in Toronto took place on July 4, 1918. For the occasion the American flag was raised over City Hall and Sir John Hendrie, lieut.-governor of Ontario, and James C. O'Brien, assistant corporation counsel of Chicago, among others, presented speeches.

Source: "Canada Observes Fourth," *New York Times*, 5 July 1918, 9.

Transparencies

A popular form of illuminated paintings and drawings presented on the Fourth of July in theatres, gardens, and public buildings during the nineteenth century. Typically transparencies depicted historic figures and events, some were pastoral settings and others scenes depicted military battles or crafts of the mechanical arts. One of the popular places in Philadelphia for viewing transparencies was **Gray's Gardens**. On July 4, 1790, "Grays' Gardens, on the banks of the Schuylkill, exhibited a noble appearance, on this delightful occasion. Language is too faint to describe this enchanting spot, this fairy ground of pleasure and festivity, where new scenes met the eye at every step. The splendid, every where diversified, illumination." On July 4, 1791, displayed there was "an emblematical transparent piece of painting, very large," titled "the Goddess of Independency." Other transparencies displayed included depictions of George Washington, Benjamin Franklin and Lafayette, "as large as life, together with several other transparent figures and landscapes, executed by eminent artists."

In New York, in the evening of July 4, 1792, "the Wigwam of Tammany Society was elegantly illuminated; together with a beautiful transparent painting of the arms of the United States, with the words Independence, fourth of July, 1776." The Mechanic Hall also displayed "an elegant transparent painting, emblematic of their craft."

On July 4, 1799, at Vauxhall Gardens in New York City, transparencies were set up outside and were displayed at sunset into the night. The garden was "brilliantly illuminated, and four grand transparencies 8 feet high" were exhibited in different parts of the grounds. One represented the "Discovery of America" by Columbus, another the "Temple of Liberty," the third "The Evacuation of New York by the British," and the fourth, "A Military Dance Round the Constitution." An advertisement for the event noted that "In one corner of the above transparency 'Envy Struck with the Thunder of Love.'"

In Boston on July 4, 1805, there were transparencies displayed in the evening of "The National and States Arms, busts of Washington and Hamilton, and figures representing Justice and Liberty, from a stage in the center of the common."

In Washington on July 4, 1810, "a grand emblematic transparency" was on display at the Washington Theatre, and in the following year at the theater "a Grand Transparency painted for the occasion by an eminent artist" was exhibited. In New York at the "Theatre in the Park," on July 4, 1814, a "transparent painting" in which "Liberty" was represented by a "Female figure, clad in robes of yellow, beneath her feet a Globe" was displayed.

In Charleston, South Carolina, on July 4, 1828, a "grand transparency of Gen. Andrew Jackson, surrounded with brilliant stars" was displayed at the Tivoli Garden.

In New York City, on July 4, 1836, at the City Saloon, "a beautiful transparency relative to the late glorious achievement of our brave countrymen in Texas [was] brilliantly illuminated in the evening." On July 3, 1876, German-Americans in Omaha, Nebraska, held a torchlight parade, and they carried a number of transparencies with the themes "A Nation of Heroes in War," "America Is Now Our Fatherland and Home," "The Immortal Trio, Columbus, Washington and Lincoln," among others.

Sources: *The Universal Asylum and Columbian Magazine* 5/1 (July 1790): 58; *Pennsylvania Gazette,* 29 June 1791 and 11 July 1792; *Daily Advertiser,* 4 July 1799, 3; *New-England Palladium,* 5 and 9 July 1805, 2 and 2, respectively; *National Intelligencer* 4 July 1810 and 1811, 3 and 3 respectively; *New-York Evening Post,* 2 July 1814, 2–3; *Charleston Courier,* 4 July 1828, 3; *New York Herald,* 4 July 1836, 2; "Patriotic Inscriptions," *Omaha Republican,* 4 July 1876, 4.

Treaty of Delaware Agency, Kansas

This treaty with the Delaware Indians and the State of Kansas was agreed upon on July 4, 1866. The legislation by Congress removed the Native American tribes from Kansas to a location "between the States of Kansas and Texas."

The preamble summarizes the provisions set in the fifteen articles which constitute the treaty. The Pacific Railroad had agreed to purchase the present Delaware Indian reservation and to pay "to said Indians the full value of all that part of their reservation." Thomas Murphy, superintendent of Indian affairs, John G. Pratt, agent for the Delawares, and William H. Watson, special commissioner, represented the interests of the United States; and John Connor, "Captain Sarcoxie," and Charles Journeycake, chiefs, and James Ketchum, James Connor, Andrew Miller, and John Sarcoxie, counselors, represented the Delaware Indians. The treaty was ratified on July 26 and "proclaimed" on August 10, 1866.

Source: *Indian Affairs, Laws and Treaties,* vol. II (*Treaties*), ed. Charles J. Kappler (Washington, D.C.: Government Printing Office, 1904), reprinted as "Treaty of Delaware Agency," Web site, 6 September 2002, <http://www.councilfire.com/treaty/treat351.html>.

Troy, New York, affray

On July 4, 1814, members of the Democrat and Federalist parties engaged in a fight brought about by political differences. News went out that as many as ten lives were lost,

but accurate accounts determined that it was "nothing more than a battle of fisty-cuffs." Firearms were fired by both sides, mostly at the flags flying that represented each faction. "Several balls having been fired through the federal standard by the democrats, some of the federalists, belonging to the rifle corps, undertook to return the compliment, and actually brought down the democratic standard, by cutting with rifle balls the two main cords which sustained it to the flag-staff."

Source: *Frederick-Town Herald,* 16 July 1814, 2.

Truman, Harry S (1884–1972)

Thirty-third president of the U.S. (1945–53). Truman was born in Lamar, Missouri, served in World War I, was elected U.S. senator in 1934 and 1940, and was vice president under Franklin D. Roosevelt. Upon the president's death in April 1945, Truman became president.

On July 3, 1946, Truman pledged on the eve of the new Philippines republic that "our two countries will be closely bound together for many years to come." On July 4, 1947, he gave an address at Monticello that focused on the Soviet disapproval of a joint European World War II recovery project. In 1948, he launched a three-day celebration of the 100th anniversary of the Washington Monument and spoke on the Monument grounds.

On July 4, 1950, due to renovations in the White House, Truman celebrated in the Blair House, the first president to do so. On July 4, 1951, Truman spoke again on the Monument grounds. His speech focused on the soldiers who had died in the Korean War, and he said the effect was similar to the events at Bunker Hill and Gettysburg. He also warned of Soviet aggression. On the even of July 4, 1952, Truman "signed a constitution giving Puerto Ricans greater self-rule." He also proclaimed July 4 as a day of national prayer. Following his presidency, Truman enjoyed celebrating the Fourth at his home town of Independence, Missouri. Occasionally he gave speeches there.

Sources: "Truman Pledges All Help to New Philippines Republic," *Washington Post,* 4 July 1946, 1; "Parade and Truman Talk Start Monument and Celebration Today," *Washington Post,* 3 July 1948, 1; Edward T. Folliard, "President Praises Achievement," *Washington Post*, 5 July 1951, 1; *Washington Post*, 4 July 1952, A1, and "Yanks Mark Fourth Around the World," 5 July 1952, 17; *Washington Post*, 5 July 1969, 2.

Tuskegee University

A prestigious African-American university which was founded on July 4, 1881, as Alabama's first normal school, Tuskegee Institute, for the education of black teachers. The land was purchased by Booker T. Washington (1856–1915) and the first class consisted of thirty students. Washington served as principal. He gave an address titled "Freedom and Service" on July 4, 1905, in Montclair, New Jersey.

Source: *Washington Evening Star*, 5 July 1905, 1.

Twenty-First Street Bridge, Birmingham, Alabama

Formally opened on July 4, 1891. The bridge spanned the railroad tracks and cost $100,000 to build. A trades parade marched through the streets and across the bridge that day.

Source: "In Alabama," *Houston Daily Post*, 5 July 1891, 1.

Tyler, John (1790–1862)

Tenth president of the U.S. (1841–45) who is best remembered on the Fourth for entertaining visitors in the White House. Tyler was born in Greenway, Virginia, graduated from William and Mary College, and served in Congress (1816–21), as governor of Virginia (1825–27), and as U.S. senator (1827–36). In 1840 he was elected vice president under Harrison. Upon Harrison's death on April 4, 1841, Tyler assumed the presidency. Subsequently, on the Fourth of July, Tyler was in the Executive Mansion entertaining guests.

In 1842, Tyler was invited to attend the July 4 celebration at McArran's Garden in Philadelphia. Although it was an assemblage that included his supporters, Tyler declined the invitation, sent a letter of regret and his views on a "plan of finance and of currency" that he had submitted to Congress. Tyler wrote, "In the administration of public affairs I seek only to carry out the end and design of that great revolution you propose to celebrate.

The happiness of the people, founded on measures calculated to advance their prosperity, should be the high object of all those entrusted by the people with the administration of their affairs." Tyler chose to be in the Executive Mansion, where on that morning he entertained children of the various Sunday schools. A local newspaper reported also that the "temperance people made a dissent [sic] upon the White House, too, and the President made a capital speech to them." On July 4, 1843, Tyler's celebration included standing under "the spacious portico" of the White House, where he acknowledged 630 students of the St. Matthew's Sunday School. As they passed by him, he "saluted the youthful group with a cordial bow, and a smile of true, sincere approval."

On July 4, 1845, Tyler gave a speech at the College of William and Mary in Williamsburg, Virginia.

Sources: "The National Anniversary," *National Intelligencer*, 6 July 1841, 3; *Niles' National Register* 12/19 (9 July 1842): 1; *New York Herald*, 6 July 1842, 2; "Fourth of July Celebration," *National Intelligencer*, 7 July 1843, 3; *Richmond Enquirer*, 8 July 1845, 4.

Tyler, Royal (1756–1826)

Playwright, writer, and poet, who was born in Boston and who composed a Fourth of July ode and "Convivial Song" in 1799 for the celebration at Windsor, Vermont. Tyler graduated from Harvard in 1776, served in the military, and wrote the "first American play which was ever acted on a regular stage by an established company of comedians." Titled *The Contrast*, it premiered at the John Street Theatre in New York City on April 16, 1786. Tyler also wrote light verse and prose for a number of publications including the *Farmer's Weekly Museum* and *Algerine Captive; or the Life and Adventures of Doctor Updike Underhill* (1797). After 1800, Tyler served his state of Vermont as chief justice of the Superior Court and continued to write throughout the years that followed.

The first stanza of the Fourth of July ode is representative of Tyler's knack for expressing content with simplicity of words:

When haughty Britons strove in vain
To bind our land with slavery's chain,

Our fathers drew their warlike swords.
Our fathers drew their warlike swords.
Immortal fields of Bennington,
Attest the laurels which they won.
Now faithless France, with impious hand,
Strikes at the glory of our land–
To arms! To arms! Each hardy son,
And earn the fame your sires have won.

Tyler's "Convivial Song" was a toast in homage to Washington:

Here's Washington, the brave, boys,
Source of all Columbia's joys,
Here's Washington, the brave, boys,
Come rise and toast him standing:
For he's the hero firm and brave,
Who all our country's glory gave,
And once again he shall us save,
Our armies bold commanding.
Here's to our native land, boys,
Land of liberty and joys,
Here's to our native land, boys,
Your glasses raise for drinking;
And he that will not drink this toast,
May he in France of freedom boast,
There dangling on a lantern post,
Or in the Rhone be sinking.

Henry Clay Lukens recalled an "Independence Day Ode" Tyler composed for the Fourth of July in 1801 and described the piece as "barbarous in rhyme," yet popular:

Feeble in literary construction, halting in metre, almost barbarous in rhyme, loud and discordant in its mirth, it is astonishing that this rude, dialectic fusing of kitchen holiday jollity with village pot-house revels should so long have held a local popularity. The spirited fife-and-fiddle movement of the verse doubtless explains its familiar toleration in certain rural communities.

The poem deserves merit for its information as to how the Fourth of July was celebrated in rural "country towns" in Massachusetts and New Hampshire. It was first printed in the *Farmer's Weekly Museum* and later reprinted in *Antiquities of Long Island* (1874).

Squeak the fife and beat the drum,
Independence day is come!!
Let the roasting pig be bled,
Quick twist off the rooster's head,
Quickly rub the pewter platter,
Heap the nut cakes fried in butter,
Set the cups and beaker glass,
The pumpkin and the apple sauce.
Send the keg to shop for brandy;

Maple sugar we have handy.
Independent, staggering Dick,
A noggin mix of swinging thick;
Sal, put on your russel skirt,
Jotham, get your boughten shirt,
To-day we dance to tiddle-diddle —
Here comes Sambo with his fiddle;
Sambo, take a draw of whiskey,
And play up Yankee Doodle frisky —
Moll, come leave your witched tricks,
And let us have a reel of six —
Father and mother shall make two;
Sall, Moll, and I stand all a row,
Sambo, play and dance with polity;
This is the day of blest equality, —
Father and mother are but men,
And Sambo is a citizen.
Come, foot it, Sal; Moll, figure in,
And, mother, you dance up to him;
Now saw as fast as e'er you can do,
And, thater, you cross over to Sambo.
— Thus we dance and thus we play,
On glorious Independence Day.
Rub more rosin on your bow,
And let us have another go —
Zounds! As sure as eggs and bacon,
Here's Ensign Sneak and uncle Deacon,
Aunt Thiah, and their Bet's behind her
On blundering mare, than beetle blinder —
And there's the Squire, too, with his lady —
Sal, hold the beast! I'll take the baby!
Moll, bring the Squire our great arm-chair,
Good folks, we're glad to see you here —
Jotham, get the great case bottle,
Your teeth can draw the corn-cob stopple —
  Ensign, Deacon, never mind;
Squire, drink until you're blind.

Sources: Evert A. Duyckinck, *Cyclopaedia of American Literature* (New York: C. Scribner, 1856) and portions reprinted on the Web site *Early American Fiction* Collection (1789–1875) <http://etext.virginia.edu/eaf> (University of Virginia Library); Gabriel Furman and Frank Moore, *Antiquities of Long Island* (New York: J.W. Bouton, 1874), 270–71; Henry Clay Lukens, "American Literary Comedians," *Harper's New Monthly Magazine* 80/479 (April 1890): 786.

Uncas, Chief of the Mohegans

A monument to Uncas was erected in his honor on July 4, 1842, in Norwich, Connecticut, and William L. Stone presented a "historical Discourse to his memory."

Sources: William L. Stone, *Uncas and Miantonomah: An Historical Discourse, Delivered at Norwich (Conn.) on the Fourth Day of July, 1842* (New York: Dayton and Newman, 1842); "The Uncas Monument," *Alexandria Gazette*, 13 July 1842, 3.

Uncle Sam

A long-standing national symbol for the United States and a popular icon on the Fourth of July that took its name from Sam Wilson, a government inspector of army provisions in 1812. Wilson was a local businessman in the Troy, New York, area. Uncle Sam's origin lies partly in legend, when in October 1812 Albert Anderson, a contractor for the army, was inspecting a meat packing plant where Sam Wilson worked. On the occasion a number of plant workers who were "overhauling the provisions purchased by the contractor for the army" inquired why the barrels were marked E.A.—U.S. It was reportedly said that E.A. stood for Albert Anderson and U.S. meant Uncle Sam Wilson (U.S. really stood for the United States). Individuals found this story to be amusing. "The joke took among the workmen and passed currently, and 'Uncle Sam' himself being present, was occasionally rallied by them on the increasing extent of his passions." The use of "Uncle Sam" spread by word of mouth and references in newspapers (see, for example, *New York Gazette and General Advertiser*, 12 May 1830). Soon those working for the army generally considered supplies received to be Uncle Sam's. Although no actual likeness of Sam Wilson exists, caricatures of Uncle Sam began appearing in various publications. Jonathan Tafel notes that the first illustration of Uncle Sam was a lithograph cartoon in 1832. By 1848 a magazine editor for the *Mechanic's Advocate* pointed out how Uncle Sam "gained favor rapidly, until it was recognized in every part of our country, and will no doubt continue a national cognomen, while the U.S. remain a nation." On July 4, 1853, at the Chestnut Street Theatre in Philadelphia, a comedy of "My Uncle Sam" was performed. At an Independence Day celebration in 1882 at Southold, Long Island, New York, it was reported that 93-year-old "S.S. Vail, well known from the earliest recollection as 'Uncle Sam,'" was in the audience.

The centennial year of 1876 was a notable occasion for Uncle Sam. In Windsor, Connecticut, the town's parade featured a carriage that had "a small boy representing 'Uncle Sam of 1776' and a man of aldermanic proportions personating 'Uncle Sam of 1876.'" On that same day in Parkersburg, West Virginia, a wagon bearing the name "Uncle Sam" paraded through the streets. The costumed man was seven feet, three inches tall. He wore "the traditional Yankee costume of swallow-tailed coat, yellow pants, six inches too short in the leg, white stove pipe hat set on the back of his head, while in his hand he held a stick and jack-knife engaged in the everlasting Yankee habit of whittling." In 1961 a Congressional act officially recognized the grave of Samuel Wilson in Oakwood Cemetery, Troy, N.Y., as a national shrine.

Sources: "Origin of Uncle Sam," *Mechanic's Advocate* 2/7 (22 January 1848): 51; *Daily News*, 4 July 1853, 2; "Observances in Other Parts of the State," *Hartford Courant*, 6 July 1876, 1; "Our Editorial Correspondence," *Wheeling Daily Register*, 10 July 1876, 2; "Southold," *Brooklyn Daily Eagle*, 6 July 1882, 2; Tafel, "The Historical Development of Political and Patriotic Images of America: A Visual Analysis of Fourth of July Cartoons in Five Newspapers."

Union

A popular name for model replica ships used in Fourth of July parades and which typically depicted the confederation of states, a symbol of federalism. One of the early *Union* replica vessels constructed was a 33-foot boat that mounted 20 guns and was placed in the **"Grand Federal Procession"** in Philadelphia on July 4, 1788. She was symbolically commanded by John Green, Capt. S. Smith, W. Belchar and Mr. Mercer and included lieutenants, four midshipmen, and twenty-five officers. According to a newspaper report, the ship's "bottom is the barge of the ship *Alliance*, and the same barge which formerly belonged to the *Serapis*, and was taken in the memorable engagement of Captain Paul Jones, of the *Bon Homme Richard*, with the *Serapis*." The construction of the ship was accomplished in less than four days. The boat was mounted on a carriage and drawn by ten horses.

A sheet of canvas was tacked all around, along the water line, and extending over a light frame, hung to the ground so as entirely to conceal the wheels and machinery. This canvas was painted to represent the sea, so that nothing incongruous appeared, to offend the eye.

The ceremonies in setting sail, receiving the pilot on board, trimming the sails to the wind according to the several courses of the line of march, throwing the lead, her arrival at Union Green, casting anchor, being hailed and welcomed with three cheers, and the Captain forwarding his dispatches to the President of the United States, &c. &c. were all performed with the strictest maritime propriety.

Another *Union* constructed was the 40-foot vessel for the parade in Baltimore on July 4, 1828, on the occasion of the laying of the first stone of the **Baltimore and Ohio Railroad**. A local newspaper reported that

it was the grand center of attraction to all eyes. She was full rigged, sails set, and streamers flying in the wind and her hull was a most beautiful specimen of Naval Architecture. The officers and crew were on deck, in the various occupations of a sailor's life. The Commander giving orders to his officers the officers with their speaking trumpets passing them to the boatswain and crew, the boatswain enforcing them with his shrill call, the sailor in the shrouds heaving the lead & singing the soundings, and the orderly bustle and regular confusion on ship-board at sea, were all done to the life.

"Union" as a shipbuilder's metaphor for the new nation of states was portrayed in other ways. In Philadelphia in 1790, a transparency (see **Transparencies**) of "the ship Union [was] elegantly lighted up, and shining with superior luster" at **Gray's Gardens**.

Sources: *Pennsylvania Gazette*, 9 July 1788; *Universal Asylum and Columbian Magazine* 5/1 (July 1790): 58; *Maryland Journal and True American*, 16 July 1828.

United States

A steamboat launched in Baltimore on July 4, 1818, from the ship yard of Flannigan and Beachem, at Fell's Point.

Source: *Maryland Herald and Hagers-Town Weekly Advertiser*, 15 July 1818, 3.

United States Building, Covington, Kentucky

The cornerstone of this building was laid on July 4, 1876. Included in the ceremony was an oration presented by William E. Arthur, who described the symbolism of the building:

It is a fitting type of the solidity of our institutions, for it is as firm as the adamantine rock from which it was hewn; it is a fitting emblem of our Federal Union, for it is Indiana marble, supported by Kentucky soil; it is a fitting memorial of the benevolence of our form of government, for it is to establish justice, diffuse intelligence, provide for the common defense, and promote the general welfare.

Source: W.E. Arthur, "The American Age Contrasted," in *Our National Centennial Jubilee* (New York: E.B. Treat, 1876).

United States Capitol

Where the U.S. Congress meets and one of the icons of democracy and freedom having a strong presence on the Fourth of July. Designed by William Thornton with modifications by Stephen Hallet and Benjamin Henry Latrobe, the cornerstone was laid by George Washington on September 18, 1793. The hand trowel that Washington used to set the cornerstone was borrowed subsequently for other cornerstone ceremonies, including the **Jackson Hall** event in Washington on July 4, 1845.

Congress first convened in the Capitol in November 1800. The first Fourth of July oration was presented in 1801 by a "Mr. Austin," a Republican, in the chamber of the House of Representatives. In the following years, numerous statesmen, cabinet members, congressmen, and other dignitaries, as well as private citizens, spoke in the Capitol on the Fourth. John Quincy Adams publicly read the Declaration of Independence and presented an oration on Independence Day in 1821. Some other noteworthy figures who spoke on the Fourth in the early years included Richard Rush (1812), attorney general; Richard Bland Lee (1819), judge; Mathew St. Clair Clarke, (1824), clerk of the House of Representatives; James Barbour (1826), secretary of war; and Francis Scott Key (1831). Typically each oration was preceded by a reading of the Declaration of Independence. Early instances of readings of the Declaration include those by Richard Bland Lee (1815), William S. Radcliff (1816), Henry Carroll (1817), Joseph Anderson (1819 and 1826), and Daniel Brent (1825).

The first significant Independence Day event for the Capitol building after the ceremony of 1793 was the laying of the cornerstone for the expansion of the Capitol wings on July 4, 1851. On that day Daniel Webster gave his final Independence Day oration while President Fillmore and the Masonic Fraternity presided over the laying of a block which inside had a "hermetically sealed" jar containing "a variety of valuable historical parchments, the coins of the United States, a copy of the oration ... by the Secretary of State, newspapers of the day, and other memorials."

Another event of equal importance occurred on July 4, 1959, when President Eisenhower dedicated the beginning of construction to extend the east front of the Capitol by thirty-two feet. The ceremony included the placing of a three-foot cube of red marble inscribed "A.D. 1959." The work was completed in 1962.

Independence Day ceremonies in the Capitol were rooted in traditions and practices established early on. When July 4 or 5 fell on a Sunday, "divine" sermons preached by clergyman took the place of civic events. On Sunday, July 5, 1846, the "Rev. Mr. Baker" preached in the Hall of the House of Representatives and President James K. Polk sat in the audience.

In the nineteenth century Congress occasionally chose to remain in session over the holiday. In 1836, a notice in the newspaper that day described only slight interest in celebrating the Fourth: "The Anniversary of Independence passed off in this city, without, it is believed, any other commemoration by individuals, or by the officers of the Government, than firing salutes at the naval and military posts. In Congress, no notice was taken of the day." Yet in 1861 when Congress met on the Fourth, there were exciting speeches and celebrations both in Congress and throughout the city.

Typically, American flags were flown over the Capitol only when Congress was in session. On July 3, 1890, the sergeant-at-arms of the Senate brought a recommendation for flying flags throughout the year on the Capitol to Senator John J. Ingalls, *president pro tempore*. After discussion Ingalls decided that four American flags would be flown from four separate non-regulation masts for the first time

on the following day the Fourth of July. The masts were placed at the bottom of the dome, and they displayed "twenty-five-foot flags" that "pointed north, south, east, and west."

The House of Representatives met on July 4, 1951, the first time on Independence Day since 1940. Seventy-five members of Congress were present. The Declaration of Independence was read and Representative John E. Rankin (D.—Miss.) made a motion that the Declaration be re-adopted, but no action was taken.

Sources: *National Intelligencer*, 3 July 1801, 6 July 1836, and 7 July 1851, 3, 3, and 2, respectively; "Congress on the 'Glorious Fourth,'" *Washington Evening Star*, 5 July 1884, 1; "The Flag Will Fly," *Los Angeles Times*, 4 July 1890, 4; "House in Brief Session Hears Declaration Read," *New York Times*, 5 July 1951, 8; *Diary of James K. Polk*, ed. Milo Milton Quaife (Chicago: A.C. McClurg, 1910; reprint, New York: Kraus Reprint Co., 1970), 2:12.

United States Constitution

The oldest federal constitution in effect, the United States Constitution is frequently referred to as the nation's "living" document, whose Revolutionary spirit and principles are put into practice and which has the flexibility to be interpreted with changing times. The Constitution became a national icon for celebration on the Fourth during the nineteenth century. The document was drafted in Philadelphia in May through September 1787, adopted by the Constitutional Convention, and signed on September 17 by George Washington. The revision of the Constitution by future generations was provided for by a series of 27 amendments of which the first 10 constitute the Bill of Rights.

It was the process of ratifying the Constitution by the thirteen states that resulted in the outbreak of conflict of Federalists, who supported the Constitution and a strong federal government, with the Anti-Federalists, who believed that state governments would be weakened if the Constitution were adopted. Even though by June 1788 a number of states had ratified the document, the tension brought about by the unification of states would endure for the next decade. In July 1788, a number of states, including Virginia and New York, had yet to approve the Constitution. Independence Day that year proved to be significant, and citizens poured fourth in the nation's streets voicing their views about the Constitution. In Albany, New York, a copy of the Constitution was burned by Anti-Federalists. Open conflict on the city streets by Federalists and Anti-Federalists resulted in the death of one individual and several others injured. In Philadelphia, the scene was tranquil. Federalist Francis Hopkinson was instrumental in creating the largest and most magnificent parade there in eighteenth century America, designed to promote the adoption of the Constitution. According to Howard H. Martin, the Constitution later took on a greater meaning in the face of increasing threats to national unity. Compared to the Declaration of Independence, the Constitution was not referred to that frequently on the Fourth. In Fairfield, New Jersey, on July 4, 1820, "the reading of the Constitution was substituted for that of the Declaration of Independence, being the fruit of the independence declared at that time." The text of the Constitution was printed in the *National Intelligencer* on 4 July 1833, 2, and in Paris on July 4, 1912, Ambassador Myron T. Herrick read portions of the document in an address to 500 guests at a banquet sponsored by the American Chamber of Commerce. Herrick explained that the Constitution "could not be changed 'by a demagogic propaganda or marred overnight by a sudden whim.'" In Tonasket, Washington, parts of the Constitution were read on July 4, 1927. The Constitution was frequently toasted at dinner celebrations during the nineteenth century.

Sources: *Connecticut Courant*, 14 July 1788, 3; "Fourth of July," *The Whig* (Bridgeton, N.J.), 17 July 1820, 3; "Herrick the Orator," *Washington Post*, 5 July 1912, 1; "Tonasket Has Crowd on 4th," *Oroville Gazette*, 7 July 1927, 1; Martin, "Orations on the Anniversary of American Independence, 1777–1876," 337.

United States Marine Band

The oldest and most important band of musicians that performed regularly on the Fourth of July. The band was established by Congress and signed into law on July 11, 1798, by John Adams. The only official performance of the band (thirty-two fifes and drums) in Philadelphia before establishing residency in Washington City occurred on July 4, 1800, when it performed under the baton of William Farr at the celebration of the Society of the Cincinnati at the City Tavern. When Thomas Jefferson assumed the presidency, he referred to the band as "The President's Own." Its first Fourth of July performance in Washington was in 1801 at the Executive Mansion (see **White House**). Although its primary mission was to provide music for the president of the United States, in years that followed the band also performed for an innumerable number of Independence Day events that included official performances in honor of heads of state and other dignitaries, dedication and inaugural ceremonies, social events in hotels, meetings of associations, dinners and balls.

The band quickly became a patriotic icon on the Fourth and played an immeasurable role enriching the musical heritage of the holiday. The ensemble was a frequent participant in ceremonies at the Capitol, with some early performances occurring in 1815, 1822, and 1833, but also at some unusual holiday affairs. On July 4, 1883, for example, the band performed between heats at the horse races at the Washington Driving Club. It was John Philip Sousa, the band's musical director in 1880–92, who developed the band into a world-renowned musical organization and composed works that are still played each year on the Fourth throughout the country. On July 4, 1894, in a parade down Madison Place by several Revolutionary societies in Washington, the band played the *Marseillaise* and saluted the statue of Lafayette. On July 4, 1908, the band performed at the dedication of the new "Municipal building" in Washington, D.C. The band helped inaugurate the city of Washington's first "safe and sane" Fourth in 1909. Another important occasion occurred on July 4, 1986, when the band performed in New York City for the rededication of the Statue of Liberty. The performance was a re-creation of the band's event under John Philip Sousa for the original dedication ceremony in 1886.

Sources: *Aurora General Advertiser*, 7 July 1800,

2; "Anniversary of American Independence," *National Intelligencer*, 4 July 1822, 2; *Washington Post*, 4 July 1883, 4; *Washington Evening Star*, 4 July 1894, 2; "Ready for Festivities," *Washington Post*, 4 July 1908, 2.

United States Mint, Philadelphia

The cornerstone for the U.S. Mint building was laid in Philadelphia on July 4, 1829. "Officers of the Mint and a number of distinguished citizens" were present. Enclosed within the stone were a number of items, including copies of the Declaration of Independence and Constitution, coins issued in 1792, and a new "half dime" coined on the morning of the 4th, "being the first of a new emission of that coin." An extension of the Mint establishment was by act of Congress on March 2, 1829.

Source: *New York American*, 9 July 1829, 2.

United States Patent Office

Established on July 4, 1836, by President Andrew Jackson, who signed the act of Congress. "Patent No. 1 went to Senator John Ruggles, of Maine, who sponsored the legislation and was an inventor" of a cogwheel for locomotives which was designed to help them function on heavy grades.

Source: "100th Year Marked by Patent Office," *Washington Post*, 5 July 1936, A3.

USS *Bennion*

This destroyer was launched on July 4, 1943, at the Boston Navy Yard. The vessel was named in honor of Captain Mervyn Sharp Bennion, who was "killed while in command of the battleship *West Virginia* when the Japanese raided Pearl Harbor."

Source: "Two Destroyers, Sub Launched in '4th' Ceremonies," *Washington Post*, 5 July 1943, 2.

USS *Chesapeake* and *Leopard* battle

The attack of the British warship *Leopard* on the USS *Chesapeake* commanded by Captain James Barron on June 22, 1807, resulted in American loss of lives, and weighed heavily on the minds of Americans who celebrated Independence Day that year. Across the country, expressions regarding the affair were published in newspapers and presented in orations. The event caused a general unification of the country. According to published accounts, the British commander demanded that four British deserters he claimed were on the *Chesapeake* be handed over to him. When Barron refused, the *Leopard* began shelling the American vessel. Three Americans were killed, eighteen others wounded. The badly damaged *Chesapeake* returned to Norfolk. On July 2 President Jefferson issued a proclamation ordering British warships out of U.S. territorial waters. On July 4 the public's rage was expressed in Independence Day ceremonies and newspapers across the nation. In Richmond **Skelton Jones** presented an impassioned oration denouncing the British, while in New York at Mayor Marinus Willett's reception at the City Hall, "the Leopold outrage was almost the sole topic of conversation." At numerous coffee houses and leading hotels throughout the city, "the necessity for a great navy and for additional harbor defenses was the subject of discussion all the afternoon."

In Baltimore, the editor of the *Moonshine* printed this sentiment:

At the moment when we are preparing to celebrate another anniversary of our emancipation, a scene of bloodshed is exhibited to our eyes, which arouses the feelings of every American. At such an outrage, patience would be pusillanimity, and silence would be cowardice. Every man who possesses the faintest spark of national pride or personal courage, every honest breast which delights to cherish the generous sentiments of valour, must rouse to its energy, and every arm must exert its power. With all the emphasis and earnestness which we can summon to our aid, we call upon the young men of our country to signalize themselves at this trying crisis.

In Washington a military parade was mustered as a show of support for the navy and the nation, while at the White House President Jefferson had invited both Federalists and Republicans to the Independence Day assemblage there because of the "patriotic feelings and unanimity called for by the times."

Sources: "Fourth of July, 1807," *Moonshine*, 23 July 1807, 1–3; *National Intelligencer*, 3 and 8 July 1807, 3 and 1 respectively; Frank Marshall White, "The 'Fourth' in New York One Hundred Years Ago," *Harper's Weekly*, 6 July 1907;

USS *Constellation*

This 38-gun frigate, the first in a line of U.S. Navy vessels having the name *Constellation*, was scheduled to be launched on July 4, 1797, in Baltimore, but the event was delayed until September 7 of that year. It was reported in a Pennsylvania newspaper that "Gen Smith (of Baltimore) in a late debate in Congress, mentioned that the *Constellation* frigate, building at that place, would be launched the 4th of July next." The *Constellation* was designed by Joshua Humphreys, was 164 feet in length, and had an illustrious tour of duty, having won a number of naval battles. She defeated the French 36-gun frigate *Insurgente* on February 5, 1799, in the West Indies and the French warship *Vengeance* on February 2, 1800, near Guadeloupe Island. On July 4, 1820, *Constellation*, referred to affectionately as the "Yankee Racehorse" due to her 14-knot cruising capability, was in New York Harbor participating in the ceremonies there and was decorated with numerous national flags. In 1853 *Constellation* was decommissioned and taken apart at the Gosport Navy Yard in Portsmouth, Virginia.

The next USS *Constellation* was launched August 26, 1854, and was the last all-sail warship built by the U.S. Navy. The ship had an illustrious history. On July 4, 1912, the Rhode Island Society of the Cincinnati voted for a resolution protesting against the proposed destruction of the old frigate. Asa Bird Gardiner, president, and others in the society urged that the ship be maintained at Narragansett Bay "as a fitting monument to the old navy." The vessel subsequently had a tour of duty in World War II and was placed in ordinary at Boston Navy Yard. In 1955 she was moved to Baltimore. On July 4, 2004, a "Sailabration" event in Baltimore harbor honored the 150th year of this last Civil War–era naval vessel still afloat.

Sources: *Pennsylvania Gazette*, 21 June 1797; "Forty-Fourth Anniversary," *New-York Gazette and General Advertiser*, 6 July 1820, 2; "Appeal for Constellation," *New York Times*, 5 July 1912, 7; Tanika White, "Ship-Shape Harbor Holiday," *Baltimore Sun*, 5 July 2004, B1, B3; "Constellation History" Web site, <http://www.constellation.org/history/frigate.html>, 10 November 2004.

USS *Constitution*

One of the most renowned naval ships in American history, which had an illustrious tour of duty. Her popularity made the ship a center of attraction when she was frequently put on display on the Fourth of July. This 44-gun frigate was launched on October 21, 1797, and was later dubbed "Old Ironsides," due to her extremely strong and thick wooden construction. During the war with the Barbary States (1801–05), *Constitution* was the flagship for the fleet under the command of Commodore Edward Preble. The ship actively participated in the War of 1812 and ably demonstrated her ability to engage the enemy. On August 19, 1812, under the command of Capt. Isaac Hull, she defeated the British 38-gun frigate *Guerrière* off Nova Scotia, and on December 29 of that year, under the command of William Bainbridge, destroyed the British 38-gun frigate *Java* off the coast of Brazil. *Constitution* was retired from service in 1882 but restored in 1927–31 and re-commissioned.

Constitution has a colorful history in Fourth of July celebrations. In 1801, in Boston, she fired off an artillery salute in the harbor. On July 4, 1828, the ship had just arrived in Boston returning from a cruise, and "fired a salute in honor of the day." Midshipmen who served on the frigate were considered celebrities. For example, on July 4, 1877, 89-year-old Daniel Lopez, perhaps the oldest sailor to serve on *Constitution*, participated in a celebration held at the Sturtevant House in New York City.

On July 4, 1834, *Constitution* was berthed at the Navy Yard between the USS *Columbus* and USS *Independence* and was a topic of discussion in and around Boston. Two days previous, a young lad had managed to get aboard and sawed off "the wooden image of General Jackson, lately placed upon it as a figure-head" and removed it. The boy escaped to New York where he decided to confess the deed. In the following year *Constitution* fired another salute in the New York Harbor.

Since 1934, *Constitution* has been based at the Charlestown Navy Yard in Massachusetts. On July 4, 1976, *Constitution* fired her cannons, the first time in 95 years, and continued her tradition of 21-gun salutes in subsequent years. In recent years, an annual turnaround cruise on the Fourth of July has become a tradition as *Constitution* is purposely repositioned at her mooring in order to control weathering and maintenance of the vessel. This event typically draws thousands of spectators. In 1990, the event was coupled with the celebrations of the Coast Guard's 200th birthday, as "the Coast Guard training bark *Eagle*, a 300-foot square-rigger, led the *Constitution* on the 10-mile sail down harbor." On board to experience the excursion was presidential Chief of Staff John Sununu, Navy Undersecretary J. Daniel Howard, and many other officials. "About 100,000 spectators lined piers and ship decks from Charlestown to Castle Island's grassy slopes, and others cheered the colorful pageant from the 1,051-foot long flight deck of the carrier *John F. Kennedy* and from more than 1,100 spectator vessels of all sizes."

The use of the name "Constitution" for a vessel was likely first in New Haven, Connecticut, at the Fourth of July celebration there in 1788. In a "grand procession" represented by the crafts of the city, a "ship Constitution" mounting twenty guns, "as large as they could carry, under full sail," was drawn by ten seamen. Later that day at a dinner given at the State House, hanging from the ceiling over the table where the dignitaries sat, was yet another "Constitution," this one "prepared with a complete sett of rigging." Some of the left over wood used in the construction of the USS *Constitution* was saved and later made into a cane that was presented by the Brooklyn, New York, Common Council to Mayor Cyrus P. Smith on July 4, 1842. The cane was described as having "a fine gold head, richly chased and engraved," and a dedication to Smith inscribed on it.

On July 4, 1843, in a Brooklyn, New York, parade, a model *Constitution*, "manned by old and young salts, was borne upon a car, and [was] followed by a portion of the Naval Apprentices." Another instance of a miniature "Constitution" in New Haven was a six-foot-long, full rigged "antique model" that was paraded on July 4, 1884. According to legend as

reported in a local newspaper, the boat "was picked up adrift in the English Channel in 1764, by a vessel bound from France to New Haven. Its first use in procession was in the New Haven parade celebrating the Declaration of Peace in 1783, and since 1838 it has not been used until today."

In 1876 at the **Centennial Exhibition** in Philadelphia a half hull model of the *Constitution* was on display as part of a Navy Department exhibit on the evolution of American naval construction. This model was one of the oldest models used by the navy and was used to instruct midshipmen at Annapolis on important vessel designs of the early navy. *Constitution* was frequently acknowledged in Independence Day celebrations such as the dinner held on July 4, 1815, in Lexington, Massachusetts, when Col. George Blake offered this toast: "Our favorite frigate *Constitution*— the eagle has lent his eye to aim her thunderbolts, and his wings to speed her flight!"

Sources: "Fourth of July at Lexington," *The Yankee*, 7 July 1815, 3; "New Haven's Centennial," 5 July 1884, 10; "New Haven," *Connecticut Courant*, 14 July 1788, 2; *New-England Palladium*, 3 July 1801, 3; *Frederick-Town Herald*, 19 July 1828, 2; "Frigate Constitution," and "The Figure Head," *National Intelligencer*, 8 and 14 July 1834, 3 and 2, respectively; "Interesting Ceremony," *Brooklyn Daily Eagle*, 5 July 1842, 2; "The Celebration Yesterday," *Brooklyn Daily Eagle*, 5 July 1843, 2; *New York Times*, 5 July 1877, 8; *Washington Post*, 5 July 1976, A14, and 5 July 1978, A1; Appelbaum, *The Glorious Fourth*, 63–64; William P. Coughlin, "In the Harbor, Boom Times for Old Ironsides," *Boston Globe*, 5 July 1990, 23; Robert C. Post, ed., *1876: A Centennial Exhibition* (Washington, D.C.: National Museum of History and Technology, Smithsonian Institution, 1976), 87.

USS *Forrestal*

On July 4, 1976, the USS *Forrestal* was host ship for the International Naval Review of the Bicentennial event in New York City. On board was President Gerald Ford, who reviewed over forty "tall ships" representing countries from throughout the world and tolled the ship's bell in honor of the day. *Forrestal* was named after James V. Forrestal (1892–1949), secretary of the navy in 1944 and secretary of defense in 1947. The vessel is a 60,000-ton, 1039-foot aircraft carrier designated CVB-59. Her keel was laid in July 1952 and she was commissioned on October 1, 1955. The ship is now out of service and located in Rhode Island.

Source: Edward Walsh, "Ford: Chief Celebrant and No. 1 Spectator," *Washington Post*, 5 July 1976, A6.

USS *George Washington*

This nuclear powered aircraft carrier was commissioned on July 4, 1992, with First Lady Barbara Bush assisting and accompanied by Secretary of Defense Dick Cheney. The vessel was built in Virginia by the Newport News Shipbuilding Company with the keel laid on August 25, 1986. With full combat load, *George Washington* displaces 97,000 tons and carries a crew of over 6,000.

Source: Bob Schieffer, "Navy Unveils New Aircraft Carrier," "CBS Evening News Transcript," 4 July 1992.

USS *Iwo Jima*

A Fourth of July celebration took place on this ship in 1983 and consisted of commanding officers of the peace-keeping force in Lebanon, who enjoyed eating a large Independence Day birthday cake. The officers included French gen. J.C. Coulion, U.S. Marine col. Timothy Geraghty, British lt. col. John Cochrane, Lebanese gen. Ibrahim Tannous, and U.S. Navy capt. Morgan France.

Source: "Peace-Keepers Attack Birthday Cake," *Washington Post*, 5 July 1983, A16.

USS *Nebraska*

The keel of the 435-foot vessel was laid on July 4, 1904, in Seattle. The boat was launched on October 7 of that year from the Moran Brothers Shipyard with 55,000 spectators in attendance.

Source: "NavSource Online: Battleship Photo Archive" Web site, <http://www.navsource.org/archives/01/14.htm>.

USS *Newcomb*

This destroyer was launched on July 4, 1943, at the Boston Navy Yard. The vessel was named for late Commodore Frank H. Newcomb, who served in the Coast Guard in the Spanish wars.

Source: "Two Destroyers, Sub Launched in '4th' Ceremonies," *Washington Post*, 5 July 1943, 2.

USS *Roosevelt*

On July 4, 1917, this vessel participated in the dedication ceremony for the new Lake Washington Ship Canal by leading "300 commercial and pleasure craft through the Ballard locks (later renamed after General Hiram Chittenden [1858–1917]) to Lake Union and Lake Washington." The *Roosevelt* previously received recognition for carrying Admiral Robert Peary (1856–1920) for his expedition to the North Pole in 1909.

Source: Patrick McRoberts, "USS Roosevelt, in Dedication Ceremony, Leads a Marine Parade through the Ballard Locks on July 4, 1917," Web site <History Link.org>.

USS *Santee*

The training ship of the United States Naval Academy, which had a long standing tradition of firing artillery salutes beginning in the 1880s.

Source: "How Annapolis Spent the Day," *Baltimore Morning Herald*, 6 July 1880, 4.

USS *Vermont*

In Boston at the Navy Yard, on July 4, 1857, "during the firing of a salute at the navy yard at noon on the fourth," the frigate *Vermont* was set on fire when "a wad was blown on board of the hull."

Source: *Alexandria Gazette*, 11 July 1857, 2.

USS *Washington*

A 74-gun ship-of-the-line, commanded by Captain John O. Creighton, that was host for a celebration on July 4, 1816, in the Mediterranean with the governor of Gilbraltar and the Dutch admiral, guests of Commodore Isaac Chauncey. *Washington* was the flagship for Commodore Chauncey's Mediterranean squadron and was on her maiden voyage. The ship was built in Portsmouth, New Hampshire, and launched on October 1, 1814. She had a distinguished tour of duty and returned to New York Harbor in early July 1818 in time to fire her cannons on Independence Day. The vessel was retired in 1820.

Sources: "Fourth of July," *Reflector*, 28 July 1818, 2; James R. Heintze, "'Tyranny and Despotic Violence': An Incident Aboard the USS *Washington*," *Maryland Historical Magazine* 94/1 (Spring 1999): 31–54.

University of Missouri at Columbia

The ceremony officially establishing the University of Missouri took place at the laying of the cornerstone of the first building on July 4, 1840, in the town of Columbia. That day there was a procession that began near the courthouse and was attended by state officials. James L. Minor, secretary of state, was honored with the keynote address. David Todd, former judge of the Circuit Court, presided over the laying of the cornerstone which was filled with various items, "including a list of the Boone County donors, a copy of the Geyer Act providing for an annual report to the secretary of state, copies of newspapers, and other memorials."

The proposal for the structure at that time described it as three stories in height with a splendid dome thirty-six feet high and two wings, for a total length of 156 feet. It was elaborated with porticos and high quality brick, with the interior made up of classrooms and a chapel.

Source: Frank F. Stephens, *A History of the University of Missouri* (Columbia: University of Missouri Press, 1962), 28–29.

Utica, Illinois, bridge collapse

On July 4, 1910, a bridge collapsed throwing 200 persons into the water. The group was watching a "tub race." At least one person was killed and thirty more injured.

Source: *New York Times*, 5 July 1910, 13.

Valentine, Joshua S.

City council member of Wilmington, Delaware, in 1854, who was put in jail for setting off firecrackers in town on July 4. The mayor of Wilmington was subsequently mobbed by citizens in protest.

Source: *Alexandria Gazette*, 8 July 1854, 2.

Valley Forge, Pennsylvania

Location northwest of Philadelphia where the Continental Army camped between December 19, 1777, and June 18, 1778, under primitive conditions resulting in great stress on the troops. Washington had established winter quarters there following his defeat at Germantown, Pennsylvania. Significant events on the Fourth of July have taken place at Valley Forge and many dignitaries and U.S. presidents have visited the site on Independence Day. On July 4, 1926, the "Star-Spangled Banner" peace chime and the National Birthday Bell were dedicated there. On July 4, 1976, a thirteen-month-long wagon train consisting of 2,500 wagons arrived at Valley Forge, and President Gerald Ford signed legislation transferring ownership of the park from Pennsylvania to the National Park Service.

Sources: *New York Times*, 5 July 1926, 5; Doug Brown, "Wagons Complete Bicentennial Trek to Valley Forge," *Washington Post*, 4 July 1976, 10, and 5 July 1976, A15.

Van Buren, Martin (1782–1862)

Eighth president of the U.S. (1837–41) who spent his Fourths mostly in the Executive Mansion entertaining guests. On July 4, 1839, Van Buren was in New York dining with members of the city's Common Council at Castle Garden. He presented a "sub-Treasury speech to a group comprised principally of Whigs." The editor of the *National Intelligencer* printed a correspondent's report that the president "making party speeches, the very moment he is receiving the honors of the constituted authorities of the whole city, is not only an act offensive, but uncivil and insulting." On that day, the U.S. Marine Band was at Piney Point, Maryland, providing music for an excursion party. At the dinner, after a toast to "The President of the United States," the band played their rendition of *Van Buren's March*.

On July 4, 1840, the young men that made up the several societies that celebrated that day marched in procession "along some of the principal streets of the city to the Mansion of the President of the United States, by whom they were politely received." Van Buren had issued an order for the day that the U.S. Marine Band "should not attend any of the Whig parties on that day, but allowed it to accompany a Locofoco procession and gathering at Shuter's Hill [outside of Washington], and to play there the whole day." The editor for the Washington *National Intelligencer* printed the following response to the order: "Such is the impartiality of the man who now, to its misery and disgrace, governs the nation."

Sources: "Editors Correspondence," *National Intelligencer*, 6 and 8 July 1839, 3 and 3, respectively; "The Fourth of July at the Potomac Pavilion, Piney Point, Md.," *National Intelligencer*, 11 July 1839, 3; "The National Anniversary" and "Bladensburg Celebration of the Fourth," *National Intelligencer*, 6 and 8 July 1840, 3 and 3, respectively.

Varnum, James M. *see* Marietta, Ohio

Vermont People's Party

Formed on July 4, 1893, in Rutland, Vermont, as a hasty response to the stock market crash a few days earlier. The initial "convention" consisted of fifteen men and the platform as reported in a local newspaper "declares for free silver, woman suffrage, and an income tax."

Source: "The Vermont People's Party," *New York Times*, 5 July 1893, 1.

Veterans Memorial Park, Cabot, Arkansas

This park was dedicated on July 4, 2001. Located on Lincoln Street, the facility was created to honor those who died in World War II and who served in the U.S. armed forces. Two granite monuments honor the service men and women.

Source: Ed Galucki, "Cabot Veterans Memorial Park Dedication Story," *Cabot Star-Herald*, as reprinted on the Web site <http://www.arklegion.homestead.com/files/by_Ed_Galucki.htm>, 4 July 2001.

Vicksburg, Mississippi, battle

Was a decisive campaign for the Civil War that was ended on July 4, 1863, when the town surrendered to Union general Ulysses S. Grant after a forty-seven-day siege. On July 4, 1864, in Philadelphia at Grover's Chestnut Street Theatre, a "grand patriotic jubilee" titled *The Seven Sisters* was presented. The presentation included a scene that depicted "the storming of Vicksburg."

The dramatic story of Vicksburg was recounted on July 4, 1889, in the *Los Angeles Times* as a notable Independence Day event. "During the siege a man could not show his head above the intrenchments without being picked off by the riflemen. A hat held for two minutes at a port-hole was riddled with 15 bullets."

In 1945 a "Carnival of the Confederacy" was instituted in Vicksburg on Independence Day "as a tribute to the European victories of American soldiers from the North and South." The event was reported to be the first time in eighty-two years the town celebrated the Fourth of July since the "investment of the city by Union troops." In 1947 General Dwight D. Eisenhower attended the Carnival as the chief speaker. He told a crowd of 50,000, including Governor Fielding L. Wright of Mississippi and an assemblage of army and navy officers, that the war their forefathers fought was the "start of a world union for peace." A two-hour parade included floats that depicted "scenes from the city's history" while squadrons of B-29s flew overhead.

Sources: "Amusements," *Philadelphia Inquirer*, 4 July 1864, 8; "The 4th of July: Capitulation of Vicksburg," *Los Angeles Times*, 4 July 1889, 7; John N. Popham, "General in Vicksburg Address," *New York Times*, 5 July 1947, 12; Duane Schultz, *The Most Glorious Fourth: Vicksburg and Gettysburg, July 4th, 1863* (New York: W.W. Norton, 2002).

Vicksburg, Mississippi, killings

On July 4, 1875, at the Vicksburg Courthouse, a fight broke out between blacks and whites resulting in death and injury. On that day an "ordinary assemblage of patriotic citizens" took place in celebration of the holiday. G.W. Davenport, clerk of the Chancery Court, organized the event. About 2000 persons were present to hear the Rev. J.C. Embry read the Declaration of Independence and Judge George F. Brown speak. James Hill, secretary of state, an African-American, addressed the crowd. "He spoke of Crispus Attucks, colored, the first martyr of the revolution," and said that "the band of white men who threw the tea overboard in Boston harbor a hundred years ago were led by a negro, a young man." That statement angered whites in the audience and after an exchange of words, a handgun was fired, and the audience stampeded toward the exits. Once on the street a number of whites, by most newspaper accounts, attacked the fleeing blacks, killing three of them—Henry Carter, James Perrin, and Allen Ross. The *New Orleans Republican* reported:

> Relate them [the facts] how you will and the horrible outrage of armed white men on peaceable negroes can not be disguised. It was not a war upon carpetbaggers. It was the murder of black[s] by the white citizens of Mississippi. We think the colored men had a right to meet as they did, and to speak, and to gain all the glory they could from history, and to eulogize the American flag to their heart's content. We think the white gentlemen had no right to be there unless peaceably disposed. We learn that a number of best citizens of Vicksburg regret the occurrence.

No arrests were made at Vicksburg.

Sources: *New Orleans Republican*, 8, 10, and 21 July; *New York Times*, 6 July 1875, 4.

Vietnam War

The United States' involvement in the conflict between South Vietnam and the North Vietnamese from 1957 to 1975 resulted in close to 46,000 American deaths and others missing in action. There were numerous demonstrations across the country to halt the U.S. support of the war. As the war progressed and more Americans died, protest gatherings and marches took place on Independence Day in order to increase public awareness of demonstrators' demands. On July 4, 1968, antiwar demonstrations took place in Philadelphia and Minneapolis. Vice President Hubert H. Humphrey speaking at Independence Hall in Philadelphia told a jeering crowd that Americans ought to be able to "walk the streets and proclaim their cause without violence." On July 4, 1974, Vietnam veterans rallied against the war at the Elipse in Washington, D.C.

Numerous popular performers became involved in the peace movement such as country music legend Johnny Cash, who in Washington, D.C., on July 4, 1993, read his patriotic poem, "Rugged Old Flag," while citizens there held flags to honor prisoners of war and servicemen missing in action since the Vietnam War. The Vietnam War influenced the production of new literary works whose authors directly tied their themes to the Fourth. Paul Goetsch cites two noteworthy works: *5th of July* (1978), by Lanford Wilson, which opened on the Fourth in 1977 and featured Kenneth Talley, who lost both legs in the war, and *Born on the Fourth of July* (1876), by Ron Kovic, that focuses on a wounded Vietnam War soldier paralyzed from the chest down. See also **Hanoi, Vietnam.**

Sources: "What's News," *Wall Street Journal*, 5 July 1968, 1; "Peace Pickets Heckle HHH in Philadelphia," *Washington Post*, 5 July 1968, A1; "Veterans Stage 2 Protests," *Washington Post*, 5 July 1974, B1–B2; Paul Goetsch, "The Fourth of July and Its Role in American Literature," *The Fourth of July: Political Oratory and Literary Reactions 1776–1876*, 41–42.

Virginia Military Institute (VMI), Lexington

The first commencement for a graduating class of VMI occurred on July 4, 1842. Sixteen graduates received their degrees that day.

Sources: "Virginia Military Institute," *Alexandria Gazette*, 14 July 1842, 2; William Couper, *One Hundred Years at V.M.I.* (Richmond: Garrett and Massie, 1939), 98–100.

Wabash and Erie Canal

The longest man-made canal system in the country during the nineteenth century, which extended 468 miles connecting Toledo, Ohio, with the Ohio River at Evansville, Indiana. The first section to Lafayette was officially completed and opened on July 4, 1843, with a special ceremony. The principal oration was given by General Lewis Cass. After paying tribute to the anniversary of the republic, he remarked, "We have come here to join in another commemoration. To witness the union of the lakes and of the Mississippi. To survey one of the noblest works of man in the improvement of that great highway of nature, extending from New York to New Orleans, whose full moral and physical effects it were vain to seek, even to conjecture." The construction of the Wabash and Erie Canal was authorized by Congress in 1827 and the canal operated until 1872. Due to competition with the railroad, the canal lost business and was eventually sold off in 1877.

Sources: *Niles' National Register* 64/24 (12 August 1843), 378–81; *The Wabash and Erie Canal* Web site, 5 April 2002, <http://www.huntingtoncounty.org/forks/canal.html>.

Virginia Military Institute, from an 1842 drawing by Cadet Charles P. Deyerle. The first commencement at VMI was held on July 4, 1842, and subsequent commencements were generally held on the Fourth from 1842 through the 1870s. Shown here are the original barracks and arsenal buildings. Manuscript Collection 191, courtesy of Virginia Military Institute Archives.

Wanamie Explosion, Pennsylvania

In the small mining town of Wanamie on July 4, 1906, ten miles south of Wilkesbarre, five boys lost their lives and two others were not expected to live, as the result of an explosion of a home-made pipe bomb. "The boys intended to give the residents of the place a celebration which they would never forget by causing an explosion which would startle the whole neighborhood." The "record-breaking firecracker" was made from iron pipe, five feet in length. It was filled with dynamite, giant powder, and stones. The boys were "ramming the pipe" when it exploded. The boys were hurled some distance away and died immediately. "The force of the explosion was so great that windows in houses near by were broken. All the victims were Lithuanians, and were employed in the mines as breaker boys or drivers."

Source: "Five Killed by Bomb," *New York Times*, 5 July 1906, 1.

War Memorial, Bladensburg, Maryland

This Korean and Vietnam war memorial, located in Prince George's County, was un-

veiled on July 4, 1983. A ceremony included speeches by local officials, including one by Congressional Representative Steny Hoyer (D.— Md.), who said, regarding the Vietnam War, "It is time to evaluate the long-term damage and repay a debt to a generation of young Americans." The monument is described as "12 feet wide and a six-sided marker." Inscribed in the stone is the U.S. Military Academy motto: "Duty, Honor, Country."

Source: Joanne Ostrow, "Memorial to Korean, Vietnam Dead Unveiled in Bladensburg Ceremony," *Washington Post*, 5 July 1983, B3.

War Memorial, Indianapolis

The cornerstone of this monument to World War I veterans was laid on July 4, 1927. Thousands of spectators were present to see the ceremony that featured Gen. **John J. Pershing** and a parade of 5000 war veterans with Pershing in the lead column. He was escorted by the "black horse troop" of Culver Military Academy. Pershing delivered a eulogy for soldiers who were killed in action and encouraged his listeners to meet their obligations as good citizens. "The patriot does not fall in the performance of his obligations either in peace or war," he said. "It is quite as easy to lose our liberty through default or neglect as it would be to lose it through failure to defend it by force of arms."

Inside the cornerstone was placed a copper box that included "the names of Indiana's 40,000 war veterans, a copy of President Wilson's declaration of war and a copy of the Versailles Treaty." According to a newspaper report, the memorial to be constructed "is the central structure in a half-mile-long downtown memorial plaza."

Source: "Indiana Lays Stone for War Memorial," *New York Times*, 5 July 1927, 14.

War Monument, Brooklyn, New York

On July 4, 1922, ground was broken for a war monument in Winthrop Park.

Source: *New York Times*, 5 July 1922, 14.

War of 1812 (1812–14)

War broke out between the United States and Great Britain as a result of naval blockades and other violations by the British of American maritime rights. The conflict was depicted in Independence Day speeches, parades, flag raisings and presentations. As the memories of the Revolutionary War era faded, a renewed importance was given to military veterans. Many towns extended invitations to them for participation in ceremonies and marching in parades. Veterans' societies were begun in many eastern states and veterans of the War of 1812 gathered together annually in many places to commemorate their heroic deeds and to share experiences.

In Washington on July 4, 1862, the highly esteemed "Soldiers of the War of 1812" assembled in the Post Office Department at 11 A.M. and marched to the White House,

where, after passing through the East Room, they called on the President in his office, and were introduced by Col. Seaton, in a brief speech. Mr. Lincoln replied appropriately, thanking them for the call. After each member had been introduced, the line was reformed, and they proceeded back to the place of meeting, where they partook of a bountiful colla-

tion prepared by Mrs. Russell at the instance of E.J. Hall, Esq., of the Post Office Department.

In Frederick, Maryland, the "United Brothers of the War of 1812" met on June 25, 1862, to make plans for "commemorating the glorious fourth of July, after the manner of their fathers." In Buffalo, New York, on July 4, 1863, "a procession of 17 veterans of the war of 1812" paraded.

In Philadelphia a group calling themselves the Soldiers of the War of 1812 assembled regularly. On July 4, 1861, the soldiers "met in the District Court room" and expressed their concern that "the Government had taken no action with regard to pensioning the infirm among them, or their widows." They later went to Independence Hall to hear the Declaration of Independence read. On July 4, 1870, they assembled in the Supreme Court Room. The meeting included electing new members, citing the names of those that had died since the last meeting, offering toasts to the nation and those that fought on its behalf, and listening to a reading of the Declaration of Independence by Col. John S. Riley. At the Fourth celebration in 1880, only a dozen members celebrated. Plans were made to admit the sons and grandsons into membership to perpetuate the organization. On July 4, 1898, they were known as the Pennsylvania Society of the War of 1812 and "had charge of the exercise at Independence Hall" that year.

New York City had a very loyal following of war veterans that assembled each year under the name Corps of Veterans of 1812. Typically their events consisted of speechmaking and flag raisings. On July 4, 1851, they met in the church at Canal and Greene Streets, and Peter J. van Pelt (1778–1861) was the orator of the day. The 1853 celebration of the Veteran Corps included an address before 54 members by "the grandson of one of the captors of **Major [John] André**, Mr. Van Boort [Wart], of Tarrytown, who very effectively revived the recollection of that incident in our national history." Independence Day in 1877 included a flag raising at dawn in the old fort in Central Park by Adjutant J. Gould Warner. Later at the Battery, "he assisted the veteran soldier David Van Arsdale in placing the banner under which he had fought 62 years ago at the top of the flag-staff." At noon 24 veterans assembled at Military Hall, No. 193 Bowery, and marched carrying the flag that was aboard the *Bonhomme Richard* in her combat with the *Serapis*, to the Sturtevant House. At the dinner, "Daniel Lopez, aged 89, who fought on board the frigate *Constitution*, danced a jig, keeping perfect time with the music."

Gradually the numbers of the veterans dwindled. Whereas in 1851 the New York veterans numbered 600 with 150 assembling that year to hear an address by the New York mayor, in 1884 on the Fourth, only eight veterans celebrated, the dinner taking place at the Sturtevant House. Similarly in Philadelphia the Society of the Veterans of 1812 were few in number. On July 4, 1884, only five members were mustered for their celebration.

Sources: Peter J. van Pelt, *A Discourse Delivered by Request of the Survivors of the Veteran Corps in the War of 1812* (New York: C.C. Childs, 1851); *New York Herald*, 6 July 1851, 1; "The Veterans," *New York Times*, 6 July 1858, 1; *The Press* (Philadelphia), 5 July 1861, 3; *Frederick Examiner*, 25 June 1862, 2; *Buffalo Express*, 6 July 1863, 3; *Washington Evening Star*, 5 July 1862, 3; "The Soldiers of the War of 1812," *Philadelphia Inquirer*, 6 July 1870, 6; *New York Times*, 5 July 1877, 8; "Veterans of 1812," *Philadelphia Inquirer*, 6 July 1880, 2; "The National Anniversary," *Washington Post*, 5 July 1884, 1; "In Liberty's Cradle," *Baltimore Herald*, 5 July 1898, 8.

Ward, Samuel Augustus (1847–1903)

Organist at Grace Episcopal Church in Newark, New Jersey, to whose tune was set the poem "America the Beautiful" by **Katharine Lee Bates**. Ward's melody was titled "Materna," was composed in 1882, and was derived from the hymn "O Mother Dear Jerusalem." "Materna" was first published on July 12 in *The Parish Choir*, a weekly church publication.

Source: Lynn Sherr, *America the Beautiful: The Stirring True Story Behind Our Nation's Favorite Song* (New York: BBS Public Affairs, 2001).

Warren, Gouverneur Kemble (1830–1882)

Commander of the Fifths Corps of the Army of the Potomac, the general is honored with a bronze statue which was unveiled on July 4, 1896, in Brooklyn, New York.

Source: *New York Times*, 5 July 1896, 24.

Warren, John (1753–1815)

Presented the first Fourth of July oration in Boston, at Faneuil Hall on July 4, 1783, encouraged both through a Boston General Court act which proclaimed in that year that "The Fourth of July shall be constantly celebrated by the delivery of a Publick oration" and replacement of Boston's annual March 5 massacre orations that commemorated the Boston Massacre in 1770 with commemorations of the nation at peace.

Warren, a medical educator and physician, was born in Roxbury, Massachusetts, and graduated from Harvard in 1771. He practiced medicine in Salem and towards the onset of the Revolutionary War held various posts as surgeon for regiments and hospitals. In 1777 he was named director of the Continental Army general hospital in Boston. Warren was instrumental in establishing Harvard Medical School and served as the school's first professor of anatomy and surgery.

Warren's political activities were limited to a few newspaper articles and his Independence Day oration in 1783. According to Stephen James, Warren was the appropriate person to present Faneuil Hall's first Fourth of July oration due to his participation in the Battle of Lexington as well as his popularity in the city. Moreover, he was the brother of the hero General Joseph Warren, who died at the battle of Lexington. His other brother Ebenezer also fought in that skirmish. In his presentation Warren spoke about the celebration of the occasion and how future generations would commemorate the day. "The generations yet unborn shall ... celebrate to the latest ages of the republic, the anniversary of that resolution of the American Congress, which gave the rights of sovereignty and independence to these United States."

Sources: John Warren, *An Oration, Delivered July 4th, 1783* (Boston: Commonwealth of Massachusetts: John Gill, 1783); James, "The Other Fourth of July," 50–57; Philip Cash, "John Warren," *American National Biography*, 22:723–24.

Washington

A popular steamboat that provided Fourth of July excursions on the Potomac River to Mount Vernon during the 1820s. The boat was owned by the New Potomac Steam Boat Company. As reported in an advertisement for an excursion on July 4, 1828, the vessel had three large cabins and could carry eighty passengers. The fee was one dollar.

Sources: *Alexandria Gazette*, 1 and 3 July 1823, 3 and 3 respectively; *National Intelligencer*, 21 June 1828, 3.

Washington, Booker T. *see* Tuskegee University

Washington Benevolent Societies

Active in Boston, New York, Philadelphia, and various towns in New England to counteract the growth of Republican influence. The Boston Washington Benevolent Society, which favored Adams, was founded in 1812 (its last meeting was July 4, 1819) by Federalists to counteract the influence of the Republicans' Washington Society (1805 to 1822), which supported the ideals of Jefferson. Each of the groups had their separate meetings, orations and dinners on the Fourth. Both societies annually exchanged antagonisms, respectively, against Adams and Jefferson. The diatribes were continued in local newspapers and the party animosities that had begun during the period of the ratification of the Constitution in the 1780s through the election of Jefferson as president in 1801 continued ever more heated. According to Charles Warren it was this party separation on the Fourth that prevented a truly national celebration from taking place.

The New York association was founded on July 12, 1808, by a number of Federalists to rival Tammany, a Republican organization. Led by Gulian C. Verplanck, the New York members frequently paraded around town in colorful apparel on the Fourth of July, and they were made up of "substantial shopkeepers and Mechanicks, of men in the middling classes, and a considerable number of old Revolutionary officers and soldiers." The society heralded George Washington, the model of "morality, piety and benevolence," but admonished "licentiousness," a characteristic often associated with common citizens. Meetings were held on Independence Day at various sites, including the North Dutch Church, and Washington Hall, their home base. Orators who spoke at society affairs on Independence Day included, for example, Gulian C. Verplanck (1809), Robert Sedgwick (1811), and **Gouverneur Morris** (1813).

The cornerstone of New York's Washington Hall, located at the corner of Broadway and Reed Streets, was laid on July 4, 1809, and included a memorable ceremony at the North Church. Isaac Sebring, president of the society, gave a brief address. "While I congratulate the Society on this occasion, I cannot but express the hope that the Hall, to be erected on the spot, may be sacredly devoted to the cultivation of friendship, of charity, of correct principles, and of ardent patriotism," he said. Robert Morris, Jr., second vice president of the society, had a copy of Washington's farewell address in hand, and Joseph Warren Brackett composed a vocal work appropriately titled "Auspicious Day" for the event. The piece was sung by "Mr. Caulfield in a style of peculiar excellence." Also, two bands of music performed for the occasion.

The political rivalry continued but abated somewhat at the end of the War of 1812. The party issues that symbolized Adams and Jefferson were finally laid to rest with the deaths of the two presidents on July 4, 1826, and a new era of nationalization in the way the holiday was celebrated took root.

Sources: *Alexandria Gazette*, 12 July 1809, 3; Washington Society, *An Historical View of the Public Celebrations of the Washington Society, and Those of the Young Republicans. From 1805, to 1822* (Boston: True and Greene, 1823); Charles Warren, "Fourth of July Myths," *William and Mary Quarterly* 2 (July 1945): 254–72; Howard B. Rock, "The American Revolution and the Mechanics of New York City: One Generation Later," *New York History* 57/3 (July 1976): 367–94; Robert W. July, *The Essential New Yorker: Gulian Crommelin Verplanck* (Durham: Duke University Press, 1951), 21–24.

Washington Flagpole, Minneapolis

Located on Hennepin Avenue across from the new Federal Reserve Bank, this monument was dedicated in 1917. The inscribed text on the base of the memorial reads:

"Presented to the City of Minneapolis as a monument to George Washington by the Monument Chapter of the Daughters of the American Revolution July Fourth 1917."

Washington, George (1732–1799)

First president of the U.S. and commander in chief of the Continental Army, who was an ardent participant in Fourth of July ceremonies and who will forever be memorialized as a result of his service to the nation. Washington was born in Westmoreland County, Virginia. His pursuits included farming and politics, first as a member of the Virginia House of Burgesses (1759–74). He developed his military prowess as a soldier in the French and Indian War. In May 1775 the Second Continental Congress named Washington as commander of the Continental Army. With the signing of the Declaration of Independence, the outbreak of war was inevitable, and through the next six years Washington's skills as a military commander were tested. In 1781 with help from French allies, General Cornwallis was forced to surrender at Yorktown, Virginia. Washington was subsequently elected United States president, serving two terms (1789–1797), after which he retired to his Virginia estate, **Mount Vernon**. Upon leaving office, Washington delivered his farewell address to the people of the nation. The address quickly became an icon of Washington's patriotism and love for country and it was publicly recited and referred to in numerous Fourth of July ceremonies in the nineteenth century.

Washington's first Fourth celebration was one he personally orchestrated. On July 4, 1778, encamped with his army at Brunswick, New Jersey, he directed his men to observe through celebration the second anniversary of the signing of the Declaration of Independence. Each troop was given an extra ration of rum and they were asked by Washington to put "green boughs" in their hats. A special artillery salute was then commenced. News of this event spread through the colonies by newspapers and personal accounts. Washington's idea for firing artillery in that celebration

may have influenced the adoption of this practice in subsequent celebrations throughout the next century.

Upon the conclusion of the war, one of the first notable tributes to Washington occurred on July 4, 1783, at the commencement exercises at the University of Pennsylvania, when the general was awarded an honorary doctor of laws degree. Although he was not there to accept the degree, six months later Washington was given the diploma when he stopped in Philadelphia on his way to Annapolis to resign his commission. Most of Washington's most memorable Fourth of July experiences occurred during his presidency at the annual celebrations held in Alexandria, Virginia, just north of Mount Vernon. These celebrations usually included a visit to the church, listening to an oration, and a dinner with toasts to and from Washington.

On July 4, 1793, Washington was in Alexandria. After attending a "divine service" in the Protestant Episcopal Church, he listened to a "discourse, suited to the occasion" by the Rev. Mr. Davis. Then the president and no less than 110 persons sat down "to an elegant dinner in Mr. Wise's long room." The 15th toast was to Washington: "The man who unites all hearts," followed by "3 cheers and 15 rounds from the 12 pounders." The president then gave a toast to the group: "Prosperity to the Town of Alexandria," and, after drinking the health of the company, retired.

Washington's fame and endearment to the American public was evidenced in newspaper articles, speeches, fireworks, and toasts. On July 4, 1853, the following editorial in the *New York Herald* noted his legacy:

> The day has again arrived when the name of Washington hangs upon every lip, and when the vastness of his fame, the amount of his self-denial, and the soundness of his patriotism fall with redoubled force upon the recollections of every one.

At the Independence Day fireworks celebration in New York in front of City Hall on July 9, 1855 (the earlier event was postponed due to rain), Washington was depicted through a pyrotechnical feat. A local newspaper reported that it was "truly a great triumph of the pyrotechnic art, covering, as it did, the whole balcony and pillared portico of City Hall. The design was a life-size figure of Washington on horseback, forming the centre of the façade of a temple, surmounted by a spread eagle in the center and by shields and urns at the corners." Throughout the nineteenth century, numerous associations named after Washington sponsored Fourth of July celebrations and published orations given on that day. These included the Washington Benevolent Societies active in Philadelphia; New York; Hanover, New Hampshire; Cambridge, Greenfield, and Worcester and other Massachusetts towns; New Brunswick, New Jersey; and the Washington Societies of Boston, Charleston, and Alexandria, Virginia.

Sources: *Pennsylvania Packet*, 14 July 1778; *Freeman's Journal*, 9 July 1783; *Virginia Gazette and Alexandria Advertiser*, 11 July 1793, 2–3; *New York Herald*, 4 July 1853, 4; "The Deferred Fireworks," *New York Times*, 10 July 1855, 4; Edward Potts Cheyney, *History of the University of Pennsylvania, 1740–1940* (Philadelphia: University of Pennsylvania Press, 1940), 140.

Washington Monument, Baltimore

The cornerstone for this 178-foot-high monument in Baltimore was laid on July 4, 1815, and is considered the first ceremony for a monument in honor of George Washington. Made out of marble, this structure sits high atop Mount Vernon Place, known as Howard's Park in 1815. The monument was designed by Robert Mills. The statue of Washington on his horse was sculpted by Enrico Causici and was installed in 1829.

The 1815 ceremony began at noon with the stone laid by James A. Buchanan, president of the Board of Managers, with assistance by Gov. Levin Winder, grand master of the Masonic Fraternity of the state, and Col. John E. Howard, president of the State Society of the Cincinnati. Thirty thousand spectators were in attendance and watched as "the different coins of the United States and the publications of the day" were deposited in the "chamber" of the stone. A "brass plate" with the following words was attached: "On the 4th of July 1815, was laid this foundation stone of the first monument to the memory of

George Washington," with the names of the managers and architect. At the end of the ceremony, "a grand salute of 100 guns were fired in quick succession by the regiment of artillery and three fires of joy by the infantry." See also **Howard's Park, Baltimore.**

Sources: *Virginia Patriot*, 8 July 1815; *Frederick-Town Herald*, 15 July 1815, 3; *A Guide to Baltimore Architecture* (Baltimore: Dorsey and Dilts, 1997).

Washington Monument, Budapest, Hungary *see* Hungary

Washington Monument, District of Columbia

The largest and best known monument in honor of the nation's first president. The cornerstone was laid on July 4, 1848. Large crowds assembled to witness the event. The dignitaries present included President James K. Polk and his cabinet, members of Congress, the diplomatic corps, officers of the army and navy, and city authorities representing Alexandria, Georgetown, and Washington. Societies represented included Rechabites, Red Men, Odd Fellows, and Free Masons, in their respective regalia. Robert C. Winthrop, Speaker of the House of Representatives, was the principal orator. He discussed the political systems of Europe and the United States and the name of George Washington being memorialized "to all free men of the two worlds."

For a number of years work on the monument had ceased, due to the Civil War and other matters. Individuals, such as Washington resident **Benjamin Brown French**, spoke out on the Fourth urging the monument be completed. It was to many a national embarrassment. In Pittsfield, Massachusetts, on July 4, 1855, a toast was offered expressing this sentiment to "The Washington National Monument — like the 'finger of scorn,' it moves slowly, but when once it is raised it must shame oppression from before it."

Through the years the monument and its grounds became a gathering place for crowds witnessing the annual fireworks displays, as well as other ceremonies. For example, a Washington monument ceremony took place on July 4, 1850, and included the laying of a block of marble by the "Corporation." The event held there on July 4, 1894, began at the Arlington Hotel as a procession headed by the United States Marine Band and the Washington Light Infantry and Battery A of the District of Columbia National Guard. E.B. Hay read the Declaration of Independence and Senators John Sherman of Ohio and Thomas Jordan Jarvis of North Carolina gave speeches which focused on easing tensions that had arisen between laborites and management.

With the building of the **Sylvan Theater** on the monument grounds in the early twentieth century, annual events that included speeches by well known persons became the norm. For example, on July 4, 1950, John Foster Dulles, special consultant to the State Department, gave a speech on the North Korean invasion of South Korea. Another noteworthy event was the first televised Fourth of July ceremony there in 1947.

Sources: "The Fourth of July in Washington — Mr. Winthrop's Oration," *National Era* 2/80 (13 July 1848): 110; *The Republic*, 4 July 1850, 3; "The Celebration of the Fourth," *Pittsfield Sun*, 12 July 1855, 2; *New York Times,* 5 July 1894, 8; *Washington Evening Star*, 5 July 1947, A3; *Washington Post*, 5 July 1950, 1.

Washington Monument, Philadelphia

In 1858 the Washington Monument Association of Pennsylvania was established for the purposes of raising funds to construct a monument in honor of George Washington. In 1869 the project was completed, with the dedication of the statue taking place on July 4. The affair was the highlight of Philadelphia's holiday events that year.

The dedication ceremony included an invocation prayer by the Rev. Albert Barnes, singing of "Hail Columbia," "Star-Spangled Banner," and "America," a presentation address by George F. Gordon, and a reception of the statue address by Daniel M. Fox, mayor.

Sources: *The Age*, 5 July 1869, 1; *New York Times*, 5 July 1869, 1.

Washington Monument, South Mountain, Boonsboro, Maryland

This monument was erected on July 4, 1827, and a rededication ceremony occurred

on July 4, 1936. The monument was first made of "native stone blocks" but has since "been rebuilt twice, the last time by the Civilian Conservation Corps."

Sources: "Washington Shaft Rededicated," *New York Times*, 5 July 1936, 22; "Go See It on the Mountain: Washington's 1st Monument," *Washington Post*, 1 July 1983, A1.

Washington Monument, Washington Rock, New Jersey

On July 4, 1867, a cornerstone for a monument to George Washington was laid under the auspices of the Washington Monument Association and was reported to be the first

Washington Monument, Boonsboro, Maryland. This first monument in honor of George Washington was built and dedicated on July 4, 1827. A rededication ceremony occurred on July 4, 1936, after the Civilian Conservation Corps had restored the structure to its original design. During the Civil War, the monument served as a Union signal station. Photograph by author.

monument built in New Jersey that commemorated the nation's first president. Washington Rock, a natural outcropping, served as a lookout point where, during the Revolutionary War, General Washington spotted the British army under General William Howe in the valley as they marched toward Westfield. With that vantage point, Washington was able to strategically maneuver his troops to cut off the retreat of Howe's forces.

Plans for the monument to Washington included a foundation "15½ feet square, from which a pedestal of the same material will rise to the height of fifty-five feet, and upon this will be reared the statue." The location of Washington's Rock is 3½ miles northeast of Plainfield. The ceremony included a procession of dignitaries and military persons and the setting of the cornerstone that contained "local newspapers and periodicals of the day," and an address by the "Grand Mason," and an oration by J. Dagget Hunt, in which he said,

> Within a decade of a century ago the army of the Federal Colonies encamped on this spot, and left here hallowed memories to those who came after them. The corner-stone laid today was laid by the Masonic Fraternity, because Washington was a member of that Order, and it had been resolved by the people of New Jersey that the monument to be erected by them should far surpass that of any other State, in beauty of design and real intrinsic value.

On July 4, 1893, the actual rock was dedicated by a delegation from Washington Camp No. 1, which sought to "preserve the rock and paint on it a representation of the Stars and Stripes." In 1913 the State of New Jersey purchased the site, and it was renamed Washington Rock State Park.

Sources: "A Monument to Washington," *New York Times*, 5 July 1867, 1; *New York Times*, 5 July 1893, 9.

Washington Musical Association

This organization was active in the nation's capitol in the 1830s. Its members numbered 40 men and women. The association celebrated on July 4, 1839, at the residence of Enoch Tucker, about 3½ miles from Washington.

Source: *National Intelligencer*, 8 July 1839, 3.

Washington; or, The Memorable Era of 1776

This drama in three parts was premiered on July 4, 1799, at the Hay-Market Theatre in Boston.

Source: *Independent Chronicle*, 1–4 July 1799, 3.

Washington Statue, Paris, France

An equestrian bronze statue of George Washington, a gift of "An Association of American Women for the Presentation of a Statue of Washington to France," was unveiled on the Place d'Iena in Paris, on July 3, 1900. The American delegation included General Horace Porter, U.S. ambassador, who gave an address in both English and French about Washington's accomplishments, and Ambassador William Franklin Draper and his family. Music was provided by Sousa's band, and national anthems of both countries were played. French minister of foreign affairs Theophile Delcassé officially accepted the statue. About Washington he said,

> When he died two nations mourned — the nation he had founded and the nation which aided him to found it — and the same crepe drapes the starred banner and the cockade of Lafayette today and the same two peoples are more united than ever and more than ever convinced that they will never cease to be so.

The statue, described as fifteen feet in height, was cast in bronze in New York City by the Henry Bonnard Bronze Co. by sculptors Daniel C. French, who modeled the figure of Washington, and Edward C. Potter, who made the horse. "Washington is represented in full military costume, taking command of the American Army at Cambridge (July 3, 1776), and dedicating his sword to the service of his country." The pedestal was made of granite and marble and was designed by Charles F. McKim, and stood fourteen feet in height. An annual tradition of placing flowers at the monument on the Fourth of July quickly took hold. The 1927 event was particularly noteworthy due to the presence of explorer Richard E. Byrd.

Sources: "Statue in Paris of Washington," *New York Herald*, 4 July 1900, 10; "Washington Statue in Paris," *New York Times*, 3 January 1900, 6; "A Franco-American Fete," *New York Times*, 4 July 1900, 6;

"France Accepts America's Gift," *Washington Post*, 4 July 1900, 7; "France Observes the Day," *New York Herald Tribune*, 5 July 1927, 8.

Washington Statue, Philadelphia

A bronze statue of George Washington was unveiled "on the Chestnut Street side" of Independence Hall on July 4, 1910. Prior to the unveiling, John Barrett of Washington, D.C., representing the International Bureau of American Republics, gave an oration that touched on "the problems and responsibilities of the United States to the Latin-American republics." There was also "patriotic music by the municipal band and singing by the children of the public schools."

Source: "Washington Statue Unveiled," *New York Times*, 5 July 1910, 18.

Washington Statue, Raleigh, North Carolina

This bronze statue, cast by William J. Hubbard of Richmond, Virginia, was unveiled on the grounds of the state capitol on July 4, 1857. The monument portrays Washington with a sword standing next to a plow that symbolizes his humble background.

Source: State Capitol/Visitor Services, North Carolina Office of Archives and History.

Washington Statues, New York

A bronze equestrian statue by Henry K. Brown was unveiled in New York City on July 4, 1856, before a crowd of 20,000. The Washington statue took four years to construct, weighed four tons and was placed on a granite pedestal "weighing one hundred tons. The whole is twenty-nine feet high, the statue being fourteen and a half feet high. It cost $30,000, and was cast in Chicopee, Mass." A newspaper reported that the statue

> was uncovered with great difficulty, and only after the assistance of a neighboring fire company had been procured. But when the canvas was fully removed, as if by magic, there went up from the vast multitude one prolonged and continuous shout of cheering, and the waving of handkerchiefs, hats and flags, with the simultaneous discharge of thousands of different species of firearms, testified the enthusiastic devotion of the American people to Washington, "The father of his country."

Statue of George Washington on the Place d'Iena in Paris, France, unveiled on July 3, 1900. Among the dignitaries present was John Philip Sousa and his band, who performed *The Stars and Stripes Forever!* Photograph courtesy of George Arnold.

Another statue of Washington was unveiled in Riverside Park on July 4, 1884, "in presence of a large number of spectators." The statue was "a present from the pupils of the public schools of the city." Gen. Viele of the Park Department gave an address, and the statue was presented by "ex-president Wood, of the Board of education." On behalf of the city, Mayor Edson officially received the statue.

Sources: *The Evening Post*, 5 July 1856, 3; *New York Times*, 5 and 7 July 1856; "The National Anniversary," *Washington Post*, 5 July 1884, 1.

Washington's Farewell Address

The text of **George Washington**'s Farewell Address was printed in newspapers, publicly recited, and toasted on the Fourth of July during the nineteenth century in reverence to the nation's first president, who died on December 14, 1799, at Mount Vernon. Washington had given his farewell address on September 19, 1796, after declining a third term as president. The text of the address quickly became one of the nation's patriotic icons.

An early reading in New York City took place at a ceremony of several societies on July 5, 1813, and was presented by William H. Bunn of the Columbian Society. Readings of the Farewell Address took place in Charleston, South Carolina, one on July 4, 1831, by Gen. Daniel Ellicott Huger at the First Presbyterian Church and another on July 4, 1832, by Thomas Lee at the Second Presbyterian Church. On July 4, 1856, it was read in Washington in Clendenin's Grove near the Glenwood Cemetery by John E. O'Brien of the Assembly Church.

On July 4, 1862, it was read by Russell Houston in the hall of the Tennessee State Capitol in Nashville. The occurrence of this reading was known as far away as Cincinnati, through an auditor's letter that was sent to a Cincinnati newspaper: "While Russell Houston, esq. read Washington's Farewell Address, the most profound attention was given. The revered words were received with deep solemnity, as a voice from the dead." Although the city was divided among Yankee and secessionist supporters, the audience for the reading consisted mostly of women, many holding flags. "Great numbers of little girls were dressed in red, white and blue, and young ladies wore the honored stripes and stars on their bosoms as badges." On July 4, 1893, the address was read by William C. Smith at a gathering of the Francis Scott Key Monument Association in Baltimore, and on July 4, 1921, it was read by Peter J. McCormick before 4000 persons at the Civic Auditorium in San Francisco.

The Farewell Address was also printed occasionally in newspapers, such as *National Intelligencer* (Washington), July 4, 1835, *Franklin Democrat* (Greenfield, Massachusetts), July 4, 1855, and *Frederick Examiner* (Frederick, Maryland), July 3, 1861. Other memorable occasions included toasts such as the one at Fork of Richland District in South Carolina on July 4, 1831: "The Farewell Address of Washington — May it make a lasting impression on the minds of the people of the U. States, and may they ever bear in mind the prophetic warning of this Father of his country."

Sources: *New York Statesman*, 3 July 1813, 2; *Charleston Courier*, 6 July 1831 and 6 July 1832, 2 and 2, respectively; *The* [Washington] *Globe*, 15 and 18 July 1831, 3 and 3, respectively; *National Intelligencer*, 4 July 1835, 2; *Franklin Democrat*, 2 July 1855, 1–2; "Celebration of the Fourth," *Washington Evening Star*, 7 July 1856, 3; "Letter from Nashville," *Cincinnati Daily Gazette*, 8 July 1862; *Baltimore Morning Herald*, 5 July 1893, 2; "Thousands in Auditorium Pay Tribute to U.S.," *San Francisco Chronicle*, 5 July 1921, 3.

Washington's Revolutionary War Headquarters, Newburgh, New York

In 1782–83, Washington established his Revolutionary War headquarters in the home of Jonathan Hasbrouck, in Newburgh, New York. On July 4, 1850, the site officially became the property of New York State and a ceremony in honor of the occasion took place. The Hon. J.W. Edmonds delivered an oration, and a flag was raised by General **Winfield Scott**, "amid the enthusiastic cheers of the multitude and the roaring of artillery. The General then addressed the vast concourse before him in a pertinent and interesting speech." He spoke about the "detestable tactics of politicians." Also, an ode ("Freemen, pause, this ground is holy") written by Mrs. J.J. Monell of Newburgh was sung. After the ceremony, the party dined at the West Point Hotel.

Today the site, located at 84 Liberty Street, has facilities where visitors can view various exhibits consisting of period furnishings, firearms, military artifacts, documents, firearms, and portraits of George and Martha Washington.

Sources: *The Literary World* 7/2 (13 July 1850): 36; *Alexandria Gazette*, 10 July 1850, 4; *New York Herald*, 6 July 1850, 1.

Washington's Tent

The headquarters tent used by General George Washington and his staff during the Revolution and later in commemorative Fourth of July celebrations. This marquee-type tent, 18 × 28 feet, was brought back to Mount Vernon after the war and after Washington's death passed to **George Washington Parke Custis,** who kept the tent at his Arlington, Virginia, residence. In 1826, on the occasion of the Fiftieth Anniversary Jubilee, he hosted a celebration that followed the ceremony held in the Capitol and used the tent to honor the memory of Washington. Made out of heavy, unbleached, woven linen, the tent was appropriately decorated: "The pillars that supported this venerated canvass were beautifully encircled with alternate wreaths of the laurel and the vine; at its head hung an original portrait of the 'Pater Patrix' [George Washington] by Sharpless [James Sharples (1751–1811)?] which has generally been esteemed the best likeness ever taken of him." Custis was asked by his guests to speak about the tent, and he responded with "a brief account of the Pretorium, from the time of its first being pitched, on the Heights of Dorchester, in 1775, to its becoming a banquetting hall for the captive chiefs of our enemy at York Town in 1781." According to Auguste Levasseur, the tent was also used at a reception honoring Lafayette at Fort McHenry. Custis eventually gave the tent to the U.S. government and it is now located in the National Museum of American History in Washington, D.C.

Sources: *Charleston Courier*, 17 July 1826, 2; Auguste Levasseur, *Lafayette in America in 1824 and 1825; or, Journal of Travels, in the United States* (New York: White, Gallaher and White, 1829), 1:163.

Watsonville, California, Band

On July 4, 1996, the Watsonville Band, conducted by Gonzalo Viales, performed a two-hour concert before 8,000 guests on the White House south lawn by invitation of President Bill Clinton. The 75-member band was given a tour of the White House and also performed in the Washington's National Independence Day Parade that day. After the band assembled on the south lawn, the musicians were welcomed by Leon Panetta, chief of staff to the president, followed by brief remarks by President Clinton. By the president's request, the band performed the *Thunderer March* by John Philip Sousa.

Source: "Washington D.C. Tour, July 4th, 1996," Web site, <http://www.edpio-assoc.com/scb/watbnd3.html>, 29 June 2000.

Webb, George James (1803–1887)

Composer, who wrote an "Ode for the 4th [of] July 1832," SATB with piano.

Source: Manuscript; score (7 pages) in the New York Public Library.

Webster, Daniel (1782–1852)

Statesman, attorney, and noted orator who spoke frequently on Independence Day, his first Fourth address in 1800 as a student at Dartmouth College and his last in 1851 as secretary of state at the Capitol cornerstone ceremony. Webster was born in Salisbury, New Hampshire, and after being admitted to the Boston bar in 1805, was elected to Congress in 1812. He appeared often before the U.S. Supreme Court in notable cases, increasing his reputation as a constitutional lawyer. In 1827 he was elected to the U.S. Senate and later served as secretary of state under Presidents William Henry Harrison and John Tyler.

Following his 1800 oration Webster spoke on the Fourth in 1802 at Fryeburg, Maine; his address was published eighty years later (Boston: A.F. and C.W. Lewis, 1882).

Webster's oration delivered at Concord,

New Hampshire, on July 4, 1806, was an enduring statement about freedom. An excerpt was published in Philadelphia thirty-one years later:

When we speak of preserving the Constitution, we mean not the paper on which it is written, but the spirit which dwells in it — Government may lose all its real character, its genius, its temper, without losing its appearance. Republicanism, unless you guard it, will creep out of its case of parchment, like a snake out of its skin. You may have a despotism under the name of a Republic. You may look on a government, and see it possess all the external modes of Freedom, and yet find nothing of its essence, the vitality of Freedom in it; just as you may contemplate an embalmed body, where art has preserved proportion and form, amidst nerves without motion, and veins void of blood.

On July 4, 1840, Webster was in Barre, Massachusetts, speaking amidst "deep thunders of applause," before an audience of 5000 at a Whig Association celebration, billed as a Grand Harrison Festival. On July 4, 1851, he gave an oration "from the stand on the East Portico of the Capitol" on the occasion of the laying of the cornerstone of the new Capitol edifice. This was his last Fourth of July oration. A newspaper reported:

Mr. Webster then rose from a chair next to President Fillmore, and approached the front of the stand. He was welcomed by the hearty cheers of the multitude, and proceeded to read the Address which he had prepared, a copy of which had been deposited in the cornerstone. He did not, however, confine himself to the manuscript, but occasionally extemporized new thoughts and other highly interesting reflections, which, together with the reading, occupied him nearly two hours.

He began his speech with the following uplifting welcome:

"Fellow-Citizens: I congratulate you, I give you joy, on the return of this Anniversary; and I felicitate you, also, on the more particular purpose of which this ever-memorable day has been chosen to witness the fulfillment. Hail! All hail! I see before and around me a mass of faces, glowing with cheerfulness and patriotic pride. I see thousands of eyes, turned towards other eyes, all sparkling with gratification and delight. This is the New world!"

A local newspaper reported:

It was a wise, elaborate, and patriotic review of the past and present condition of our country, and comprised the recital of much statistical data. There was probably less in it intended or adapted to merely entertain the hearer than in any other oration ever delivered on a like occasion; but more to interest, to arouse us to a right appreciation of our true condition and destiny as a nation.

Webster was frequently honored by name at Fourth of July dinners. For example, in Philadelphia, on July 4, 1833, at a public dinner hosted by "The Friends of American Industry and the City Administration," the following toast was spoken: "Daniel Webster — formerly the New Hampshire farmer, now the great Colossean of the North-eastern Hemisphere."

On July 4, 1853, Timothy Bigelow gave an address at the Old South Church in Boston and commemorated the statesman: "But though the republic is safe even when the great citizens are removed, we cannot forget today the death, a few months since, of her greatest statesman," he said. "The mountains of New Hampshire gave Daniel Webster to America, and his character and conduct always bore the colossal imprint of his birthplace." In Faneuil Hall, where the dinner was held, there was a "large historical picture representing Mr. Webster," delivering a speech, hanging on the hall wall "opposite the entrance," as well as a "marble bust of Mr. Webster appropriately draped with the national colors" on display.

Sources: "At Philadelphia," *National Intelligencer*, 13 July 1833, 3; "Extract from an Oration," *Poulson's American Daily Advertiser*, 10 July 1837, 2; *New Bedford Mercury*, 10 July 1840, 1; *National Intelligencer*, 7 and 8 July 1851, 3 and 2, respectively; "The Celebration Yesterday," *Boston Evening Transcript*, 5 July 1853, 2.

Webster, Fletcher (1813–1862)

Lawyer, soldier, and eldest son of Daniel Webster, who delivered a stirring oration in Boston on July 4, 1846, of which Fletcher was cited as having "the moral courage to assert great truths in a community where they can win little applause." His topic was the lawfulness of war and the duty of the citizen to obey the government, and his position directly opposed "fanatical reformers" and advocates of the "Peace Party."

Webster was born in Portsmouth, New Hampshire, and graduated from Harvard College in 1833. His father instructed him in law, and after being admitted to the bar he was private secretary for his father's service as secretary of state. His professional positions included secretary of legation in China in 1843, a member of the Massachusetts legislature in 1847, and surveyor of Boston's port in 1850–61. In 1861 he entered the Civil War as colonel of the 12th Massachusetts Regiment.

Webster's oration (Boston: Eastburn, 1846) represented a departure from typical orations of his day — those that focused on the American interest in greatness, deference to the founding fathers, the glorious past, and projected future. According to a reviewer writing in the *Boston Daily Advertiser*, Webster wrote the oration as a response to Charles Sumner's oration on peace the year before. In Webster's piece, he immediately brought attention to "some weak-minded but well disposed New England ministers," who opposed going to war with England in 1812 and through their influence, "peace became a sort of cant among us, and it was hazardous to one's reputation to intimate that war, terrible as may be its evils, is nevertheless sometimes just and necessary." Moreover, these "canting ministers, strolling spinsters, and beardless youths" referred to George Washington as an "inhuman butcher" and presented themselves as "the sole authoritative expounders of the precepts of the divine law. We are unable to determine what it is safe to eat or to drink, when to rise up or sit down, unless some of these self-constituted guides condescend to inform us." Webster viewed this "new morality" as a serious threat to the country. Selecting war and loyalty as his topic, he presented a carefully worded and extensive rationale supporting his notion that while peace is preferred, "war is not morally wrong" and that it is the duty of the citizen to answer the government's call when asked. Death on the battlefield was an acceptable price to pay:

No doubt, philanthropy [the new morality]
may weep over the wounded and the dying;
but it is no great evil to die. It is appointed unto all men to die, and, so far as the death itself is concerned, it matters not whether it comes a few months earlier or a few months later, on the battle-field or in our own bedchambers. The evil is not in dying, but in dying unprepared. If prepared,— and the soldier, fighting by command of his country in her cause, may be prepared,— it is of little consequence whether the death come in the shape of sabre-cut or leaden bullet, or in that of disease or old age.

Ironically Webster was killed on August 30, 1862, at the second battle of Bull Run.

Sources: "An Oration Delivered before the Authorities of the City of Boston in the Tremont Temple, July 4, 1846," *Boston Daily Advertiser*, 6 July 1846; *Brownson's Quarterly Review* 3 (October 1846): 493–518; Charles Cowley, "Colonel Fletcher Webster," *Bay State Monthly* 1/3 (March 1884): 143–49; "A Reminiscence of Col. Fletcher Webster," *Bay State Monthly* 3/1 (April 1885): 38; "Fletcher Webster," *The National Cyclopaedia of American Biography*, 13:169.

West Philadelphia Institute

On July 4, 1853, the cornerstone of this building was laid.

Source: *Daily News*, 4 July 1853, 2.

West Point, United States Military Academy

West Point has an illustrious history of celebrating the Fourth of July with orations, readings of the Declaration of Independence, and events that included military parades, dinners and music provided by the United States Military Academy Band.

In 1802, President Thomas Jefferson signed legislation establishing the U.S. Military Academy. From 1817 to 1833, Col. Sylvanus Thayer, the "father of the military academy," served as superintendent. He upgraded academic standards, instilled military discipline and emphasized honorable conduct. West Point graduates gained experience and recognition during the Mexican and Indian wars, and during the Civil War they dominated the highest ranks on both sides.

Ceremony and ritual, as well as pride and patriotism, have always been of the highest order of those associated with West Point. The academy was formally opened on July 4, 1802. The day began with a federal salute from Fort

View of the Hudson River from Trophy Point at West Point, New York. The U.S. Military Academy formally opened on July 4, 1802, and was a popular destination for visitors on the Fourth of July. Photo courtesy of the United States Military Academy.

Clinton "which was echoed by the adjacent mountains." The artillery under the command of Lieut. R.W. Osborne paraded, and it was reported that "the troops, by their soldierly appearance, and conduct in performing the different military evolutions, did honor to themselves." Later "the gentlemen of the corps of Engineers and Artillery, who compose the Military Academy, under the command of Major Jonathan Williams" joined those from the garrison for dinner. The evening concluded with a salute from Fort Clinton followed by "a handsome display of fire works."

The U.S. Military Academy Band was first organized under the direction of Richard Willis, prominent musician, composer and inventor of the E-flat keyed bugle. The band's first annual concert was given on July 4, 1817, at the ruins of Fort Putnam at West Point. On of the more notable concerts occurred on July 4, 1876, when the band performed at the

United States' Centennial celebration in Philadelphia.

In 1826 a one-hundred-year-old tradition of a graduating cadet presenting an oration on the Fourth of July began. William Maynadier, class of 1827, met with his class at the house of Mr. John Winfield, "about two miles from the Point," where he spoke. In the audience was "a soldier of '76" who recalled to the cadets "the battles in which he had been engaged, and the wounds he had received in defending the sacred rights of his country." After the address, a number of toasts were drunk, "after which the class returned to camp."

In 1830, the cadets celebrated Independence Day on Saturday, July 3. They marched to the chapel "preceded by their excellent band," and displaying their banners. Cadet Williams of Georgia read the Declaration of Independence. The choir sang the Marseilles

Hymn and Henry Clay, Jr., delivered the "annual oration," which was reported "bright with the glow of enthusiasm, as he felt and thought to convey to his auditory, the stirring influence of his theme — the love of Liberty."

Other cadets who gave speeches on the Fourth of July at the academy included Joseph Ritner (1829), Leslie Chase (1837), William W. McCreery (1859), Peter Smith Michie (1862), William David O'Toole (1864), Arthur Sherburne Hardy (1868), Charles A.L. Totten (1872), Joseph Lavialle Donovan (1890), John McAuley Palmer (1891), William Baker Ladue (1893), Herbert Arthur White (1894), George H. Shelton (1895), Frank C. Boggs (1897), R.N. Campell (1905), Enoch Barton Garey (1907), Raphael Robert Nix (1908), Creswell Carlington (1909), Benjamin Fiery Hope (1913), Edward William Garbisch (1924), and Herbert G. Sparrow (1930).

West Point cadets also participated in other significant local celebrations. On July 4, 1850, they sponsored a ball in honor of the celebration held at **Washington's Revolutionary War Headquarters** in Newburgh, New York, and General Winfield Scott, who participated. The affair took place at the West Point Hotel and was reported as "a very brilliant and happy occasion."

A description of the West Point ceremony on July 4, 1894, is an example of what must have been typical during the 1890s. The cadets gathered in full dress uniforms, the upper classmen wearing white trousers and gloves and the plebes in gray undress uniforms. "Seats had been provided beneath the old elms where the graduation exercises are held. Upon a small boxlike platform, tastefully decorated with the Stars and Stripes, sat the Chairman, Cadet Haydon Y. Grubbs, Chaplain Allen, Cadet J.M. Hinkley, Jr., and Cadet George H. Shelton, who delivered the oration." A prayer by Chaplain Allen opened the exercises. Hinkley read the Declaration of Independence, followed by an oration by Shelton that was described as a "masterpiece." At noon, "a national salute was fired by a detachment of cadets in the artillery park." A 1908 program listed a special "Cadet Mess dinner of cream of chicken, olives, radishes, roast boneless turkey, giblet sauce, new carrots and peas, potatoes au gratin, vanilla ice cream, grape juice punch, and wine cake."

Sources: *United States Oracle*, 20 July 1802, 3–4; "Fourth of July and West Point," *National Intelligencer*, 12 July 1830, 2; *The Statesman* 5/55 (11 July 1826); *New York Herald*, 6 July 1850, 1; "General View of the Day," *New York Times*, 5 July 1876, 4; "The Fourth at West Point," *New York Times*, 5 July 1895, 3; Robert D. Moon, "Chronology of the USMA Band, 1803–1991" (West Point: Special Collections and Archives Division, U.S. Military Academy Library, 1991).

Western Reserve Boundary Marker

A northwest boundary stone of the Western Reserve near Poland, Ohio, and located on State Line Road, was dedicated on July 4, 1967, in Ottawa County, Ohio.

Sources: Meredith B. Colket, "The Story Behind the Stone," copy in Western Reserve Historical Society Library 9 pp.; Poland Township Government Web site, <www.polandtownship.org>.

Westminster Presbyterian Church, Baltimore

The opening of this church occurred on July 4, 1852, and John Chester Backus (1810–1884) delivered a "discourse" for the occasion.

Source: *A Discourse Delivered at the Opening of the Westminster Presbyterian Church, Baltimore, July 4, 1852* (Baltimore: S. Guiteau, 1852).

White House

Located in Washington, D.C., the White House serves as the residence of the U.S. presidents, and was referred to in the nineteenth century as the President's House or Executive Mansion. As a national icon, the White House generated special interest among Americans, especially during the nineteenth century. Although the first president to inhabit the mansion was John Adams in 1800, it was **Thomas Jefferson** who, on July 4, 1801, held the first Fourth of July celebration there. This event is especially significant not only as part of the history of the White House but also because it helped to establish important traditions for future Fourth of July celebrations there. Jefferson gave public receptions that allowed common citizens and dignitaries alike to assemble inside the residence and to meet the president. Other presidents continued that tradition. Exceptions occurred only when the president or members of his family were ill or if the chief executive was out of town. Some of the visitors included large groups representing associations. Occasionally brief addresses were made both by the president and the spokesperson for the groups.

Jefferson also initiated the importance of having music as a part of the celebrations there. On July 4, 1801, the first Independence Day performance there of the **United States Marine Band** took place. Among the pieces performed was appropriately the "President's March." At noon Jefferson welcomed all the heads of departments, civil and military officers, foreign officials, Cherokee chiefs, and citizens into his residence. Refreshments were served until 2 P.M., and guests enjoyed the "martial and patriotic airs" played by the band under the direction of William Farr. At 4 P.M. the group shared dinner together, likely at a local hotel. Toasts were presented each with a "discharge of artillery" from one of the frigates in the Potomac River. "Hail Columbia! Happy Land" was sung by Captain Thomas Tingey after a toast to "the day, and those who value it."

A White House tradition also included the president and first lady and friends watching the city fireworks from the White House balcony.

Sources: *National Intelligencer*, 6 July 1801, 2; Mrs. Samuel Harrison Smith (Margaret Bayard), *The First Forty Years of Washington Society*, ed. Gaillard Hunt (New York: Scribner's, 1906), 30.

Whitehouse, Ohio, Park Statue

Located in Whitehouse, Ohio, this statue was dedicated on July 4, 1900, and honors those who fought in the Civil War. The statue was renovated in 1979. Whitehouse, named after Edward Whitehouse, who donated the land for the Village Green, is located in Lucas County and has a population of slightly over 2500 persons.

Source: "Village History," in Whitehouse Historical Society Web site, 11 September 2002, <http://www.historicalsociety.whitehouse.oh.us>.

Whitfield, James Monroe (1822–1871)

Abolitionist and African-American poet, born in Exeter, New Hampshire, who wrote "Ode for the Fourth of July" for his collection *America and Other Poems* (Boston, 1853). It was this collection that established Whitfield's career as an abolitionist and prominent supporter of the emigration of blacks. Whitfield wrote letters to the *Frederick Douglass Paper* and served as a delegate to Martin Delany's National Emigration Convention, held in Cleveland in 1854. Another book of poetry is titled *Poems* (1846). Whitfield moved to California in 1862 and later spend time in Oregon and Idaho, before finally settling in San Francisco. In 1867 Whitfield published a history of America and slavery titled *A Poem* and dedicated the work to Philip A. Bell, editor of the *Elevator*, a local publication.

Source: Johnnella E. Butler, "James Monroe Whitfield," *American National Biography*, 23: 265–66.

Whittier, John Greenleaf (1807–1892)

Celebrated poet and abolitionist who wrote poetry for the 1876, 1883 and 1888 Independence Day celebrations. His six-stanza "Centennial Hymn" was written specifically for the opening of the **Centennial Exposition** in Philadelphia, May 10, 1876, and was sung by a thousand voices of the Centennial Choral Society. The music was composed by John Knowles Paine, a professor of music at Harvard, and was described by a newspaper reporter as a "sweet melody accompanied by simple harmonies, which rolled forth upon the air like the gently moving billows of an old Ocean in her most peaceful mood."

The work was well received, and a number of other performances of the work occurred elsewhere on July 4, 1876. For example, at the celebration held in the Congregational Church in Washington, D.C., the piece was "finely rendered by the choir," In Cumberland, Maryland, it was sung by a choir of fifty under the direction of Joseph P. Wiesel at the town's grandstand, and at Denver, Colorado, at the park, it was sung by the Handel and Haydn Societies.

"Our Country" was read at Woodstock, Connecticut, on July 4, 1883, and printed in the *New York Times* on the following day. This multi-stanza poem was a social statement that freedom should be extended to African-Americans and Native Americans deserve to have their grievances addressed. Privileges of education should be extended to all children.

> We give thy natal day to hope,
> O Country of our love and prayer!
> Thy way is down no fatal slope,
> But up to freer sun and air.
> Tried as by furnace-fires, and yet
> By God's grace only stronger made,
> In future tasks before thee set
> Thou shalt not lack the old-time aid.

On July 4, 1888, Whittier's poem "One of the Signers," written in memory of Gov. **Josiah Bartlett** of Amesbury, Massachusetts, was read "simultaneously on the unveiling of his statue" in Amesbury and at Roseland Park in **Woodstock, Connecticut**.

> (first stanza)
> O storied vale of Merrimac!
> Rejoice through all thy shade and shine,
> And, from his century's sleep, call back
> A brave and honored son of thine!

Sources: *Our National Centennial Jubilee: Orations, Addresses and Poems Delivered on the Fourth of July, 1876*, ed. Frederick Saunders (New York: E.B. Treat, 1877); "Uncle Sam's Birthday," *Cumberland Alleganian Times*, 6 July 1876, 1, 4; "The Fourth," *Daily Rocky Mountain News*, 6 July 1876, 1, 4; "Celebration at the Congregational Church," *Washington Evening Star*, 5 July 1876, 4; *New York Times*, 5 July 1883, 4–5; *New York Times*, 5 July 1888, 4; Edith Louise Markham, "Poetry Written for the Opening Exercises and the Fourth of July Celebration at the 1876 Centennial Exhibition in Philadelphia" (M.A. thesis, University of North Carolina at Chapel Hill, 1950); *The Poetical Works of John Greenleaf Whittier*, 4 vols. (New York: AMS Press, 1969), 367–71.

Wilcox, Ella Wheeler (1850–1919)

Prolific poet who was presented with a badge by the Army of Tennessee Society at its meeting held in Madison, Wisconsin, on July 4, 1872. Her poem "After the battles are over" was written and read for the occasion. It received an ovation, and Union General Philip H. Sheridan, who was in the audience, exclaimed, "If this goes to that girl's heart, it will do her good; if it goes to her head it will spoil her." Wilcox, born in Johnstown Center, Wisconsin, was a frequent contributor to numerous magazines and newspapers, including the *New York Mercury, Leslie's Weekly*, and *Waverly Magazine*. Her best-known collection of poems was *Poems of Passion* (1883), which was first rejected by a publisher in Chicago who believed it to be immoral.

Sources: *New York Times*, 6 July 1872, 1; Ella Wheeler Wilcox Society Web site <http://www.ellawheelerwilcox.org/>.

Wilkes, Charles (1798–1877)

Naval officer and explorer who gave the first Fourth of July celebration west of the Missouri River in 1841 at a site near Sequalitchew Lake (now Pierce County), Washington. Wilkes, born in New York City, attended private schools, where he studied the sciences. In 1818 he joined the navy as a midshipman and in 1826 was promoted to lieutenant. His interest in exploration led to his appointment as commander of a Pacific expedition in 1838 that took him to Tuamotus, Tahiti, Samoa, Australia, Fiji, and Hawaii. By April 1841, Wilkes had arrived off the Oregon coast and with his men spent the following 5 months exploring and charting the northwest area. On July 4, 1841, he provided a July Fourth holiday for his men. He reported,

> Wishing to give the crew a holiday on the anniversary of the declaration of our independence, and to allow them to have a full day's folic and pleasure, they were allowed to barbecue an ox, which the company's agent had obligingly sold me. They were permitted to make their own arrangements for the celebrations, which they conducted in the following manner.
>
> All was bustle and activity on the morning of the 5th, as the 4th fell upon Sunday. Before 9 o'clock all the men were mustered in clean white frocks and trousers, and all, including the marines and musicians, were landed shortly after, to march to the scene of festivity, about a mile distant. The procession was formed at the observatory, whence we all marched off, with flags flying and music playing, Vendovi and the master-at-arms bringing up the rear. Vendovi was dressed out after the Fiji fashion. Two brass howitzers were also carried on the prairie to fire the usual salutes.

On July 5, 1906, a commemorative celebration of that first Fourth of July celebration took place near the original site. A monument was unveiled to permanently mark the site. Six societies, including the Pierce County

Pioneer Association, sponsored the event. A number of speeches were given, including "The Revolutionary Idea" by C.H. Hanford, "Dr. J.P. Richmond's Participation in the Original Celebration," by A. Atwood, "Historical Places and Occasions," by Washington governor Albert Edward Mead, who said, "No less valiant, no less rugged, no less far-seeing than the Puritan fathers were the pioneers of the Pacific Northwest. The time will come when such historic spots as that on which we stand will be revered and honored as Plymouth Rock today." Perhaps the most noteworthy presentations were those by Capt. Thomas Mountain, the only survivor of the Wilkes expedition, and Chief Slugamus Koquilton, the only known survivor of Wilkes' celebration. Chief Koquilton said,

> We were glad to see the white people. Long before that time the Indians did not know about anything of that kind. The country did not belong to any nation, just belonged to the Lord; it was for all the people. The celebration here made the Indians feel good; all felt good towards the white people. It makes me feel good to see so many people come here today, and to see you all so happy.

The monument, covered with an American flag, was unveiled, and the group sang the "Star-Spangled Banner," led by Dudley Eshelman, of Tacoma, Washington.

Sources: *United States Exploring Expedition* (Philadelphia: C. Sherman, 1840); *Commemorative Celebration at Sequalitchew Lake* (Tacoma, Wash.: Vaughan and Morrill, 1906); Allan Carpenter, *The Encyclopedia of the Far West* (New York: Facts on File, 1991), 135; Roberta A. Sprague, "Charles Wilkes," *American National Biography*, 23: 394–96.

Williamsburg, Virginia

The town shares a tradition of Independence Day celebrations beginning with the first public reading of the Declaration of Independence on July 25, 1776. On July 4, 1827, a commemoration of the day occurred at a Williamsburg church with W.H. Wilmer, president of the College of William and Mary, offering the prayer, followed by a dinner at the "former residence of Judge Prentis." Attending the affair was John Tyler, member elect to the U.S. Senate.

In recent times, reenactments, parades,

public readings of the Declaration of Independence, musket and artillery salutes, and other events have highlighted the historic life in Colonial Williamsburg. In 1980, there was a fife and drum corps parade, and costumed soldiers fired muskets and cannons. In 2003 as the country's largest live interactive history museum, reenactors played the roles of Patrick Henry, Thomas Jefferson, John and Abigail Adams, Marquis de Lafayette, and Martha Washington. The event included aerial fireworks, eighteenth century children's games, and music representing the Revolutionary War era. During the 1950s, Williamsburg residents celebrated a second Fourth of July on July 25 to commemorate the first public reading.

Sources: *Virginia Gazette*, 26 July 1776; *Richmond Enquirer*, 24 July 1827, 1; *New York Times*, 4 July 1871, 2; "Second 'July 4,'" *Washington Post*, 25 July 1951, B2; Suzanne Donner, "Notes Celebrating the Fourth of July," *New York Times*, 22 June 1980, section 10, 3.

Wilson, Woodrow (1856–1924)

Twenty-eighth president of the U.S. (1913–21) and popular speaker on the Fourth of July. Wilson, a democrat, graduated from Princeton in 1879 and Johns Hopkins University in 1886. In 1910, he was elected governor of New Jersey, and in 1913 inaugurated president. Wilson was known for his progressive reform, his leadership of the country during World War I, and his efforts to gain U.S. support for the League of Nations. After 1919, he suffered a series of heart attacks that left him greatly incapacitated.

Wilson was an ardent participator in Fourth of July events. As president of Princeton University he attended the Jamestown Exposition in Norfolk, Virginia, on July 4, 1907, and presented a speech on the author and signers of the Declaration of Independence, noting that whereas Jefferson and his colleagues asserted that all men have the right to liberty, "each generation must form its own conception of what liberty is." In 1911, Wilson gave an Independence Day address at Ocean Grove, New Jersey, on the occasion of the inauguration of the new amusement park attractions there.

Wilson's first Independence Day event as

president occurred in 1913 in Gettysburg, Pennsylvania, where he gave an address to 10,000 veterans, some of whom "spoke unfavorably of it." Although a good speech, they said Wilson failed to catch the sentiment of the day. After only forty-six minutes there, he left for Harrisburg, Pennsylvania.

On July 4, 1914, Wilson was at Independence Hall in Philadelphia and gave a speech on the meaning of the Declaration of Independence, mentioning the famous line, "Our country, right or wrong." On Independence Day in 1916 he presented a speech at the dedication of the **American Federation of Labor building** in Washington, D.C. He spoke about labor issues and cautioned his listeners that there was more to working than merely wages. "He is working for some persons whom he loves," he said, "for some community that he wishes to assist, for some nation that he is ready to serve and defend." The president's obligation, Wilson noted, is to recognize the labor movement and the idea that labor contests should be settled through negotiation, "candid and dispassionate conference with regard to the points at issue."

In 1918, Wilson gave a speech at an "international Fourth of July celebration" held at Mount Vernon. Wilson spoke about the need to bring all nations together to declare independence and to send that message to Germany. A reporter noted "the men who ruled the German nation had heard their doom in words which they could not misunderstand."

On Independence Day in 1919 Wilson was on board the *George Washington* returning from a trip to Europe. He addressed the passengers saying that America had met its vision for safeguarding freedom of the nation and the world. He acknowledged the soldiers who fought in World War I and commented on the plurality of immigrants that make up the nation.

A number of Independence Day honors were bestowed on Wilson. On July 4, 1918, the city of Florence, Italy, conferred the honor of "the freedom of the city on President Wilson" for his efforts in the war. On July 4, 1924, a tablet erected to the memory of President Wilson was unveiled on Quay Wilson in Geneva. On July 4, 1931, in Poznah, Poland, he was honored by a presentation of a memorial statue of him, designed by Gutzon Borglum and given by renown pianist Ignace Paderewski to the people of Poland.

Sources: "The Author and Signers of the Declaration of Independence," *North American Review* 186 (September 1907); "Ocean Grove: Fast Losing Its Identity As Merely a Tenting Place," *New York Times*, 2 July 1911, X2; "Gettysburg Cold to Wilson's Speech," *New York Times*, 5 July 1913, 1; *New York Times*, 5 July 1914, 1, 3; *New York Times*, 5 July 1918, 1, 9 and 11, and 5 July 1924, 6, and 5 July 1931, 1; *The Papers of Woodrow Wilson*, ed. Arthur S. Link (Princeton, N.J.: Princeton University Press, 1981), 37:353–58.

Winthrop, Beckman (1874–1940)

Inaugurated governor of Puerto Rico (1904–07) on July 4, 1902. His platform promised "the extension of the school system, the building of roads, and the impartial execution of all laws." Winthrop was born in Orange, New Jersey, graduated from Harvard in 1897, and was appointed judge of the Court of First Instance in the Philippines in 1903.

Sources: "Porto Rico's New Governor," *New York Times*, 5 July 1904, 6; "Beckman Winthrop," *National Cyclopaedia of American Biography*, 35:247–48.

Winthrop, Robert Charles (1809–1894)

A celebrated orator who was keenly interested in the Fourth of July and as Speaker of the House of Representatives gave an address on July 4, 1848, on the occasion of the laying of the cornerstone for the **Washington Monument** in Washington, D.C. Born in Boston, Winthrop, an attorney, served in Congress as a representative and senator from Massachusetts, from 1840 to 1850. He was a strong Unionist who agreed in principal to opposing the spread of slavery. He often spoke at historical events, including the centennials of the Boston Tea Party (1773) in 1873 and the battle of Yorktown (1781) in 1881. A contemporary account of his 1848 Independence Day oration in *The Merchants' Magazine* describes it as

> happy in conception, scholarly and felicitous in style, every page glows with a chastened eloquence, and a noble and generous patriotism that must have made a deep impression upon the minds and sympathies of all who listened

to its delivery. It is free from all party narrow-
ness of view, and furnishes a truthful and
beautiful portrait of the saviour of his country—the immortal Washington. It is as nearly
faultless as any human performance can well
be.

The editor of *Niles' National Register* said,
"He spoke of the grandeur of the occasion,
and of the appropriateness of the day, the illustrious dead, the august assembly, and the
fitness of the present crisis for such an event,
when the millions of Europe's oppressed sons
are rising to assert the rights of man. His closing remarks were a fervid allusion to the monument which was about to rise."

In 1858 Winthrop expressed his concern
about Independence Day falling on a Sunday
and the holiday typically celebrated on the following day. He proposed in a letter published
in the *New York Times* that when July 4 fell on
a Sunday, the celebration should take place on
July 3 to coincide with the date George Washington assumed command of the Continental
Army (3 July 1775) so as to "combine the commemoration of those two great events."

On July 4, 1876, at Boston's Music Hall,
Winthrop gave an oration titled "The Centennial of Independence."

Sources: *Merchants' Magazine and Commercial
Review* 19/4 (October 1848): 464; *National Intelli-
gencer*, 6 July 2 and 4, and 8 July 1848, 3; *New York
Times*, 9 July 1858, 4; *Niles' National Register* 74, 12
July 1848, 32; "The Centennial Fourth," *Boston Eve-
ning Transcript*, 5 July 1876, 1–3.

Women and the Fourth of July

The Fourth of July served as a catalyst
for social and political change for women. In
antebellum America, women were generally
excluded from direct participation in Independence Day ceremonies. Lacking a right for
exercising a voice in political affairs, females
were typically confined to domestic activities.
In the eighteenth century, the ceremonies and
dinners held on the Fourth were exclusively
men's affairs. Following the Revolutionary
War, women struggled to bring about greater
freedom and equality across an extensive social sphere and to have a greater voice in political life. One of the early conversations regarding women's roles in the new nation

occurred between John and Abigail Adams,
just prior to the issuance of the Declaration of
Independence. She had asked her husband in
a letter she wrote on 31 March 1776 not to
forget the importance of women when "independency" is declared. "If particular care and
attention is not paid to the Laidies we are determined to foment a Rebellion and will not
hold ourselves bound by any Laws in which
we have no voice, or representation." Within
twenty years, the status of women increasingly
became a topic of conversation. The *New-
Hampshire Spy* noted in 1789 that regarding
the Fourth, "the ladies have no share in the joy
of the day; no, poor souls, they must tarry at
home, to watch their fires and to stand ready
with their buckets and bags, for fear of accident." Elias Boudinot stated in an oration he
gave on July 4, 1793, in Elizabeth, New Jersey, that "the Rights of Women are no longer
strange sounds to an American ear. They are
now heard as familiar terms in every part of
the United States." The advent of republicanism that accompanied Thomas Jefferson's election to the presidency in 1800 helped spark
opportunities for women to have some participation in Fourth ceremonies, notably in trade
union parades.

Irregardless of social conventions at that
time, some groups of women chose to gather
independently on the Fourth of July. One of
the earliest recorded events occurred on July 4,
1800, in New York City, when a group of females met "to celebrate, in [their] own way,
the glorious and ever memorable day" and to
drink toasts to their "fathers, husbands, and
brothers." Another similar event occurred on
July 4, 1819, at Mossy Spring, Kentucky, when
some women prepared their own dinner,
"seated themselves on the grass" and heard an
oration by a "Mrs. Mead." The ladies then
offered thirteen "resolutions," not toasts, for
they thought the latter would "be deemed un-
feminine."

Although women received training in
elocution in their formative years, public
speechmaking was generally frowned upon.
There were exceptions, however. On July 4,
1822, for example, an unnamed female was
designated "orator of the day" in Windham,

Vermont. Following her speech, the audience also heard the Declaration of Independence read by "a number of young ladies, 'representing the confederated States of the Union.'"

Women were applauded occasionally for public speaking when their speeches preceded the presentation of handmade flags to military units. Their addresses were carefully prepared and some were printed in newspapers. On July 4, 1801, for example, in Lancaster, Pennsylvania, "the ladies of Lancaster presented to the Volunteer republican Blues an elegant standard, exhibiting the American Eagle grasping a thunderbolt, from which issued streams of lightning darting on the symbols of slavery." The presentation was accompanied by a patriotic address. Another similar address on a presentation of a flag occurred on July 4, 1826, in Quincy, Massachusetts, by Caroline Whitney. Such addresses were eloquently framed and instructive. When **Eletia Hubball**, accompanied by six of her female friends, presented a flag to the Company of Light Infantry, commanded by Capt. Nicholas Blasdell, at Alexandria, Virginia, on July 4, 1821, she said,

> Our motives in addressing you on this occasion are not to excite in you a sense of noble daring, or a just appreciation of your rights as freemen. The songs of freemen want no incentives to action: Liberty and honor are inate principles, fostered by paternal care. They have nobly will'd and bravely dared. The historic page records the noble achievements, and gallant actions in their country's cause; on the ocean and on the land their prowess stands pre-eminent; the haughty foe has struck his proud flag to our brave and hardy tars, and bent his proud crest to the strong arm of your brothers in arms. From pole to pole, the goddess of liberty has proclaimed the merited applause of her sons.

It was during the temperance, abolition and education movements that women first began to organize and to hold public meetings freely. Under the guise of temperance issues, especially the importance of teaching children abstinence, women's groups held separate celebrations on the Fourth. For example, on July 4, 1842, a Ladies' Total Abstinence Tea Party was held at the Apollo Hall in Washington, D.C., and the occasion included speech making and performances of vocal and instrumental music.

The single most important event that paved the way for women's freedom and equity was the First Women's Rights Convention, held at **Seneca Falls**, New York, in July 1848, when Elizabeth Cady Stanton presented her Declaration of Sentiments of equal rights for women, modeled on the Declaration of Independence. Stanton's Declaration was one of the seminal documents of the suffrage movement that ultimately led to the adoption of the 19th amendment to the Constitution, which was ratified in August 1920. Following the Civil War there were a number of events that also helped the movement to gain momentum. On July 4, 1867, the Friends of Universal Suffrage met in South Salem, Massachusetts, and Susan B. Anthony publicly read the Declaration of Sentiments. On July 4, 1871, the Massachusetts Woman's Suffrage Association met at Framingham Grove, and Lucy Stone and others gave speeches.

Another important occasion took place on the nation's centennial, July 4, 1876, when the Declaration of Sentiments was presented once again by members of the National Women Suffrage Association which met at "Dr. Furness' church, corner of Broad and Locust Street." Susan B. Anthony, Mrs. Matilda Joslyn Gage, Elizabeth Cady Stanton, and other leaders of the movement were there. Many gave speeches. Early that day Anthony and Gage were at the public ceremony at Independence Square. After Richard Henry Lee had finished reading the Declaration of Independence, the two women pushed their way through the crowds and presented an "engrossed copy"—about three feet in length and "tied with ribbons of various colors"—of the declaration to Michigan senator Thomas W. Ferry, "who received it with a courteous bow," although he was quite surprised. Afterward the two women went to the steps of Independence Hall where Anthony read from the text "to an assembled multitude."

On July 4, 1895, the first "woman's day celebration" took place at Chautauqua, New York, when females dressed in yellow and heard an oration on "the new woman" by woman's rights advocate the Rev. Charles C. Albertson of Jamestown, New York. On July 4, 1913, a group of suffragettes assembled at Long Beach, New York, for speechmaking to the bathers. They brought with them a "1776 campaign wagon." One of the speeches was written on cards displayed on a "big yellow tripod" positioned close to the water while Mrs. Wilmer Kearns presented her "voiceless speech" while standing in the ocean. She wore a bathing suit, with "'Votes for Women' on a yellow cap on her head, and wearing a yellow sash." The campaign wagon "carried a yellow umbrella and was decorated with banners, and the suffragettes themselves were equipped with 'Votes for Women' parasols or yellow bags for the suffrage papers. Miss Irene Davidson was in a Minute Man's costume." On July 4, 1917, suffragettes demonstrated in front of the White House. Great strides had been made by the time the Nineteenth Amendment, which gave women the right to vote, became law in August 1920.

Sources: "Fourth of July," *New-Hampshire Spy*, 13 June 1789, 53; *American Citizen and General Advertiser*, 10 July 1800; *National Intelligencer*, 17 July 1801, 3; *Commentator* (Frankfort, Kentucky), 30 July 1819, 1–2; *Alexandria Gazette*, 7 July 1821, 2; *National Intelligencer*, 23 July 1822, 3; *Columbian Sentinel*, 22 July 1826, 1; "City News," *National Intelligencer*, 6 July 1842, 3; *Westfield Newsletter*, 7 July, 1847, as reported in Anne Marie Hickey, "The Celebration of the Fourth of July in Westfield, 1826–1853," *Historical Journal of Massachusetts* 9/2 (1981): 42; *New York Times*, 5 July 1867 and 5 July 1871, 8 and 4, respectively; "Woman's Day at Chautauqua," *New York Times*, 5 July 1895, 3; "Suffrage Talk Amid Waves," *New York Times*, 5 July 1913, 9; "Events of the War 13 Years Ago Today: July 4, 1917," *Washington Post*, 4 July 1930, 5; *History of Woman Suffrage*, ed. Elizabeth Cady Stanton, Susan B. Anthony and Matilda Joslyn Gage (New York: Arno, 1969), 3:40–43; Francis D. Cogliano, *Revolutionary America, 1763–1815* (New York: Routledge, 2000).

Women's Municipal League of New York City

Held a gala but unusual affair in which Native American actors who were performing in Longfellow's "Hiawatha" were at the recreation pier located on East Twenty-Fourth Street receiving "cigarettes of peace." They were presented to the Indians, "as the oldest residents of the country," by Stephen Merritt,

"the oldest resident of the Chelsea district." Miss Amelia Ives, representing the league, was in charge of the affair. "The city furnished patriotic decorations and the front of the building was decorated with lights at night, when there was an orchestra to provide dance music. The Boy Scouts were in attendance to see that things went smoothly."

Source: "Hiawatha at Pier Dance," *New York Times*, 5 July 1913, 9.

Women's Peace Union of the Western Hemisphere

On July 4, 1925, this organization presented a "Declaration of Independence from War" at Battery Park, in New York City:

> We therefore declare that mankind is, and of right ought to be, free and independent of and absolved from all allegiance to war; that the women of this country in particular, now that they are possessed of political power, wish, and indeed are bound to use, that power for the annihilation of war; that all connection between our own government and war should be totally dissolved, by making war illegal and impossible; and that we hereby contract an eternal allegiance with peace and with all those everywhere who have pledged themselves to the repudiation of war, to last as long as this world shall endure. And for the support of this declaration, with a firm reliance on the protection of Divine Providence, we mutually pledge to each other our lives, our fortunes and our sacred honor.

The Women's Peace Union was established in 1921 when American and Canadian women met at Niagara Falls, New York. Records of the association are held at Swarthmore College.

Source: "Pacifists in Battery Park," *New York Times*, 5 July 1925, 18.

Woodstock, Connecticut

One of the most important towns for Fourth of July celebrations in New England after the Civil War due to the varied content of the ceremonies and their distinguished participants. Annually, Woodstock hosted many presidents, popular politicians, dignitaries, writers and poets. Roseland Park, a popular lakeside resort in Woodstock, was officially opened on July 4, 1877, and given to the town by Henry C. Bowen, editor of the *New York*

Independent. Many of the events were held there.

For the 1877 Fourth of July opening of Roseland Park, thousands of persons assembled there for the gala celebration that included speeches by ex-governor Daniel H. Chamberlain of South Carolina, who spoke about the "Presidential Southern policy," Senator James G. Blaine (Maine), who addressed the audience on the Mexican policy of the government, Cyrus Northrop of Yale College, who spoke on the Revolution of 1776 and its results, and Theodore L. Cuyler of Brooklyn, who addressed the crowd on temperance. There were also poetry readings, one by Oliver Wendell Holmes, who read his poem "The Ship of State, Above Her Skies Are Blue," and a poem by Mrs. Mary Clemmer, read by Charles F. Richardson. "The principal sentiment of the poem was a tribute to the founder of Roseland Park." It was this combination of political speeches mixed with literary recitations which set the tradition for future celebrations there. Activities at Roseland typically included games in the afternoon following the ceremonies and fireworks in the evening.

The park consisted of 60 acres bordering on a lake. Dining tables and refreshment stands were located in various parts of the park. "A boat and bathing house on the lake is one of the prominent structures of the park." For the dedication ceremony a stand had been erected "beneath the shade of a group of fine trees."

On July 4, 1879, the celebration took place at Bowen's Roseland Cottage House. No less than seven dignitaries spoke. Topics speakers chose included finances, "rural life," New England, "political progress," and higher education. One of the notable presentations was that by Senator Orville H. Platt of Connecticut, who spoke about the "heresy of state sovereignty and to the growth of the country and good government since 1861." Platt discussed the weakening of state power and that at the federal level the "disbandment of the Army" followed the Civil war.

On the Fourth in 1885, Gov. Henry B. Harrison spoke, and James McCosh, president of Princeton College, gave a "[l]ong address on 'What an American University Should Be.'" A "Nation's Birthday Hymn" by the Rev. J.E. Rankin was read, as well as a poem entitled "Daybreak" by Maurice Thompson. "Joaquin Miller's verses describing Horace Greeley's ride with Hank Monk were read." On July 4, 1889, President Harrison spoke in Woodstock.

On July 4, 1890, the Rev. William Hayes Ward delivered "a most graphic poem dealing with the Johnstown flood" titled "The South Fork Fishing Club." Senator Joseph R. Hawley presented an address titled "The Day We Celebrate," designed to set the public straight regarding the pension question.

Independence Day 1892 was a significant event at Woodstock. Thomas J. Morgan, Indian commissioner, presented an address that encouraged conferring citizenship upon Native Americans.

On July 4, 1894, the celebration at Roseland Park was a gallant affair that included a welcome speech by Congressman Charles A. Russell, an address by St. Clair McKelway, editor of *The Brooklyn Eagle*, Congressman Walker of Massachusetts, the Rev. M. Woolsey Stryker, president of Hamilton College, and **Galusha A. Grow**, ex–Speaker of the House. McKelway's speech was considered "the most important address delivered" and focused on how money interests affect the administration of law. "The worst evil this Nation has ever ended was the sale of human beings. The worst evil this Nation has not yet ended is the sale of law. The movement against this evil must become affected by a moral interest." The event also included a song by Harriet Prescott Spofford, sung to the tune of "Yankee Doodle," and poems by S.W. Foss of Somerville, Massachusetts, and Richard Benton of Hartford, Connecticut.

Sources: *Baltimore Bee*, 5 July 1877, 1; *New York Times*, 5 July 1877, 1; *Baltimore Morning Herald*, 5 July 1879, 1; "The Woodstock Holiday," *New York Times*, 5 July 1879, 3; "By the Nation," *Philadelphia Inquirer*, 6 July 1885, 2; "The Day at Woodstock," 5 July 1890, 2, and 8 and 5 July 1894, 8; "Mr. Bowen's Mild Celebration," *New York Times*, 5 July 1892, 2.

Woodward's Gardens, San Francisco

The site for the first reported daytime fireworks in the United States on July 5, 1880.

A local newspaper reported that the idea for having fireworks during daylight hours originated in Japan and was brought over by a "government official." The event, which took place on the amphitheater grounds, drew a crowd of 10,000 spectators who sang the "Star-Spangled Banner" at the moment the "first bomb" was lit and exploded 200 feet above their heads. The pyrotechnical display featured "a perfectly formed turtle gyrating in the air causing an immense deal of amusement by its natural movements and brilliant colors." With the start of the **Safe and Sane** movement in the early twentieth century, daylight fireworks were organized in a number of cities.

Source: "Flying Figures," *San Francisco Chronicle*, 6 July 1880, 5.

Worcester, Massachusetts

City where a citizens' protest occurred on July 4, 1855, and a spectacular fire occurred on July 4, 1901, at the Walker Ice Company. Citizens demonstrated against city officials who refused to fund the town's Fourth of July celebration in 1855. The fire in 1901 attracted 20,000 spectators and was believed to have been caused by fireworks set off by Walker workers.

Sources: *New York Times*, 7 July 1855, 3; *Worcester Telegram*, 4 July 1901, reported in Roy Rosenzweig, *Eight Hours for What We Will: Workers and Leisure in an Industrial City, 1870–1920* (Cambridge: Cambridge University Press, 1983), 154–55.

World Trade Center Attack

The most devastating single act of war against mainland United States occurred on September 11, 2001, when Arab terrorists hijacked four commercial airliners and crashed three of them into buildings in New York City and Washington. Two planes were flown into the World Trade Center towers, a third plane crashed into the Pentagon in Arlington, Virginia, and a fourth crashed into a rural area in western Pennsylvania, the latter a result of a heroic attempt by passengers to subdue the hijackers. These events shocked the nation and led to intense security measures initiated by the federal government and the war on terrorism launched by President George W. Bush.

The following Independence Day, July 4, 2002, was a day of remembrance and of great magnitude as the nation expressed tributes and engaged in memorial services to all those who lost their lives. Amidst heightened security across most major cities in the country and not withstanding renewed anxiety over possible terrorist threats, Americans celebrated with a greater sense of unity, spirit and patriotism. President Bush, speaking in Ripley, West Virginia, at Courthouse Square, said Americans should accept the threat of terrorism but not let it interfere with "celebrating our freedom." They need to "go about their business knowing full well that our government is doing everything we can to protect them," he said. Air patrols by fighter jets took place in the skies over some major cities. Extra police were on duty in Washington, D.C., and electronic surveillance and sensors for radioactivity monitored key events. Memorial Bridge was closed and designated access points to the Mall were set up. In New York, armed counter-terrorist teams were on guard while in Dallas, "a single entry checkpoint to the downtown site of its fireworks celebration" was set up. About 150,000 persons were scanned with metal-detection wands. The Federal Aviation Administration banned flights over the Statue of Liberty, Mount Rushmore and the Gateway Arch in St. Louis. In Boston, those attending the concert at the Hatch Shell were videotaped, and some 10,000 persons passed through screening checkpoints. In Pennsylvania, a largest ever truck-inspection program was in place checking for suspicious cargo.

Meanwhile, from San Diego to Boston, Americans were eager to demonstrate their patriotism and fly the Star Spangled Banner. Celebrations in major cities went off with a sense of renewed verve and hope. In Washington, headliners Aretha Franklin, Chuck Berry, and Lee Ann Womack, performed with the National Symphony Orchestra on the West Lawn of the Capitol. Shanksville, Pennsylvania, held its first Fourth of July parade ever to honor the crash victims of United Airlines Flight 93. Across America signs "Remembering the Heroes of 9–11" were placed on fire trucks, and editorials on September 11 were eagerly published in newspapers as a way of demonstrating resilience and kindness. In New York a float that featured a reenactment of firefighters raising the American flag in the World Trade Center rubble brought tears to participants and spectators alike while an Air Force F-117A Nighthawk stealth fighter participated in a "patriotic flyover." In Northville, Michigan, a "Star-Spangled Banner" sing-along took place along a two-mile section of Main Street. On July 6, 2002, a "Star Spangled Symphony Spectacular" took place in Clarksburg, Maryland, on the Lockheed Martin Grounds to honor the eleven Montgomery County citizens who were lost in the September 11 tragedy. In Juneau, Alaska, the Filipino community there entered a float in the city parade that was "designed to resemble images of the rubble of the World Trade Center." Because of the collapse of the World Trade Center, Lee Greenwood's 1984 hit "God Bless the U.S.A." was as popular as Irving Berlin's "God Bless America." At Monticello, seventy immigrants were sworn in as American citizens. Meanwhile, although some celebrations were cancelled in Kuwait and Vienna, most events abroad went forward albeit with caution.

In Philadelphia that day Secretary of State Colin Powell was awarded the 2002 Philadelphia Liberty Medal "for his leadership in the war on terrorism, his efforts in the Middle East and his concern for human rights." At the ceremony Powell said, "The terrorists thought they could keep us from celebrating the Fourth of July. They were wrong. We are here, and we will remain." On July 4, 2004, a cornerstone for a new **Freedom Tower** was laid to honor those who lost their lives.

Sources: *Baltimore Sun*, 5 July 2002, 1; Mary Claire Dale, "2002 Philadelphia Liberty Medal Goes to Colin Powell," *Associated Press State and Local Wire*, 5 July 2002; Judy Keen, "USA Must Accept Terrorism Threat, Bush Says," *USA Today*, 5 July 2002, 2A; Rochelle Sharpe, "Security to Be Intense for Holiday," *USA Today*, 3 July 2002, 3A; "Firefighters' Trade Center Flag Mock-up Draws Applause, Tears," *Associated Press State and Local Wire*, 5 July 2002; J.R. Moehringer, "Celebrating Freedom," *Los Angeles Times*, 5 July 2002, A1.

World War II *see* Pearl Harbor, attack by Japanese

World's Columbian Exposition of 1893

Held in Chicago, this international exhibition celebrated the 400th anniversary of the discovery of America by Christopher Columbus. Also referred to as the Chicago World's Fair, legislation to authorize the exposition was introduced in Congress in 1890 and signed into law that year by President Benjamin Harrison. The exposition was international in scope and formally opened on May 1, 1893, and closed on October 30 of that year. The fair was located in Jackson Park and drew enormous crowds. The Fourth of July was one of the best attended days of the fair, and crowds numbering over 100,000 were pleased with the varied opportunities for fun, such as musical presentations by several bands, flag waving, fireworks, electric fountains, and the interesting exhibitions of international culture, as well as domestic agriculture and machinery. The Ferris Wheel, commonly enjoyed on the Fourth today at most theme parks, was invented by George Ferris for the fair and had its Independence Day premiere there. An original flag that sailed on board the ship that John Paul Jones "sailed with the authority of Congress" was seen waving from a carriage in the parade that entered the gates of the fair grounds. Other carriages carried Mayor Monroe Heath, various city officials, and members of the Liberty Bell Committee. That day four choirs numbering 500 each were stationed at various places and led onlookers in the singing of a medley of patriotic tunes. In the evening fireworks were "set off from floats anchored in Lake Michigan" and included "rockets, bombs, floating stars, and various set pieces."

Sources: "For the Fourth," *Los Angeles Times*, 29 June, 1893, 2; "Closed with the Fireworks" and "Patriotism in the Very Air," *New York Times*, 5 July 1893, 5.

Worthington, Ellis

Wrote "Ode for the Temperance Celebration" in Dedham, Massachusetts, on July 4, 1842. The piece was sung to the tune "America." First line: "Hail! Day of Glory, Hail!"

Source: Broadside, "Ode for the Temperance Celebration..." (Dedham, Mass.: 1842).

Wyoming Valley Massacre, Pennsylvania

On July 3, 1778, Sir John Butler and a group of Loyalists and Indians swept through Wyoming Valley. Over 350 settlers were killed. About 40 survivors were massacred after having surrendered. Occasionally the event has been remembered on Independence Day. On July 4, 1876, in Parkersburg, West Virginia, according to a newspaper report, a wagon in a parade there "drawn by sixteen oxen carried a log cabin, in which the family was being tomahawked by Indians, representing the massacre of Wyoming Valley."

At the centennial celebration of the event on July 3, 1878, President **Rutherford Birchard Hayes** was there and addressed a crowd of 60,000. "The procession of military and civil societies was more than four miles long and passed in review before President Hayes and Governor [John F.] Hartranft." Secretary of the Treasury John Sherman and U.S. Attorney General Charles Devens, as well as Gov. John Hartranft, also made speeches.

Sources: "Our Editorial Correspondence," *Wheeling Daily Register*, 10 July 1876, 2; "Washington News and Gossip," *Evening Star*, 5 July 1878, 1.

Yankee Chronology; or, Huzza for the Constitution!

Written by William Dunlap (1766–1839) and performed on July 4, 1812. The work consists of "A musical interlude, in one act, to which are added, the patriotic songs of The Freedom of the Seas, Yankee Tars," and an interlude on the frigate *Constitution*.

Source: *Yankee Chronology; or, Huzza for the Constitution!* (New York: W. Dunlap, 1812).

Yellowstone region

The first recorded Fourth of July celebration in the Yellowstone region was held a few miles north of Fort Yellowstone at Livingston, Montana, in 1883, shortly after the Northern Pacific Railroad had laid tracks in the area. The first Independence Day celebration in Yellowstone National Park occurred in 1887, a year after the U.S. Army's arrival there to take charge of it for thirty years until the National Park Service was established. The event included the raising of the flag at Camp Sheridan (later Fort Yellowstone) and a speech by E.C. Waters, who later operated the Yellowstone Lake Boat Company. "We ... gather today to pay our kindly respects to the dear old flag and ... may it ever be protected in this National Park by as gallant a commander and troops as today are its protectors." According to local newspapers, celebrations were held at Mammoth Hot Springs in 1901, 1903, 1913, and 1916. These events typically included sporting contests, such as horse races, as well as speeches, music, and fireworks. The 1916 Fort Yellowstone event included an artillery salute of 48 guns with a baseball game between the hotel's employees and the soldiers. Today large-scale celebrations are not held in Yellowstone; fireworks are not allowed in national parks and the large crowds that are typically there to enjoy the park in July prohibit such events. "For many, the chance to come to Yellowstone and see and smell a geyser's steamy plume or hike a high-country meadow glowing with wildflowers or catch a brief glimpse of a grizzly bear or wolf or herd of bison is a fine way to celebrate the birth of our nation, a nation that has given the world its best idea, national parks."

Sources: "Fourth of July at Fort Yellowstone," Web page, National Park Service, <http://.nps.gov/yell/jun-30pr.htm>; *Livingston Enterprise*, July 1901; *Gardiner Wonderland*, July 1903.

Yippies Anti-Marijuana Laws March and Celebration

First started in Washington, D.C., on July 4, 1968, as a way to garner support for repealing all anti-marijuana laws. Through the years demonstrators met on the Mall and Lafayette Park. Their demonstrations were often referred to as "smoke-ins," and each typically drew over 500 persons. On July 4, 1977, protestors held up signs such as "Free Dope" and "Get High, U.S.A.," while tossing Frisbees and listening to rock music. On July 4, 1982, at Lafayette Park, a "10-foot long facsimile of a marijuana cigarette" was displayed as nine persons were arrested "on charges of sale and possession of marijuana." On July 4, 1983, the Yippies were barred from using the park because a coalition of counter-demonstrators, consisting of about 200 persons, including District of Columbia City Council members and members of Concerned Citizens for Drug and Alcohol Abuse, reserved the area. The Yippies had their meeting on the sidewalk in front of the White House.

Sources: Stephen J. Lynton, "Calm Fourth," *Washington Post*, 5 July 1977, A6; *Washington Post*, 5 July 1981, B5; Peter Perl, "A Fine Fourth," *Washington Post*, 5 July 1982, A1, A7; Edward D. Sargent, "Celebration of Family Life at Park Leaves Yippies Out in the Rain," *Washington Post*, 5 July 1983, B3.

Zambelli Fireworks Internationale

Founded in 1893 in New Castle, Pennsylvania, and one of the oldest and largest fireworks companies in America. Antonio Zambelli brought the craft over to America when he emigrated from Cassarta, Italy. The fireworks were based on secret recipes that dated from the 14th century. Billing themselves as "the first family of fireworks," Antonio's son George, Sr., took over the business in 1946. Each year the firm produces more than 3,500 shows. George Zambelli, Sr., died in 2003.

Sources: Michelle Massie, "Obituary: George Zambelli Sr. Headed One of Oldest Fireworks Companies," *Pittsburgh Post-Gazette.com*, 27 December 2003; Gianni DeVincent Hayes, *Zambelli: The First Family of Fireworks* (Forest Dale, Vt.: Paul S. Eriksson, 2003).

Zanesville, Ohio, Masonic Hall

On July 4, 1857, the cornerstone for this building was laid. The activities that day began with the firing of artillery. About 2000 persons assembled in town from outlying areas via local railroads.

Source: *Daily Ohio State Journal*, 7 July 1857, 2.

APPENDIX: THE DECLARATION OF INDEPENDENCE OF THE THIRTEEN COLONIES

In CONGRESS, July 4, 1776.

The unanimous Declaration of the thirteen United States of America,

When in the Course of human Events, it becomes necessary for one People to dissolve the Political Bands which have connected them with another, and to assume among the Powers of the Earth, the separate and equal Station to which the Laws of Nature and of Nature's God entitle them, a decent Respect to the Opinions of Mankind requires that they should declare the causes which impel them to the Separation.

We hold these truths to be self-evident, that all Men are created equal, that they are endowed by their Creator with certain un-alienable Rights, that among these are Life, Liberty and the pursuit of Happiness — That to secure these Rights, Governments are insti-tuted among Men, deriving their just Powers from the consent of the governed, that when-ever any Form of Government becomes de-structive of these ends, it is the Right of the People to alter or to abolish it, and to insti-tute new Government, laying its Foundation on such Principles, and organizing its Powers in such Form, as to them shall seem most likely to effect their Safety and Happiness. Prudence, indeed, will dictate that Govern-ments long established should not be changed for light and transient Causes; and accordingly all experience hath shewn, that Mankind are more disposed to suffer, while Evils are suffer-able, than to right themselves by abolishing the Forms to which they are accustomed. But when a long Train of Abuses and Usurpations, pursuing invariably the same Object, evinces a Design to reduce them under absolute Despotism, it is their Right, it is their Duty, to throw off such Government, and to provide new Guards for their future Security. Such has been the patient Sufferance of these Colonies; and such is now the Necessity which con-strains them to alter their former Systems of Government. The History of the present King of Great-Britain is a History of repeated In-juries and Usurpations, all having in direct Object the Establishment of an absolute Tyranny over these States. To prove this, let Facts be submitted to a candid World.

He has refused his Assent to Laws, the most wholesome and necessary for the public Good.

He has forbidden his Governors to pass Laws of immediate and pressing Importance, unless suspended in their operation till his As-sent should be obtained; and when so sus-pended, he has utterly neglected to attend to them.

He has refused to pass other Laws for the

Accommodation of large Districts of People, unless those People would relinquish the Right of Representation in the Legislature, a right inestimable to them, and formidable to Tyrants only.

He has called together Legislative Bodies at Places unusual, uncomfortable, and distant from the Depository of their public Records, for the sole Purpose of fatiguing them into Compliance with his Measures.

He has dissolved Representative Houses repeatedly, for opposing with manly Firmness his Invasions on the Rights of the People.

He has refused for a long Time, after such Dissolutions, to cause others to be elected; whereby the Legislative powers, incapable of Annihilation, have returned to the People at large for their exercise; the State remaining in the mean time exposed to all the Dangers of Invasion from without, and Convulsions within.

He has endeavoured to prevent the Population of these States; for that Purpose obstructing the Laws for Naturalization of Foreigners; refusing to pass others to encourage their Migrations hither, and raising the Conditions of new Appropriations of Lands.

He has obstructed the Administration of Justice, by refusing his Assent to Laws for establishing Judiciary Powers.

He has made Judges dependent on his Will alone, for the Tenure of their offices, and the Amount and Payment of their Salaries.

He has erected a Multitude of new Offices, and sent hither Swarms of Officers to harass our People, and eat out their Substance.

He has kept among us, in Times of Peace, Standing Armies, without the consent of our Legislatures.

He has affected to render the Military independent of and superior to the Civil Power.

He has combined with others to subject us to a Jurisdiction foreign to our Constitution, and unacknowledged by our Laws; giving his Assent to their Acts of pretended Legislation:

For quartering large Bodies of Armed Troops among us:

For protecting them, by a mock Trial, from punishment for any Murders which they should commit on the Inhabitants of these States:

For cutting off our Trade with all Parts of the World:

For imposing Taxes on us without our Consent:

For depriving us, in many Cases, of the Benefits of Trial by Jury:

For transporting us beyond Seas to be tried for pretended Offences:

For abolishing the free System of English Laws in a neighbouring Province, establishing therein an arbitrary Government, and enlarging its Boundaries, so as to render it at once an Example and fit Instrument for introducing the same absolute Rule into these Colonies:

For taking away our Charters, abolishing our most valuable Laws, and altering fundamentally the Forms of our Governments:

For suspending our own Legislatures, and declaring themselves invested with Power to legislate for us in all Cases whatsoever.

He has abdicated Government here, by declaring us out of his Protection and waging War against us.

He has plundered our Seas, ravaged our Coasts, burnt our Towns, and destroyed the Lives of our People.

He is, at this Time, transporting large Armies of foreign Mercenaries to compleat the Works of Death, Desolation and Tyranny, already begun with circumstances of Cruelty and Perfidy, scarcely paralleled in the most barbarous Ages, and totally unworthy the Head of a civilized Nation.

He has constrained our fellow Citizens taken Captive on the high Seas to bear Arms against their Country, to become the Executioners of their Friends and Brethren, or to fall themselves by their Hands.

He has excited domestic Insurrections amongst us, and has endeavoured to bring on the Inhabitants of our Frontiers, the merciless Indian Savages, whose known Rule of Warfare, is an undistinguished Destruction, of all Ages, Sexes and Conditions.

In every stage of these Oppressions we have Petitioned for Redress in the most humble Terms: Our repeated Petitions have been answered only by repeated Injury. A Prince, whose Character is thus marked by every act which may define a Tyrant, is unfit to be the Ruler of a free People.

Nor have we been wanting in Attentions to our British Brethren. We have warned them from Time to Time of attempts by their Legislature to extend an unwarrantable Jurisdiction over us. We have reminded them of the Circumstances of our Emigration and Settlement here. We have appealed to their native Justice and Magnanimity, and we have conjured them by the Ties of our common Kindred to disavow these Usurpations, which, would inevitably interrupt our Connections and Correspondence. They too have been deaf to the Voice of Justice and of Consanguinity. We must, therefore, acquiesce in the Necessity, which denounces our Separation, and hold them, as we hold the rest of Mankind, Enemies in War, in Peace, Friends.

We, therefore, the Representatives of the UNITED STATES OF AMERICA, in General Congress, Assembled, appealing to the Supreme Judge of the World for the Rectitude of our Intentions, do, in the Name, and by the Authority of the good People of these Colonies, solemnly Publish and Declare, That these United Colonies are, and of Right ought to be, FREE AND INDEPENDENT STATES; that they are absolved from all Allegiance to the British Crown, and that all political Connection between them and the State of Great-Britain, is and ought to be totally dissolved; and that as FREE AND INDEPENDENT STATES, they have full Power to levy War, conclude Peace, contract Alliances, establish Commerce, and to do all other Acts and Things which INDEPENDENT STATES may of right do. And for the support of this Declaration, with a firm Reliance on the Protection of divine Providence, we mutually pledge to each other our Lives, our Fortunes, and our sacred Honor.

[New Hampshire]
Josiah Bartlett, Wm Whipple, Matthew Thornton

[Massachusetts]
John Hancock, Saml Adams, John Adams, Robert Treat Paine, Elbridge Gerry

[Rhode Island]
Steph Hopkins, William Ellery

[Connecticut]
Roger Sherman, Samuel Huntington, Wm Williams, Oliver Wolcott

[New York]
Wm Floyd, Phil Livingston, Frans Lewis, Lewis Morris

[New Jersey]
Richd Stockton, Jno Witherspoon, Fras Hopkinson, John Hart, Abra Clark

[Pennsylvania]
Robt Morris, Benjamin Rush, Benja Franklin, John Morton, Geo Clymer, Jas Smith, Geo Taylor, James Wilson, Geo Ross

[Delaware]
Caesar Rodney, Geo Read, Thom McKean

[Maryland]
Samuel Chase, Wm Paca, Thos Stone, Charles Carroll of Carrollton

[Virginia]
George Wythe, Richard Henry Lee, Th Jefferson, Benja Harrison, Thos Nelson, Jr., Francis Lightfoot Lee, Carter Braxton

[North Carolina]
Wm Hooper, Joseph Hewes, John Penn

[South Carolina]
Edward Rutledge, Thos Heyward, Junr., Thomas Lynch, Junor., Arthur Middleton

[Georgia]
Button Gwinnett, Lyman Hall, Geo Walton

BIBLIOGRAPHY

American National Biography. Ed. John A. Garraty and Mark C. Carnes. 24 vols. New York: Oxford University Press, 1999.

An American Time Capsule: Three Centuries of Broadsides and Other Printed Ephemera. Washington, D.C.: Rare Books and Special Collections Division, Library of Congress. Web site, <http://memory.loc.gov/ammem/rbpehtml/pe home.html>.

Appelbaum, Diana Karter. *The Glorious Fourth: An American Holiday, an American History*. New York: Facts on File, 1989.

Branham, Robert James, and Stephen J. Hartnett. *Sweet Freedom's Song: "My Country 'Tis of Thee" and Democracy in America*. New York: Oxford University Press, 2002.

Clark, J. Bunker, ed. *American Keyboard Music through 1865*. Boston: G.K. Hall, 1990.

_____. *The Dawning of American Keyboard Music*. New York: Greenwood Press, 1988.

Dennis, Matthew. *Red, White, and Blue Letter Days: An American Calendar*. Ithaca: Cornell University Press, 2002.

Encyclopedia Americana. 30 vols. Danbury, Conn.: Grolier, 1999.

Encyclopedia of American History: Bicentennial Edition. Ed. Richard B. Morris. New York: Harper and Row, 1976.

The Encyclopedia of New York City. Ed. Kenneth T. Jackson. New Haven: Yale University Press for the New-York Historical Society, 1995.

The Folklore of American Holidays. 3rd ed. Ed. Hennig Cohen and Tristram Potter Coffin. Detroit: Gale, 1999.

The Fourth of July: Political Oratory and Literary Reactions 1776–1876. Ed. Paul Goetsch and Gerd Hurm. Tübingen: Gunter Narr Verlag, 1992.

Gerber, Scott Douglas, ed. *Declaration of Independence: Origins and Impact*. Washington, D.C.: CQ Press, 2002.

Hawken, Henry A. *Trumpets of Glory: Fourth of July Orations, 1786–1861*. Granby, Conn.: Salmon Brook Historical Society, 1976.

Hay, Robert P. "Freedom's Jubilee: One Hundred Years of the Fourth of July, 1776–1876." Ph.D. dissertation, University of Kentucky, 1967.

Heintze, James R. "Orations, Speeches, and Readings of the Declaration of Independence in Washington, D.C. and Surrounding Towns on the Fourth of July: 1801–1876." Washington, D.C.: the author, 2001.

James, Stephen Elliot. "The Other Fourth of July: The Meanings of Black Identity at American Celebrations of Independence, 1770–1863." Ph.D. dissertation, Harvard University, 1997.

Martin, Howard Hastings. "Orations on the Anniversary of American Independence, 1777–1876." Ph.D. dissertation, Northwestern University, 1955.

Memoirs of John Quincy Adams, Comprising Portions of His Diary from 1795 to 1848. 12 vols. Ed. Charles Francis Adams. Freeport, N.Y.: Books for Libraries Press, 1969.

The National Cyclopaedia of American Biography. New York: James T. White, 1898; 1949; reprint, Ann Arbor: University Microfilms, 1967.

Tafel, Jonathan Leigh. "The Historical Development of Political and Patriotic Images of America: A Visual Analysis of Fourth of July Cartoons in Five Newspapers." Ph.D. dissertation, Ohio State University, 1979.

Travers, Len. *Celebrating the Fourth: Independence Day and the Rites of Nationalism in the Early Republic*. Amherst: University of Massachusetts Press, 1997.

Wolfe, Richard J. *Secular Music in America 1801–1825: A Bibliography*. 3 vols. New York: New York Public Library, 1964.

INDEX

Numbers in *bold italics* represent primary entries in the encyclopedia